STUDIES IN

HOMOSEXUALITY

A GARLAND SERIES

Edited with
Introductions by

Wayne R. Dynes
Hunter College, City University
of New York

and Stephen Donaldson

Contents of Series

I	Homosexuality in the Ancient World
II	Ethnographic Studies of Homosexuality
III	Asian Homosexuality
IV	Homosexuality and Homosexuals in the Arts
V	History of Homosexuality in Europe and America
VI	Homosexuality: Discrimination, Criminology, and the Law
VII	Lesbianism
VIII	Homosexual Themes in Literary Studies
IX	Homosexuality and Medicine, Health, and Science
X	Homosexuality and Government, Politics, and Prisons
XI	Homosexuality and Psychology, Psychiatry, and Counseling
XII	Homosexuality and Religion and Philosophy
XIII	Sociology of Homosexuality

VOLUME II

Ethnographic Studies of Homosexuality

Edited with Introductions by
Wayne R. Dynes
Hunter College, City University of New York
and Stephen Donaldson

Garland Publishing, Inc.
New York & London 1992

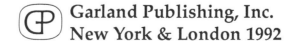

Library of Congress Cataloging-in-Publication Data

Ethnographic studies of homosexuality / edited by Wayne R. Dynes and Stephen Donaldson.
p. cm. — (Studies in homosexuality ; v. 2)
A collection of previously published journal articles.
Includes bibliographical references.
ISBN 0-8153-0547-8
1. Homosexuality—Cross-cultural studies. I. Dynes, Wayne R. II. Donaldson, Stephen. III. Series.
[DNLM: 1. Cross-Cultural Comparison—collected works. 2. Ethnic Groups—collected works. 3. Homosexuality—history—collected works. WM 615 S933]
HQ76.25.E84 1992
306.76'6—dc20
DNLM/DLC 92-14694
for Library of Congress CIP

Printed on acid-free, 250-year-life paper
Manufactured in the United States of America

General Introduction

Over the past quarter century powerful currents of research and writing on homosexuality, lesbianism, and bisexuality have rippled through widening channels, finding outlets in scores of journals affiliated with more than a dozen disciplines. While this increase in the volume of publications signals a welcome lessening of the taboo on the subject and a growing sense of its importance, this profusion makes it difficult for even specialists to monitor the progress of scholarship in its many domains. Much of the key material in this area has appeared in hard-to-locate and often unlikely appearing academic periodicals, which have escaped even diligent indexers and bibliographers. Moreover, not a few of these journals appeared in very limited issues and cannot be found today even in the larger research libraries.

To make more accessible to the reader the classic, the pioneering, and the most recent outstanding articles of scholarly work in a wide variety of disciplines, this series gathers a selection of such articles, reprinting them in thirteen volumes organized by discipline. Sifting through thousands of journal articles, the editors have chosen for republication works of scholarly distinction without attempting to impose any uniform ideological perspective on a field still characterized by lively controversies. Dates of original publication of the selections included in these volumes span the twentieth century, from Erich Bethe's landmark 1907 article on Dorian pederasty in *Rheinisches Museum* to current articles embodying the latest techniques of archival research and conceptual analysis. In some cases, it has been impossible to obtain permission to reprint material we felt worth inclusion; Haworth Press, for example, declined to permit republication of any articles from the *Journal of Homosexuality*. Fortunately, that periodical is widely available so that its absence does not detract from our goal of furnishing important but hard-to-find research.

The earlier situation in which work on homosexuality typically found its home in the social sciences and in medicine has significantly broadened, with important work in history, the humanities, and the arts. Attention has also shifted from the isolated individual to the interaction of the gay/lesbian/bi person with his/her peers. Increased attention has also been devoted to cultural representations in novels and poetry, films and popular music.

Each individual volume brings together the best article-length scholarship on homosexuality from that discipline and will save the specialist a great deal of time and effort. Each volume is self-contained; at the same time, the entire series is designed so that the reader seeking a broad understanding of the phenomena of homosexualities and their cultural, literary, and historical manifestations can make profitable use of the volumes representing other disciplines.

The introduction to each volume examines the history of the discipline(s) represented and its approaches to the study of homosexuality, critiques the development of research in the field, notes milestones in the evolution of thought and research, raises methodological issues, discusses conceptual questions, and suggests directions for future investigation and developments in the field. These introductions allow the reader from outside the discipline to survey and appreciate the issues raised. At the same time specialists will find a constructive critique of the state of their discipline as well as an appreciation of its contributions to the overall development of gay, lesbian, and bisexual scholarship. Appended to each introduction is a survey bibliography of important book-length works in that field.

Introduction

The academic discipline of anthropology took shape in the 1860s under L. H. Morgan in the United States and E. B. Tylor in England, but it can trace its roots to the comparative study of human societies adumbrated by the fifth-century B.C. Greek historian Herodotus. The new discipline soon acquired disparate branches in physical anthropology, which deals with the evolution of the hominid line; archaeology, the study of material remains; linguistics, with the task of recording and analyzing the speech of nonliterate peoples; and cultural anthropology, which took up an older tradition of ethnography and settled down to specialize in comparative investigation of human cultures. Originally these fields tended to address what pioneering anthropologists thought were the "lower races." In the 1930s, however, Robert Redfield and his associates began the study of the folk society of peasants, forming a bridge to more recent fieldwork within the host society itself.

In the course of the twentieth century anthropology absorbed influences from behavioral psychology, Freudian psychoanalysis, Marxism, ecology, ethology and primatology, semiotics, area studies, and even literary criticism. From a small, holistic discipline, American anthropology greatly expanded in the 1960s and 1970s, stimulated by an infusion of federal financial support. The field became increasingly fragmented and did not develop a central body of theory or unified approach.

Cultural anthropologists generally assume culture to be the main determinant of behavior, resisting encroachments from ethology, genetics, and (most recently) sociobiology, which emphasize uniformity and biological determinism. By contrast, anthropologists tend to value cultural diversity, accepting pluralism as an unalloyed good. But what is culture? A major cleavage in contemporary anthropology is between materialists who, influenced by the Marxian tradition, tend to trace the determining features of culture to socioeconomic factors (which vary enormously owing to differences of technology and ecology), and symbolists, who focus on concepts and ideas cherished by the culture, including myths.

Recently, with their traditional hunting grounds, the unspoiled preliterate cultures, dwindling, some anthropologists have turned their techniques on the large American city, creating "urban anthropology" in a domain which had been the prime turf of sociology. Faced with such territorial raids, sociologists retaliated by invading the Third World, compounding still further the question of anthropology's identity as a discipline.

Anthropology entered the popular imagination through the massive creation of Sir James George Frazer, *The Golden Bough* (1890-1915), a work criticized by professionals because it was derived from secondary sources and retained strong elements of Eurocentric judgmentalism. In America a new model based on fieldwork and cultural relativism was championed by Franz Boas. Even better known were his pupils Ruth Benedict and Margaret Mead, who were sexually involved with each other as well as with other women. Mead became a pundit of sorts, commenting widely on topical matters and discounting the usual assumption that the American way of life was the only valid one.

The growth of "green" environmentalist groups in industrial societies, with their concept of appropriate technology, stimulated interest in native peoples—especially those of North America and the Amazon—now no longer perceived as backward but having lessons to teach for the future. The rise of a gay and lesbian American Indian movement reawakened knowledge of the indigenous tradition of the berdache, as examined by Will Roscoe herein.

Today anthropology as a separate discipline in Western university faculties is widely perceived as an example of division of labor, with sociologists taking the European and North American cultural zone, area studies the developing and advanced Asian nations, and anthropology left with the villages not yet reached by television. And yet, sustained by their own rich tradition, anthropologists may ask different questions or examine different aspects than would the sociologist. When it addresses American society, the work of Gilbert Herdt and Kath Weston does so from the standpoint of anthropology rather than of sociology. Moreover, anthropology retains a noble ambition of interpreting the whole of human culture and not just particular zones thereof.

Anthropology and Homosexuality

In general, classical cultural anthropologists addressed kinship and social structure rather than personal matters like sexuality, and homosexuality in particular escaped the framework of their investigations. In the preanthropological stage of encounter with tribal society many travelers collected anecdotal evidence for same-sex behavior, but this data has tended to be neglected by professionals. Many anthropologists seem to have tacitly accepted a version of the noble-savage myth: indigenous peoples could not be contaminated with such a decadent Western vice as same-sex behavior, hence one need not bother to ask about it. A few recorded it, either on the basis of personal predilections or through a wish to rationalize colonial expropriation. Others collected relevant data, but refrained from publishing it. Some worried about their personal reputations. Male anthropologists were reluctant to inquire about lesbian practices or found such inquiry taboo. Frequently, Western assumptions governed the inquiry; a classic instance is William Davenport asking Melanesians if they knew anyone who had no sexual desire for women, but only for men. No one did, so Davenport concluded there was no homosexuality. Later he learned that homosexual activity was nearly universal among his subjects, but simply did not supplant heterosexuality. Often natives of cultures with a gender-differentiated type of homosexuality no longer consider those persons who were born male but who have ritually left their gender to still be males, and hence answer questions about sex between males in the negative.

Native reticence about sex in general or particular practices, especially ritual and shamanic homosexuality, is occasionally a handicap. Even more of a problem is previous encounter with Western sexual repression in the form of missionaries, teachers, government officials, and others; natives are quick to pick up the emotional reactions of these visitors to native homosexuality as shameful, amusing, or evil. In numerous instances, direct and often successful efforts at suppression of native practices had already taken place before the ethnographers arrived.

Nevertheless, a considerable body of observations of homosexual practices among preliterate peoples did accrue. Paolo Mantegazza, a professor in Florence, in 1885 published *The Sexual Relations of Mankind*, in which he emphasized the variety of sexual customs found in humankind. Calling sodomy "shameful above all," "vice against nature," and "unclean and revolting," Mantegazza cited fourteen cases of it (or cross-gender behavior) among the indigenous peoples of the Americas.

The following year Sir Richard Burton issued his translation of the *Thousand Nights and a Night* with a lengthy appended "Terminal Essay" containing 42 pages on pederasty, outlining his theory of a "Sotadic Zone" extending to the South Sea Islands and the New World at the time of its discovery, where "the Vice is popular and endemic."

The Finnish anthropologist Edward Westermarck included a substantial chapter on "Homosexual Love" in his *Origin and Development of Moral Ideas* (1906–08) showing the variability of same-sex relations around the globe.

In 1911 Ferdinand Karsch-Haack published the 668–page *Das gleichgeschlechtliche Leben der Naturvölker*, the first book devoted to the subject of homosexuality among preliterate societies (significantly, in German, the "nature peoples"). This work abounds in excerpts from primary materials in a number of languages. Unfortunately, many of these sources, which could provide comparisons over time with the contemporary cultures being studied by present-day anthropologists, have suffered signal neglect.

Many of the early reports of European observers were biased, not only in the telling but even more importantly in the omission, reflecting the missionary and government auspices under which these observers operated. Anthropologists, too, tended to remain inattentive to subgroups which might engage in homosexual behavior.

The Human Relations Area Files were established at midcentury at Yale University to compile world culture traits. The materials accumulating there were utilized by anthropologist Clellan S. Ford in his 1951 collaboration with Frank A. Beach in *Patterns of Sexual Behavior*, constituting a major breakthrough. The authors found that 64 per cent of the societies for which records were available to them tolerated or encouraged homosexual behavior; such behavior was also noted in primates and other animals.

Following Ford and Beach, anthropologists took a new look at the berdache phenomenon among native American tribes. In the seventies scholars formed the Anthropological Research Group on Homosexuality, which published a newsletter and later changed its name to the Society of Lesbian and Gay Anthropologists.

Methodologically, anthropology displays some major discrepancies between initial and subsequent ethnographies of a single culture by different researchers, casting doubt on the reliability of such observations (the so-called "Rashomon effect"). In some cases, of course, the apparent discrepancy reflects the targeting of different aspects of the culture or a somewhat different geographical focus. Moreover, tribal societies are not static, as one tends to think, but evolve, so that discrepancies between earlier and later ethnographies may simply mirror a pattern of ongoing change. Many cultures are being contaminated by acculturation, and tribal informants have learned to respond to an investigator's expectations. The "initiatory" homosexuality of many cultures may be closed to outsiders and hence denied.

A survey of the current data on homosexuality in preliterate cultures shows a striking lack (except among Arthur Sorenson's Indians of the northwest Amazon) of the androphile type of relationship (involving pairs of adults, both considered to be of the same gender, of roughly equal social status, and reciprocal in their behavior) which dominates today's industrialized Western world. Situational homosexuality does occur among African and South American all-male hunting bands roaming far from their families. Ethnographers have also found numerous instances of adolescent experimentation and occasional dominance-enforcement homosexuality among warrior tribes, but they have rarely described ephebophilia (except among the Nkundo of Africa and the native Hawaiian aristocracy), possibly because they were not aware of it as constituting a distinct type. (Ephebophilia is the attraction to males in the seventeen to twenty-one age range.) Broadly speaking, anthropologists have found two major systems: one gender-differentiated and the other age-differentiated.

Shamanism and the Gender-differentiated System

The gender-graded or "berdache" systems may be the remnants of a once-existing cultural sphere which spread across the northern plains of Asia, colonized the Western Hemisphere from Siberia, and sent offshoots to the coastal and litoral societies of the eastern Pacific and Indian Oceans, including Polynesia. This is a pattern in which the passive partner receives a summons from spirits or perceives signs that he must give up his manhood in favor of a not-man status (sometimes described as feminine, sometimes as a third gender), which remains a lifelong assignment; he may assume special healing or religious functions as a shaman or perform other special functions for the tribe; usually he engages in limited or complete cross-dressing. His sexual partner, whom he may marry, could be any adult male of the tribe (not another berdache); in this type of arrangement the insertive role is not extraordinary, only the receptive one.

Native Americans, whose institution of berdachehood has attracted the most sustained attention, accepted gender diversity in a religious context, assigning its origins to the spirit world, which overruled the biological sex of the berdache. Like their Siberian counterparts, berdaches acted as shamans and healers, seers, and prophets. Berdaches, called "two-spirited" by some tribes, also served as teachers, adoptive parents, and mediators. Subject to repression from Christian intolerance, the institution went underground; in some tribes it disappeared, while in a few it has continued to the present, and in others the tradition is being revived.

Shamanism is a feature of the Paleo-Siberian peoples, including not only Siberia but also Alaska. Anthropologists have noted a widespread human idea that special powers or gifts are associated with interstitial or ambiguous persons, including mixed-gender individuals. Where division of labor in the tribe is by gender, the shaman serves as artist and intellectual. The "calling" to shamanhood may take place at any point in life, and far from being limited to males, often shows a predominance of females. Other areas reporting cross-dressing shamans include Kalimantan on Borneo, Celebes (Indonesia), and Vietnam.

In Tahiti most villages had a single *mahu*, who engaged in nonreciprocal sex as the orally receptive partner with young bachelors of the village; see Robert Levy's article, included herein. The Philippine archipelago shows numerous instances of gender-differentiated homosexuality, with the transvestites especially involved in entertainment activities; the *banci* of eastern Java are similar. Comparable roles for females appeared in the Philippines but not in Tahiti.

Reports have also placed the male gender-differentiated type in the upper Amazon basin and the lower extremity of South America. Females who gave up their original gender-identity appeared among the Eskimos, the Plains Indians, and in South American tribes; these women would become warriors and hunters and marry standard females. Sometimes they had reputations for spiritual power and prophesy. See Paula Gunn Allen's and Evelyn Blackwood's articles, included herein.

In India the devotees of the Hijra sect seem to belong to the gender-differentiated tradition, working as entertainers and with a definite spiritual dimension as worshippers of the Mother Goddess. Custom requires Hijras to surgically remove the male organs, after which they are regarded as females, but the timing of the operation is subject to omens and many Hijras, therefore, regard themselves as preoperative transsexuals. In Thailand the *katoey* (gatuhy) fills the gender-differentiated role, but without shamanistic vestiges in that Buddhist country. Herodotus reported on the *enarees*, diviners who seem to have formed an effeminate priesthood among the Scythian inhabitants of southern Russia and the present-day Ukraine in the first millennium B.C.

The eastern coast of Africa has also reported gender-differentiated homosexuality, some of it tied to possession cults, most notably among the Otoro, Moro, Nyima, Tira, Korongo, and Mesakin; in West Africa the Fanti and Wolof are so inclined; in central Africa the Basangye's *kitesha* form a third gender; the south African Thonga seem to have had elements of the gender-differentiated type (mixed with age-graded, as is occasionally the case with other African tribes).

The possession cults of Afro-Brazilian and Afro-Caribbean societies (not primitive, if underdeveloped) show gender-differentiated adepts. As this example shows, shamanistic homosexuality is not limited to pre-literate cultures. In a different, secularized form it remains widespread in the more advanced cultures today, constituting the dominant mode of homosexuality in Latin America, much of Mediterranean Europe, and much of the Far East, while manifesting as a minority model in androphilic cultures of or derived from northern Europe. In these "advanced" areas, however, it appears to have lost its extraordinary spiritual aura and any claim to gifts of healing or prophecy.

Initiation and the Age-differentiated System

The other major type of homosexual organization found in preliterate cultures has sometimes merited the term "initiatory" since it is used to mark the transition from boy to man or from one stage of boyhood to another rather than to ascribe a permanent non-man role to the passive partner. The initiation may be a brief, one-time-only situation, or it may stretch over a period of years. (We are familiar with examples of the latter from the highly literate cultures of ancient Athens and the early modern Japanese samurai.) There appears to be a high correlation between initiatory homosexuality and masculinized warrior societies.

In some cultures the initiatory function receives little emphasis, but the age-differentiated, transitory nature of the homosexuality remains paramount. As a general feature of the type, the older partner, who is the penetrator, passes on his knowledge and power to the younger, who is temporarily the penetrated. The adult commonly relates to adults of the opposite gender like any other adult male of that culture.

Bernard Sergent, a follower of Georges Dumézil, has recently claimed that Indo-European warriors practiced initiatory pederasty prior to their dispersion (and for some, such as the Greeks, afterwards) in the third millennium B.C. This thesis has remained controversial, for homosexuality is unknown to the orally transmitted Rig-Vedic legends of the warrior class (Kshatriya) descendants of the Indo-European Aryans who invaded ancient India (though the Rig-Veda in the form known to us is dated no earlier than 1500 B.C., and the Brahmins who assumed custody of the tradition may have deleted such references), and Greek pederasty seems to have originated in Crete in historical times, though there is evidence for ritual initiation as part of the Cretan practice, which could have roots in an older tradition. On the other hand, the warlike Celts were said by Athenaeus and others to have preferred boys to women, and there are suggestions of initiatory functions in this system. The ancient historians Ammianus Marcellinus and Procopius attested that some Germanic warriors of the Roman era commonly indulged in pederastic acts. Surviving pre-Christian Nordic literature contains no references to pederasty; the practices of the pre-Christian Slavs are unknown.

Gilbert Herdt noted ritualized age-graded homosexuality among the Australians (some of whom took boy-wives while themselves ephebes—older teens—awaiting heterosexual marriage) and it was he who documented the most commonly cited practices of overt—and mandatory—initiatory homosexuality, those of the Melanesian Sambia, where knowledge of the cult was taboo for women. There teenagers who are between puberty and the age of marriage (nineteen) "implant" their semen in boys between nine and puberty, so that it may take root and spread its male virtue through their growing bodies, on the analogy of seed which must be planted before it can grow to produce fruit. The act of penetration of the boy is seen as masculinizing him rather than feminizing him. As a result Herdt's Sambians engaged in exclusive homosexuality for some ten years before turning to exclusive heterosexuality at the point of marriage. One advantage of this system to the males was that their brides were considerably younger, having just passed menarche. See the excerpt from Herdt's 1984 book reprinted herein.

Eastern Javanese warriors kept boys called *gemblakan*, but these men prized the boys' feminine characteristics. The pre-European-contact Hawaiian warrior chiefs kept masculine ephebes, called *aikane*, procured at about seventeen, for sexual and romantic purposes.

In Mexico, the Spanish conquistadors noted the presence of boy prostitution, though it is not clear if the boys were active partners with transvestitic lowlanders or passives (or perhaps even actives in the ephebophilic mode) with older "normal" males. For a contemporary report on Mexico, see Joseph Carrier's 1976 article herein. Alves da Silva reported homosexuality in the puberty rites of Amazon Basin Indians.

In Africa, age-differentiated homosexuality has characterized the Azande of the Sudan (see E. E. Evans-Pritchard's article, reprinted herein), the Bantu-speaking Fang, and the ephebophilic Nkundo.

Among literate cultures today, pederasty remains common throughout the Islamic world and in a number of Asian countries (Thailand, the Philippines, Japan), though in the "advanced" nations it has lost its initiatory function just as the gender-differentiated type has lost its shamanic role; though heavily stigmatized, it continues to exist clandestinely in Western societies.

Cultural Diffusion?

Scholars have suggested that such conceptual models of homosexuality as the gender- and age-differentiated types have spread from culture to culture; this is almost certain to have been the case in Polynesia. We can easily document today the spread of androphilic ideas to literate cultures previously unfamiliar with them. Another hypothesis is that of submerged *Kulturkreise*, surviving island remnants of what used to be more cohesive geographical patterns, the main parts of which have been extirpated by Christianity, colonialism, and modernization. A good example is the remnants of the North American berdache institution which are islands within a sea of Euro-American culture.

Some scholars favor economic-ecological considerations as a starting point for explanations of the distribution of types of homosexuality, observing that initiatory/age-graded relationships tend to accompany warrior cultures (though certainly not uniformly, as the absence of that type from among American Indian tribes attests). Stephen O. Murray has also suggested that scholars look to differences in social structure, associating Polynesian gender-differentiated cultures with all-powerful chiefs and pervasive slavery, while age-differentiating Melanesian warriors were more egalitarian among themselves. Several scholars have argued that in Melanesia ritualized homosexuality, along with proscribed times for heterosexual intercourse, lowered the birthrate.

Sociobiology and Evolution

The process of human evolution having long been a major focus of anthropology, it should not be surprising that anthropologists would take some interest in the question of the evolutionary nature (if any) of homosexuality. The physical anthropologists have had nothing to say on this topic, but sociobiologists, whose intellectual roots lie outside of but parallel to the discipline (both sharing sources in ethology and primatology as well as an allegiance to Darwin), have spilled quite a bit of ink on the matter. To them it is an outstanding theoretical challenge to explain a behavior which leaves no progeny behind. G. Evelyn Hutchinson developed a theory of heterozygote advantage, which may apply best to bisexuality, in 1959. James D. Weinrich in 1976 developed kin-selection theory to account for gender-differentiated types of homosexuality. Other types of homosexuality, such as the age-differentiated type in which the participants all eventually marry, situational homosexuality, adolescent experimentation, and dominance-enforcement, do not have significant effects on reproductive rates and thus do not pose puzzles for evolutionary theorists. The most difficult challenge for Darwinians would be exclusive androphilia, but this may be too recent a widespread development to have had noticeable evolutionary consequences.

Conclusions

How can anthropology contribute to the study of homosexuality? Until very recently, it has mainly helped to refute various homophobic theories, such as that homosexuality is the product of a decadent and declining civilization, that it is unknown to "natural peoples" and hence itself unnatural, that it is universally abhorrent, the product of certain family psychodynamics, a degenerative disease, an aristocratic vice, a hormonal failure, or a contagious perversion.

As we discard these shopworn ideas, however, anthropology may help us to develop a better understanding of what homosexuality is and is not. Clearly, same-sex behavior of some type or other seems to be found in all but the tiniest cultures, and therefore may legitimately lay claim to the status of a universal component of the human behavioral repertoire. In its organization and details, however, it is equally clear that variability is the rule and that the culture prescribes the parameters. What is intriguing is the *limited* number of forms of organization displayed, a fact which calls out for theoretical explication.

Meanwhile, we may pause and reflect over the raised status of the shaman, the male-bonding effects of ritual homosexual initiation, the universal male participation rate in some tribes of Melanesia, the lack of lifelong effects on any of the participants' (except for the berdaches') sexuality, the refusal to single out the homosexually insertive males and label them any differently from males in general, the wide acceptance of homosexual relations with adolescents or prepubic boys, and, most provocatively, the general lack of reciprocity and "equality" in the relationships described.

Anthropological literature has given us much less material on lesbianism, but that should encourage researchers to redouble their efforts to find it. Depending on the results of that search, the theories of male homosexuality and of lesbianism may have to diverge.

Time is running out; when the last tribal Papuan can tune in to the "Gay Liberation Hour" with his satellite dish, traditional field work will be at an end.

Bibliography

Baumann, Hermann. *Das doppelte Geschlecht: Studien zur Bisexualität in Ritus und Mythos*. Berlin: Dietrich Reimer Verlag, 1955.

Blackwood, Evelyn, ed. *Anthropology and Homosexual Behavior*. Binghamton, NY: Haworth Press, 1986.

Bleibtreu-Ehrenberg, Gisela. *Mannbarkeitsriten: zur institutionellen Päderastie bei Papuas und Melanesiern*. Berlin: Ullstein, 1980. Idem. *Der Weibmann: Kultischer Geschlechtswechsel im Schamanismus; eine Studie zur Transvestition und Transsexualität bei Naturvölkern*. Frankfurt: Fischer, 1984.

Carpenter, Edward. *Intermediate Types among Primitive Folk*. 2nd ed. London: George Allen and Unwin, 1911.

Greenberg, David F. *The Construction of Homosexuality*. Chicago: University of Chicago Press, 1988.

Herdt, Gilbert H. *Guardians of the Flutes*. New York: McGraw-Hill, 1981. Idem, ed. *Ritualized Homosexuality in Melanesia*. Berkeley: University of California Press, 1984.

Karsch-Haack, Ferdinand, *Das gleichgeschlechtliche Leben der Naturvölker*. New York: Arno Press, 1975 (originally Munich: Ernst Reinhardt, 1911).

Levy, Robert Isaac. *Tahitians: Mind and Experience of the Society Islands*. Chicago: University of Chicago Press, 1973.

Murray, Stephen O., ed. *Male Homosexuality in Central and South America*. New York: Gai Saber, 1987. Idem, *Oceanic Homosexuality*, New York: Garland Publishing, 1992.

Schneebaum, Tobias. *Wild Man*. New York: Viking Press, 1979.

Sergent, Bernard. *L'homosexualité initiatique dans l'Europe ancienne*. Paris: Payot, 1986.

Weston, Kath. *Families We Choose: Lesbians, Gays, Kinship*. New York: Columbia University Press, 1991.

Williams, Walter L. *The Spirit and the Flesh: Sexual Diversity in American Indian Culture*. Boston: Beacon, 1986.

Contents

Lesbians in American Indian Cultures
Paula Gunn Allen 1

Sexuality and Gender in Certain Native American Tribes: The Case of Cross-Gender Females
Evelyn Blackwood 23

Cross-Cultural Codes on Twenty Sexual Attitudes and Practices
Gwen J. Broude and Sarah J. Greene 39

The North American Berdache
Charles Callender and Lee M. Kochems 61

Cultural Factors Affecting Urban Mexican Male Homosexual Behavior
Joseph M. Carrier 89

Sexual Subordination: Institutionalized Homosexuality and Social Control in Melanesia
Gerald W. Creed 111

Polynesia's Third Sex: The Gay Life Starts in the Kitchen
Bengt and Marie Therese Danielsson 132

Institutionalized Homosexuality of the Mohave Indians
George Devereux 136

Homosexuality in Sub-Saharan Africa: *An Unnecessary Controversy*
Wayne Dynes 166

Sexual Inversion among the Azande
E. E. Evans-Pritchard 168

Must We Deracinate Indians to Find Gay Roots?
Ramón A. Gutiérrez 175

On Male Initiation and Dual Organisation in New Guinea
Per Hage 182

Ritualized Homosexual Behavior in the Male Cults of Melanesia, 1862-1983: An Introduction
Gilbert H. Herdt 191

Berdache: A Brief Review of the Literature
Sue-Ellen Jacobs 273

Subject Honor and Object Shame: The Construction of Male Homosexuality and Stigma in Nicaragua
Roger N. Lancaster 289

A Cult Matriarchate and Male Homosexuality
Ruth Landes 304

The Community Function of Tahitian Male Transvestitism: A Hypothesis
Robert I. Levy 316

Fuzzy Sets and Abominations
S.O. Murray 326

Stigma Transformation and Relexification: "Gay" in Latin America
Stephen O. Murray and Manuel Arboleda G. 330

Sentimental Effusions of Genital Contact in Upper Amazonia
Stephen O. Murray 339

Mistaking Fantasy for Ethnography
Stephen O. Murray 353

The Zuni Man-Woman
Will Roscoe 358

Sexual Inversion among Primitive Races
C. G. Seligmann 371

Acknowledgments 376

Index 379

PAULA GUNN ALLEN

LESBIANS IN AMERICAN INDIAN CULTURES

I. Introduction

The Lesbian is to the American Indian what the Indian is to the American–invisible.[1] Among the Sioux there were women known as the "manly-hearted women" who, it seems, functioned as warriors. Whether they were Lesbians is not mentioned in references to them. Indeed, their existence was a pretty well kept secret, and little is made of it. Among the Cherokee there were women known as Beloved Women who were warriors, leaders, and influential council members. But among the Cherokee, all women had real influence in tribal matters until reorganization was necessitated by American removal attempts. It is not known, however, whether the Beloved Women were Lesbians.

In my reading about American Indians, I have never read an overt account of Lesbians, and that reading has included hundreds of books and articles.[2] The closest anyone has come, to my knowledge, is a novel by Fred Manfred entitled *The Manly-Hearted Woman*, and though its protagonist dresses as a man and rejects her feminine role, and though she marries a woman, the writer is very explicit: she and her "wife" do not share intimacies–a possibility which seems beyond the writer's ability to envision. Indeed, she eventually falls in love with a rather strange young warrior who is possessed of enormous sexual attractiveness (given him by spirit-power and a curious genetic circumstance). After the warrior's death, the Manly-Hearted Woman divorces her wife and returns to woman's garb and occupation, discarding the spirit stone which has determined her life to that point.[3]

Because there are few direct references to Lesbians or Lesbianism among American Indians that I am aware of, much of my discussion of them here is necessarily conjectural. The conjectures are based on secure knowledge of American Indian social systems and customs which I have gathered from study and from personal information on the American Indian people–of whom I am one–and on my knowledge of Lesbian culture and practice.

Certainly, the chances that aboriginal American women formed affectional alliances are enormous. There was a marked tendency among many of the tribes to encourage virginity or some version of chastity among pubescent women; this tendency was rarely found with respect to the sexual habits of married women, however, and it referred to intercourse with males. Nothing is said, to my knowledge, about sexual liaisons between women, except indirectly. It is equally likely that such relationships were practiced with social sanction, though no one is presently talking about this. The history of Native America is selective; and those matters pertaining to women that might contradict a Western patriarchist world view are carefully selected out.

Some suggestions about how things were in "time immemorial," as the old folks refer to pre-contact times, have managed to find their way into contemporary literature about American Indians. Many tribes have recorded stories concerning daughters born to spirit women who were dwelling alone on earth. These daughters then would become the mothers of entire tribes. In one such tale, first mother was "born of the dew of the leaf of the beautiful plant."[4] Such tales point to a time prior to the advent of the patriarchy. While historical and archeological evidence suggest that this time pre-dated European contact in some regions of the Western Hemisphere, the change in cultural orientation was still proceeding. The tribes became more male-oriented and more male-dominated as acculturation accelerated. As this process continued, less and less was likely to be said by American Indians about Lesbians among them. Indeed, less and less about women in any position other than that sanctioned by missionaries was likely to be recorded.

There are a number of understandings about the entire issue that will be important in my discussion of American Indian women—heterosexual or Lesbian. It is my contention and belief that those two groups were not nearly as separate as modern Lesbian and straight women are. My belief is based on my understanding of the cultures and social systems in which women lived. These societies were tribal, and tribal consciousness, with its attendant social structures, differs enormously from that of the contemporary Western world.

This difference requires new understanding of a number of concepts. The concept of family, the concept of community, the concept of women, the concept of bonding and belonging, and the concept of power were all distinctly understood in a tribal matrix;

and those concepts were/are very different from those current in modern America.

The primarily Spirit-directed nature of the American Indians must be understood before the place of women, and the place of Lesbians, will be comprehensible. Without that understanding, almost anything about American Indians will seem trivial, obscure, or infuriating. To put it simply, the tribes believed that all human and non-human activities were directly related to the Spirit world. They believed that human beings belonged in a universe that was alive, intelligent, and aware, and that all matters were as much in the province of the Spirits as of human beings.

This perception was not based on fantasy or on speculation. It did not spring from some inarticulate longing planted deep within the savage breast by some instinctive human need to understand and manipulate reality. That scholars and folklorists can believe that it did testifies to their distance from a tribal world. In fact, the American Indian people, of whatever tribe, grounded their belief in the Spirit world firmly upon their own personal, direct and communal experience. Those who are traditionals today still place the same construction on actual events. They speak directly to a Spirit being, as directly as you might speak to a lunch companion.

Because this is so, their understanding of bonding, sexual relationships, power, familial order, and community was quite different from a modern Christian's view. Included in one's family were a number of Spirit people. Among those who shared intimately in one's personal and private reality were one or more personal Spirit guides; on the advice of these guides rested many of the decisions and activities in which any person engaged.

II. Family and Community in American Indian Life

Much of modern society and culture among American Indians results from acculturation. Christianity has imposed certain imperatives on the tribes, as has the growing tendency to "mainstream" Indians through schooling, economic requirements, and local, state, and federal regulation of their lifestyles. The Iroquois, for example, changed the basic structure of their households after the American Revolution. The whiteman determined that they had defeated the Longhouse (the term denoting Iroquois tribal groupings, or the

Iroquois nation as a whole)—though they had not even fought the Iroquois. Social disorder of enormous magnitude ensued. Handsome Lake, a Seneca prophet, received a series of visions that were to help his people accommodate to the whiteman. The central relationship of mother-daughter was thus destroyed, for Handsome Lake decreed that a woman should cleave to her husband and they should share a dwelling separate from her mother's (clan) longhouse.[5]

Among American Indians, Spirit-related persons are perceived as more closely linked than blood-related persons. Understanding this primary difference between American Indian values and modern Euro-American Judeo-Christian values is critical to understanding Indian familial structures and the context in which Lesbians functioned. For American Indian people, the primary value was relationship to the Spirit world. All else was determined by the essential nature of this understanding. Spirits, gods and goddesses, metaphysical/occult forces, and the right means of relating to them, determined the tribes' every institution, every custom, every endeavor and pastime. This was not peculiar to inhabitants of the Western Hemisphere, incidentally; it was at one time the primary value of all tribal people on earth.

Relationship to the Spirit world has been of primary value to tribespeople, but not to those who have studied them. Folklorists and ethnographers have other values which permeate their work and their understandings, so that most of what they have recorded or concluded about American Indians is simply wrong. Countless examples could illustrate this basic misunderstanding, but let me share just one, culled from the work of one of the more influential anthropologists, Bronislaw Malinowski. His massive study of the Keres Pueblo Acoma presumably qualified him as an authority on mother-right society in North America. In *Sex, Culture and Myth* Malinowski wrote: "Patrilocal households are 'united households,' while 'split households' are the exclusive phenomena of matrilocal mother-right cultures."[6] While acknowledging that economic considerations alone do not determine the structure of marriage patterns, Malinowski fails to recognize marriage as a construct founded on laws derived from conversations with Spirits. The primary unit for a tribe is not, as he suggests, the household; even the term is misleading, because a tribal "household" includes a number of individuals who are clan rather than blood relatives. For non-tribal people, "household" typically means a unit composed of a father, mother, and offspring—though contemporary living arrangements often deviate from that stereotyped conception. A tribal household might encompass assorted blood-kin, medicine society "kin," adoptees, servants, and visitors who have a clan or supernatural claim on membership although they are biologically unrelated to the rest of the household. Writing about tribal societies in Oceania, Malinowski wrote: "Throughout Oceania a network of obligations unites the members of the community and overrules the economic autonomy of the household."[7] To a tribal person, the very notion of the household's autonomy appears to be nonsensical. To exemplify his view of tribal practices, Malinowski cites the Trobriand Islanders' requirement that a man give approximately half of his produce to his sister(s) and another portion to other relatives, thus using only the remainder for "his own household" which, Malinowski concedes, is largely supported by the wife's brother(s) and other relatives. I mention this example from a tribe which is not American Indian, because Malinowski himself encourages generalization: "Economic obligations," he continues, which "cut across the closed unity of the household could be quoted from every single tribe of which we have adequate information."[8]

Malinowski and other researchers have dismissed the household as an economic unit, but have continued to perceive households from the viewpoint of the nuclear family—father, mother(s), and offspring. He remains within the accepted, biased European understanding of "household" when he states:

> The most important examples [of split-households] come from the communities organised in extreme mother-right, where husband and wife are in most matters members of different households, and their mutual economic contributions show the character of gifts rather than of mutual maintenance.[9]

The case of matrifocal-matrilocal households only seems extreme when one defines "household" in terms that do not allow for various styles of bonding. Malinowski believes that this "extreme mother-right" method of housing people is exceptional. He does concede that it results from conditions found in high-level cultures, rather than in "primitive" ones[10] — which is an extremely interesting observation. But in making it, he again relies on some assumptions that are not justified by available evidence.

If "household" signifies housing and food-provision systems, then the living arrangements of American Indians pose numerous problems, the matter of father-right versus mother-right being only one. In fact, people were inclined to live wherever they found themselves, if living signifies where you stash your belongings, where you take your meals, and/or where you sleep. Throughout North America, men were inclined to have little personal paraphernalia, to eat wherever they were when meal-time came, and to sleep in whatever spot was convenient when they were tired. Clan, band, and medicine-society affiliations had a primary bearing on these arrangements, as did the across-the-board separation of the sexes practiced formally or informally by most tribes.

Malinowski's view assumes that households may take various forms, but that in any case they are unified to the extent that they may be spoken of as "mine" by a male who is husband to a woman and claims to be the father of her children. The "extreme" case of the "split household" occurs when a man who is identified as a woman's husband does not contribute to her economic life except by giving presents. This notion of "household" is pretty far from any held by tribal people with which I am familiar. Even among contemporary American Indians, a male who is identified as the husband of the lady of the house may not be (and often is not) the father of her children. But according to Malinowski, "The most important fact about such extreme matriarchal conditions [as among the Pueblo and several other groups cited] is that even there the principle of social legitimacy holds good; that though the father is domestically and economically almost superfluous, he is legally indispensible and the main bond of union between such matrilineal and matrilocal consorts is parenthood[sic]."[11]

Carefully examined, the foregoing observation makes no sense; even if it did, it suggests that even though fatherhood is irrelevant in the home or office, a male remains indispensible because his presence (which may be very infrequent) confers legitimacy on something. Indeed.

Analyses like those of Malinowski can only be explained by the distortive function of cultural bias. A Pueblo husband is important because husbands are important. But I have known many "husbands" who had several "wives" and could claim that a number of women (who might or might not be claimed as wives) were the mothers of their children. And this remains the case despite some two to five hundred years of Christian influence. As an old Laguna woman has said in reference to these matters in the long ago, "We were very careless about such things then."

Actually, the legitimacy of motherhood was determined by its very existence. A woman who gave birth was a mother as long as she had a living child, and the source of a household's legitimacy was its very existence. American Indians were and are very mystical, but they were and are a very practical people.

While there can be little question about the fact that most women married, perhaps several times, it is important to remember that tribal marriages bore little resemblance to Western concepts of that institution. Much that has been written about marriage as practiced among American Indians is wrong.

Among many tribes divorce was an easy matter for both women and men, and movement of individuals from one household to another was fluid and essentially unconstrained. There are many exceptions to this, for the tribes were distinct social groups; but many had patterns that did not use sexual contraint as a means of social control. Within such systems, individual action was believed to be directed by Spirits (through dreams, visions, direct encounter, or possession of power objects such as stones, shells, masks, or fetishes). In this context it is quite possible that Lesbianism was practiced rather commonly, as long as the individuals cooperated with the larger social customs. Women were generally constrained to have children, but in many tribes, child-bearing meant empowerment. It was the passport to maturity and inclusion in woman-culture. An important point is that women who did not have children because of constitutional, personal, or Spirit-directed disinclination had other ways to experience Spirit instruction and stabilization, and to exercise power.

"Family" did not mean what is usually meant by that term in the modern world. One's family might have been defined in biological terms as those to whom one was blood-kin. More often it was defined by other considerations; spiritual kinship was at least as important a factor as "blood." Membership in a certain clan related one to many people in very close ways, though the biological connection might be so distant as to be practically nonexistent. This facet of familial ordering has been much obscured by the presence of white Christian influence and its New Testament insistence that the term "family" refers to mother, father and children, and those others who are directly related to mother and father. In this construct, all persons who can point to common direct-line ancestors are in some sense related, though the individual's distance from that ancestor will determine the "degree" of relationship to other descendants of that ancestor.

Among many American Indians, family is a matter of clan membership. If clan membership is determined by your mother, and if your father has a number of wives, you are not related to the children of his other wives unless they themselves happen to be related to your mother. So half-siblings in the white way might be unrelated in an Indian way. Or in some tribes, the children of your mother's sister might be considered siblings, while those of your father's brother would be the equivalent of cousins. These distinctions should demonstrate that the concept of *family* can mean something very different to an Indian than it does to a non-Indian.

A unified household is one in which the relationships among women and their descendants and sisters are ordered. A split household is one in which this is not the case. A community, then, is an ordering of sister-relationships which determine who can depend on whom for what. Male relationships are ordered in accordance with the maternal principle; a male's spiritual and economic placement and the attendant responsibilities are determined by his membership in the community of sisterhood. A new acquaintance in town might be asked, "Who is your mother?" The answer identifies the person and determines the ensuing relationship between the questioner and the newcomer.

Again, community in the non-Indian modern world tends to mean people who occupy a definable geographical area and/or who share a culture (life-style) or occupation. It can extend to mean people who share an important common interest—political, avocational, or spiritual. But "community" in the American Indian world can mean those who are of a similar clan and Spirit; those who are encompassed by a particular Spirit-being are members of a community. In fact, this was the meaning most often given to the concept in traditional tribal cultures. So it was not impossible that members of a community could have been a number of women who "belonged" to a given medicine society, or who were alike in that they shared consciousness of a certain Spirit.

III. Women and Power

Any discussion of the status of women in general, and of Lesbians in particular, cannot hope for accuracy if one misunderstands women's power in tribal societies. It is clear, I think, that the ground we are here exploring is obscure: women in general have not been taken seriously by ethnographers or folklorists, and what explorations have been done have been distorted by the preconceptions foisted on us by a patriarchal world-view, in which Lesbians are said not to exist, and women are perceived as oppressed, burdened, and powerless.

In her discussion of the "universal" devaluation of women, Sherry Ortner, for example, cites the Crow, a matrilineal American Indian tribe which placed women rather highly in their culture. Ortner points to the fact that Crow women were nevertheless required to ride "inferior" horses during menstruation, and were prohibited from participating in ceremonies during their periods. She cites anthropologist Robert Lowie who reported that Crow women were forbidden to open one particular medicine bundle which "took precedence not only of other dolls but of all other Crow medicines whatsoever."[12] Ortner marshalls this and other impressive evidence to support her claim that Crow women were believed to be inferior to men. But I suspect that the vital question is not whether women have been universally devalued, but when and how and why this came about. I further suspect that this devaluation has resulted from the power which women are perceived to have, and that evidence supporting this contention is at least as massive as the evidence of our ignominy.

Ortner again cites Lowie, who wrote: "Women. . . [during menstruation] formerly rode inferior horses and evidently this loomed as a source of contamination, for they were not allowed to approach either a wounded man or men starting on a war party."[13] Ortner continues in this vein, concluding that women are devalued even among the matrilineal Crow, because menstruation is seen as "a threat to warfare, one of the most valued institutions of the tribe, one that is central to their self-definition. . . ."[14]

Ortner apparently follows Lowie in assuming that menstruation was perceived as dirty and contaminating by tribal people, and that they saw it in the same light in which it was viewed by patriarchal peoples. Thus, she concludes that the Crow prohibited women at prescribed times from certain activities because of a belief that menstruation is unclean. The truth of the matter is quite different. Tribal people view menstruation as a "medicine" of such power that it can cause the death of certain people, i.e., men on the eve of combat.

Menstruating (or any other) Crow women do not go near a particularly sacred medicine bundle, and menstruating women are not allowed among warriors getting ready for battle, or those who have been wounded, because women are perceived to be possessed of a singular power, most vital during menstruation, puberty, and pregnancy, that weakens men's powers—physical, spiritual, or magical. The Crow and other American Indians do not perceive signs of womanness as contamination; rather they view them as so powerful that other "medicines" may be cancelled by the very presence of that power.

The Oglala Holy Man John Lame Deer has commented that the Oglalas do not view menstruation, which they call *isnati* (dwelling alone), as "something unclean or to be ashamed of." Rather it was something sacred; a girl's first period was greeted by celebration. "But," he continues, "we thought that menstruation had a strange power that could bring harm under some circumstances. This power could work in some cases against the girl, in other cases against somebody else. . . ."[15]

Lois Paul has found similar notions in the context of a peasant culture. In her essay "Work and Sex in a Guatemalan Village," she discusses the power that menstruation, pregnancy and menarche are believed to possess. She notes the belief of the peasant Pedranos (in Guatemala) that menstruating women can seriously impair a man's health, or even kill him by stepping over him or putting menstrual blood in his food.[16]

Power, among tribal people, is not perceived as political or economic, though status and material possessions can and often do derive from it. Power is conceived of as being supernatural and paranormal. It is a matter of spirit, involvement, and destiny. Woman's power comes automatically, hers by virtue of her femaleness, her natural and necessary fecundity, and her personal acquaintance with blood. The Arapaho felt that dying in war and dying in childbirth were of the same level of spiritual accomplishment. In fact, there are suggestions in the literature on ritualism and tribal ceremony that warriors and male initiates into medicine societies gain their supernatural powers by imitating ritually the processes that women undergo naturally.

The power of women can only be controlled and directed by other women, who necessarily possess equal power. A woman who is older is more cognizant of what that power entails, the kinds of destruction it can cause, and the ways in which it can be directed and used for good. Thus, adolescent women are placed under the care of older women, and are trained in manners and customs of modesty so that their powers will not result in harm to themselves or the larger community. Usually, a woman who has borne a child becomes an initiate into the mysteries of womanhood, and if she develops virtues and abilities beyond those automatically conferred on her by her nature, she becomes a medicine woman. Often, the medicine woman knows of her destiny in early childhood; such children are watched very carefully so that they will be able to develop in the way ordained for them by the Spirits. Often these children are identified by excessive "sickliness," which leads them to be more reflective than other children and which often necessitates the added vigilance of adults around them.

Eventually, these people will enter into their true profession. How and when they do so will vary tribe by tribe, but they will probably be well into their maturity before they will be able to practice. The Spirit or Spirits who teach and guide them in their medicine work will not appear for them until they have stabilized. Their health will usually improve, and their hormone-enzyme fluctuations will be regularized. Very often this stabilization will occur in the process of childbearing and nursing, and this is one reason why women usually are not fully accepted as part of the woman's community until after the birth of a first child. Maternity was a concept that went far beyond the simple biological sense of the word. It was the prepotent power, the basic right to control and distribute goods because it was the primary means of producing them. And it was the perfect sign of right spirit-human relationship. Among some modern American Indians this principle is still accepted. The Keres, for example, still recognize the Deity as female, and She is known as Thought Woman, for it is understood that the primary creative force is Thought.

As Leslie Silko of Laguna put it in opening her novel *Ceremony:*

> Ts'its'tse'nako, Thought-Woman,
>
> is sitting in her room
>
> and whatever she thinks about
>
> appears.

She thought of her sisters,
Nau'ts'ity'i and I'tcts'ity'i,
and together they created the Universe
this world
and the four worlds below.

Thought-Woman, the spider,
named things
and as she named them
they appeared.[17]

Women have great power that is unique to them. This power must be carefully controlled lest it upset the tribal applecart. This concept concerning the supernatural power of women has undergone changes since contact. At Zuni and Hopi, for example, the Deity, who was once perceived as female, has been seen as male in recent times, having passed through a phase of androgyny.[18] The Deity at Laguna, Ts'its'tsi'nako, Thought Woman, has two "descendants" or "sisters," Nau'ts'ity and I'tcts'ity'i. Somewhere along in the Myth of Creation, I'tcts'ity'i, referred to as "she," is suddenly referred to as "he." An interesting parallel occurs within the Pueblo religious structure, where the Cacique/Hochin is (or are) always referred to as *yaya,* mother, though a male always holds these positions. Yet the title derives from Iyetico, Beautiful Corn Woman, who is our mother. Iyetico returned to *Shipap* because of the men's disobedience. She didn't exactly abandon her children, but she removed herself from their presence, leaving with them her symbol and link, *lariku,* "corn mother," and the protection of the *cacique.* At least, that's how the current story goes. One suspects that Iyetico didn't leave–that she was abandoned. The men's disobedience led to some disastrous consequences; perhaps the most disastrous (and least talked about) consequence was the increase in violence toward Keres women as the Keres tribes have moved from the rule of Iyetico to the patriarchy.

IV. Lesbians in Tribal Life

Lesbianism and homosexuality were probably commonplace among the old Indians. But the word Lesbian, when applied to traditional Indian culture, does not have the same meanings that it conveys today. The concepts are so dissimilar as to make ludicrous attempts to relate the long-ago women who dealt exclusively with women on sexual-emotional and spiritual bases to modern women who have in common an erotic attraction for other women.

This is not to make light of the modern Lesbian, but rather to convey some sense of the enormity of the cultural gulf that we must confront and come to terms with when examining any phenomenon related to the American Indian. The modern Lesbian sees herself as distinct from "society." She may be prone to believe herself somehow out of sync with "normal" women, and often suffers great anguish at perceived differences. And while many modern Lesbians have come to see themselves as singular but not sick, many of us are not that secure in our self-assessment. Certainly, however we come to terms with our sexuality, we are not in the position of our American Indian fore-sister who could find safety and security in her bond with another woman because it was perceived to be destined and nurtured by non-human entities, and was therefore acceptable and respectable (albeit, perhaps terrifying) to others in her tribe.

Simple reason dictates that Lesbians did exist in tribal cultures, for they exist now. Because they were tribal people, the terms on which they existed must have been suited to the terms of tribal existence. And women were not perceived to be powerless; their power was great and was perceived to be great by women and men.

Spheres of influence and activity in American Indian cultures were largely divided between the sexes: there were women—goddesses, mothers, sisters, grandmothers, aunties, shamans, healers, prophets and daughters; and there were men—gods, fathers, uncles, shamans, healers, diviners, brothers, sons. What went on in one group was often unknown to the other.

There were points of confluence, of course, such as in matters pertaining to mundane survival; family-band-clan groups interacted in living arrangements, in the procural or production of food, weaponry, clothing, and living space, and in political function. Men and women got together at certain times to perform social and ceremonial rituals, or to undertake massive tasks such as hunts, harvests, or wars. There were certain reciprocal tasks they performed for one another. But in terms of any real sense of community, there were women and there were men.

In such circumstances, Lesbianism and homosexuality were

probably commonplace. Indeed, same-sex relationships may have been the norm for primary pair-bonding. Families did not consist of traditional nuclear units in any sense. There were clans and bands or villages, but the primary personal unit tended to include members of one's own sex rather than members of the opposite sex.

Women spent a great deal of time together, outside the company of men. Together they spent weeks in menstrual huts; together women tilled their fields, harvested wild foods and herbs, ground grains, prepared skins, smoked or dried foodstuffs, and just visited. Women spent long periods together in their homes and lodges while the men stayed in mens' houses or in the woods, or were out on hunting or fishing expeditions. Young women were often separated from the larger groups for periods of months or years, as were young men. It seems likely that a certain amount of sexual activity ensued. It is questionable whether these practices would be identified as Lesbian by the politically radical Lesbian community of today; for while sex between women probably occurred regularly, women also regularly married and raised children—often adopting children if they did not have any. There were exceptions to this rule. The Objibway, for example, recorded several examples of women who lived alone by choice. These women are not said to have lived with other women; they lived alone, maintaining themselves and shunning human society.

The women who shared their lives with women did, as a matter of course, follow the usual custom of marrying. The duration of marriage and the bonding style of marriage differed among tribes. Many peoples practiced serial monogamy; others acknowledged the marriage bond but engaged in sexual activities outside of it. Adultery was not a generally recognized concept in American Indian cultures, although some tribes did punish severely a woman who "transgressed" the marriage bond. Among many tribes paternity was not very important; one was identified by the identity of the mother and her clan. This practice was widespread in North America at the time of contact and today persists in many regions, including the southwestern United States.

Because traditional American Indian women spent the preponderance of their time with women, and because attitudes toward sex were very different from modern Western views, it is likely, in my opinion, that Lesbianism was an integral part of American Indian life. This seems reasonable given the fact that Lesbianism is a widespread practice even in cultures which have more rigid notions about "appropriate" sexual and bonding behavior. However, relationships among women did not depend only on opportunity. Lesbianism must be viewed in the context of the spiritual orientation of tribal life.

The prototypical relationship in this sphere was that of sister to sister. Silko makes this apparent in her account of Indian myth: Ts'its'tsi'nako, Thought Woman, thought of her sisters, and together they created the Universe, this world and the four worlds below. This concept posits that the original household, the proto-community, was founded on sisterhood. It was based on the power of Creative Thought, and it was that Thought—of three sisters, united—which gave rise to all creation.

It may be possible to distinguish between those women who took advantage of the abundant opportunities to form erotic bonds with other women, and those women whose relationships with women were as much a matter of Spirit-direction as of personal preference (though the two were one in some senses).

It might be that some American Indian women could be seen as "dykes," while some could be seen as "Lesbians," if you think of "dyke" as one who bonds with women in order to further some Spirit and supernatural directive, and "Lesbian" as a woman who is emotionally and physically intimate with other women. (The two groups would not have been mutually exclusive.)

The "dyke" (we might also call her a "ceremonial Lesbian") was likely to have been a medicine woman in a special sense. She probably was a participant in the Spirit (intelligence, force-field) of an Entity or Deity who was particularly close to earth during the Goddess period (though that Deity is still present in the lives of some American Indian women who practice Her ceremonies and participate actively and knowingly in Her reality). Signs of this Deity remain scattered all over the continent: Snake Mound in Ohio is probably one such holdover. La Virgin de Guadalupe is another. There are all sorts of petroglyphs, edifices, and stories concerning some aspect of Her, and Her signs are preserved in much of the lore and literature of many tribes.

American Indian tradition holds that one who is chosen/directed by the Spirits for a particular task must carry out that task. Whoever does not do so is subject to physical and/or psychological destruction. This is not, by the way, because Spirits are naturally vindictive, but rather because it is the nature of supernatural/paranormal power to act; if it is denied proper expression, it will express inappropriately, and this might (and often does) result in dire events to the chosen one, her loved ones and/or her people.

Essentially, the way is dependent on the kind of power the woman possesses, the kind of Spirit to whom she is attached, and the tribe to which she belongs. Her initiation will take the course that that of males takes: she will be required to pass grueling physical tests; she will be required to lose her mundane persona and transform her soul and mind into other forms. She will be required to follow the lead of Spirits and to carry out the tasks they assign her. For a description of one such rite, Fr. Bernard Haile's translation and notes on the Navajo Beautyway/Nightchant is instructive. Such stories abound in the lore and literature of the American Indian people.[19] They all point to a serious event which results in the death of the protagonist, her visit to the Spirit realms from which she finally returns, transformed and powerful. After such events, she no longer belongs to her tribe or family, but to the Spirit teacher who instructed her. This makes her seem "strange" to many of her folk, and, indeed, she may be accused of witchcraft, though that is more likely to be charged at present than it was in days gone by. (I might note here that among American Indians men are often accused of the same thing. Tales of evil sorcerers abound; in fact, in my reading, they seriously outnumber the tales about sorceresses.)

The Lakota have a word for some of these women, *kǒskalaka,* which is translated as "young man," and "woman who doesn't want to marry." I would guess that its proper translation is "Lesbian" or, colloquially, "dyke." These women are said to be the daughters (the followers/practitioners) of *wiya numpa* or Doublewoman. Doublewoman is a Spirit/Divinity who links two women together making them one in Her power. They do a dance in which a rope is twined between them and coiled to form a "rope baby."[20] The exact purpose or result of this dance is not mentioned, but its significance is clear. In a culture that values children and women because they bear them, two women who don't want to marry (a man) become united by the power of *wiya numpa* and their union is validated ("legitimized," in Malinowski's sense) by the creation of a rope baby. That is, the rope baby signifies the potency of their union in terms that are comprehensible to their society, which therefore legitimizes it.

It is clear that the *kǒskalaka* are perceived as powerful, as are their presumed male counterparts, the *winkte.* But their power does not constitute the right "to determine her own and others' actions" as Jane Fishburne Collier defines the concept.[21] Rather, it consists of the ability to manipulate physical and non-physical reality toward certain ends. When this power is used to determine others' actions, it at least borders on "black magic" or sorcery.

To clarify the nature of the power I am talking about, let us look briefly at what Lame Deer has to say about the *winkte.* Lame Deer is inclined to speak rather directly, and tends not to romanticize either the concept of power as it is understood and practiced by his people, or the *winkte* as a person who has certain abilities that make him special.

He says that a *winkte* is a person who is a half-man and half-woman, perhaps even a hermaphrodite with both male and female organs. In the old days, *winktes* dressed like women and lived as women. Lame Deer admits that though the Lakotas thought people are what nature, or dreams, make them, still men weren't happy to see their sons running around with *winktes.* Still, he says that there are good men among the *winktes,* and that they have special powers. He took Richard Erdoes (who was transcribing his conversation for their book, *Lame Deer: Seeker of Visions*) with him to a bar to interview a *winkte.* He asked the man to tell him all about *winktes,* and the *winkte* told Lame Deer that "a *winkte* has a gift of prophecy and that he himself could predict the weather." The Lakota go to a *winkte* for a secret name, and such names carry great power, though they are often off-color. "You don't let a stranger know [the secret name]," he says. "He would kid you about it."[22] A *winkte*'s power to name often won the *winkte* great fame, and usually a fine gift as well.

The power referred to here is magical, mysterious and sacred. That does not mean that its possessors are to be regarded as a priestly-pious people, for this is hardly the case. But it does mean that those who possess "medicine power" are to be treated with a certain cautious respect.

It is interesting to note that the story—one of the few reliable accounts of persons whose sexual orientation differs from the heterosexual—concerns a male, a *winkte.* The stories about *kǒskalaka* are yet to be told. It seems to me that this suppression is a result of a series of coincidental factors: the historical events connected with the conquest of Native America; the influence of Christianity and the attendant brutal suppression of medicine people and medicine practices; the patriarchal suppression of all references to power held by women; Christian notions of "proper" sexual behavior; and, recently, a deliberate attempt on the part of American Indian men to suppress all knowledge among their own people of the traditional place of women as powerful medicine people and leaders in their own right. The medicine-Lesbian (to coin a term) has become anathema; her presence must remain hidden until all power she held has been totally blanketed by silence. It is to prevent what I believe to be a serious tragedy that this article is being written. We must not allow this conspiracy of silence to prevent us from discovering who we have been and who we are. We must not forget the true source of our being, nor its powerfulness, and we must not allow ourselves to be deluded by patriarchal perceptions of power which inexorably rob us of our true power. As Indian women, as Lesbians, we must make the effort to understand clearly what is at stake, and this means that we must reject all beliefs that work against ourselves, however much we have come to cherish them as we have lived among the patriarchs.

V. Conclusion

Womanculture is unregulated by males, and is misperceived by ethnographers. Perhaps this is so because it is felt—at least among ethnographers' tribal informants—that it is wise to let "sleeping dogs lie." There may also be fear of what power might be unleashed if the facts about American Indian Lesbianism were discussed directly. A story that has recently come to my attention might best clarify this statement.

Two white Lesbians, feminists and social activists, were determined to expand their activities beyond the Lesbian and Feminist communities, and to this end became involved in an ecological movement that centered on American Indian concerns. In pursuit of this course, they invited a Sioux medicine man to join them, and arranged to pick him up from the small rural town he was visiting. When he saw them, he accused them of being Lesbians, and became very angry. He abused them verbally, in serious and obscene terms. They left him where he was and returned home, angry and confused.

A certain amount of their confusion was a result of their misperception of Indians and of this particular medicine man. I have friends in the primarily white Lesbian community who seem to think that Indian men, particularly medicine men, are a breed apart who are "naturally just." Like other Americans, Indians are inclined to act in ways that are consistent with their picture of the world, and, in this particular Indian's picture, the world was not big enough for Lesbians. The women didn't announce their sexual preference to him, by the way; but he knew a *kǒskalaka* when he saw one, and reacted accordingly.

A friend who knew the women involved asked me about this encounter. She couldn't understand why the medicine man acted the way he had. I suspect that he was afraid of the Lesbian's power, and I told her that. An American Indian woman to whom I recounted the story had the same reaction. *Kǒskalaka* have singular power, and this medicine man was undoubtedly aware of it. The power of the *koskalaka* can (potentially, at least) override that of men, even very powerful medicine men such as the one in my story. I know this particular man, and he is quite powerful as a medicine man.

Not so long ago, the American Indians were clearly aware of the power that women possessed. Even now there are those among traditionals (those who follow the old ways) who know the medicine power of women. This is why a clear understanding of the supernatural forces and their potential in our lives is necessary. More than an interesting tour through primitive exotica is to be gained.

Before we worry about collecting more material from aborigines, before we join forces with those who are in a position to destroy us, and before we decide, like Sherry Ortner, that belief in ancient matriarchal civilization is an irrational concept born of conjecture and wish, let us adjust our perspective to match that of our foresisters. Then, when we search the memories and lore of tribal peoples, we might be able to see what eons and all kinds of institutions have conspired to hide from our eyes.

The evidence is all around us. It remains for us to *dis*cover what it means.

NOTES

[1] I use the term American Indian, rather than Native American. While Native American was the usage introduced on college campuses in the Sixties and Seventies, American Indian is the preferred term of Indian communities and organizations.

[2] Jonathan Katz, in *Gay American History* (New York: Crowell, 1976), included a chapter on "Native Americans/Gay Americans, 1528-1976"

(pp. 281-334). Fourteen entries in that chapter relate to women. Several of these refer to Indian women who dressed in male clothing. Others cite studies or accounts of the Kutenai Indians (Claude E. Schaeffer, 1811), the Mohave (George Devereux, 18??), the Crow (Edwin T. Denig, 1855-56), the Klamath (Leslie Spier, 1930), the Yuma (C. Daryll Forde, 1931), and the Kaska (J.J. Honigmann, 1964) which document or suggest the existence of Lesbian relationships. Other entries cite Indian legends involving Lesbian relationships.

[3] Frederick Manfred, *The Manly-Hearted Woman* (New York: Bantam, 1978).

[4] Hamilton A. Tyler, *Pueblo Gods and Myths* (Norman: University of Oklahoma Press, 1964), pp. 116-124.

[5] For a detailed discussion of this, see Anthony Wallace, *The Life and Death of the Seneca* (New York: 1969), and "The Law of the Great Peace of the People of the Longhouse [Iroquois]" and "Now This Is Gaiwiio," in *Literature of the American Indian*, Thomas Sanders and Walter Peek, eds. (New York: Glencoe Press, 1973).

[6] Bronislaw Malinowski, *Sex, Culture, and Myth* (New York: Harcourt, Brace & World, Inc., 1962), p. 12.

[7] Malinowski, p. 12.

[8] Malinowski, p. 12.

[9] Malinowski, p. 13.

[10] Malinowski, p. 13.

[11] Malinowski, p. 13.

[12] Sherry B. Ortner, "Is Female to Male as Nature Is to Culture," in *Woman, Culture and Society*, Michelle Zimbalist Rosaldo and Louise Lamphere, eds. (Stanford: Stanford University Press, 1974), pp. 65-71.

[13] Ortner, p. 70.

[14] Ortner, p. 70.

[15] John (Fire) Lame Deer and Richard Erdoes, *Lame Deer, Seeker of Visions: The Life of a Sioux Medicine Man* (New York: Simon and Schuster, Touchstone Books, 1972), pp. 148-149.

[16] Lois Paul, "Work and Sex in a Guatemalan Village," in Rosaldo and Lamphere, pp. 293-298. Paul's article discusses these concepts in a peasant culture, that is, one which exists in an agricultural, pastoral environment, and whose social structure is based on perceived relationship to the land. This type of culture occupies a niche which might be thought of as halfway between industrial, urban people and tribal, Spirit-centered people.

[17] Leslie Marmon Silko, *Ceremony* (New York: Viking Press, 1977), p. 1.

[18] Anthony Purley, "Keres Pueblo Concepts of Deity," *American Indian Culture and Research Journal* (Los Angeles: University of California, 1974, I:1), pp. 28-30.

[19] See John Bierhorst, ed., *Four Masterworks of American Indian Literature: Quetzal coatl/The Ritual of Condolence/Cuceb/The Night Chant* (New York: Farrar, Straus and Giroux, 1974). Fr. Haile's work is included in Leland C. Wyman, ed., *Beautyway: A Navajo Ceremonial* (New York: Bollingen Series LIII-Pantheon Books, 1975).

[20] Elaine A. Jahner and J. DeMollie, *Lakota Belief and Ritual,* Part III, "Narratives" (Lincoln: University of Nebraska Press, 1980).

[21] Jane Fishburne Collier, "Women in Politics," in Rosaldo and Lamphere, p. 90.

[22] Lame Deer, p. 150.

[23] Joan Bamberger, "The Myths of Matriarchy: Why Men Rule in Primitive Society," in Rosaldo and Lamphere, pp. 260-271.

Sexuality and Gender in Certain Native American Tribes: The Case of Cross-Gender Females

Evelyn Blackwood

Ideological concepts of gender and sexuality arise from cultural constructions and vary from culture to culture. The female cross-gender role in certain Native American tribes constituted an opportunity for women to assume the male role permanently and to marry women.[1] Its existence challenges Western assumptions about gender roles. Some feminist anthropologists assume that it is in the nature of sex and gender systems to create asymmetry in the form of male dominance and female subservience and to enforce corresponding forms of sexual behavior.[2] Because kinship and marriage are closely tied to gender systems, these social structures are implicated in the subordination of women. The existence

I am particularly grateful to Naomi Katz, Mina Caulfield, and Carolyn Clark for their encouragement, support, and suggestions during the development of this article. I would also like to thank Gilbert Herdt, Paula Gunn Allen, Sue-Ellen Jacobs, Walter Williams, Luis Kemnitzer, and Ruby Rohrlich for their insightful comments on an earlier version.

1. The term "berdache" is the more common term associated with the cross-gender role. It was originally applied by Europeans to Native American men who assumed the female role, and was derived from the Arabic *bardaj*, meaning a boy slave kept for sexual purposes. I prefer the term "cross-gender," first used by J. M. Carrier, particularly for the female role. See J. M. Carrier, "Homosexual Behavior in Cross-Cultural Perspective," in *Homosexual Behavior: A Modern Reappraisal*, ed. Judd Marmor (New York: Basic Books, 1980), pp. 100–122.

2. Sherry B. Ortner and Harriet Whitehead, eds., *Sexual Meanings: The Cultural Construction of Gender and Sexuality* (Cambridge: Cambridge University Press, 1981); Gayle Rubin, "The Traffic in Women: Notes on the 'Political Economy' of Sex," in *Toward an Anthropology of Women*, ed. Rayna R. Reiter (New York: Monthly Review Press, 1975), pp. 157–210.

[*Signs: Journal of Women in Culture and Society* 1984, vol. 10, no. 1] of the female cross-gender role, however, points to the inadequacies of such a view and helps to clarify the nature of sex and gender systems.

This study closely examines the female cross-gender role as it existed historically in several Native American tribes, primarily in western North America and the Plains. It focuses on western tribes that shared a basically egalitarian mode of production in precolonial times,[3] and for which sufficient data on the female role exist. Although there were cultural differences among these groups, prior to the colonial period they all had subsistence-level economies that had not developed significant forms of wealth or rank. These tribes include the Kaska of the Yukon Territory, the Klamath of southern Oregon, and the Mohave, Maricopa, and Cocopa of the Colorado River area in the Southwest. The Plains tribes, by contrast, are noteworthy for the relative absence of the female cross-gender role. Conditions affecting the tribes of the Plains varied from those of the western tribes, and thus analysis of historical-cultural contexts will serve to illuminate the differing constraints on sex and gender systems in these two areas.

Ethnographic literature has perpetuated some misconceptions about the cross-gender role. Informants frequently describe the institution in negative terms, stating that berdache were despised and ridiculed. But ethnographers collected much of the data in this century; it is based on informants' memories of the mid- to late 1800s. During this period the cross-gender institution was disappearing rapidly. Thus, twentieth-century informants do not accurately represent the institution in the precontact period. Alfred Kroeber found that "while the [berdache] institution was in full bloom, the Caucasian attitude was one of repugnance and condemnation. This attitude . . . made subsequent personality inquiry difficult, the later berdache leading repressed or disguised lives."[4] Informants' statements to later ethnographers or hostile white officials were far different from the actual attitude toward the role that prevailed in the precolonial period. An analysis of the cross-gender role in its

3. Much feminist debate has focused on whether male dominance is universal, or whether societies with egalitarian relations exist. For a more comprehensive discussion of egalitarian societies, see Mina Davis Caulfield, "Equality, Sex and Mode of Production," in *Social Inequality: Comparative and Developmental Approaches*, ed. Gerald D. Berreman (New York: Academic Press, 1981), pp. 201–19; Mona Etienne and Eleanor Leacock, eds., *Women and Colonization: Anthropological Perspectives* (New York: J. F. Bergin, 1980); Eleanor Burke Leacock, *Myths of Male Dominance: Collected Articles on Women Cross-Culturally* (New York: Monthly Review Press, 1981); Karen Sacks, *Sisters and Wives: The Past and Future of Sexual Inequality* (Westport, Conn.: Greenwood Press, 1979); Rayna R. Reiter, ed., *Toward an Anthropology of Women* (New York: Monthly Review Press, 1975); and Eleanor Burke Leacock and Nancy O. Lurie, eds., *North American Indians in Historical Perspective* (New York: Random House, 1971).

4. Alfred L. Kroeber, "Psychosis or Social Sanction," *Character and Personality* 8, no. 3 (1940): 204–15, quote on p. 209.

proper historical context brings to light the integral nature of its relationship to the larger community.

Cultural Significance of the Female Cross-Gender Role

Most anthropological work on the cross-gender role has focused on the male berdache, with little recognition given to the female cross-gender role. Part of the problem has been the much smaller data base available for a study of the female role. Yet anthropologists have overlooked even the available data. This oversight has led to the current misconception that the cross-gender role was not feasible for women. Harriet Whitehead, in a comprehensive article on the berdache, states that, given the small number of cross-gender females, "the gender-crossed status was more fully instituted for males than for females."[5] Charles Callender and Lee Kochems, in a well-researched article, base their analysis of the role predominantly on the male berdache.[6] Evidence from thirty-three Native American tribes indicates that the cross-gender role for women was as viable an institution as was the male berdache role.[7]

The Native American cross-gender role confounded Western concepts of gender. Cross-gender individuals typically acted, sat, dressed, talked like, and did the work of the other sex. Early Western observers described the berdache as half male and half female, but such a description attests only to their inability to accept a male in a female role or vice versa. In the great majority of reported cases of berdache, they assumed the social role of the other sex, not of both sexes.[8] Contemporary theorists, such as Callender and Kochems and Whitehead, resist the idea of a complete social role reclassification because they equate gender with biological sex. Native gender categories contradict such definitions.

5. Harriet Whitehead, "The Bow and the Burden Strap: A New Look at Institutionalized Homosexuality in Native North America," in Ortner and Whitehead, eds. (n. 2 above), pp. 80–115, quote on p. 86.

6. Charles Callender and Lee M. Kochems, "The North American Berdache," *Current Anthropology* 24, no. 4 (1983): 443–56.

7. These tribes by area are as follows: Subarctic—Ingalik, Kaska; Northwest—Bella Coola, Haisla, Lillooet, Nootka, Okanagon, Queets, Quinault; California/Oregon—Achomawi, Atsugewi, Klamath, Shasta, Wintu, Wiyot, Yokuts, Yuki; Southwest—Apache, Cocopa, Maricopa, Mohave, Navajo, Papago, Pima, Yuma; Great Basin—Ute, Southern Ute, Shoshoni, Southern Paiute, Northern Paiute; Plains—Blackfoot, Crow, Kutenai.

8. See S. C. Simms, "Crow Indian Hermaphrodites," *American Anthropologist* 5, no. 3 (1903): 580–81; Alfred L. Kroeber, "The Arapaho," *American Museum of Natural History Bulletin* 18, no. 1 (1902): 1–150; Royal B. Hassrick, *The Sioux: Life and Customs of a Warrior Society* (Norman: University of Oklahoma Press, 1964); Ronald L. Olson, *The Quinault Indians* (Seattle: University of Washington Press, 1936); Ruth Murray Underhill, *Social Organization of the Papago Indians* (1939; reprint, New York: AMS Press, 1969).

Although the details of the cross-gender females' lives are scant in the ethnographic literature, a basic pattern emerges from the data on the western tribes. Recognition and cultural validation of the female cross-gender role varied slightly from tribe to tribe, although the social role was the same. Among the Southwestern tribes, dream experience was an important ritual aspect of life and provided success, leadership, and special skills for those who sought it. All cross-gender individuals in these tribes dreamed about their role change. The Mohave *hwame* dreamed of becoming cross-gender while still in the womb.[9] The Maricopa *kwiraxame* dreamed too much as a child and so changed her sex.[10] No information is available for the development of the female cross-gender role (*tw!nnaek*) among the Klamath. It was most likely similar to the male adolescent transformative experience, which was accomplished through fasting or diving.[11] Dreaming provided an avenue to special powers and also provided sanction for the use of those powers. In the same way, dreams about the cross-gender role provided impetus and community sanction for assumption of the role.

The female candidate for cross-gender status displayed an interest in the male role during childhood. A girl avoided learning female tasks. Instead, as in the case of the Cocopa *warrhameh*, she played with boys and made bows and arrows with which to hunt birds and rabbits.[12] The Mohave *hwame* "[threw] away their dolls and metates, and [refused] to shred bark or perform other feminine tasks."[13] Adults, acknowledging the interests of such girls, taught them the same skills the boys learned. Among the Kaska, a family that had all female children and desired a son to hunt for them would select a daughter (probably the one who showed the most inclination) to be "like a man." When she was five, the parents tied the dried ovaries of a bear to her belt to wear for life as protection against conception.[14] Though in different tribes the socializing processes varied, girls achieved the cross-gender role in each instance through accepted cultural channels.

Upon reaching puberty, the time when girls were considered ready for marriage, the cross-gender female was unable to fulfill her obligations

9. George Devereux, "Institutionalized Homosexuality of the Mohave Indians," *Human Biology* 9, no. 4 (1937): 498–527.

10. Leslie Spier, *Yuman Tribes of the Gila River* (Chicago: University of Chicago Press, 1933).

11. Leslie Spier, *Klamath Ethnography*, University of California Publications in American Archaeology and Ethnology, vol. 30 (Berkeley: University of California Press, 1930).

12. E. W. Gifford, *The Cocopa*, University of California Publications in American Archaeology and Ethnology, vol. 31, no. 5 (Berkeley: University of California Press, 1933).

13. Devereux (n. 9 above), p. 503.

14. John J. Honigmann, *The Kaska Indians: An Ethnographic Reconstruction*, Yale University Publications in Anthropology, no. 51 (New Haven, Conn.: Yale University Press, 1954), p. 130.

and duties as a woman in marriage, having learned the tasks assigned to men. Nonmarriageable status could have presented a disadvantage both to herself and to her kin, who would be called upon to support her in her later years. But a role transfer allowed her to enter the marriage market for a wife with whom she could establish a household. The Mohave publicly acknowledged the new status of the woman by performing an initiation ceremony. Following this ceremony she assumed a name befitting a person of the male sex and was given marriage rights.[15] At puberty, the Cocopa *warrhameh* dressed her hair in the male style and had her nose pierced like the men, instead of receiving a chin tattoo like other women.[16] These public rites validated the cross-gender identity, signifying to the community that the woman was to be treated as a man.

In adult life cross-gender females performed the duties of the male gender role. Their tasks included hunting, trapping, cultivating crops, and fighting in battles. For example, the Cocopa *warrhameh* established households like men and fought in battle.[17] The Kaska cross-gender female "dressed in masculine attire, did male allocated tasks, often developing great strength and usually becoming an outstanding hunter."[18] The Mohave *hwame* were known as excellent providers, hunting for meat, working in the fields, and caring for the children of their wives.[19] Cross-gender females also adhered to male ritual obligations. A Klamath *tw!nnaek* observed the usual mourning when her long-time female partner died, wearing a bark belt as did a man.[20] Mohave *hwame* were said to be powerful shamans, in this case especially good at curing venereal disease.[21] Many other cross-gender females were considered powerful spiritually, but most were not shamans, even in the Southwest. Cross-gender females did not bear children once they took up the male role. Their kin considered them nonreproductive and accepted the loss of their childbearing potential, placing a woman's individual interests and abilities above her value as a reproducer.[22]

In most cases ethnographers do not discuss the ability of cross-gender females to maintain the fiction of their maleness. Whitehead suggests that women were barred from crossing over unless they were, or at least pretended to be, deficient physically.[23] However, despite some reports that cross-gender women in the Southwest had muscular builds, unde-

15. Devereux (n. 9 above), pp. 508–9.
16. Gifford (n. 12 above).
17. Ibid., p. 294.
18. Honigmann (n. 14 above), p. 130.
19. Devereux (n. 9 above).
20. Spier, *Klamath Ethnography* (n. 11 above), p. 53.
21. Devereux (n. 9 above).
22. Ibid.; Gifford (n. 12 above); Honigmann (n. 14 above).
23. Whitehead (n. 5 above), pp. 92–93.

veloped secondary sexual characteristics, and sporadic or absent menstruation,[24] convincing physical evidence is noticeably lacking. In fact, the Mohave *hwame* kept a husband's taboos with regard to her menstruating or pregnant wife and ignored her own menses.[25] That such may have been the case in other tribes as well is borne out by the practice of the Ingalik cross-gender female. Among the Alaskan Ingalik, the *kashim* was the center of men's activities and the place for male-only sweat baths. The cross-gender female participated in the activities of the *kashim*, and the men were said not to perceive her true sex.[26] Cornelius Osgood suggests that she was able to hide her sex, but, as with the Mohave, the people probably ignored her physical sex in favor of her chosen role. Through this social fiction, then, cross-gender females dismissed the physiological functions of women and claimed an identity based on their performance of a social role.

Gender Equality

Women's ability to assume the cross-gender role arose from the particular conditions of kinship and gender in these tribes. The egalitarian relations of the sexes were predicated on the cooperation of autonomous individuals who had control of their productive activities. In these tribes women owned and distributed the articles they produced, and they had equal voice in matters affecting kin and community. Economic strategies depended on collective activity. Lineages or individuals had no formal authority; the whole group made decisions by consensus. People of both sexes could achieve positions of leadership through skill, wisdom, and spiritual power. Ultimately, neither women nor men had an inferior role but rather had power in those spheres of activity specific to their sex.[27]

24. C. Daryll Forde, *Ethnography of the Yuma Indians*, University of California Publications in American Archaeology and Ethnology, vol. 28, no. 4 (Berkeley: University of California Press, 1931), p. 157; Gifford (n. 12 above), p. 294; Devereux (n. 9 above), p. 510.

25. Devereux (n. 9 above), p. 515.

26. Cornelius Osgood, *Ingalik Social Culture*, Yale University Publications in Anthropology, no. 53 (New Haven, Conn.: Yale University Press, 1958).

27. Based on ethnographic data in Honigmann (n. 14 above); Gifford (n. 12 above); Leslie Spier, *Cultural Relations of the Gila and Colorado River Tribes*, Yale University Publications in Anthropology, no. 3 (New Haven, Conn.: Yale University Press, 1936), *Klamath Ethnography* (n. 11 above), and *Yuman Tribes* (n. 10 above); Theodore Stern, *The Klamath Tribe* (Seattle: University of Washington Press, 1966); Alfred L. Kroeber, *Mohave Indians: Report on Aboriginal Territory and Occupancy of the Mohave Tribe*, ed. David Horr (New York: Garland Publishing, 1974), and *Handbook of the Indians of California*, Bureau of American Ethnology Bulletin no. 78 (Washington, D.C.: Government Printing Office, 1925); William H. Kelly, *Cocopa Ethnography*, Anthropological Papers cf the University of Arizona, no. 29 (Tucson: University of Arizona Press, 1977); Lorraine M. Sherer, *The Clan System of the Fort Mohave Indians* (Los Angeles: Historical Society of Southern California, 1965).

Among these tribes, gender roles involved the performance of a particular set of duties. Most occupations necessary to the functioning of the group were defined as either male or female tasks. A typical division of labor allocated responsibilities for gathering, food preparation, child rearing, basket weaving, and making clothes to women, while men hunted, made weapons, and built canoes and houses. The allocation of separate tasks to each sex established a system of reciprocity that assured the interdependence of the sexes. Because neither set of tasks was valued more highly than the other, neither sex predominated.

Gender-assigned tasks overlapped considerably among these people. Many individuals engaged in activities that were also performed by the other sex without incurring disfavor. The small game and fish that Kaska and Klamath women hunted on a regular basis were an important contribution to the survival of the band. Some Klamath women made canoes, usually a man's task, and older men helped women with food preparation.[28] In the Colorado River area, both men and women collected tule pollen.[29] Engaging in such activities did not make a woman masculine or a man feminine because, although distinct spheres of male and female production existed, a wide range of tasks was acceptable for both sexes. Because there was no need to maintain gender inequalities, notions of power and prestige did not circumscribe the roles. Without strict gender definitions, it was then possible for some Native American women to take up the male role permanently without threatening the gender system.

Another factor in creating the possibility of the cross-gender role for women was the nature of the kinship system. Kinship was not based on hierarchical relations between men and women; it was organized in the interest of both sexes. Each sex had something to gain by forming kin ties through marriage,[30] because of the mutual assistance and economic security marital relations provided.[31] Marriage also created an alliance between two families, thereby broadening the network of kin on whom an individual could rely. Thus, marriage promoted security in a subsistence-level economy.

The marriage customs of these tribes reflected the egalitarian nature of their kinship system. Since status and property were unimportant, marriage arrangements did not involve any transfer of wealth or rank

28. Julie Cruikshank, *Athapaskan Women: Lives and Legends* (Ottawa: National Museums of Canada, 1979); Spier, *Klamath Ethnography* (n. 11 above).

29. Gifford (n. 12 above).

30. The five tribes discussed here varied in forms of kinship, but this variation did not have a significant effect on the relations between the sexes. Lacking rank or wealth, kinship groups were not the focus of power or authority, hence whether a tribe was matrilineal or patrilineal was not as important as the overall relationship with kin on either side.

31. John J. Honigmann, *Culture and Ethos of Kaska Society*, Yale University Publications in Anthropology, no. 40 (New Haven, Conn.: Yale University Press, 1949), and *Kaska Indians* (n. 14 above).

through the female. The small marriage gifts that were exchanged served as tokens of the woman's worth in the marriage relationship.[32] Furthermore, because of the unimportance of property or rank, individuals often had a series of marriages, rather than one permanent relationship; divorce was relatively easy and frequent for both women and men.[33] Marriages in these tribes became more permanent only when couples had children. Women were not forced to remain in a marriage, and either partner had the right to dissolve an unhappy or unproductive relationship.

This egalitarian kinship system had important ramifications for the cross-gender female. A daughter's marriage was not essential for maintenance of family rank; that is, a woman's family did not lose wealth if she abandoned her role as daughter. As a social male, she had marriage rights through which she could establish a household and contribute to the subsistence of the group. Additionally, because of the frequency of divorce, it was possible for a married cross-gender female to raise children. Evidence of cross-gender females caring for their wives' offspring is available only for the Mohave *hwame*. Women in other tribes, however, could also have brought children into a cross-gender marriage, since at least younger offspring typically went with the mother in a divorce.[34] A cross-gender woman might acquire children through marriage to a pregnant woman, or possibly through her wife's extramarital relationships with men. Cross-gender couples probably also adopted children, a practice common among heterosexual couples in many tribes.

Details from the Mohave help to illuminate the cross-gender parent/child relationship. The Mohave believed that the paternity of an unborn child changed if the pregnant woman had sex with another partner; thus, the cross-gender female claimed any child her wife might be carrying when they married. George Devereux states that such children retained the clan affiliation of the previous father.[35] But the clan structure of the Mohave was not strongly organized and possessed no formal authority or ceremonial functions.[36] The significant relationships were those developed through residence with kin. Thus, children raised in a cross-gender household established strong ties with those parents. The investment of parental care was reciprocated when these children became adults. In this way the cross-gender female remained a part of the network of kin through marriage.

32. Spier, *Klamath Ethnography* (n. 11 above); J. A. Teit, "Field Notes on the Tahltan and Kaska Indians: 1912–15," *Anthropologica* 3, no. 1 (1956): 39–171; Kroeber, *Handbook* (n. 27 above); Gifford (n. 12 above).

33. Kelly (n. 27 above); Spier, *Klamath Ethnography* (n. 11 above).

34. Kelly (n. 27 above).

35. Devereux (n. 9 above), p. 514.

36. Kelly (n. 27 above); Forde (n. 24 above).

Sexual Relations in the Cross-Gender Role

Sexual behavior was part of the relationship between cross-gender female and the women they married. Although the cross-gender female was a social male, Native Americans did not consider her sexual activity an imitation of heterosexual behavior. Her sexual behavior was recognized as lesbian—that is, as female homosexuality. The Mohave were aware of a range of sexual activities between the cross-gender female and her partner—activities that were possible only between two physiological females. Devereux recorded a Mohave term that referred specifically to the lesbian love-making of the *hwame* and her partner.[37] The Native American acceptance of lesbian behavior among cross-gender females did not depend on the presence of a male role-playing person; their acceptance derived instead from their concept of sexuality.

Native American beliefs about sexuality are reflected in the marriage system. Theorists such as Gayle Rubin have implicated marriage as one of the mechanisms that enforce and define women's sexuality. According to Rubin, the division of labor "can . . . be seen as a taboo against sexual arrangements other than those containing at least one man and one woman, thereby enjoining heterosexual marriage."[38] Yet in certain Native American tribes other sexual behavior, both heterosexual and homosexual, was available and permissible within and outside of marriage. Homosexual behavior occurred in contexts within which neither individual was cross-gender nor were such individuals seen as expressing cross-gender behavior.[39] Premarital and extramarital sexual relations were also permissible.[40] Furthermore, through the cross-gender role, women could marry one another. Sexuality clearly was not restricted by the institution of marriage.

Native American ideology disassociated sexual behavior from concepts of male and female gender roles and was not concerned with the identity of the sexual partner. The status of the cross-gender female's partner is telling in this respect. She was always a traditional female; that is, two cross-gender females did not marry. Thus, a woman could follow the traditional female gender role, yet marry and make love with another woman without being stigmatized by such behavior. Even though she was the partner of a cross-gender female, she was not considered homosexual or cross-gender. If the relationship ended in divorce, heterosexual marriage was still an option for the exwife. The traditional female gender role did not restrict her choice of marital/sexual partners. Consequently,

37. Devereux (n. 9 above), pp. 514–15.

38. Rubin (n. 2 above), p. 178.

39. See Forde (n. 24 above), p. 157; Honigmann, *Kaska Indians* (n. 14 above), p. 127.

40. Spier, *Klamath Ethnography* (n. 11 above), and *Yuman Tribes* (n. 10 above); Kroeber, *Handbook* (n. 27 above).

individuals possessed a gender identity, but not a corresponding sexual identity, and thus were allowed several sexual options. Sexuality itself was not embedded in Native American gender ideology.

Women on the Plains

The conditions that supported the development and continuation of the cross-gender role among certain western tribes were not replicated among the Plains tribes. Evidence of cross-gender females there is scant while reports of male berdache are numerous. Whitehead suggests that the absence of cross-gender females resulted from the weakness of the cross-gender institution for women.[41] A more plausible explanation involves the particular historical conditions that differentiate the Plains tribes from the western tribes. Yet it is precisely these conditions that make accurate interpretation of women's roles and the female cross-gender role much more difficult for the Plains tribes.

The Plains Indian culture of nomadic buffalo hunting and frequent warfare did not develop until the late eighteenth and early nineteenth centuries as tribes moved west in response to the expansion and development of colonial America. The new mode of life represented for many tribes a tremendous shift from an originally settled and horticultural or hunting and gathering life-style. With the introduction of the horse and gun, the growth of the fur trade, and pressure from westward-moving white settlers, tribes from the east and north were displaced onto the Plains in the late 1700s.[42] As the importance of hide trade with Euro-Americans increased in the early 1800s, it altered the mode of production among Plains tribes. Increased wealth and authority were accessible through trade and warfare. Individual males were able to achieve greater dominance while women's social and economic autonomy declined.[43] With the growing importance of hides for trade, men who were successful hunters required additional wives to handle the tanning. Their increasing loss of control in this productive sphere downgraded woman's status and tied her to marital demands. Recent work on the Plains tribes, however, indicates that this process was not consistent; women maintained a degree of autonomy and power not previously acknowledged.[44]

41. Whitehead (n. 5 above), p. 86.

42. Gene Weltfish, "The Plains Indians: Their Continuity in History and Their Indian Identity," in Leacock and Lurie, eds. (n. 3 above).

43. Leacock and Lurie, eds. (n. 3 above); Alan Klein, "The Political-Economy of Gender: A 19th Century Plains Indian Case Study," in *The Hidden Half: Studies of Plains Indian Women*, ed. Patricia Albers and Beatrice Medicine (Washington, D.C.: University Press of America, 1983), pp. 143–73.

44. See Albers and Medicine, eds.

Early ethnographic descriptions of Plains Indian women were based on a Western gender ideology that was contradicted by actual female behavior. Although traditional Plains culture valued quiet, productive, nonpromiscuous women, this was only one side of the coin. There was actually a variability in female roles that can only be attributed to women's continued autonomy. Beatrice Medicine provides an excellent discussion of the various roles open to women among the Blackfoot and Lakota. Such roles included the "manly-hearted woman," the "crazy woman" (who was sexually promiscuous), the Sun Dance woman, and the chief woman or favorite wife.[45] According to Ruth Landes, Lakota women served in tribal government and were sometimes appointed marshalls to handle problems among women. Most Plains tribes had women warriors who accompanied war parties for limited purposes on certain occasions, such as avenging the death of kin, and who received warrior honors for their deeds.[46] As Medicine states, "These varied role categories . . . suggest that the idealized behavior of women was not as rigidly defined and followed as has been supposed."[47]

The presence of a variety of socially approved roles also suggests that these were normative patterns of behavior for women that need not be construed as "contrary" to their gender role. Warrior women were not a counterpart of the male berdache, nor were they considered cross-gender.[48] Ethnographers' attributions of masculinity to such behavior seem to be a product of Western beliefs about the rigid dichotomization of gender roles and the nature of suitable pursuits for women. That men simply accepted females as warriors and were not threatened by such behavior contradicts the notion that such women were even temporarily assuming the male role.[49] The men's acceptance was based on recognition of the women warriors' capabilities as women.

There were individual Plains women in the nineteenth century whose behavior throughout their lives exemplified a cross-gender role. They did not always cross-dress, but, like Woman Chief of the Crow, neither did they participate in female activities. They took wives to handle their households and were highly successful in hunting and raiding activities. They were also considered very powerful. Of these women, the Kutenai cross-gender woman always dressed in male attire and was re-

45. Beatrice Medicine, " 'Warrior Women'—Sex Role Alternatives for Plains Indian Women," in Albers and Medicine, eds., pp. 267–80; see also Oscar Lewis, "Manly-Hearted Women among the North Piegan," *American Anthropologist* 43, no. 2 (1941): 173–87.

46. Ruth Landes, *The Mystic Lake Sioux* (Madison: University of Wisconsin Press, 1968).

47. Medicine, p. 272.

48. Sue-Ellen Jacobs, "The Berdache," in *Cultural Diversity and Homosexuality*, ed. Stephen Murray (New York: Irvington Press, in press); Medicine, p. 269.

49. On male acceptance of women warriors, see Landes.

nowned for her exploits as warrior and mediator and guide for white traders. Running Eagle of the Blackfoot lived as a warrior and married a young widow. Woman Chief became the head of her father's lodge when he died and achieved the third highest rank among the Crow. She took four wives.[50] Particularly since no records of earlier cross-gender women have been found, these few examples seem to constitute individual exceptions. What then was the status of the female cross-gender role among Plains tribes?

Part of the difficulty with answering this question stems from the nature of the data itself. Nineteenth-century observers rarely recorded information on Plains Indian women, "considering them too insignificant to merit special treatment."[51] These observers knew few women and only the more successful males. "Those who did become known were women who had acted as go-betweens for the whites and Indians,"[52] such as the Kutenai cross-gender female. Running Eagle and Woman Chief were also exceptional enough to be noticed by white traders. Except for the Kutenai woman, none of the women are identified as berdache in nineteenth-century reports, although all were cross-gender. Observers seem to have been unable to recognize the female cross-gender role. Indeed, no nineteenth-century reports mention cross-gender females among even the western tribes, although later ethnographers found ample evidence of the role.

Ethnographers had no solid evidence of the female cross-gender role among Plains Indians. Several factors may help to explain this discrepancy. White contact with Plains tribes came earlier than with the western tribes and was more disruptive. The last cross-gender females seem to have disappeared among Plains tribes by the mid-nineteenth century, while in the Southwest this did not occur until the end of the century, much closer to the time when ethnographers began to collect data. Discrepancies also arise in informants' stories. The Kutenai denied the existence of cross-gender females among them, in contradiction with earlier evidence, and yet willingly claimed that such women lived among the Flathead and Blackfoot.[53] The Arapaho told Alfred Kroeber that the

50. Edwin Thompson Denig, *Of the Crow Nation*, ed. John C. Ewers, Smithsonian Institution, Bureau of American Ethnology, Bulletin no. 151, Anthropology Papers no. 33 (Washington, D.C.: Government Printing Office, 1953), and *Five Indian Tribes of the Upper Missouri*, ed. John C. Ewers (Norman: University of Oklahoma Press, 1961); Claude E. Schaeffer, "The Kutenai Female Berdache: Courier, Guide, Prophetess, and Warrior," *Ethnohistory* 12, no. 3 (1965): 193–236.

51. Patricia Albers, "Introduction: New Perspectives on Plains Indian Women," in Albers and Medicine, eds. (n. 43 above), pp. 1–26, quote on p. 3.

52. Katherine Weist, "Beasts of Burden and Menial Slaves: Nineteenth Century Observations of Northern Plains Indian Women," in Albers and Medicine, eds. (n. 43 above), pp. 29–52, quote on p. 39.

53. Harry H. Turney-High, *Ethnography of the Kutenai*, Memoirs of the American Anthropological Association, no. 56 (1941; reprint, New York: Kraus Reprint, 1969), and

Lakota had female berdache, but there is no corroborating evidence from the Lakota themselves.[54] Informants were clearly reticent or unwilling to discuss cross-gender women. In her article on Native American lesbians, Paula Gunn Allen suggests that such information was suppressed by the elders of the tribes.[55] Most information on Plains Indian women was transmitted from elder tribesmen to white male ethnographers. But men were excluded from knowledge of much of women's behavior;[56] in this way much of the data on cross-gender females may have been lost.

The record of Plains cross-gender females remains limited. Certain social conditions may have contributed to the small number of women who assumed the role in the nineteenth century. During the 1800s the practice of taking additional wives increased with the men's need for female labor. This phenomenon may have limited women's choice of occupation. The pressures to marry may have barred women from a role that required success in male tasks only. The practice of sororal polygyny particularly would have put subtle pressures on families to assure that each daughter learned the traditional female role. Indeed, there were said to be no unmarried women among the Lakota.[57] Furthermore, given the constant state of warfare and loss of able-bodied men, the tribes were under pressure merely to survive. Such conditions in the 1800s discouraged women from abandoning their reproductive abilities through the cross-gender role. In fact, among the Lakota, women who insisted on leading men's lives were ostracized from the group and forced to wander by themselves.[58] Knowledge of the female cross-gender role may have persisted, but those few who actually lived out the role were exceptions in a changing environment.

The Demise of the Cross-Gender Role

By the late nineteenth century the female cross-gender role had all but disappeared among Native Americans. Its final demise was related to a change in the construction of sexuality and gender in these tribes. The dominant ideology of Western culture, with its belief in the inferior

---

The Flathead Indians of Montana, Memoirs of the American Anthropological Association, no. 48 (1937; reprint, New York: Kraus Reprint, 1969).

54. Kroeber, "The Arapaho" (n. 8 above), p. 19.

55. Paula Gunn Allen, "Beloved Women: Lesbians in American Indian Cultures," *Conditions: Seven* 3, no. 1 (1981): 67–87.

56. Alice Kehoe, "The Shackles of Tradition," in Albers and Medicine, eds. (n. 43 above), pp. 53–73.

57. Hassrick (n. 8 above).

58. Jeannette Mirsky, "The Dakota," in *Cooperation and Competition among Primitive Peoples*, ed. Margaret Mead (Boston: Beacon Press, 1961), p. 417.

nature of the female role and its insistence on heterosexuality, began to replace traditional Native American gender systems.

Ideological pressures of white culture encouraged Native American peoples to reject the validity of the cross-gender role and to invoke notions of "proper" sexuality that supported men's possession of sexual rights to women. Communities expressed disapproval by berating the cross-gender female for not being a "real man" and not being properly equipped to satisfy her wife sexually. In effect, variations in sexual behavior that had previously been acceptable were now repudiated in favor of heterosexual practices. Furthermore, the identity of the sexual partner became an important aspect of sexual behavior.

The life of the last cross-gender female among the Mohave, Sahaykwisa, provides a clear example of this process. According to Devereux, "Sahaykwisa . . . was born toward the middle of the last century and killed . . . at the age of 45. Sahaykwisa had at a certain time a very pretty wife. Other men desired the woman and tried to lure her away from the *hwame*." The men teased Sahaykwisa in a derogatory manner, suggesting that her love-making was unsatisfactory to her wife in comparison to that of a "real man." They ridiculed her wife and said, "Why do you want a transvestite for your husband who has no penis and pokes you with the finger?"[59] Such derision went beyond usual joking behavior until finally Sahaykwisa was raped by a man who was angered because his wife left him for Sahaykwisa. The community no longer validated the cross-gender role, and Sahaykwisa herself eventually abandoned it, only to be killed later as a witch. By accusing the cross-gender female of sexual inadequacy, men of the tribe claimed in effect that they had sole rights to women's sexuality, and that sexuality was appropriate only between men and women.

Conclusion

In attempting to fit the Native American cross-gender role into Western categories, anthropologists have disregarded the ways in which the institution represents native categories of behavior. Western interpretations dichotomize the gender roles for each sex, which results from erroneous assumptions about, first, the connection between biology and gender, and, second, the nature of gender roles. Callender and Kochems state, "The transformation of a berdache was not a complete shift from his or her *biological* gender to the opposite one, but rather an approximation of the latter in some of its social aspects."[60] They imply that anatomy

59. Devereux (n. 9 above), p. 523.
60. Callender and Kochems (n. 6 above) p. 453 (italics mine).

circumscribed the berdache's ability to function in the gender role of the other sex. Whitehead finds the anatomical factor particularly telling for women, who were supposedly unable to succeed in the male role unless deficient physically as females.[61] These theorists, by claiming a mixed gender status for the berdache, confuse a social role with a physical identity that remained unchanged for the cross-gender individual.

Knowing the true sex of the berdache, Native Americans accepted them on the basis of their social attributes; physiological sex was not relevant to the gender role. The Mohave, for example, did not focus on the biological sex of the berdache. Nonberdache were said to "feel toward their possible transvestite mate as they would feel toward a true woman, [or] man."[62] In response to a newly initiated berdache, the Yuma "began to feel toward him as to a woman."[63] These tribes concurred in the social fiction of the cross-gender role despite the obvious physical differences, indicating the unimportance of biological sex to the gender role.[64]

Assumptions regarding the hierarchical nature of Native American gender relations have created serious problems in the analysis of the female cross-gender role. Whitehead claims that few females could have been cross-gender because she assumes the asymmetrical nature of gender relations.[65] In cultures with an egalitarian mode of production, however, gender does not create an imbalance between the sexes. In the western North American tribes discussed above, neither gender roles nor sexuality were associated with an ideology of male dominance. Women were not barred from the cross-gender role by rigid gender definitions; instead, they filled the role successfully. Although cross-gender roles are not limited to egalitarian societies, the historical conditions of nonegalitarian societies, in which increasing restrictions are placed on women's productive and reproductive activities, strongly discourage them from taking on the cross-gender role.

Anthropologists' classification of gender roles as dichotomous has served to obscure the nature of the Native American cross-gender role. For Whitehead, the male berdache is "less than a full man" but "more than a mere woman,"[66] suggesting a mixed gender role combining elements of both the male and the female. Similarly, Callender and Kochems

61. Whitehead (n. 5 above), p. 92.

62. Devereux (n. 9 above), p. 501.

63. Forde (n. 24 above), p. 157.

64. Data on the Navajo *nadle* are not included in this article because the Navajo conception of the berdache was atypical. The *nadle* was considered a hermaphrodite by the Navajo—i.e., of both sexes physically—and therefore did not actually exemplify a cross-gender role. See W. W. Hill, "The Status of the Hermaphrodite and Transvestite in Navaho Culture," *American Anthropologist* 37, no. 2 (1935): 273–79.

65. Whitehead (n. 5 above), p. 86.

66. Ibid., p. 89.

suggest that the berdache formed an intermediate gender status.[67] Native conceptualizations of gender, particularly in the egalitarian tribes, do not contain an invariable opposition of two roles. The Western ideology of feminine and masculine traits actually has little in common with these Native American gender systems, within which exist large areas of overlapping tasks.

The idea of a mixed gender role is particularly geared to the male berdache and assumes the existence of a limited traditional female role. Such a concept does not account for the wide range of behaviors possible for both the male and female gender roles. By contrast the term cross-gender defines the role as a set of behaviors typifying the attributes of the other sex, but not limited to an exact duplication of either role. Attributes of the male berdache that are not typical of the female role—for example, certain ritual activities—do not indicate a mixed gender category. These activities are specialized tasks that arise from the spiritual power of the cross-gender individual.

The term "cross-gender," however, is not without its problems. Sue-Ellen Jacobs suggests that a person who from birth or early childhood fills this variant role may not be "crossing" a gender boundary. She prefers the term "third gender" because, as among the Tewa, the berdache role may not fit either a male or female gender category but is conceived instead as another gender.[68] Kay Martin and Barbara Voorheis also explore the possibility of more than two genders.[69] Certainly the last word has not been spoken about a role that has confounded researchers for at least one hundred years. But it is imperative to develop an analysis of variant gender roles based on the historical conditions that faced particular tribes since gender systems vary in different cultures and change as modes of production change.

Department of Anthropology
San Francisco State University

67. Callender and Kochems (n. 6 above), p. 454.

68. Sue-Ellen Jacobs, personal communication, 1983, and "Comment on Callender and Kochems," *Current Anthropology* 24, no. 4 (1983): 459–60.

69. M. Kay Martin and Barbara Voorheis, *Female of the Species* (New York: Columbia University Press, 1975).

Cross-Cultural Codes on Twenty Sexual Attitudes and Practices[1]

Gwen J. Broude and Sarah J. Greene
Harvard University

The purpose of this article is to present a set of twenty codes measuring a variety of sexual attitudes and practices, along with ratings for each code on 200 societies. The codes were developed for a long-range study on styles of male-female attachment. The goals of the study have been to examine the patterning of opposite-sex relationships in cross-cultural perspective and to isolate any social structural or psychological antecedents that might help to explain variations in heterosexual relationships from one culture to the next. We have been testing hypotheses relating to these two goals and wished to make the full set of codes and ratings on sexual attitudes and practices, constructed in the course of our own work, available to other researchers who are interested in the cultural management of human sexuality. Our intent here, then, is to extend the body of cross-cultural data on sexual beliefs and behaviors rather than to propose any theories or test any hypotheses concerning the cultural handling of sexuality.

Sample

The codes appearing in this article were rated on Murdock's and White's (1969) Standard Cross-Cultural Sample. Among the reasons for using this sample are the following:

The Standard Sample consists of 186 societies, each of which represents a different and independent culture cluster within the major world areas. The sample was constructed with the specific aim of minimizing the problems of diffusion and historical contamination that have characterized other cross-cultural samples. For this reason, care was taken that the societies in the sample be geographically and linguistically unrelated.

The societies in the Standard Sample have also been defined in terms of both specific locality and ethnographic present. An exhaustive bibliography has been provided for the entire set of societies. All of this means that the researcher is relatively confident that different sets of codes using the Standard Sample will have been rated on the same population at more or less the same point in time.

Finally, a number of anthropologists have recently confined themselves to the Standard Sample in the rating of new sets of codes. Therefore, we wished to continue this trend of having a variety of codes rated on a single sample of societies.

SELECTION OF VARIABLES FOR CODING

The choice of specific sexual attitudes and practices to be coded was dictated by two considerations; the first being the goals of the research in which we were engaged, and the second being the state of the ethnographic data on sex.

In terms of the research aims, it was one of our intentions to explore the degree to which the patterning of sexual attitudes and practices is consistent within a society. That is, we wanted to determine whether or not societies tend to be generally permissive or restrictive, or generally secure or anxious in their management of sexuality in its many manifestations. The degree to which cultures exhibit regularity in the patterning of sexual beliefs and behaviors has been examined by other researchers, notably Brown (1952); Heise (1967); Minturn, Grosse, and Haider (1969); and Stephens (1972). These studies, however, confined themselves to a consideration of the relationships among a limited set of variables, and we hoped to be able to re-examine the issue of cultural consistency with an expanded and more representative set of sexual attitudes and practices. For this reason, it was our goal to construct as exhaustive a set of codes as possible within the limitations of what was available in the ethnographic literature.

It should be noted that a number of attitudes and practices for which we have constructed codes have also been rated in other cross-cultural work on sexuality. Minturn, Grosse, and Haider (1969) have published scales dealing with divorce, rape, and homosexuality; we have also focused on these variables. Attitudes toward premarital sex, which are also rated in the present article, have been coded by John T. Westbrook (Murdock 1963) and by George W. Goethals and John W. M. Whiting (Palfrey House n.d.). We decided to construct new codes for these variables for two reasons. First, the scales found in other studies were not rated on the Standard Sample, so that the ratings for those codes would have had to be augmented at a minimum. This would have introduced the problem of reliability, as we had some difficulty at times in understanding the underlying rationale for rating particular societies on some of these codes. In any event, we wished to make some modifications in the available scales to better suit our own interests and also to better reflect the data at hand. We, therefore, started from scratch in our construction of scales although we were in some ways duplicating the efforts of other researchers.

PROBLEMS WITH ETHNOGRAPHIC DATA

It was mentioned that the choice of variables to be coded and utilized in our research project was to some degree dictated by the state of the ethnographic literature. The process of code construction and rating is always difficult in cross-cultural research; however, studies dealing with sexual attitudes and practices face a special set of challenges. In the first place, information of any sort on sexual habits and beliefs is hard to come by, and is a result of a number of factors. The area, to begin with, is not conducive to participant-observation: interviews or questionnaires can clearly be awkward to conduct under certain circumstances; and the ethnographic reporting of sexual matters has not always been considered an appropriate undertaking. When data do exist concerning sexual attitudes and practices, they are often sketchy and vague; what is more, such information is usually suspect in terms of its reliability, either because of distortions on the part of the subjects or because of biases introduced by the ethnographer. Informants may exaggerate or understate regarding their sexual views and activities, depending upon dominant cultural values and also upon personal motives. The propensities of the anthropologist himself are sometimes more insidious. Some field workers are plainly uncomfortable about sexual matters. At the other extreme are the anthropologists whose frank admiration of sexual freedom overshadows their capacity to discern the jealousies and anxieties of the people themselves. And, to a greater extent than is true of other areas of social structure, personality, or behavior, many anthropologists simply neglect any mention of sexual customs because the reporting of such matters is not customary in the traditional ethnography.

The pecularities of the ethnographic data on sex, then, influenced the range and kinds of attitudes and practices which were coded, the form of the scales themselves, and also the procedure that was followed in the isolation of variables and code construction and rating.

CODE CONSTRUCTION AND RATING

Because of the special problems presented by cross-cultural data on sex, choice of specific attitudes and practices to be coded was preceded by a preliminary review of the ethnographic literature to determine what kinds of sexual beliefs and behaviors were described often enough and in enough detail to be useful for cross-cultural codes. We relied here, as in all subsequent data collection, on the bibliographies provided by researchers using the Standard Sample (Barry and Paxson 1971; Murdock and Morrow 1970; Murdock and Provost 1973; Murdock and White 1969). Supplementary data were also taken from the Human Relations Area Files. This initial survey of the ethnographic data generated a list of some 35 sexual attitudes and practices for which we felt that codes could be written and ratings obtained for a reasonable number of societies in our sample.

We then took verbatim notes on 50 Standard Sample societies for each of the 35 attitudes and practices which we had isolated. From these notes, we constructed a rough set of codes and independently rated the 50 societies on these scales. The codes were then revised on the basis of discussions concerning problems and disagreements encountered in the initial coding attempt. Codes were sometimes expanded to include more detailed discriminations and were sometimes collapsed because of the sketchiness of the data. Wording also had to be modified to reflect the realities represented in the ethnographic material. Verbatim notes were then taken for the remaining Standard Sample societies and these were rated on the revised set of codes. When codes still presented problems, they were further modified; in these cases, the whole sample was recoded on the final scale.

All societies were rated independently by the two authors on all codes. All ratings were checked for agreement between the two judges. Disagreements were discussed, each coder citing evidence in the verbatim notes that led to her rating. The final rating for each code on each society was a product either of initial agreement or of consensus between the two coders after discussion; if no consensus could be reached, the rating was omitted.

PROBLEMS WITH SPECIFIC CODES

While difficulties with specific codes were largely ironed out by revision of the scales themselves, a number of problems could not be resolved by modification of the scales because their origins rested in the data. The two most serious difficulties were identified with the "present-absent" scales and the frequency scales.

"Present-absent" codes always present the problem that, while the existence of a particular trait or behavior is relatively easy to determine, its absence is not. When a trait is not specifically designated by the ethnographer as absent, the coder either has to infer its absence or to omit any rating for the culture, and this leads to highly skewed distributions where most societies are coded as present or "not ascertainable."

Concerning the present set of codes, we tried to avoid the "present-absent" code, but this was not always possible because the data did not permit any other kinds of distinctions. Therefore, when we did have to resort to the use of this type of code, we generally rated a practice as absent only if this was explicitly stated in the ethnography. Where this convention was ignored, this is stated in the code itself.

The second problem which was encountered in the ethnographic data was the pervasiveness of imprecise and often misleading wording regarding the frequencies of various sexual attitudes and practices. The problem particularly affected the coding of frequencies of premarital sex, extramarital sex, and homosexuality. The most troublesome example of imprecision or ambiguity in reports on frequencies of a behavior is the statement that a practice is "not uncommon." "Not uncommon" could mean almost universal, very common, or typical. Our solution to this difficulty was twofold. First, we attempted to so construct the scales on frequencies that one item would, in fact, include very common to typical. Further, we incorporated the actual wording "not uncommon" into the scales themselves.

Inspection of the twenty codes on sexual attitudes and practices reveals a number of other problems with the rating of cross-cultural management of sexuality. Some of the codes are general, for example those on importance or frequency of homosexuality, while others are highly detailed, the clearest instance of this being the wife-sharing scale. In some cases, the items on a scale are not strictly ordered; in some cases, the "distance" between items is not comparable on a specific code.

In point of fact, the codes, as a set, tend to reflect neither ideal distributions nor ideal codes, but rather, ethnographic reality. They were constructed on the basis of what was available in the literature and, while this clearly has its drawbacks, we feel that this particular set of codes represents our best effort given what there is to work with in the ethnographic material.

CODES

The final set of twenty codes measuring a variety of sexual attitudes and practices appears below. The coded data appear in Table I following the code descriptions. The list of variables included in this article was reduced from the original 35 attitudes and practices to the present twenty scales for two reasons.

Thirteen of the original codes were dropped because they could not be rated on a large enough sample of societies. These codes dealt with one or another aspect of masturbation, heterosexual play in childhood, modesty in bathing and toilet habits in adulthood, and machismo. Our display of affection code could be rated on a reasonable number of societies, but the code itself was inadequate. It attempted to discriminate between societies that allowed displays of affection in public and those that did not. The discrimination could not be made with any degree of reliability based upon the data at hand. The remaining twenty codes, then, represent the specific sexual attitudes and practices that we felt could be codified with confidence out of the total range of beliefs and behaviors described in the ethnographic literature.

Scale	*Frequency Dist.*	*Percent*	*Cumulative Percent*
Column 1: Talk about Sex			
1 = Adolescents and adults talk explicitly and without inhibition about sexual matters in front of anyone, including children	19	28.4	28.4
2 = Talk about sex except in front of children	3	4.5	32.8
3 = Talk about sex except in front of specific categories of people (e.g., kin, elders, opposite sex)	17	25.4	58.2
4 = Talk about sex only with small group of intimates (e.g., age-mates, friends)	10	14.9	73.1
5 = Talk about sex always shameful, offensive, improper; euphemisms always used	18	26.9	100.0
	67		
Column 2: Attitude Toward Desirability of Frequent Sex in Marriage			
1 = Abstinence undesirable; frequent sex desirable; no concept of abstinence	12	17.1	17.1
2 = Abstinence desirable under some circumstances (e.g., occasional sex taboos); otherwise frequent sex desirable	42	60.0	77.1
3 = Sexual intercourse desirable in moderation; excesses unhealthy, bad, debilitating, but abstinence also undesirable in extremes	6	8.6	85.7
4 = Too much sexual intercourse is undesirable, bad, debilitating; abstinence admired	10	14.3	100.0
	70		
Column 3: Belief that Sex is Dangerous			
1 = Sexual intercourse never considered dangerous; sex always normal and natural	14	37.8	37.8
2 = Sexual intercourse dangerous to specified categories of people (e.g., shamans, unmarried, prepubescent)	4	10.8	48.6
3 = Unusual or unsanctioned sexual intercourse dan-			

Scale	*Frequency Dist.*	*Percent*	*Cumulative Percent*
Column 1: Talk about Sex			
gerous (e.g., sex at the wrong time, in the wrong place, using the wrong technique)	10	27.0	75.7
4 = Sexual secretions are dangerous; cleansing important after sexual intercourse	2	5.4	81.1
5 = Sexual intercourse is always dangerous; ritual purification always accompanies sexual activity	7	18.9	100.0
	37		
Column 4: Foreplay			
1 = Present: prolonged non-coital activity before sexual intercourse (e.g., kissing, caressing, fondling)	21	53.8	53.8
2 = Minimal: Some, but not elaborate or extensive non-coital activity	4	10.3	64.1
3 = Absent: no non-coital activity; intercourse is perfunctory	14	35.9	100.0
	39		
Column 5: Age at which Clothing Begins to be Worn (Male)			
1 = Never: adults wear no clothing	6	14.3	14.3
2 = Adulthood	1	2.4	16.7
3 = At puberty	9	21.4	38.1
4 = Before puberty but after toddler stage	21	50.0	88.1
5 = At toddler stage	1	2.4	90.5
6 = At birth or soon after	4	9.5	100.0
	42		
Column 6: Age at which Clothing Begins to be Worn (Female)			
1 = Never: adults wear no clothing	4	7.5	7.5
2 = Adulthood	2	3.8	11.3
3 = At puberty	7	13.2	24.5
4 = Before puberty but after toddler stage	29	54.7	79.2
5 = At toddler stage	7	13.2	92.5
6 = At birth or soon after	4	7.5	100.0
	53		
Column 7: Attitude Toward Premartial Sex (Female)			
1 = Premarital sex expected, approved; virginity has no value	34	24.1	24.1
2 = Premarital sex tolerated; accepted if discreet	29	20.6	44.7
3 = Premarital sex mildly disapproved; pressure towards chastity but transgressions are not punished and non-virginity ignored	24	17.0	61.7
4 = Premarital sex moderately disapproved: virginity valued and token or slight punishment for non-virginity	12	8.5	70.2
5 = Premarital sex disallowed except with bridegroom	6	4.3	74.5

Scale	*Frequency Dist.*	*Percent*	*Cumulative Percent*
Column 1: Talk about Sex			
6 = Premarital sex strongly disapproved: virginity required or stated as required (virginity tests, severe reprisals for non-virginity, e.g., divorce, loss of brideprice)	36	25.5	100.0
	141		
Column 8: Frequency of Premarital Sex (Male)			
1 = Universal or almost universal: almost all males engage in premarital sex	64	59.8	59.8
2 = Moderate: not uncommon for males to engage in premarital sex	19	17.8	77.6
3 = Occasional: some males engage in premarital sex but this is not common or typical	11	10.3	87.9
4 = Uncommon: males rarely or never engage in premarital sex	13	12.1	100.0
	107		
Column 9: Frequency of Premarital Sex (Female)			
1 = Universal or almost universal: almost all females engage in premarital sex	56	49.1	49.1
2 = Moderate: not uncommon for females to engage in premarital sex	19	16.7	65.8
3 = Occasional: some females engage in premarital sex but this is not common or typical	16	14.0	79.8
4 = Uncommon: females rarely or never engage in premarital sex	23	20.2	100.0
	114		
Column 10: Who Initiates Sexual Activity (Premarital)			
1 = Women always take the initiative in making sexual advances	6	17.6	17.6
2 = Women usually take the initiative but men sometimes do	0	0	17.6
3 = Both sexes take the initiative with more or less equal frequency	11	32.4	50.0
4 = Men usually take the initiative but women sometimes do	5	14.7	64.7
5 = Men always take the initiative; women never do	12	35.3	100.0
	34		
Column 11: Double Standard in Extramarital Sex			
1 = Single standard prevails: extramarital sex allowed for both husband and wife	13	11.2	11.2
2 = Double standard: extramarital sex is allowed for husband but condemned for wife	50	43.1	54.3
3 = Double standard: extramarital sex is condemned for both sexes but wife's activities are more severely punished (e.g., husband is scolded but wife is divorced)	26	22.4	76.7

Scale	Frequency Dist.	Percent	Cumulative Percent
Column 1: Talk about Sex			
4 = Single standard: extramarital sex condemned for both sexes and punished equally severely	27	23.3	100.0
	116		
Column 12: Frequency of Extramarital Sex (Male)			
1 = Universal or almost universal: almost all men engage in extramarital sex	7	12.7	12.7
2 = Moderate: not uncommon for men to engage in extramarital sex	31	56.4	69.1
3 = Occasional: men sometimes engage in extramarital sex but this is not common	6	10.9	80.0
4 = Uncommon: men rarely or never engage in extramarital sex	11	20.0	100.0
	55		
Column 13: Frequency of Extramarital Sex (Female)			
1 = Universal or almost universal: almost all women engage in extramarital sex	7	12.5	12.5
2 = Moderate: not uncommon for women to engage in extramarital sex	25	44.6	57.1
3 = Occasional: women sometimes engage in extramarital sex but this is not common	9	16.1	73.2
4 = Uncommon: women rarely or never engage in extramarital sex	15	26.8	100.0
	56		
Column 14: Wife Sharing			
1 = Extramarital sex of any kind allowed for wives	4	3.6	3.6
2 = Wife lending and/or exchange institutionalized *vis a vis* a woman and a group of men (e.g., any man in husband's age grade, husband's clansmen)	11	10.0	13.6
3 = Wife lending and/or exchange institutionalized *vis a vis* some specific man other than husband (e.g., brother-in-law)	5	4.5	18.2
4 = Wife lending and/or exchange only on occasion and specifically for sexual satisfaction	7	6.4	24.5
5 = Wife lending and/or exchange occurs for reason that benefits husband (e.g., wife exchanged in return for labor, money)	3	2.7	27.3
6 = Wife lending and/or exchange occurs on a one-time basis for a specific purpose over and above sexual satisfaction (e.g., hospitality, alliance, ceremonial)	13	11.8	39.1
7 = No wife lending or exchange allowed	67	60.9	100.0
	110		
Column 15: Attitude Toward Rape			
1 = Accepted, ignored	10	25.0	25.0
2 = Ridiculed	4	10.0	35.0
3 = Mildly disapproved: token fine or punishment	8	20.0	55.0

Scale	*Frequency Dist.*	*Percent*	*Cumulative Percent*
Column 1: Talk about Sex			
4 = Strongly disapproved: severe punishment (e.g., severe whipping, exile, death)	18	45.0	100.0
	40		
Column 16: Frequency of Rape			
1 = Absent	8	23.5	23.5
2 = Rare; isolated cases	12	35.3	58.8
3 = Common; not atypical	14	41.2	100.0
	34		
Column 17: Male Sexual Aggressiveness			
1 = Men are diffident, shy about making sexual overtures	6	9.2	9.2
2 = Males do not make sexual overtures, but this is not due to diffidence	9	13.8	23.1
3 = Men typically forward in sexual overtures, but these are verbal as opposed to physical	26	40.0	63.1
4 = Men are physically aggressive in sexual overtures, but this is solicited and/or desired by women	7	10.8	73.8
5 = Men's sexual advances are occasionally hostile (e.g., rape, unsolicited sleep-crawling, forced intercourse with wives)	7	10.8	84.6
6 = Men are typically hostile in their sexual advances; overtures are rough or aggressive and not solicited or desired by women (e.g., grabbing at sexual organs)	10	15.4	100.0
	65		
Column 18: Attitude Toward Homosexuality			
1 = Accepted, ignored	9	21.4	21.4
2 = No concept of homosexuality	5	11.9	33.3
3 = Ridiculed, scorned, but not punished	6	14.3	47.6
4 = Mildly disapproved, considered undesirable, but not punished	5	11.9	59.5
5 = Strongly disapproved and punished	17	40.9	100.0
	42		
Column 19: Frequency of Homosexuality			
1 = Absent, rare	41	58.6	58.6
2 = Present, not uncommon	29	41.4	100.0
	70		
Column 20: Impotence			
1 = Absent: incidence of and/or concern about impotence absent or atypical	8	20.0	20.0
2 = Present: incidence of and/or concern about impotence present (women complain about partner's impotence; charms, magic, etc. to cure impotence or promote virility; fear of impotence a pervasive preoccupation)	32	80	100.0
	40		

TABLE 1

Coded Data on Sex Attitudes and Practices

Area	Society	1	2	3	4	5	6	7	8	9	10
001	Hottentots	-	2	-	1	-	-	-	2	2	-
002	Kung	3	4	-	1	-	-	-	-	-	-
003	Thonga	-	2	-	-	-	-	1	1	1	-
004	Lozi	-	-	-	-	-	-	4	-	-	-
005	Mbundu	2	-	-	-	-	-	6	-	-	-
006	Suku	-	-	-	-	-	-	-	-	-	-
007	Bemba	-	1	5	-	-	-	1	-	-	-
008	Nyakyusa	4	-	4	-	-	-	5	-	-	-
009	Hadza	-	-	-	-	-	-	1	1	1	-
010	Luguru	-	-	-	-	-	-	-	-	-	-
011	Kikuyu	-	-	1	-	-	4	6	3	3	-
012	Ganda	1	2	-	-	4	3	3	2	2	-
013	Mbuti	1	-	-	-	-	-	1	1	1	-
014	Nkundo	4	2	3	1	-	-	2	-	-	-
015	Banen	-	-	-	-	-	-	-	-	-	-
016	Tiv	-	1	-	-	-	-	3	-	-	-
017	Ibo	3	-	3	-	3	3	6	-	3	-
018	Fon	3	-	-	1	-	-	4	2	3	-
019	Ashanti	-	-	-	-	-	-	2	-	-	-
020	Mende	-	-	-	-	-	-	-	-	-	-
021	Wolof	-	-	-	-	-	-	6	-	-	-
022	Bambara	-	2	3	-	-	-	-	1	1	-
023	Tallensi	1	4	1	-	2	2	1	3	3	-
024	Songhai	4	-	-	-	-	-	2	1	-	-
025	Fulani	-	-	-	1	-	-	3	1	-	-
026	Hausa	-	-	-	-	-	4	3	-	-	-
027	Massa	-	-	-	-	-	-	-	-	-	-
028	Azande	-	2	3	-	-	-	1	1	1	5
029	Fur	-	-	-	-	-	-	4	2	2	-
030	Nuba	5	-	-	-	-	-	1	1	1	-
031	Shilluk	-	2	5	-	-	-	1	1	1	-
032	Mao	-	-	-	-	-	-	4	-	-	-
033	Kaffa	-	-	-	-	-	-	-	-	-	-
034	Masai	-	-	-	3	-	-	1	1	1	-
035	Konso	4	4	-	-	4	5	3	2	2	-
036	Somali	-	4	-	-	-	-	6	4	4	-
037	Amhara	-	-	-	-	4	4	6	-	4	-
038	Bogo	-	-	-	-	-	-	-	-	-	-
039	Nubians	-	-	-	-	-	-	-	-	-	-
040	Teda	-	-	-	-	-	5	6	-	-	-

Area	Society	11	12	13	14	15	16	17	18	19	20
001	Hottentots	1	-	-	4	4	-	-	1	2	-
002	Kung	3	3	3	4	-	-	-	-	-	-
003	Thonga	2	-	-	7	-	-	3	-	1	2
004	Lozi	4	-	-	7	-	-	-	-	-	-
005	Mbundu	4	-	-	-	-	-	2	5	2	-
006	Suku	-	-	-	7	-	-	-	-	-	-
007	Bemba	-	-	-	-	-	-	-	-	-	1
008	Nyakyusa	2	2	2	-	-	-	-	-	1	2
009	Hadza	1	-	-	7	1	3	6	-	-	-
010	Luguru	-	-	-	-	-	-	-	-	-	-
011	Kikuyu	3	-	4	-	4	-	2	5	1	2
012	Ganda	2	-	-	7	-	-	-	-	-	-
013	Mbuti	2	2	-	7	-	1	4	5	1	-
014	Nkundo	3	2	2	2	4	1	-	-	2	-
015	Banen	-	-	-	2	-	-	-	-	-	-
016	Tiv	2	-	-	6	-	-	-	-	-	2
017	Ibo	-	-	-	5	-	-	-	-	-	-
018	Fon	-	-	-	-	-	-	-	4	2	2
019	Ashanti	-	-	-	-	-	-	-	-	-	-
020	Mende	1	-	-	3	-	-	-	-	-	2
021	Wolof	2	-	-	-	-	-	-	-	2	2
022	Bambara	2	-	-	7	-	-	-	-	-	2
023	Tallensi	3	-	-	-	3	-	3	-	-	-
024	Songhai	-	2	-	-	4	-	-	-	-	-
025	Fulani	2	-	-	7	-	-	-	-	-	2
026	Hausa	4	-	-	-	-	-	-	-	-	2
027	Massa	-	-	-	-	-	-	-	-	-	-
028	Azande	2	-	-	7	4	2	3	1	2	2
029	Fur	3	-	-	-	4	-	3	-	-	-
030	Nuba	2	-	-	7	-	-	5	-	-	2
031	Shilluk	2	-	-	2	4	-	3	-	-	1
032	Mao	-	-	-	-	-	-	-	-	-	-
033	Kaffa	-	-	-	-	-	-	-	-	-	-
034	Masai	1	-	-	2	-	-	-	-	-	-
035	Konso	2	-	-	-	-	-	-	3	2	-
036	Somali	2	-	-	7	-	-	5	-	-	-
037	Amhara	-	-	-	-	-	-	5	1	2	2
038	Bogo	-	-	-	-	-	-	-	-	-	-
039	Nubians	-	-	-	-	-	-	-	-	-	-
040	Teda	-	-	-	-	3	3	-	-	-	-

TABLE 1 (continued)

Area	Society	1	2	3	4	5	6	7	8	9	10
041	Tuareg	-	-	-	1	-	-	1	1	1	-
042	Riffians	-	-	-	-	-	-	6	-	-	-
043	Egyptians	5	1	1	-	-	-	6	4	4	-
044	Hebrews	-	2	5	-	-	-	6	-	-	-
045	Babylonians	-	2	-	-	-	-	6	-	-	-
046	Rwala	-	-	-	-	-	-	6	-	-	-
047	Turks	5	-	-	-	-	-	6	-	-	-
048	Gheg	-	-	-	-	-	-	6	-	-	-
049	Romans	-	-	-	-	-	-	-	-	-	-
050	Basques	-	-	-	-	-	-	-	-	-	-
051	Irish	-	2	-	3	6	6	6	4	4	-
052	Lapps	-	2	-	-	6	6	1	1	1	-
053	Yurak	-	-	-	-	-	-	-	-	-	-
055	Abkhaz	-	-	-	-	-	-	6	-	4	-
056	Armenians	-	-	-	-	-	-	-	-	-	-
057	Kurd	3	-	5	-	6	6	6	-	-	-
058	Basseri	-	-	-	-	-	-	6	4	4	-
059	Punjabi	-	1	-	-	-	-	6	4	4	5
060	Maria Gond	-	2	5	-	-	4	2	-	1	-
061	Toda	1	1	-	2	-	-	2	1	1	-
062	Santal	-	-	-	-	-	-	2	2	2	-
063	U. Pradesh	-	-	-	-	-	-	-	-	-	-
064	Burusho	-	-	-	-	-	-	-	4	4	-
065	Kazak	-	-	-	-	-	-	5	1	2	-
066	Mongols	-	-	-	-	-	-	-	-	4	-
067	Lolo	-	-	-	-	-	-	2	1	1	-
068	Lepcha	1	1	1	2	4	4	1	2	2	4
069	Garo	-	-	-	-	4	4	2	1	1	5
070	Lakher	-	2	3	-	-	-	1	1	1	3
071	Burmese	-	-	1	-	-	-	3	1	1	-
072	Lamet	-	2	-	-	-	-	1	1	1	-
073	Vietnamese	-	-	-	-	-	-	3	-	-	-
074	Rhade	-	-	-	-	-	-	-	-	-	-
075	Khmer	5	-	-	-	-	-	5	3	4	-
076	Siamese	3	-	-	-	4	4	6	4	4	-
077	Semang	-	-	3	-	-	-	-	2	2	-
078	Nicobarese	-	-	-	-	-	-	1	1	1	-
079	Andamanese	-	-	-	-	-	-	2	1	1	-
080	Vedda	-	-	-	-	4	4	5	3	3	-
081	Tanala	-	-	-	-	4	4	3	1	4	-

Area	Society	11	12	13	14	15	16	17	18	19	20
041	Tuareg	3	3	-	-	-	-	3	-	1	2
042	Riffians	3	-	-	7	-	-	-	-	2	-
043	Egyptians	-	4	4	7	-	-	1	-	2	2
044	Hebrews	2	-	-	7	4	-	-	5	2	-
045	Babylonians	2	-	-	-	4	-	-	5	2	2
046	Rwala	2	-	-	7	4	-	3	5	1	2
047	Turks	2	4	4	7	-	-	-	-	-	2
048	Gheg	2	-	-	-	-	-	-	-	-	-
049	Romans	-	2	2	-	-	-	-	-	-	-
050	Basques	-	-	-	-	-	-	-	-	-	-
051	Irish	-	4	4	7	-	-	-	-	1	-
052	Lapps	-	4	4	7	-	-	-	-	-	-
053	Yurak	-	-	-	-	-	-	-	-	-	-
055	Abkhaz	2	-	-	7	4	-	-	5	1	-
056	Armenians	-	-	-	-	-	-	-	-	-	-
057	Kurd	-	-	-	-	-	-	-	-	1	-
058	Basseri	-	-	-	7	-	-	-	-	-	-
059	Punjabi	2	-	-	7	-	-	-	5	2	-
060	Maria Gond	-	-	-	-	-	-	-	-	-	2
061	Toda	1	-	-	2	-	-	-	-	-	-
062	Santal	4	-	-	7	-	-	-	-	-	-
063	U. Pradesh	-	-	-	-	-	-	-	-	-	-
064	Burusho	-	4	4	7	-	-	-	-	-	-
065	Kazak	1	2	2	7	4	3	-	-	-	2
066	Mongols	4	-	-	6	-	-	-	-	-	-
067	Lolo	-	-	-	-	-	-	-	-	-	-
068	Lepcha	1	3	3	1	1	3	3	2	1	1
069	Garo	4	-	-	7	-	-	3	-	-	-
070	Lakher	2	-	4	-	4	2	6	-	-	2
071	Burmese	3	-	-	-	-	-	-	3	2	-
072	Lamet	-	-	-	-	-	-	3	-	-	-
073	Vietnamese	-	2	2	-	-	-	-	-	-	-
074	Rhade	-	-	-	-	-	-	-	-	-	-
075	Khmer	4	-	-	7	-	2	-	-	-	-
076	Siamese	-	-	-	-	-	-	2	-	-	1
077	Semang	4	-	-	7	-	-	-	-	-	-
078	Nicobarese	-	-	-	-	-	-	-	-	-	-
079	Andamanese	1	2	2	-	-	-	-	-	1	-
080	Vedda	-	4	4	7	-	-	-	-	-	-
081	Tanala	4	-	-	7	-	3	-	1	2	2

TABLE 1 (continued)

Area	Society	1	2	3	4	5	6	7	8	9	10
082	N. Sembilan	-	-	-	-	-	-	-	-	-	-
083	Javanese	5	-	1	-	4	4	3	1	3	-
084	Balinese	1	-	3	1	-	-	2	1	1	4
085	Iban	-	2	-	-	-	-	2	2	2	-
086	Badjau	1	-	-	1	3	4	3	3	3	-
087	Toradja	-	-	-	-	-	-	-	-	-	-
088	Tobelorese	-	-	-	-	-	-	-	-	-	-
089	Alorese	1	2	-	1	-	-	3	3	3	3
090	Tiwi	-	-	-	-	-	-	-	-	-	-
091	Aranda	-	-	-	-	-	-	-	-	4	-
092	Orokaiva	-	2	-	-	-	-	3	-	-	-
093	Kimam	-	-	5	-	-	-	2	1	1	1
094	Kapauku	5	2	-	-	4	4	4	1	1	3
095	Kwoma	-	2	-	3	1	1	4	1	1	1
096	Manus	4	-	-	3	-	4	6	4	4	-
097	Lesu	3	-	-	3	-	-	-	1	1	-
098	Trobrianders	-	2	-	1	-	4	2	1	1	3
099	Siuai	-	4	-	3	1	2	4	1	1	4
100	Tikopia	4	-	-	-	-	-	3	1	1	-
101	Pentecost	5	2	-	-	-	-	-	-	-	-
102	Fijians	-	-	-	-	3	4	-	-	-	-
103	Ajie	-	-	-	-	-	-	-	-	-	-
104	Maori	1	-	-	-	3	3	1	1	1	-
105	Marquesans	-	-	-	3	-	-	1	-	-	-
106	Samoans	1	-	-	-	3	3	2	1	1	-
107	Gilbertese	-	-	2	-	-	-	6	-	-	-
108	Marshallese	1	2	-	-	4	4	1	1	1	5
109	Trukese	3	2	-	3	4	4	1	1	1	5
110	Yapese	-	4	-	1	-	-	2	1	1	-
111	Palauans	-	-	-	-	4	4	1	1	1	-
112	Ifugao	3	1	-	1	-	-	1	1	1	5
113	Atayal	-	-	-	-	-	-	-	-	-	-
114	Chinese	-	-	-	-	-	-	6	2	4	-
115	Manchu	-	-	-	-	-	4	4	-	2	-
116	Koreans	3	-	-	-	-	-	3	-	-	-
117	Japanese	5	-	-	3	-	-	4	-	3	-
118	Ainu	-	-	-	2	-	-	2	1	1	-
119	Gilyak	-	-	-	1	-	-	1	-	-	-
120	Yukaghir	5	-	-	-	-	-	1	1	1	-
121	Chukchee	1	-	1	1	-	-	2	1	1	-

Area	Society	11	12	13	14	15	16	17	18	19	20
082	N. Sembilan	-	-	-	-	-	-	-	-	-	-
083	Javanese	4	2	4	7	-	-	-	-	-	-
084	Balinese	-	-	-	-	-	-	-	-	-	-
085	Iban	-	-	3	-	-	-	4	1	2	-
086	Badjau	-	-	-	-	-	-	-	3	1	-
087	Toradja	-	-	-	-	-	-	-	-	-	-
088	Tobelorese	-	-	-	-	-	-	-	-	-	-
089	Alorese	3	2	-	7	-	2	3	2	1	-
090	Tiwi	2	1	1	-	-	-	-	-	-	-
091	Aranda	2	-	-	6	-	-	-	-	-	-
092	Orokaiva	3	-	-	6	-	-	3	-	-	-
093	Kimam	4	-	-	4	-	-	2	-	-	-
094	Kapauku	2	-	2	7	-	-	6	-	-	-
095	Kwoma	-	1	1	7	4	-	2	5	1	-
096	Manus	-	-	-	7	-	-	6	4	1	-
097	Lesu	1	1	1	1	-	1	3	2	1	-
098	Trobrianders	3	2	2	7	1	-	3	3	1	-
099	Siuai	2	-	3	7	-	1	4	-	1	-
100	Tikopia	3	-	4	7	-	-	5	-	2	-
101	Pentecost	-	-	-	-	-	2	-	-	-	-
102	Fijians	2	2	2	6	-	-	-	-	-	-
103	Ajie	-	-	-	-	-	-	-	-	-	-
104	Maori	4	-	-	-	-	-	-	-	-	-
105	Marquesans	-	-	-	-	-	-	-	-	2	-
106	Samoans	4	2	2	7	2	-	3	-	2	-
107	Gilbertese	2	-	-	2	-	-	-	-	-	-
108	Marshallese	-	-	-	3	-	3	3	5	1	-
109	Trukese	2	2	2	2	2	-	3	2	1	1
110	Yapese	-	-	-	-	-	-	-	-	-	-
111	Palauans	4	-	-	5	-	-	-	-	-	-
112	Ifugao	4	-	-	7	3	2	6	-	1	-
113	Atayal	-	-	-	-	-	-	-	-	-	-
114	Chinese	2	3	-	7	-	-	-	-	-	-
115	Manchu	1	-	-	2	-	-	-	-	-	-
116	Koreans	2	-	-	7	-	-	-	-	-	2
117	Japanese	-	-	-	-	-	-	-	-	1	-
118	Ainu	-	-	-	-	-	-	-	-	-	-
119	Gilyak	-	-	1	2	-	2	-	4	1	-
120	Yukaghir	-	-	-	-	-	-	3	-	-	-
121	Chukchee	1	-	-	4	3	-	-	1	2	-

TABLE 1 (continued)

Area	Society	1	2	3	4	5	6	7	8	9	10
122	Ingalik	3	-	-	2	-	-	2	1	1	4
123	Aleut	-	-	3	-	-	-	-	-	-	-
124	C. Eskimo	-	-	-	-	-	-	-	-	-	-
125	Montagnais	5	-	-	-	-	-	4	2	2	-
126	Micmac	5	1	-	-	-	-	6	-	-	-
127	Saulteaux	-	1	2	3	-	-	2	2	2	3
128	Slave	5	-	-	-	-	-	3	1	2	-
129	Kaska	4	3	-	1	4	4	3	2	2	3
130	Eyak	-	2	1	-	-	-	6	-	4	-
131	Haida	-	-	-	-	-	-	4	1	2	-
132	Bellacoola	1	3	1	-	-	-	-	-	-	-
133	Twana	-	2	-	-	-	-	6	3	4	5
134	Yurok	5	2	3	-	-	-	2	-	-	-
135	Pomo	-	-	-	1	-	-	-	-	-	-
136	Yokuts	-	-	-	-	-	-	-	-	-	-
137	Paiute	-	2	-	-	-	-	1	-	-	4
138	Klamath	-	-	-	-	-	-	6	-	3	-
139	Kutenai	-	4	-	-	-	-	3	3	3	-
140	Gros Ventre	3	-	-	-	-	-	6	-	-	-
141	Hidatsa	-	-	-	-	-	-	-	1	-	-
142	Pawnee	1	2	-	-	3	3	6	1	3	-
143	Omaha	-	1	-	-	4	5	3	4	4	-
144	Huron	-	-	-	-	-	-	1	1	1	3
145	Creek	-	4	-	-	-	-	2	-	-	-
146	Natchez	-	2	-	-	-	-	1	1	1	-
147	Comanche	-	-	-	-	-	-	2	1	1	1
148	Chiricahua	5	3	-	-	-	-	6	2	4	-
149	Zuni	-	-	-	-	-	4	-	-	-	5
150	Havasupai	-	2	2	-	4	4	3	2	2	5
151	Papago	1	-	-	-	4	4	3	3	3	-
152	Huichol	-	2	-	-	-	4	3	2	2	-
153	Aztec	-	-	-	-	-	-	6	-	-	-
154	Popoluca	-	-	-	-	-	-	-	1	1	-
155	Quiche	5	-	-	-	-	-	6	-	-	-
156	Miskito	-	-	-	-	-	-	-	-	-	-
157	Bribri	-	2	-	-	-	4	-	-	-	-
158	Cuna	5	4	-	3	-	-	6	4	4	-
159	Goajiro	-	3	-	1	-	-	6	2	3	-
160	Haitians	4	2	1	-	4	4	3	1	1	-
161	Callinago	-	-	-	-	-	-	-	-	-	5

Area	Society	11	12	13	14	15	16	17	18	19	20
122	Ingalik	-	1	3	7	4	3	6	-	1	-
123	Aleut	-	-	-	-	-	-	-	-	-	-
124	C. Eskimo	-	-	-	4	1	-	-	-	-	-
125	Montagnais	3	-	-	-	1	-	-	-	-	-
126	Micmac	-	4	4	7	-	-	-	-	-	-
127	Saulteaux	2	-	-	-	-	-	4	-	-	1
128	Slave	3	2	-	7	2	-	-	-	1	-
129	Kaska	4	2	3	4	1	-	4	4	2	-
130	Eyak	4	-	-	4	-	-	-	-	-	-
131	Haida	4	-	-	2	-	-	-	-	-	-
132	Bellacoola	-	-	-	-	-	-	-	-	-	-
133	Twana	2	-	-	7	-	-	3	-	-	-
134	Yurok	-	-	-	6	-	-	-	1	2	-
135	Pomo	-	-	-	-	-	-	-	-	-	-
136	Yokuts	3	-	-	-	-	-	-	-	-	-
137	Paiute	4	2	2	-	-	-	3	-	-	-
138	Klamath	3	4	4	-	-	-	-	-	2	2
139	Kutenai	2	4	4	7	1	-	5	5	1	-
140	Gros Ventre	2	-	-	6	-	-	1	-	-	-
141	Hidatsa	-	-	-	6	4	3	5	-	-	-
142	Pawnee	-	-	-	5	-	-	-	-	1	-
143	Omaha	4	-	-	-	-	1	-	-	2	-
144	Huron	1	-	2	6	-	-	3	-	-	-
145	Creek	-	-	-	-	-	-	-	-	1	-
146	Natchez	2	-	4	6	-	-	-	-	-	-
147	Comanche	2	-	-	-	2	3	1	5	1	-
148	Chiricahua	3	2	2	7	4	2	-	5	-	2
149	Zuni	-	-	-	-	-	-	-	-	2	-
150	Havasupai	3	-	-	-	3	-	1	5	2	-
151	Papago	3	2	2	7	3	-	3	1	2	-
152	Huichol	4	2	2	7	-	1	-	-	1	-
153	Aztec	2	-	-	-	-	-	-	-	-	-
154	Popoluca	-	-	-	-	-	-	-	-	-	-
155	Quiche	4	-	-	7	-	-	-	-	-	2
156	Miskito	-	-	-	-	-	-	-	-	-	2
157	Bribri	-	-	-	-	-	-	-	-	-	-
158	Cuna	-	2	2	7	4	2	2	5	1	-
159	Goajiro	2	-	-	7	-	-	3	5	2	-
160	Haitians	3	-	-	7	-	-	-	3	2	2
161	Callinago	2	2	3	-	3	3	6	-	-	-

TABLE 1 (continued)

Area	Society	1	2	3	4	5	6	7	8	9	10
162	Warrau	-	-	-	-	-	-	-	-	-	-
163	Yanomamo	-	2	-	-	-	-	-	-	-	-
164	Carib	-	-	-	3	4	4	1	1	1	-
165	Saramacca	3	-	1	-	3	3	2	2	2	-
166	Mundurucu	-	-	-	-	-	-	-	-	-	-
167	Cubeo	5	-	-	-	3	5	-	3	3	1
168	Cayapa	-	-	-	-	3	3	2	3	2	1
169	Jivaro	5	2	2	-	-	-	2	1	1	-
170	Amahuaca	-	-	-	-	-	-	-	-	-	-
171	Inca	-	2	-	-	-	-	-	-	-	-
172	Aymara	-	-	-	-	5	5	1	1	1	3
173	Siriono	-	-	1	-	1	1	2	1	1	-
174	Nambicuara	1	2	-	-	-	-	-	-	-	-
175	Trumai	1	3	-	-	1	1	2	1	1	5
176	Timbira	-	2	-	-	1	1	-	1	3	-
177	Tupinamba	-	-	-	-	-	-	1	1	1	-
178	Botocudo	-	-	-	-	-	-	-	-	-	-
179	Shavante	4	1	1	-	1	-	-	4	4	-
180	Aweikoma	1	2	1	1	-	-	1	1	1	3
181	Cayua	-	-	-	-	-	-	-	-	-	-
182	Lengua	-	-	-	-	-	-	-	-	-	-
183	Abipon	-	-	-	-	-	-	-	4	4	-
184	Mapuche	3	3	-	3	-	-	2	1	1	-
185	Tehuelche	-	-	-	-	-	-	-	-	-	-
186	Yahgan	2	2	-	-	-	-	6	4	4	-
	Alternates										
011A	Chagga	-	-	-	-	-	-	3	-	-	-
029A	Katab	-	-	-	-	-	4	5	-	-	-
038A	Dorobo	3	-	-	-	-	-	1	-	-	-
046A	Lebanese	4	-	-	-	6	6	6	2	-	-
060A	Chenchu	-	-	-	-	-	-	-	-	-	-
068A	Sherpa	-	-	-	-	-	-	1	-	1	-
090A	Murngin	3	-	-	1	-	-	5	1	1	3
095A	Wogeo	2	2	5	1	-	-	2	1	1	-
106A	Pukapuka	1	1	4	1	-	-	1	1	1	5
138A	Washo	-	-	-	-	-	-	-	-	-	-
141A	Crow	3	2	-	-	-	-	3	-	-	-
149A	Navaho	3	4	3	3	4	5	4	-	-	3
175A	Bororo	-	-	-	-	-	-	-	-	-	-
179A	Caraja	-	-	-	-	-	5	-	-	-	-
183A	Mataco	-	-	-	-	4	4	1	1	1	1

Area	Society	11	12	13	14	15	16	17	18	19	20
162	Warrau	-	-	-	-	-	-	-	-	-	-
163	Yanomamo	2	2	2	3	-	3	-	-	-	-
164	Carib	2	-	-	-	-	-	3	-	-	-
165	Saramacca	-	1	1	1	-	-	-	-	-	2
166	Mundurucu	3	2	2	7	1	3	6	-	-	-
167	Cubeo	2	2	2	7	-	-	2	-	1	2
168	Cayapa	-	3	-	7	-	-	1	-	1	-
169	Jivaro	2	-	-	7	-	-	-	-	1	-
170	Amahuaca	-	-	-	-	-	-	-	-	-	-
171	Inca	4	-	-	7	-	-	-	-	-	-
172	Aymara	3	2	2	-	-	1	4	-	-	-
173	Siriono	3	2	2	2	3	2	-	1	1	-
174	Nambicuara	2	2	2	3	-	-	-	3	1	-
175	Trumai	3	2	3	-	1	3	6	-	1	-
176	Timbira	-	-	-	6	-	1	3	-	1	-
177	Tupinamba	2	-	-	7	-	-	-	-	-	-
178	Botocudo	-	-	-	-	-	-	-	-	-	-
179	Shavante	2	4	4	3	-	-	-	-	1	1
180	Aweikoma	1	1	1	1	-	-	4	-	1	-
181	Cayua	-	-	-	-	-	-	-	-	-	-
182	Lengua	-	-	-	-	-	-	-	-	-	-
183	Abipon	2	-	-	7	-	-	-	-	-	-
184	Mapuche	2	-	-	7	-	-	3	-	-	-
185	Tehuelche	-	-	-	-	-	-	-	-	-	-
186	Yahgan	4	3	3	7	-	-	-	5	-	-
	Alternates										
011A	Chagga	-	-	-	-	-	-	-	-	-	2
029A	Katab	-	-	-	-	-	-	-	-	-	-
038A	Dorobo	-	-	-	-	-	-	-	-	-	-
046A	Lebanese	-	4	-	7	-	-	-	4	-	-
060A	Chenchu	-	-	-	-	-	-	-	-	-	-
068A	Sherpa	4	-	-	7	-	-	-	-	-	-
090A	Murngin	4	2	2	6	-	2	1	-	-	-
095A	Wogeo	3	1	1	7	-	-	2	-	-	-
106A	Pukapuka	4	-	-	7	-	-	-	2	1	2
138A	Washo	-	-	-	-	-	-	-	-	-	-
141A	Crow	2	2	2	6	-	-	5	-	-	-
149A	Navaho	2	-	-	-	1	3	6	-	-	1
175A	Bororo	-	-	-	-	-	-	-	-	-	-
179A	Caraja	-	-	-	-	-	2	-	-	-	-
183A	Mataco	3	-	-	7	-	-	2	-	-	-

NOTE

1. This research was made possible by a grant from the National Institutes of Health, Grant #HD 07806-01.

BIBLIOGRAPHY

Barry, H., III, and L. Paxson. 1971. Infancy and Childhood: Cross Cultural Codes 2. Ethnology 10: 446-508.

Brown, J, S. 1952. A Comparative Study on Deviations from Sex Mores. American Sociological Review 17: 135-46.

Heise, D. R. 1967. Cultural Patterning of Sexual Socialization. American Sociological Review 32: 726-39.

Minturn, L., M. Grosse, and S. Haider. 1969. Cultural Patterning of Sexual Beliefs and Behavior. Ethnology 8: 301-18.

Murdock, G. P. 1967. Ethnographic Atlas. Pittsburgh.

Murdock, G. P., and D. O. Morrow. 1970. Subsistence Economy and Supportive Practices. Ethnology 9: 302-330.

Murdock, G. P., and C. Provost. 1973. Factors in the Division of Labor by Sex: A Cross-Cultural Analysis. Ethnology 12: 203-25.

Murdock, G. P., and D. R. White. 1969. Standard Cross-Cultural Sample. Ethnology 13: 329-69.

Palfrey House. n.d. Cross-Cultural Codes. Harvard University.

Stephens, W. N. 1972. A Cross-Cultural Study of Modesty. Behavior Science Notes 7: 1.28.

SUPPLEMENTARY BIBLIOGRAPHY

The following ethnographic sources were used as supplementary texts in the coding procedure.

1: *Nama Hottentots*

Murdock, G. P. 1936. Our Primitive Contemporaries. New York.

8: *Nyakyusa*

Wilson, M. 1959. Communal Rites of the Nyakyusa. London.

12: *Ganda*

Mair, L. 1965. An African People in the Twentieth Century. New York.

Murdock, G. P. 1936. Our Primitive Contemporaries. New York.

21: *Wolof*

Ames, D. 1959. Selection of Mates. Continuity and Change in African Cultures, ed. W. R. Bascom and M. J. Herskovits, pp. 156-68. Chicago.

36: *Somali*

Lewis, I. M. 1962. Marriage and the Family in Northern Somaliland. East African Institute of Social Research. East African Studies 15. Kampala, Uganda.

46: *Rwala*

Raswan, C. R. 1947. Black Tents of Arabia. New York.

61: *Toda*

Murdock, G. P. 1936. Our Primitive Contemporaries. New York.

73: *Vietnam*

Coughlin, R. J. 1965. Pregnancy and Childbirth in Vietnam. Southeast Asian Birth Customs: Three Studies in Human Reproduction, eds. D. V. Hart *et al.* New Haven.

77: *Semang*

Murdock, G. P. 1936. Our Primitive Contemporaries. New York.

105: *Marquesans*

Suggs, R. C. 1971. Sex and Personality in the Marquesas. Human Sexual Behavior, ed., D. S. Marshall and R. C. Suggs, pp. 163-86. Princeton.

119: *Gilyak*

Chard, C. S. 1961. Sternberg's Materials on the Sexual Life of the Gilyak. Anthropological Papers of the University of Alaska 10: 13-23.

159: *Goajiro*
Watson, L. 1973. Marriage and Sexual Adjustment in Goajiro Society. Ethnology 12: 153-62.
168: *Cayapa*
Altschuler, M. 1971. Cayapa Personality and Sexual Motivation. Human Sexual Behavior, ed., D. S. Marshall and R. C. Suggs, pp. 38-58. Princeton.
46a: *Lebanese*
Melikian, L. H., and E. T. Prothro. 1954. Sexual Behavior of University Students in the Arab Near East. Journal of Abnormal and Social Psychology 49: 59-64.
149a: *Navaho*
Reichard, G. 1928. Social Life of the Navaho Indians. New York.
183a: *Mataco*
Fock, N. 1963. Mataco Marriage. Folk 5: 91-101.

CURRENT ANTHROPOLOGY Vol. 24, No. 4, August-October 1983

The North American Berdache[1]

by Charles Callender and Lee M. Kochems

THE BERDACHE among North American Indians may be roughly defined as a person, usually male, who was anatomically normal but assumed the dress, occupations, and behavior of the other sex to effect a change in gender status. This shift was not complete; rather, it was a movement toward a somewhat intermediate status that combined social attributes of males and females. The terminology for berdaches defined them as a distinct gender status, designated by special terms rather than by the words "man" or "woman." Literal translations of these terms often indicate its intermediate nature: halfman-halfwoman (Grinnell 1962, vol. 2:39), man-woman (Bowers 1965:167), would-be woman (Powers 1977:38).

The word "berdache" is used here as a generic term for this status throughout North America north of Mexico. The distinctions made by Martin and Voorhies (1975:95–100) seem unnecessary. While variation characterized the institution, it included a common core of traits. Although "berdache" originally designated a male, its etymology became irrelevant long ago, and it is used here for both sexes.

Although accounts of berdaches go back to the 16th century (Katz 1976:285–86), broad surveys of this status have appeared only in recent years. A few American anthropologists briefly summarized its features for North America generally or specifically for the Plains tribes (e.g., Benedict 1934:263; Linton 1936:480; Lowie 1924*b*:245–46). The most provocative early treatment, published in 1940 by Kroeber (1952:313–14), included a call for general syntheses. It drew almost no response. Except for a note by Angelino and Shedd (1955) centering on definitions of the status, anthropologists (e.g., Hoebel 1949:459; Mead 1949:129–30; 1961:1452) continued to limit their treatment to brief statements that differed little from earlier summaries. The recent large-scale examinations, beginning with Jacobs (1968), continued with Forgey's (1975) analysis of berdaches among the northern Plains tribes. Katz (1976:281–334) published a large collection of ethnographic data about homosexuality in general among American Indians, with comments from an explicitly gay standpoint. The new perspectives implicit in this recent work become very evident with Whitehead's (1981) analysis. Broad syntheses appeared earlier among European anthropologists, who usually treated the berdache status as one aspect of a more widespread pattern of institutionalized transvestism (e.g., Baumann 1950, 1955; Bleibtrau-Ehrenberg 1970) and concentrated on phenomena outside North America. Signorini (1972), however, focusses explicitly upon berdaches.

Evidence for a cross-cultural examination of the berdache status is scanty, fragmentary, and often poor in quality. Still existing in a few societies, more or less covertly (Fire 1972:149–50; Forgey 1975:67), berdaches began to disappear soon after European or American control was established. Most accounts are retrospective, based on memory or tradition and describing phenomena no longer subject to observation. The waning of this status was a complex process in which the hostility of Western outsiders who were outraged by its open display and public acceptance was only one factor, if a very potent one. However, this cultural bias strongly skewed the gathering of information. Descriptions of berdaches sometimes contain much more denunciation than data (e.g., Dumont in Swanton 1911:100; Gatschet 1891:67; McCoy 1976). The extent to which bias determined what observers saw and reported is evident in accounts of 17th-century Illinois berdaches. Marquette (1900:129), a neutral observer, and Liette (1947:112–13), who was prejudiced, agree on little except transvestism. Sometimes the biases of editors or publishers came into play, excising data (e.g., in the London edition of James 1823) or coyly switching into Latin (e.g., Kroeber 1902:20; Lowie 1910:42), a form of evasion less destructive than Catlin's (1973, vol. 2:214–15) taking refuge in hopelessly garbled Sauk (Ives Goddard, personal communication). Indians who absorbed the biases of the dominant culture became reticent about berdaches or denied their former existence (cf. Gayton 1948:106; Lurie 1953).

The berdache status is occasionally confused with other conditions that partly resembled it. These include forcing female dress upon males who showed extreme cowardice in warfare; homosexuality; and hermaphroditism.

Observers sometimes interpreted berdaches as cowardly men upon whom transvestism was imposed as a sign of disgrace (Bradbury 1904:64–65; Powers 1877:132). This practice did exist among some societies in the upper Midwest. Illinois men who deserted during military action had to dress like women but could rehabilitate themselves by demonstrating courage (Bossu 1972:82). Lurie (1953:71) describes the similar punish-

[1] We gratefully acknowledge the aid of Cynthia Beall, Ives Goddard, Italo Signorini, and Elisabeth Tooker, who provided information or made suggestions that are incorporated in this article.

CHARLES CALLENDER is Associate Professor of Anthropology at Case Western Reserve University (Cleveland, Ohio 44106, U.S.A.). Born in 1928, he was educated at the University of Chicago (Ph.B., 1948; M.A., 1954; Ph.D., 1958). He has taught at the American University in Cairo (1961–63) and the University of Delaware (1963–65) and has done fieldwork among the Fox, Sauk, Potawatomi, and Kenuz. His research interests are social organization, gender relations, American Indians, and the Middle East. He has published *Social Organization of the Central Algonkian Indians* (1963) and a number of articles about American Indians.

LEE M. KOCHEMS is a Ph.D. candidate in the Department of Anthropology at the University of Chicago. He was born in 1958 and received his B.A. and M.A. from Case Western Reserve University in 1980. His research interests are gender relations, the construction of the person, and East African pastoralists.

The present paper was submitted in final form 25 XI 82.

ment of a Winnebago warrior who had compounded his offense by claiming war honors after his flight. Santee Dakota youths who had never joined a war party could be forced to wear dresses at social dances (Landes 1968:206–7; Pond 1889:245–46). This usage seems a more intense form of the widespread custom of shaming males who were reluctant to fight by calling them women (e.g., Wallace and Hoebel 1952:273). Restricted to a few societies, in which berdaches also existed, it shared with the latter only the feature of transvestism. Forcibly imposed by human agents, this form of cross-dressing lacked the supernatural validation often attached to berdaches, was a mark of disgrace, and was temporary or potentially subject to change. The status it denoted was thus clearly distinct from that of the berdache.

Its frequent equation with homosexuality, even by explicitly gay writers (e.g., Russo 1981:218), distorts the sexual aspects of berdachehood. Certain interests were often believed to foreshadow the assumption of this status, but only one account (Gayton 1948:236) cites homosexual behavior. Rather than homosexuals' becoming berdaches, many berdaches, perhaps most of them, became homosexual; but their sexual partners were always nonberdaches. Evidence for homosexual activity unrelated to this status is abundant (Devereux 1937:498–500; Forde 1931:147; Holder 1889:625; Honigmann 1954:129–30; Jones 1907:141; Lowie 1910:223; Osgood 1958:222–23). North American homosexuality transcended berdaches; though they were its most visible and—except for their spouses—its most consistent participants, their orientations could be bisexual or heterosexual.

Berdaches were often confounded with intersexual persons. Early observers who called them hermaphrodites sometimes assumed they were truly intersexual (Hennepin 1903:167–68; Membre 1922:131–59; Le Moyne du Morgues 1875:7–8; cf. Lafitau 1724:52). Morfi confessed his uncertainty on this point (Newcomb 1961:74). Font (1966:105) recorded his original impression that Yuma berdaches were intersexed and his later discovery of the error. Stevenson (1902:37) suggested that observers may have misunderstood such native terms as "half-man-halfwoman." One factor in the persistence of the hermaphrodite label may have been doubt about an alternative. Denig (1961:187–88) applied it to Crow berdaches even while pointing out that they were defined by their behavior rather than their anatomy.

The sharp distinction between berdaches and intersexes urged by Angelino and Shedd (1955:124–25) is easily drawn at the conceptual level but harder to apply when examining the literature. Some cultures clearly separated the two statuses. Mead's (1961:1452) account of a boy who was classed as a berdache only after he was determined to be anatomically male indicates that the Omaha made such a distinction. Other cultures blurred the line by assigning berdaches and intersexes to the same status (Ray 1932:148; Spier and Sapir 1930:220–21; Steward 1941:253; 1943:338; cf. Forgey 1975:2–3). The Navaho treated them as a single category but linguistically separated intersexes ("real *nadle*") from berdaches ("those who pretend to be *nadle*") and prescribed somewhat different rules of behavior for them (Hill 1935). Perhaps cultures that merged the two statuses generally separated them into different subclasses, but the evidence is no longer recoverable. While the data prevent drawing a clear and consistent distinction between berdaches and intersexes, most berdaches were anatomically normal and were culturally defined.

DISTRIBUTION

Scanty, fragmentary, and unsatisfactory as most of the data are, they provide reasonably good evidence for the berdache status among the 113 groups listed in table 1. The evidence for its existence among another eight groups seems insufficient or ambiguous. One instance each was reported for the Coeur d'Alene (Ray 1932:18) and Slave (Honigmann 1946:84), but descriptions of both persons as truly intersexual cloud the existence of a real berdache category in either culture. Bella Coola accounts of Haida women who dressed like men and hunted (McIlwraith 1948, vol. 2:95–96) are not confirmed by Haida sources. Tlingit statements combine denials that berdaches existed with an apparent assertion of their periodic reincarnation in a certain clan (de Laguna 1954:178). While Kardiner (1945:56–57, 88) said the Comanche prohibited transvestism, his reference to "effeminate" men who did the work of women suggests that berdaches may have existed in a covert form, as among the Pima (Hill 1938), but more information is needed to resolve this question. One possible instance from the Kinugmiut Eskimo (Ray 1975:89, 97) is inconclusive. Goddard (1978:231) cautiously notes indications of berdaches among the Delaware. Boyce (1978:283) raises the possibility that Tuscarora men who were poor hunters and followed other occupations might have been berdaches. Practice among the Creek is uncertain. Romans (1964:97) reported male homosexuality, but not berdaches; Underhill (1953:34) described the latter without citing a source; and Adair's (1966:25) reference to a woman rumored to be a hermaphrodite is not decisive.

Explicit denials that are not contradicted by other evidence have been reported for only nine groups: Cahuila (Drucker 1937:29, 49), Chimariko (Driver 1939:347, 465), Cochiti (Lange 1959:15), Karok (Driver 1939:347, 465), Maidu (Voegelin 1942:134, 228), Serrano (Drucker 1937:27), Walapai (Drucker 1941:218; McKennon in Kroeber 1935); Wappo (Driver 1936:200), and Yavapai (Drucker 1941:163; Gifford 1936:296). Their significance is uncertain; similar denials are recorded for cultures known to have had berdaches. Driver is openly skeptical about the Chimariko and Karok statements; neither Drucker nor McKennon seems satisfied with the Walapai denials; and Drucker stresses the Cahuila and Serrano reluctance to discuss any sexual matters.

Direct evidence for the presence or absence of the berdache status does not seem available for other groups—a statement necessarily qualified by the possibility that we missed references. The significance of silence is hard to assess. It can stem from very diverse causes. For many of these cultures, destroyed very early and poorly known in every respect, the absence of references means very little. Other cultures in this group are well known, but those who described them may not have asked about berdaches; informants may have been reluctant to offer information; or the status may have been forgotten. That silence cannot automatically be interpreted as evidence that the status was absent is shown by the relatively well-described Winnebago, who would fall into this category except for Lurie's (1953) article. Yet to assume that it existed unless denials were recorded is equally dangerous. When specific references are lacking, our discussion of the distribution of the berdache status rests on three assumptions: First, a group whose neighbors were culturally similar and had berdaches probably had them; thus one may reasonably assume their probable presence among the Kickapoo, Missouri, and Yanktonai. Second, if detailed accounts of a culture by several observers over a period of time are consistently silent, berdaches probably did not exist. Third, if references are lacking for a large cluster of adjacent cultures that are fairly well known, the probability is that berdaches were not present.

The berdache status existed over a large area extending from California to the Mississippi Valley and upper Great Lakes, with scattered occurrences beyond it (fig. 1). If probably distributed rather more widely than the maps indicate, it still seems to have been far from universal. In terms of culture areas, using Driver's (1969) classification, berdaches were ubiquitous in California and the Great Basin except for a few scattered groups that are poorly known or whose denials, as noted, are not entirely convincing. With similar exceptions they characterized the Plains and Prairies, except for the south. Their distribution in the Southwest and the Northwest Coast seems to have been decidedly less pervasive than in the four culture areas first noted. References are scantiest for the Arctic, Subarctic, Plateau, and East.

It might seem predictable that the berdache status should fade out toward the north, among band societies with a less complex level of sociocultural organization (cf. Opler 1965:111). This assumption may be unjustified. The distributional pattern in North America shows little correlation between this status and the level of social organization. Almost universal among band societies of the Great Basin, even in the Subarctic it extended beyond the limits one might expect. Possibly its attenuation and disappearance in the north rested on the specific nature of Arctic and Subarctic subsistence economies, to which the contribution of males was too valuable to promote their transformation. A significant point, perhaps, is that the berdaches recorded for all Subarctic groups except the Ojibwa included females, who hunted, and only female berdaches are reported for the Kaska and Carrier.

The relative absence of berdaches among Plateau groups also seems predictable, perhaps deceptively so. Whatever the reasons, the extent to which this seems a Plateau characteristic is reflected in their concentration among marginal groups that

TABLE 1

NORTH AMERICAN CULTURES RECOGNIZING THE BERDACHE STATUS

1. Achumawi (Voegelin 1942: 134–35)
2. Acoma (Hammond 1882: 346)
3. Aleuts (Bancroft 1874, vol. 1: 92; Dall 1897: 402–3)
4. Arapaho (Kroeber 1902: 19–20)
5. Arikara (Holder 1889: 623)
6. Atsugewi (Voegelin 1942: 134–35)
7. Assiniboine (Lowie 1910: 42)
8. Bannock (Steward 1943: 385)
9. Bella Bella (McIlwraith 1948, vol. 1: 45–46)
10. Bella Coola (McIlwraith 1948, vol. 1: 45–46)
11. Blackfoot (Turney-High 1941: 128)
12. Caddo (Newcomb 1961: 301)
13. Carrier (McIlwraith 1948, vol. 1: 45–46)
14. Cheyenne (Grinnell 1962, vol. 2: 39–42; Hoebel 1960: 77)
15. Chilula (Driver 1939: 347)
16. Chiricahua Apache (Opler 1965: 111)
17. Choctaw (Bossu 1962: 169; Romans 1962: 82–83)
18. Chumash (Costanso 1910: 137; Harrington 1942: 32)
19. Coahuiltecans (Cabeza da Vaca in Katz 1976: 285)
20. Coast Salish (Barnett 1955: 149; Teit 1900: 321)
21. Cocopa (Drucker 1941: 163; Gifford 1933: 294)
22. Costanoan (Harrington 1942: 32)
23. Crow (Denig 1961: 187–88; Holder 1889; Lowie 1935: 48, 312–13; Simms 1903)
24. Eyak (Birket-Smith and de Laguna 1938: 206)
25. Flathead (Teit 1930: 384; Turney-High 1937: 85)
26. Fox (Michelson 1927: 257)
27. Gabrieleño (Harrington 1942: 32)
28. Gros Ventre (Holder 1889: 623)
29. Haisla (Olson 1940: 200)
30. Hidatsa (Bowers 1965: 166–68, 323–27)
31. Hopi (Beaglehole and Beaglehole 1935: 44; Fewkes 1892: 11)
32. Hupa (Driver 1939: 347)
33. Illinois (Liette 1947: 112–13; Marquette 1900: 129)
34. Ingalik (Osgood 1958: 219, 261–63)
35. Iowa (Lurie 1953: 711)
36. Ipai (Drucker 1937: 27)
37. Juaneño (Kroeber 1925: 647)
38. Kalekau (Essene 1942: 31, 65)
39. Kaniagmiut (Bancroft 1874, vol. 1: 82; Dall 1897: 402–3)
40. Kansa (Dorsey 1890: 386; Say in James 1823: 129)
41. Karankawa (Newcomb 1961: 74)
42. Kaska (Honigmann 1954: 129–30)
43. Kato (Driver 1939: 347; Essene 1942: 31)
44. Kitanemuk (Harrington 1942: 32)
45. Klamath (Spier 1930: 51–53; Voegelin 1942: 134–35)
46. Kutenai (Spier 1935: 26–27; Turney-High 1941: 128)
47. Laguna (Parsons 1923: 272; 1939: 53)
48. Lassik (Essene 1942: 31, 65)
49. Lillooet (Teit 1906: 267)
50. Lipan Apache (Gifford 1940: 66)
51. Luiseño (Boscana 1978: 54; White 1963: 146–47)
52. Mandan (Bowers 1950: 272, 296, 298)
53. Maricopa (Drucker 1941: 163; Spier 1933: 242–43)
54. Mattale (Driver 1939: 347)
55. Menomini (Skinner 1913: 34)
56. Miami (Trowbridge 1938: 68)
57. Miwok (Gifford 1926: 333)
58. Modoc (Ray 1963: 43)
59. Mohave (Devereux 1937; Kroeber 1925: 478–79; Drucker 1941: 173)
60. Natchez (Swanton 1911: 100)
61. Navaho (Hill 1935; Mathews 1897: 70)
62. Nez Perce (Holder 1889: 623)
63. Nisenan (Beals 1933: 376)
64. Northern Paiute (Gayton 1948: 174; Lowie 1924*b*: 283; Steward 1933: 238; Stewart 1941: 405)
65. Nootka (Drucker 1951: 333)
66. Nomlaki (Goldschmidt 1951: 387)
67. Ojibwa (Coues 1897: 163–65; Kinietz 1947: 155–57; McKenney 1827: 314–15)
68. Omaha (Fletcher and La Flesche 1911: 132–33; Dorsey 1890: 379)
69. Osage (Fletcher and La Flesche 1911: 132–33)
70. Oto (Irving 1888: 120–33; Whitman 1969: 50)
71. Papago (Drucker 1941: 163; Underhill 1969: 186–87)
72. Patwin (Kroeber 1925: 293; 1932: 272)
73. Pawnee (Dorsey and Murie 1940: 108)
74. Pima (Drucker 1941: 63; Hill 1938)
75. Plains Cree (Mandelbaum 1940: 256–57)
76. Pomo (Gifford 1926: 333)
77. Ponca (Dorsey 1890: 379; Howard 1965: 142–43)
78. Potawatomi (Landes 1970: 190–91, 195–96)
79. Quapaw (St. Cosme in Kellogg 1917: 360)
80. Quileute (Olson 1936: 99)
81. Quinault (Olson 1936: 99)
82. Rogue River (Barnett 1937: 185)
83. Salinan (Harrington 1942: 32; Mason 1912: 174; Hester 1978: 502)
84. Santa Ana Pueblo (Gifford 1940: 66, 168)
85. Santee Dakota (Landes 1968: 32, 57, 66, 112–13)
86. Sauk (Catlin 1973, vol. 2: 214–15; Keating 1825: 216)
87. Shasta (Holt 1946: 317; Voegelin 1942: 134–35)
88. Shoshoneans (Steward 1941: 252–53; 1943: 338)
89. Shoshoni (Shimkin 1947; Steward 1943: 271)
90. Sinkaietk (Cline 1938: 137, 149)
91. Sinkyou (Driver 1937: 347)
92. Siuslaw (Barnett 1937: 185)
93. Southern Paiute (Driver 1937: 90, 129; Drucker 1941: 173; Lowie 1924*b*: 282; Stewart 1944: 405)
94. Teton Dakota (Hassrick 1964: 122; Mirsky 1937: 416–17)
95. Thompson (Teit 1900: 321)
96. Timucua (Le Moyne du Morgues 1878: 7–8)
97. Tipai (Drucker 1941: 173)
98. Tolowa (Driver 1939: 347; Gould 1978: 131, 134)
99. Tubatulabal (Driver 1937: 90; Voegelin 1938: 47)
100. Ute (Gifford 1940: 55, 136; Lowie 1924*b*: 282–83; Stewart 1940: 298)
101. Washo (Steward 1941: 485)
102. Winnebago (Lurie 1953)
103. Wintu (Voegelin 1942: 134)
104. Western Apache (Gifford 1940: 66, 136, 168)
105. Wishram (Spier and Sapir 1930: 229–21)
106. Wiyot (Driver 1937: 347; Elsasser 1978: 159)
107. Yana (Sapir and Spier 1943: 275)
108. Yankton (Dorsey 1890: 467)
109. Yokuts (Gayton 1948: 66, 106, 236; Wallace 1978*a*: 455; 1978*b*: 466)
110. Yuki (Foster 1944: 183, 186; Powers 1877: 132–33)
111. Yuma (Forde 1931: 157; Gifford 1931: 56)
112. Yurok (Kroeber 1925: 46)
113. Zuni (Parsons 1916; Stevenson 1902: 37–38)

adjoined other culture areas where the status was more common.

In the East, berdaches are documented for the lower Mississippi Valley among the Natchez, Caddo, Choctaw, and Quapaw; they also characterized the Timucua. References for other cultures, vague and uncertain at best, seem limited to the Creek, Delaware, and Tuscarora. The status might have been widespread in the past, disappearing soon after contact. It seems improbable, however, that reports as detailed as those for the Iroquois and covering so long a time period would never have mentioned berdaches if these had existed. Elisabeth Tooker (personal communication) interprets this silence as indicating their possible absence. We agree. The berdache status, then, seems to have been surprisingly absent, undeveloped, or very obscure throughout the East except for its southern fringe.

Another region, smaller in extent, in which references to berdaches are unexpectedly absent centers on the southern Plains with adjacent Prairie and Southwest cultures. The Comanche, as noted, are a debatable case, but their prohibition of transvestism, a cardinal trait of the status, seems to indicate hostility toward it. If berdaches were actually absent, the causes are obscure, particularly since they characterized most of the surrounding cultures and were prominent in the northern Plains.

Another distributional aspect is the limited occurrence of female berdaches, reported for only 30 groups: Achumawi, Atsugewi, Bella Coola, Carrier, Cocopa, Crow, Haisla, Ingalik, Kaska, Klamath, Kutenai, Lillouet, Maricopa, Mohave, Navaho, Nootka, Northern Paiute, Papago, Quinault, Shasta, Shoshoneans, Tipai, Ute, Washoe, Western Apache, Wintu, Wiyot, Yokuts, Yuki, and Yuma. They may also have characterized the Flathead and Haida. Male berdaches are not reported for the Carrier, Kaska, and Kutenai; the uncertain Haida reference mentions only women. Even more strongly than the berdache status as a whole, its female variety tended to concentrate in western North America, restricted to the Subarctic, Northwest Coast, Plateau, Great Basin, California, and Southwest (fig. 2). The only exception is a single instance reported for the Crow. Female berdaches tended to be more prevalent in less complex societies and those in which agriculture was absent or less important.

NUMBERS

Berdaches are usually described as rare or uncommon; numbers, if given, are few. Holder (1889:623) reported six among the Gros Ventre, five among the Teton Dakota, four for the Flathead, two for the Nez Perce, and one for the Shoshoni. Kroeber (1925:66) estimated that one Yurok man in a hundred assumed this status. Except among groups limiting the status to women, female berdaches tended to be much rarer than their male counterparts.

Early accounts that mention their frequency consistently describe berdaches as more numerous. Cabeza de Vaca (Katz 1976:285) reported many of them among the Coahuiltecans between 1528 and 1533. Le Moyne du Morgues (1875:7–8) said they were quite common among the Timucua in 1564. In 1769–70 Costanso (1910:137) reported them present in every Chumash village. Henry in 1799–1800 (Coues 1897:347–48) credited the Hidatsa with many berdaches, and Maximilian (1906:354) gave a similar account for the Crow around 1832. In 1822 Boscana (1978:54) reported a second-hand account that they were very numerous among the Yuma before a plague

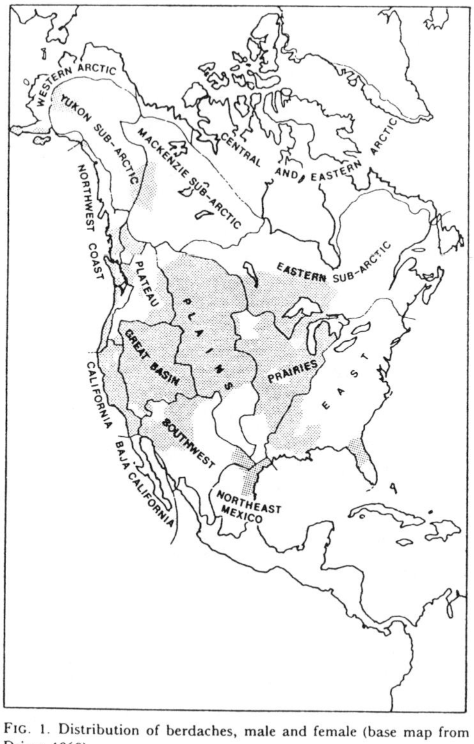

FIG. 1. Distribution of berdaches, male and female (base map from Driver 1969).

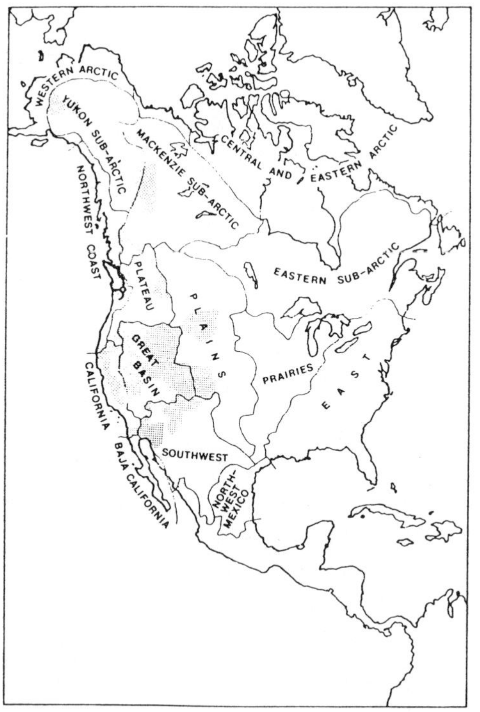

FIG. 2. Distribution of female berdaches (base map from Driver 1969).

reduced their numbers. Perhaps these reports should be treated skeptically; yet when information is available for a specific group over time the number of berdaches dwindles rapidly. Maximilian's statement that in 1832 the Crow had many may be compared with Holder's reporting five in 1889 (1889:622–23), Simms's counting three in 1902 (1903:580–81), and Lowie's meeting only one (1924*b*:243–44). Hidatsa traditions held that their tribe once had as many as fifteen to twenty-five; Bowers's (1965:166–67) informants could remember only two in the generation before theirs. Grinnell (1962, vol. 2:39) said the Cheyenne had five, later dwindling to two, with the last one dying in 1879. Since overall population was also decreasing, the proportion of berdaches may have remained fairly constant, up to a point. Some early accounts suggest, however, that berdaches had a significant social role whose importance diminished as other factors combined to discourage the assumption of this status. Bowers (1965:168) attributes their disappearance among the Hidatsa to the disintegration of the religious system to which they were linked. While it seems unlikely that berdaches were ever numerous, they were probably once more common than later accounts indicate.

TRANSVESTISM

Male berdaches usually adopted the dress and hairstyle of women. References to their imitating women's voices and using their forms of speech, if these differed from men's, are less common, but this may reflect gaps in reporting rather than actual frequency. Female berdaches usually dressed as men. Transvestism was one of the most widespread and significant features of the status, often marking the final stage of gender transformation (cf. Lurie 1953:708). Yet it was neither universal nor invariable.

Transvestism was prohibited by the Pima, whose male berdaches imitated the speech, behavior, and postures of women but wore men's dress (Hill 1938:339), and by the Comanche (Kardiner 1945:56–57, 88), if they had berdaches. Female berdaches retained women's dress among the Achumawi, Atsugewi, Klamath, and Shasta (Spier 1930:51–53; Voegelin 1942:134–35), although no compulsion was reported and the male variety in these societies cross-dressed. The Crow female berdache carried weapons but dressed as a woman (Denig 1961:195–200). Grinnell's description of Cheyenne berdaches as dressing like elderly men (1962, vol. 2:39) was probably a misunderstanding (cf. Hoebel 1960:27). Accounts of male Shasta berdaches conflict, Voegelin (1942:134–35) describing transvestism but Holt (1946:317) denying it. Some societies permitted individual choice. While intersexual Navahos had to dress like women, unmarried berdaches of either sex dressed as they wished. Free choice is reported for male berdaches among the Northern and Southern Paiute (Gayton 1948:174; Lowie 1924*b*:282; Stewart 1941:405), for the female variety among the Wintu (Voegelin 1942:134), and for all Shoshonean berdaches (Steward 1941:252–53; 1943:385).

Male berdaches sometimes assumed the dress proper to their anatomic sex in certain contexts. The Navaho required those who married to dress as men, whether their spouses were male or female (Hill 1935:273, 275–76). One condition that could evoke this shift was undertaking an action defined as specifically male. Miami and Osage berdaches who joined a war party intending to fight had to wear male clothing until they returned (Fletcher and La Flesche 1911:133; Trowbridge 1938:68). Among the Western Mono some alternated by occupation, dressing like women when gathering but changing to men's attire to hunt. Gayton's (1948:174) suggestion that this practice may have distinguished men who had undergone a partial transformation from those who had completed this and always dressed like women could perhaps be extended to other societies in which a berdache assumed this status gradually, with the

complete adoption of women's clothing marking the end of the process. Landes (1970:198–202) describes a Potawatomi example. Such an assumption could reduce some of the variation evident in the data.

A further consideration bearing on the variability reported in dress is that most of the data were gathered after American control had been imposed. Some deviations from the general pattern of transvestism reflect attempts by officials to stamp out the institution by forcing male berdaches to dress as men (Bowers 1965:315; Simms 1903:580). American attitudes also promoted native hostility toward transvestism. Teit's (1930:384) statement that occasionally Flathead male berdaches briefly assumed male dress to please the men illustrates this pressure. The last Winnebago berdache wore a combination of male and female clothing because his brothers threatened to kill him if he completed the transformation (Lurie 1953:708). It seems, then, a valid generalization that in traditional North American societies and under ordinary circumstances a berdache usually cross-dressed. Yet some of the variability reported in the literature was a traditional attribute of the status.

OCCUPATIONS

Berdaches often followed the occupations of the gender whose dress they assumed. This was another particularly widespread feature of their status, one of the traits most often cited and, like transvestism, one of the most significant. A boy's interest in women's occupations and his propensity for engaging in these might be interpreted as signs that he would become a berdache and were sometimes advanced as the causal factors promoting change in gender status. Parsons (1939:38) said that a Pueblo male who did women's work beyond a point—the point not specified—had to become a berdache. Similar significance was seen in a girl's interest in work assigned to men.

Male berdaches are consistently described as exceptionally skilled in women's work, often as better than women. Among the Crow they had the largest and best-appointed lodges and were excellent sewers and the most efficient cooks (Simms 1903:581). This proficiency, noted by observers as well as informants, was another attribute of their status (Boscana 1978:54; Bowers 1965:167; Devereux 1937:513–14; Hassrick 1965:123; Hill 1935:275; Howard 1965:142–43; Kroeber 1952:313; Landes 1968:112–13; 1970:195–96; Linton 1936:480; Lowie 1935:48; Lurie 1953:708–10; Mathews 1897:215; Mirsky 1937:416–17; Parsons 1916:523; Underhill 1969:186). Accounts of their employment by local Whites or acculturated Indian families are also evidence to this point (Holder 1889:624; Landes 1970:198–202; Steward 1941:253). Admiration for their skill centered on crafts and housework rather than agriculture, although some references note their value as gatherers. Apparently female berdaches showed a similar pattern of excelling in male activities, with hunting most often cited (Devereux 1937:515; Honigmann 1954:129–30). Denig (1961:195–203) described Woman Chief as at least equal to any Crow man as a hunter; significantly, she was able to support four wives.

Further evidence that berdaches were considered exceptionally productive is the fact that households based on marriage between a man and a male berdache were exceptionally well-to-do, more prosperous than those founded on male/female unions (Bowers 1965:167; Devereux 1937:513–15; Stevenson 1902:38). So were extended families that included an unmarried berdache. The Navaho regarded such a family as particularly fortunate, since it was assured of wealth (Hill 1935:274). Even berdaches who constituted single-person households seem to have been well-off (Hassrick 1964:121–22; Landes 1968:324; Mirsky 1937:416–17).

Several observers attributed the productivity of male berdaches to their greater strength (Boscana 1978:45; Bowers 1965:167; Stevenson 1902:310–11; Underhill 1969:186–87). Cabeza da Vaca (Katz 1976:285) and Simms (1903:580–82) described them as unusually strong or robust even by comparison with other men. Stevenson (1902:310) called the berdache Wewha the strongest person at Zuni and perhaps the tallest. A Potawatomi berdache was said to be taller than most men (Landes 1970:200). Statements crediting berdaches with unusual size or strength are not frequent enough to provide evidence for a general tendency. That male berdaches were stronger than women seems reasonable, given their larger body size. This may have increased their productivity; but the crafts in which they were most often described as excelling did not require particular strength, nor does this explanation account for the hunting skill of female berdaches. Bowers's (1965:167) emphasis on their freedom from pregnancy and child care echoes Stevenson (1902:37), who estimated that a Zuni berdache could do almost twice as much work as a woman. This advantage again seems an insufficient explanation for excellent craftsmanship. Another possible factor in their productivity may have been industry, a trait often imputed to them (e.g., Devereux 1937:513–14; Stevenson 1902:38); perhaps berdaches had to try harder.

Perhaps this tendency to excel in the occupations assigned to their status also reflected belief in the supernatural powers often ascribed to this. Among the Dakota such supernatural beings as Double-Woman, who ordered men to become berdaches, were associated with proficiency in such activities as quillworking and could confer this talent upon women who experienced visions of them. Explicitly cited by Landes (1970:36–37, 41) and Mirsky (1937:416–17), the association of berdache skills with supernatural power can probably be extended to other cultures. Hassrick (1964:133) describes the items made by Teton Dakota berdaches as "highly desirable" and "eminently marketable." Whether these products were valued simply for their craftsmanship or whether their desirability rested in part on associations with the supernatural, their exchange provided income and was probably an important factor in the prosperity even of single berdaches.

Another important component of their economic role and a significant element in the prosperity often attributed to berdaches rested on the intermediate nature of their gender status, allowing them to combine activities proper to men and to women and maximize their economic opportunities. Mead (1961:1452) characterized the male berdache among the Navaho and Teton Dakota as "a totally self-sufficient 'household' capable of both male and female activities." Voegelin (1942:134–35) credits female berdaches among the Atsugewi, Shasta, and Wintu with this freedom; male berdaches had the same latitude among the Bannock (Steward 1943:385) and some Northern Paiute (Gayton 1948:174). Navaho berdaches of either sex could undertake men's and women's work (Hill 1935:275). Male berdaches are often described as hunting. While reporting that the Navaho forbade them this activity, Hill (1935:275) named it among their occupations; Gifford (1940:168) reported it for the western Navaho berdaches. The apparent contradiction between Mirsky's (1937:416–17) description of Teton Dakota berdaches as combining household work with hunting and Hassrick's (1964:121) argument that their inability to compete as hunters impelled them to adopt berdache status could be resolved by assuming that their hunting was limited and—if such a term is proper—noncompetitive; but we suspect that Hassrick assumed this inability from their status. Linton's (1936:480) statement that among the Plains tribes the husband of a male berdache was taunted for trying to obtain a wife who would hunt and keep house indicates that berdache status did not preclude hunting. Hunting is clearly implied in Cabeza da Vaca's report that Coahuiltecan berdaches, who also did the work of women, used bows (Katz 1976:285). While it seems improbable that one person could effectively carry on both kinds of work on a regular basis, a berdache's ability when necessary to alternate or combine the occupational roles associated with male and female genders would have increased his productivity.

A source of income limited to male berdaches involved specific duties tied to their status. They performed special services in a number of cultures. Accounts seldom specify compensation for these, but the examples described suggest that this practice was probably widespread. Teton berdaches received horses as payment for the secret names they were asked to give children (Fire 1972:217). Among the California cultures in which they were responsible for burial and mourning rituals they were paid for their services (Kroeber 1925:497, 500–501). Still another service peculiar to their status that may have required compensation was their use as go-betweens, facilitated by their ability to move freely between males and females (Mead 1932:189).

WARFARE

Berdache status is often described as a sanctuary for males who were unable or unwilling to accept the role of warrior (Benedict 1939:572; Hoebel 1949:459; Linton 1936:480; Marmor 1965:13; Mead 1961:1452; Mirsky 1937:416–17; Underhill 1969:186). Hassrick (1964:121–22) cast this interpretation in terms of what he called "sissies" and "mamma's boys" who could not face the hardships of hunting and warfare. Fear of warfare is sometimes advanced as the primary reason for assuming the status (Underhill 1953:54; cf. Devereux 1937:517–18). Apparently formulated by anthropologists examining the Teton Dakota, this analysis of the male berdache does not really hold up when extended to North America generally. In our opinion the evidence, considered in its entirety, casts doubt upon this traditional view as valid even for the northern Plains.

No correlation is discernible between the existence of male berdaches and the prevalence or significance of warfare. Their status was as characteristic of the Hopi and Zuni as of the northern Plains tribes, and, granting that the Western Pueblos were less peaceful than they have sometimes been described, they differed qualitatively in this respect from the Teton. Very warlike societies, such as the Iroquois, could lack berdaches, who were at best obscure and perhaps altogether absent in the southern Plains.

Men who feared war did not have to assume berdache status. Information about this group is slight, but its existence is indicated by several sources, including Linton's (1936:480) comment that berdaches had higher status than men who failed as warriors. Further evidence is provided by the measures to shame them, described in the first section of this article, superficially resembling the cross-dressing feature of the berdache status but sharply distinguished from it in concept. Also relevant here, we think, is Catlin's account of the young Mandan men he called "dandies," whom the warriors despised. Whatever their sexual orientation may have been—and we doubt that his reference to them as "gay and tinselled bucks" (1973, vol. 1:112–14) should be taken in the contemporary sense—they were obviously not berdaches.

Berdache status, usually assumed at adolescence or foreshadowed earlier, was occasionally embraced by an established warrior. Tixier (1940:234) describes such an event among the Osage; Irving (1888:120–22) gives an Oto example. De Smet (1904:1017) met such a man among the Crow. A similar interpretation may apply to the Osage berdache described below, except that he continued warrior activity. These incidents seem to have been rare; but so were berdaches.

The frequent exclusion of male berdaches from warfare seems to us best analyzed as part of a widespread but variable prohibition against their engaging in certain actions defined as specifically male. Sometimes this prohibition was a cultural rule; sometimes it was individual practice. It was neither universal nor absolute. Illinois berdaches fought but were forbidden to use bows, symbolic of maleness (Marquette 1900:129). As we have seen, the Miami required them to dress as males when going to war (Trowbridge 1938:68), and a similar practice may be inferred for the Osage on the basis of the account of a young man who, returning as leader of a successful raid, was supernaturally revealed to be a berdache and accepted this status, although he continued to act as a war leader and in this capacity dressed as a man (Fletcher and La Flesche 1911:133). The Crow berdache Lowie knew had fought (1935:8). Henry (Coues 1897:163–65) described a berdache who acted as rear guard for a group of Ojibwa, fighting off a Dakota war party while his companions retreated. This was the Yellow Head, whose "disgusting advances" later outraged John Tanner (1956:89–91) and whom Whitehead (1981:108) cites as an example of an unsuccessful berdache. When the leader of a Hidatsa war party that came upon three Dakota women decided to count coup upon them, one "woman" revealed himself as a berdache and drove off the warriors with a digging stick, his threats aided by their leader's arrow's failing to penetrate his robe (Bowers 1965:256). It is also clear that berdache status did not ensure safety from enemy attack (cf. Kurz 1937:211).

In contexts outside warfare, berdaches were capable of violent behavior contradicting naive assumptions that they were necessarily gentle by nature (cf. Underhill 1953:54). The Yellow Head, whom Henry described as troublesome when drunk, lost an eye in a fight (Coues 1897:53). Mohave berdaches might assault unfaithful husbands or men who ridiculed them (Devereux 1937:510–14). The berdache Wewha was imprisoned for a year for attacking three policemen trying to make an arrest at Zuni (Parsons 1939:65).

In some societies, berdaches fought. In others, although not fighting, they had significant roles in the war complex. They accompanied warriors to carry supplies among the Natchez and Timucua (Dumont in Swanton 1911:110; Le Moyne du Morgues 1878:7–8), to herd the horses taken from the Spanish among the Karankawa (Newcomb 1961:74). Cheyenne war parties often invited berdaches to accompany them (Grinnell 1962, vol. 2:40–41); besides treating the wounded, they had custody of scalps, carried these into camp, and ran the dance that followed the raiders' return. The Teton Dakota consulted berdaches to divine their success in projected battles (Grinnell 1956:237–38; Hyde 1937:147).

Rather than a group of males who feared warfare, berdaches were closely tied to the war complex in a number of societies and perhaps even a crucial part of it. Admitting that direct evidence for his argument is lacking, Hoebel (1960:77) suggests that the Cheyenne attributed the success of a war party to its inclusion of a berdache, whose stored-up unexpended virility was essential for this end. We do not entirely accept Hoebel's precise argument, although we agree that by rejecting the kinds of power normally accessible to males berdaches might be regarded as acquiring special and potent kinds of power that could affect military actions, among other activities. We do think that Hoebel has discerned much more of the actual relationship between berdaches and warfare than those who formulated or accept the traditional analysis. Further evidence for such an association is provided by Bowers (1965:108, 327), who points out that Hidatsa men became berdaches through visions sent by the Holy Women, supernatural beings closely associated with warfare and aiding young warriors; and he attributes their disappearance to the end of warfare and the collapse of the ceremonial structure associated with it.

Female berdaches did not emulate male behavior by becoming warriors. Gifford's (1933:5) report that this was one of their attributes among the Cocopa, not confirmed by accounts of other River Yuman groups, is explicitly denied for the Mohave (Devereux 1937:518–19). The female Kutenai berdache fought (Spier 1935:26–27), and Woman Chief achieved high rank as a Crow warrior (Denig 1961:195–200), but their activity in the war complex was exceptional for their status and differed only in scale from that of occasional nonberdache woman warriors.

SEXUALITY

Sexual behavior is the aspect of the berdache status in which the reticence of informants most often combines with the prudery of observers to obscure actual practice and in which suppositions have been most frequent. Early European observers, when aware that berdaches were not intersexual, tended to assume that men who dressed and acted like women were necessarily homosexual (cf. Lafitau 1724:52). That this belief, reflected in their use of the word "berdache," was sometimes only an assumption is shown by Dumont's 18th-century account of the Natchez (Swanton 1911:100): "as among these people [the Natchez], who live almost without religion and without law, libertinism is carried to the greatest excess, I will not answer that these barbarians do not abuse this pretended chief of the women [berdache] and make him serve their brutal passions." Most later observers continued to hold this view, at least implicitly. Yet if often accurate, the assumption that berdaches were homosexual is oversimplified. Like their other attributes, sexual behavior was variable and very complex.

Questioning whether homosexuality was an integral feature of berdache status, Kroeber (1952:313) pointed out that informants emphasized its social aspects—transvestism and occupations—rather than sexual behavior. This emphasis, prominent in the literature, could reflect reluctance to offend Western sensibilities rather than indicating the native view. Most accounts of Crow berdaches stress social behavior, yet Holder (1889) obtained explicit data about sexual practices. Mohave informants gave Devereux (1937) detailed descriptions of homosexual activity. The Yellow Head's intentions toward Tanner (1956:89–91) were very clear. Homosexual exploits were an important attribute of berdaches among the Santee, who claimed these were too lewd to describe to Landes (1968:112–13). Noting this Santee contrast with the Potawatomi emphasis on berdaches' concern with "proper" female behavior, she interprets this as a cultural difference (1970:198–202). While reticence cannot be ignored as a factor potentially skewing anthropologists' perceptions of the native view of berdaches, it seems possible that if some cultures considered homosexual activity a significant aspect of this status, others did not.

Most descriptions of berdache sexual behavior stress homosexuality. This involved intercourse with persons of the same anatomical sex, but not with other berdaches, and entailed relations ranging in form from casual promiscuity to stable marriages. Information is, as usual, unsatisfactory. Many sources are silent. Most of them specify little more than that berdaches lived with persons of the same sex or say they never married without describing other relationships. Even statements about marriage seldom note its nature or frequency. Enough data are available for a few societies to discern or infer certain recurring patterns. Promiscuity apparently characterized Santee and Teton Dakota berdaches, who were not allowed to marry men or even to establish relatively long-term sexual relationships (Hassrick 1964:121–22; Landes 1968:32; Mirsky 1937:416–17). Catlin's Sauk account (1973, vol. 2:214–15), also implying promiscuity, suggests that their sexual partners were young men, perhaps not yet married, although it seems likely a berdache's lovers also included married men. We think this was one common pattern. Both casual relations and marriage are reported for some societies. Holder (1889:624) implies that Crow berdaches seldom married, but apparently it was not forbidden; the female berdache in this tribe married women. Papago berdaches, who could marry, often lived alone and received male lovers (Underhill 1969:186–87). Among the Navaho they were free to pursue any kind of relationship, including marriage (Hill 1935). Brittle, unstable marriages are described for Mohave berdaches (Devereux 1937:157) and may be inferred for the Ojibwa (Tanner 1956:89–91). Stable unions, reported for the Yuma (Forde 1931:157), also characterized the Hidatsa, whose berdaches usually married older men, childless, who had difficulty keeping wives, and if the husband also had female wives insisted upon a separate lodge (Bowers 1965:166–68). A Hidatsa berdache could develop a complete family by adopting children, either village orphans or war captives taken by his relatives, of whom he was considered the mother. Among the Cheyenne (Hoebel 1960:77) and Luiseño (Boscana 1978:54), berdaches could only be auxiliary wives.

Although direct evidence for this conclusion is scanty, we suspect that homosexual relations with berdaches were generally accepted as long as they did not obstruct "normal" marriages or, in some cultures, take the form of these. Concern with preventing any interference with the child-producing male/female unions necessary to perpetuate a society would center most intensely upon marriage and could explain those cultures that prohibited formal unions with berdaches. Bowers's description of the husbands of Hidatsa berdaches, cited above, is suggestive; even when marriage was strongly encouraged, the husbands were relative failures maritally or already had female wives. Moreover, the relatively few indications that sexual relations with berdaches drew disapproval usually focus on marriage rather than casual affairs. This emphasis seems clear in Linton's (1936:480) account of the ridicule directed at the husband of a Plains berdache. Devereux (1937:513–18) attributes the instability of Mohave berdache marriages to the derision their spouses experienced; affairs with them did not draw this response.

This analysis might also explain the anomalously vehement denunciations of sexual relations with berdaches attributed to the Teton Dakota. Mirsky (1937:416–17), describing berdaches as "passive" homosexual males, reported that the Teton ostracized their "active" counterparts. If the latter terms designate the sexual partners of berdaches, their ostracism seems improbable; Forgey (1975:3–4) argues that berdaches served the needs of "active" homosexuals. Perhaps Mirsky meant nonberdache males who were exclusively homosexual and refused to marry. Hassrick (1964:122) cites a man's warning to his son that relations with a berdache will draw punishment in the afterlife. Since his informant simultaneously described homosexual intercourse as the culminating step in their transformation, berdaches obviously found sexual partners. Unless such warnings were an empty form, it seems probable that they were actually directed against long-term relationships rather than intercourse or, if really addressed to young boys, as Lame Deer (Fire 1972:149) seems to imply, were meant to discourage close associations with berdaches that might lead to assuming the same status.

Accounts of the modes of intercourse practiced by male berdaches in the homosexual context are very rare. Kroeber (1902:19–20) describes anal intercourse performed upon Arapaho berdaches. Holder (1889:625) notes its practice by the Crow without indicating whether the context was heterosexual or homosexual and nonberdache; he insists that berdaches limited themselves to fellation of their partners. Devereux (1937: 511–15), who credits Mohave berdaches with both practices—which also characterized heterosexual intercourse in their culture—is the main authority on the forms of intercourse for female berdaches. Among the Mohave these were limited to digital manipulation of the sexual partner and to various techniques producing vulvic contact. He denies the practice of cunnilingus, to which Mohave men were extremely averse; while women might not share this aversion, female berdaches imitated male behavior. Vulvic contact, perhaps common among other groups, is implied by Jones's (1907:141) account of a sexual encounter between two nonberdache women. The Kutenai female berdache is said to have used an artificial phallus to convince her wife she was actually a man (Schaeffer 1976:294).

If homosexuality is the orientation most often described or assumed for berdaches, it is not the only one recorded or implied. Kroeber (1952:312) suggested that some of them may have found transvestism—including general social behavior—satisfying in itself. Benedict (1934:263) held that the status included some men who were impotent or had a weak sexual drive. Both suggestions draw some support from the ethnographic evidence. Osgood (1958:261–62) concluded that his information about Ingalik berdaches suggested asexuality. Teit's (1930:38) denial that Flathead berdaches were homosexual, corroborated by Turney-High's (1937:85) later study, may also have held for their Nootka counterparts (Drucker 1951:331). The Pima prohibited homosexuality (Hill 1938:339). None of these accounts describe heterosexual behavior. Descriptions of individual berdaches among the Plains Cree (Mandelbaum 1940:256–57), Chiricahua Apache (Opler 1965:111), and Bella Coola (McIlwraith 1948, vol. 1:45–46) include denials of any overt sexual activity. Fletcher and La Flesche's (1911:182) statement that Omaha berdaches "must sometimes become subject to gross actions" hints at homosexuality but implies that only some of them engaged in this. We conclude, then, that the berdache category included some essentially asexual persons; perhaps certain cultures even defined this orientation as proper.

Other accounts ascribe heterosexual behavior to berdaches, either exclusively or as part of a general bisexual orientation. Olson (1940:288) described those of the Haisla as entirely heterosexual, male berdaches marrying women and female berdaches men. The sexual partners of one male Quinault berdache were elderly women (Olson 1935:99). McIlwraith (1948, vol. 2:45–46) reported that some male Bella Bella and Bella Coola berdaches married women. One male Osage berdache had a wife (Fletcher and La Flesche 1911:133). Although Navaho intersexes were restricted to male sexual partners, their berdaches were essentially bisexual, engaging in sexual relations with males and females (Hill 1935:276). So were Illinois berdaches, whom Liette (1947:112–13) described as homosexuals who also had intercourse with women. Informants said a Crow berdache occasionally had sex with women, although he denied it (Holder 1889:624). Spier (1930:50–53) described a bisexual female Klamath berdache. If the Mohave account of a woman who turned heterosexual after her rape by the husband of a woman she was courting sounds rather too much like a male fantasy, reports of her earlier earnings as a prostitute suggest a bisexual capacity (Devereux 1961:416–25). One of Steward's Shoshonean informants said his great-grandfather had been a berdache (Steward 1941:253); so was the grandfather of a Navaho berdache (Hill 1935:273).

Besides reports of open heterosexual behavior that was culturally approved or at least viewed neutrally, some accounts describe berdaches as engaging in this surreptitiously. Discounting a Yurok suggestion that transvestism afforded males sexual access to women without rousing suspicion, Kroeber (1952:314) accepted this as an occasional possibility. Miami berdaches may have taken similar advantage of their status (Trowbridge 1938:68). Stevenson (1902:37–38) recorded a parallel belief among the Zuni. To her statement that Zuni berdaches never married women she added the qualification that they seldom had sexual relations with them; and while discounting rumors that the berdache Wewha had fathered several children she believed one child to be his. Tixier (1940:23) noted rumors that an Osage berdache was the lover of the chief's wife.

Evaluating this scattered information about heterosexual behavior presents special problems. Some of it is obviously hearsay, of uncertain reliability. Another factor complicating an assessment of its significance is uncertainty about the time in an individual's life when heterosexual behavior occurred. A berdache usually entered this status at adolescence but could do so as an adult and after marriage; or, rarely, might move from it back into a normal gender status. The female Kutenai berdache had a husband before her transformation and later marriages to women (Spier 1935:26–27). Some Mohave women became berdaches after experiencing difficult deliveries (Devereux 1937:507–8). Spier (1930:51–53) describes two Klamath men who withdrew from the berdache status but says nothing about their sexual activity while in it. Yet, even with these reservations, it seems necessary to conclude that a number of berdaches were bisexual while they held this gender status. At first sight, indeed, the extent of their bisexuality seems surprising, but, here again, the intermediate nature of the status could well have been expressed sexually as it was in occupations and dress.

ONTOGENY

Most accounts of the processes by which individuals became berdaches center around two themes. One view, relatively secular and matter-of-fact, describes them as entering this status in childhood by showing interest in the work of the other gender and by associating with its members. This behavior led their parents to dress and treat them as berdaches and their societies to accept them as such. The second and more widespread view is that the status required supernatural validation, usually in the form of a vision and generally occurring at adolescence or later, resulting in a public transformation of gender status.

Still other modes of recruitment are reported for a few groups. Several accounts describe berdaches as chosen, in infancy or very early childhood, and trained for their role. Kaska couples who wanted a daughter to become a hunter dressed her as a boy and gave her masculine work (Honigmann 1954:129–30). The Luiseño, who valued berdaches as auxiliary wives for their chiefs, selected certain male infants for this purpose (Boscana 1978:54). Bancroft (1874, vol. 1:82), citing Langsdorff and Sauer as sources, said Kaniagmiut women chose their handsomest and most promising sons for this status, which provided wives for wealthy men. The most divergent account, Hammond's (1882) report that each Pueblo feminized one of its most virile adult males through a combination of continuous horseback riding and incessant masturbation, seems best interpreted as a misunderstanding, perhaps stimulated by too enthusiastic a search for parallels with the Scythians.

Statements that male war captives were forced to become berdaches seem mostly an anthropological myth. Extrapolating from Iroquois reports, Carr (n.d.:18–19, 33) explained berdaches as captives assigned to agricultural work. Angelino and Shedd (1955) based their argument that berdaches included feminized captives on the rhetoric used by Iroquois orators to describe their political relations with the Delaware (cf. Goddard 1978:223), interpreting this imagery literally and transferring it to an entirely different context. Apart from flaws in method, both hypotheses are handicapped by the complete lack of evidence for Iroquois berdaches. A Tlingit account suggesting an attempt to force homosexual relations upon a captive male did not involve berdache status (de Laguna 1960:155). The references in Hill's novel *Hanta yo* (1979) to sodomizing male enemies are entirely fictional, according to Powers (1979:825), who explains these as an invention based upon Hill's misunderstanding of Dakota. Evidence for this method of recruitment consists of a single Winnebago instance, which Lurie's (1953:710) informants apparently regarded as exceptional.

The distribution of the two major processes is indicated in table 2. A few groups appear in both lists because sources disagree. Emphasis on childhood behavior may also be inferred for cultures requiring a formal test to determine whether a boy who liked women's work was really destined for berdachehood. The Papago placed such a child in a brush windbreak containing basketry material as well as a bow and arrow and set fire to the enclosure; choosing the basketry as he fled ensured his future as a berdache (Underhill 1969:186–87). Similar tests involving objects symbolizing male and female work are reported for the Pima (Hill 1938:339–40), some Ute (Stewart 1944:298), and one Shoshonean group (Steward 1941:253). A Klamath incident rather similar in form occurred in adolescence and coincided with a vision experience (Spier 1930:51–53).

Belief in visions may also be inferred when not explicitly reported. Pawnee and Yankton berdaches (Dorsey 1890:67; Dorsey and Murie 1940:108) were influenced by the moon, a frequent source of transformation visions among neighboring cultures. Marquette's Illinois account (1900:129), silent about such visions, strongly implies them.

Descriptions of transformation visions, mostly obtained from Prairie and Plains tribes, usually involve female supernaturals. The most widespread was the moon, reported for the Omaha, Sauk, and Winnebago, implied for the Yankton and Pawnee, and inferable for the Iowa, Kansa, Osage, Oto, and Ponca, whose term for berdache, ***mixuga***, is glossed as "instructed by the moon" (Fletcher and La Flesche 1911:132). The female deity associated with Miami berdaches may also have been the moon, given their use of the term "white face" for the status (Trowbridge 1938:68). The moon, then, had a paramount role in berdache visions among the Dhegiha and Chiwere Siouans, the Pawnee, and some Algonquian tribes. In Omaha accounts, the most detailed, it held a burden strap in one hand and a bow and arrow in the other; and when the dreamer reached for the bow, quickly crossed its arms and tried to force the burden strap on him, sealing his status as a berdache (Fletcher and La Flesche 1911:132–33).

Double-Woman, similarly important for Santee and Teton Dakota berdaches, was particularly skilled in women's work. Women who had visions of her became, like berdaches, expert in this, or, alternatively, could become seducers of men (Lowie 1916:118–19; Wissler 1916:92). Like the moon among the Omaha, Double-Woman offered Teton men a choice between male and female implements, the latter making them berdaches. Hidatsa berdaches dreamed of Village-Old-Woman or deities that she created, Woman Above and the Holy Women, or of a loop of sweetgrass (Bowers 1965:166–67, 323–30). Women who dreamed of them entered the Holy Women society, which also included the berdaches. Among the Mandan, transformation dreams came from Old Woman Above or other holy women; later, the dreamer picked up porcupine quills or a rope in the forest (Bowers 1950:272, 298).

Supernatural elements in gender transformation were probably more important than the accounts emphasizing childhood interests suggest. Reporting that Hidatsa boys who showed any signs of effeminacy were classed with girls and brought up as such, Biddle (Jackson 1962:537) completely missed this aspect of the process. While the Hidatsa thought boys who showed inordinate interest in women's occupations were more likely to dream of the deities who ordered males to become berdaches, this behavior was discouraged, even forbidden; the transformation occurred among young men and required repeated visions (Bowers 1965:105–6, 115, 130). Omitting the supernatural aspects of Illinois berdaches and describing their status as one automatically assigned to boys interested in women's vocations, Liette (1947:112–13) greatly distorted their social role. Supernatural validation could be rather covert, and informants could view the transformation process very differently. Like some of his Mohave informants, Devereux (1937:501–3) emphasized the secular view, concentrating on children's behavior. Yet Drucker (1941:173) and Kroeber (1925:7–8) reported that dreams preceded this behavior and were believed to produce it. Some of Devereux's informants described a supernatural experience in the form of dreams coming to the embryo in the womb. The Mohave transformation came in later childhood, when the family of an incipient berdache secretly prepared an initiation ceremony which, if accepted by the child, certified its status.

In societies lacking visions, mythological sanctions may have substituted for them, although the figures involved were usually hermaphrodites rather than berdaches. The Bella Coola regarded Sxints, a supernatural hermaphrodite, as the prototype of the berdaches, who were somehow affected by him (McIlwraith 1948, vol. 1:45–46). The Navaho closely associated the berdache/intersex category with the hermaphrodite twins born to First Man and First Woman, important mythical figures who invented pottery and other artifacts associated with women (Hill 1935:273–74; Mathews 1897:70, 217; Reichard 1950, vol. 4:140). The transvestite-hermaphrodite had a prominent role in Zuni myths and ceremonies (Cushing 1896:401; Parsons 1916:524–25; Stevenson 1902:37) and figures in rituals at Acoma (Parsons 1939:540, 765) and among the Hopi (Titiev 1972:153, 214–15). One Tipai culture hero was a transvestite (Gifford 1931:12, 56). Transvestite episodes involving the culture hero as trickster were widespread in North America (e.g., Jones 1907:315–31). The Sinkaietk cited one of these as the precedent for their berdaches (Cline 1938:149). That mythical sanction could be significant seems demonstrated by the Oto, who described Elk as the first transvestite and whose berdaches came from the Elk clan (Whitman 1969:50).

Another indication that berdache status, even when described as attained by entirely secular processes that did not involve vision experience, still included important supernatural aspects centers on the skills typically associated with it. In North American cultures, exceptional ability itself usually signified supernatural power. The Navaho belief that their berdaches were predestined to be wealthy and control wealth illustrates this point. Despite Devereux's secular emphasis, he notes that Mohave berdaches, especially females, were exceptionally powerful shamans and points out parallels in the processes leading to the two statuses (1937:516).

The secular and supernatural views of the processes leading to berdachehood are inherently neither contradictory nor mutually exclusive. Incipient berdaches might well have shown, interests foreshadowing their future transformation, but we doubt that cultures automatically assigned such children to the berdache category. Evidence that parents might discourage this prefiguring behavior (Bowers 1965:105–6; Denig 1961:187–88;

TABLE 2

MAIN FACTORS LEADING TO BERDACHE STATUS

CULTURE	CHILDHOOD INTERESTS	VISION EXPERIENCE
Achumawi (Voegelin 1942: 134–35)	. . .	x
Arapaho (Kroeber 1902: 19–20)	. . .	x
Assiniboine (Lowie 1910: 42)	. . .	x
Bella Bella (McIlwraith 1948, vol. 1: 45–46)	x	
Bella Coola (McIlwraith 1948, vol. 1: 45–46)	x	. .
Cocopa (Drucker 1941: 163; Gifford 1933: 294)	x	x
Crow (Denig 1961: 187–88; Simms 1903: 580–81)	x	. .
Flathead (Teit 1930: 384)	. . .	x
Hidatsa (Jackson 1962: 531; Bowers 1965: 105–6)	x	x
Illinois (Liette 1947: 112–13)	x	. . .
Ingalik (Osgood 1958: 262–63)	x	. . .
Iowa (Lurie 1953: 711)	. . .	x
Kansa (Say in James 1823: 129)	. . .	x
Mandan (Bowers 1950: 272, 296)	. . .	x
Maricopa (Drucker 1941: 163; Spier 1933: 242–43)	. . .	x
Miami (Trowbridge 1938: 68)	. . .	x
Mohave (Devereux 1937: 501–3; Drucker 1941: 173; Kroeber 1925: 478)	x	x
Ojibwa (Kinietz 1947: 155–56; McKenney 1827: 314–15)	. . .	x
Omaha (Dorsey 1890: 379; Fletcher and La Flesche 1911: 132)	. . .	x
Osage (Fletcher and La Flesche 1911: 132–33)	. . .	x
Oto (Irving 1888: 120–22)	. . .	x
Ponca (Dorsey 1890: 379; Howard 1965: 142–43)	x	x
Potawatomi (Landes 1970: 190–91)	. . .	x
Santee Dakota (Landes 1968: 57)	. . .	x
Sauk (Keating 1825, vol. 1: 216)	. . .	x
Teton Dakota (Hassrick 1964: 122; Powers 1977: 58–59)	. . .	x
Ute (Stewart 1940: 298)	. . .	x
Winnebago (Lurie 1953: 70)	. . .	x
Yokuts (Gayton 1948: 236)	x	. .
Yuma (Forde 1931: 157)	. . .	x
Zuni (Parsons 1916: 526–27)	x	. . .

Simms 1903:580–88) or be reluctant to admit its implications (Devereux 1937:508) suggests there must have been some point at which the transformation had to be accepted and made formal. From this point of view, perhaps, a vision was equivalent to the brushwood test or the Mohave initiation ceremony as an event that fixed a berdache's destiny beyond doubt. Yet to assume that a vision simply sanctioned or validated a disposition that had already shown itself (e.g., Meyer 1977:75) seems an extreme oversimplification. Transformation visions could come unexpectedly. Omaha men sometimes tried to conceal them, unsuccessfully, or even killed themselves to escape their destiny (Dorsey 1890:379; Fletcher and La Flesche 1911: 132–33). As noted earlier, men who had achieved warrior status sometimes had visions directing their transformation. Berdache-type visions often offered the dreamer a choice between alternatives, with his selection determining his future; yet the significance of his choice might be clear only in retrospect. Osage accounts credit the supernaturals with surprising trickery and deceit (Fletcher and La Flesche 1911:133). One youth, offered his choice of weapons, selected a battle-axe as the most manly of these, only to find that near his village it became a hoe. The meaning of the bow-or-burden-strap choice offered Omaha men by the moon was obvious, but dreamers did not choose the strap; it was forced upon them as they tried to seize the bow.

A neglected aspect of the selection process involves statements that only members of certain social groups could become berdaches. While all Hidatsa boys were discouraged from showing behavior predisposing them toward receiving visions from female deities, in fact berdache status was potentially open not to all males, but only to those whose fathers or brothers owned ceremonial rights to bundles associated with these (Bowers 1965:168). Mandan practice was similar (Bowers 1950:502). One of Devereux's informants claimed that generally only members of prominent Mohave families could acquire the status (1937:502). If the Tlingit did have berdaches, they had to belong to a particular clan (de Laguna 1954:178), as among the Oto (Whitman 1969:50). Other societies may have had similar restrictions even if these were not general.

SOCIAL POSITION

The attitudes toward berdaches reported for North American cultures varied from awe and reverence through indifference to scorn and contempt. We attribute this diversity to declining esteem, influenced by Western views. Some early accounts (e.g., Le Moyne du Morgues 1878:7–8) describing the status as scorned seem explicable as expressions of the European reaction rather than actual native views. Attitudes toward berdaches may have varied in the past. Certainly their absence could be interpreted as evidence of hostility toward the status. The ambivalent Mohave views reported by Devereux (1937) could represent disapproval of the claims of anatomical transformation made by their berdaches, rather than contamination by the Western outlook. With these reservations, we hold that statements ascribing low status to berdaches generally represent shifts away from older and very different views.

Statements that the status carried high prestige use remarkably similar terms for societies widely separated in space and time. Thus, the Navaho regarded berdaches as holy and sacred (Hill 1935:297), the Hidatsa as mysterious and holy (Bowers 1965:326–27). Lowie's description of Assiniboin berdaches as *wakan* (1910:42) corresponds almost precisely with Marquette's assertion over two centuries earlier that their Illinois counterparts passed for *manitus* (1900:129). Ascriptions of low status seem less convincing. References to them as unproductive or lazy (Birket-Smith and de Laguna 1938:206; Gifford 1940:136, 138) conflict sharply with the productivity usually stressed as one of their main attributes. A southern Ute claim that berdaches "were kept hard at work at tasks reserved for women" (Opler 1940:147) seems a pejorative reinterpretation of this attribute and of the standard occupational aspect of their status. Such statements, resembling the Western bias evident in Stephen's (1936:276) reference to berdaches as "abominable," seem to be a reappraisal of the status, in retrospect, under its influence. Lurie (1953:708) wrote on this point, "Most informants felt that the berdache was at one time a highly honored and respected person, but that the Winnebago had become ashamed of the custom because the white people thought it was amusing or evil." Hill (1935:274) found this shift occurring among the Navaho. In traditional Indian societies, berdaches were respected, perhaps feared, because their condition manifested power given them by the supernatural. Perhaps strongest in societies where visions sanctioned their status, this attitude also characterized other groups such as the Navaho.

The supernatural power of berdaches apparently manifested itself in the gender-mixing attributes of their status rather than in distinctive public roles apart from these. They did not hold formal offices. Occasional suggestions of a close association with chieftainship (Boscana 1978:54; Tixier 1940:34), perhaps most explicit in Marquette's (1900:129) report that Illinois councils decided nothing without their advice, resemble early accounts of transvestites from the Circum-Caribbean area (Guerra 1971:48–49, 55) but are too fragmentary to indicate a general pattern. A few accounts note distinctive ritual functions. Berdaches conducted burials among several California tribes (Gayton 1948:46, 236; Kroeber 1925:497–501; Voegelin 1942:134–35) and the Timucua (Le Moyne du Morgues 1878:7–8). In Zuni ceremonies they took the role of the transvestite/hermaphrodite (Parsons 1916:325; Stevenson 1902:37–38). Some cultures assigned them ritual duties as part of the war complex (Grinnell 1962, vol. 2:37–38; Underhill 1969:186–87). Most reports emphasize the intensity and extent of their ritual participation rather than any distinctive features. Navaho male berdaches were very active in ritual, but their activities did not differ in kind from those of other men (Hill 1935:275)—another indication of their ability to mix gender-related behavior. They were the most active Hidatsa ritual group, taking part in every ceremony, but shared these activities with the postmenopausal women who also belonged to the Holy Women society except that, being stronger, berdaches were responsible for certain duties such as selecting and raising the poles for the Sun Dance (Bowers 1965:167, 326). Berdaches might be shamans, although this was usually an individual attribute rather than a property of their gender status. Even when characteristic of all berdaches, as among the Mohave and Yurok, shamanism was not limited to them (Devereux 1937:516; Kroeber 1925:46).

The importance or significance of their power for the societies to which berdaches belonged apparently lay in beliefs that this could extend beyond the individuals belonging to this status to affect others. Intimations of this attitude in Landes's (1970:195–202) discussion of the Potawatomi are somewhat more pronounced in Hoebel's (1960:77) analysis of Cheyenne beliefs and are explicit in Navaho statements that their prosperity and even their existence as a people depended upon berdaches (Hill 1938:274).

CONCLUSIONS

The transformation of a berdache was not a complete shift from his or her biological gender to the opposite one, but rather an approximation of the latter in some of its social aspects, effecting an intermediate gender status that cut across the boundaries between gender categories. A male berdache, who might be referred to as "she," could be called a man (Stevenson 1902:87) but not a woman. Usage here resembled the current

Western practice of using "she" for a male performing in drag but not labelling him a woman. In noting this parallel we are not equating the two statuses and would reject their identification except insofar as berdache status could be called a performance. The native view here seems illustrated by the Zuni, who buried male berdaches in women's dress but men's trousers on the men's side of the graveyard (Parsons 1916:528).

Transformation was anatomically circumscribed. No matter how successfully a male berdache imitated the social behavior of a woman, he could not become one physiologically, lacking her reproductive capacities, unable to menstruate or conceive. Nor could a female berdache impregnate women. Indian societies sharply rejected claims that berdaches had transcended their anatomical sex in any sense other than the social. The acceptable limits of transformation were represented by Hidatsa berdaches, who became mothers by adopting children. The female Kutenai berdache's pretense that she had physiologically become a male was exposed by her brother (Schaeffer 1976:296).

The Mohave openly ridiculed their male berdaches for insisting that female terms be used for their sexual organs and for their simulations of menstruation, pregnancy, and childbirth and taunted female berdaches for lacking penises (Devereux 1937:510–13). The only possible exception to limiting transformation was the apparent belief among the Mohave and other River Yuman cultures that female berdaches did not menstruate or did so only sporadically. Yet assuming at least a partial lack of the female reproductive process, while perhaps facilitating their practice as shamans, did not define them as men. A Mohave man who had intercourse with a pregnant woman could become her child's father and give it membership in his clan. The same assertion by a female berdache who acquired a pregnant wife was rejected; the child belonged to the clan of its biological father (Devereux 1937:514). Her male counterpart who claimed he had given birth to a stillborn infant had to bury the supposed corpse privately; public cremation, implying acceptance of his pretense, was not permitted.

Berdaches who observed the anatomical limits bounding their gender status gained acceptance and respect. Yet in another sense these restrictions expanded social opportunities for male berdaches—who, as nonwomen, free of menstrual pollution, enjoyed the status advantages of women who had passed menopause and could take nonmale roles in ritual contexts—and were probably an important factor in the mixing of gender features in their social behavior.

The berdache status allowed men to combine roles assigned to male and female genders, mixing aspects of these categories. Cross-dressing, perhaps their most consistently observed gender feature, was not universal and was assumed voluntarily. Regulations forcing them to wear men's clothing for specifically male activities are a significant indication of their potential ability to cross and recross the social boundaries between the two main gender categories. The occupations associated with berdache status, perhaps its most important attribute, also crosscut these boundaries. They permitted a combination of male and female work which, given their freedom from child care, let them achieve exceptional productivity. This gender mixing may have given them credit for supernatural power that translated into their outstanding craft skills. Certainly it facilitated their role as go-betweens, which rested on their freedom to mingle with both sexes. A potential for gender mixing in activities relating to warfare is not surprising. Individual nonberdache women often crossed gender boundaries in this area. The role of male berdaches in the war complex sometimes approximated that of male or female warriors but sometimes resembled that of noncombatant women without being identical to it. Their sexual behavior again mixed aspects of gender categories and in a sense transcended their limits. Conventionally taking the role of women in intercourse with men, many also had sex with women. Their privileged sexual status was most explicitly described for the Navaho, who permitted them any form of sexual intercourse with either sex (Hill 1935:276). Finally, their ritual activity, often associated with the vision-based power on which their transformation frequently rested, also depended on their definition as nonwomen. Hill's (1935:276) conclusion that Navaho berdaches "enjoy more opportunities for personal and material gratification than the ordinary individual" can be extended to other North American cultures even if, as he points out, not all berdaches took advantage of these. Opportunities for female berdaches, except perhaps among the Navaho, seem to have been fewer.

A berdache thus transcended the boundaries of a gender category that was biologically and culturally defined to attain an intermediate gender status biologically the same but culturally redefined. Crossing the boundary between these gender categories was not a single process or a one-directional movement. Berdache status included a continuing crossing of this boundary, in both directions, to such an extent that we prefer to characterize the status as gender mixing rather than gender crossing. Like the opportunities open to those who adopted this status, these gender-mixing features seem much more pronounced among male berdaches. Among the Navaho, at least, they also sharply distinguished the status of berdaches from that of intersexes, who were not allowed to cross back.

In examining the berdache status and its attributes we have not directly addressed the reasons for its existence. This issue involves two closely interwoven problems: why persons became berdaches and why North American cultures gave this mixed gender status formal recognition. Most explanations offered by American anthropologists cluster around two hypotheses, neither of them satisfactory.

One hypothesis describes berdachehood as a status instituted specifically for homosexuals. Implicitly held by those who class it as a form of institutionalized homosexuality, this position has also been adopted by some gay writers. It was presented most explicitly and in greatest detail by Devereux (1937) in his study of the Mohave. Devereux equated berdaches with homosexuals, using the terms interchangeably. He specified homosexual inclination as the factor impelling Mohave individuals to become berdaches. To answer the second problem, he argued that formal recognition of the berdache status had advantages for Mohave society. Publicly identifying homosexuals and making them an institution gave them a protected status. At the same time, it forced them into the open and robbed homosexuality of its glamor as something secret and forbidden. Requiring homosexuals to dress like the other gender prevented their misrepresenting themselves to seduce and recruit unsuspecting heterosexuals. It also allowed heterosexuals to satisfy passing impulses toward sexual experiment without jeopardizing their normal status. Anyone who had sexual relations with a berdache was only a temporary bisexual, apparently even someone who spent most of his life having sex with berdaches. These practices, according to Devereux, promoted overall social health by localizing the homosexual "disorder."

This hypothesis, in all its forms, embodies an archaic view of homosexuality as equivalent to defective gender and defines it in terms of transvestism and occupation rather than sexual activity. The homosexual bent that Devereux ascribed to incipient male berdaches manifested itself as intense interest in women's activities, not as the homosexual behavior occasionally characterizing other Mohave boys. Throughout their range, berdaches had intercourse only with nonberdaches. Nonberdache males could have intercourse with women, with berdaches, and with each other. Sexual partners for nonberdache women similarly included men, female berdaches, and one another. Perhaps only berdaches, free of pressures to marry heterosexually, could be exclusively and permanently homosexual, but their status did not preclude heterosexual behavior. Our position, stated earlier, is that homosexuality was a secondary phenomenon following from assuming berdache status rather than precipitating this decision. We agree with Whitehead (1981:97) that North American Indian definitions of gender generally reversed the criteria used in Western societies: they emphasized occupational pursuits and social behavior rather than choice of sexual object, which in itself was not sufficient to change gender status.

The second hypothesis explains berdaches as men who were unable to meet the demands of the warrior role or strongly averse to the aggressive male role in general (e.g., Driver 1969:441; Hoebel 1949:459; Linton 1936:480). A variant blaming berdaches on overprotective mothers, suggested for the Teton Dakota by Hassrick (1964:121–22), was extended to the northern Plains by Forgey (1975:12) and attributed to the Mohave in a novel by McNichols (1944:170–71). Proponents of these arguments apparently share the implicit assumption—explicit in Forgey (1975:3–4)—that North American societies recognized two sharply distinct gender categories, male and female, and automatically assigned to the female category those males who did not show the features of social behavior defining their own gender category. Earlier we rejected the view that men who feared war became berdaches as incompatible with the evidence. Some berdaches fought; some nonberdache males did not; nor, for that matter, did most female berdaches. Berdache status was not a complete rejection of the male role; gender mixing was one of its essential features. Formulated for societies that lacked female berdaches, this hypothesis attempts to account for only the male variety. Even if inverted to explain the women entering this status as "too aggressive for feminine pursuits" (Whitehead 1981:98), we doubt that this characterization fits them unless one accepts hunting as a form of aggression. We doubt the assumed dichotomy between aggressive males and nonaggressive females. Aggressive Blackfoot women may have been called manly-hearted (Lewis 1941) but were clearly defined as women.

European anthropologists, on the other hand, have approached the berdache status from a very different perspective, as part of a much more widespread pattern of institutionalized transvestism that they examine as a primarily religious phenomenon. Their approach often emphasizes its androgynous aspects' uniting such oppositions as male and female and, by so doing, attaining completion or "totality" and acquiring power (Signorini 1972:159–60). They also stress links between this status and deities who are themselves bisexual or androgynous. Eliade (1965:116), referring to Siberian shamanism, suggests that ritual homosexuality "is believed to be at once a sign of spirituality, of commerce with gods and spirits, and a source of sacred power." As this example suggests, these analyses are often drawn from other parts of the world and applied to the berdache institution. Similarly, Baumann's (1950, 1955) extended discussion of such phenomena generally concentrates on areas outside North America. Signorini (1972:159), coming from this intellectual tradition but directly examining berdaches, holds that the sexual ambiguity attached to their status drew respect because they were believed to possess qualities superior to those of a normal individual or at least particular qualities their societies needed for their own ends.

Granting that gender mixing seems closely related to sexual ambiguity, we would further concede that a general disposition to ignore this European tradition and concentrate on individual psychological motivations has been a major analytical weakness in discussions of the berdache status by American anthropologists. Yet we have some reservations about this approach. Particularly, we doubt that the European analysis can be transferred to North America without distorting the berdache status. Some ethnographic accounts describe berdaches as an essentially secular phenomenon. We agree with Signorini (1972:156) that this secular emphasis may reflect the fieldworker's interpretation or, for that matter, informants' lack of knowledge. Yet in some cultures berdaches may have been secular. Religious concepts consonant with those stressed by the European school of thought are scattered throughout American Indian cultures but seem much less systematized. Perhaps this effect reflects the fragmentary nature of the data and more research would uncover far-reaching connections. Thus, Signorini points out (p. 159) how well the berdache status fits the Earth-female/Sky-male dualism that suffused Omaha culture. It also seems to us that the general North American concepts of individual relations with the supernatural allowed many persons to obtain various kinds of superior qualities, of which the attributes of berdaches were a very important variety but not necessarily superior to other kinds. The status was usually separated from shamanism or from a priesthood, where this existed, and it had very important economic implications. Nevertheless, the similarities between our views and Signorini's seem very strong, including his emphasis (p. 160) on the ability of berdaches to move between male and female occupations with economic advantage and their function as talismans.

Whitehead's (1981) recent and provocative reanalysis of the berdache status differs significantly from earlier studies and represents still a fourth hypothesis. We agree with important parts of her argument, including her stress on occupation and prestige, and with her analysis of the criteria used for defining gender in North America. Emphasizing the social and cultural context of berdachehood seems a more productive approach than analyses based on speculation about individual motivation, usually phrased in psychosexual terms that are embedded in Western cultural attitudes. Certainly the status itself must be understood before one can comprehend the reasons individuals adopted it. Our major disagreements with Whitehead center on her specific hypotheses explaining the relative infrequency of female berdaches and the social approval extended to the male berdache status.

Pointing out that while occupational gender crossing by men led to their transformation into berdaches, Whitehead notes (pp. 90–91) that women who crossed social gender boundaries to engage in such male activities as hunting and warfare were not defined as berdaches. She argues that transformation was more difficult for females. The biological component of gender had greater significance for women, whose reproductive capacity in the form of menstrual and parturient blood threatened males, their activities, and supernatural power in general. She holds that almost all reports of female berdaches come from the Southwest, where gender crossing included "a mystique of anatomical change" (p. 92). River Yuman groups, believing that women who became berdaches did not menstruate, therefore assumed they lacked the female reproductive process. Without the physiological factor that inhibited the assumption of berdache status by women elsewhere, the occupational component in definitions of gender could promote their transformation.

Women's reproductive capacity may have inhibited the incidence of female berdaches; certainly some factor did. But, if rare, they occurred more widely than Whitehead assumes and were not concentrated in the Southwest. The anatomical-change mystique that accompanied berdache status, for both sexes, among River Yuman cultures seems to have been a local elaboration without wider significance, viewed with at least partial disapproval on its home ground and strongly repressed elsewhere. We agree with Whitehead that hunting and warring by women represented a crossing of social gender boundaries (or, in our terms, a mixing of gender aspects) but see a significant difference between these two activities as they related to berdachehood. In some cultures hunting did not redefine the gender status of women; in others, we suspect, this activity promoted their transformation. Female berdaches typically hunted, but participation in warfare was not an attribute of their status and apparently did not affect gender definitions for women.

Among the Mohave, where hunting was an important occupation for female berdaches, it was nonberdache women who took part in warfare, accompanying their husbands or brothers in the same manner Grinnell (1962, vol. 2:44–47) described for the Cheyenne. Women who gained honor and prestige through warfare were usually not the women who became berdaches when this status was open to them. Given Whitehead's emphasis on occupational prestige, could it not be argued that women who engaged in high-prestige male activities like warfare but remained within their gender category had higher status in their societies than women who became berdaches, and that this difference in prestige might explain the infrequency of transformations among women?

Examining social approval of the male berdache status, Whitehead argues (pp. 101–9) that the "permissiveness" of North American cultures in accepting individual variations in behavior for which supernatural sanction was claimed actually centered upon occupations that were relevant to prestige and closely associated with gender. The regular economic activities of women included the production of important durable goods that figured in gift exchange and in trade. Women who made these articles and circulated or exchanged them could acquire wealth and social prestige in their own right, particularly if age and marital status gave them control over the services of other women. Except for male fear of female blood, the boundary between male and female occupations was not strongly "defended," and occasional crossings of this line were acceptable. Extending Lewis's (1941) description of the wealthy and powerful Piegan women called "manly-hearted" to the entire northern Plains, Whitehead concludes that very successful women approached successful males in prestige and surpassed unsuccessful men. A boy who could not aspire to success in the male occupational sphere could seek another form of success through women's occupations. She writes (pp. 108–9):

> Stated broadly, the culturally dominant American Indian male was confronted with a substantial female elite not perceivable as simply dependents of powerful men. Within such a context, the response to feminine transgressions into the traditional male sphere (hunting, warfare) was amazingly dispassionate: A woman who could succeed at doing the things men did was honored as a man would be. . . . What seems to have been more disturbing to the culture—which means, for all intents and purposes, to the men—was the possibility that women, within their own department, might be onto a good thing. It was into this unsettling breach that the berdache institution was hurled. . . . Through him, ordinary men might reckon that they still held the advantage that was anatomically given and unalterable.

We agree that the individual abilities or powers acquired through the vision quest or sanctioned by more diffuse beliefs were not entirely random and tended to emphasize skills that may broadly be called occupational. The relation of occupations to systems of prestige and to definitions of gender in North America seems beyond argument. Yet these personal abilities were not equal any more than visions were. The ideology enveloping berdaches, seen in their frequent description as holy, transcended a simple confirmation of their right to engage in high-prestige occupations that involved crossing gender boundaries, just as their status itself transcended gender categories. Perhaps crossing these boundaries required unusually strong endowment with power; perhaps, as we hold, the primary locus of their holiness and power was the gender mixing that characterized their status.

Concurring with Whitehead that North American women acquired prestige in their own right and that the female elite did not derive its position from men, we do not agree that their status was generally based on the production of durable prestige goods. Apparently this activity was the foundation for their position among northern Plains cultures. The early incorporation of eastern Prairie tribes into the fur trade and the consequent influx of European goods crippled the native production of these items; yet a female elite persisted. It was also evident among the Iroquois, where its status rested on control of agricultural production and the distribution of food (Brown 1975). We suspect that an examination of other areas in North America would uncover still other bases for women's position. This objection may seem minor but has significant implications. Perhaps men of the Plains and western Prairie cultures did promote the male berdache status to assert their superiority over women in an occupational sphere defined as female and associated with prestige. The absence of berdaches in their culture suggests that Iroquois men did not use this strategy—or that Iroquois women did not permit it. This last suggestion, entirely speculative, raises an issue we consider important: Could berdaches have been successful in this occupational sphere without the consent and cooperation of women?

The literature suggests that women reacted favorably to male berdaches and found them helpful. Tanner's outraged reaction to the Yellow Head's pursuit only amused his Ojibwa hostess, who welcomed the berdache, "very expert in the various employments of the women" (1956:89–91) and obviously a much more valuable asset to the household than Tanner—perhaps even a better hunter. Women's approval could exceed that of men. When a Zuni male decided to become a berdache, it was the men of his lineage who were unhappy; its women were favorable because he would remain a resident of their household and increase its work force (Stevenson 1902:31). Perhaps women encouraged and promoted the status of male berdache, while "defending" their side of the occupational boundary by insisting that men who crossed it had to go through a transformation.

This speculation raises our fundamental disagreement with Whitehead's position that men were considered superior in worth to women throughout North America and that men determined cultural practices. Systems of prestige existed for men and for women, with the male system the more visible, the more public, and the more often described. Outsiders often overlooked the female system (Brown 1975:239–40). The greater visibility of the male system does not mean it was actually dominant or alone determined policy. Grinnell (1962, vol. 1:103, 128), who characterized Cheyenne women as masterful, described them as the rulers of the camp. Black Hawk (1955:107–8) thought it important that women of his Sauk band supported his actions.

The male and female systems of prestige sometimes intermeshed, with a husband and wife working together to enhance their joint status. At certain points either gender could move into the other's prestige system: women by going to war, men by doing women's work. As far as berdache status carried prestige, this aspect was usually much stronger among its male members. The gender-mixing activities of male berdaches, as noted earlier, seem much less prominent among the female variety. In both aspects, the female counterparts of male berdaches were not female berdaches, but women who behaved in some respects like men without changing their gender status. Rather than interpreting this as a restriction imposed upon such women by their reproductive capacity, we view it as a privilege confined to women and suggest that it was at their insistence that men who entered their occupational sphere had to shift to an intermediate gender status, accomplished by the mixing of attributes of the two gender categories within their culture.

Comments

by GISELA BLEIBTREU-EHRENBERG
Grevelsberger Weg 17, 5307 Wachtberg-Villip, Federal Republic of Germany. 12 III 83

This thorough and informative paper deserves a more detailed commentary than can be written in two pages. Therefore I must confine myself to purely critical observations, which makes what follows sound rather brusque. I hope the authors will understand my problem. This is not to deny the value of their paper in general.

1. A worldwide phenomenon such as that of (cultic or secularized) costume and sex change can, of course, be profitably studied as a regional one, but this should be done only if the aspects which transcend the regional are discussed at the same time. This the article does not do. (Not even virtually identical instances from Central and South America are included.)

2. The berdache phenomenon, basically religious, has been secularized under the influence of the "white man's way," and this has occurred in different ways and—more particularly—to varying degrees among the various tribes. This explains the heterogeneous and often irreconcilable picture that exists at the present time. (The article tries to go the other way and deduce certain norms concerning the status and social significance of the berdache from present-day circumstances. The methodological error of this approach becomes clear when one realizes what nonsensical results it would produce if applied to cultures which are neither primitive nor without written history.)

3. There is no discussion of the ambivalence we must assume exists in the psyche of the person chosen to be a transvestite. It is precisely here, however, that there is an indication of the social (value) change in the overall social assessment of the berdache phenomenon which might throw light on the effects of a great sexual and cultural conflict.

4. The conclusion that the berdache phenomenon is generally friendly towards women is not really supported by the large amount of evidence presented. (I am forced by lack of space to omit examples which clearly oppose this point of view.) In any case, the occurrence of a berdache everywhere in ritual where one would expect to find a woman raises the suspicion that there has been a reduction in the social and ritual function of women in the course of a social development which began long before the arrival of the Europeans.

by HARALD BEYER BROCH
Ethnographic Museum, University of Oslo, Oslo, Norway. 6 IV 83

This article provides a long-needed summary of our accumulated knowledge of the institution of berdache in North America as well as a systematic, well-edited presentation of major theoretical interpretations offered by anthropologists. I fully agree with the authors that, although homosexuality is closely related to berdache status, the variation is too great to permit a direct correlation. In this context, homosexuality should be regarded as a secondary phenomenon following from elaborations of berdache roles. The authors could perhaps have paid more attention to the possibilities of "moving in and out of statuses" or what we might call situational role behavior.

Two issues should be stressed in reference to both past and present distributions of the berdache status. I believe that there are indications that both male and female berdaches may have existed among northern Indians such as the Chipewyan, Dogrib, Kutchin, and Hare. Crowe (1974:72–90) offers information about Slave Woman, a strong, courageous individual and a mediator in peace negotiations between her own and other Athapaskan tribes. She devoted a significant portion of her life, leaving her family to do so, to this effort. Among other women mentioned were a Metis woman living on the Liard River (described as a physically powerful person, dressed in deerskin and with a knife at her belt) and a female leader of Arctic Red River Kutchins who traded at Fort Good Hope. While our information from this ethnographic region about the existence of the berdache status is scanty, this may well be due either to the interview techniques of most early ethnographers or to the reluctance of the Indians to talk about such practices. The fact that no berdache was present in a particular band at a particular time does not mean that the status was not recognized or that people would not have known how to react when they encountered one. During my own fieldwork among the Hare in 1972–73, I observed a youth performing a role that I interpret to be in accord with that of a berdache, and I found that his behavior was well understood by those with whom he interacted, though it had a situational character and was limited to an all-Indian male setting (Broch 1977). I consider it likely that this exclusiveness is a result of the modernization processes occurring within the Hare community. That the berdache institution disappeared so rapidly from ethnographic reports may indicate a reluctance on the part of informants to reveal their knowledge of it, but it may also be due to the expansion of the behavioral repertoire of the potential berdache. With modernization and Western influence, males could find gratification within new trades (as full-time handicrafters, schoolteachers, cooks, etc.), and females were gradually let into important political positions on band and settlement councils. This latter development is not contrary to the traditional recognition of women as important members of, and as important decision makers in, for instance, Hare society, although the openness of their political performance *is* new.

If the berdache institution was indeed absent among Northern Athapaskans, it does not follow that this was because of the specific nature of Arctic and Subarctic subsistence economies. Too often the role of the male hunter of large game is given exaggerated importance, while the hunting and snaring of small game, activities in which women took part and which were equally critical to household and band viability, are ignored. Furthermore, when trapping was introduced, a male staying at the base camp or going along but concentrating on skinning and preparing furs and food would have been a great asset, especially to the best hunters. This is, incidentally, the role taken by some old men, not regarded as berdaches, in current Hare bush adaptations.

by JUDITH K. BROWN
Oakland University, Rochester, Mich. 48063, U.S.A. 8 IV 83

Callender and Kochems have provided a valuable compendium of descriptive material that will encourage further research concerning the berdache. I would like to mention one additional instance: the berdache among the Kwakiutl (Ford 1941:129–32). Callender and Kochems's interesting speculation that the male berdache depended upon "the consent and cooperation" of the women of his society receives some confirmation from the Kwakiutl account.

Why were female berdaches so rare? Recent research on the aversive reaction of certain game animals to the odor of menstrual blood is suggestive (March 1980, Nunley 1981, Kitahara 1982). Since hunting was an important attribute of female berdaches, perhaps recruitment was limited to women with amenorrhea. The incompatibility of hunting with the care of babies and small children (Brown 1970) may also be relevant.

The nonoccurrence of the berdache requires further investigation. Callender and Kochems identify one well-documented case: the Iroquois, a society notable for the separateness of the sexes in daily life (see Morgan 1962[1851]). The role of the go-between, so typical of the berdache in other sex-segregated societies (see Thayer 1980), was here taken by the older Iroquois women. One example is provided by Parker (1968) in his description of the cornhusking bee that traditionally followed the harvest; here was one opportunity for matrons to note the relative industry of those eligible to marry and to arrange matches accordingly.

In many traditional societies, the woman past childbearing was viewed as transformed into a being very like a man (Kerns

1979). Occasionally possessing special spiritual powers, often becoming the go-between between the world of women and the world of men (Brown 1982), more proficient than novices at performing the work of women, the matrons in some societies resemble the male berdache. The parallels are curious. Whereas all societies contain aging women, why did some also have berdaches?

It is disappointing that Callender and Kochems fail to indicate how Thayer's (1980) findings, which deal only with the berdache among the Indians of the northern Plains, fit into the scheme for all of North America which they present, and how both in turn are related to the hypotheses suggested for worldwide samples by Munroe, Whiting, and Hally (1969), Munroe and Munroe (1977), and Munroe (1980). A synthesis of all these studies would be welcome indeed.

by NANCY DATAN
Department of Psychology, West Virginia University, Morgantown, W.Va. 26506, U.S.A. 5 IV 83

This comprehensive survey of the North American berdache status makes the reader wish that the Nacirema—that wide-ranging American tribe whose habits were recorded by Miner in the *American Anthropologist* in 1956—had come in for a mention. The "exotic bias" of anthropology, while it reveals the diversity of the human condition, may mask the diversity within one's own tribe. I would suggest that a major contribution of this survey is how much it shows us of ourselves in the mirror of tribal cultures. For example, the status of berdache as prestigious has its parallel in Western culture in the figure of Teiresias, the seer of Greek myth who assumed both male and female form, declared to Zeus that of ten parts of sexual pleasure men had one and women nine, and was struck blind by Hera and then compensated by Zeus with second sight and great length of life (see Datan n.d. for a discussion of androgyny and the life cycle). Parallels with contemporary American customs include the relative invisibility of the female berdache, the frequent extension of male privilege to the male berdache (which may be the "factor" these authors seek to explain the inhibition of "the incidence of female berdaches"), and the exclusion of male berdaches from warfare. Gender and its ambiguities have been part of Western civilization from the taboo in Leviticus against putting on clothing of the opposite sex to the contemporary fascination with the movie *Tootsie*—and not merely with the irony on which the plot turns (that a male actor cross-dresses to become a female star), but with the effect of the role upon the actor himself. Anthropology offers the student of human behavior a chance to appreciate the range of human variation, but it should not overlook the lessons to be learned from human commonalities.

Finally, I must take issue with the authors' concluding discussion of prestige and gender. They dispute Whitehead's claim that men ranked above women in prestige, arguing that the male prestige system is more visible and public and thus more often described. It is commendable to call attention to the often overlooked female prestige system, but it is implausible to argue that women may have less visible prestige but an equal claim on dominance, as it must also be posited that women are content with power so subtle that its effects are difficult to detect. It is far more parsimonious, though less pleasing, to concede that women have unequal access to power.

by GARY GRANZBERG
Department of Anthropology, University of Winnipeg, Winnipeg, Manitoba, Canada R3B 2E9. 29 III 83

Callender and Kochems present a useful tabulation of berdache material. However, because of certain weaknesses in methodology and theory, the full ethnographic and ethnological value of their work is not realized.

With regard to ethnographic understanding, I would like to have seen a fuller appraisal of previous tabulations (to which several brief allusions are made) and a clearer statement of how this effort builds upon and improves that which went before it. Perhaps there is improvement in defining the principal attributes of the institution and in appraising its incidence and variations, but without adequate analysis of prior work the quality of the contribution remains too much a matter of conjecture. This is doubly lamentable in that a more critical appraisal of the various accounts of the berdache status (most of which, the authors acknowledge, are secondhand) might have gone far toward allaying the skepticism that has arisen in the wake of questions about the validity of another celebrated institution, cannibalism (Arens 1979).

With regard to ethnological understanding, I am not persuaded that the authors' theory about the meaning of berdache status should be taken any more seriously than any other. They argue that the institution arises largely as a function of females' domination of social life and monopolization of the ability to adopt the other gender's role behavior without having to assume new gender status. No cross-cultural data are marshalled to put this hypothesis in jeopardy. Rather, acceptance or rejection of it depends largely upon which side we are inclined to support in a political argument about the relative power of male vs. female in society. Here again, a splendid opportunity is missed. The authors could have used their data to further our understanding of the neglect by anthropologists of the woman's perspective in social life and the consequences of this neglect for theory building (Leacock 1981). But the material relevant to this is presented only at the very end of the article, almost as an afterthought.

In spite of these shortcomings, the authors' review is provocative, raises a number of important issues, and constitutes a useful, concise summary of a vast field of data.

by DAVID HOLMBERG
Anthropology/Women's Studies/Asian Studies, Cornell University, Ithaca, N.Y. 14853, U.S.A. 11 IV 83

This detailed reassessment of the evidence on the berdache status is a welcome refinement of our knowledge that will direct future ethnological efforts and reorient our reading of previous accounts. Callender and Kochems reexpress several of Whitehead's observations on berdaches and the sex-gender systems of North American Indians (and correct a number of overgeneralizations common to the literature on berdaches) but disagree with her on several points. I will touch (sympathetically) on only three. In assessing Whitehead's emphasis on the occupational correlates of berdache status, they propose that the sacred powers attributed to the berdache have an independent (although not unrelated) value. This is an intriguing and important suggestion, yet Callender and Kochems leave us dangling: What were these powers? Why are "mixed-genders" powerful? How do they fit into religious symbology? How do they relate to the sex-gender system? Did men and women have equal access to this role and its concomitant powers? A discussion of these aspects could enrich and supplement Whitehead's interpretation. Second, they allude to the possibility that women's independent abilities to achieve status may be based on something more than production and control of "prestige goods." Here the implicit distinction between "exchange value" and "use value" of goods may be overdrawn, for food has important exchange value in feasting and prestige systems. Rather, what is called for is further ethnographic elaboration of the place of women in Indian systems of exchange and social organization. Third, Callender and Kochems address Whitehead's view that culture in North America is a male construct, and they argue that women were as much generators of culture as respondents to a given system. This is certainly possible—if we allow women creativity in the accumulation of prestige, why not in the generation or regeneration of culture?—but references to brief observations on the Iroquois, Cheyenne, and Sauk do not constitute an alternative model of total sex-gender systems or really support their assertion. However, Callender and Kochems, through judicious attention to ethnography, do pose problems, by demonstrating greater diversity than is commonly recognized, for interpretations. Overall, it appears to me that Whitehead, by framing her discussion in terms of general comparative issues in the anthropology of sex and gender, and Callender and Kochems, by thoroughly examining the data, have together set the stage for yet other reassessments of the berdache status. Their essays should be read in tandem.

Following Callender and Kochems's rigorous mapping of the berdache status, intensive comparison between regions seems called for. Berdaches *and their absence and variations* must be situated in particular sociocultural constellations and then compared. Above all, the commonly neglected domains of kinship and social organization require consideration. It might be appropriate to compare negative cases with positive ones, beginning with the Iroquois, to whom Callender and Kochems regularly allude. Attention to the absence of berdaches in what Murdock dubbed a "quasi-matriarchy" might clarify the ethnographic and interpretive issues. Finally, as Callender and Kochems stress, the tricksterish character and sacred powers of the berdache need further development. They have, however, overlooked Thayer's (1980) contribution to this aspect of the problem.

by ÅKE HULTKRANTZ
Seglarvägen 7, S-181 62 Lidingö, Sweden. 1 IV 83

Of all the papers on the American Indian berdache institution this is definitely one of the best in that it calmly and judiciously discusses different approaches without advocating any particular solution. Considering the fact that the article is directed to a wide anthropological readership, it would have been even better if the etymology of the term had been illuminated. Briefly, the word *berdache* or *bardache* was first used by the French in New France and originates from the Arabic word *bardaj*, "slave" (Marquette 1900[1674]: n. 26).

The authors prefer—at least in most cases—a cultural definition of berdaches and deal extensively with their intermediate position in society. This kind of evaluation, which is, of course, correct, has recently inspired Miller (1982) to an interpretation of berdache status in structural terms. Miller's article, which has appeared too recently to be discussed by Callender and Kochems, offers the devoted structuralist much "thinking," but for most of us it is probably a bit trying to learn that "bear beliefs can be compared with those associated with the berdache, since both of them seem to relate to the overall definition of humanness" (Miller 1982:276).

The authors rightly point out that many have been called berdaches who really never belonged to this group. From my own field experiences among the Wind River Shoshoni in the 1940s and '50s, I can report that there were several groups of single men who, because of their permanent abstinence from sexual relations, constituted categories of their own: (1) impotent men who were refused by women (of such a fellow it was said that "he has got his mind wrong, he is nobody, not recognized"); (2) men who were cowards in war, who in former days were derogatorily classed with women; (3) visionaries who remained unmarried indefinitely out of fear that exposure to menstruation would destroy their relations with the guardian spirits; (4) men who longed to become women, lived with women (without any sexual relationship), and imitated their ways of talking and moving; (5) berdaches (none alive during my visits to the Shoshoni), who dressed like women and performed both male and female tasks. These latter persons, called *tïwaša:'* ("dried-up penis"), held a respected place in society. Only men were berdaches among the Shoshoni. As far as I know they were never married to other men. I was unable to learn whether any of these five categories was associated with homosexual practices.

The occurrence of the berdache institution among the Wind River Shoshoni may strengthen the interpretation of its presence among the Comanche, who, as we know, separated from these Shoshoni just a couple of hundred years ago. As both Shimkin and I have shown, the connections between the two tribes have remained strong right up to our own time.

Although my documentation is insufficient, it was implied by one of my Shoshoni informants that a person became a berdache through a dream or vision. This informant distinguished between those who assumed the status of "half-women" because they wished to do so and those who were true berdaches as a result of visionary experiences. These two processes correspond closely to Callender and Kochems's two versions of berdache ontogeny, although only the latter seems to have been institutionalized among the Shoshoni.

This is apparently the more usual approach to the berdache phenomenon in North America. European scholars have, as the authors emphasize, favoured a religious interpretation. This may, according to my (European!) understanding, be a correct opinion. If, with Lowie (1940:312), we consider the vision quest a "democratized shamanism" and change of sex is a trait common to both the vision quest and shamanism, then it is possible to see American berdachism as a variation of an ancient shamanic practice. (Limits of space prohibit me from discussing the possible causes of this behaviour.) This is, of course, just a suggestion, but it deserves further contemplation. It is in any case a remarkable fact that among the Yurok all berdaches were shamans (Kroeber 1925:46).

by SUE-ELLEN JACOBS
Women Studies, University of Washington, Seattle, Wash. 98195, U.S.A. 6 IV 83

This analytical synthesis of published and unpublished accounts of the berdache status provides many valuable new ways of understanding a widespread North American cultural phenomenon that has been misunderstood by Euro-Americans for several hundred years. One of the problems underlying this misunderstanding has been a tendency for writers to disregard the cultural context for a trait that is widespread among societies in so culturally heterogeneous an area as North America. Callender and Kochems have shown us that by examining the cultural category in contexts of occurrence (as reported in various descriptive writings) it is possible to describe the wide range of endogenous expressions.

"Berdache" is defined in the *Random House Dictionary* as "a man who adopts the dress and social role of a woman." The *Oxford English Dictionary* leads from "berdache" to several other terms, one of the last being "catamite . . . a boy kept for unnatural purposes." Summarizing the OED, and as I noted in 1968 (following Angelino and Shedd 1955), "the English word berdache comes from the French word *bardash;* furthermore, the French derived their term from the Italian *bardascia*, which was taken from Arabic *bardaj;* and the latter borrowed from the Persian word *bardah:* in all cases meaning a 'kept boy' or 'male prostitute.' " There have been several attempts by anthropologists to reduce the confusion created by application of the term "berdache" to a whole host of behaviors that fall outside of standard categorizations of women's and men's behavioral norms. Now, Callender and Kochems have given us an anthropological definition that ought to work in all North American Indian cultures in which the conception of a third gender exists. I wonder if this will help untangle the confusion one still finds in reading the older literature. They have managed to give us many examples of contextual definitions and descriptions of and attitudes toward third genders (in the form of mixed-gender role enactments and categorical conceptualizations), gender switching (e.g., transvestism) and homosexuality. The composite picture which shows differences between these phenomena is becoming clearer because of their work. Unfortunately, we are still left with a post-hoc analysis of a series of cultural categories (now to be lumped under the term "berdache") that seems to have begun "to disappear soon after European or American control was established." (I qualify their statement with "seems to have" because there is evidence that the berdache status continues to exist in some societies, even though it may be "underground.") The term "berdache" has been applied to the aforementioned categories in the past, but if we follow the proposed definition here it will not be so applied to transvestism and homosexuality, and it will include women as well as men who are gender-mixed.

In the list of tribes for which berdaches have been reported, the Tewa (Rio Grande Pueblo peoples), whom I listed in 1968, have been left out, presumably because of unreliability of sources. After ten years of research into published information available on the Tewa, I support this exclusion on those grounds. However, my ethnographic research has uncovered some interesting information. Among some Tewa of New Mexico, the concept of *quetho* continues to be acknowledged. According to Tewa elders, a *quetho* comes into being because its genitals were exposed to the full moon at a critical time during early infancy. *Quethos* have special qualities, identifiable when the child is quite young: special relationships to deities or supernatural forces; a mid-gender or androgynous personality, with "gentle" qualities prevailing; and resistance to full adolescent socialization into traditional men's or women's roles. According to these same elders, *quethos* should be raised "to be who they are"; such child-rearing practices ideally place the burden of enculturation to proper third-gender (i.e., *quetho*) behavior and body of cultural knowledge on an adult *quetho*. *Quethos* are designated as a third gender and are clearly distinguished from homosexual men and women. Homosexuals are, according to informants, "mixed-up people who can be cured." The only *quethos* these elders have recognized are individuals who appear to be males because of dress, names, and other "normal" male markers. When questioned about the genitals of *quethos* (a hard subject to pursue because of the sense of privacy that prevails on such matters in normal conversation, though it is a subject of jokes in other situations), I was told that *quethos* are "like women and men in their private parts." In various studies of Tewa origin stories and myths regarding supernatural beings, one finds reference to androgynous people. The pronoun used most often to refer to contemporary *quethos* is "she." Pronoun reference to animals and people who are not personally known to the speaker sometimes takes the form "she or he or whatever it may be." *Quethos* may be bisexual, homosexual, heterosexual, or trisexual (i.e., having sexual relationships with women, men, and *quethos*), and the same is true for non-*quethos*. This of course, refers to sexual activity, not personal characteristics or role assignments. Further elaboration on this matter will have to be reserved for another place (Jacobs n.d.).

I applaud Callender and Kochems for their detailed work and respect the theoretical direction their work follows. They also are to be commended for providing useful departure points for further research. A few statements in the article puzzle me, however. They say that the distribution of berdaches in the Southwest "seems to have been decidedly less pervasive than in the four culture areas first noted," but on their list they include the Navajo, Hopi, Zuni, Papago, Pima, and Yuma. They do not list the Apache (whom Stewart listed in 1960) or the Pueblos (whom Hay referred to in 1963). Given the distribution of cultures in the Southwest, the proportional occurrence of berdache status (as they have defined it) could have been as high in the Southwest as in other culture areas. They state that berdaches "did not hold formal office," yet they cite a case in which a "female berdache" was a chief. What they may mean is that when berdaches held formal offices it was incidental to their gender status. Still, being responsible for funerary activities, the naming of children, and other ritual duty assignments (examples they have given of roles) may well have conferred formal office according to tribal concepts of "office."

I am particularly impressed with Callender and Kochems's clear recognition that among many Indian peoples women's and men's systems of prestige "sometimes intermeshed" and, further, that in some societies women's approval of certain men's behaviors was necessary for those behaviors to be tolerated in the community. I agree with them in their disagreement with Whitehead's position regarding the relative worth of women and men. There is abundant ethnographic evidence that men and women used to have comparable worth in many North American Indian societies. That this is not true in some communities of recent years is evidence of adoption of Euro-American values on this matter.

Although the Tewa elders with whom I have spoken would not assign a male or female sex to *quetho*, I pushed the point further on a number of occasions, asking if women were ever *quethos*. The answer was no. Then I asked if men were the only ones who were *quethos*. Again, the answer was no. In trying to force a categorization of *quethos* as women or men (or female or male), I only exasperated my Tewa friends, who do make a clear distinction between *quethos*, homosexuals (gay men and women), women, men, and those who on ceremonial occasion dress in the attire of their opposite sex. If the Tewa do this, along with others (including their neighbors the Navajo), is it not possible that we are still asking the wrong questions because in Euro-American culture we have a difficult time accepting that there can be a genuinely conceptualized third gender that has nothing to do with transvestism or homosexuality? If I went by the verbal accountings of elders only, the *quetho* would not fit Callender and Kochems's definition of a berdache. Going on accounts given by others, the characterizations of *quethos* begin to look more like characterizations of contemporary gay males, particularly. My observations confirm this latter. No reference or observation indicates that *quethos* or gay men publicly wear clothing of "the opposite sex," however. In this situation, definitions of gender emphasize not only "occupational pursuits or social behavior, rather than choice of sexual objects," but also personal characteristics of the individual. That there is conflicting information regarding *quethos* when one compares statements of elders with those of younger people is, to me, another example of local adoption of Euro-American values. The fit of *quetho* to Callender and Kochems's definition remains to be judged in ethnohistorical and contemporary sociocultural contexts, as has been done by these authors in examining other indigenously defined third genders.

by ALICE B. KEHOE
Department of Sociology, Anthropology and Social Work, Marquette University, Milwaukee, Wis. 53233, U.S.A. 26 II 83

At last, a thorough, sensitive, and sensible survey of the berdache status, *sensu stricto*. I agree with Callender and Kochems, though I can expand somewhat on their conclusion.

Speaking from the point of view of the northern Plains Indians, it should be borne in mind that Algonkian and Siouan languages, unlike the Indo-European ones, do not require the specification of the sex of nouns. Sexual categorization is thus not subconsciously as compelling to Algonkian- or Siouan-speakers as it is to speakers of Indo-European languages; it is easier for Plains Indians to think of sexual categorization as a relatively minor attribute. The compelling gender categorization for Algonkian-speakers is animate versus inanimate, and because "animate" is fundamentally the presence of Power (in European scientific terminology, vitalism), the degree of Power inherent in a being is one of its major attributes.

As Callender and Kochems note, there tends to be an association of the moon as a female deity with berdaches. Unpublished notes by the late Claude E. Schaeffer describe a Blackfoot holy man named Four Bears who died about 1889 and who was described by two of Schaeffer's informants as deriving power from the moon. To signify the source of his power, Four Bears dressed as a woman when, and only when, performing as a holy person, and one of his rites included obliging young men on whom he was conferring good luck to suckle his nipple. This symbolic crossing of sexual categorizations by a nonberdache emphasizes, it seems to me, the importance of nongenital connotations to Plains Indian sexual-category symbols.

Callender and Kochems's critique of Whitehead's assumption that men were considered superior to women in Indian societies is well supported both in the literature, allowing for bias in earlier works (Kehoe 1983), and in contemporary Indian groups. As I argued in an earlier paper (Kehoe 1976), the Blackfoot attribute spiritual blessings to the mediation of women: only women can open medicine bundles, and the Sun Dance requires a holy woman to serve as its focus. Blackfoot myths describe the major medicine powers (bundles) as coming to their people through the agency of women. To the Blackfoot, men:women::nature:culture, the myth of the primeval marriages describing women enjoying a civilized home while men were suffering like beasts, unable to cook or to clothe or shelter themselves. Siouan myths and rituals similarly cast women as the medium through which spiritual power can flow to men (Kehoe 1970). Thus Plains Indian women did not need to "insist," as Callender and Kochems phrase it, that men who wished to gain proficiency and possibly status in women's occupations remove themselves from the sexual category "man"; the ideology of the societies excluded men from the status of those humans who *normally inherently* are imbued with power to reproduce civilization, both its carriers and its crafts. A person who has been gifted with some of this reproductive power, that of producing a civilized home with its furnishings, but not all of it—not the capacity to produce children—obviously occupied an intermediate status. The notion that berdaches were likely to be wealthy could be the result of observations that, as in our own societies, capable and hardworking but childless adults are generally more affluent than those supporting children, or it could stem from the supposition that persons gifted beyond the normal capacities of their class will be materially fortunate.

A minor addendum: Miller (1974) is relevant to discussion of the Iroquois.

by JOHANN KNOBLOCH
Venusbergweg 34, D-5300 Bonn 1, Federal Republic of Germany. 2 IV 83

Having read this very informative article, I have a lot of questions:

1. What is the origin of the term "berdache"? I haven't been able to find an explanation of this term even in Stoutenburgh's *Dictionary of the American Indian* or the Encyclopedia Britannica.

2. Is there any documentation of a belief in the transmigration of souls among these tribes? If there were, it seems possible to me that a berdache could be a man with a feminine soul—and this "mistake" might be manifested in feminine behavior during childhood which would be noticed by the adults in the child's environment and by the child in his later life.

3. If berdaches give children secret names, might it be because they have more experience in things of the other world?

4. The position of berdaches could be defined more precisely by noting which terms of women's speech they use and which not. For instance, Roman men swore by Jupiter (*mediusfidius*) and women by Castor, Jupiter's son (*ecastor*).

by MARGOT LIBERTY
1149 Pioneer Rd., Sheridan, Wyo. 82801, U.S.A. 10 IV 83

1. Berdache status and cultural definition may be gone, but male transvestism in the northern Plains is not: a Northern Cheyenne example dating from the 1960s has left vivid memories on the reservation and in bordering non-Indian communities.

2. The economic and social value of the berdache role seems indeed likely to have arisen in Plains cultures with the rise of labor needs in producing tanned and ornamental robes and other leather goods for trade. Thus berdache frequency probably increased after such trade became prevalent, from an earlier hunting baseline in which "the contribution of males was too valuable to promote their transformation."

3. The supernatural power widely attributed to berdaches in the northern Plains may perhaps have included the transfer of sacred power from senior priest to novice priest through mutual homosexual intercourse with a berdache intermediary, as has been reported for shared heterosexual intercourse in several northern Plains societies.

4. The existence of any widespread "female elite" in Plains cultures after the adoption of horses is doubtful. Using the four criteria of (1) subsistence contribution/economic control, (2) political power roles, (3) supernatural power roles, and (4) personal physical autonomy, I have argued that for Plains Indian women the quality of life deteriorated drastically in the classic equestrian period. It is hard to agree with Grinnell that Cheyenne women were generally masterful "rulers of the camp" when they were widely subject to nasal amputation for alleged marital unfaithfulness, as well as to gang rape for disobedience to their brothers, and prone to suicide (Hanging Woman Creek is a well-known watercourse in southern Montana named for a Cheyenne episode). Role variability is the key to understanding here (see Liberty 1979, 1982).

by WILLIAM K. POWERS
Department of Anthropology, Rutgers University, New Brunswick, N.J. 08903, U.S.A. 28 III 83

The berdache status is still viable in Lakota society, although transvestism is less so because whites consider it unacceptable (or it is obfuscated owing to acceptable trends in unisexual dress). The role of go-between in amorous affairs is current, the berdache (*winkte*) customarily being a female's cross-cousin. *Winktes* are characterized as robust: they walk long distances carrying heavy loads through severe weather. They perform occupations considered female, working long hours without complaining. They are regarded as intelligent, kind, thoughtful human beings who take care of the old and feeble. In contrast, "homosexuals" are ridiculed by males, and vivid descriptions of homosexual behavior are frequently the subject of conversation at all-male drinking parties. Older people view *winktes* in their traditional roles without stigma; younger people associate them with homosexuality.

Hassrick's interpretation of berdaches as "sissies" and "mamma's boys," however, is inconsistent with Lakota ideology: *winktes* are *wakan*, "sacred." Some receive instructions in visions from Anuk ite ("Double Face"), a symbol of proper and improper marital behavior (Powers 1977), who offers them a choice (she never orders them). M. N. Powers (1980) reports that *winktes* also are influenced by the moon and dream of menstruating women and *pte winkte*, a "dry buffalo cow." Devereux betrays his own ethnocentrism when he states that berdaches receive "protection" through institutionalization and that cross-dressing prevents berdaches from "recruiting" unsuspecting heterosexuals. Similarly, Hassrick's contention that berdaches were "punished" in the afterlife and Lame Deer's idea that a boy should refrain from long-term relationships with them are clearly non-Indian.

It is unlikely that fear of hunting and war figured as a reason for becoming a berdache; *winkte*s participated in both. Today individual *winkte*s usually hunt alone for deer or small game and do not join in hunting parties. Perhaps in the past the same was true.

I agree with the authors' preference for "gender mixing" over "gender crossing" because "mixing" may be in fact short-term. Equally provocative is their reference to the fact that an American performer "in drag" may be a "she" but never a "woman." (This would be impossible in Lakota, where sexually differentiated pronouns do not exist and anyone "in drag" would always be *winkte*.) While the authors would not compare the two cultures "except insofar as berdache status could be called a performance," there are some cases in which the comparison can be made: some short-term gender mixing could indeed be called a performance. We can thus distinguish between the berdache and the *heyoka* (Lakota for "contrary"), who frequently dresses or speaks in the manner of a female. Thus the distinction between *winkte* and *heyoka* is contextual, not categorical. If the gender mixing is temporary, there is no reason to assume either that homosexuality leads to berdache status or that homosexuality is a secondary phenomenon following the assumption of berdache status. Perhaps in some societies the berdache has no sexual connotation at all. We are certainly not ready to assume in our society that college men are potential homosexuals because of their transvestite performance in, say, a Princeton Triangle show.

I also support the authors' position that assumption of berdache status does not necessarily have any bearing on the overworked equation of "male" with "superior" and "female" with "inferior," which certainly does not hold for the Lakota, as M. N. Powers (1982) has recently shown.

Berdache status will continue to be controversial not because it suggests sexual "aberration," but because its history is so sketchy. It is perhaps an appropriate commentary on our society that we become concerned with the sexual customs of "tribal" people just at a time when we question what is proper and what is not in our own sexuality. Today our preoccupation with legalizing sexual behaviors that have been stigmatized as "perverse" and the proliferation of scholarship on the social and cultural construction of gender are cases in point. Callender and Kochems are to be congratulated on their timely contribution. The article is a welcome addition to the study of human sexuality, mixed or not.

by ALICE SCHLEGEL
Department of Anthropology, University of Arizona, Tucson, Ariz. 85721, U.S.A. 11 IV 83

Callender and Kochems have done an impressive job of ferreting out and synthesizing available material on the berdache phenomenon. The material they bring together gives rise to two important theoretical questions. First, is institutional transvestism more widespread in North America than in other world regions, and, if so, why? Second, how do we account for the distribution of male only, female only, and both-sex berdaches? (Admittedly, in this type of historical reconstruction, where one depends on often casual remarks by observers, there is always the chance that the distribution as reported is an artifact of reportage rather than a reflection of ethnographic reality.)

The first question cannot be answered by analyzing data in this paper, as it deals only with North America. For the second, however, Callender and Kochems provide some hints. They propose that male transvestism was absent from the Arctic and Subarctic because male labor was too valuable to have been lost; later they remark that freedom from child care allowed the male berdache to be more productive than the normal female (to this we can add freedom from the energy drains of pregnancy and lactation). Clearly, a thread of economic causality runs through their work, although it has not been developed into a hypothesis.

The hypotheses they discuss all ask why certain people become berdaches, not why the institution exists at all. The homosexual hypothesis and the weakling (inability to assume male roles) hypothesis are clearly wrong. Furthermore, these deal with psychological dispositions that are just as applicable to idiosyncratic transvestism as to the institutionalized form. The European explanation, that the berdache combines male and female powers into a unity of spiritual power, illuminates some but not all cases, as Callender and Kochems point out. Whitehead's hypothesis of occupational prestige has more credibility in their eyes, but I concur with their criticism of this hypothesis, which rests on an assumption that men were considered superior to women throughout North America. Compared with other world regions, this is a region of widespread parity of the sexes, particularly in gathering (as opposed to hunting) and horticultural societies.

While they do not develop an explanatory hypothesis, I would like to use their data to propose one. There are three classes of societies with the berdache status: those in which it has been reported for men only, those in which it has been reported for women only, and those in which it has been reported for both sexes. The first class greatly outnumbers the other two. While this could be an artifact of reporting, it could also reflect reality. Given permissiveness within a society toward sex-role transfer, it may be that men are more likely to suffer sex-role dysfunction than women. I find this less plausible than another argument, which is that where reproduction is a matter of grave concern, as it generally is in societies with small and fluctuating populations, societies are unfriendly toward the loss of a fertile woman from the reproductive pool. The same would be even more true of matrilineal societies, where the matrilineage might resist the loss of a reproductive member.

Several of the female-berdache societies are matrilineal: Crow, Kaska, Navaho, and Western Apache. In none of these is there a strong lineage or clan structure, compared with matrilineal Pueblos or Central or Eastern matrilineal tribes. The case of the Kaska is instructive. Honigmann (1954:129–30) notes that families will turn a daughter into a berdache only if they have no son. This is permitted but not entirely approved. Female transvestism is generally not institutionalized to the same degree as male: for example, while the Mohave male berdache undergoes a special initiation ceremony, the female berdache does not. This may reflect some ambivalence toward the female berdache even in societies that tolerate her.

My hypothesis is that male berdaches are tolerated or encouraged where two conditions obtain: (1) female labor is highly valued and (2) there is an actual or potential shortage of female labor. As to the first, female labor could be valuable either because women make a large contribution to subsistence or because women produce a craft item that is highly valued for exchange. The first case includes gathering and most horticultural societies in North America, while the second includes such societies as the Pueblos, where women produced valuable pottery, and postcontact Plains and Navaho, where women produced valuable beadwork and rugs, respectively. Female berdaches are tolerated, but probably not encouraged, in societies where (1) females make a lesser contribution to production than men and (2) male labor is in actual or potential short supply. In essence, this hypothesis states that the institution of the berdache is a mechanism by which societies with uncertain sex ratios can regulate their labor supply, giving them a greater flexibility than exists in societies where one's sex is the only determinant of one's gender. The concentration of berdache societies seems to be in western and central North America, where foraging and marginal horticulture provided a less certain food supply and militated against the growth of large stable populations.

I did a cross-cultural test of female contribution to subsistence, one element of this hypothesis, using data from Barry and Schlegel (1982). I tested societies with male berdaches only against those with female berdaches present (with or without the male form) for high versus low contribution to subsistence. High-contribution societies are those in which women contribute 35% or more to subsistence (the mean is 35.5%). The sample with information on both female contribution and the berdache status contains 18 societies (see table 1). The results did not reach the level of significance; however, the distribution is not inconsistent with this hypothesis. I did not include production of high-value crafts in the test, as there is no coded measure for this. There is also no coded measure for actual or potential shortage of female labor, an essential feature of this hypothesis. With such a restricted set of societies to work with as the North American societies that practice institutionalized transvestism, an analysis along these lines should not be too difficult.

by ITALO SIGNORINI
Istituto di Etnologia, Università di Roma, Rome, Italy. 5 IV 83

We owe a debt of gratitude to Callender and Kochems for their brilliant revival of discussion of the subject of transvestism in North America. Much has been said on the subject but not in an analytic vein. Their work considers the phenomenon exhaustively and distinguishes it from homosexuality, which is properly considered something that transcends transvestism. It also considers berdache variations, spread, and connections, and this is in itself a great achievement. It does not, however, take up the problem of why the institution exists—what its original meaning is—although at several points, especially in the discussion of ontogeny, it does break new interpretive ground in which the religious aspect seems clear. The authors say that "the primary locus of [berdaches'] holiness and power was the gender mixing that characterized their status," but the cause-and-effect relationship should be explained. The authors express reservations about "European" interpretations (e.g., Baumann 1950, 1955; Eliade 1971) that consider berdache as part of a much more widespread pattern of institutionalized transvestism, a primarily religious phenomenon in which special value is given to androgyny as the conjunction of the male/female opposition. The authors' reservations are based on the consideration that "some ethnographic accounts describe berdache as an essentially secular phenomenon," that "religious concepts consonant with those stressed by the European school of thought are scattered throughout American Indian cultures but seem much less systematized," and that "North American concepts of individual relations with the supernatural allowed many persons to obtain various kinds of superior qualities, of which the attributes of berdaches were a very important variety but not necessarily superior to other kinds." It strikes me that their reservations are weakly grounded, particularly since they themselves emphasize a set of elements that tend in this very direction:

1. Supernatural powers are attributed to berdaches, and they have specific ritual responsibilities (funerals, conferring of secret names, warfare, and others) that in some societies are also performed by women who have passed the menopause, that is, are no longer impeded by impurity and are "naturally" gender-mixed.

2. The ***necessity*** that a group have berdaches is apparent, and not just in special cases such as that of the Tlingit, who believe berdaches are reincarnated in a given clan, or the 17th-century Yuma, who had a rule that there always be *four* berdaches (Alarcón 1565:368). There is constant concern to identify individuals who show ambiguous sexual tendencies and push them into the role of berdaches. There is also concern to guarantee that the role be "filled" through the means of a "call" (dream or vision) on the part of supernatural beings, in some cases with the support of myth.

3. The very element of gender mixing, which the authors rightly see as a defining feature of berdaches and which they distinguish from gender crossing, points to the fact that what is being sought is a conjunction of sexual opposites. (Since this is normally linked with the presence of androgynous supernatural beings, it would certainly require further attention than it has had so far [see Kluckhohn 1960:52; Baumann 1950].) The authors provide much information on this subject. They also mention female divinities connected with the "call" to take up the role of berdache, and this agrees perfectly with Baumann (1950:23), who says that transvestism sometimes aims simply at uniting the physical and spiritual qualities of the two sexes, while at other times it aims at adjusting to a supernatural being that is androgynous or of *the opposite sex*. Moreover, Eliade (1971:100) noted that "wholeness" may be expressed by any pair of opposites (female-male, visible-invisible, sky-earth, light-dark), a notion not infrequently found in North America. Eliade goes on to say (p. 106) that the union of the two sexes can be achieved on the level of symbol or expressed ritually and hence concretely and that "there is a full range of intermediate types." I should add that the berdache status is a cultural element like any other. It may spread to other groups and may be integrated by the receiving groups in ways that are very different from those of the groups that spread it.

The fact remains, however, that transvestism may be considered in a strictly North American context only in terms of limited aims. Otherwise the phenomenon has to be considered in a broader perspective (the rest of the American continent alone provides abundant material) and in comparative terms.

Some marginal remarks: It is surprising that no reference is made to Munroe, Whiting, and Hally (1969), who examined the hypothesis that institutionalized male transvestism tends to appear in societies "that make minimum use of sex as a discriminating factor in prescribing behavior" and not in those

TABLE 1

SEX OF BERDACHES AND FEMALE CONTRIBUTION TO SUBSISTENCE

Female Subsistence Contribution	Sex of Berdaches: Ethnographic Atlas Code: Male only	Sex of Berdaches: Ethnographic Atlas Code: Female present	Sex of Berdaches: Standard Sample Code: Male only	Sex of Berdaches: Standard Sample Code: Female present
High	7	7	6	2
Low	4	4	5	5

SOURCE: Barry and Schlegel (1982).

that "maximize sex distinction" (p. 38). This hypothesis may help to explain certain blanks in the distribution of the phenomenon and to explain its connection with individual tendencies, a connection that, formulated in another fashion, is properly rejected by the authors as an "extreme oversimplification."

A final point: The text says that the Iroquois certainly did not have berdaches because there is absolutely no mention of the phenomenon in the literature. Actually, de Charlevoix speaks of it (1744:4–5).

by ANDREW STRATHERN
Institute of Papua New Guinea Studies, Box 1432, Boroko, Papua New Guinea. 25 IV 83

This is a very level-headed and praiseworthy approach to a complex and puzzling phenomenon. The berdache status, itself varying considerably from culture to culture, shows an intermediate logical possibility between the genders "male" and "female." The authors quite rightly argue that it is to be understood first in terms of social and cultural logic and only secondarily in terms of individual psychological motivations. This status is not found in the two societies of Papua New Guinea where I have worked, but basic ideas of gender crossing and gender mixing are found, and these appear to be the secular bases from which the institution was constructed among North American Indians. In Hagen the idea of gender crossing is quite explicit: insofar as a woman can do things that make her "big," or "prestigeful," she is gaining access to something which is stamped as "male." Conversely, a male who shows weakness or does not perform as he should is described as "rubbish" and as tending towards the "female." Activities normally performed by women do not, however, necessarily have to be avoided by men. For example, women ordinarily and predominantly roll the thread which is used to make aprons and head-nets for men, but a few men also do this and are praised for their industry rather than looked down upon. Similarly, among the Wiru, a woman who undertakes men's work in gardening is praised for her strength; women are also praised in both societies for their strength in their own spheres of work, such as pig keeping and childbearing. It is clear that prestige attaches to success in these activities, but in Hagen a further sphere of prestige specific to men is constructed from an ideology of ceremonial exchange.

Actual transvestism is quite different from the above, as is the actual incidence of intersexuality or sex change. Transvestism in Hagen and Wiru has solely to do with making political statements: women are dressed as men to say "Even our women are as strong as your men," or men dressed as women to say "You are arguing that our men are weak as women, but you will see." It is confined to ceremonial contexts. As to intersexuality, I know of two cases from Wiru. In one the person acted as a man and married a wife but could never impregnate her; his rudimentary penis was too small. Nevertheless, they stayed as husband and wife, and the husband was a great fighter and worker. In the other case the intersexual desired to be a woman and was not short of suitors because, again, she was a strong worker (something Wiru intersexuals are known for). In Hagen I know of one case: a girl decided she was really a boy as she grew up and indeed is now accepted as a man and is married, again without children. In 1964 I also saw one man who wore a headcloth as women do and walked about with the women, despite the fact that he was heavily bearded and middle-aged. His activities were tolerated with amusement by other men.

My point in citing these anecdotes is to reinforce the suggestion that it is not in isolated individual cases of sex change or sex ambiguity that the origin of berdache-type institutions is to be sought, but in the social logic of gender construction. Nevertheless, there has to be a social psychology which is capable of explaining how individuals are inducted into the status and why there are many or few people holding it. Materialist and idealist answers are likely to run in counterpoint here.

Reply

by CHARLES CALLENDER and LEE M. KOCHEMS
Cleveland, Ohio, U.S.A. 18 V 83

Addressing 15 comments, often overlapping, poses problems of organization that we think are best handled by grouping the information and opinions they contain into three topical categories: the berdache institution itself, methodology, and explanatory hypotheses.

The berdache institution. Trying to achieve a contextual definition of berdache status, we consciously omitted any etymological discussion of the word "berdache," a label originally applied by outsiders to the phenomena examined here. Semantic change has now confined the term to this context, which the word's earlier pejorative meaning distorted. We overlooked Hultkrantz's point, apparently concurred in by Jacobs and underlined by Knobloch's question. The statements by Hultkrantz and Jacobs, if not entirely agreeing, seem sufficient; Guerra (1971:43) gives a slightly different etymology for the Spanish form, *bardaje*.

Our delineation of berdache distribution needs less redrawing than we expected, with the northern Athabaskans the most important exception. We unfortunately missed Broch's (1977) article documenting berdache status among the Hare. While his Chipewyan, Dogrib, and Kutchin examples may have been similar to the Piegan "manly-hearts," that berdaches were probably widespread among northern Athabaskans (cf. Rogers 1981:27) seems likely. We would now move the Slave from doubtful to definite and revise our statement about the attenuation of berdache status in the Subarctic.

Signorini notes that Charlevoix ascribed berdaches to the Iroquois. We don't have this reference but had rejected a similar statement in his *Journal of a Voyage to North America* (1923[1720]:73–74) as unreliable, not supported by Jesuits who worked among Iroquois groups and conflicting with the omission of the Iroquois in Lafitau's comparable passage (1724:603–4). We might add that Loskiel's (1794:11) report of homosexuality among the Delaware and apparently the Iroquois (Katz 1976:290) did not describe berdache behavior. The case for the absence of berdaches among Iroquois cultures is strong. Kehoe points out that Miller (1974) reached a similar conclusion. Brown terms it "clearly documented."

We agree with Hultkrantz that the Wind River Shoshoni berdache status strengthens the case for its presence among the closely related Comanche, but this remains a probability rather than a certainty.

Although Jacobs disagrees that berdache distribution in the Southwest seems less pervasive than in some other areas, we think the evidence at hand supports our conclusion. Berdaches are not documented for the Plateau Yumans, the Eastern Pueblos, or the Jicarilla and Mescalero Apache.

Turning to comments about berdache characteristics, Powers's description of these among the Lakota (Teton Dakota) provides richly detailed ethnographic data for ready comparison with information from other cultures. His clarification of related problems raised by earlier studies of this culture has far-reaching implications. Powers explicitly denies that their accounts of prejudice against berdaches, often cited in the literature, express native Lakota sentiments. These pejorative statements have a very different significance when seen as contamination by American views.

Knobloch asks whether belief in the transmigration of souls might have provided an explanation for berdaches as men with feminine souls. Such a belief, if it existed, was not widespread. The concept of a feminine soul in a male body seems to us essentially Western, explicitly advanced by Ulrichs to explain homosexuals as a third sex (DeCicco 1981:33) and still held in some quarters (cf. Russo 1981:55). As for Knobloch's other questions, belief in their special supernatural power underlay the Lakota practice of asking berdaches to name children. Hassrick (1971:273) reports a belief that these names might confer long life. Powers (1977:38), however, relates this practice to another belief, that berdaches had "auspicious powers related to childbirth and child-rearing." We don't have specific information about the speech forms that berdaches used.

Liberty's suggestion that northern Plains priests might have transferred power to each other through the mediation of a berdache with whom both had sexual intercourse is provocative, but we have no confirming evidence.

Jacobs properly objects to our poorly worded statement that berdaches did not hold formal offices. We should have said that they did not hold formal political offices directly related to their gender status. DuMont's (Swanton 1911:100) tantalizingly fragmentary reference to a Natchez berdache as "this pretended chief of the women" might imply an exception, but his meaning is unclear. We also agree with Jacobs that the roles berdaches performed as such could have been defined as offices.

Much research obviously remains to be done on defining berdache status and delineating its functions. Hultkrantz's report that the Shoshoni defined berdaches as one of five recognized categories of men who abstained from heterosexual relations has important implications. An untrained observer might have extended the berdache label to some of these other categories, which still other societies may have merged. Definitions of berdaches probably varied by culture more than the literature suggests, and some persons it describes as berdaches may not have been defined as such.

Jacobs's description of the Tewa *quetho*, a status that does not fit our definition of berdache, raises further problems. Did other North American cultures have categories like the *quetho*? Should the definition be reworded to include *quetho* status, or was this a different development that perhaps inhibited the appearance of berdaches? One possible solution is to shift emphasis to berdaches as one widespread variety of gender mixing, which also subsumed such statuses as the *quetho* and included temporary contextual or situational gender mixing behavior by nonberdache males. The Blackfoot holy man cited by Kehoe, performing in this capacity, cross-dressed and simulated lactation when conferring power on other men. Powers describes temporary gender mixing by the Lakota *heyoka*. Broch, whose Hare example shows shifts into and out of berdache behavior, suggests that we might have given more attention to situational role behavior, which we agree is significant.

Holmberg's call for intensive comparison of variations in the berdache institution by culture area and for comparing cultures with berdaches and those lacking these defines another important direction for research. Brown, agreeing with this last point, suggests that one common berdache function, that of go-between, was assumed among the Iroquois by older women, who arranged marriages. While their role does not seem really comparable to the carrying of messages by berdaches, we agree with her emphasis on the parallels between berdaches and postmenopausal women.

Another set of unresolved problems concerns postcontact changes in berdache status. If knowledge of its traditional forms has many gaps, information about its current forms is even more limited. Powers's and Broch's accounts, taken together, illustrate the range of contemporary berdache behavior. Liberty's Cheyenne example shows the persistence even of transvestism, its least viable aspect. A very basic problem—here we again agree with Jacobs—involves the definition of berdache status when only some of its traditional features are evident. Powers describes it as clearly viable among the Lakota, even without transvestism. Landes describes Santee Dakota (1969:112–13) and Potawatomi (1970:26, 195–98) males interested in some aspects of women's work who informants agreed would have become berdaches in the past; here the status seems no longer viable. At what point, then, do berdaches go underground but persist, and at what later point does their behavior become vestigial? The factors modifying or destroying the status, very complex and indirect as well as obvious, also need more attention. We agree with Broch's suggestion that contact may also have introduced or redefined occupations that made the assumption of berdachehood unnecessary.

Methodology. Bleibtreu-Ehrenberg's comment, involving conceptual and methodological issues, seems to stress the latter. Our disagreement with her is pronounced. While ultimately concerned with gender mixing on a broad scale, we limited this first phase of our study to North America, where it was common (perhaps even, as Schlegel notes, particularly widespread), where the cultures shared enough features to facilitate comparison, and where we had better control of the literature. Before undertaking a broader study we wanted to reach a definition of its North American forms. This explicitly limited aim, carrying some disadvantages, offers important compensations and is legitimate. In deducing features of berdache status, we used data from every time period, evaluating these and trying to filter out the effects of postcontact changes as well as the errors or biases of observers. This method seems preferable to assuming that all variations in the status result from Western contact. Our general avoidance of individual psychology, discussed below, was deliberate and justified. Finally, the few statements we found describing women as hostile toward berdaches (e.g., Romans 1962:82–83) were brief, unconvincing, and sometimes derivative.

Datan wishes we had mentioned the Nacirema. We did, implicitly, throughout the article. Most accounts of berdaches were written by Nacirema, lay or anthropologist, many of whom insisted on viewing or analyzing them in Nacirema terms. Unless we completely misunderstand her, Datan perpetuates this cultural attitude by equating berdaches with *slauxesomoh*, a subgroup whom Nacirema social scientists defined as very rare and whose male members they viewed as gender-defective and rather like females, a condition often blamed on their mothers but sometimes regarded as contagious. The Theban seer Teiresias, as we recall, turned into a woman when, encountering two copulating snakes, he killed the female; and returned to male form seven years later when, under similar circumstances, he killed the male. We class this as gender crossing, rather than gender mixing.

Granzberg's comment is puzzling. While criticizing us for not having written a different article, his perceptions of this one seem unique, even his calling it a tabulation. We admit that it includes two tables. Of the "previous tabulations" he wanted us to appraise more fully, the only really comparable article is Jacobs (1968). Where we cover the same points, we are in essential agreement. Katz (1976), as we pointed out, is a compilation of documents about American Indian homosexuality, and not comparable. Forgey (1975), as we also pointed out, covers the northern Plains, not North America. We noted our agreements and disagreements with Signorini (1972) and Whitehead (1981). We could have gone through Benedict (1934), pointing out errors sentence by sentence, but this seemed unnecessary. His reference to Arens also puzzles us. Does he view berdaches as a myth? If he means that the sources have to be evaluated with care, so they do; as we noted. We did not argue that females dominated social life among American Indians. The questions with which we ended were suggested directions for future research, not our central hypotheses.

Explanatory hypotheses. The explanatory hypotheses most explicitly discussed in the comments include one specific problem, the rare occurrence of female berdaches. Otherwise they center on the berdache institution as a whole.

Three comments suggest reasons female berdaches were rarer than males. Datan's suggestion that male berdaches tended to have male privileges, apparently based on an equation with American homosexuals, does not explain the difference in frequency. Brown cites studies based on experiments at feeding stations for deer, showing that they avoid food scented with human blood and suggesting that menstruating females would draw a similar reaction. These contexts don't seem really equivalent. Given the importance of hunting as an occupation for female berdaches, however, and perhaps adding the Mohave statements that they did not menstruate (much), this hypothesis, if confirmed, would be significant. We are most attracted by Schlegel's hypothesis that societies concerned with reproduction would not encourage the loss of fertile females from the breeding pool. The evidence, as she notes, seems to support her subsidiary argument that repression or discouragement of female berdaches was strongest where strong matrilineal descent groups existed.

The four broad explanatory hypotheses for the berdache institution—psychological, economic, religious, and gender-construction—may be used as alternatives or combined. We see each of these as an important aspect of the status.

We rejected the psychological approach, explicitly when considering its two subsidiary hypotheses and implicitly by silence. Thayer (1980:288) also rejects it, arguing that it takes berdache behavior out of its cultural context, emphasizing its genital aspects (a point Kehoe also notes) and reducing it to a form of sexual activity. We would add two further criticisms. Grounded in Western folk beliefs about gender, homosexuality, and transvestism, this approach well illustrates Sahlins's (1976:75) point that the "etic" in cultural analysis is usually the "emic" of the anthropologist's society. Moreover, it seldom attempts to explain more than individual motivations for assuming the status.

We are surprised that this approach has drawn very little defense in the comments, except perhaps those noting our failure to discuss the articles by Munroe, Whiting, and Hally (1969) and Munroe and Munroe (1977). The former study concludes that transvestism is most common in societies with relatively few sex distinctions and suggests that these conditions facilitate gender crossing. While we dislike its terminology, the argument seems reasonable. Munroe and Munroe (1977), more explicitly psychological in approach, conclude that male transvestism is highly correlated with subsistence economies to which males make greater quantitative contributions. This seems unlikely. Given a normal sex ratio, one would expect such societies to discourage the practice. Without supporting data, the argument cannot be evaluated, but we reject its explicit premise that berdache status is an "escape mechanism" from the "rigorous male role" and the implicit assumption that a male berdache did only women's work.

In rejecting most applications of the psychological approach, we are not denying the importance of this aspect of the berdache status, but expressing dissatisfaction with the concepts and techniques this approach uses. We agree with Strathern that "there has to be a social psychology which is capable of explaining how individuals are inducted into the status and why there are many or few people holding it" but haven't yet found it.

A second explanatory hypothesis is economic. Schlegel notes the clear thread of economic causality running through the article. The junior author wanted to develop this into a hypothesis; the senior author had reservations. Schlegel also points out (very tactfully) a major weakness in our treatment of this aspect. Emphasizing the economic advantages berdaches derived from their status and the gender-mixing activities attached to it, we did not examine these from the standpoint of their societies. She does so, impressively, arguing that berdache status is essentially "a mechanism by which societies with uncertain sex ratios can regulate their labor supply." One of us doubts that her hypothesis will meet all cases. Liberty's comment supports it, but Broch points out that our linking of the attenuation of the institution with the specific nature of Subarctic subsistence economy rests on a misunderstanding of its sexual division of labor. We both agree that the line of research Schlegel has outlined, which has the further merit of accounting for the presence or absence of female berdaches, is a very important one to pursue.

Another explanatory hypothesis approaches berdache status as essentially a religious phenomenon. One form, not covered in the article, is Thayer's (1980) analysis of the northern Plains berdache, which, as several comments note, we had overlooked. Thayer sees the berdache as "straddling" the worlds of men and women. He describes them as "interstitial," in Douglas's sense, being both male and female and neither male nor female. This feature gave them power to mediate between men and women and, through the visions that validated their status, to mediate between the human and divine worlds. We agree with Thayer in some respects. A weak point in his argument is the ambivalence he postulates in cultural attitudes toward berdaches among northern Plains tribes. Admitting that this was not evident among the Cheyenne, he draws his specific examples from the Lakota. But Powers's comment indicates that the ambivalence described for the Lakota was intrusive, Western in origin, and not indigenous. We are not certain that berdaches mediated between men and women, apart from acting as go-betweens. Although they could be shamans, only some of them had this role, and in spite of their resemblances to shamans we would not call them such. In any case, many other persons had vision experiences, and some of these also mediated with the supernatural.

Bleibtreu-Ehrenberg, Hultkrantz, and Signorini criticize our reservations about the religious approach in general. We agree that berdache status was a religious phenomenon and is legitimately examined as such. The reservations we expressed center on our view that its analysis in terms of any single dimension is not incorrect, but incomplete.

Hultkrantz's suggestion that berdache status is "a variation of an ancient shamanistic practice" obviously deserves consideration. But even if this was its origin, it has added other dimensions, and not only through Western contact. Often tied to vision experience, the status also existed in societies where visions were much less important or even absent. All Yurok shamans *were* berdaches; but shamanism, monopolized by women and male berdaches, was an important source of income in Yurok society, whose elite (Pilling 1978:112) emphasized wealth and property.

Signorini, after a disarming opening, presses a vigorous (and entirely fair) attack, using as weapons berdache characteristics we had emphasized. His first point is that berdaches had supernatural powers and specific ritual responsibilities. They did, but the latter seem not to have been universal and we are not sure the former were. His second point is also very important; many North American societies regarded berdaches as essential. But again, not all societies held this view. Third, he holds that gender mixing, as "a conjunction of sexual opposites," is normally linked with deities who are androgynous or the reverse of the gender-mixer's anatomical sex. We grant the existence of a widespread religious complex that subsumes gender mixing as an aspect. But gender mixing, as Strathern's comment indicates, may also be entirely secular. In American Indian cultures the divine world tended to suffuse the secular, and many forms of behavior had both aspects. Their analysis may stress either aspect.

Signorini observes that berdache status, as it spread, could be integrated in various ways into cultures. This point, added to his earlier statement about the status's "original meaning," may elucidate the crux of our disagreement with him, Hultkrantz, and probably Bleibtreu-Ehrenberg. We are not dealing with the institution's original meaning or attempting to determine this. Whether we should be doing so is another issue. We are concerned with the status in the recent historical past. Perhaps we could negotiate a truce, based on mutual recognition that, within a broad range of agreement, they and we are concentrating on somewhat different problems and thus emphasizing slightly different aspects. And while we hold that an analysis in terms of a single dimension is incomplete, we concede that limiting our analysis to North America opens us to a similar criticism.

The fourth approach to berdache status is analysis in terms of gender construction. Strathern, whose comment directly addresses this point, describes examples of secular gender mixing and gender crossing in New Guinea, which we welcome as indications that such phenomena may be a significant element in the berdache institution.

Within this overall approach, the issue of gender-related status asymmetry in North America seems the most controversial. Jacobs, Kehoe, Powers, and Schlegel take positions similar to ours. Perhaps we could infer Broch's agreement as well, given his statement that the *openness* of political performance among Hare women is new. This agreement, particularly by those who have done fieldwork among American Indians, strengthens our perception that Whitehead's model in this respect is essentially based on Western concepts. Liberty takes a very different position that, opposing ours, also disagrees with Whitehead. Having read only the more popular version (1982) of her published argument, we respect her position but are far from complete acceptance of it.

Holmberg, whose comment also centers on gender construction (and notes the status asymmetry issue), concentrates on three points where we disagree with Whitehead's analysis of the berdache status. In all three, our knowledge of American Indian cultures led us to mistrust the logic of Whitehead's model of gender, production, and prestige in North America, which seemed to rest on far too narrow a data base and, in spite of her excellent discussion of gender, to include many concepts that were basically Western and not really transferable (cf. K. Brown 1982). We are not yet ready to propose an alternative model. Holmberg's points are important. Besides demonstrating again that berdache status obviously needs further study, they mark out directions for future research on the total sex-gender systems of North American societies.

References Cited

ADAIR, JAMES. 1966. *History of the American Indians.* Edited by Samuel Cole Williams. New York: Argonaut Press.

ALARCÓN, F. 1565. "Relatione della navigatione & scoperta che fece il Capitano Fernando Alarchone per ordine dello illustrissimo signor don Antonio di Mendozza vice re della nuova Spagna, data in Colima, porto della nuova Spagna," in *Delle navigationi et viaggi,* vol 3. Edited by G. B. Ramusio, pp. 363–67. Venice. [IS]

ANGELINO, HENRY, and CHARLES L. SHEDD. 1955. A note on berdache. *American Anthropologist* 57:121–26.

ARENS, WILLIAM. 1979. *The man-eating myth: Anthropology and anthropophagy.* Oxford University Press. [GG]

BANCROFT, HUBERT HOWE. 1874. *The native races of the Pacific states of North America.* Vol. 1. New York: D. Appleton.

BARNETT, H. G. 1937. *Culture element distributions 7: Oregon Coast.* Anthropological Records 1(3).

———. 1955. *The Coast Salish of British Columbia.* Eugene: University of Oregon Press.

BARRY, HERBERT, III, and ALICE SCHLEGEL. 1982. Cross-cultural codes on contribution by women to subsistence. *Ethnology* 21:165–88. [AS]

BAUMANN, HERMANN. 1950. *Der kultische Geschlechtswandel bei Naturvölkern.* Zeitschrift für Sexualforschung (Frankfurt/M.) 1.

———. 1955. *Das doppelte Geschlecht.* Berlin.

BEAGLEHOLE, ERNEST, and PEARL BEAGLEHOLE. 1935. *Hopi of the Second Mesa.* American Anthropological Association Memoir 44.

BEALS, RALPH L. 1933. *Ethnology of the Nisenan.* University of California Publications in American Archaeology and Ethnology 31(6).

BENEDICT, RUTH. 1934. Anthropology and the abnormal. *Journal of General Psychology* 10:59–82.

———. 1939. Sex in primitive society. *American Journal of Orthopsychiatry* 9:570–75.

BIRKET-SMITH, KAJ, and FREDERICA DE LAGUNA. 1937. *The Eyak Indians of the Copper River delta, Alaska.* København: Levin and Munksgaard.

BLACK HAWK. 1955. *Ma-ka-tai-me-she-kia-kiak, Black Hawk: An autobiography.* Edited by Donald Jackson. Urbana: University of Illinois Press.

BLEIBTREU-EHRENBERG, GISELA. 1970. Homosexualität und Transvestition im Schamanismus. *Anthropos* 65:189–228.

BOSCANA, GERONIMO. 1978. *Chinigchinich.* Banning, Calif.: Malki Museum Press.

BOSSU, JEAN-BERNARD. 1962. *Jean-Bernard Bossu's travels in the interior of North America 1751–1762.* Translated and edited by Seymour Feiler. Norman: University of Oklahoma Press.

BOWERS, ALFRED. 1950. *Mandan social and ceremonial organization.* Chicago: University of Chicago Press.

———. 1965. *Hidatsa social and ceremonial organization.* Bureau of American Ethnology Bulletin 194.

BOYCE, DOUGLAS W. 1978. "Iroquoian tribes of the Virginia–North Carolina coastal plain," in *Handbook of North American Indians,* vol. 15. Edited by Bruce G. Trigger, pp. 282–89. Washington, D.C.: Smithsonian Institution.

BRADBURY, JOHN. 1904. *Travels in the interior of America in the years 1809, 1810, and 1811.* (*Early western travels,* edited by Reuben G. Thwaites, vol. 14.) Cleveland: Arthur H. Clark.

BROCH, HARALD B. 1977. A note on berdache among the Hare Indians of northwestern Canada. *Western Canadian Journal of Anthropology* 7:95–101. [HBB]

BROWN, JUDITH K. 1970. A note on the division of labor by sex. *American Anthropologist* 72:1073–78. [JKB]

———. 1975. "Iroquois women: An ethnohistorical note," in *Toward an anthropology of women.* Edited by Rayna R. Reiter, pp. 235–51. New York: Monthly Review Press.

———. 1982. Cross-cultural perspectives on middle-aged women CURRENT ANTHROPOLOGY 23:143–56. [JKB]

BROWN, KYLE ELAINE. 1982. Your context or mine? A feminist analysis examined. Unpublished M. Sc. paper, London School of Economics, London, England.

CARR, LUCIEN. n.d. The mounds of the Mississippi Valley, historically considered. Reprinted from *Memoirs of the Kentucky Geological Survey 2.*

CATLIN, GEORGE. 1973. *Letters and notes on the manners, customs, and conditions of the North American Indians.* 2 vols. New York: Dover.

CHARLEVOIX, PIERRE-FRANÇOIS-XAVIER DE. 1744. *Histoire et description générale de la Nouvelle France.* Vol. 6. Paris: Nyon. [IS]

———. 1923 (1720). *Journal of a voyage to North America.* Vol. 2. Edited by Louise Phelps Kellogg. Chicago: Caxton Club.

CLINE, WALTER. 1938. "Religion and world view," in *The Sinkaietk or southern Okanogan.* Edited by Leslie Spier, pp. 131–49. (General Series in Anthropology 6.) Menasha, Wis.: George Banta.

COSTANSO, MIGUEL. 1910. *The narrative of the Portola expedition of 1769–1770.* Edited by Adolph Van Hemeri-Engert and Frederick J. Teggard. (Publications of the Academy of Pacific Coast History 1[4].) Berkeley: University of California Press.

COUES, ELLIOTT. 1897. *New light on the early history of the greater Northwest: The manuscript journals of Alexander Henry and of David Thompson, 1799–1814.* New York: Francis P. Harper.

CROWE, K. J. 1974. *A history of the original peoples of northern Canada.* Montreal: McGill–Queen's University Press. [HBB]

CUSHING, FRANK HAMILTON. 1896. *Outlines of Zuni creation myths.* Bureau of American Ethnology Annual Report 13.

DALL, WILLIAM H. 1897. *Alaska and its resources.* Boston: Lee and Shepart.

DATAN, NANCY. n.d. Androgyny and the life cycle: The Bacchae of Euripides. *Journal of Imagination, Cognition, and Personality: The Scientific Study of Consciousness.* In press. [ND]

DECICCO, JOHN P. 1981. "Definition and meaning of sexual orientation," in *Nature and causes of homosexuality: A philosophical and scientific inquiry.* Edited by Noretta Koertge, pp. 51–67. New York: Haworth Press.

DE LAGUNA, FREDERICA. 1954. Tlingit ideas about the Indian. *Southwestern Journal of Anthropology* 10:172–79.

———. 1960. *The story of a Tlingit community: A problem with relationships between archaeological, ethnological, and historical methods.* Bureau of American Ethnology Bulletin 172.

DENIG, EDWIN T. 1961. *Five Indian tribes of the upper Missouri.* Edited by John C. Ewers. Norman: University of Oklahoma Press.

DE SMET, PIERRE JEAN. 1904. *Life, letters, and travels of Father de Smet among the North American Indians.* Edited by Hiram Martin

Chittendon and Alfred Talbot Richardson. Vol. 3. New York: Francis P. Harper.

DEVEREUX, GEORGE. 1937. Institutionalized homosexuality of the Mohave Indians. *Human Biology* 9:498–527.

———. 1961. *Mohave ethnopsychiatry: The psychic disturbances of an Indian tribe*. Washington, D.C.: Smithsonian Institution.

DORSEY, GEORGE A., and JAMES R. MURIE. 1940. *Notes on the Skidi Pawnee society*. Field Museum of Natural History Anthropological Series 27(2).

DORSEY, J. OWEN. 1890. *A study of Siouan cults*. Bureau of American Ethnology Annual Report 11.

DRIVER, HAROLD E. 1936. *Wappo ethnography*. University of California Publications in American Archaeology and Ethnology 36(3).

———. 1937. *Culture element distributions 6: Southern Sierra Nevada*. University of California Anthropological Records 1(2).

———. 1939. *Culture element distributions 10: Northwest California*. University of California Anthropological Records 1(6).

———. 1969. *Indians of North America*. Chicago: University of Chicago Press.

DRUCKER, PHILIP. 1937. *Culture element distributions 5: Southern California*. University of California Anthropological Records 1(1).

———. 1941. *Culture element distributions 12: Yuman-Piman*. University of California Anthropological Records 6(3).

———. 1951. *The northern and central Nootkan tribes*. Bureau of American Ethnology Bulletin 144.

ELIADE, MIRCEA. 1965. *Mephistopheles and the Androgyne: Studies in religious myth and symbol*. Translated by J. J. Cohen. New York: Sheed and Ward.

ELSASSER, ALBERT B. 1978. "Wiyot," in *Handbook of North American Indians*, vol. 8. Edited by Robert F. Heizer, pp. 155–63. Washington, D.C.: Smithsonian Institution.

ESSENE, FRANK. 1942. *Culture element distributions 20: Round Valley*. University of California Anthropological Records 8(1).

FEWKES, W. WALTER. 1892. A few Tusayan pictographs. *American Anthropologist* 5:9–26.

FIRE, JOHN, with RICHARD ERDOES. 1972. *Lame Deer, seeker of visions*. New York: Simon and Shuster.

FLETCHER, ALICE C., and FRANCIS LA FLESCHE. 1911. *The Omaha tribe*. Bureau of American Ethnology Annual Report 27.

FONT, PEDRO. 1966. *Font's complete diary of the second Anza expedition*. Translated from the original Spanish manuscript and edited by Herbert Eugene Bolton. (*Anza's California expeditions*, edited by H. E. Bolton, vol. 14.) New York: Russell and Russell.

FORD, CLELLAN. 1941. *Smoke from their fires: The life of a Kwakiutl chief*. New Haven: Yale University Press. [JKB]

FORDE, C. DARYLL. 1931. *Ethnography of the Yuma Indians*. University of California Publications in American Archaeology and Ethnology 28(4).

FORGEY, DONALD G. 1975. The institution of berdache among the North American Plains Indians. *Journal of Sex Research* 11:1–15.

FOSTER, GEORGE M. 1944. *A summary of Yuki culture*. University of California Anthropological Records 5(3).

GATSCHET, ALBERT B. 1891. *The Karankawa Indians, the coast people of Texas*. Archaeological and Ethnological Papers of the Peabody Museum 1(2).

GAYTON, ANNA H. 1948. *Yokuts and Western Mono ethnography*. University of California Anthropological Records 10(1–2).

GIFFORD, EDWARD WINSLOW. 1926. *Clear Lake Pomo society*. University of California Publications in American Archaeology and Ethnology 18(2).

———. 1931. *The Kamia of Imperial Valley*. Bureau of American Ethnology Bulletin 97.

———. 1933. *The Cocopa*. University of California Publications in American Ethnology and Archaeology 31(5).

———. 1936. *Northeastern and western Yavapai*. University of California Publications in American Archaeology and Ethnology 34(4).

———. 1940. *Culture element distributions 12: Apache-Pueblo*. University of California Anthropological Records 4(1).

GODDARD, IVES. 1978. "Delaware," in *Handbook of North American Indians*, vol. 15. Edited by Bruce G. Trigger, pp. 213–39. Washington, D.C.: Smithsonian Institution.

GOLDSCHMIDT, WALTER. 1951. *Nomlaki ethnography*. University of California Publications in American Archaeology and Anthropology 42(4).

GOULD, RICHARD A. 1978. "Tolowa," in *Handbook of North American Indians*, vol. 8. Edited by Robert F. Heizer, pp. 128–36. Washington, D.C.: Smithsonian Institution.

GRINNELL, GEORGE B. 1956. *The fighting Cheyennes*. Norman: University of Oklahoma Press.

———. 1962. *The Cheyenne Indians*. 2 vols. New York: Cooper Square.

GUERRA, FRANCISCO. 1971. *The pre-Columbian mind*. London: Seminar.

HAMMOND, WILLIAM A. 1882. The disease of the Scythians (Morbus Feminarum) and certain analogous conditions. *American Journal of Neurology and Psychiatry* 1:339–55.

HARRINGTON, JOHN P. 1942. *Culture element distributions 19: Central California coast*. University of California Anthropological Records 7(1).

HASSRICK, ROYAL B. 1964. *The Sioux*. Norman: University of Oklahoma Press.

HAY, HENRY. 1963. Review of the Hammond Report. *Homophile Studies* 6:1–21. [SJ]

HENNEPIN, LOUIS. 1903. *A new discovery of a vast country in America*. Edited by Reuben G. Thwaites. Chicago: A. C. McClurg.

HESTER, THOMAS ROY. 1978. "Salinan," in *Handbook of North American Indians*, vol. 8. Edited by Robert F. Heizer, pp. 500–504. Washington, D.C.: Smithsonian Institution.

HILL, RUTH BEEBE. 1979. *Hanta yo: An American saga*. New York: Doubleday.

HILL, WILLARD WILLIAMS. 1935. The status of the hermaphrodite and transvestite in Navaho culture. *American Anthropologist* 37:273–79.

———. 1938. Note on the Pima berdache. *American Anthropologist* 40:338–40.

HOEBEL, E. ADAMSON. 1949. *Man in the primitive world: An introduction to anthropology*. New York: McGraw-Hill.

———. 1960. *The Cheyennes: Indians of the Great Plains*. New York: Holt, Rinehart and Winston.

HOLDER, A. B. 1889. The bote: Description of a peculiar sexual perversion found among North American Indians. *New York Medical Journal* 50:623–25.

HOLT, CATHERINE. 1946. *Shasta ethnography*. University of California Anthropological Records 3(4).

HONIGMANN, JOHN H. 1946. *Ethnography and acculturation of the Fort Nelson Slave*. Yale University Publications in Anthropology 33.

———. 1954. *The Kaska Indians: An ethnographic reconstruction*. Yale University Publications in Anthropology 51.

HOWARD, JAMES H. 1965. *The Ponca tribe*. Bureau of American Ethnology Bulletin 195.

HYDE, GEORGE E. 1937. *Red Cloud's folk*. Norman: University of Oklahoma Press.

IRVING, JOHN TREAT. 1888. *Indian sketches taken during a U.S. expedition to make treaties with the Pawnee and other tribes of Indians in 1833*. New York: Putnam.

JACKSON, DONALD. Editor. 1962. *Letters of the Lewis and Clark Expedition, with related documents 1783–1854*. Urbana: University of Illinois Press.

JACOBS, SUE-ELLEN. 1968. Berdache: A brief review of the literature. *Colorado Anthropologist* 1:25–40.

———. n.d. As if in a dream: Images of change at San Juan Pueblo. MS. [SJ]

JAMES, EDWIN. 1823. *Account of an expedition from Pittsburgh to the Rocky Mountains in the years 1819 and '20, by order of the Hon. J. C. Calhoun, Sec'y of War: under the command of Major Stephen H. Long*. Philadelphia: H. C. Carey and I. Lea.

JONES, WILLIAM. 1907. *Fox texts*. Publications of the American Ethnological Society 1.

KARDINER, ABRAM. 1945. *The psychological frontiers of society*. New York: Columbia University Press.

KATZ, JONATHAN. 1976. *Gay American history: Lesbians and gay men in the U.S.A.* New York: Crowell.

KEATING, WILLIAM H. 1825. *Narrative of an expedition to the source of St. Peter's river, Lake Winnepeck, Lake of the Woods, etc. etc. performed in the year 1823 under the command of Stephen H. Long, Major U.S.T.E.* Vol. 1. Philadelphia:H. C. Carey and I. Lea.

KEHOE, ALICE B. 1970. The function of ceremonial sexual intercourse among the northern Plains Indians. *Plains Anthropologist* 15:99–103. [ABK]

———. 1976. Old Woman had great power. *Western Canadian Journal of Anthropology* 6:68–76. [ABK]

———. 1983. "The shackles of tradition," in *The hidden half*. Edited by Patricia Albers and Beatrice Medicine. Washington, D.C.: University Press of America. [ABK]

KELLOGG, LOUISE PHELPS. Editor. 1917. *Early narratives of the Northwest*. New York: Scribner.

KERNS, VIRGINIA. 1979. Social transition at menopause. Paper presented at the 78th annual meeting of the American Anthropological Association, Cincinnati, Ohio. [JKB]

KINIETZ, W. VERNON. 1947. *Chippewa village: The story of Katikitegon*. Cranbrook Institute of Science Bulletin 25.

KITAHARA, MICHIO. 1982. Menstrual taboos and the importance of hunting. *American Anthropologist* 84:901–3. [JKB]

KLUCKHOHN, C. 1969. "Recurrent themes in myths and mythmaking," in *Myths and mythmaking*. Edited by H. A. Murray, pp. 46–60. Boston: Beacon Press. [IS]

KROEBER, ALFRED L. 1902. *The Arapaho*. American Museum of Natural History Bulletin 18.

———. 1925. *Handbook of the Indians of California*. Bureau of American Ethnology Bulletin 78.

———. 1932. *The Patwin and their neighbors*. University of California Publications in Archaeology and Ethnology 29(4).

———. 1935. Editor. *Walapai ethnography*. Memoirs of the American Anthropological Association 2.

———. 1952. *The nature of culture*. Chicago: University of Chicago Press.

KURZ, RUDOLPH F. 1937. *Journal of Rudolph Friedrich Kurz: An account of his experiences among fur traders and American Indians on the Mississippi and Missouri rivers during the years 1846 to 1852*. Edited by J. N. B. Hewitt. Bureau of American Ethnology Bulletin 115.

LAFITAU, JOSEPH FRANÇOIS. 1724. *Moeurs des sauvages ameriquains, comparées aux moeurs des premiers temps*. Vol. 1. Paris: Saugrain l'ainé.

LANDES, RUTH. 1968. *The Mystic Lake Sioux*. Madison: University of Wisconsin Press.

———. 1970. *The Prairie Potawatomi*. Madison: University of Wisconsin Press.

LANGE, CHARLES R. 1959. *Cochiti, a New Mexico pueblo, past and present*. Austin: University of Texas Press.

LEACOCK, ELEANOR BURKE. 1981. *Myths of male dominance: Collected articles on women cross-culturally*. New York: Monthly Review Press. [GG]

LE MOYNE DU MORGUES, JACQUES. 1875. *Narrative of Le Moyne, an artist who accompanied the French expedition to Florida under Laudonniere, 1564*. Translated by Frederick B. Perkins. Boston: James R. Osgood.

LEWIS, OSCAR. 1941. The manly-hearted woman among the North Piegan. *American Anthropologist* 43:173–87.

LIBERTY, MARGOT. 1979. "Plains Indian women through time: A preliminary overview," in *Lifeways of intermontane and Plains Montana Indians*. Edited by Leslie B. Davis, pp. 137–50. (Occasional Papers of the Museum of the Rockies 1.) Bozeman, Montana: Montana State University. [ML]

———. 1982. Hell came with horses: The changing role of Plains Indian women through time. *Montana: The Magazine of Western History* 32(3):10–19. [ML]

LIETTE, PIERRE. 1947. "Memoir of Pierre Liette on the Illinois country," in *The western country in the 17th century*. Edited by Milo Milton Quaife. Chicago: Lakeside Press.

LINTON, RALPH. 1936. *The study of man*. New York: D. Appleton-Century.

LOSKIEL, GEORGE HENRY. 1794. *History of the mission of the United Brethren among the Indians of North America*. London: The Brethren's Society.

LOWIE, ROBERT H. 1910. *The Assiniboine*. Anthropological Papers of the American Museum of Natural History 4, pt. 1.

———. 1916. *Dance associations of the Eastern Dakota*. Anthropological Papers of the American Museum of Natural History 11, pt. 2.

———. 1924*a*. *Notes on Shoshonean ethnography*. Anthropological Papers of the American Museum of Natural History 20, pt. 3.

———. 1924*b*. *Primitive religion*. New York: Liveright.

———. 1935. *The Crow Indians*. New York: Farrar and Rinehart.

———. 1939. *Ethnographic notes on the Washo*. University of California Publications in American Archaeology and Ethnology 36(5).

———. 1940. 2d edition. *An introduction to cultural anthropology*. New York: Rinehart.

LURIE, NANCY O. 1953. Winnebago berdache. *American Anthropologist* 55:708–12.

McCOY, ISAAC. 1976. "His presence was so disgusting," in *Gay American history*. Edited by Jonathan Katz, p. 300. New York: Crowell.

McILWRAITH, T. F. 1948. *The Bella Coola Indians*. 2 vols. Toronto: University of Toronto Press.

McKENNEY, THOMAS A. 1827. *Sketches of a tour to the Lakes, of the character and customs of the Chippeway Indians*. Baltimore: Fielding Lucas, Jun'r.

McNICHOLS, CHARLES L. 1967. *Crazy weather*. Lincoln: University of Nebraska Press.

MANDELBAUM, DAVID G. 1940. *The Plains Cree*. Anthropological Papers of the American Museum of Natural History 37(2).

MARCH, KATHRYN. 1980. Deer, bears, and blood: A note on nonhuman animal response to menstrual odor. *American Anthropologist* 82:125–27. [JKB]

MARMOR, JUDD. 1965. "Introduction," in *Sexual inversion*. Edited by Judd Marmor, pp. 1–24. New York: Basic Books.

MARQUETTE, JACQUES. 1900(1674). "Of the first voyage made by Father Marquette toward New Mexico, and how the idea thereof was conceived," in *The Jesuit Relations and allied documents*, vol. 59. Edited by Reuben G. Thwaites. Cleveland: Burrows.

MARTIN, M. KAY, and BARBARA VOORHIES. 1975. *Female of the species*. New York: Columbia University Press.

MASON, J. ALDEN. 1912. *The ethnology of the Salinan Indians*. University of California Publications in American Archaeology and Ethnology 10(4).

MATHEWS, WASHINGTON. 1897. *Navaho legends*. Memoirs of the American Folklore Society 5.

MAXIMILIAN, ALEXANDER P. 1906. "Travels in the interior of North America," in *Early western travels*, vol. 22. Edited by Reuben G. Thwaites. Cleveland: Arthur H. Clark.

MEAD, MARGARET. 1932. *The changing culture of an Indian tribe*. New York: Columbia University Press.

———. 1949. *Male and female: A study of the sexes in a changing world*. New York: William Morrow.

———. 1961. "Cultural determinants of sexual behavior," in *Sex and internal secretions*. Edited by William C. Young, vol. 2, pp. 1433–79. Baltimore: Williams and Wilkins.

MEMBRE, ZENOBIUS. 1922. "Narrative of LaSalle's voyage down the Mississippi, by Father Zenobius Membre, Recollect," in *The journeys of Rene Robert Cavelier Sieur de la Salle*. Edited by Isaac Joslin Cox, pp. 131–59. New York: Allerton.

MEYER, ROY W. 1977. *The village Indians of the upper Missouri*. Lincoln: University of Nebraska Press.

MICHELSON, TRUMAN. 1925. The mythical origin of the White Buffalo Dance of the Fox Indians. *Bureau of American Ethnology Annual Report* 40, pp. 23–289.

MILLER, JAY. 1974. The Delaware as women. *American Ethnologist* 1:507–14. [ABK]

———. 1982. People, berdaches, and left-handed bears: Human variation in Native America. *Journal of Anthropological Research* 38:274–87. [ÅK]

MINER, HORACE. 1956. Body ritual among the Nacirema. *American Anthropologist* 58:3. [ND]

MIRSKY, JEANNETTE. 1937. "The Dakota," in *Cooperation and competition among primitive peoples*. Edited by Margaret Mead, pp. 382–427. New York: McGraw-Hill.

MORGAN, LEWIS HENRY. 1962(1851). *League of the Iroquois*. New York: Corinth Books. [JKB]

MUNROE, ROBERT. 1980. Male transvestism and the couvade: A psycho-cultural analysis. *Ethos* 8:49–59. [JKB]

MUNROE, ROBERT, and RUTH MUNROE. 1977. Male transvestism and subsistence economy. *Journal of Social Psychology* 103:307–8. [JKB]

MUNROE, ROBERT, JOHN W. M. WHITING, and DAVID HALLY. 1969. Institutionalized male transvestism and sex distinctions. *American Anthropologist* 71:87–91. [JKB, IS]

NEWCOMB, W. W., JR. 1961. *The Indians of Texas from prehistoric to modern times*. Austin: University of Texas Press.

NUNLEY, M. CHRISTOPHER. 1981. Response of deer to human blood odor. *American Anthropologist* 83:630–34. [JKB]

OLSON, RONALD L. 1936. *The Quinault Indians*. University of Washington Publications in Anthropology 6(1).

———. 1940. *Social organization of the Haisla of British Columbia*. University of California Anthropological Records 2(5).

OPLER, MARVIN K. 1940. "The Southern Ute of Colorado," in *Acculturation in seven American Indian tribes*. Edited by Ralph Linton. New York: D. Appleton-Century.

———. 1965. "Anthropological and cross-cultural aspects of homosexuality," in *Sexual inversion*. Edited by Judd Marmor, pp. 108–23. New York: Basic Books.

OSGOOD, CORNELIUS. 1958. *Ingalik social culture*. Yale University Publications in Anthropology 53.

PARKER, ARTHUR C. 1968. "Iroquois uses of maize and other food plants," in *Parker on the Iroquois*. Edited by William N. Fenton, book 1, pp. 1–119. Syracuse: Syracuse University Press. [JKB]

PARSONS, ELSIE CLEWS. 1916. The Zuni la'mana. *American Anthropologist* 18:521–28.

———. 1923. *Laguna genealogies*. Anthropological Papers of the American Museum of Natural History 19, pt. 5.

———. 1939. *Pueblo Indian religion*. Chicago: University of Chicago Press.

PILLING, ARNOLD. 1978. "Yurok," in *Handbook of North American Indians*, vol.8. Edited by Robert F. Heizer, pp. 137–54. Washington, D.C.: Smithsonian Institution.

POND, GIDEON H. 1889. Dakota superstitions. *Minnesota Historical Society Collections* 2:215–55.

POWERS, MARLA N. 1980. Menstruation and reproduction: An Oglala case. *Signs* 6:54–65. [WKP]

———. 1982. Oglala women in myth, ritual and reality. Unpublished doctoral dissertation, Rutgers University, New Brunswick, N.J. [WKP]

POWERS, STEPHEN. 1877. *Tribes of California*. U.S. Geographical and Geological Survey of the Rocky Mountain Region, Contributions to North American Ethnology 3.

POWERS, WILLIAM K. 1977. *Oglala religion*. Lincoln: University of Nebraska Press.

———. 1979. The archaic illusion. *American Indian Art* 5:68–71.

RAY, DOROTHY JEAN. 1975. *The Eskimos of Bering Strait, 1650–1898*. Seattle: University of Washington Press.

RAY, VERNE F. 1932. *The Sanpoil and Nespelem*. University of Washington Publications in Anthropology 5.

———. 1963. *Primitive pragmatists: The Modoc Indians of northern California*. Seattle: University of Washington Press.

REICHARD, GLADYS A. 1950. *Navaho religion: A study of symbolism*. New York: Bollingen Foundation.

ROGERS, EDWARD S. 1981. "History of ethnological research in the Subarctic Shield and Mackenzie borderlands," in *Handbook of North American Indians*, vol. 16. Edited by June Helm, pp. 19–29. Washington, D.C.: Smithsonian Institution.

ROMANS, BERNARD. 1962. *A concise natural history of East and West Florida*. Gainesville: University of Florida Press.

RUSSO, VITO. 1981. *The celluloid closet: Homosexuality in the movies.* New York: Harper and Row.

SAHLINS, MARSHALL. 1976. *Culture and practical reason.* Chicago: University of Chicago Press.

SAPIR, EDWARD, and LESLIE SPIER. 1943. *Notes on the culture of the Yana.* University of California Anthropological Records 3(3).

SCHAEFFER, CLAUDE E. 1976. "The Kutenai female berdache," in *Gay American history.* Edited by Jonathan Katz, pp. 293–98. New York: Crowell.

SHIMKIN, DMITRI B. 1947. *Childhood and development among the Wind River Shoshone.* University of California Anthropological Records 5(5).

SIGNORINI, ITALO. 1972. "Transvestitism and institutionalized homosexuality in North America." *Atti del XL Congresso Internazionale degli Americanisti,* vol. 2. Genova: Tilgher.

SIMMS, S. C. 1901. Crow Indian hermaphrodites. *American Anthropologist* 5:580–88.

SKINNER, ALANSON. 1913. *Social life and ceremonial-bundles of the Menomini Indians.* Anthropological Papers of the American Museum of Natural History 13.

SPIER, LESLIE. 1930. *Klamath ethnography.* University of California Publications in American Archaeology and Ethnology 30.

———. 1933. *Yuman tribes of the Gila River.* Chicago: University of Chicago Press.

———. 1935. *The Prophet Dance of the Northwest and its derivatives: The source of the Ghost Dance.* (General Series in Anthropology 1.) Menasha, Wis.: George Banta.

SPIER, LESLIE, and EDWARD SAPIR. 1930. *Wishram ethnography.* University of Washington Publications in Anthropology 3, pt. 3.

STEPHEN, ALEXANDER. 1936. *The Hopi journals of Alexander M. Stephen.* Edited by Elsie Clews Parsons. Vol. 1. New York: Columbia University Press.

STEVENSON, MATILDA G. 1902. *The Zuni Indians: Their mythology, esoteric societies, and ceremonies.* Bureau of American Ethnology Annual Report 23.

STEWARD, JULIAN H. 1933. *Ethnography of the Owens Valley Paiute.* University of California Publications in American Archaeology and Ethnology 33, pt. 3.

———. 1941. *Culture element distributions 13: Nevada Shoshone.* University of California Anthropological Records 4(2).

———. 1943. *Culture element distributions 23: Northern and Gosiute Shoshoni.* University of California Anthropological Records 8(3).

STEWART, OMER C. 1941. *Culture element distributions 1: Northern Paiute.* University of California Anthropological Records 4(3).

———. 1944. *Culture element distributions 28: Ute-Southern Paiute.* University of California Anthropological Records 6(4).

———. 1960. Homosexuality among the American Indians and other native peoples of the world. *Mattachine Review* 6(2):13–19. [SJ]

SWANTON, JOHN R. 1911. *Indian tribes of the Lower Mississippi Valley and adjacent coast of the Gulf of Mexico.* Bureau of American Ethnology Bulletin 43.

TANNER, JOHN. 1956. *A narrative of the captivity and adventures of John Tanner.* Edited by Edwin James. Minneapolis: Ross and Haines.

TEIT, JAMES. 1900. *The Thompson Indians of British Columbia.* American Museum of Natural History Memoir 2, pt. 4.

———. 1906. *The Lillouet Indians.* American Museum of Natural History Memoir 4, pt. 5.

———. 1930. *The Salishan tribes of the western plateau.* Bureau of American Ethnology Annual Report 5.

THAYER, JAMES STEEL. 1980. The berdache of the northern Plains: A socioreligious perspective. *Journal of Anthropological Research* 36:287–93. [JKB, DH]

TITIEV, MISCHA. 1972. *The Hopi Indians of Old Oraibi.* Ann Arbor: University of Michigan Press.

TIXIER, VICTOR. 1940. *Tixier's travels on the Osage prairies.* Edited by John Francis McDermott. Norman: University of Oklahoma Press.

TROWBRIDGE, CHARLES C. 1938. *Meearmeear traditions.* Edited by Vernon Kinietz. Occasional Contributions from the Museum of Anthropology of the University of Michigan 7.

TURNEY-HIGH, HARRY HOLBERT. 1937. *The Flathead Indians of Montana.* American Anthropological Association Memoir 8.

———. 1941. *Ethnography of the Kutenai.* American Anthropological Association Memoir 56.

UNDERHILL, RUTH M. 1953. *Red man's America.* Chicago: University of Chicago Press.

———. 1969. *Social organization of the Papago Indians.* Columbia University Contributions to Anthropology 30.

VOEGELIN, ERMINIE W. 1938. *Tubatulabal ethnography.* University of California Anthropological Records 2(1).

———. 1942. *Culture element distributions 20: Northwest California.* University of California Anthropological Records 7(2).

WALLACE, ERNEST, and E. ADAMSON HOEBEL. 1952. *The Comanches: Lords of the south Plains.* Norman: University of Oklahoma Press.

WALLACE, WILLIAM J. 1978*a*. "Southern valley Yokuts," in *Handbook of North American Indians,* vol. 8. Edited by Robert F. Heizer, pp. 448–61. Washington, D.C.: Smithsonian Institution.

———. 1978*b*. "Northern valley Yokuts," in *Handbook of North American Indians,* vol. 8. Edited by Robert F. Heizer, pp. 462–70. Washington, D.C.: Smithsonian Institution.

WHITE, RAYMOND C. 1963. *Luiseño social organization.* University of California Publications in American Archaeology and Ethnology 8(2).

WHITEHEAD, HARRIET. 1981. "The bow and the burden strap: A new look at institutionalized homosexuality in native North America," in *Sexual meanings: The cultural construction of gender and sexuality.* Edited by Sherry B. Ortner and Harriet Whitehead, pp. 80–115. New York: Cambridge University Press.

WHITMAN, WILLIAM. 1969. *The Oto.* Columbia University Contributions to Anthropology 28.

WISSLER, CLARK. 1916. *Societies and ceremonial associations in the Oglala division of the Teton-Dakota.* Anthropological Papers of the American Museum of Natural History 11.

Serials

▪ *Mediterranean Language Review* is a new journal aimed at stimulating and promoting inquiry into the linguistic and cultural history of the Mediterranean, with special reference to the following research areas: (1) linguistic interaction among the languages of the Mediterranean; the typology of linguistic and cultural borrowing; present and past channels of linguistic diffusion in the Mediterranean; (2) lesser-known Mediterranean languages, especially hybrid languages or dialects, e.g., Maltese, Cypriot Arabic, Jewish languages, South Italian Greek, Romany, etc.; terminal languages; languages spoken by minority groups, particularly such as are definable by reference to ethnic, religious, and professional dimensions; (3) aspects of ethnic, political, social, and economic history relevant to the present linguistic and dialectal profile of the Mediterranean; and (4) *linguae francae*, examined synchronically and diachronically. The first volume is expected to appear towards the end of May 1983 and will contain the following contributions:

Introductory Essay: Aspects of Mediterranean Linguistics (Henry and Renée Kahane)

The Present State of the Study of Turkisms in the Languages of the Mediterranean and the Balkan Peninsula (Andreas Tietze)

Lateral, Marginal, Peripheral Zone: Three Key-Terms of Spatio-Temporal Linguistics (Yakov Malkiel)

God-Wishes in Syrian Arabic (Charles A. Ferguson)

Some Problems in Judezmo Linguistics (David M. Bunis)

Language and Culture of the Jews of Tripolitania: A Preliminary View (Harvey Goldberg)

Is Karaite a Jewish Language? (Paul Wexler)

The *MLR* is published and distributed by Otto Harrassowitz Verlag, D-6200 Wiesbaden, 1 Taunusstrasse 6, Postfach 2929, West Germany; the cost of single copies is DM 48. For further information, write: Paul Wexler and Alexander Borg, Department of Linguistics, Tel-Aviv University, Tel-Aviv, Israel 69978.

▪ *PAX*, the newsletter of the Association for Anthropological Diplomacy, Politics, and Society, has recently appeared for the first time and will be issued twice a year (Winter and Summer). Subscription is by membership in the association. Please write: Mario D. Zamora, Department of Anthropology, College of William and Mary, Williamsburg, Va. 23185, U.S.A.

Archives of Sexual Behavior, Vol. 5, No. 2, 1976

Cultural Factors Affecting Urban Mexican Male Homosexual Behavior[1]

Joseph M. Carrier, Ph.D.[2,3]

Some aspects of the mestizoized urban culture in Mexico are linked to male homosexuality in support of the theory that cultural factors play an important role in the kind of life styles and sex practices of males involved in homosexual behavior. The following factors are considered relevant: the sharp dichotomization of gender roles, dual categorization of females as good or bad, separate social networks maintained by males before and after marriage, proportion of unmarried males, and distribution of income. One result of the sharp dichotomization of male and female gender roles is the widely held belief that effeminate males generally prefer to play the female role rather than the male. Effeminacy and homosexuality are also linked by the belief that as a result of this role preference effeminate males are sexually interested only in masculine males with whom they play the passive sex role. The participation of masculine males in homosexual encounters is related in part to a relatively high level of sexual awareness in combination with the lack of stigmatization of the insertor sex role and in part to the restraints placed on alternative sexual outlets by available income and/or marital status. Males involved in homosexual behavior in Mexico operate in a sociocultural environment which gives rise to expectations that they should play either the insertee or insertor sex role but not both and that they should obtain ultimate sexual satisfaction with anal intercourse rather than fellatio. In spite of cultural imperatives, however, individual preferences stemming from other variables such as personality needs, sexual gratification, desires of wanted partners, and amount of involvement may override the imperatives with resulting variations in sexual behavior patterns.

KEY WORDS: homosexuality; cross-cultural; Mexican; effeminate; masculinity; heterosexuality.

[1]Presented to Symposium on Homosexuality in Crosscultural Perspective, 73rd Annual Meeting of the American Anthropological Association, Mexico City, November 23, 1974.
[2]Gender Identity Research Group, UCLA School of Medicine, Los Angeles, California.
[3]Address reprint requests to Joseph M. Carrier, 17447 Castellammare Drive, Pacific Palisades, California 90272.

INTRODUCTION

The objective of this report, which suggests how some aspects of the mestizoized urban culture in Mexico may be linked to male homosexual behavior, is to provide additional evidence in support of the theory that cultural factors play an important role in the determination of the kind of life styles and sex practices of males involved in homosexual behavior.

Although the focus of the report is on the urban population in Mexico, the cultural factors discussed are also believed to be relevant to the homosexual behavior of males living in mestizoized rural settings. Those Mexican males living in Indian cultures or in mestizoized rural cultures still essentially following the Indian way of life are believed to be influenced by a different set of cultural factors.

The report is divided into three parts. The first presents a description of the cultural setting into which Mexican males are born and raised. The second suggests how cultural factors appear to be linked to homosexual behavior in Mexico. The last presents a general discussion of the major findings. The description of the cultural setting is based on the literature available on the Mexican family and on the Mexican National Census of 1970. The linking of the cultural factors to the observed behavior and the general discussion are for the most part based on data gathered by the author in Mexico during the past 6 years.

It should be noted that in this report the terms *sex role* and *gender role* will be used to describe different behavioral phenomena. As Hooker (1965) points out, they "are often used interchangeably, and with resulting confusion." Following her suggestion, the term *sex role,* when homosexual practices are described, will refer to "typical sexual performance" only. "The gender connotations (M-F) of these performances need not then be implicitly assumed." The term *gender role* will refer to the "expected attitudes and behavior that distinguish males from females."

THE CULTURAL SETTING

The following is a description of those aspects of the cultural setting considered to be particularly relevant to male homosexual behavior in Mexico. It relies essentially on the findings presented by Peñalosa (1968) and McGinn (1966) but also includes some items not cited in their papers as well as some of the author's analyses of Mexican Census (1970) data. Peñalosa made an extensive study of the available literature on the family in Mexico for his review paper on Mexican family roles. McGinn used the available literature and drew on his own research findings from fieldwork in Guadalajara for his paper, which provides a general description of "normative marriage and family roles as found in middle-class Mexico today." Both researchers conclude that there have been few systematic studies of marriage and family roles in Mexico. Among others, Peñalosa cites Ramos (1962), Paz (1950), Bermudez (1955), Diaz-Guerrero (1961), Piñeda (1963), Ramirez (1961), and Lewis (1959); McGinn basically cites the same sources but notes that the "most complete study" discussed in his paper is an unpublished one by Villaseñor (1964).

Before turning to the descriptive material, it should be noted that the roles described represent the normative cultural ideals of the dominant Mexican national culture of the mestizoized majority of the population. For a critical review of these "normative cultural ideals," see the polemical essay by Kinzer (1973).

Importance of Manliness

The Mexican mestizo culture places a high value on manliness. One of the salient features of the society is thus a sharp delimitation between the roles played by males and females. Role expectations in general are for the male to be dominant and independent and for the female to be submissive and dependent.

The continued sharp boundary between male and female roles in Mexico appears to be due in part to a culturally defined hypermasculine ideal model of manliness, referred to under the label *machismo*. The ideal female role is generally believed to be the reciprocal of the macho (male) role.

Machismo is most often characterized by the attributes of the *macho* male. In thinking about manliness, a Mexican male may thus measure himself, his sons, and his male relatives and friends against such attributes as courage, dominance, power, aggressiveness, and invulnerability. The following statement by a Mexican boxer (quoted in Ross, 1966) illustrates how *machismo* may be conceptualized:

> *Machismo* means manhood. To the Mexican man *machismo* means to have the manly traits of honor and dignity. To have courage to fight. To keep his word and protect his name. To run his house, to control his woman, and to direct his children. This is *machismo*, to be a man in your own eyes.

As a noun *macho* is defined in English as "a male animal; in particular, a he-goat," and as an adjective as "masculine, vigorous, robust, male" (Velázquez, 1967). Although not all males in Mexico (probably not even a majority) aspire to actually play the *macho* role in its extreme form, the available evidence suggests that the folk concept of *machismo* continues to operate as one of the principal forces dominating the learned part of gender role for Mexican males.

As a consequence of the high status given manliness, Mexican males from birth onward are expected to behave in as manly a way as possible. Peñalosa sums it up as follows: "Any signs of feminization are severely repressed in the boy." McGinn concludes: "The young Mexican boy may be severely scolded for engaging in feminine activities, such as playing with dolls or jacks. Parents verbally and physically punish 'feminine' traits in their male children . . . ." He also notes that in a recent study of the Mexican family in Guadalajara, Villaseñor found that 94 of the 100 middle-class mothers making up her sample believed it important for a boy "to be manly." The importance of manly behavior continues throughout the life span of Mexican males.

Dual Categorization of Females

Another salient feature of Mexican society is a belief system that leads to the categorization of females as being either "good" or "bad." A "good" woman is represented as being basically the reciprocal of the *macho* male; that is, she must be submissive and dependent. Prior to marriage, according to the normative cultural ideal, she must also be chaste and faithful. After marriage she must continue to be faithful and should not demonstrate excessive sexual interest even in her husband. The categorization "good" thus comes down to a basic belief that a woman cannot be considered a prime sexual target and still be considered good. A woman is therefore labeled "bad" precisely because she is primarily thought of by males as being immediately exploitable as a sexual outlet. It is interesting to note that even female prostitutes are apparently responsive to the cultural ideal about female passivity. Roebuck and McNamara (1973), for example, reporting on female prostitution in a Mexican border city, noted that they played "a more feminine and passive role" in the houses of prostitution which only the Mexican men patronized.

A related aspect of the "good-bad" dichotomization of females is the double standard of sexual morality allowed Mexican males. The double standard begins prior to marriage. In the Mexican courtship system the prospective bride is labeled a *novia*, the prospective groom a *novio*.[4] The period of courtship may last 5 years or more. Since she may one day be his wife and the mother of his children, a *novia* must in the eyes of her *novio* fall into the category "good"; she obviously cannot be considered a sexual target prior to marriage. Under existing mores, however, at the same time a Mexican male is courting a *novia* he may have a series of sexual contacts with whatever outlets are available. Girlfriends considered appropriate for sexual seduction are referred to as *amigas;* lovers are referred to as *amantes.* After marriage the double standard is maintained and the husband may continue to seek sexual outlets in addition to his wife.

Several of the author's Mexican respondents claimed that they did not consider it important for their *novias* to be chaste and faithful. Their feelings were that this aspect of courtship is breaking down in the large urban areas. They nevertheless still believed it to be an important factor for most Mexican males.[5]

[4] There is no counterpart to this system in the United States. The Mexican couple can be said to have an understanding. McGinn notes that "this arrangement is more serious than the American steady system, yet less formal than an engagement."

[5] Some preliminary data gathered by Taylor (1974) suggest that heterosexual anal intercourse — considered to be a common occurrence by his Mexico City respondents — may be used in Mexico as "a method of maintaining the female's status as a vaginal virgin during courtship and a common form of birth control."

Separate Social Networks

A third relevant feature of Mexican society is the separate network of friends retained by males after marriage. Peer group relationships, of particular importance in adolescence, may remain essentially unchanged by marriage. Peñalosa sums it up as follows:

> In social life a Mexican man's marital status is of little practical importance, as a man carries on virtually the same sort of social life after marriage as he did before — and one in which the women have little part.

Social relationships of Mexican males tend to be all male in character both before and after marriage. Men feel free to spend a lot of their spare time with their male friends rather than with their wives.

Drinking establishments in Mexico — cantinas, bars, and nightclubs — are popular locations where Mexican males spend some of their free time away from their families. With few exceptions, these establishments by convention are restricted to male customers. Females who go generally have working relationships as dance hostesses and/or prostitutes. They obviously fall into the "bad" category. A "good" woman in Mexico would never be seen in a public drinking establishment, except possibly in cities which have hotel bars or nightclubs for tourists. Even there, however, a Mexican woman would have to consider herself "liberated" in order to frequent such establishments on any regular basis.

Proportion of Unmarried Males

A fourth relevant characteristic of Mexican society is the proportion of single males past the age of puberty. Although in any given age group the proportion that is single varies over time and within and between counties, states, or regions, marriage patterns in Mexico at present lead to a sizable percentage of males not marrying until in their late 20s. In a recent National Census (1970) the proportion of single males distributed in the total population by age groups between 12 and 39 were as follows:

Age group	Percent single
12-14	99.3
15-19	94.7
20-24	61.2
25-29	27.2
30-34	13.8
35-39	9.2

Of the male population 12 years of age and older, 44% were unmarried at the time of the census.

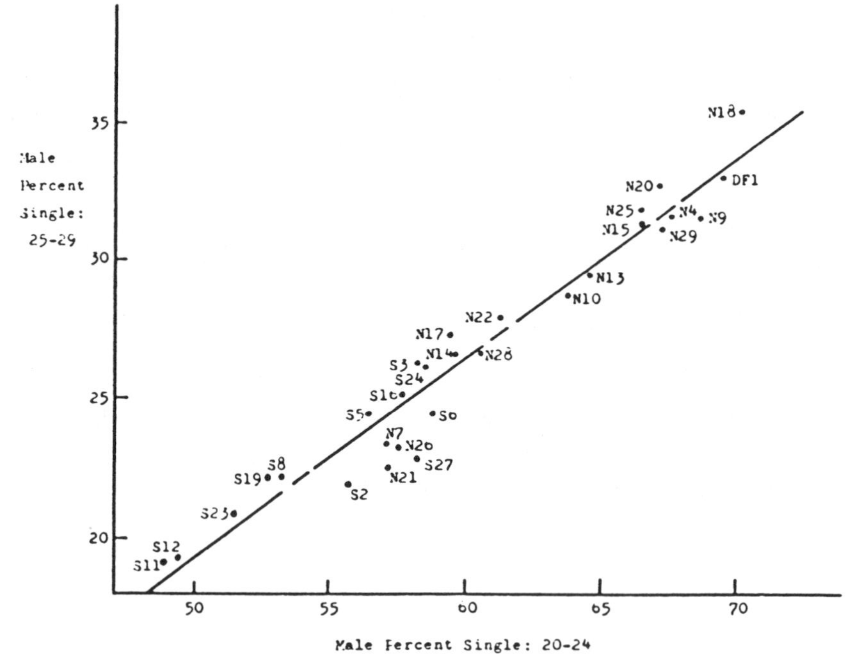

Fig. 1. Percent single male age group 20-24 vs. percent single male age group 25-29 in Mexico by states and Federal District (D.F.) according to 1970 census. The states of Yucatan, Campeche, and Quintana Roo are combined as the Yucatan Peninsula states (S19); the territory of Baja California south is combined with Baja California north (N20). The remaining states are Sonora (N18), Sinaloa (N15), Chihuahua (N10), Coahuila (N17), Nuevo Leon (N9), Tamaulipas (N13), Durango (N22), Nayarit (N25), Jalisco (N4), Colima (N29), Zacatecas (N21), Aguascaliente (N28), San Luis Potosi (N14), Queretaro (N26), Guanajuato (N7), Michoacan (S6), Mexico (S2), Morelos (S24), Hidalgo (S16), Tlaxcala (S27), Puebla (S5), Veracruz (S3), Guerrero (S11), Oaxaca (S8), Chiapas (S12), and Tabasco (S23).

Differences between Mexican states in proportions of single males for two age groups in 1970 (20-24 and 25-29) are shown in Fig. 1. A significant part of the variation shown may be explained by two factors: marriage customs and migration between states. As seen in Fig. 1, the states showing the lowest percentage of single males (clustered in the lower left quadrant of the figure and thus below the national average) are located in the southern region of the country whereas the states showing the highest percentage (clustered in the upper right quadrant) are located in the northern region. A major difference between these two regions is the continuing influence of Indian cultures on varying but sizable segments of the population in the south as opposed to the north. The connection between the influence of Indian cultures and the relatively smaller percentage of single males in the south relates to the fact that males influenced by Indian cultures, judging from the available ethnographic evidence (Wauchope, 1969), generally marry in their late teens and early 20s. Members of the male population living under the influence of the mestizoized Mexican national culture, on the other hand, are not pressured by their society to marry at an early age.

Internal migration is another explanatory factor of the differences shown in Fig. 1. There is a high degree of association between states with relatively higher percentages of single males and states with net gains in population from out-of-state migrants. The three northern central states (N7, N21, and N26) having smaller proportions of single males and experiencing little or no influence from Indian cultures show net losses of population from migration in the 1970 census.

Increased urbanization may help explain part of the higher percentage of single males but cannot account for the higher proportions generally found in the northern states. An examination of the 1960 census data of the state of Jalisco showed no correlation between the degree of urbanization in *municipios* (an administrative area roughly comparable with the U.S. county) and the proportions of single males found in given age groups.

Finally it should be noted that, while single, a large majority of Mexican males – a little over 80% according to the 1970 census – continue to live in some kind of family grouping. This pattern apparently holds true even when single males are in their late 20s or 30s. The available data suggest that the only way a single male is able to move away from his family, even if he wants to and can afford to, is to move to another area.

Distribution of Income

The final characteristic of Mexican society to be considered is distribution of income. In Mexico inequalities in income distribution combined with high birth rates result in large segments of the urban as well as rural population living on incomes that barely provide the basic necessities of life. Although urban dwellers generally fare better than rural folk, the available data suggest that a majority in both parts of the population still tend to be in marginal situations economically. Leyva (1970) presents estimates in a recent study, for example, which show that 66% of the urban families in Mexico live on 1500 pesos or less per month ($120 or less per month U.S. equivalent) in family groupings averaging five members. Comparable estimates of the rural families show that 90% live on 1500 pesos or less per month in family groupings averaging 5.5 members.

A significant outcome of the inequitable distribution of income in Mexico is the crowding suggested by the census data which show that a little over two-thirds of the Mexican population in January 1970 were living in one- or two-room dwellings. Although the percentage of inhabitants living in one- or two-room dwellings in urban areas is less than in rural areas, urban crowding is nevertheless impressive. For example, in Mexico's second largest urban area, Guadalajara, 43% of the population in 1970 were living in one- and two-room dwellings. Leyva (1970) presents a comparison of population density per room for a number of countries. Mexico ranks among the highest in the world. The average number of persons per room in Mexico in 1960 was estimated by the Mexican National Institute of Housing to be 2.6 in urban areas and 3.4 in rural areas. Comparable figures for the United States are 0.6 in urban areas and 0.7 in rural areas.

CULTURAL FACTORS AND HOMOSEXUAL BEHAVIOR

The following presents ways in which the cultural factors described above appear to be linked to homosexual behavior in Mexico. It is based primarily on data gathered by the author (1) in Guadalajara over a period of 1½ years, from the fall of 1969 to the spring of 1971, and (2) in a number of urban areas in the northwestern, central, and southwestern parts of Mexico during relatively short visits over a 4-year period from the summer of 1968 to the summer of 1972. It is also based on information provided by five U.S. respondents who have had extensive homosexual experiences in Mexico for 10 or more years and on the findings made by Taylor (1974) in Mexico City and by Ingham (1968) in a rural setting in central Mexico.

Effeminate Males and Homosexuality

In the masculine-oriented Mexican society, one result of the sharp dichotomization of male and female gender roles is the widely held belief that effeminate males basically prefer to play the female role rather than the male. The link between male effeminacy and homosexuality is the additional belief that as a result of this role preference effeminate males are sexually interested only in masculine males with whom they play the passive sex role. Although the motivations of males participating in homosexual encounters are unquestionably diverse and complex, the fact remains that in Mexico cultural pressure is brought to bear on effeminate males to play the passive insertee role in sexual intercourse, and a kind of *de facto* cultural approval is given (that is, no particular stigma is attached to) masculine males who want to play the active insertor role in sexual intercourse.[6]

The beliefs linking effeminate males with homosexuality are culturally transmitted by a vocabulary which provides the appropriate labels, by homosexually oriented jokes and word games (*albures*), and by the mass media. The links are established at a very early age. From early childhood on, Mexican males are made aware of the labels used to denote male homosexuals and the connection is

[6] Although sexual intercourse between males in Mexico may be anal or oral, the author's data suggest that anal intercourse is generally preferred over fellatio.

Table I. Interviewee Hearing of Homosexual Joking

	Frequency of response (%)				
How often heard[a]	Daily	1-2/wk	1-2/mo	Never	Sample No.
At home	0	9	33	58	45
With friends[b]	35	36	25	4	48
At school	16	42	19	23	31
At work	30	46	11	13	37

[a]The question asked respondents was "How often (at the above-named locations) has conversation turned to joking (or comments) about homosexuals?"
[b]Unfortunately, no distinction was made between hearing jokes with straight and with homosexual friends.

always clearly made that these homosexual males are guilty of unmanly effeminate behavior.

Evidence in support of the link between effeminacy and homosexuality will be presented. The homosexual vocabulary, jokes and word games, and mass media will be briefly examined first. This will be followed by a presentation of the author's data on the effeminate male target.

The Homosexual Vocabulary

A large number of Spanish terms are used in Mexico to describe male participants in homosexual encounters. In popular usage the terms clearly distinguish the passive effeminate participants from the active masculine participants. Only the passive effeminate terms, however, also denote a participant homosexual. An equivalence is always made between the effeminate male and the homosexual male.

The only popular, reasonably polite words used to designate a homosexual male are *maricón* and *raro.* Both denote a male effeminate as well as homosexual. The first definition of *maricón* is "sissy" (Velázquez, 1967). Colloquially it is used to mean "fairy" or "queer," i.e., homosexual. *Raro* translated into English can mean "strange," "odd," or "queer." Used in a certain context with a certain inflection, it can also suggest an effeminate homosexual male.

The Spanish words most often used to describe participants in homosexual encounters are *puto, joto,* and *mayate.*[7] It is the consensus of my informants, however, that, though widely known, they are derogatory vulgar words and generally are not used in polite company. *Puto* and *joto* designate passive effeminate

[7]*Puto* is probably the word most often used in graffiti. I have seen it more often than any other word scribbled on the walls of bathrooms in cantinas, public buildings, and houses in all parts of Mexico.

participants. *Mayate*, on the other hand, designates the active masculine participant but does not connote him homosexual. As used, *mayate* designates (1) a male who likes to wear loud, flashy clothes, (2) a male prostitute for other males, and (3) any male who takes the active insertor sex role in homosexual intercourse. There are many more words to designate participants in homosexual encounters. However, most of them (40 out of 44) designate effeminate male participants only. And none of them, according to my informants, is widely known and used.

Homosexual Jokes and Word Games

Homosexually oriented jokes and word games are pervasive in Mexican society. During my years of fieldwork in Mexico, I frequently observed such interchanges during business transactions, on walks around downtown areas and in local neighborhoods, and in bars and cantinas. This impression was supported by a large majority of my respondents in Guadalajara, as shown in Table I, who reported observing and/or participating in such joking among friends (96%), at work (87%), and at school (77%). Although not a majority, close to one-half (42%) reported hearing such joking at home. Ingham (1968) also reports frequent homosexual joking and word games in a rural Mexican setting, so they are not just an urban pehenomenon. Finally, it should be noted that in Mexico male homosexuality is treated in a joking way by such mass media as television, movies, stage shows, and comic books.

The focus of the homosexual jokes and word games is on the behavior of the effeminate passive male. The following examples provide some idea of the content and the variety of situations in which they take place. It is important to note that while most of the jokes and word games occur between men they also occur between men and women.

The following observations were made in Guadalajara. One afternoon, while waiting for my car to be repaired, I observed a 30-year-old mechanic and his 18-year-old helper trading homosexual jokes centered around the possibility that the younger man was a desirable sex object for *jotos*. On another occasion, in a small cantina one night in the *Zona Roja* (an area set aside in most large urban areas in Mexico for dance bars, houses of prostitution, and cantinas) I observed a well-dressed middle-aged man play a lengthy homosexually oriented word game with one of the bar girls. She had started the word game with this known customer by suggesting that since he had not paid much attention to her during recent visits he must be more interested in men. An individual male may also play the buffoon while with a group of male friends. An informant reported, for example, that in his school in Guadalajara a boy may remark to a pretty girl when she walks by: "If I were *really* a man, I would like to go around with you." His male friends respond by laughing and whistling, and calling him *Papacito*. The implication of the label is that he is both handsome and desirable. This is then likely to trigger off a set of jokes about *jotos*.

Another informant, who to my knowledge had had no homosexual contacts, reported the following sequence of events between him and his *amiga.* He claimed it to be typical of the way girls joke with their boyfriends about the possibility of the boy being a *joto.* While talking to his *amiga* one evening about 9 o'clock just outside the main entrance to her house in Guadalajara, her mother called to her to come in. She ignored the call. A second call came. Worrying that the mother might get angry with him, he told his *amiga* that he had better leave so she could obey her mother and go inside. His *amiga* responded by saying:"*Ay tu*!" — the literal translation and implication of the exclamation being that "*you* (are a *joto* too)." He then responded by saying: "Do you really think so!" The conversation then went back and forth with the *amiga* implying that he wanted to leave because he was afraid of her and preferred boys.

The Mass Media and Homosexuality

In the mass media of Mexico, homosexuality either is handled as a joke or is ridiculed and condemned, but the connection is always made between homosexuality and effeminate males. For example, from time to time on Sunday afternoons I watched the most popular variety show on Mexican television, *Siempre Domingos.* A skit depicting homosexual males as weak, passive, and effeminate was often included in the show. This same general theme was also presented in the stage shows of a popular variety theater in Guadalajara and was followed by homosexual characters, when included, in Mexican movies. *Los Superfrios,* a popular Mexican comic book series, devoted an issue in November 1970 to the story of a Mexican general and his attempts to interest his effeminate son in girls.

The most denigrating view of homosexuality in the mass media is presented by a tabloid newspaper published every Wednesday in Mexico City and distributed throughout Mexico. It is called *ALARMA!* and focuses on grisly murders, rapes, scandals, and highway accidents all over Mexico. I saw copies of it in practically every home I visited in Guadalajara. During the year and a half I read the publication it had considerable reporting about homosexual activity in Mexico and the United States, and at least once a month it had a banner headline about homosexuals. In the headlines and reportage the same general viewpoint was usually maintained, namely, that homosexual males are degenerate, vicious, immoral, and *effeminate.*

The Effeminate Male Target

The author's data support the notion that from an early age onward effeminate males in Mexico are targeted as sexual objects for other males and are expected to play the passive insertee sex role in anal intercourse. Of the 47 respondents in Guadalajara who could be rated, 18 responded affirmatively to

Table II. Comparison of Respondents' Effeminacy Scores as a Child and Prepubertal Homosexual Contacts with Postpubertal Males[a]

Effeminacy score	Prior to first ejaculation sexual contact with postpubertal male		
	Yes	No	Totals
High	17	1	18
Low	9	20	29
Totals	26	21	47

[a]The adjusted ϕ coefficient is equal to 0.87. $\chi^2 = 18.07$ (1 df, $p < 0.001$).

several of the following criteria indicating preadolescent effeminacy – remembered self as effeminate, played with dolls, cross-dressed one or more times, experienced desire at least once to be female, and had little or no interest in sports. All but one of the respondents scoring on the effeminate side as a child (17 of 18) had, prior to their first ejaculation, sexual contacts with older postpubertal males. Thirteen of the 17 had contacts between 5 and 10 years of age. In comparison, as shown by Table II, only nine of 29 males scoring on the masculine side (31%) had, prior to their first ejaculation, sexual contacts with postpubertal males.

Effeminacy in males is observable at a very early age. Green (1968, 1974), for example, reports American parents being able to "clearly identify cross-gender behavior at the age of 3 years or younger." Moreover, as previously noted, in Mexico the adult population – sensitized by the folk concept of *machismo* – may be particularly aware of effeminate behavior in prepubertal males.

Setting aside the question of their effeminacy as children, of those respondents asked about the kind of sexual technique utilized in their prepubertal homosexual eccounters (22 of 26), all but one reported that they had played the passive insertee sex role. One reported that only his genitals had been fondled. Of the 21 who reported that they had played the passive sex role, a majority claimed they had been anally penetrated by the penis of their older male partner. About one-third claimed their partner had performed sexual intercourse in some way between their thighs. The encounters reported were more than a casual one-time sexual experience for most respondents. A majority (21 of 26) had, on different occasions, two or more sexual experiences with their older male partners, six having had sexual experiences with the same partner for 1 year or longer.

Following the onset of puberty, effeminate males continue to be sexual targets for other males because of their effeminacy. The consensus of my effeminate respondents in Guadalajara is that regardless of whether they are at school, in a movie theater, on the downtown streets, in a park, or in their own neighborhood they are sought out and expected to play the passive sex role by more masculine males. As one 14-year-old respondent put it, in response to the question of where he had looked for sexual contacts during the year prior to the interview, "I didn't have to search for them . . . they looked for me (*ellos me buscan a mí*)."

The notion of effeminate males as sexual targets is also supported by the fact that effeminacy is used by Mexican males to cue other males as to their availability as sexual objects. The phenomenon of males with varying degrees of effeminacy exaggerating it to lure wanted male sexual partners has been observed by the author, particularly in the setting of cantinas, throughout Mexico. Further confirmation of the phenomenon is provided by the experiences of both effeminate and masculine respondents in Guadalajara and by American male homosexual respondents who have traveled extensively in Mexico.

Masculine Male Participants

The other side of the coin is represented by masculine male participants in homosexual encounters. Given the fact that effeminate males in Mexico are assumed homosexual and thus considered available as sexual outlets, how do the cultural factors contribute to the willingness of masculine males to play the active insertor sex role? The available data suggest that, insofar as the social variables are concerned, their willingness to participate in homosexual encounters is due in part to the relatively high level of sexual awareness that exists among males in the society. This is in combination with the lack of stigmatization of the insertor sex role and in part with the restraints that may be placed on alternative sexual outlets by available income and/or by marital status.

Sexual Awareness

The high level of sexual awareness among males in Mexico appears to be partly the result of the sexual stimuli presented them from birth onward by the scolding, joking, and public media. They are thus sensitized to many different kinds of sexual relationships. By the time they reach puberty, they are especially aware of the availability and acceptability of effeminate males as alternative sexual outlets. According to Taylor (1974), in both heterosexual and homosexual relationships "a very common term referring to people who are in love is *enculado* or *entwined by the anus* (*el culo*)."

The acceptance and desirability of sexual intercourse in Mexican society are further enhanced by the fact that adolescent males are pressured while in their early teens — often at the first signs of puberty — by their brothers, male cousins, and/or friends to prove their masculinity by having heterosexual intercourse with either prostitutes or available neighborhood girls. The Guadalajara data show, for example, that a majority of the respondents rating themselves as regular or very masculine in early adolescence (18 of 20) had heterosexual intercourse between the ages of 14 and 18, the median age being 16. Moreover, about one-third of those respondents rating themselves slightly or very effeminate (seven of 22) reported they also had tried heterosexual intercourse under pressure of peers or relatives.

Finally, awareness of the body's daily functions and needs, including the sexual, is heightened under the crowded family circumstances in which a majority of the population live. Body contact and/or sexual joking between male members of the family sleeping in the same bed or close together is apparently not unusual, nor is their knowledge about sexual intercourse. It is of interest to note that the prepubertal homosexual contacts of several respondents, which took place over extended periods of time, occurred while sleeping in the same bed with postpubertal relatives.

Lack of Stigmatization

As implied in the above discussion on effeminate males and homosexuality, masculine males who play the active insertor role in homosexual encounters do not appear to be generally conceptualized as *homosexuals* in Mexico. This lack of stigmatization provides prospective active participants with the important feeling that their masculine self-image is in no way threatened by their playing of the active sex role. There is no doubt some level of same-sex sexual involvement where even a masculine male may be labeled deviant, particularly if he develops a pattern of nonassociation with females, but at the very least, as Paz (1950) has noted, "masculine homosexuality is regarded with a certain indulgence [in Mexico] insofar as the active agent is concerned." The following observations made by the author in many different parts of Mexico support the notion that a great deal of tolerance is extended to those masculine males who utilize passive males as alternative sexual outlets.

One indication of the degree of acceptance accorded the active sex role in Mexico is suggested by the fact that masculine males appear to rarely take offense at the approaches made by effeminate males. A surprising feature of their behavior is the way in which they handle the attention given them by males who so openly and obviously express their sexual interest. Rather than showing anger or no reaction at being approached, the targeted males if not interested will most likely be amused. Moreover, instead of feeling that their masculinity is threatened, many apparently feel it is supported and possibly even enhanced by the attention. A hostile reaction may occasionally be triggered but usually only if an approach is made at what would be considered an inappropriate place or time, e.g., in front of parents or relatives at home or in some kind of group situation where individual attention might be embarrassing.

Another indication of the kind of acceptance given active participants is suggested by respondents' reports that "masculine" boys talk with each other about their "active" sex experiences with effeminate boys. These conversations take place among groups of friends at school, for example, rather than just between several intimate friends in secret. Although active males may be no more willing than passive males to relate their involvement in homosexual encounters to parents and siblings, they nevertheless continue to participate with the belief that the active sex role does not have the same kind of shame connected with it as does the passive. Their expectation is to be accepted with far more tolerance than are their penetrated sexual partners.

Still another indication of the kind of acceptance accorded the active sex role is suggested by the fact that these males are often willing to engage in much the same kind of sexual foreplay with their passive male partners as would be expected with their female partners and may also allow their genitals to come into contact with those of the effeminate males. Although the percentage of the author's "active" respondents in Guadalajara claiming to restrict foreplay one way or another with their "passive" partners is not small, the fact remains that almost one-half said they regularly engaged in open-mouth kissing with their male partners and a little over two-thirds allowed other males' genitals to come into contact with their own. A majority of the respondents who played the passive and active-and-passive sex roles claimed that *almost all* of their active partners participated in open-mouth kissing and allowed genital contact.

It appears, however, that a larger percentage of the active group are more concerned about open-mouth kissing than genital contact with another male and are more concerned about having their anus or buttocks touched than either kissing or genital contact. Penetration from the rear represents such a threat to some active participants that when sleeping with another male they try to sleep only on their back.

Relative Costs of Sexual Outlets

The relative money costs of alternative sexual outlets may be an important factor in helping determine the demand for one particular outlet in a sexual marketplace where a large number of prospective buyers may have their choices limited by income. In Mexico, the amount of income available to a majority of males for the pursuit of sexual outlets is extremely limited. As previously noted, inequalities in the distribution of income are such that a majority of Mexican families must live on incomes that barely provide the basic essentials of food, shelter, and clothing.

A comparison of alternative sexual outlets for Mexican males playing an insertor sex role suggests that the lowest-cost outlet is generally offered by males willing to play the insertee sex role. The "insertor" males may prefer to have sexual intercourse with females. Given their limited incomes, however, a large percentage may find that on those occasions when their sexual need is high and their available cash is low, effeminate males are acceptable sexual outlets.

The major cost difference between female and "insertee male" sexual outlets is the price charged for sexual intercourse. Males playing the passive sex role usually offer their sexual services free. Some females may also provide their sexual services free. Because of the good-bad dichotomization of females in Mexico, however, a majority must play the role of prostitute in the sexual marketplace and levy a charge. Effeminate homosexual males in Mexico may solicit favors from their sexual partners in cash or kind, but they rarely do this as the sole source of financial support. Moreover, when favors are solicited there appears to be an age and income differential, with the effeminate male being younger and/or poorer than the male playing the active role. Male prostitutes in Mexico usually play only the active sex role.

Marital Status

The marital status of Mexican males appears to have an important effect on the type of sexual outlets they choose over time. Prior to marriage, the dual categorization of females into those that are sexual targets (*amigas, amantes*, and *prostitutas*) and those that are not (*novias*) requires Mexican males to spend a lot to time socializing with females (*novias*) who by social convention can usually offer no sexual outlet. Given the relatively late age at which a large percentage marry (as many as one-third still single in their late 20s), it follows that during the years of high sexual activity a majority of Mexican males wanting sexual contacts must turn to outlets other than their *novias*. Since they may offer sexual intercourse at little or no cost, females who are willing to play the *amiga* role — that is, girlfriends considered appropriate for sexual seduction — are probably first choices as sexual outlets for Mexican males. However, not enough females seem willing to play the *amiga* role to the point of sexual intercourse because current mores about the importance of virginity prior to marriage lead the families of Mexican females to push them in the direction of playing *only the novia role.* The assurance of virginity is the principal reason for the chaperon system, and, although this system may be losing its hold somewhat, the available data suggest that Mexican males still give great weight to virginity when they assess females as prospective brides. Mexican girls who have sexual adventures prior to marriage run the risk of spoiled reputations and thus problems in making good marriages.

Females with spoiled reputations probably make up the largest group of premarital sexual outlets for Mexican males. They may play the role of prostitute (*puta*), lover (*amante*), or commonlaw wife. Regardless of the role played, however, certain monetary costs are generally associated with these possible sexual outlets. And these costs, as noted above, may operate as a factor limiting the kind and number of sexual contacts any given male may have with females in this group.

A third and potentially cost-free group of premarital sexual outlets available to Mexican males is made up of other males willing to play the passive insertee role in sexual intercourse, as noted above.

Following marriage, Mexican males have a legitimate outlet for sex: their wives. Because of the double standard allowed males both before and after marriage, however, if desired they may continue to maintain sexual contacts begun while still courting. This is facilitated by the separate network of friends retained by them after marriage. As noted previously, men feel free to spend time away from work and family socializing with male friends. They may also feel free to continue previous sex contacts and/or develop new ones. These extramarital sexual contacts may be only with females. *They may also include or be only with other males.* For example, in response to the question "Do you think many married men have sex with other males after being married?" 92% of my respondents questioned in Guadalajara (46 of 50) replied "yes." And close to two-thirds (33 of 50) reported that they had had sexual intercourse with one or more married males. Most were not sure of the total number of married contacts they had had since they did not necessarily know the marital status of each partner.

DISCUSSION

An important finding of this study is that males involved in homosexual behavior in Mexico operate in a sociocultural environment which gives rise to expectations that they should play either the active (insertor) or passive (insertee) sex role but not both, and that they should obtain ultimate sexual satisfaction with anal intercourse rather than fellatio. By and large as a result of the sharply defined gender roles in the society, the general belief exists that effeminate males are passive and penetrable, like females; that masculine males are active and impenetrable; and that the anus may provide sexual pleasure like the vagina. Participants in homosexual encounters are thus motivated by their environment to establish a sex role preference and to focus on anal intercourse. The effects of environment, however, must be viewed as being functionally interrelated with personality variables. As Hooker (1961) has suggested, the relations between sociocultural and personality variables "in determining the commitment to, and patterns of, adult homosexuality are complex. For many, the stability of the commitment appears to be a function of the interaction of both sets of variables."

Although data are not available with which to estimate the percentage of the population involved, the cultural factors and homosexual behavior described above suggest that a relatively large percentage of Mexican males, perhaps a majority, participate in homosexual encounters at one time in their lives. The dichotomization of sex roles suggests further that there are probably considerable differences in the degree and kind of involvement between participants according to sex role preferred and practiced over time.[8]

Cultural traditions in sexual partnerships in mestizoized Mexico prescribe the insertor sex role in anal intercourse for "masculine" males interested in homosexual outlets. This appears to be particularly relevant for the age set of single males between puberty and the late 20s. The only cultural proscription is for "masculine" males to play the passive sex role.

The passive sex role is by inference — through the cultural equivalence of effeminacy with homosexuality — prescribed for "effeminate" males. It becomes a self-fulfilling prophecy of the society that effeminate males (a majority?) are eventually, if not from the beginning, pushed toward exclusively homosexual behavior. The Guadalajara data (Carrier, 1972) substantiate that some do engage in heterosexual intercourse and some marry and set up households, but they probably are a minority of the identifiably effeminate males in the mestizoized segment of the Mexican population.

In spite of the cultural imperatives for those participating in homosexual encounters to play either one sex role or the other, and to utilize anal sexual techniques, individual preferences stemming from a number of other variables such as personality needs, sexual gratification, desires of wanted partners, and amount of involvement may override the imperatives, with resulting variations in sexual behavior patterns. For example, the Guadalajara interview data show that at the time of interview (see Table III) a little over one-fourth of the respondents (15 of 53) preferred to play both sex roles, 4% (two of 53) had no sex role preference, 8% (four of 53) preferred oral-genital contacts, and 2% (one of 53) preferred mutual masturbation.[9] Furthermore, most of the respondents had had some oral-genital contacts, and close to one-fourth had experienced mutual masturbation.

The data also show that while a majority of respondents maintained their sexual preferences and practices over time, a sizable percentage changed them (Table III) from those carried out during their first sustained year of homosexual experiences. For example, a little over 40% of those playing the anal active sex role and close to one-fourth of those playing the anal passive sex role during their first sustained year had over time incorporated the opposite sex role into their sexual repertoire. A significant aspect of the behavior of those who change, however, is that they usually do not play both sex roles with the same partner. They *rank* prospective partners as to whether they are more masculine or more effeminate than themselves. If thought more masculine, the prospective partner

[8] For a detailed comparison of participants by sex role played, see Carrier (1971).

[9] No inferences about the distribution of the Mexican male population participating in homosexual encounters by sex role preference can be made from the interview data since sex role preference was a criterion for the selection of respondents.

Table III. A Percentage Comparison of Respondents' Sexual Preference and Majority of Homosexual Experiences at Time of Interview[a]

At time of interview	Anal: Active	Anal: Active and passive	Anal: Passive	Total[b]
Sexual preference				
Anal				
Active	59	44	0	26
Active/passive	41	33	23	28
Passive	0	0	77	32
Oral	0	0	0	8
Masturbation (mutual)	0	0	0	2
No preference	0	23	0	4
Total	100	100	100	100
Majority of homosexual experiences				
Anal				
Active	59	22	0	22
Active/passive	41	78	23	36
Passive	0	0	77	32
Oral	0	0	0	8
Masturbation (mutual)	0	0	0	2
Total	100	100	100	100
Median age of respondents at time of interview	24	20	21	22
Median years between first sustained year and time of interview	8	5	5	5
Sample No.	17	9	22	53

[a]Grouped by major homosexual activity first sustained year following first ejaculation. For example, the first column shows that of the respondents who were "anal active" in a majority of their first-year experiences, 59% by preference and practice were still anal active at time of interview; 41% had changed and incorporated both sex roles between first year and time of interview.

[b]The total includes four respondents whose major homosexual activities during the first sustained year following first ejaculation were oral-genital and one respondent whose major sexual activity was mutual masturbation. Their sexual preference and majority of homosexual experiences at time of interview remained the same as first-year experiences.

is generally rated active sexually; if more effeminate, passive sexually. Once this judgment is made – and assuming it is made correctly, i.e., there is concordance between degree of masculinity and predicted sex role – they then play the appropriate opposite role. There is a low probability that *both* active and passive anal intercourse are practiced by *both* participants in a given homosexual encounter in Mexico.

From the available data, a judgment cannot be made about the stability of the relationship between sex and gender roles in mestizoized Mexico. In general, however, the participants with the most rigidly developed sex-typed interests appear least likely to change their sexual preferences and practices over time. That is, those participants with strongly developed female sex-typed interests *through early socialization* continue to maintain those interests and to either exclusively or primarily play the passive sex role, and *vice versa*. Further, the data on family relationships support this notion in that the more observably effeminate a male the more likely his mannerisms will become accepted by his family in the long run, and pressures to change are diminished. For the masculine male, i.e., the male with strongly developed male sex-typed interests and masculine bearing, the family pressures more likely strengthen his masculine choices.

More data need to be generated on those males who over time play both the active and passive sex roles. At least two basically different behavior patterns are suggested by the data. On the one hand, there are males who from the very beginning appear to have little or no developed preference, despite the cultural imperatives. But there are other males who have a preference from the beginning and thus for a given time period play only one role. As they expand their sexual experiences over time, however, they may start to play the opposite role, thus discovering in one way or another that there is pleasure associated with both sex roles. They may also discover that a certain amount of cognitive dissonance results as a consequence of playing both roles. This would seem to be particularly true for those males who conceptualize themselves as masculine and play a masculine gender role around family, friends, and work associates.

Available data suggest that the males playing both sex roles tend to be more like those who play only the active role than like those who play only the passive. They tend, for example, to be more interested in masculine-type activities, to have had more heterosexual contacts, and to be more interested in their masculine image than males who only play the passive sex role. They also tend to maintain the belief that at an appropriate age they will marry and set up a household. An important factor underlying the behavior patterns of participants who play both sex roles over time may be the need to reduce the dissonance generated by the inconsistency between masculine self-concept and the social judgment that the passive sex role is effeminate.

Despite the fact that there are no legal sanctions in Mexico against consenting adult males having sexual congress in private, the general public tends to view homosexuality with considerable disapproval. The net effect of this attitude is that every effort is made by the Mexican law authorities to keep behavior which might be interpreted as homosexual, i.e., effeminate male behavior, as invisible as possible. One result of this policy is that steady pressure — harassment by both uniformed and plainclothes policemen — is exerted on any insitution or location in which obvious (effeminate) homosexual males congregate. Offending establishments are closed or threatened with closure if they do not change their policies; locations such as movie theaters, parks, and steam baths are from time to time infiltrated by policemen and arrests are made.[10] However, although the number of males searching for male sexual partners may diminish at the locations harassed by the police, the penalty levied on those caught is not considered particularly severe (a small fine rather than imprisonment) unless the arrest becomes publicly known. The searching males may move to a new location or re-establish more discreet behavior at the harassed location. There is some evidence that as of the fall of 1974 this policy may be changing. Respondents recently interviewed by the author suggest, for example, that harassment by law authorities is increasing in Guadalajara and Mexico City. It is perhaps relevant that in describing the composition of terrorist groups the Mexican President noted in September 1974 that, among other things in their background, there is "a high incidence of masculine and feminine homosexuality . . ." (Fourth State of the Nation Report, 1974).

Counterposed to the Mexican society's generally disapproving attitude toward homosexuality is the fact that it appears to accept the inevitability of homosexual contacts between men. There seems to be a wide acceptance of the reality that most males have multiple sexual outlets when single and have sexual outlets over and above those provided by the wife when married. Although not socially approved, these extramarital outlets are nevertheless generally accepted as long as they are carried out with a certain amount of discretion. As previously indicated, homosexual contacts between males are thought no better or worse than other kinds of sexual outlets which do not carry social approval, this understanding of course being essentially extended only to those playing the insertor sex role.

An accommodation takes place not only between families and their effeminate sons and brothers but also between the society at large and effeminate males. The principal tactic of accommodation common both to the family and the society at large is for genuine effeminate behavior to be kept as much out of sight as possible. In families, and especially in family gatherings, the effeminate male tries as best he can to behave in a masculine way. If he has sexual contacts with males rather than females, he has them discreetly. The fact that the contacts are taking place is ignored by all parties concerned. Outside the family, effeminate males generally try to make as masculine a presentation as possible — particularly at work and with "straight" friends. The social tension created by the attempted concealment of real effeminate behavior appears to be relieved by the widespread joking about effeminate males and homosexuality which occurs with such frequency among "masculine" males in Mexico.

[10]This explains in part why there are so few exclusively homosexual meeting places. Another important factor is the fear of being seen going into such places. The most common term used to express this fear is *quemar* (to burn) – one's reputation is likely to be burned or scorched.

ACKNOWLEDGMENTS

The author would like to express his thanks to Dr. Evelyn Hooker for a careful reading of an original draft and many helpful suggestions. Helpful comments were also received from members of the gender identity research group at UCLA's School of Medicine and from members of the American Anthropological Association Symposium on Homosexuality in Crosscultural Perspective held in Mexico City, November 23, 1974.

REFERENCES

Carrier, J. (1971). Participants in urban Mexican male homosexual encounters. *Arch. Sex. Behav.* 1(4): 279-291.
Carrier, J. (1972). Urban Mexican male homosexual encounters: An analysis of participants and coping strategies. Unpublished doctoral dissertation, University of California, Irvine.
Fourth State of the Nation Report (1974). *Separata: Mexican Newsletter*, No. 21, September 1, 1974, p. 5.
Green, R. (1968). Childhood cross-gender identification. *J. Nerv. Ment. Dis.* 147: 500-509.
Green, R. (1974). *Sexual Identity Conflict in Children and Adults*, Basic Books, New York.
Hooker, E. (1961). The homosexual community. In Gagnon, J. H., and Simon, W. (eds.), *Sexual Deviance*, Harper and Row, New York, p. 169.
Hooker, E. (1965). An empirical study of some relations between sexual patterns and gender identity in male homosexuals. In Money, J. (ed.), *Sex Research: New Developments*, Holt, New York, pp. 24-25.
Ingham, J. (1968). Culture and personality in a Mexican village. Unpublished doctoral dissertation, University of California, Berkeley.
Kinzer, N. (1973). Priests, machos and babies: Or, Latin American women and the Manichaean heresy. *J. Marriage Family* 35: 300–311.
Leyva, J. (1970). El problema habitacional. In *El Perfil de Mexico en 1980*, Vol. 2, Siglo XXI Editores, S. A., Mexico, D.F.
McGinn, N. (1966). Marriage and family in middle-class Mexico. *J. Marriage Family* 28: 305-313.
Mexican Census (1970). *IX Censo General de Poblacion: 1970*, Direccion General de Estadistica, Mexico, D.F.
Peñalosa, F. (1968). Mexican family roles. *J. Marriage Family* 30: 680-689.
Paz, O. (1950). *The Labyrinth of Solitude: Life and Thought in Mexico*, Grove Press, New York.
Roebuck, J., and McNamara, P. (1973). Ficheras and free-lancers: prostitution in a Mexican border city. *Arch. Sex. Behav.* 2(3): 231-244.
Ross, S. (1966). *Is The Mexican Revolution Dead?*, Knopf, New York, p. 386.
Taylor, C. (1974). Preliminary report on homosexual subculture in Mexico. Presented to American Anthropological Association Symposium on Homosexuality in Crosscultural Perspective, Mexico City, November 23, 1974, mimeographed.
Velázquez, M. (1967). *Spanish and English Dictionary*, Follett, New York.
Wauchope, R. (1969). *Handbook of Middle American Indians: Ethnology*, Parts 1 and 2, University of Texas Press, Austin.

SEXUAL SUBORDINATION: INSTITUTIONALIZED HOMOSEXUALITY AND SOCIAL CONTROL IN MELANESIA[1]

Gerald W. Creed
City University of New York Graduate Center

Like food and shelter, sex is a basic human need that different societies satisfy in manifold ways. Compared with other topics, however, anthropologists have provided relatively few studies of sexuality. Even holistic ethnographies skim over or ignore sexual behavior and are not admonished for it. Anthropologists assume that all other dimensions of social behavior are socially constructed but, for whatever reasons, they disregard the social construction of sexuality and exclude it from social analysis. The roots of this bias are deep. As Malinowski's (1929) study of Trobriand sexual customs aptly demonstrates, early British ethnographers treated sexuality as an independent issue divorced from its broader political context. Influenced by the colonial administration's concern with tribal politics, British ethnographers conceptually divided the world into separate public and private spheres (e.g., Fortes and Evans-Pritchard 1940). They located the political issues which concerned them in the public sphere and cloistered away sexual behavior in the private realm where it could be justifiably ignored.

If anthropologists have had difficulty treating sexuality in general, dealing with the sexual practices they were taught to abhor (such as homosexuality) was almost impossible. Although the tenet of cultural relativism entreats us to perceive our subject matter objectively, there is something about sexual issues, particularly those Western culture regards as "deviant," that prohibits us from putting aside our own feelings and inhibitions. Anthropologists deal with this problem in two ways. First, one may throw relativism to the wind and accept the moralistic values of one's own society. For example, Williams (1936:158) refers to "sodomy" among the Keraki as an "unnatural practice" and a "perversion." Second, and potentially more damaging to scholarship, is to maintain a relativistic stance but ignore sexual practices that pose a threat. Thus, Evans-Pritchard hesitated reporting homosexual activity among the Azande. Even though he published several articles and books on the Azande, he (Evans-Pritchard 1970) only recently discussed their homosexual proclivities. Another version of this avoidance is manifested earlier in the research process when fieldworkers simply avoid investigating sensitive issues such as homosexuality, or do not pursue them as extensively as they would other issues. Kenneth Read (1980:184), reflecting on his own fieldwork among the Gahuku-Gama, admits that a more insistent investigation might have uncovered homosexual activity. That researchers are now admitting such omissions and oversights is a reflection of changing attitudes in our own society.

In order to grasp the broader political and social importance of sexuality we must reject the old public/private dichotomy and realize that the private is political. Cohen (1969) took a giant step in this direction when he suggested that developing states used sexual regulations to gain political control of their citizenry, and since then many studies (Rowbotham 1973; Zaretsky 1976; Ortner 1978) have pursued the connection between sexuality and politics. Cohen (1969:664) suggested that "there is 'something' about sexuality that renders people vulnerable to control through it." This "something" may include the radically individualistic view of sexuality; the perception of sexuality as something so private and so personal means that controlling sexuality is virtually synonymous with controlling the individual. Furthermore, if we assume that every sex act contains an element of domination and subordination, then by controlling the occurrence of sex—by structuring who can have sex with whom and how—the inherent individual qualities of dominance and subordination can be generalized and assigned to particular groups of a population. Thus, we might view the insistence on heterosexuality as a way of ensuring male social and economic hegemony. Similarly, where homosexuality is a socially prescribed institution, we might look for a pattern of domination and subordination between those involved. Ritualized/institutionalized homosexuality in New Guinea I view as a mechanism of social control that operates to perpetuate a system of inequality based on sex and age. New Guinea ethnographers (Kelly 1976; Herdt 1981; Van Baal 1966) have suggested similar ideas but they have not pursued or supported these suggestions. I will attempt to specify some of the ways in which ritualized homosexuality actually subordinates and controls women and young men.

INSTITUTIONALIZED HOMOSEXUALITY IN MELANESIA

"Ritualized homosexual practices, usually introduced in male initiation, are virtually universal throughout the Papuan Gulf, extending from Anga groups (e.g., Menya, Sambia, Baruya) and the Fly headwaters west to Prince Hendrik Island and including fringe areas such as the Papuan Plateua (e.g., Etoro, Kalule) and Nomad River" (Herdt and Poole 1981:8). As the above quotation suggests, the practice of homosexuality in New Guinea is widespread, highly structured, and culturally regulated. The particulars of this practice may vary from society to society, but there is a general skeleton of beliefs and actions that characterize the institution across Melanesia. Here, I will describe the anatomy of this common skeleton and then flesh out the particulars of several cases.

Institutionalized homosexuality is rooted in a belief that the attributes of masculinity are not innate in male biology but acquired through strict adherence to a ritualized regimen. This is in contradistinction to femininity which is acquired naturally by women without such effort. Taking some liberties with old anthropological terminology, we might say that femaleness is an ascribed characteristic while maleness is an achieved one. The essence and focus of this maleness invariably is semen. Once this premise is accepted, the logical conclusion is clear; males must acquire semen in order to become real men. Basically, this is what ritualized homosexuality is all about; promoting masculine development by transferring semen from the haves to the have-nots.

This is always accomplished through a highly structured process. It usually takes place in the context of initiation rites, so that we must examine ritualized homosexuality in tandem with other aspects of male initiation. Even the sexual act itself is highly structured; there are restrictions on who may have sex with whom and what role an individual may play in sexual encounters. Kinship and age factors structure the phenomenon such that certain categories of kin are prohibited from having homosexual relations while other categories of male relatives may be prescribed. The younger partner in a homosexual episode must always receive the semen from the older male, but as a boy ages he graduates to the role of inseminator and eventually moves into a period of heterosexuality, marriage, and child-rearing.

Malekula

Although this paper focuses on New Guinea, it behooves us to first examine Malekula, an island in Eastern Melanesia, since there is documentation of homosexual activity there from a relatively early period, and the pattern is similar to that described above. Layard's (1942) monograph and the posthumous edition of Deacon's (1934) fieldnotes together give a basic account of homosexual practices in the northern area of Malekula known as the Big Nambas. This area was not the primary fieldwork site of either ethnographer; Layard's work was concerned with the small northeastern island of Voa, and Deacon spent most of his time in the southwest of the island, making only a brief visit to the Big Nambas (Deacon 1934:xxii).

Both accounts suggest that the Malekula pattern of homosexual activity conforms in several ways to that found in New Guinea. Deacon (1934:260, 267) writes that up until the time a boy assumes his bark belt, which is the badge of the adult male, he is a "boy lover" to some older man. Once he assumes his belt this bond is terminated and he takes a "boy lover" himself. Neither Deacon nor Layard indicate the ages of boys at the time of their initial homosexual initiation, nor the age at which they receive the bark belt and graduate to homosexual dominants. Both authors are also unclear about how long men continue in the role of dominant inseminator, although some passages suggest that such involvements continue throughout adult life (Deacon 1934:260-262). Furthermore, neither ethnographer is clear about the ideology surrounding homosexual activities. Deacon (1934:262) relates that homosexual practices are believed to cause the boy's "male organ" to grow strong and large, and he assumes that this "male organ" is the penis. Recent work in New Guinea, however, has revealed a belief in an internal "semen organ" which swells up as semen acquired in homosexual intercourse accumulates there (Herdt 1981:217). The possibility exists that a similar mythical anatomical structure is the referent of the Malekulan "male organ." If so, this would make the connection between homosexuality and the transfer of semen which neither Deacon not Layard makes explicit. Layard (1942:489) does say that ritualized homosexual practices constitute "a transmission of male power by physical means" but he does not say that semen is the vehicle of this transmission.

Two characteristics distinguish the Big Nambas case from the general pattern described above: the close, often monogamous relationship between a boy and his adult inseminator; and the existence of what appears to be hereditary chiefs. Unfortunately, neither author gives much information on the basis of chiefly authority or the benefits of chiefly privilege. Deacon (1934:49-50) superficially notes that chiefs owe their influence and power to their opportunities for acquiring greater wealth, but he does not elaborate on how they come into these opportunities. Chiefly status is important to an understanding of homosexuality because chiefs may take on many boy lovers just as they may acquire many wives. Deacon does not investigate this interface of high status, wealth, and sexual access. Furthermore, he (Deacon 1934:170) does not tell us whether the quality of the homosexual relationships between a chief and his boy lovers is any different from that experienced by the rest of the population whose homosexual involvements appear to be monogamous.

Deacon's description of the quality of the average homosexual relationship is the strong point of his analysis. After the decision to hold circumcision rites, the father of a candidate will seek out someone to act as guardian to his son. After these arrangements have been made the guardian has exclusive sexual rights over his ward. He becomes the boy's "husband" and their relationship is very close. The boy accompanies his guardian everywhere and if one of the two should die the survivor would mourn him deeply (Deacon 1934:261). Layard's description of homosexuality is primarily quoted from Deacon's account.

The Transfly

Reports from the Trans-Fly area of Papua New Guinea suggest that the intimate monogamous dimension found in the Big Nambas is absent. The primary sources on this area are Williams (1936) and Landtman (1927). The latter is disappointing with regard to homosexuality—the author (Landtman 1927:237) merely mentions that "sodomy" is practiced within the context of initiation as a means to make youth strong and tall. Even this statement is confounded by the fact that initiation is not a single event among the Kiwai. Youths are initiated separately into each of the great secret ceremonies as they occur, none of which has exclusive reference to the initiates (Landtman 1927:237).

Williams's account of the Keraki is much more informative with regard to homosexuality. Although he uses derogatory expressions such as "unnatural practice" and "perversion," he gives an informed account of the institution. He (Williams 1936:158) relates that sodomy was fully sanctioned by male society, universally practiced, and that homosexuality was actually regarded as essential to a boy's bodily growth. Boys are initiated at the bull-roarer ceremony at about the age of thirteen. On the night of the ceremony the initiate is turned over to a youth of the previous group of initiates who introduces the boy to homosexual intercourse. In all cases noted by William (1936:188), the older youth was the mother's brother's son or the father's sister's son of the new initiate. After this, the boy is available to fellow villagers or visitors of the opposite moiety who wish to have homosexual relations with him. During this time the initiates live together in a seclusion hut for several months, during which they are supposed to grow rapidly with the aid of homosexual activities. At the end of the seclusion the youth becomes a "bachelor." He associates more freely with the elders and shows an increased interest in hunting, but he continues to play the passive role in homosexual relations for a year or so.

Near the end of this period the initiates go through a ceremony of lime-eating. Lime is poured down their throats and the severe burns that result are thought to neutralize the effects of homosexual intercourse; i.e., to ensure that the young men do not become pregnant. After this, a youth's compulsory service as a passive homosexual partner comes to an end. He is then entitled to adopt the opposite role when the next batch of boys is initiated into the bull-roarer (Williams 1936:200-203). "It is commonly asserted that the early practice of sodomy does nothing to inhibit a man's natural desires when later on he marries; and it is a fact that while the older men are not debarred from indulging, and actually do so at the bull-roarer ceremony, sodomy is virtually restricted as a habit to the *setiriva* [bachelors]" (Williams 1936:159).

Like Deacon and Layard, Williams emphasized the role of homosexuality in growth and development without explicitly connecting this function to the transfer of semen. On the other hand, no alternative explanation connecting homosexuality and growth is offered. Williams (1936:204) suggests that "the real motive is presumably self-gratification and although the idea of promoting growth is actually present . . . we may be sure that sodomy could get on very well without it." While this conclusion is perhaps a bit extreme, it directs our attention to the actual physical and erotic aspects of homosexuality which are often overlooked when it is treated as institutionalized behavior. Institutionalized homosexuality is still sex and it may still serve a pleasurable function. Analyses that neglect this fact are incomplete.

Marind-Anim

To the west of the Keraki are the Marind-anim, a coastal group studied by Van Baal (1966). The Marind occupy a vast territory extending along the entire southeastern coast of Irian Jaya. They are the epitome of what Wagner (1972:19) calls the "flamboyant coastal cultures." Homosexuality is prescribed for an extended period of about six years with boys engaging in anal intercourse. According to Van Baal's (1966:147) description this period probably begins when the boy is between seven and fourteen years old. Van Baal suggests that boys are subjected to both the sexual desires of their appointed mentors, usually their mother's brother, as well as the desires of the age-grade of youths above them. Thus, Marind custom seems to combine generalized sexual access with the idea of a single homosexual partner.

Actually, Van Baal's descriptions are not explicit about the details of homosexuality. He does not pay any attention to the distinction between active and passive roles within homosexual relations and, consequently, he does not document the transition from one role to another. Certain statements do suggest such a transition, however, when examined in the context of the male life cycle. A boy is given a mentor at the onset of puberty and "the relationship between the boy and his mentor is a homosexual one, the *binahorevai* [mentor] having the right to use him" (Van Baal 1966:118). At about the same time the boy moves into the *gotad*—a ritual seclusion hut. The boy spends his days here but joins his mentor in the men's house at night where they sleep next to one another. When the boy's hair is long enough to be plaited into an elaborate hairdo, which is the pride of the Marind male, he is promoted to the age-grade of *wokraved,* where he stays for the next two or three years. According to Van Baal (1966:147) "the *wokraved* is called a girl, a qualification apparently referring to his role in the homosexual relationship with his *binahor*-father (and possibly with his older mates in the gotad)." This suggests that the *wokraved* plays the passive role in anal intercourse. It is confirmed by Van Baal's (1966:495) statement that the mother's brother might be seen as a mother substitute who promotes the boy's growth by depositing semen in his body.

Following the stage of *wokraved,* the adolescent young man becomes *ewati.* He remains in this age-grade for about three more years or until just before marriage, whereupon he leaves the *gotad.* "The promotion to *ewati* is a big event in the boy's life. It implies an important change in status . . . The *ewati* is, to all intents and purposes, a man . . . and he need no longer obey his *binahorevai.* However, he is in no hurry to marry as he finds much gratification in his status of *ewati*" (Van Baal 1966:151-152). Based upon the pattern of the other societies examined, we might suspect that the termination of the youth's obedience to his mentor spells the end of their homosexual relationship as well. It is also likely that the *ewati*'s reluctance to marry and leave the *gotad* is due to the fact that some of the "gratification" he finds in his status is his new role as the dominant inseminator to a new group of *wokraved.* This suggestion, however, is not obvious from Van Baal's description.

Van Baal (1966:166) is explicit about the general transition to heterosexuality. Eventually the *ewati* arranges for marriage, becomes an adult man, and leaves the *gotad.* "To be married is the wish of every man; in Marind-anim opinion the unmarried male is a poor wretch." Thus, the Marind conform to the general cycle from homosexuality to heterosexuality, though it seems that Marind men may continue to engage in homosexual sodomy throughout their life. The ideological underpinnings of homosexuality among the Marind also conform to our general pattern. Like the residents of the Big Nambas and the Transfly, the Marind believe homosexual relations promote the growth and development of boys. Unlike Layard's and Williams's descriptions, however, Van Baal's account states explicitly that this growth is attributed to the transfer of semen. Recent studies of the Papuan Plateau are even more insistent about semen being the pivotal issue of the homosexual cult.

The Papuan Plateau

Our knowledge of homosexuality on the Plateau comes to us from the work of Kelly (1976, 1977) and Schieffelin (1976) who conducted fieldwork among the Etoro and Kaluli, respectively. Homosexuality is also practiced by the Onabasalu and Bendamini but the researchers of these areas have not yet published any account of homosexuality there. The homosexual activities of the Onabasalu are known to us through a reference to them in Kelly's description of the Etoro. Based on personal communication with the fieldworker, Ernst, Kelly (1977:16) relates that Onabasalu initiation is focused on masturbation and the smearing of semen over the initiates' bodies. According to Ernst, the Onabasalu formerly practiced oral intercourse and some Onabasalu boys were actually initiated at Etoro seclusion houses.

Schieffelin's (1976) description of the Kaluli is organized around an eloquent analysis of the *Gisaro* ceremony. The *Gisaro* is an exotic ritual drama in which dancers/singers from one longhouse community visit another community where they sing songs recalling some painful and depressing memory of their hosts. In a successful *Gisaro,* someone in the audience will be moved to such grief and sorrow that he will grab a torch and burn the dancer. Schieffelin treats the ceremony as a celebration of social reciprocity and believes that the theme of reciprocity is the basic current flowing through all of Kaluli society.

Unfortunately, Schieffelin does not pursue the theme of reciprocity when dealing with homosexuality. He simply explains homosexuality as an extreme expression of maleness within a context of male-female opposition. On the other hand, Schieffelin (1976:123) claims that relationships between Kaluli men and women are unusual, by New Guinea standards, for their lack of hostility and for their affection. Why then, do we not find this extreme expression of maleness in New Guinea societies with greater sexual antagonism, such as those in the Highlands proper? Schieffelin is not concerned with such questions.

The characteristics of Kaluli maleness are concentrated in semen. Semen has a magical quality that promotes physical growth and mental understanding. Boys must, therefore, acquire semen in order to grow and develop masculine qualities. "When a boy is eleven or twelve years old he is engaged for several months in homosexual intercourse with a healthy older man chosen by his father . . . Men point to the rapid growth of adolescent youths, the appearance of peachfuzz beards, and so on as the favorable results of this child-rearing practice" (Schieffelin 1976:124). Schieffelin does not tell us how much older this "older man" is or what criteria guide his selection, but he (Schieffelin 1976:126) does reveal that during periods of seclusion in the ceremonial hunting lodge, "homosexual intercourse was practiced between the older bachelors and the younger boys to make them grow, some boys and men developing specific liaisons for the time." Is this in addition to the homosexual relationship arranged by the boy's father? If so, how does it articulate with that relationship? Again, Schieffelin does not discuss the details.

Actually, Schieffelin says little beyond a basic statement of the relationship between homosexuality and adolescent development but, lest we criticize him for this, we should recall that his analysis is concerned with *Gisaro,* not with ritualized homosexuality, and his limited attention to homosexual practices makes sense in this context. At the end of the book, Schieffelin (1976:222) makes a connection between the generative role of homosexual intercourse in this world and the vitalizing, regenerative role that the *Gisaro* ritual plays in the "unseen world." In a report devoted to examining the *Gisaro,* Schieffelin tells the reader only enough about homosexuality to ensure that the symbolic connection between the two is grasped.

Kelly's (1976) descriptions of Etoro homosexuality are also circumscribed by his particular interests. He examines Etoro society from a structural perspective and his investigation of homosexuality provides another clue in his search for the underlying structural characteristics of Etoro social structure. In his well-known article on witchcraft and sexual relations, Kelly treats homosexual and heterosexual activities together, since they both represent a transfer of "life force" from one individual to another. In the case of homosexual intercourse the passive boy is the beneficiary of the life force transferred to him in semen. In the case of heterosexual intercourse the unborn child is the recipient of this life force, since the Etoro believe that the semen deposited in the womb combines with the female's blood to form the child. Kelly (1976:41) suggests that witchcraft and sexual relations occupy analogous structural positions within the Etoro conceptual system since they both constitute modes on interaction through which life force is transmitted from one human being to another.

Kelly (1976:52) stresses the role of homosexual intercourse in supplying boys with adequate life force/semen to ensure their proper growth and maturity. To this end, a boy is inseminated through oral intercourse by a single inseminator from about the age of ten until he is fully mature and has a manly beard, usually around his early to mid-twenties. Initiation appears to take place during the later portion of this period. Kelly (1976:47) states that "youths are initiated into manhood in their late teens or early twenties when they are physically mature (although not fully bearded)." About every three years, all young men who have reached this stage of development go to a seclusion lodge and cannot be seen by women. The previous group of initiates, who are now completely mature, also reside at the lodge, but Kelly does not say whether they engage in sexual relations with the neophytes. He (Kelly 1976:47) does say that a "generalized insemination of the youths by older men takes place at the seclusion lodge," but the reader is unsure if the previous group of initiates are part of this group of "older men." Kelly is also not specific regarding how long the seclusion lasts, but, upon reaching maturity the Etoro initiate will become the inseminator of a new young neophyte, preferably his wife's (or his wife-to-be's) brother.

In his study of Etoro social structure, Kelly (1977) has more to say about the preference for the wife's brother as a homosexual partner. Here Kelly (1977:2) attempts to demonstrate that the principle of siblingship is as important as the principle of descent, and that Etoro social structure can be viewed as the outcome of managing these two contradictory principles. Kelly's discussion of homosexuality in this book is minimal and submerged under detailed description of the kinship system. Regarding homosexuality, he focuses primarily on the preference for the sister's husband as her brother's inseminator. If this ideal is achieved, then a married sister and her younger brother have equivalent relationships of sexual partnership to the same man. The relationship between the sister's husband and her unmarried brother is "exceptionally strong" and sexual relations between the two continue until the younger marries and starts inseminating his own wife's brother (Kelly 1977:183). Kelly (1977:270) uses the Etoro organization of homosexuality as an example of the principle of siblingship, in this case, as it is mediated by an affine.

The Sambia

Herdt's (1981) analysis of the Sambia—occupants of the narrow river valleys in the remote Eastern Highlands—is the only full-length study of a New Guinea society concerned primarily with institutionalized homosexuality. Ironically, this narrow focus gives the impression that institutionalized homosexuality is a system unto itself, concerned only with the construction of gender identity—a suggestion that flies in the face of the anthropoligical tenet that culture is integrated. We would be better informed of the importance of homosexuality if we were given more information about its connection to kinship, politics, economics, etc. The only connection that Herdt really stresses is the role of homosexuality in reproducing a warriorhood—a warriorhood that is reproduced sufficiently in other New Guinea societies without the aid of homosexual activities (Meggitt 1977).

The narrow focus of Herdt's analysis is the product of two factors. First, his definition of culture as "the cognitive system of values, norms, and rules influencing perception and behavior" is mentalistic and allows him (Herdt 1981:12) to give short shrift to material connections. Second, Herdt's goal is to discover the subjective experience of homosexuality for individuals by focusing on verbal behavior, especially idioms. His (Herdt 1981:11) primary concern is with intimate communication; what particular men in particular circumstances said to him in particular. Putting aside the question of whether or not one person can actually understand another's "subjective experience," there is still the question of the value of such an exercise. As a rule, anthropologists are not interested in individual idiosyncrasies but in social generalities.

Herdt discusses Sambia homosexuality in terms of stages of "masculinization." The Sambia believe that masculine attributes develop when young men acquire sufficient semen. By this point in the paper it should come as no surprise that the Sambia think that semen must be acquired by ingesting it in homosexual oral intercourse. Around the age of seven to ten years old, a boy is separated from his mother and subjected to painful and traumatic rituals directed toward purging the initiates of female contamination. Once purged, the initiates embark upon a period of consuming semen intended to provide them with the requisite for masculine development. Fellatio becomes a way of life and elders reiterate that boys should ingest semen every night (Herdt 1981:235). Boys must consume a lot of semen in order to build a reservior of maleness and strength that will last a lifetime.

The appearance of male physical traits around the age of fourteen to sixteen is taken as proof that the boy has ingested enough semen. He is promoted to the status of bachelor and required to serve as the dominant inseminator for a new group of initiates. This period leads into marriage, usually to a pre-menarche girl. The young wife may practice fellatio on her husband but the new couple cannot engage in vaginal intercourse. During a period of about a year or two then, a man can be truely bisexual, continuing to have oral sex with young initiates as well as his wife. Once the wife's menarche occurs, however, they begin coitus and homosexual activities should cease (Herdt 1981:252).

As the bachelor approaches coitus and fatherhood, which is the peak of manhood, his ritual practices are shifted to defend and maintain the manliness already acquired. For example, men begin drinking white "milk" sap after each occasion of heterosexual intercourse as a means of replacing ejaculated semen (Herdt 1981:251). But one wonders why milk sap is not used as the original source of semen for initiates. This enigma should have prompted Herdt to look for other possible functions of the homosexual relationship which could not be replaced by milk sap consumption, such as the subordinate-dominant relationship between homosexual partners, which is affirmed in the sexual exchange.

Herdt (1981:320) views homosexual contacts as powerful personal experiences that inculcate masculinity and further the unfinished process of male "separation-individuation." "Ritualized homosexuality reinforces the rigidity of the masculine ethic, it allows for no exceptions in the race for acquiring maleness" (Herdt 1981:322). In Herdt's (1981:305) terms, ritualization homosexuality is a process of "radical resocialization," a kind of "ritualized gender surgery" that replaces the gender identity a boy acquires at the hands of his mother with the appropriate masculine gender identity. Herdt does not say why homosexuality is the means of "radical resocialization" nor how other societies, which have to deal with the same problem, manage without it.

HOMOSEXUALITY AND SOCIAL CONTROL

Herdt's suggestion follows Burton and Whiting's (1961) explanation of male initiation as "psychological brainwashing." They (Burton and Whiting 1961:90-91) suggest that puberty rites replace the feminine identity acquired by boys during the intense period of mothering with the appropriate masculine identity. Male initiation in general and ritualized homosexuality in particular are obviously connected to the formation of masculine gender identity, but restricting the role of homosexuality to this one function is a mistake. In fact, what Herdt (1981) calls the "radical resocialization" of boys may not be as necessary as he thinks. While the first several years of a boy's life are dominated by his mother, during this time he is continually confronted with the gender polarization around him. Despite the closeness of his mother he could not be oblivious to the sexual divisions that define his environment. Furthermore, he is probably continually indoctrinated in the correct behavior for the different sexes—a mother surely reminds her young son of his sex and the behavior appropriate to it.

Ritualized homosexuality doubtless cements and guarantees the correct gender identity, but here I suggest a broader function of homosexual initiation—that it is a powerful component in a system of social control. This notion actually encompasses the former argument since indoctrination of the acceptable gender identity is the first line of attack in keeping individuals within the boundaries delineated and accepted by society. A closer examination, however, reveals that ritualized homosexuality may serve to control more than individual psychology. Institutionalized homosexuality is a mechanism of control that operates to perpetuate a system of inequality based on sex and age. It supports the status and position of older men over and against women and young men. Kelly (1976:51) made a similar suggestion about the structural role of sexual relations and witchcraft in producing an elementary system of inequality based on sex and age, but he does not explain how the actual practice of homosexuality contributes to such a system. Herdt (1981:13) also suggests that initiation separates women and children as a class and reproduces the social order but, as mentioned above, his analysis is restricted to an examination of gender identity and he does not specify any of the actual connections between homosexual practices and the oppression of young men and women.

Male homosexuality may seem completely removed from anything having to do with women, but, paradoxically, this separation and isolation are related to the control and subordination of women in several ways. First, the secrecy which in most cases surrounds the male homosexual cult (the Marind-anim seem to be the only exception) keeps women ignorant of male activities. This ignorance itself is a powerful controlling mechanism. Men state that women have no idea of male ritual activities and in most of the societies discussed above initiates are instructed not to reveal any of the secrets they learn. Williams (1936:185) states that young Keraki initiates were threatened with execution if they revealed any ritual secrets. Furthermore, the seclusion of small boys in initiation huts and their reappearance after the period of rapid adolescent development is intended to impress upon women the power of the male cult. Schieffelin's (1977:126) account of the Kaluli, for example, states that young men were strictly secluded from women for periods of up to fifteen months. "The young men emerged from seclusion decked in their brightest finery, so handsome and so much grown, it is said, that their own relatives didn't recognize them." A more explicit example of the manipulation of ignorance revolves around the use of the bull-roarer, a noise maker used by some societies in the context of male initiation and ritualized homosexuality. The bull-roarer makes a strange noise which can be heard by women and children. They know that it is connected with men's activities but they have no idea of its source (Williams 1936:192). Such ignorance of male ritual activity is easily turned into fear of its apparent power, and this fear ensures female submission.

Practitioners themselves actually view homosexual activity as a statement of male superiority over females. Van Baal (1966:489) says that Marind male pride and superiority find their fullest expression in homosexual rites. These rites stress the absolute superiority of the male sex. This expression, however, is a fiction that men are determined to maintain. Men are well aware that they depend upon women, not only for their substantial contribution to subsistence, but, more importantly, for their reproductive power. Among the Kaluli a man can develop the connections and influence that render him fully effective in his life only through a relationship with a woman (Schieffelin 1977:128). Similarly, among the Sambia only the birth of a child confirms complete manhood, and one's success in fathering children is an important gauge of one's prestige and social status (Herdt 1981:52). Thus, as Van Baal (1966:949) points out, the venerated power of men is not all it is pretended to be. "These self-sufficient males need the females and they know it; only they do not care to admit it." The conflict between the fiction of all-powerful masculinity and the reality of female reproductive power gives rise to masculine ritual and dogma that reinforces the former in face of the latter. Ritualized homosexuality is the critical element of the male defense system—they use it to deny their dependence upon women. Among the Sambia this is taken so far as the elaboration of a myth of male parthenogenesis which asserts that the female sex itself was the product of male homosexual intercourse (Herdt 1981). By denying the power of women, men are able to justify and assert their own authority and control. Men may try to demonstrate in many ways their ability to live without women, but male homosexuality is particularly effective in this regard since it denies the need for women in the area where women are most powerful—sexuality.

The contradiction between the myth of all-powerful masculinity and the reality of female reproductive power is paralleled within the male sex itself in terms of age. The social status and influence that come with age are well documented in the New Guinea literature. Van Baal (1966:115), for example, states that "relative age is important in Marind society. It finds expression in the somewhat exalted position of elderly people and in the system of age grades among adolescents." Herdt (1981:35) also affirms that age is a fundamental principle of hamlet organization among the Sambia, as well as one of the primary sources of power and prestige. On the other hand, older men are not blind to the energy, vitality and determination possessed by youth. In fact, they may formally recognize it. In Marind society, for example, the important position of elders is juxtaposed to a special emphasis on youth: "what counts is youth and life" (Van Baal 1966:171). Similarly, Schieffelin (1977:125) points out that the Kaluli recognize that virgin youths and unmarried young men are the best hunters not only because of their greater speed, stamina and sharpness of eye, but also because animals may be more likely to appear before them. If we accept the suggestion that homosexuality affirms masculine supremacy in the face of female power, we must also investigate the possibility that it operates in the parallel contradiction between the ideal of adult supremacy and the reality of youthful vitality.

The ways in which male initiation in general may help ensure adult ascendancy over younger males are numerous and intermittently intertwined with the control of females. The same strategy of enforced ignorance used against women is also employed against youth. Very young boys are as ignorant of male cult secrets as their mothers are. Even as they grow and begin to learn the secrets of manhood, they are in no position to challenge the accumulated wisdom and knowledge of older adult men. As Meillassoux (1960:49) suggests regarding African elders, the authority of the elders rests on withholding knowledge, and it is this which supports and justifies the control of youth's labor products. Herdt's (1981:45) account supports this suggestion. He points out that the distinguished position of Sambia elders is based on their accumulated knowledge; they hold ritual secrets that younger men have not learned and this knowledge gives them enormous power to constrain the actions of younger men. Keraki adults also restrict the knowledge of young men. According to Williams (1936) young boys learn some of the myths of the male cult in the context of initiation, but they may remain ignorant of other myths until much later in their life. Williams (1936:199) offers a poignant example of how knowledge is regulated. Bamboo pipes are revealed to initiates as the source of a mysterious, unknown sound they heard as children. After demonstrating the use of the pipes, adults give the initiates their own pipes and tell them to blow, but the boys may blow until they pass out without producing a sound since they have been given a plain tube without the almost invisible splint responsible for the noise. Thus, this step in initiation removes some of the ignorance which boys share with their mothers, but not necessarily all of it.

As young boys become more aware of male ritual secrets through the process of initiation, new and additional mechanisms of control must be found to replace ignorance. In the societies examined here the very process of enlightenment—initiation into the homosexual cult—contains the new means of control. Initiation reveals to boys the powerful secret of male homosexuality, but the ideological underpinnings of this institution perpetuate their subordination. Ideologically locating "strength" in semen means that boys, like women, lack strength and are, therefore, weak and inferior. Furthermore, by denying that semen is acquired naturally and insisting that it is a limited good which can only be acquired from someone already possessing it, adult males make boys not only completely inferior to their seniors, but also absolutely dependent upon them for status mobility. In such a situation, as Herdt (1981:51) realizes, strength, maleness and manliness become virtually synonymous with conformity to the ritual routine. "Boys and youths alike must conform: either that, which rewards manhood, or else oblivion by weakness, female contamination, or death" (Herdt 1981:242).

Equating semen with strength and other masculine qualities is an economical controlling ideology since, at the same time that it affirms the ascendancy of males over females, it also denies boys the chance to capitalize automatically on the favorable position of their sex. They can acquire the prerequisite for domination only by subordinating themselves to those who already have semen and following their ritual dictates. These dictates may include painful purging rites since the dogma of institutionalized homosexuality not only denies boys strength but also maintains that they are full of female weakness. A boy could not come from his mother's womb and go through an intense period of mothering without being infected by female pollution. Therefore, boys must be separated from this debilitating female influence and may have to go through purging rites, such as nose-bleeding, to remove existing female contamination.

While the removal of feminine influence may be the stated purpose of the early stages of initiation, ritualized homosexuality may actually be a mechanism to maintain the feminine quality of youth as a way of perpetuating their inferiority. This suggestion challenges the established anthropological interpretations of initiation rituals as simply rites of passage which make boys into men (e.g., Van Gennep 1960, Turner 1967). While this is the recognized emic purpose of ritualized homosexuality, descriptions of the phenomenon suggest that it may be a means of maintaining control of growing boys and maturing young men by emphasizing their femininity and forcing them to play a role in homosexual intercourse analogous to that of women in heterosexual activity.[2] In so doing adult men support their own superior position against the potential challenge or psychological threat of a new generation. Dundes (1976:232) points out that homosexual initiatory practices actually feminize the initiates but he seems unaware that initiates are already feminized to a certain extent by their association with their mothers. More accurately, enforced homosexuality capitalizes on the existing femininity of initiates and maintains it through homosexual intercourse in order to subordinate and control younger men and boys. Dundes is interested in psychological identity, and while he insightfully recognizes the component of feminization involved in ritualized homosexuality, he does not make the connection between feminization and subordination and control.

This feminine quality of the passive partner in homosexual initiation is also suggested by Etoro kinship terminology which refers by the same kin term to a brother and a sister, who are equally appropriate sexual partners for an older male (Kelly 1977:182). Van Baal (1966:147) offers more explicit evidence. Marind mockingly call young initiates "girls" in reference to their role in homosexual relationships. In sexually polarized societies the association of young males with females must have extensive ramifications.

The anthropological interpretation of homosexual rituals as rites of passage simplifies the complex and gradual process of masculine development. By looking at initiation ceremonies as signalling the transition from boyhood to manhood, investigators may overlook the continuing age and status differentials which separate men throughout the life cycle. Becoming a "man"/adult in New Guinea societies is only one step in the larger process of achieving status, prestige, and a prominant position in society. Ritualized homosexuality, then, is not just a rite of passage but an integrated segment in the lifelong process that takes young boys from childhood, through a period as semen recipients, then through a period as semen providers, to a time of heterosexual marriage and fathering children. Concomitantly, ritualized homosexuality assures the authority and superiority of those at the end of this cycle by subordinating those at the beginning and ensuring that they remain differentiated with no pretensions of status before their time.

The transition from semen recipient to semen donator, which is a general characteristic of institutionalized homosexuality, is also intelligible when viewed as part of a system of social control. The ideology of ritualized homosexuality describes semen as a limited good which boys acquire and then dissipate during the remainder of their lives. Logically then, those who have just acquired their store of semen through a period of homosexuality must have the most semen, and, by extension, the most strength. Switching to the role of dominant inseminator for an extended period depletes a young man of much of this newly acquired treasure and perhaps undermines any ambitions he might have as a consequence of his new found maturity. The institutionalized transition to semen provider forces those who have the most semen/strength to dissipate it for the benefit of the next group of initiates. In exchange they are able to dominate the prepubescent initiates who are dependant upon them for semen. Ideally, this subordinate relationship should continue after the initiates reach maturity, but as an added safety measure they will be forced to deplete their store of semen/strength for the next age grade, thereby ensuring their continued subordination to their seniors and the perpetuation of the system. The system thus creates and maintains a structured hierarchy in which each age grade is subordinate to the next oldest age grade.

Psychologically this arrangement also provides an emotional outlet for energetic teenagers who, according to Herdt (1981:323), "feel their growing strength and want to test their power." No doubt they also feel anger and resentment about the abuse they suffered during initiation at the hands of their seniors. The transition to the dominant position in homosexual activities is a way of directing this dangerous combination of strength and anger away from their seniors toward those who are younger. According to Herdt (1981:56), Sambia elders actually assert that young initiates must become "strong" and "angry" because of what has been done to them, then "they can do something equally laden with power: they are encouraged to channel that anger and relax their tight penises by serving as dominant fellateds (for the first time) of younger initiates."

This quotation also suggests that anger and strength are not the only feelings being orchestrated by ritualized homosexuality. The suggestion that boys "relax their tight penises" represents a recognition of the developing libido of maturing boys. By requiring that these urges be satisfied in homosexual relations, older men defend their own monopoly over women and thereby assure their own ascendancy in a system that emphasizes marriage and fatherhood as important measures of social status. The importance of wives in New Guinea is well documented in the literature. For our purposes it is sufficient to note that wives are a valuable resource. Marriage extends a man's network of social relations and provides him with a productive laborer and childbearer. Older men can maximize their own access to this resource by prohibiting younger men from having heterosexual relations and directing their developing sex drive toward young boys. As Herdt (1981:322) points out, "all sexual contact is regulated . . . ritualized homosexual contacts cordon bachelors directing their erotic impulses."

If this is an objective of institutionalized homosexuality, then the early stage of the institution may be seen not so much as a way of masculinizing the new initiates, but as a way of using new initiates to satisfy and pacify the next older age grade and thereby keep them under control. This suggestion is further supported by the general improvement in living conditions that accompanies the transition to inseminator. As initiates graduate to this stage of their life they are usually released from many of the obligations and abuses they endured during the stage of passive homosexual service. For example, among the Marind the *ewati* has an enjoyable, gratifying role and is in no hurry to marry (Van Baal 1966:151-152). The relative ease of the *ewati's* life, combined with the sexual gratification he receives from the new group of initiates, may temporarily obviate the *ewati's* desire for a wife or female sexual partner. Consequently, young females are available to older men.

If this is true we would expect to find a marriage pattern in which very young girls marry older men. This is what Kelly (1977) found historically for the Etoro; girls were traditionally married at about ten to twelve years old to men approximately ten years their senior. Kelly (1977:169) explains this age differential as a consequence of an imbalanced sex ratio. The sex ratio is obviously important, but Kelly would do well to also investigate the connection between this marriage pattern and the organization of ritualized homosexuality. I am not suggesting that ritualized homosexuality necessarily causes a certain marriage pattern, only that there may be a connection between the two that is worth examining. Western researchers have overlooked such connections because they see homosexual activities and heterosexual practices such as marriage as diametrical opposites rather than integrated components of a larger system. As Lindenbaum (n.d.) points out, this problem is further aggravated by "a method of analysis that proceeds to some degree with one sex at a time, when . . . gender is the mutual product of men and women acting in concert."

The arguments made so far regarding homosexuality revolve around the issue of controlling or influencing behavior. This same issue has been discussed more extensively with regard to initiation practices in general, and the role of initiation in socializing and disciplining initiates is well known. Burton and Whiting (1961:85) state that "regardless of the relative strength of infantile dependance, there remains a need for initiation to exercise authority over boys." Similarly, Williams (1936:247) suggests that Keraki initiation rites serve an expressly disciplinary function: "while he [the new initiate] is elevated, he must be humbled. He enters at the bottom of the class and must be taught to know his place." According to Van Baal's (1966:142) description of the Marind a first disciplining begins as soon as boys become initiates in the seclusion hut. "Living in a kind of gang, the boys drill each other on the basis of the rule that the juniors are at the beck and call of their seniors, and have to win complete acceptance by living up to the rules." Ritualized homosexuality fits nicely into this general initiatory objective. Thus, Van Baal (1966:149) concludes "that the elements of disciplining and of being subservient to others, also in homosexual relationships prevail." Herdt is even more explicit. He (Herdt 1981:56) says that "the act of ritualized fellatio confirms the respective statuses of bachelor and initiate alike, and it establishes a definite pattern of eroticism, dominance, and subordination in their interactions for years to come."

Obedience and conformity are not necessarily the only socially desireable results of homosexual practices. Older adults also accrue political and economic benefits. We have already noted how institutionalized homosexuality reserves the economic contribution of women for older men, but there may be other economic benefits as well. In societies where older adults act as inseminators there are benefits that accompany this dominant role. Among the Big Nambas, for example, from the time a father selects a "husband" for his son until the time the boy takes on the status of an adult male, his mentor has absolute sexual rights over him and would be extremely jealous of any other man having intercourse with the boy. In fact, Deacon (1934:261) claims that the older man will hardly let the boy out of his sight. However, a man may sell his rights to his boy-lover for a short period of time. This suggests a situation of privatized sexual rights which can be sold, or more accurately, rented out by a boy's "husband" for the "husband's" economic benefit.

Not surprisingly, these sexual rights go hand in hand with other service obligations, the most significant of which is the requirement that the boy work in his "husband's" garden. Deacon does not discuss the extent of this garden labor, but he (Deacon 1934:261) does say that this labor contribution is the reason chiefs acquire many boy-lovers, which suggests that the work is significant. Finally, a boy's mentor also receives compensation directly from his boy-lover and the boy's father. At some point after the seclusion period the boy must purchase his bark belt (the badge of adulthood) from his mentor with coconuts and tobacco. The homosexual relationship between the two continues until this payment is made (Deacon 1934:267). In addition, at the conclusion of the period of seclusion the father of the initiate gives his son's mentor "a very considerable payment of pigs" (Deacon 1934:262).

Van Baal notes similar benefits which accrue to the dominant inseminator. He (Van Baal 1966:845) says that the guardian enjoys many privileges and the lavish provisions he must make for the feasts given in honor of his wards are well balanced by the services they render him. "It is the boy's duty to assist his *bihahor*-father [his homosexual guardian] in gardening and hunting, to fetch coconuts for him and to render him various small services" (Van Baal 1966:148). The initiate's servitude is guaranteed by the fact that the transition to the next age grade, which terminates his sexual and economic service to his guardian, requires the co-operation of his guardian in arranging the relevant feasts. As Van Baal (1966:161) succinctly puts it, "whether he likes it or not, he has to conform to the prescribed patterns of behavior." The economic dimension of this arrangement is even more obvious in cases where the guardian is childless. A man in this situation may prefer to have the boy as a helper for as long as possible and may therefore delay the necessary feasts (Van Baal 1966:149).

Among the Keraki the primary inseminators are not older adults but the next older age grade of youths. However, the services required of initiates by their homosexual partners appear to establish a pattern of servitude that extends into adulthood. Williams (1936:189) states that all the functionaries at an initiation ceremony, one of which is an initiate's primary inseminator, have special relationships to the initiate and continue to have claims on his services. The initiate is never supposed to refuse their requests. In this sense, semen and manhood may be seen as gifts which place the recipient in a situation of almost permanent indebtedness to the giver. Such indebtedness establishes a relationship of subordination and obligation which may last a lifetime. The only compensation for this predicament is the opportunity they have to balance their own indebtedness by subordinating a younger group of initiates in the same manner.

The subordination of those who are younger as compensation for one's own subordination points to one of the most efficient characteristics of homosexuality as a social control mechanism—it is self perpetuating. The major investments are required of boys at a young age. By the time young men are at an age to offer resistance they are vested in the system, some of the benefits are already beginning to flow their way and they need only wait for time to take them to the most favored positions. This progression undercuts any identification with women who are forever destined to a subordinate position. Were young men to grow impatient, the rules and relationships indoctrinated via ritualized homosexuality provide a continual restraint.

The suggestion that institutionalized homosexuality is primarily a social control mechanism is essentially a functional explanation; as such it suffers from the usual problems and failings of functionalist theory. Perhaps the greatest pitfall of functional explanations is that they do not explain why a certain cultural phenomenon, in this instance homosexuality, is the means utilized to achieve a particular effect, in this case the control of women and youth and the perpetuation of a social hierarchy based on sex and age. In other words, if we accept the suggestion that homosexuality is a mechanism of social control we still do not know why it is used in some societies and not in others.

Lindenbaum (n.d.) offers some enlightening suggestions in this regard. She sees a connection between sister exchange and ritualized homosexuality and suggests that the latter is a sort of bride service. According to Lindenbaum, a striking aspect of societies with ritualized homosexuality is that the pattern of marriage is sister exchange with no payment of brideprice. In such a situation semen is a kind of covenant that keeps the sister exchange system intact. Lindenbaum's discussion points out the important role of material valuables and ceremonial exchange in brideprice societies. In the Highlands proper, not semen exchange but the ceremonial exchange of shells, feathers, pigs, etc. is the center of attention. Marriage arrangements are cemented with brideprice valuables and ritual is directed toward the making of men of status rather than the formation of masculine men.

This suggests that the relative paucity or absence of material wealth may be an important variable in accounting for the occurrence of institutionalized homosexuality. Where substantial amounts of material valuables and wealth are available, social ascendancy and control can be ensured by monopolizing that wealth. Where such wealth is absent, other means of control must be found and monopolized, and naturally occurring bodily substances are readily available alternatives. Semen is particularly well suited for the task since it naturally excludes women and children. In support of this suggestion, the societies with ritualized homosexual practices examined here do not appear to have vast amounts or numerous types of material wealth, nor do they seem overly concerned about such issues. Herdt (1981:52) actually states that the Sambia "have few material means of gaining control." Furthermore, as Lindenbaum (n.d.)

points out, when such items do become available they are utilized for brideprice payments, and sister exchange as a marriage pattern and ritualized homosexuality begin to break down in tandem. This argument still does not tell us why homosexuality developed or why it was institutionalized into the male cult. These are historical questions that require and deserve more extensive research. However, the focus on material wealth points out one variable that may figure substantially in the answers to these questions.

Lindenbaum's (n.d.) analysis is also instrumental in showing the explanatory potential of comparisons with New Guinea societies which do not exhibit a ritualized homosexual complex. Generally, researchers interested in homosexuality treat it as a single type of behavior and compare it cross-culturally (e.g., Broude and Greene 1976; Carrier 1980). In response to this approach Whitehead (1981:81) claims that many cases of homosexuality (the modern United States, the berdache, the New Guinea examples, etc.) are very different "animals" and not really comparable. While such comparisons are not worthless, we can learn more about the New Guinea cases by comparing them instead with nonhomosexual New Guinea societies. As Lindenbaum's paper demonstrates, our best clues to understanding homosexuality in New Guinea may be the other differences that distinguish homosexual and nonhomosexual societies within this culture area. More comparisons of this type must be attempted.

Discussion

The intention of this paper is not to answer all the perplexing questions surrounding ritualized/institutionalized homosexuality in New Guinea, but to examine existing accounts of the phenomenon, and to demonstrate that its role as a social control mechanism has been underestimated or at least underinvestigated. In this attempt I have shown that institutionalized homosexuality is not an independent phenomenon that can be understood or explained in isolation. It is an aspect of culture integrated with the position of women, the ideology of pollution, the stratification of males by age, as well as the economic organization of the society. Obviously, these are not the only connections between homosexuality and the rest of social life. As a conclusion I will mention a few of the questions and issues that must be pursued if a complete or holistic understanding of ritualized homosexuality is to be achieved.

First and foremost, more reliable and comparable ethnographic descriptions must be compiled. Much of the existing literature is old and, due to the divergent interests of the ethnographers, the extent of their concern with homosexuality is highly variable. When they do discuss the phenomenon their descriptions focus on different aspects or issues and therefore undermine comparative and generalizing endeavors. The usual problems encountered when working with other people's data are even more troublesome when such time differences and such variation of focus are prominent. In addition, older accounts are often unclear about the source of their information and whether or not they are referring to extant customs.

Only when we have a larger, more uniform ethnographic base will we be able to make generalizations about homosexuality in New Guinea or, conversely, make any suggestions about the variations in the practice within New Guinea. Just because several societies have institutionalized homosexuality does not mean that it serves the same role or function in each. The variations we have noted in the practice of homosexuality, such as the length of time a boy is subjected to it (from several months among the Kaluli to several years among the Etoro), or the differences between the "monogamous"-type arrangement between a boy and an adult inseminator and the situation where one or more youths from the next older age grade act as inseminators, may be related to other sociocultural differences.

Even contemporary research does not adequately address certain issues, such as the articulation of institutionalized homosexuality with the kinship system. We have seen repeatedly that kinship relations are important concerns in establishing homosexual involvements. Kelly (1976) pointed out that the Etoro preference for the wife's brother as a homosexual partner is an example of the principle of siblingship, and there are probably other kinship connections worth examining. In sexually polarized societies such as the ones we are dealing with here, each "pole" must socially reproduce itself. We have already discussed how the organization of institutionalized homosexuality helps ensure the continuity of a male cult, but homosexual relations may also act to maintain and perpetuate an ideology of relatedness or "kinship" between generations within the male cult. In this way semen and homosexuality are to the male cult what blood and fatherhood are to the lineage—the means of descent.

Interesting in this regard is the fact that among the Etoro, the personal characteristics which a youth develops as he matures are believed to correspond to those of his primary inseminator. "If a man is strong, vigorous in his advanced years, a proficient hunter and trapper, and/or courageous warrior, then his protege will possess identical qualities and abilities upon attaining manhood" (Kelly 1976:46). According to Layard's (1942) description of the Big Nambas, this kind of connection may transcend several generations. He (Layard 1942:489) believes that the act of homosexuality represents a transmission of male power by physical means; this power does not come simply from the active partner but from the ancestors in direct succession through each generation. Indeed, since semen is a limited good passed down the generations, the semen men have now is the same semen possessed by their male ancestors. Elsewhere, Layard (1959:111) states that homosexual anal intercourse among the Big Nambas symbolizes "continuity with the ancestoral ghosts in the male line."

Alternatively, one might view homosexual relationships as cross-cutting ties that bind together various kin groups. For example, among the Sambia all kin are taboo with regard to fellatio. As a rule, fellatio is permissible only with males from "outside one's security circle," that is with "unrelated, potentially hostile males" (Herdt 1981:238). Similarly, Kelly (1977:91) states that a boy gets his life giving force in semen from individuals outside his lineage. Thus, homosexuality can be interpreted as somewhat analogous to the institution of marriage as explained by alliance theory—homosexual connections may ally potentially hostile groups. Unfortunately, the existing ethnographies do not discuss the role of homosexual relationships/connections in conflict or conflict resolution, but neither do they deny such a connection. The more general point is that in societies where kin relations are crucial to social organization the connections between kinship and institutionalized homosexuality have not been adequately investigated.

Another issue that needs attention is the issue of cultural change. As Lindenbaum (n.d.) points out, "the systematic interconnectedness of the various aspects of culture [is] best illuminated at moments of transformation." Apart from her paper, however, most studies treat homosexuality statically as an unchanging institution. In some societies rituals of homosexuality are disappearing (Godelier 1976), others are experiencing increasing exposure to societies and traditions that do not condone homosexuality and may even be hostile to such behavior. These dynamics obviously contribute to the current situation regarding homosexuality.

Change and contact are not merely recent developments. Deacon's (1934:22) early account of Malekula discusses the massive depopulation of whole districts caused by labor migration to large plantations. Such processes have become even more important and extensive in recent years. Kelly (1976:53) mentions in a footnote that young Etoro men were anxious for him to arrange work for them as contract laborers on the coast. Even among the more isolated Sambia, Herdt

(1981:179) notes that young men have been leaving their hamlets for temporary work on coastal plantations since the 1960s. He estimates that twenty percent of unmarried males currently journey to the coast and remain for two to four years. Anthropologists have noted how the unusual circumstances of labor migration give rise to temporary periods of homosexuality (e.g., Hogbin 1946:205-206, Mead 1930:193-199, Malinowski 1929:472) but the effect of such movements on those who carry a belief in ritualized homosexuality with them has not been investigated.

Labor migration is both a symptom and a cause of increasing involvement in a cash economy, yet the general impact of cash on homosexuality has not been addressed. The introduction of wage labor is a major metamorphosis that may put economic power in the hands of young workers. The effect of cash is, therefore, an important area to investigate in regard to the suggestion that homosexuality is a mechanism for controlling youth by denying them power. How does this new economic resource effect the youth's role in homosexual relations and his social status in general? Herdt (1931:46) mentions that the introduction of a cash economy and coffee production among the Sambia have led to the acceptance of the entreprenurial big man, but he does not mention the effect of this on the practice or ideology of homosexuality.

Labor migration and participation in a cash economy are manifestations of the broader issue of colonial and foreign intervention. Another major manifestation is pacification. The recreation of a warriorhood is referred to repeatedly in attempts to account for ritualized homosexuality, especially by Van Baal and Herdt. Van Baal (1966:160) asserts that the creation of a "warlike spirit" is one of the primary objectives of male initiation. Herdt (1981:315) repeatedly suggests that the crux of ritualized homosexuality, and the male cult in general, is the creation of warriors. He (Herdt 1981:50) also acknowledges, however, that Australian officials succeeded in completely pacifying the Sambia in 1968 and that fighting among the Sambia and their neighbors came to an end at that time. If homosexuality and warfare are as intertwined as Herdt and Van Baal suggest, it is inconceivable that pacification did not affect the practice or ideology of homosexuality. If there was no effect, then that fact in itself needs explanation.

The impact of colonial administration is not limited to warfare and migration. Kelly (1977:169) notes that the colonial government prohibited "child marriages" among the Etoro in 1966. As a result the average age at marriage for both men and girls increased about six years. Since marriage is a general point when homosexual activities are curtailed, one might expect that this legislation led to a prolonged period of homosexuality, but Kelly does not mention it.

The creation of tribal councils is another change that might influence the practice of homosexuality. Like wage labor, the creation of tribal councils opens up new avenues of power and influence for young men. Consequently, it might effect existing power relations between the generations. Herdt (1981:46) tells us that such councils were set up among the Sambia, but he does not discuss any ramifications for intergenerational relations or homosexuality.

Finally, the problem of missionary activity should be investigated. Needless to say, Christian missionaries do not look favorably on homosexuality. The impact of their moralizing and evangelizing might provide enlightening information about the nature and importance of ritualized homosexuality. For example, we might look for a relationship between the presence of missionaries and the degree of secrecy that shrouds homosexual practices.

In order to address these questions we surely must do more research on the topic but we must go beyond static studies, narrowly focused on homosexuality. Institutionalized homosexuality, like all sexuality everywhere, is embedded in other social arenas and changes as these other dimensions of society change. As Ross and Rapp (1981:54) point out, "sexuality both generates wider social relations and is refracted through the prism of society. As such, sexual feelings and activities express all the contradictions of power relations—of gender, class, and race." This paper has concentrated specifically on the interaction of homosexual activities with the power relations between the sexes and between the generations. These are still only a few strands in the web of connections between homosexuality and other aspects of culture. If we hope to grasp the complexity of this web we must broaden our scope and look at the multitude of interrelations between sex and society. Simultaneously, we must extend our time frame and adopt a processual view that can accommodate change.

Ross and Rapp, drawing upon Geertz's onion imagery, eloquently summarize these issues. They (Ross and Rapp 1981:54) state that "in sexuality as in culture, as we peel off each layer (economics, politics, families, etc.) we may think that we are approaching the kernel, but we eventually discover that the whole is the only 'essence' there is. Sexuality cannot be abstracted from its surrounding social layers." Only when we succeed in connecting ritualized homosexuality to all the surrounding social layers of New Guinea society will we come close to understanding its "essence."

NOTES

1. I am grateful to Professor Mervyn Meggitt for comments on an earlier version of this paper and to Professor Shirley Lindenbaum for providing me with a copy of her yet unpublished paper. Her paper is to be published soon in a collection of essays devoted to ritualized homosexuality in Melanesia edited by G. Herdt. At the time of my research I did not have access to the other unpublished papers to be included in that volume.
2. The attribution of feminine and despicable qualities to only the passive partner in a homosexual encounter is also found in nonhomosexual New Guinea societies (e.g., Whiting 1941:51), and in other culture areas such as the Mediterranean (e.g., Brandes 1981:232-233).

BIBLIOGRAPHY

Brandes, S. 1981. Like Wounded Stags: Male Sexual Ideology in an Andalusian Town. Sexual Meanings: The Cultural Construction of Gender and Sexuality, eds. S. Ortner and H. Whitehead, pp. 216-239. Cambridge.
Broude, G. J., and S. J. Greene. 1976. Cross-cultural Codes on Twenty Sexual Attitudes and Practices. Ethnology 15:409-429.
Burton, R. V., and J. W. M. Whiting. 1961. The Absent Father and Cross-Sex Identity. Merrill-Palmer Quarterly of Behavior and Development 7:85-95.
Carrier, J. M. 1980. Homosexual Behavior in Cross-Cultural Perspective. Homosexual Behavior: A Modern Reappraisal, ed. J. Marmor, pp. 100-122. New York.
Cohen, Y. A. 1969. Ends and Means in Political Control: State Organization and the Punishment of Adultery, Incest, and the Violation of Celibacy. American Anthropologist 71:658-687.
Deacon, B. A. 1934. Malekula: A Vanishing People in the New Hebrides. London.
Dundes, A. 1976. A Psychoanalytic Study of the Bullroarer. Man 11:220-238.
Evans-Pritchard, E. E. 1970. Sexual Inversion Among the Azande. American Anthropologist 72:1428-1434.
Fortes, M., and E. E. Evans-Pritchard. 1940. Introduction. African Political Systems, eds. M. Fortes and E. E. Evans-Pritchard, pp. 1-23. Oxford.
Godelier, M. 1976. Le sexe comme fondement ultime de l'ordre social et cosmique chez les Baruya de Nouvelle-Guinee. Sexualité et Pouvoir, ed. A. Verdiglione, pp. 268-306. Paris.
Herdt, G. 1981. Guardians of the Flutes. New York.
Herdt, G., and F. J. P. Poole. 1981. Sexual Antagonism: The Intellectual History of a Concept in the Anthropology of Melanesia. Paper presented at the annual meeting of the American Anthropological Association, Los Angeles.
Hogbin, H. I. 1946. Puberty to Marriage: A Study of the Sexual Life of the Natives of Wogeo, New Guinea. Oceania 16:185-209.
Kelly, R. C. 1976. Witchcraft and Sexual Relations: An Exploration in the Social and Semantic Implications of the Structure of Belief. Man and Woman in the New Guinea Highlands, eds. P. Brown and G. Buchbinder, pp. 36-53. Special publication of the American Anthropological Association.
——— 1977. Etoro Social Structure: A Study in Structural Contradiction. Ann Arbor.
Landtman, G. 1927. The Kiwai Papuans of British New Guinea. London.
Layard, J. 1942. Stone Men of Malekula. London.
——— 1959. Homo-eroticism in Primitive Society as a Function of the Self. Journal of Analytic Psychology 4:101-115.

Lindenbaum, S. (n.d.) Socio-Sexual Forms in Transition in Melanesia: An Overview. Ritualized Homosexuality in Melanesia, ed. G. Herdt, (in press).
Malinowski, B. 1929. The Sexual Life of Savages in North-Western Melanesia. New York.
Mead, M. 1930. Growing Up in New Guinea. New York.
Meggitt, M. J. 1977. Blood is Their Argument. Palo Alto.
Meillassoux, C. 1960. Essai d'interpretation de phénomène economique dans les sociétés traditionelles d'auto-subsistance. Cahiers d'Etudes Africaines 1:38-67.
Ortner, S. 1978. The Virgin and The State. Feminist Studies 4:37-62.
Read, K. E. 1980. Other Voices. Novato, California.
Ross, E. and R. Rapp. 1981. Sex and Society: A Research Note from Social History and Anthropology. Comparative Studies in Society and History 23:51-72.
Rowbotham, S. 1973. Woman's Consciousness, Man's World. New York.
Schieffelin, E. 1976. The Sorrow of the Lonely and the Burning of the Dancers. New York.
Turner, V. W. 1967. Betwixt and Between: The Liminal Period in *Rites de Passage*. The Forest of Symbols, ed. V. Turner, pp. 93-111. Ithaca.
Van Baal, J. 1966. Dema. The Hague.
Van Gennep, A. 1960 (1909). The Rites of Passage, trans. M. K. Vizedom and G. L. Gaffee. Chicago.
Wagner, R. 1972. Habu: The Innovation of Meaning in Daribi Religion. Chicago.
Whitehead, H. 1981. The Bow and the Burden Strap: A New Look at Institutionalized Homosexuality in Native North America. Sexual Meanings: The Cultural Construction of Gender and Sexuality, eds. S. Ortner and H. Whitehead, pp. 80-115. Cambridge.
Whiting, J. W. M. 1941. Becoming a Kwoma. New Haven.
Williams, F. E. 1936. Papuans of the Trans-Fly. Oxford.
Zaretsky, E. 1976. Capitalism, the Family and Personal Life. New York.

They are called 'Mahu' in French Polynesia, 'Fakaleitis' in Tonga and 'Fa'a Fafines' in the Samoas They are the true transvestites, the Third Sex of Polynesia, with a life-style which, in the case of the Samoans, has been thrust upon them from birth through custom. PIM prints their story, not as a sideways glance at a situation which has been the butt of comedians for years, but as a serious study of a phase of life in the Islands. Husband and wife authors Bengt and Marie Therese Danielsson in Tahiti write about the Mahu, Robin Pierson tells the Samoans' story and a Tonga correspondent brings out both the sad and the glad side of the Third Sex.

POLYNESIA'S THIRD SEX: THE GAY LIFE STARTS IN THE KITCHEN

IN TAHITI

Ever since its discovery Tahiti has enjoyed a worldwide reputation for being the *Island of Love*, and the earliest European visitors all describe in the most glowing terms the islanders' untrammeled promiscuity, their unashamed public intercourses and their artful strip-tease shows. Another amusing example of this general permissiveness was recorded in 1789 by Lieutenant George Mortimer of the British ship Mercury which, on her way to the American Northwest coast to engage in the fur trade, made a short call at Tahiti.

As Mortimer himself tells the story, during a *heiva* show, one of the mates, "took it into his head to be very much smitten with a dancing girl, went up to her, made her a present of some beads and other trifles, and rather interrupted the performance by his attentions. But what was his surprise, when the performance was ended, and after he had been endeavouring to persuade her to go with him on board our ship, which she consented to, to find that this supposed damsel, when stripped of her theatrical paraphernalia, was a smart, dapper lad! The Otaheiteans on their part enjoyed the mistake so much that they followed us to the beach with shouts and repeated peals of laughter".

This anecdote from Mortimer's *Observations and Remarks made during a Voyage to the Islands*, which appeared in 1791, is the first published account we have of a Tahitian *mahu* transvestite.

Shortly afterwards a group of ministers and brethren from the London Missionary Society arrived on the scene and succeeded gradually in converting the Tahitians to their puritan and sectarian form of the Protestant faith.

A traditional Tahitian *mahu* (right) with his lady's bicycle and one of his many female friends. The picture was taken in the early 1930s by a staff member of Honolulu's Bishop Museum.

Yet today, 180 years later, in spite of all the attempts made by the church and civilian authorities to stamp out all the obscene and lascivious practices that delighted the early navigators, the mahu is still a popular and honoured member of every village throughout the Society Islands. Similar comedies of error – where love's labour is definitely lost – are also constantly being reenacted, and produce always bursts of laughter among the Tahitian spectators.

Under other names, true transvestites have existed from immemorial times in most other Polynesian islands. The most complete and detailed coverage of this fascinating subject can be found in a book which we wrote in the early 1950s and which has often been reprinted since then – *Love in the South Seas*.

A typical Tahitian mahu begins at an early age to associate and play with girls and stays at home to do household chores, while the other boys go fishing with their fathers. When reaching puberty, he will start wearing women's clothes, including brassiere. The use of jewellery and cosmetics is also common today in more sophisticated places like Papeete.

An adult mahu will gladly do the cooking and look after babies. But above all he loves to sew, mend, wash and iron clothes. He will spend most of his considerable leisure time in the company of the womenfolk whose manners and voices he will imitate. If he dances – which he usually does with consummate skill and grace – he is invariably a member of the female team.

Although nobody will object if a mahu chooses to live alone, most individuals belonging to this distinct social category prefer to be inmates of a family household. As a matter of fact, the mahu transvestites are much sought after as maids.

Europeans often take for granted that they are all homosexuals which is not the case. Those who are (and they may form the majority) observe as a rule great discretion and modesty. Lasting liaisons are rare and the most common pattern for a mahu is to have occasional, furtive contacts, usually with adolescents still at an experimenting, exploratory stage of their sexual development.

This leaves, however, a small number of mahu transvestites who must be described as indifferent or asexual. Bisexual individuals are not totally unknown, and some have even sired children, but all available evidence indicates that such blatantly heterosexual behaviour represents only short episodes in their lives.

In sharp contrast to the basically negative attitude towards homosexuals in our Western societies, the individuals in Polynesia who follow the traditional mahu way of life are not only tolerated but meet with general approval and praise. We can even go one step farther and say that there exists a definite social pressure to produce individuals with this deviant behaviour.

However, a very important point here which should be born in mind is that there must never be more than one mahu in each village or community. This unwritten law, as well as the fact that a new mahu will always emerge in the case of a vacancy due to death or departure, show even more clearly that we have to do with a sociological and not a biological phenomenon.

How it all started, we shall, of course, never learn, since there are no scientifically-valid traditions or legends, explaining the origin of this time-honoured institution. The only thing we can do, therefore, is to speculate about its possible psychological significance and social implications. The best hypothesis will be found in Professor Robert L. Levy's excellent study *Tahitians, Mind and Experience in the Society Islands* (University of Chicago Press, 1973), based on several years of intensive field work in Tahiti and Huahine, carried out in the native language.

His conclusions are briefly that the Polynesians, like all other peoples, need models and that a mahu is a sort of negative image that helps the boys to become men, or real males, by showing them in a particularly striking manner the sex role which they must **not** choose.

Although the venerable mahu institution survived for almost 200 years, in spite of the constant opprobrium of all church and government dignitaries, there are now many signs that it will eventually disappear as a result of the brutal modernisation process – also called "progress" – to which Tahiti and the other Society Islands have been exposed during the last 15 years, or so. What is happening, ironically enough, is that the rising tide of Western type homosexual prostitution is rapidly engulfing the native style mahu transvestites. Like thousands of other Polynesians they have migrated to the Sodom and Gomorra called Papeete, where they are all bewildered and lost, since the French laws and European customs which prevail there are utterly incomprehensible. Having no other means of making a living in this new harsh environment, the mahu transvestites sooner or later resort to the expediency of selling their favours to the numerous foreign homosexual tourists.

Several bars and night clubs now openly cater to this special category – for which the special word *raerae* has been coined – even to the point of organising beauty contests for the title of *Miss Tane*, or *Miss Male*. The ultimate stage in this westernisation of the Tahitian sexual customs is the recent emergence of lesbian prostitutes whose behaviour all real mahu transvestites, of course, disapprove of as being definitely abnormal . . .

IN SAMOA

Mention the words *fa'a fafine*, and most Samoans giggle. Ask them what the words mean, and they'll tell you, "like a lady, you know, 50-50". Many think this definition is sufficient in explaining the large fellows who speak so sweetly, dress so finely, and carry a purse, but it doesn't, not quite. For the Third Sex in Samoa is unique – fa'a fafines don't choose to be gay, they are raised that way.

It so happens, that the children of Samoa are their families' work force, and a continuous stream of tasks are bestowed upon them from the time they cease being babies, until they have children of their own.

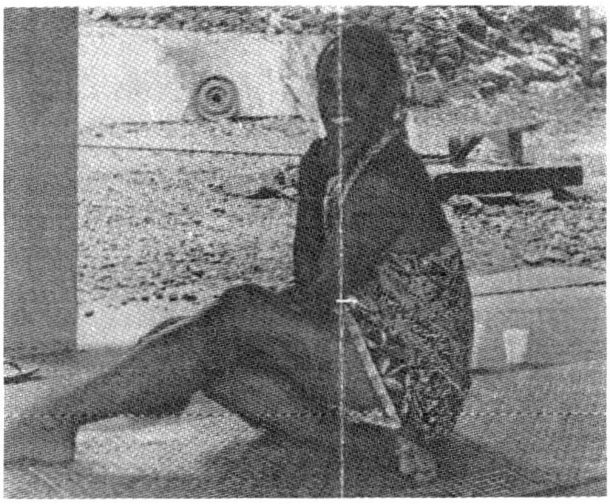

A Samoan *fa'a fafine* turns on a warm smile for the camera.

Boys and girls tasks are segregated, integrating children into an accepted role within their community and family at an early age. Occasionally, a family may have an abundance of male children, which means there is a disparity in the work-load, and, basically, that the woman of the household needs more help.

At times like this, Samoan parents often find that little boys can do girls' work quite adequately, hence, the problem is solved – the labour remains equally distributed, and most importantly, it gets done.

So the young boys grow up doing women's work, associating primarily with women, therefore picking up feminine mannerisms and traits, and gradually they develop into fa'a fafines – like a lady, while at the same time, being very different from a lady.

Yet, an effeminate young man, who reaches maturity wearing women's clothing, is often disconcerting to the male members of his family, to the village priests he is sinful, and it is usually the school authorities who exert pressure on the individual to tone down his style while attending high school. But having been raised as a woman from day one onward, the individual's identity is established, and a transition at this stage would be difficult to make. Besides, regardless of the changes the young man may make outwardly or inwardly, he has already been labelled as a fa'a fafine, making it extremely difficult to be anyone else in the eyes of his community and family. So, even though pressured during adolescence, most fa'a fafines continue to emerge and grow into the role they have been placed in. In other words, the fa'a fafine traits in most of these individuals do not die, but rather come into full bloom.

Many of the fa'a fafines of Samoa have lived, attended school or have been employed in the United States, and the general consensus is that it's a lot easier to be a fa'a fafine in Samoa. The practice of raising a boy child as a girl is accepted in Samoa and generally the end product is accepted also, as long as the individual isn't too blatant about it. But many are blatant. Feeling quite comfortable masquerading as women, and doing remarkably well at it, they're bucking powerful family and societal pressures, which is something that not many Samoans have the courage to do.

Others, who hold high positions within the community, have acquired a subdued fa'a fafine-type appearance, making them more acceptable to the general populus. Yet even these people will most probably stay within their role as fa'a fafines for the rest of their lives, for as with many things on the island, everyone knows your background, making it difficult to change, but acceptable to remain as you are.

Each Sunday afternoon, a unique gathering takes place in downtown Fagatongo in American Samoa. Superficially, the scene is that of a small club meeting. The minutes from last week's meeting are read, donations to the club's treasury are commended, and new fund-raising projects are discussed. Some of the group's members are extravagantly dressed for this informal gathering. Some sport immaculately-groomed coiffures, heavy makeup and long gowns, while others are more casual in *lava-lavas* tied discreetly above the chest. Sitting close to one of the more elegant individuals, a small hint of a heavy beard becomes apparent. The laughter that emanates from the group comes in giggles — deep throated and husky, yet giggles just the same. It's the weekly meeting of the *Tamua Stars,* American Samoa's first and only fa'a fafine organisation.

The group represents the emergence of individual fa'a fafines who have accepted their unique roles and are striving to strengthen their own self-image within that role. They gather together to share their problems, their joys and to counsel others, especially younger fa'a fafines to make their unique path a smoother one.

In June, the Tamua Stars of American Samoa, along with *The My Girls,* the fa'a fafine organisation of Western Samoa, was to host the fa'a fafines of New Zealand for a gala, including a beauty contest, a fashion show, and an array of sports competitions. At a similar event last Christmas, the New Zealanders shone the brightest, but they probably found a bit of competition this year from the lovelies of American and Western Samoa.

Generally, the island's fa'a fafines are considered responsible and efficient employees and students, and having no sexual interest in women or their fellow fa'a fafines, they seldom marry, but instead provide intimate diversity for some Samoan males.

Though not readily nor openly discussed, the original function of the village fa'a fafines was to introduce young men into the art of love-making. Though this practice seems to have rapidly diminished, the fa'a fafines are still a source of pleasure in the Samoan society.

They see themselves as vehicles of happiness and good feelings which they endeavour to share with others. To many it may seem that these men have been dealt an unfair hand by their family and society, but even a bad hand can result in an enjoyable game if the player's attitude is a positive one. The general open and candid manner displayed by the fa'a fafines of Samoa is refreshing and they are a source of delight to the majority of those living among them.

IN TONGA

Outside, men both young and old peered through openings in the foliage-screened front windows of the Dateline Hotel in Tonga's capital, Nukualofa. At the front door, a young, effeminate man collected happily a *one pa'anga* cover charge for those going in. Inside, a standing-room crowd looked on.

The occasion was the annual *Fakaleiti Ball,* an event that has become popular with both Tongans and foreign visitors to Nukualofa. Although the event was more toned-down this year than in the past, it still provided plenty of interest and a chance for Tonga's more visible *fakaleitis* to strut their stuff.

The beauty pageant format, used last year at Joe's Hotel, was discarded with the movement of the ball to the Dateline, Tonga's main tourist hotel, which has a much less rowdy reputation.

Instead, each of the five main participants was introduced and performed a dance routine on the hotel's main dance floor, surrounded by tables of interested spectators.

The audience was in good humour as participants performed their routines in outfits that ranged from short shorts and long nylons to long gowns with low necklines and even in-

'I was born to be like this'

When he was young, he liked to play with girls. But now, at 18, he still finds the ways of women more attractive to him. Because of this, he is occasionally taunted and has lost most of his male Tongan friends.

But, says Longosai Fineanganofa, "I was born to be like this".

Longosai is the youngest of a group of Tongan Fakaleiti *who openly flaunt their femininity, usually in the small park area in front of the International Dateline Hotel, on the beachfront in Nukualofa. He is the youngest of a young group. He calls his friends of 30 "old".*

But the Dateline scene has been a good one for him in the two years he has enjoyed it since finishing school. In addition to Tongan fakaleiti *friends, he now corresponds with friends all over the world.*

But at times, it is obvious that he is restless and concerned about his future.

"Those who understand my life don't talk badly about me, but some, they hate me," Longosai said. "I've been to New Zealand and Fiji and you get used to the way people treat you. But for myself, I want to stay in Tonga.

"I just can't change myself. Sometimes I think to myself 'why was I born to be like this?' But there's nothing I can do. Some people were born to be white and I was born to be like this."

Although Longosai has kept some of his female friends from his schooldays, he has few male friends. Many of his friends in Tonga are from the expatriate or papalangi *community, because, "They show more interest in me".*

He is an only child. Longosai's parents were separated and he has lived most of his life with his grandmother. He enjoys a good relationship with his family and lives at home most of the time.

"My parents leave me alone," he said. At home, he often fulfils the woman's role, cooking and sewing among his other chores.

Most of the time, Longosai keeps late days, going out in the evening and not returning home until early morning. Although he has never encountered trouble with the Tongan police, some of his friends have, he said. Tongan law prohibits two males from having sexual relationships with one another and some of his friends have been prosecuted, he said.

When his friends gather along the beach, the main topic of conversation is usually men, Longosai said. Some nights the group just gathers to talk. On other nights, they dress in women's clothes and wear makeup, moving along the beach to meet customers from the hotel or other visitors who might be interested in spending the night with them. When a cruise ship calls at Queen Salote wharf for an overnight visit, or a naval warship puts into port, Longosai stays busy, he said.

Generally, it is a style of life that satisfies Longosai. Financially, and in terms of gifts he often receives from overseas friends he has made, Longosai lives a comfortable life. "I could easily find a job," Longosai explains. "But I still enjoy this life."

Another hotel near the ocean, Joe's Hotel, is also a gathering place for the fakaleiti *group. Once a year, the group holds a beauty contest at the hotel, each* fakaleiti *posing as a beauty contest winner from some other part of the world, such as "Miss Africa". The contests are popular among Tongans and expatriates, with Joe's usually jammed for the beauty finals.*

This Tongan *fakaleiti* was unlucky enough to lose his wig during a performance at Nukualofa's International Dateline Hotel.

cluded one belly-dancing costume. One dancer, performing to a recorded version of *The Way We Were,* attracted wolf whistles and wows until a saucy jerk of the head sent his expensive wig flopping onto the floor. Then the audience roared.

Although word of the event did not circulate well among the island's *papalangi* community, limiting their attendance, a large group of hotel guests bolstered the number of foreigners in attendance. Some of them plainly did not know what to think of the event. Most missed the irony when a local *fokisi,* Tongan prostitute, danced a *lakalaka* — a traditional Tongan dance — to raise money for her *fakaleiti* friends.

Money from the cover charge and the fund-raising dances will be used to hold a party for the *fakaleiti* community and their friends, a spokesman said.

The audience proved to be well behaved through the performances. One drunk stumbled out onto the floor to harass one of the performers, but found himself quickly being escorted away by a grey-uniformed policeman.

The crowd, including many friends and relatives of the performers, was predominantly a female one. When the house band turned back to its own brand of Polynesian Rock after the last dance routine, the spectators were not to be denied their chance to dance. Finding not enough male partners, the women simply danced with each other.

There were plenty of partners outside the hotel, peering in trying to get a good view of the dance floor. But they would not pay the one pa'anga cover charge to come inside.

INSTITUTIONALIZED HOMOSEXUALITY OF THE MOHAVE INDIANS

BY GEORGE DEVEREUX

Department of Anthropology, University of California

THE present body of data has been obtained during three visits to the Mohave Indians, who live at present at Parker, Arizona and Needles, California. Both towns are part of their former habitat.

In view of the fact that equivalent data are largely absent, even from the Yuma who are the next of kin of the Mohave, the present paper will be limited to a discussion of Mohave data.

Mohave sex-life is entirely untrammelled by social restraint and no phase of sex, with the exception of procreation and the introduction to the status of an acknowledged homosexual, has been surrounded with any appreciable amount of observances.

Homosexuality among the Mohave has been reported by the earliest travellers in that region.[1] Although there is little or no objection to homosexuality among the Mohave at present there is no avowed homosexual living on the reservation. This is not surprising in view of the fact that the Mohave at present number less than 500, according to information obtained from the Superintendent of the Colorado River Indian Agency. Nevertheless gossip will have it that certain persons indulge in secret homosexuality. Three men, two of whom are uterine brothers, are at present accused of active and passive homosexuality. One of the two half-brothers is said to be highly intelligent. His adolescence appears to have been somewhat peculiar. At the age of seventeen or eighteen he acted "funny, like a woman." They even accuse him of active sex-relations with a white man, while he was at a certain Indian School outside of the reservation.

[1] FORDE, C. DARYLL. Ethnography of the Yuma Indians. *University of California Publications in American Archaeology and Ethnology,* Vol. 28, page 96 (quoting the old Spanish traveller FONT), 1931.

His uterine brother lives in the same house with another man suspected of homosexuality. They are usually referred to as each other's wives and are said to indulge in rectal intercourse.

All the above-mentioned men are in their early thirties. None of them however has officially submitted to the transvestite initiation ceremony.

Casual homosexual relations in early childhood were frequent in the past and, according to my informants, seem to be on the increase at the present time. "Nowadays the kids at school don't get a chance to play with the opposite sex and therefore they go off into the bushes and copulate with other boys or other girls." But even in the past mutual masturbation, urinating competitions, measurements of phalli, etc., have been quite frequent. Complete nudity and lack of any kind of supervision, especially of boys, who remained naked until they reached puberty, combined with incessant sexual talk on the part of adults, must have furthered the desire for sex-experience. Water-games were especially favorable for sexual intimacy, which, however, seldom if ever led to actual sex-relations in the water because the Mohave believe that intercourse in the water causes a certain disease in women.

Children banded off in mixed groups composed of boys as well as girls. They exhibited their genitalia, poked fun at each other's conformation and referred to each other by sobriquets derived from the size or conformation of their respective genitalia, such as "sharp, crooked, blunt or stubby penis". Not seldom older boys got hold of one of their comrades, pulled back his foreskin and smeared mud on the exposed gland. Mutual masturbation was not absent but rather uncommon. Older boys, however, often performed forced rectal intercourse on their younger playmates. Fellatio was rare, but not entirely absent.

Masturbating and urinating competitions were frequent. In masturbating competitions both the shortness of the time required to cause ejaculation and the distance at which the sperma was projected was taken into consideration. Urinating competitions consisted of urinating figures and letters on the ground.

Adults seldom had sexual intercourse with children of their own sex, although betrothal of young girls to old men or seduction of very young boys by adult women was not rare.

A Walapai Indian of about twenty-five years of age went to hunt with a twelve year old Walapai boy. He was an inveterate homosexual and had intercourse with the boy in a wash. When they returned to the settlement the boy had such pains in his rectum that he could not sit down. His parents menaced him with a whipping if he did not sit down. They also refused to give him food until then, thinking he was being naughty. At last the boy broke down and confessed the events of the hunting expedition. The parents prosecuted the offender, who ran away into the Mohave territory, because the Walapai speak a similar language and are really of our own kind. They held a trial at Kingman. The Mohave policeman from Parker went to arrest the man. He found him at Topock and brought him back handcuffed. He was sent to prison.

No similar Mohave case has been reported, and the Walapai Indian's actions were severely condemned.

Homosexual activities of children were not considered to be truly homosexual, but dismissed as mere infantile naughtiness. Nor was the man in the case-history about to be reported considered a homosexual.

Kwiskwinay had been sentenced to a term in prison, for burying alive the newborn child of his sister, partly because that was the customary way of killing half-breeds, and partly because his sister's Mexican husband deserted her and denied the paternity of the child. In prison Kwiskwinay had anal intercourse with a white prisoner. "First the white man 'bent over', then I did", he has been reported as saying. Upon his release he often complained of diarrhoea, explaining that the great phallus of the white man hurt him. A niece of Kwiskwinay describes him as a "kind man, but d- - -n impulsive". (It may be noted here that according to information obtained from the Mohave, as well as from the late Anna Israel-Nettle M. D., the genitalia of the Mohave male are small in size when compared to the genitalia of the average Caucasian or to the size of the vagina of Mohave women.)

Another example of what is not considered homosexuality by the Mohave will be drawn from the early life-history of future shamans. Such boys are very unruly and not seldom "pull back their penis between their legs and then display themselves to women, saying 'I too am a woman, I am just like you are' "

TYPES OF HOMOSEXUALS

The Mohave recognize only two definite types of homosexuals. Male transvestites, taking the rôle of the woman in sexual intercourse, are known as alyha·. Female homosexuals, assuming the rôle of the male, are known as hwame·.[2] Their partners are not considered homosexuals,

[2] Kroeber, A. L. Handbook of the Indians of California. *Bureau of American Ethnology,* Bulletin No. 78, p. 748, 1925.

and from the evidence of our case-histories appear to have been invariably persons of bisexual tendencies, who did not go through any formal initiation and were not designated by any special name.

While there exists no mention of any transvestite Mohave culture-hero comparable to the culture-hero of the kindred Kamia,[3] homosexuality and the initiation-ceremonies thereto pertaining are mentioned in the creation-myth—the only other section dealing with things sexual being concerned with procreation and the intimately related puberty ceremonies.

The following account was obtained from the late N̄ahwera, an almost senile singer, said to be the last person to know the transvestite initiation songs. It has been further expanded by several other informants. Neither the above-mentioned singer nor the informants in question were homosexuals.

"From the very beginning of the world it was meant that there should be homosexuals, just as it was instituted that there should be shamans. They were intended for that purpose. While their mothers are pregnant, they will have the usual dreams forecasting the anatomic sex of their child. Thus the mothers of alyha· dream of arrow-feathers and other male appurtenances, while the mothers of hwame· dream of feminine regalia such as beads, etc." (This is curious in view of the fact that beginning with the sixth (lunar) month of elapsed pregnancy the foeti are said to be conscious and dream of their future destinies, sharing to a certain extent their dreams with their mothers, and vice versa.) "At the same time the dreams of their mothers will also contain certain hints of the future homosexual proclivities of the child about to be born." (No data as to the nature of these "hints" could be obtained.) "For several years following birth these homosexual tendencies will remain hidden. They will come to the fore, however, previous to puberty: that is, the time when young persons become initiated into the functions of their sex, such as hunting or cooking, respectively. None but young people will become berdaches as a rule. Their tendencies will become apparent early enough to cause them to be tattooed in accordance with the tattooing pattern pertaining to their adopted sex. Once a young person started off 'right' there is no danger of his or her becoming homosexual (alyha· or hwame·) even if occasional unions with homosexuals should occur. They will feel toward their possible transvestite mate as they would feel toward a true woman, respectively man."

This point is crucial. The transvestite must attempt to duplicate the behavior-pattern of his adopted sex and make "normal" individuals

---

[3] Gifford, E. W. The Kamia of Imperial Valley. *Bureau of American Ethnology*, Bulletin No. 97, p. 12, 1931.

of his anatomic sex feel toward him as though he truly belonged to his adopted sex. Forde[4] describes this situation very accurately. "When he (i.e. the transvestite) came out of the dream, he put his hand to his mouth and laughed four times. He laughed with a woman's voice and his mind was changed from male into female. Other young people noticed this and began to feel toward him as to a woman."

Any person who dreamt about becoming a transvestite while in the maternal womb may turn into one. They then attend to the occupation-pattern of their adopted sex, except that female transvestites may not be tribal or war-leaders. Social status however seemed to play a certain rôle. One female informant, herself a member of a chiefly family, stated that only persons classified as ipa tahana (person really, i.e. member of a prominent family) became transvestites, as a rule. Conversely it was said that only "normal" persons possessing special powers, especially shamans specializing in the cure of venereal diseases and credited with special luck in love, may secure transvestite spouses.

OTHER DETERMINANTS OF HOMOSEXUALITY

Beyond the factor of predestination, other factors also influenced the decision of certain persons to become transvestites.

"The chief may hold gatherings and people became transvestites through his (spiritual) power." This statement has never been explained. "In recent times a certain youth at Needles became a homosexual through listening to the alyha· songs of N̄ahwera, who sang his songs at feasts and funerals." (Any song may be sung on those occasions.) "That youth was a relative of my husband. Eventually he got sores about his rectum and died. Now N̄ahwera does not like to sing his songs any more."

"A boy may begin to act strangely just as he is about to reach puberty. At that time other boys try to act like grown-ups and imitate their elders. They handle bows and arrows, ride horses and hunt, and make love to little girls. These boys, however, will shun such tasks. They pick up dolls and toy with metates just as girls do. They refuse to play with the toys of their own sex. Nor will they wear a breech-clout. They ask for skirts instead. They will watch a woman's gambling game which we call the Utah-game—as though they were under a spell. This game will fascinate them. They will try to participate in this game whenever they see it." (This game consists in throwing four dice, one of which is called "male" because it is painted black, and another "female", because it is painted red. The fall of these dice is accompanied by much obscene comment. When the red die falls on top of the black one comments like "this woman is actively copulating with her mate" are made.)

---

[4] FORDE, C. DARYLL. *Op. cit.*, p. 157.

"Girls will act just the opposite. They like to chum with boys and adopt boys' ways. They throw away their dolls and metates, and refuse to shred bark or perform other feminine tasks. They turn away from the skirt and long for the breech-clout."

"Their parents will eventually notice this strange behavior and comment upon it. 'Well, he may be a boy, but he seems to be more interested in the ways of women'. Corresponding comments are made about boyish girls. Parents and relatives will sometimes try to bully them into normal behavior—especially the girls, but they soon realize that nothing can be done about it. 'If our child wishes to go that way, the only thing we can do is make it adopt the status of a transvestite.' They are not proud of having a transvestite in the family, because transvestites are considered somewhat crazy."

After the above information had been obtained a trip was taken to Needles by the present writer, his interpreter and his chief informant, to obtain the four alyha· songs from Ñahwera. The following is his account. The songs themselves are in a very old-fashioned Mohave, almost unintelligible to the younger generation and consisting of mere catchwords, in accordance with the customary Mohave style of singing.

Ever since the world began at the magic mountain Avi-kwame· it was said that there would be transvestites. In the beginning, if they were to become transvestites, the process started during their intra-uterine life. When they grew up they were given toys according to their sex. They did not like these toys however. At the beginning, the God Matavilye died at Avi-kwame·, not because he had to die, but because he wanted to set mankind an example. There is the house. He is on his death-bed and people are all around him. He tells them that their lives would be different, and some among them would turn into transvestites. Then Matavilye died. All the people went their own way but Matavilye loved mankind so much that, although he was already on his way to heaven, he returned to be cremated in our fashion. Had he not returned to us, we would have been just like the Whites: evil, cruel and grasping. He cared for us so much that he returned to be cremated on earth. If a ghost comes to visit the earth he does it because he likes the earth very much. If from underneath the cremation pit a whirlwind rises, it means a soul went in there, because it thought so much of the earth. Then all things begin in that death-house. When there is a desire in a child's heart to become a transvestite that child will act different. It will let people become aware of that desire. They may insist on giving the child the toys and garments of its true sex, but the child will throw them away and do this every time there is a big gathering. Then people prepare a skirt of shredded bark for the boy or a breech-clout for the girl. If they give them the garments worn by other members of their sex they will turn away from them. They do all they can to dissuade girls who show such inclinations. But if they fail to convince her they will realize that it cannot be helped. She will be chumming with men and be one of them. Then all those who have tried to change her conduct will gather and agree that they had done all that could be done and that the only thing for them to do was to give her the status of a transvestite.

These female transvestites (hwame·) are like lewd women who also throw away their house-keeping implements, and run wild. These songs are called alyha· kwayum or alyha· kupama and are for boys. The singer refers to himself as Pameas and describes their actions in these songs.

These are the four songs.

(1) Akueña / ahvayatco / kwetokoñe / kanava / avera / tovara / ku-añaye / huyaytatkohav / touama / iðauav / vovaa / iðaui / kanava / avakwiðaui / avavono / kaviya / epatcomitcam / tcoom / kwaava / eekanava / veevaua /

(1′) To twist / make dress / front part / tell of it / finished / wants it / light (bright) / take up the skirt and tie it in front / around / take / (describing immediate action) / take / tell of it / all listening / now all hear / then / people gathered there / all / hear / tell of it / standing.

(1″) This song describes how to put on a skirt and tie the string around the waist and how not to tie it on the side. Now all are here to see and hear and if you cannot help acting that way, then act that way, so that all may see what you are.

(Interpreter comments: "This transvestite fellow is now as happy as a bug, because he got a skirt.")

(2) Pamekwa / ñiha / lakuye / ñivatce / iðoma / ñivatce / nalye / ava / hiðaua / mataramkutcatc / hatciñe / kopama / kwi-yahve / tcinvakwa / ava / hevatce / nalya / .

(2′) People / by being looked at / proud / traipse or waddle / turning to / that side / they / all hear / a flat stretch of ground which is still damp / unmenstruated girl / dancing back and forth / dances stooping / even if girl (unmenstruated) / feels / she dances / that side / .

(2″) This describes the hwame· (?) who, proud of being stared at, traipses and dances back and forth in a stooped posture over a flat stretch of damp land. That is how she acts if she is to be a true hwame· (?).

(3) ñikatño / memkwiya / ñikatcivas / viya / ñikatco / ðoraviya / ivamavi / ivaua / iðaua voova / iðaua / ñikatcolok / isto / ivatce / nalya / ðauave / veðeye / kaanava / toomtcoya-toomtcoðome / amayamtcuya / kaanava / hatciñma / kopama / itcavono / ihatim / añoorä / ñorávo-vonova / ñoravova / hatciñekwo / ava / hañorám / vono / kawimaava /

(3′) Advances / stalking / advances / furtively / advances / sneakingly / reaches / there / stands and takes it / takes it / furtively cuts in pieces / gathers / backing / away / takes it / comes back / tells of it. / Divides them (dice) / tosses up / tells of it / girl / stoops (dances) / gathers / will split / paints / in the act of painting / ready to paint / girl (unmenstruated) / hear / in the act of painting / can't make "her" (male transvestite is meant) do otherwise / .

(3") (This song refers to the attraction of the split-stick dice-game for the future male transvestite.) "He advances stealthily toward the willow, he stands there and cuts the branches and gathers them up. He tells about it. He divides them up, he tosses them up and tells the girls about it. He stoops, gathers the pieces, splits them, paints them and the girls hear of it. He cannot do otherwise".

(Interpreter's comment: "If he were a man he would be painting arrows, not dice.")

(4) Hatom / askilye askilyem / kaanavam / kunovum / awi / askilaskil / vonokowi /

(4') Spit / marks / zig-zags / tells of it / tells of it / ? / marks / doing it.

(4") This song describes the patterns painted on the dice.

The nature of the present songs is perhaps doubtful. They were said to describe the ceremony of initiation, and indeed the songs quoted by Kroeber[5] are somewhat different, However Kroeber also mentions songs to which the transvestite dances. Whether these are the songs in question is open to debate. The remark "anyone is free to learn these songs and the ceremony" leads the present writer to believe that these songs are sung during the initiation. The question is one on which he would not care to dogmatize. N̄ahwera was senile and toothless. The presence of the main informant was necessary, because he had heard the songs before and could pronounce the words clearly after hearing them. However, the fact that the latter was a shaman and believed to be a witch so excited N̄ahwera that ever since he avoided the three of us to the great amusement of the reservation.

The ceremony in question appears to have been a sanctioning of the inevitable, which is typical of almost any human society.

The scene at the initiation is vividly described in these songs. The future transvestite is the centre of interest. Just what rôle the chance of "showing off" at any price may play in the psychology of a child entering upon this momentous decision, need not be discussed here.

CEREMONY OF INITIATION

We possess three accounts of the ceremony in question. The general patterns of all accounts are similar, but the differences are by no means negligible. It is suggested tentatively that Mohave ritualism is extremely

[5] KROEBER, A. L. *Op cit.*, p. 748.

loose, and that in the case of a comparatively rarely performed semi-private ceremony considerable variations were likely to occur. Furthermore the time element must be taken into consideration. The ceremony in question has not been performed for several decades. It has been thought best to quote all available versions.

The following account has been published by Kroeber.[6]

Four men who have dreamed about the ceremony are sent for, and spend the night in the house, twisting cords and gathering shredded bark for the skirt the prospective *alyha* will thereafter wear. The youth himself lies, with two women sitting by him. As they twist the cords, the men sing:

ihatnya vudhi........ roll it this way.
ihatnya va'ama....... roll it that way.

When the petticoat nears completion:

istum................ I hold it.
icham............... I place it.
hilyuvik............. it is done.
havirk............... it is finished.
ka'avek.............. hear!
kidhauk.............. listen!

These songs the singers dreamed when they were with the god Mastamho, and during the night they tell and sing of how they saw him ordering the first performance of this ceremony.

In the morning the two women lift the youth and take him outdoors. One of the singers puts on the skirt and dances to the river in four steps, the youth following and imitating. Then all bathe. Thereupon the two women give the youth the front and back pieces of his new dress and paint his face white. After four days he is painted again and then is an *alyha.* Such persons speak, laugh, smile, sit, and act like women. They are lucky at gambling, say the Mohave, but die young. It is significant that a variety of venereal sickness which they treat is also called *alyha.*

Sometimes, but more rarely, a girl took on man's estate, among both Yuma and Mohave, and was then known as *hwami,* and might marry women. There was no ceremony to mark her new status.

The next two accounts were obtained by the present writer.

The first was obtained from an old woman of about eighty, who was not herself a hwame·. She stated that she had heard of this ceremony from a woman who in her youth used to be on friendly terms with an alyha·. "She always thought that this alyha· was really a woman, until the transvestite lifted something one day and as the fibers of the bark-

[6] KROEBER, A. L. *Op. cit.,* pp. 748-749.

skirt parted his penis became visible. My friend was aghast when she noticed that her *girl-friend* had a penis and testes. This transvestite told her about the ceremony, and she told me about it." (It is to be suspected that the "astonishment" was a mere flower of speech, in view of the fact that sex and transvestites are regularly discussed.)

"The ceremony was held on a flat stretch of land. The crowd foregathered on both sides of the terrain. On one side were the women with the skirt and on the other the boy with the singer. The singer sang and the boy danced. When this part of the ceremony was over, the singer explained to the boy every part of the feminine wearing apparel. Since not all women know how to make a dress, the singer had chosen beforehand some capable woman to make the initiate's dress. The alyha· was then taken to the river where he bathed. He kept his old name. He did not assume the gentile name which is borne by the females in every lineage. I don't know whether or not they held ceremonies for the hwame·. I knew a hwame· once. She was dressed like a woman but she was married to other women. I have never seen the ceremony myself. They don't hold it any more."

This informant also stated that the hwame· did not change their name for a name of the male type, which is obviously a mistake, as is apparent from the name of the hwame· Sahaykwisa (contraction of masahay: childless girl or woman; and matwisa·: soul or shadow, i.e. girl's shadow, which is a typically male name.)

It is true however that no male transvestite adopted a gentile name. Tampering with gentile affiliations and with the quasi-sanctity of the perpetuation of the lineages and of the tribe, by dragging it into the humoristically viewed homosexual cluster, would have been repulsive to the Mohave.

In ancient times the hwame· wore male garments.

The next account was obtained from a "normal" male shaman, an unusually well informed and willing informant. He derived most of his knowledge on this subject from a long friendship with the late Kuwal, who had married several alyha·. Kuwal's history will be reported at the end of the present paper.

"The boys who became alyha· were initiated fairly early. They did not have their noses pierced, because they did not go through the male puberty ritual." (This would place the tranvestite initiation as early as the tenth or eleventh year of age.) A subsidiary informant also claimed that if a man was found to have submitted to rectal intercourse he was compelled to undergo the initiation, but this statement has been unanimously discredited. (Curiously enough, it was said that some women became hwame· after having borne a child.)

"When the child was about ten years old his relatives would begin discussing his strange ways. Some of them disliked it, but the more intelligent began envisaging an initiation ceremony. They prepared in secret the female wearing apparel. There was no singing, lest the boy should discover what was going on. Then they asked a singer to perform the ceremony on a certain day. They did not want the boy to know of it ahead of time. The ceremony was meant to take him by surprise. It was considered both an initiation and an ultimate test of his true inclinations. If he submitted to it he was considered a genuine homosexual. Word was sent to various settlements, inviting people to attend the ceremony. They wanted them to see it and become accustomed to seeing the boy in a woman's dress." (Such "accustoming" feasts were also held when someone lost an eye.) "The time and place were set by mutual accord of the boy's family and relatives. There was no feasting, only a gathering which was held early in the morning. If the boy acted in the expected fashion during the ceremony he was considered an initiated homosexual, if not, the gathering scattered, much to the relief of the boy's family."

"The singer drew a circle in the centre of the track with a pointed stick. The boy was led by two women, usually his mother and maternal grandmother, since women have more to do with children than the males, into the centre of the circle. If the boy showed willingness to remain standing in the circle, exposed to the public eye, it was almost certain that he would go through with the ceremony. The singer, hidden behind the crowd, began singing the songs. As soon as the sound reached the boy he began to dance as women do. Gradually the singer approached the dancer. The dance-steps do not change, except insofar as the boy plays a pantomime in accordance with the text of the songs. Were the boy unwilling to become a homosexual officially, he would refuse to dance. As it is, the song goes right to his heart and he will dance with much intensity. He cannot help it. After the fourth song he is proclaimed a homosexual. The same women who led him into the circle, accompanied by other women, take him down to the Colorado River. After a bath he receives his skirt. He is then led back to the dance-ground, dressed as a woman and the crowd scatters. The same ceremony is enacted for the hwame who then dons the breech-clout."

As may be seen from the three versions presented they are complementary rather than divergent, except for minor details.

The effects of the ceremony were permanent. Just how far the chance of making a display of himself in front of a crowd of adults may have swayed a boy with some bisexual tendencies, is not easy to decide.

The initiated transvestites then assumed a name befitting a person of the opposite sex. They resented afterwards being called by their former names. The Mohave change their names fairly often and resent being called by their discarded names. "They get tired of their old names." A curious feature of Mohave name-giving may be mentioned here. Persons often assume names which are a slur on or a reference to the opposite sex, or an uncomplimentary remark upon certain habits of other persons. A certain man is known by the name of hiθpan utce· (vagina charcoal) and a woman called herself hama utce· (testicle charcoal) in retaliation.

It is emphatically stated by the Mohave that the ceremony did not operate the change in the initiate's personal habits. It was merely a test and a public acknowledgment of the shift from one sex to the other. I pointed out elsewhere that the Mohave believe that at creation and during the early periods of the mythical era there existed sexually undifferentiated stages. Thus it was not too great an effort for them to believe in the reality of such a shift.

Nowadays homosexuals do not don the garb of the opposite sex. The woman responsible for the first version of the above ceremony made the following statement.

"Years ago I knew a man who was very effeminate. He did not go through the ceremony, because it was no longer held. He always sat down the way women do and disposed his breech-clout the way women do when they sit in the Turkish posture, or with one leg folded (or tucked) under them. He probably thought he was concealing his vulva. One of my relatives was a hwame·. She had small breasts and wore a breech-clout." (She had stated that no hwame· wore a breech-clout. Cf. above.)

Since the hwame· rode and hunted, she had to wear the male garb. Sahaykwisa however wore a skirt and shoes, because occasionally she was prostituted to white men. She had big breasts, but never bore a child. One informant stated that alyha· "had red stripes painted across their bellies", red being the women's paint par excellence. Sahaykwisa occasionally painted herself black, like a warrior on the warpath.

No mention is made of any physiological deformity in homosexuals. The "small breasts" referred to above were bigger than those of an immature girl, and were probably termed small in comparison with the big pendulous breasts of the average Mohave woman. The woman informant and others stated that the hwame· menstruated only sporadically, but were not certain about it. No hwame· ever bore a child after assuming that status. The same woman informant stated that the alyha· had no erection, which is disproved by the case history of Kuwal. There is no mention of an abnormal clitoris. The most careful and repeated inquiry over a period of several years did not elicit any suggestion of anal masturbation in the case of alyha·. Both vaginal and clitoridal masturbation was practiced by both normal and homosexual women. It was stated that the alyha· had erections during anal intercourse, whenever it was performed upon them, but resented it if their partners touched their erect penes, although letting them manipulate them in the flaccid state. Whether all alyha· had emissions of sperma during anal intercourse performed on them has never been ascertained.

PHYSIOLOGICAL PATTERN ASSUMED BY HOMOSEXUALS

One of the most peculiar aspects of institutionalized homosexuality is the imitation of the physiological pattern of the assumed sex by homosexuals. They resented any normal nomenclature applied to their genitalia. Alyha· insisted that their penis (moδar) be called a clitoris (havalik), their testes (hama·), labia maiora (havakwit), and their anus (hivey), vagina (hiθpan). The hwame· equally resented any reference to the fact that they had vulvae, but it was not stated that they insisted on a corresponding male terminology. It is interesting to note that according to anatomic and embryologic observations the penis and clitoris, the rectum and the vagina, the scrotum and the labia are histologically of the same origin, the rectum and the vagina being formed from the hind gut of the embryo.

Since homosexuals resented such references, they were often teased in that fashion. "Just as a man would not like to be told he had a cunnus or a woman that she had a penis, so an alyha· resented references to his penis, and a hwame· remarks upon her vagina." (A certain Mohave man, upon being asked by his wife to bring her some water, exclaimed: "Perhaps I have a cunnus and should don your skirt too. Give me your skirt and you can have my breech-clout and go hunting.") "You can tease an hwame·, because she is just a woman, but if you tease an alyha·, who has the strength of a man, he will run after you and beat you up. He will assault you many days later, if he could not catch you at once." "A certain man passing by the house of an alyha· said to him in jest, 'How is your penis today?' 'Not penis, cunnus', replied the alyha· angrily. 'Well then, how big is your cunnus?' the man replied, using the word "erection" instead of "big". The alyha· picked up a club and for one or two weeks tried to assault the man whenever he saw him."

Intercourse with an alyha· is surrounded by an etiquette all of its own, to which the partner had better conform "lest one should get into all sorts of trouble."

"This is what Kuwal, who had several alyha· wives, told me," the shaman said. "Kuwal had rectal and oral intercourse with his alyha· wives, but if you copulate too often rectally with an alyha· he will get hemorrhoids, just as our women do when we have too much anal intercourse with them. You may play with the penis of your *wife* when it is flaccid. I often did it, saying, 'Your cunnus is so nice and big and your pubic hair is nice and soft to touch'. Then my alyha· wife would loll about, giggling happily like this, 'hhh'. *She* was very much pleased with herself and me. *She* liked to be told about her cunnus. When alyha· get an erection, it embarrasses them, because the penis sticks out between the loose fibers of the bark-skirt. They used to have erections when we had intercourse. Then I would put my arm about them and play with the erect penis, even though they hated it. I was careful not to laugh aloud, but I chuckled inwardly. At the pitch of intercourse the alyha· ejaculate."

"Kuwal used to tell about these things in public. When we asked him why he did not tell his alyha· wife that *she* had an erection, he used to say, 'I would not dare do it. *She* would kill me. I never dared touch the penis in erection, except during intercourse. You'd court death if you did it otherwise, because they would get violent if you play with their erect penis too much'."

It is noteworthy that in English all Mohave refer to an alyha· as *she* and to a hwame· as *he*. This becomes quite confusing to the field-worker, at times, but also proves the highly institutionalized character of this cultural complex.

When an alyha· found a husband, he would begin to imitate menstruation. He took a stick and scratched himself between the legs until blood was drawn. This he referred to as "catamenial flow" and submitted to the whole set of puberty observances, then as well as during subsequent "menstruations". According to the Mohave pattern, when a man marries an unmenstruated girl he has to share a great deal of her puberty taboos when she menstruates for the first time. Since the alyha· claimed this to be his first menstruation, the husband had to submit *nolens volens* to the whole set of observances.

Even more curious are the pretensions of alyha· concerning their hypothetical pregnancies. When they decided to become "pregnant" they ceased faking menstruations. They observed the customary pregnancy taboos as rigidly or even more so than normal women, conforming to many obsolescent customs even, and compelling their husbands to observe their share of taboos, as befits expectant fathers. They publicly boasted of their pregnancy, even though many Mohave women deny being pregnant, even when it has become obvious to all and sundry that they were pregnant. This gave rise to never ending jests, but the alyha· paid no attention to them. In only one way did they fail to conform to the usual pregnancy pattern. Having no other means at their disposal, they continued oral and rectal intercourse with their husbands, even though the former is alleged to harm the foetus' glottis and the latter his bowels. In the absence of their husbands they stuffed rags and bark under their skirts, in increasing quantities, to make their abdomen protrude. In due time they made a decoction of mesquite beans which is said to cause sever constipation. They drank this decoction by sucking it through their teeth, which acted as a sieve and prevented the swallowing of bean-fragments.

Eventually they had severe abdominal pains for a day or two, which they dubbed labour-pains. When the faeces could not longer be withheld the alyha· went into the bushes and defecated sitting over a hole in the traditional posture of parturating women. They had no assistants, and leaned therefore against a tree, as did women who were in travail before any feminine help could be obtained. The faeces were said to be thick, dry and friable and caused a bleeding of the rectum. They then pretended that stillbirth had taken place and buried the faeces and a little log. After that they returned to the house and claimed to have given birth to a stillborn child. They had to pretend it was a stillbirth, because stillborn babies are buried whereas those dying are cremated publicly, and "such ceremonies are past joking". Yet people would hear the alyha· wailing and mourning for the imaginary child. They clipped their hair and compelled their husbands to clip their hair in the fashion befitting the mourners. Since the Mohave never made any preparations for birth, because boys and girls had to have different cradles, no problem arose from the disposal of empty cradles.

"People used to tease me about my wives' imaginary children," Kuwal is reported as saying. "When I walked about with friends and spoke with regret of the real children I had once and of my beautiful Cocopa and Yuma wives who were real women, they used to say, 'We know all about your beautiful wives. You married those alyha· and believed them when they scratched themselves and pretended to be menstruating, or when they were pregnant with a pillow.' Or else they would kick a pile of animal dung and say, 'Those are your children'. And yet I had real children once and they died. Were they not dead they would now take care of me in my old age."

COURTSHIP

Alyha· were not courted like ordinary girls. The man did not go to the alyha·'s house or to the house of his parents, and sleep beside him in chastity for a night or two, before leading him away to his home. They were courted at gatherings like widows, divorcées or lewd women (kamaloy). Either the man or the alyha· may initiate the flirtation. It is not impossible however that for the sake of creating a comical situation, a thing paramount in the Mohave pursuit of sexual pleasure, on occasion a man went through the habitual courtship for an alyha·, because it appealed to his sense of the preposterous. Casual meetings also led to such unions. "A man went to swim. In the water an alyha· seized his penis. 'What do you want,' the man asked briskly. He was so angry that later on he went to the house of the alyha· and asked him how his penis was that day." (Cf. above for the rest of the incident.)

At dances even boys who had no intention of marrying an alyha· played around with them, as though they were flirtatious women. "In the end some of them made up their minds to become the husbands of an alyha·".

Once they were married the alyha· made exceptionally industrious wives. At every step the Mohave emphasize the lure of feminine occupations for future alyha·, a point which has hitherto been neglected in the study of precipitating causes in homosexuality. We shall come back to this point later. At any rate the certitude of a well-kept home may have induced many a Mohave to set up house with an alyha·. Having a well-kept house is not an easy problem among the Mohave who have young wives. "Girls cannot be counted upon to settle down", a woman said. The desire for good food and a well-kept household induced many Mohave to marry older women, even their former mothers-in-law, because old women were anxious to work hard to please their young husbands and make up by good food for their aged charms.

Divorcing an alyha· was not an easy matter. "They are so strong that they might beat you up", Kuwal used to say. "Some men who had enough of it tried to get rid of them politely, alleging barrenness of the alyha·. But no alyha· would admit such a thing. They would begin to fake pregnancy."

It may be said that the Mohave indulge in so much anal intercourse with women, that being the proper way to prepare immature girls for marriage, and even later on "even though the rectum of a woman is just like a man's rectum", and also indulge in so much fellatio, that they were able to obtain as much pleasure with an alyha· wife as with a woman. (hivey añie·nm, anus intercourse; ya tcahaetk, fellatio).

That, combined with the incessant search for new thrills in travel, war, love and humour, induced Mohave men to set up housekeeping with alyha· wives.

However, since the husband of the alyha· had to bear the brunt of the jokes that flew right and left in his presence, such unions were not stable, even when compared to the very unstable normal marriages. They seldom teased the alyha· himself. "He was an alyha·, he could not help it." But the husband of an alyha· had no such excuse and was fair game to all and sundry.

Returning to the hwame· they had no possibility of duplicating the male physiological pattern except in a single instance. The Mohave believe that by intercourse with an already pregnant woman the paternity of the child changes. Whenever a hwame· succeeded in getting a pregnant woman, she claimed the paternity of the child and took care of it with pride and loved it very sincerely. However the tribe did not recognize the change in gentile affiliation in that case, as it did in the case when a pregnant woman left her husband for another man. As we said before, gentile continuity is past joking.[7]

Intercourse between the hwame· and her wife was varied in scope, ranging from digital immission and fake intercourse with the wife in supine posture and the hwame· on top, to a special posture referred to as

---

[7] Devereux, Georg. Der Begriff der Vaterschaft bei den Mohave Indianern. *Zeitschrift für Ethnologie,* in press, 1937. Contains a discussion of fictitious and plural paternities where promiscuous women are involved.

hiθpan kuδape (vaginae split). The wife was stretched out in the supine posture. The hwame· lies with her head in the opposite direction, one of her legs under the wife's body, the other on top of it. In this posture of interlocking scissors the vulvae touched. Sometimes the posture was modified and the torsoes brought close together. No cunnilinctus (hiθpan ata·uk) was ever practiced among the Mohave, although they know that it occurs among the Whites. This absence is due to the horror of the vaginal odor. Kuwal often got into trouble by exclaiming, "Phew, you women smell like fish".

The hwame· got their wives usually at dances or by visiting girls and married women during the day. They never dared to try the ordinary courtship, because of the girl's parents.

The hwame· were excellent providers and took pride in dressing up their wives. Sahaykwisa who was a shaman earned good money and went to the length of prostituting herself to Whites to be able to keep her wives in comfort. Living with an industrious hwame· may have held some lure for a woman who had some experience with flighty, lazy and spendthrift husbands. "In their free time the hwame· would attend gatherings, and speak of the genitalia of their wives and mistresses as do salacious men. But then, no one ever expected a hwame· to behave herself. She would sit among the men and describe the vulva and the pubic hair of her wife."

Naturally the hwame· did not observe their own menses, but submitted to the taboos of the husband of a menstruating or pregnant wife.

Hwame· were divorced by their wives more often than they divorced them. Divorce consists simply of leaving the spouse. Their wives were usually teased until they could not bear it any longer, and naturally a hwame· was not physically in a position to fight with strong men. However Sahaykwisa once made the pretence of going on the warpath against the abductor of her wife, and since she was at the same time a shaman capable of witchcraft, she was comparatively safer than most other hwame· who were not feared.

No alyha· is reported ever having had intercourse with a woman. Some women however turned hwame· after they had a child. It was hinted that painful childbirth may not have been foreign to this decision. Occasionally a hwame· was raped or even prostituted, as was the case with Sahaykwisa.

PSYCHOLOGICAL PATTERNS

Transvestites were said to be lucky at gambling, and the Mohave did not share the belief of some other Yuman tribes that they died young. Transvestites were exceptionally powerful shamans, especially the hwame·. Kroeber's statement that the alyha· cured the venereal disease known as alyha· could not be substantiated by the present writer. It would be impossible in the present article to go into the psychological reasons of this alleged superiority of power, except for two hints. Shamanism is linked with weird things and odd behavior, including pre-natal phantasies and homicidal and suicidal impulses, the latter caused by longing for permanent reunion with the ghosts of the beloved victims of their witchcraft, with whom they have intercourse in dream. This situation has been roughly outlined in an article of the present writer on Mohave Soul Concepts.[8] The other hint refers to the intra-uterine and birth-phantasies of shamans, described by Roheim[9] and Kroeber[10] and not unlike similar phantasies of schizophrenics, according to verbal confirmation of the present writer's impressions by Dr. Bettina Warburg.

Conversely, shamans specializing in the cure of hikupk (syphilis), were lucky in love and had no difficulty in obtaining homosexual spouses. Kuwal was a hikupk shaman.

Homosexuals, according to the belief that witches always bewitch persons they are fond of sexually and otherwise, mainly bewitched persons of their own anatomic sex, and dreamed of intercourse with the ghosts of their victims. This was not harmful as would be the case if they were not shamans, in which case they would be afflicted with the dread ghost-weylak disease. For a normal person to dream of homosexual relations also causes weylak, which is usually fatal. Our woman informant's daughter, aged about 40, died of this disease shortly after she reported the following dream to the present writer: "I dreamt women wanted to have intercourse with me. They were close relatives or friends. I knew they were women, but they acted like men. They pulled my skirt up, threw me and tried to get on top of me. I fought them off and intercourse was never performed on me. I expect to get very sick,

---

[8] DEVEREUX, GEORGE. Mohave soul concepts. *American Anthropologist*, n.s., Vol. 39, 1937.

[9] ROHEIM, GEZA. Psycho-Analysis of primitive cultural types. *The International Journal of Psycho-Analysis*, Vol. 13, pts. I-II, pp. 187-188, 193-194, 1932.

[10] KROEBER, A. L. *Op. cit.*, p. 754. Cf. also KROEBER, A. L. Earth-Tongue, a Mohave. In "American Indian Life". E. C. Parsons, Ed. Pp. 190, 201, 1925.

because the fact that they were relatives makes the dream doubly bad." (Men never allow women to get on top of them, which happens only when women abuse a dead-drunk man.)

Turning to the status of homosexuals, we shall find that it is of a somewhat complex nature. They were, so far as the alyha· are concerned, rather peaceful persons, except when taunted. Interpreter stated, "My husband is far too kind. I always tell him that he is so stupidly kind that if anyone wished to have rectal intercourse with him, he would go down on all four and spread his buttocks." (The man in question is not a homosexual, but a person of an exceptionally kind and sunny disposition, even for a Mohave, which is a great deal to say.)

The alyha· were said to be cowards. The word "malyhaek" (thou art a coward) clearly shows this belief. It may not be beside the point to recall in this connection the lure feminine pursuits are said to possess for the alyha· and the fact that the Mohave were exceptionally warlike and adventuresome and prized bravery above many other virtues, and next to power obtained in dream. Except when retaliating for a raid they used to declare war upon their enemies—a procedure unknown among most aboriginals—and stood their ground to the last man against overwhelming forces. War was sport and the use of horses or guns was considered despicable. The last abortive raid of a few Mohave and Yuma against the united Maricopa and Pima, most of the latter armed with guns and on horseback, is strictly comparable to the last stand of the three hundred Spartans. Cowards were despised, and all men expected to participate in raids. Such demands were not made upon alyha·. I do not suggest that this might have had something to do with the decision of some faint-hearted boy who became an alyha·, but the possibility may be given consideration. As alyha· they could take the position of women at the yakkiδaalyk, or welcome feast for warriors returning from a raid. At that feast old women, who have lost a relative in the battle, would taunt those who did not go to war in the following manner: They prepared a penis of wood with bark wrapped around it, or merely twisted the front of their fiber-skirt into a protuberance, and walked through the crowd, poking those who had remained home between the legs, saying, "You are not a man but an alyha·". The alyha· themselves indulged in this practical joke, using mostly the above-mentioned stick, or an old club.

The alyha· and hwame· never went to war, although on occasion women insisted on accompanying a beloved husband or brother on the raid.

To call a person a "homosexual" when he is not, is a bad insult and is fiercely resented. The Mohave feel certain that a white woman whom they know and who is rather businesslike and intellectual is a hwame·. The expression "thou art a coward" (whose stem is alyha·) may be used however as a friendly taunt, or even as a joke.

The present writer's woman interpreter used to complain of his allegedly reckless driving and was called "malyhaek" by the author. She got even with him on one occasion, by inducing her cousin to drive the author and the main male informant, who were lying on the platform of an old truck, at top speed over impossible roads, shouting back at him "malyhaek". The male informant being equally afraid during that trip, author and informant kept on shouting at each other "thou art a coward" until we were all too hoarse from shouting and laughter to continue.

As a rule official homosexuals were not teased. The Mohave believe in temperamental compulsions and consider that "they cannot help it". The brunt of the inevitable joking was borne by their spouses who had no such excuse. "Kuwal married his alyha· wives because the transvestites are lucky at gambling and their luck extends to their spouses. He was a great gambler. But when people teased him about his alyha· wives he used to get angry." Some of them become so accustomed to having homosexual spouses that they don't care for normal spouses any more. We have already stated that alyha· perform fellatio. Yet when a woman asked Kuwal to allow her to perform fellatio upon him, he refused. "My penis got feelings", he objected. The woman became very angry and said, "You don't like me. You let other women (i.e. the alyha·) do it to you."

Yet, for reasons already described, alyha· had no difficulty in obtaining husbands. The essential adventuresomeness of the Mohave character, combined with their completely humoristic attitude toward sex, except where procreation is involved, together with the aforementioned reasons of economic comfort and convenience, induced many a man to become the spouse of an alyha· at least for a short time. After the dissolution of such union they could always find real wives.

Not so the hwame·. Even though women are more flighty and loose, according to the testimony of the Mohave, they were less willing to live with a hwame·. This may not be entirely due to the fact that they did not derive complete satisfaction from digital manipulations. Men not seldom shunned them afterwards, especially because these hwame· were not always young and old women are supposed to have a *sui generis* odor. Even when a young man married an old woman people said to him, "Now no young woman will want you again. You will have the smell of an old woman about your person." Furthermore the physically weaker hwame· could not protect her by physical violence against the jests of the community. The lack of satisfaction from sexual relations without children, of whom the Mohave are inordinately fond, may have been an additional factor in the brittleness of this relationship.

Nor were homosexuals considered adequate spouses. "He must be awfully hard up to marry a womanly man", or, "No man must want her, so she went to live with a hwame·", were current comments upon such unions. Nor did the community set too much faith upon their sexual satisfactions. "What can be the matter with that woman? She is quite terrible. What does she think she gets from that hwame· husband of hers?" they said about women who married hwame·. As to men, who lived with alyha· people wondered if "they really thought they were having intercourse with a woman."

Perhaps because of the greater difficulty they experienced in finding a substitute, the hwame· were more devoted spouses than were the alyha·. Here again they conform to the current pattern of their adopted sex. Mohave men are more faithful than are women, and it appears from my suicide statistics[11] that women seldom, if ever, commit suicide over the desertion of a lover, even though they kill themselves more often—or rather try to kill themselves more often—than men do at the death of a spouse. They seem to be less ready to reconcile themselves to the inevitable.

Last of all the hwame· is not safe from being raped by a practical jester, especially when she is drunk, while drunken men are seldom raped by women.

Altogether it will become apparent from the two detailed case histories about to be quoted, that the lot of the hwame· is infinitely harder than that of the alyha·.

[11] DEVEREUX, GEORGE. Mohave Suicide. Typescript report in possession of the Committee for the Study of Suicide, Inc., New York City.

SOCIAL ASPECTS

Socially speaking Mohave civilization acted wisely perhaps in acknowledging the inevitable. This airing of the abnormal tendencies of certain individuals achieved several aims. It deprived certain modes of atypical behaviour of the glamour of secrecy and sin and of the aureola of persecution. It enabled certain persons swaying on the outskirts of homosexuality to obtain the desired experience and find their way back to the average tribal pattern without the humiliation of a moral Canossa. It created what is known as an "abscess of fixation" and localized the disorder in a small area of the body social. Last of all the very publicity given to their status did not permit homosexuals to insinuate themselves into the confidence of normal persons under false colors and profit by some temporary unhappiness of the latter to sway them. They had to compete with normal blatant sexuality not in the dark groves of Corydon and Sappho but in the open daylight, on the acknowledged playground of normal sexuality, i.e. at gatherings and feasts. This arrangement, while safeguarding homosexuals from the dangers of persecution, also made their unsuccessful courtships doubly painful because of the very publicity given to it. In creating metaphorically speaking, "reserved quarters", for permanent homosexuals and for the passing whim of bisexually inclined active male homosexuals and passive female ones, they gave the latter an opportunity to satisfy their passing longings, and left the door wide open for a return to normalcy.

As for the homosexuals, the alyha· poking cowards with a bark phallus and calling him a coward, only half realising his own awkward unhappiness, serves to epitomize the whole, rather sad, picture of the status of the homosexual in almost any society.

CASE HISTORIES

It may not be unnecessary to recall here that male homosexuals were allowed among many American Indian tribes to assume officially the status of a woman. Data are very incomplete however, and seldom include actual case histories. For that reason the following two case histories have been reported with every obtainable detail, in the hope that comparable data would be obtained from other native races.

Both case histories were obtained from the same male informant, who had known in his youth Kuwal very intimately and was also acquainted with Sahaykwisa whose adventures were common knowledge at that time. He was one of the men who brought in her corpse after she was killed by drowning. Informant never had any homosexual experiences himself. The case histories were checked against the testimony of other informants, and all details were found to be correct.

Kuwal's picture may be seen in Kroeber's *Handbook of the Indians of California,* plate 65, (c), between pages 728-729. He was the last Mohave who wore a stick through his nasal septum.

The case of Kuwal

This case was reported to the present writer by the shaman Hivsu· Tupoma, who had known Kuwal in his youth.

"If you marry an alyha· you will have a hard time when you try leaving him, because he has the strength of a man and may beat you up," Kuwal told me once. Then he told me the following story:

"After I married that alyha· I went to a dance where I met a pretty girl who wanted to marry me. I liked her and flirted with her which made my alyha· wife angry. 'You carried on with me while I was having my menses and now I am pregnant', the alyha· said to me. So I continued to live with him, but carried on with the girl secretly. At last the alyha· found out about it and got very angry with me. I told him he could not bear a child anyway and went to live with my relatives.

"I had some trouble with my relatives too. I used to say when the women came near me, 'Phew, you smell like fish'. One day my hostess became very angry with me and began throwing things at me when I said it during breakfast. 'If we smell so bad you get out of here', she said. I ran away but later came back and continued to live with them. The alyha· went on looking for me and people warned me he would beat me if he found me. One day he came to the house and beat me so hard it almost laid me out. Having thus satisfied his revengeful nature he went home. I thought that this fight had appeased him and I left my relatives and went to live with that girl. A few days after my marriage the alyha· turned up at my house and wanted to fight with my wife. He was accompanied by a number of men who wanted to enjoy the sight. I was in the house and heard the noise of a fight. My wife and the alyha· were fighting in the yard outside. The alyha· was stronger than she was, being a man, but he pretended to be a weak woman and fought like women do. He did not use all his strength. He could have beaten up my wife quite easily, but he let my wife throw him several times. The men who had accompanied him were standing around snickering and shouting. They shouted to my wife, 'Be careful, *she* is with child and you might hurt the child'. My wife got very indignant and began shouting at them: 'Ah, just as you say. *She* is with child indeed. This thing here cannot have a child. *She* got a penis and testes.'

"The mother and grandmother of my wife who were sitting near by got very angry and shouted at the men, 'You brought *her* here because you knew that my daughter was no match for *her*.' 'If you throw *her* pull off *her* penis and testes', they told my wife. When the alyha heard these references to his genitalia he became very angry. He picked up a log from the camp-fire and almost succeeded in setting fire to the roof. Then he picked up a stick and tried to beat my wife with it. He might have killed her had not the men who came with him have interfered. I could not have interfered myself because a man should never mix in the quarrels of women. They got hold of the alyha· and led him away, comforting him all the while. 'You will find another husband,' they told him. They teased him the way men tease amorous women. They flirted with him."

Kuwal used to get quite melancholy when he recalled his real wife. "One time I really got a real woman and had a child by her, but the child died. Had the child lived I would now be living with it." Kuwal was very proud of having had a real child. It made him angry when people teased him and told him when he was with a crowd that he never had anything but alyha· wives. Kuwal's alyha· wives were mostly Yuma and only one of them was a Mohave. The Mohave one belonged to the Mu·θ gens. (The screw-bean gens.)

Kuwal used to get very angry when people kicked the dung of animals and said it was his children and told him he had believed his alyha· wives when they were pregnant with things stuffed under their skirts.

After a while Kuwal got himself another alyha· wife. This is the story he told me about that wife of his.

"I lived with that alyha· for a while, but someone succeeded in alienating his affection. Once the alyha·'s mind was made up to leave me, he began finding fault with me on every occasion. 'You copulate with me all the time,' he said. 'That ought to be enough for you, but when you go to gamble—which you do all the time—you also copulate with other women. You should be satisfied with me alone'. Of course the alyha· said all this only because he had made up his mind to leave me.

"In the end we went to a dance one night and the alyha· eloped with another man. I was glad to be rid of him, but thought I would pretend to be very angry, just for the sake of fun. I painted my face black, the way men on the warpath or husbands out for revenge do. Then I said: 'I will go after my *woman* and fight for *her*'. I just said it for fun, but a lot of men came with me to see what would happen. They said it would be very funny. We went to that man's house and I said to him, 'I came to fight for my woman'. At once we began to fight. The alyha· stood there looking at us, yelling and wailing like a woman. 'Peleleley!' the alyha· was yelling. The crowd was shouting lustily 'Pey-pey-pey!' They were enjoying themselves. 'Your penis is too short', the alyha· shouted. 'It is just like a clitoris'. When the men heard this they laughed. They shouted 'Pey-pey!' even louder. But the alyha· was getting very angry. 'When you were untrue to me, I did not quarrel with you, but now that I left you for another man you come and fight. Who do you think you are, anyway,' he said. The alyha· got so angry that he picked up a stick and fell foul on me, while I was fighting with *her* husband. But the men interfered, because they were afraid the stick would hurt me. They got hold of the alyha· and patted his buttocks, the way one pats a woman's buttocks. The alyha· began to giggle. 'Why don't you behave yourself,' he told them. 'Why do you try to put your hand into my vagina?' At last her husband and I stopped fighting and we went home, quite exhiliarated with the fun we had."

I heard Kuwal tell me this story just as I told it to you. He is dead now. He was a close friend of mine and always told me stories about his alyha· wives.

The case of Sahaykwisa

This case was reported by Hivsu· Tupoma, additional data having been obtained from Tcatc.

Sahaykwisa, a full blood Mohave woman of the ñoltc gens was born toward the middle of the last century and killed toward the end of the century apparently at the age of forty-five. She was a shaman specializing in the cure of venereal diseases, and therefore was said to be lucky in love. She began to practice witchcraft at the age of twenty-five, but was not accused of it until five years later, according to some of the informants. She was said never to have menstruated, but was feminine in appearance and had large breasts. She wore a short skirt (erroneously described by one informant "like a man") and was "rich" enough to wear shoes. At that time Mohave women wore Mother Hubbards and went barefoot. The Mohave refer to her as *he*. With regard to the statement that she never menstruated it may not be unnecessary to state that if she did menstruate she would certainly have told no one about it. One of her former wives is still alive. Her name is ñoltc. She could not be consulted because she resents any allusion to her homosexual venture.

It is not clear whether or not Sahaykwisa had been initiated into the status of a transvestite. Opinions differ. At any rate she is consistently referred to as a hwame· which would suggest that she did submit to that ceremony.

Sahaykwisa had at a certain time a very pretty wife. Other men desired the woman and tried to lure her away from the hwame·. "Why do you want a transvestite for your husband who has no penis and pokes you with the finger?" they said. The wife, however, remained stubborn: "That is all right for me if I want to remain with her." Eventually the suitor gave up and left her alone. Soon another man began paying attentions to her, trying to induce her to leave the transvestite. "She has no penis, she is just like you are. If you remain with her no 'other' man will want you afterwards." Eventually the wife eloped with this man, because she liked him well, although her transvestite husband provided well for her, planting and doing all the man's work. (No man does feminine work, unless he marries an unmenstruated child, who does not know how to look after the household.) When Sahaykwisa's wife ran away, the transvestite began attending dances and flirted with the girls. A man who saw her flirt with them said chaffingly, "Why don't you leave those women alone? You cannot do anything with them anyway." Behind her back people nicknamed her Hiθpan kuδape, which means split vulvae, and refers to one of the postures female homosexuals assume during coitus. This is a bad insult and no one dared call her that to her face.

Despite all this banter the wife who had left the transvestite was less satisfied with her male husband and eventually returned to the transvestite. The man did nothing about it.

When the transvestite attended dances with *his* wife, he used to sit with the men and boast in a manly fashion, describing the genitalia of his wife. In the meantime people profited by it to tease the girl about her relationship with the transvestite, saying that Sahaykwisa had neither a penis nor testes. "If I don't copulate with you and your husband both!" one of them exclaimed. "She got just what you got. But don't tell your husband I told you so, because your husband will be angry with me." In the end the girl grew tired of being an object of derision. She told her husband about it. The transvestite became very angry, and told the girl to go away and leave the house. "If you tell me to go, I shall go," the girl said and left forthwith.

Eventually Sahaykwisa got herself another wife. People also teased this woman. In the meantime the girl who had been Sahakwisa's former wife got married again, but people still teased her and her male husband. "Just poke her with your finger, that is what she likes, use your finger, that is what she is accustomed to. Do not waste your penis on her," people advised the man. (The Mohave seldom practice digital intromission, because it makes the hands smell bad.) In turn Sahaykwisa's former wife teased the transvestite's present spouse. "I know very well what you are getting. She pokes her finger into your vagina. Mine still hurts because her fingernails scratched me." The transvestite's present wife complained to her husband, but all Sahaykwisa would deign to reply was, "Never mind what she tells you. She wants to come back to me, that is all". The wife insisted that that was not so, but Sahaykwisa told her that she knew better and let it go at that.

Eventually Sahaykwisa and her present wife met her former wife and the latter's husband at a dance. Again the former wife teased the present one. The latter felt that she had enough of it and wanted to fight. The men present encouraged the women who soon stopped exchanging insults and began to fight. The husband and the transvestite both remained seated in the very dignified posture befitting men when women fight over them. The crowd, however, jeered at Sahaykwisa. "The hwame· is proud now. She thinks perhaps she got a penis." At last a practical joker pushed the fighting women on top of Sahaykwisa and the three of them rolled about in the dust. Some time afterwards the transvestite's wife felt she could not bear the jesting any longer and deserted her *husband*.

Sahaykwisa was very much disappointed and grew resentful. She painted her face black, as befits a warrior on the warpath or a man about to track down the seducer of his wife. She also took her bow and her arrows and went away. She must have had another woman on her mind, for instead of going to the house of the unfaithful wife, she visited another camp where she met with a very bad reception. The woman she wanted to visit jeered at her, and addressed her as one woman addresses another woman. "She thinks maybe that bows and arrows suit her. She thinks she is a man". Sahaykwisa was unruffled. "Yes, I can shoot game for you," she said and left. She felt encouraged because the Mohave say that if a girl insults her suitor, the latter may be certain that he will win her in the end. A few days later Sahaykwisa visited that woman once more and asked her to grind corn for her, which is what young brides do as soon as they got married. Surprisingly enough the woman complied with this request. The news spread like wildfire. "I bet she will get herself another wife.

What can be the matter with these women to fall for a transvestite?" people commented. Indeed, the third time Sahaykwisa visited the woman she eloped with her, leaving her husband for the sake of the hwame·. The husband, a man of about thirty-five years of age called Haqau did nothing about it. "He could not very well fight with a transvestite," informant commented.

Sahaykwisa's ability to obtain wives did not surprise the tribe. She was, it must be remembered, a shaman curing venereal diseases, and by definition lucky in love. Apart from that magical luck she earned considerable money by her practice of "medicine" (and by prostitution to the Whites, certain informants assert). At any rate she was a good provider, worked hard and took great pleasure in bedecking her wives with beads and pretty clothes.

In the end the third wife abandoned her too and returned to her former husband. Haqau took her back, not without some hesitation, "because she had lowered herself by becoming the wife of a transvestite." In addition to that people warned Haqau that he was in danger of being bewitched by Sahaykwisa who was now a full-fledged shaman, and one frequently accused of witchcraft. "She will get even with you," people said.

Sahaykwisa lived on the southern outskirts of the town of Needles, while Haqau and his wife lived on the northern fringe of that town.

Once more Sahaykwisa picked up her bow and arrows and went to the camp of Haqau. She did not enter it however. She stood at a certain distance from it, looking at the camp. She did this several times, thinking of how she could bewitch the girl. People noticed her and realized what sort of mischief she was up to. They warned Haqau, but the man was not afraid and took it in a spirit of jest. "Let her come", he said. "Next time she comes I will show her what a real penis can do." The next time he ambushed her in the bushes, tore off her clothes and raped her. Then he left her in the bushes and returned to his camp. Sahaykwisa stood up and left without a word.

Never again did Sahaykwisa take a wife. By that time she had already bewitched several women she was in love with and segregated their ghosts at "her own place" where she had intercourse with them in her dreams, in the approved Mohave witchcraft fashion.

After her rape by Haqau she became a drunkard and began craving men. Not seldom, when she was drunk, some men dragged her to a convenient place and farmed her out to various men, including certain Whites, at so much the intercourse. By that time she was on the down grade and considered fair game, in the way lewd women (kamaloy) are. She fell in love with an elderly man by the name of Tcuhum, who belonged to her own gens (ñoltc). Tcuhum, however, refused to have intercourse with her. "You are a man," he said. Thereupon she bewitched him, because she loved him and wanted to have intercourse with his ghost in her dreams. Tcuhum died without confessing who had bewitched him—"he wanted to become her victim" people commented, referring to certain Mohave beliefs on witchcraft. Then Sahaykwisa started an affair with Tcuhum's son Suhuraye, aged about forty or forty-five. She had an affair at the same time also with a friend of Suhuraye, a certain Ilykutcemiðo·, of the o·tc gens, aged fifty. The three of them took a trip together to a certain place about thirty miles north of Needles and worked there.

By that time Sahaykwisa began to long for her beloved victim's company, and like most Mohave bewitchers she began to look for a chance of being killed, for only a murdered shaman will join the ghosts of his victims in the other world. She used to get drunk, and while under the influence of alcohol she used to tell of the people she had bewitched. During that trip she became drunk again and told her lovers how she bewitched Tcuhum. She boasted of it until the two men picked her up and threw her into the Colorado river where she drowned.[12]

At that time Hivsu· Tupoma, the writer's informant lived at Needles. Two weeks after the killing people saw buzzards on the sandbank and, after investigating, they discovered the partly decomposed body of Sahaykwisa. Informant and a number of others brought the corpse back to the Mohave settlement and cremated it in the customary fashion. People thought for a while that she had jumped into the river while she was drunk. But even when they found out that it had been murder no one did anything about it, because witches should be killed, and witches *want* to be killed anyway.

It is said that Sahaykwisa never bewitched her next of kin, as most shamans do, but Tcuhum at least was a member of her own gens. I have pointed out elsewhere the connection between witchcraft, incest and suicide in Mohave belief.[13]

NOTES ON OTHER TRIBES

Data on other Yuman tribes are scanty or non-existent. The following divergencies from the Mohave pattern may be noted.

The Maricopa (and other tribes of the Gila River who speak Yuman languages ?) believe in a mountain inhabited by a Homosexual Supernatural. This mountain gambles with a Homosexual Mountain of their arch-foes, the Yuma, and a human male belonging to the tribe protected by the losing mountain becomes a homosexual. The Yuma and Maricopa when they drew up in battle-formation called each other women or homosexuals. One becomes a homosexual by dreaming of the Homosexual Mountain. Men approve of male transvestites, but they make women uneasy. (SPIER, LESLIE. Yuman Tribes of the Gila River, *Chicago,* 1933, pp. 6, 242-243.)

The Northeastern and Western Yavapai know only of a Tonto transvestite of whom they claim to be afraid. (GIFFORD, E. W. The Northeastern and Western Yavapai. *University of California Publications in American Archaeology and Ethnology,* vol. 34, 1936, p. 296.)

The Cocopa female transvestites had their noses pierced. Except for their genitalia their bodies had a male appearance. They fought in battles. (GIFFORD, E. W. The Cocopa. *University of California Publications in American Archaeology and Ethnology,* vol. 31, 1933, p. 294.)

---

[12] DEVEREUX, GEORGE. Mohave soul concepts. Cf. footnote 8.

[13] DEVEREUX, GEORGE. Mohave Suicide. Cf. footnote 11.

The Kamia believed in a transvestite culture-hero who taught them agriculture. (GIFFORD, E. W. The Kamia. *Bureau of American Ethnology,* Bulletin 97, 1931, p. 12.)

The Yuma female transvestites had either undeveloped or male secondary sex-characteristics. They dreamt of weapons. (FORDE, C. DARYLL. *Op. cit. University of California Publications in American Archaeology and Ethnology,* vol. 28, 1931, p. 157.) Their creation myth contains an incident in which a male inserts his penis into the woman's anus, and, upon being urged to insert it into her vagina, inserts his testes into her vulva. (HARRINGTON, J. P. A Yuma account of origins. *Journal of American Folk-Lore,* vol. 21, 1908, p. 334.)

The rest of the data corroborate our Mohave data. In every instance the attraction of the occupations of the opposite sex is stressed.

HOMOSEXUALITY IN SUB-SAHARAN AFRICA

AN UNNECESSARY CONTROVERSY

by Wayne Dynes

In recent years we have heard a good deal of the notion that sub-Saharan Africa (and especially West Africa, from which the great majority of American Blacks stem) was originally free of the "taint" of homosexuality. According to this view, the European conquerors imposed same-sex behavior on black Africa during the colonial era to degrade the subject peoples. Hence, homosexual conduct among American Blacks must be regarded as part of the lingering burden of servitude, a "white vice" forced on healthy people to drag them down. Apart from the invidious claim that homosexuality is a vice or a disadvantage, the citations below show that it has been as charcteristic of the African continent as any other. In fact, a number of our sources enable us to trace the history of same-sex customs back before the beginning of colonial rule.

Seventy years ago Ferdinand Karsch-Haack noted that the mistaken belief in the absence of homosexual behavior in sub-Saharan Africa surfaces with surprising frequency in the ethnological literature, being embraced by some writers as a virtual article of faith. The German authority suggested two reasons for the persistence of this illusion. First, homosexual customs are often part of the religious or private life of tribal peoples, and therefore not readily disclosed to the visitor, whose presence might profane them or violate a taboo. Certainly, visits of a few days or weeks, which were typical of many informants, scarcely suffice to break through this reticence. From the absence of data, generally reflecting only a superficial inquiry, the visitor rashly concludes — following the principle of *argumentum e silentio*—that homosexuality is unknown. Europeans have often held that "sodomy" is a vice of advanced, even decadent civilizations. The Africans, being innocent "children of nature" must be exempt from such corruption. Claims of this kind, far from showing any appreciation of African cultures, belong to the "natural sense of rhythm" school of patronizing pseudo-praise. A further irony lies in the fact that, far from forcing homosexual behavior on their recalcitrant subjects, Europeans—especially missionaries—are responsible for teaching them that "filthy" practices, previously a part of everyday life, were something to be ashamed of. Thus the homophobia occasionally voiced by some contemporary African spokespeople would appear itself to share in the crippling legacy of colonial subjugation that the new leaders claim to have shed. Unfortunately, as so often happens, it is the victim—the African homosexual or lesbian—who bears the brunt of disapproval.

What is the origin of the belief that the Africans were originally exempt from homosexuality? It can be traced to Chapter XLIV of Edward Gibbon's celebrated *Decline and Fall of the Roman Empire* (1781). After describing the prevalence of sodomy in Mediterranean lands and elsewhere, the historian writes: "I believe, and hope, that the negroes, in their own country were exempt from this moral pestilence." A century later Sir Richard Burton inadvertently helped to reinforce the myth of African sexual exceptionalism by drawing the boundaries of his "Sotadic Zone" (where homosexuality was widely practiced and accepted) to exclude sub-Saharan Africa.

For the majority of the following references we are indebted to Stephen Wayne Foster, who has been conducting research on homosexuality in the Third World for a number of years. Additions from readers will be very welcome. The entries are confined to sub-Saharan Africa, since North Africa has an entirely different culture, one belonging integrally to the world of Islam.

Abraham, Roy Clive. *Dictionary of the Hausa Language*. London, 1962, p. 624.

Ajayi, J.F.A., and Michael Crowder (eds.). *History of West Africa*. 2 vols. London, 1972-73, I, p. 444.

Ambrogetti, P. *La vita sessuale nell'Eritrea*. Rome, 1900, pp. 15-19.

Barth, Heinrich. *Travels and Discoveries in North and Central Africa*. 2 vols. London, 1857-58, II, p. 39

Baumann, Hermann. *Das doppelte Geschlecht: Ethnologische Studien zur Bisexualität in Ritus und Mythos*. Berlin, 1955.

Baumann, Oskar. "Conträre Sexual-Erscheinungen bei der Neger-Bevölkerung Zanzibars." *Zeitschrift für Ethnologie*, 31 (1900), pp. 668-70.

Beattie, John et al. *Spirit Mediumship and Society in Africa*. New York, 1969, pp. xxv and 143.

Brincker, H. "Charakter, Sitten und Gebräuche speciell der Bantu Deutsch-Sudwestafrikas." *Mitteilungen des Seminars fur Orientalische Sprachen an der K. Friedrich-Wilhelms-Universität zu Berlin*, 3 (1900), Abt. 3, pp. 66-92.

Bryk, Felix. *Voodoo-eros*. Trns. M. F. Sexton. New York, 1964, pp. 226. (also known as *Dark Rapture*. Translated A. J. Norton. New York, 1939, pp. 149-53).

Burton, Sir Richard F. *A Mission to Gele*. London, 1966, p. 2

______. *Zanzibar: City, Island, Coast*. 2 Vols. London, 1872, I, p. 419

Butts, June. "Is Homosexuality a Threat to the Black Family?" *Ebony* (April 1981), pp. 138-40, 142-44.

Christensen, James Boyd. *Double Descent Among the Fanti*. New Haven, 1954, pp. 92-93, 143.

Colson, Elizabeth. *Marriage and the Family Among the Plateau Tonga of Northern Rhodesia*. Manchester, 1958, pp. 139-40.

Damberger, Christian Frederick. *Travels Through the Interior of Africa...* Boston, 1801, pp. 157-59.

Dannert, Eduard. *Zum Rechte der Herero, insbesonderes uber ihr Erb- und Familienrecht*. Berlin, 1906.

Dapper, Olfert. *Eigentliche Beschreibung von Afrika...* Amsterdam, 1671.

______. *Umbständliche und eigentliche Beschreibung von Afrika...* 2 vols. Amsterdam, 1670, II, p. 41. (repr. New York, 1967).

Davidson, Basil. *The African Genius*. Boston, 1970, p. 73.

Davidson, Michael. *Some Boys: A Homosexual Odyssey*. London, 1970, pp. 181-96, 205-16.

Drieburg, J. H. *The Lango*. London, 1923, p. 110

Evans-Pritchard, Edward E. *Kinship and Marriage Among the Nuer*. New York, 1951, pp. 108-09.

______. "Sexual Inversion Among the Azande." *American Anthropologist*, 72

(1970), pp. 1428-34.

______. *Witchcraft, Oracles and Magic Among the Azande.* Oxford, 1937, p. 56.

______. (ed.). *Man and Woman Among the Azande.* London, 1974, pp. 123-25

Falk, K. "Homosexualität bei den Eingeborenen in Südwest-Afrika." *Archiv für Menschenkunde,* 1 (1925), pp. 202-14.

Ford, Clellan S. (ed.). *Cross-cultural Approaches.* New Haven, 1967, p. 212.

______, and Frank Beach. *Patterns of Sexual Behavior.* New York, 1951, pp. 130-33.

Gamble, David P. *The Wolof of Senegambia.* London, 1957, pp. 55, 80.

Gamst, Frederick C. *The Qemant: A Pagan-Hebraic Peasantry of Ethiopia.* New York, 1969, p. 106.

Gide, Andre. *Journals.* Trans. J. O'Brien. New York, 1955, vol. I, p. 335.

Goldschmidt, Walter. *Sebei Law.* Berkeley, 1967, pp. 136-68.

Gorer, Geoffrey. *African Dances.* New York, 1962, pp. 36-141, 176.

Graere, A. *L'art de guérir chez les Azande.* Brussels, 1929, p. 362.

Groves, Charles Pelham. *The Planting of Christianity in Africa.* 4 vols. London, 1948-64, III, p. 93.

Gunther, John. Inside Africa. New York, 1955, pp. 523, 560.

Hambly, Wilfred D. *The Ovimbundu of Angola.* Chicago, 1934, p. 181.

______. *Source-book for African Anthropology.* Chicago, 1937, pt. II, pp. 426-27, 500.

Hanry, Pierre. *Erotisme africain: le comportement sexuel des adolescents guinéens.* Paris, 1970.

Herskovits, Melville Jean. *Dahomey, An Ancient West African Kingdom.* 2 vols. New York, 1938, I, pp. 239-42, 288-89.

______. "A Note on 'Woman Marriage' in Dahomey." *Africa,* 10 (1937), pp. 335-41.

Irle, J. *Herero: Ein Beitrag zur Landes-, Volks- und Missionskunde.* Gütersloh, 1906, p. 58.

Johnson, Frederick. *English-Swahili Dictionary.* London, 1969, pp. 94, 127, 138, 242, 424.

Junod, Henri A. *The Life of a South African Tribe.* 2 vols. New York, 1962, I, pp. 98, 492-95. [Thonga tribe; first issued in 1912.]

Kardiner, Abram. *The Individual and His Society.* New York, 1939, pp. 218, 265-66, 287, 296-97, 303, 312-15, 331-21.

Karsch-Haack, Ferdinand. *Das gleichgeschlechtliche Leben der Naturvölker.* Munich, 1911 (repr. New York, 1975). [Copiously documented from reports of travelers, missionaries and anthropologists; pp. 116-84 (male homosexuality); 471-84 (lesbianism)]

Kolb, Peter. *The Voyage of P. K. to the Cape of Good Hope.* In: *The World Displayed.* 4th ed. London, 1774-78. vol. 4.

Krapf, Ludwig. *A Dictionary of the Suahili Language.* London, 1882, pp. 68, 95, 266, 333.

LaFontaine, Jean Sybil. *The Gisu of Uganda.* London, 1959, pp. 34, 60-61.

Lasnet, Alexandre. "Notes d'ethnologie et de médecine sur les Sakalaves du Nord-Ouest." *Annales d'Hygiène et de Médecine Coloniales,* II (1889), pp. 471-97. [Madagascar]

Laubscher, Barend J. F. *Sex Custom and Psychopathology: A Study of South African Pagan Natives.* New York, 1957, pp. 23, 25, 31, 257-59, 283-84.

Lawrance, Jeremy C. D. *The Iteso.* New York, 1957, pp. 107, 160-61. [Uganda].

Lipton, Ralph. *The Tanala: A Hill Tribe of Madagascar.* Chicago, 1933, p. 298-99.

Makin, William James. *Red Sea Nights.* London, 1932, p. 58.

"Male Homophile in Black Africa, The." *ONE Magazine,* 4 (Feb. 1965), pp. 22-25. [translated from *Arcadie,* Nov. 1954]

Martin, Maurice. *Au coeur de l'Afrique équatoriale (journal d'un officier).* Lille, 1912, pp. 139-60, 164, 187-88.

Morris, Donald R. *The Washing of the Spears: A History of the Rise of the Zulu Nation under Shaka and its Fall in the Zulu War of 1879.* New York, 1965, pp. 35-36, 46, 51-52, 54, 66, 107-07, 117, 279-81, 287-88, 587.

Milner, Alan (ed.). *African Penal Systems.* New York, 1969, pp. 301-02.

Nadel, Siegfried F. *A Black Byzantium: The Kingdom of Nupe in Nigeria.* London, 1942, p. 152.

______. *The Nuba.* New York, 1947, pp. 242,285, 300, 394-96.

Oboler, R. S. "Is the Female Husband a Man? Woman/Woman Marriage Among the Nandi of Kenya." *Ethnology,* 19 (1980), pp. 69-88.

Opler, Marvin K. (ed.) *Culture and Mental Health: Cross-cultural Studies.* New York, 1959, p. 362.

Paulitschke, Philipp. *Ethnographie Nordost-Afrikas.* 2 vols. Berlin, 1893-96, I, p. 172.

Prins, Adriaan H. J. *The Swahili-speaking Peoples of Zanzibar and the East African Coast.* London, 1961, p.99.

Purchas, Samuel. *Purchas His Pilgrimes.* 20 vols. Glasgow, 1905-07. IX (1906), p. 260.

Rachewiltz, Boris de. *Black Eros: Sexual Customs of Africa from Prehistory to the Present Day.* Trans. P. Whigham. New York, 1968, pp. 191, 280, 282.

Reade, Winwood. *Savage Africa.* London, 1864, p. 424.

Roberts, Brian. *The Zulu Kings.* New York, 1975, pp. 86-87.

Seligman, Charles G. and Brenda Z. *Pagan Tribes of the Nilotic Sudan.* London, 1932, pp. 506-07, 515.

Schapera, Isaac. *A Handbook of Tswana Law and Custom.* London, 1938, p. 278.

______. *The Khoisan Peoples of South Africa.* London, 1951, pp. 242-43.

Signorini, Italo. "Agonwole agyale: il matrimonio tra individui dello stesso sesso negli Nzema del Ghana sud occidentale." *Rassegna italiana di sociologia,* 12 (1971), pp. 529-45.

Smith, Edwin W., and Andrew M. Dale. *The Ila-speaking Peoples of Northern Rhodesia.* 2 vols. London, 1920, I, p. 373, II, P. 74.

Steele, Edward, and A. C. Madan (eds.). *A Handbook of the Swahili Language as Spoken at Zanzibar.* London, 1885, pp. 274, 283, 382.

Steinmetz, S. R. (ed.). *Rechtsverhältnisse von eingeborenen Völker in Afrika und Ozeanien.* Berlin, 1903.

Strobel, Margaret. *Muslim Women in Mombasa, 1890-1975.* New Haven, 1979, pp. 1656, 169.

Talbot, Percy Amuary. *The Peoples of Southern Nigeria.* 4 vols. Oxford, 1926, III, p. 766.

Tessmann, Günther. "Die Homosexualität bei den Negern Kameruns." *Jahrbuch für sexuelle Zwischenstufen,* 21 (1921), pp. 121-38.

Trumbull, Colin M. *Wayward Servants: The Two Worlds of the African Pygmies.* New York, 1965, p. 122.

Wagner, Gunter. *The Bantu of North Kavirondo.* 2 vols. London, 1949, I, pp. 108-09. [Kenya]

Weeks, John L. "Anthropological Notes on the Bangala of the Upper Congo River." *Journal of the Anthropological Institute of Great Britain and Ireland,* 39 (1909), pp. 97-136, 416-59 (esp. pp. 448-49).

Weyer, Edward M., Jr. *Primitive Peoples Today.* Garden City, N.Y., 1959, p. 166.

Wilson, Monica. *Good Company: A Study of the Nyakusu Age-Villages.* London, 1951, pp. 87-88, 196-97.

Sexual Inversion among the Azande

E. E. Evans-Pritchard
Oxford University

Male and female homosexual relationship seems to have been common among the Azande in past times. Between males it was approved of in the bachelor military companies. Between females it is said to have been a frequent, though highly disapproved of, practice in polygamous homes. [Sudan (southern); Azande; sexual inversion]

Accepted for publication 16 January 1970.

It is beyond question that male homosexuality, or rather a sexual relationship between young warriors and boys, was common in pre-European days among the Azande, and as Czekanowski (1924:56), citing Junker (1892: 3–4), has pointed out, there is no reason to suppose that it was introduced by Arabs as some have thought. All Azande I have known well enough to discuss this matter have asserted also that female homosexuality (lesbianism) was practiced in polygamous homes in the past and still (1930) is sometimes. This paper brings together information about both practices and presents translations of a few texts on the subject taken down from Azande of the Sudan forty years ago.

Before European rule was imposed on the Azande there was a good deal of fighting between kingdoms (Evans-Pritchard 1957b, 1957c). Part of the adult male population of each kingdom was organized in military companies of *abakumba* 'married men' and *aparanga* 'bachelors'; the same companies, besides their military functions, served at courts in various capacities and were called on for labor in the royal and princely cultivations (Evans-Pritchard 1957a). In this account we do not have to refer again to the companies of married men. It was the custom for members of bachelor companies, some of whom would always be living in barracks at court, to take boy-wives. This was undoubtedly brought about by the scarcity of marriageable women in the days when the nobility and also the richer commoners kept large harems and were able to do so because bridewealth was hard to come by and they were able to acquire it more easily than poorer men. Most young men consequently married late—well into their twenties and thirties—and, because girls were engaged (in a legal sense married) very young, often at birth, the only way youths could obtain satisfaction from a woman was in adultery. But that was a very dangerous solution to a young man's problem, for the fine his father would have to pay was heavy—twenty spears and a woman, which meant in effect the payment of two women to the husband; it sometimes happened that the husband was so enraged that he refused compensation and chose instead to mutilate the offender, cutting off his ears, upper lip, genitals, and hands. So, the risk being too great, it was the custom for cautious bachelors in the military companies who were living at court, if they were not content to masturbate—a practice to which no shame is attached, though a young man would not do it in public—to marry boys and satisfy their sexual needs with them. A youth of position in his company might have more than one boy (*kumba gude*). To these boys their warrior mates were *badiya ngbanga* 'court lovers.'

That it was on account of the difficulties of getting satisfaction in heterosexual relationships that boy marriage was a recognized temporary union is, I believe, shown by the fact that boy marriage has in post-European times entirely disappeared. It is true that the military companies disappeared also; but Azande, I think rightly, attribute the giving up of the custom to its having become easier for youths to marry and, in the general breakdown of morals and of the suppression of customary punishments, to indulge in adultery and fornication. Boy marriage was owing, Azande say, to *zanga ade* 'lack of women.' As one man put it, "What man would prefer a boy to a woman? A man would be a fool to do so. The love of boys arose from lack of women." So the Azande in my day spoke of it as *kuru pai* 'old custom,' though I have never heard anyone speak of sleeping with a boy with distaste—at worst it is regarded as something of a joke; even in my time one heard it said of a man that he used to be some well-known older man's boy much as we in England might say that someone at school was fag to some celebrity. It should also be made clear that, as in ancient Greece, so far as one can judge, when the boy-wives grew up and when they and their husbands married females they had a normal married life like everyone else. There were no urnings in the modern European sense.

The custom of boy marriage had died out before I first visited Zandeland, and as direct observation no longer was possible, I had to rely on statements about the past, but such statements by senior men were unanimous. I have pointedly used the terms "wife," "husband," and "marriage," for, as the texts will make clear, the relationship was, for so long as it lasted, a legal union on the model of a normal marriage. The warrior paid bridewealth (some five spears or more) to the parents of his boy and performed services for them as he would have done had he married their daughter; if he proved to be a good son-in-law they might later replace the son by a daughter. Also, if another man had relations with his boy he could, I was told, sue him at court for adultery.

The boys were "women": "*Ade nga ami,*" they would say, "we are women." A boy was addressed by his lover as *diare* 'my wife,' and the boy addressed him as *kumbami* 'my husband.' The boys used to eat out of sight of the warriors in the same way as women do not eat in the presence of their husbands. The boys performed many of the smaller services a woman performs daily for her husband, such as gathering leaves for his ablutions, gathering leaves for his bed, drawing water and breaking off firewood for him, helping him in hoeing his father's cultivations, bearing messages for him, and bringing him cooked provisions from his home to court to supplement those provided by the prince; but he did not cook porridge for him. With regard to these services it should be borne in mind that a young man at court had no mother or sisters to look after him there. Also, the boy-wife carried his husband's shield when on a journey. It should be understood that he performed these services lest it might be thought that the relationship was entirely of a sexual nature; it will be appreciated that it had an educational side to it. With regard to the sexual side, at night the boy slept with his lover, who had intercourse with him between his thighs (Azande expressed disgust at the suggestion of anal penetration). The boys got what pleasure they could by friction of their organs on the husband's belly or groin. However, even though there was this side to the relationship, it was clear from Zande accounts that there was also the comfort of a nightly sharing of the bed with a companion.

The word "boy" (*kumba gude*) must, it would appear, be interpreted liberally, for as far as I could judge from what I was told the lads might have been anywhere between about twelve and twenty years of age. When they ceased to be boys they joined the companies of warriors to which their at-one-time husbands belonged and took boys to wife on their own account; so the period of marriage was also one of apprenticeship. I cannot present figures for boy marriages, but the practice was certainly both accepted and common. I obtained lists of a succession of such marriages from several senior men but there would be little profit after this lapse of time (sixty-five years after King Gbudwe's death) in recording just strings of names.

Before giving the texts it should be further stated that some members of the noble ruling class indulged in homosexual intercourse. In the main these were those young sons of princes who hung about court till their fathers saw fit to give them wives and districts to administer. They kept well away from their fathers' harems and took commoner boys as servants and for sexual pleasure. It appears also that a prince, however many wives he might have, might sleep with a boy rather than by himself during the night before consulting the poison oracle, for intercourse with a woman was taboo on these occasions. It was said that *kumba gude na gberesa nga benge te* 'a boy does not spoil the poison oracle.' Otherwise I have heard of only one senior prince—deposed by the administration—who, although he had several wives, still habitually slept with boys. For this and other reasons he was regarded by Azande as slightly crazy. One must not jump to conclusions, as Czekanowski did on what Junker had recorded about boys accompanying a Zande prince wherever he went; all kings and princes are accompanied by pages who are treated by their masters with notable indulgence in contrast with the severe aloofness with which their seniors are usually treated.

Text (Evans-Pritchard 1963a:277–280) was taken down from Kuagbiaru, a man well acquainted with the court life of the past who had himself been a boy-wife and, as head of a company of warriors at the court of Prince Gangura, several times a husband to boys.

> In the past men used to have sexual relations with boys as they did with wives. A man paid compensation to another if he had relations with his boy. People asked for the hand of a boy with a spear, just as they asked for the hand of a maiden of her parents.[1] All those young warriors who were at court, all had their boys. Those huts of the young men which were around the court, all their boy-loves were in those huts. They built their huts large and long, and there were many youths to each hut, each in his own place, together with their captain. Their boy-loves also slept in the huts. When night fell they all kindled fires in front of their husbands' beds, each kindled a fire in front of his lover's bed. When the young warriors began to be very hungry at court they sent their boy-loves to their [the boys'] parents to fetch food for them. Their boy-loves went and returned with fine lots of porridge and cooked fowls and beer. The relatives of a boy escorted him [when he was married] in the same way as they escorted a bride [on her marriage] to her husband with much good food. However, the boys did not cook porridge for their lovers themselves; they

cooked manioc and sweet potatoes for their lovers. It was their mothers [the boys'] who cooked porridge in their homes, and nice meats; and some of them cooked fowls. They collected all these lots of food together where their husbands were. All these youths and their loves, there was no forgetfulness of the boys' part about giving food to the lovers. But that porridge which they gave them, they broke off part of it together with part of the meats to hide it for their husbands, for they were like wives.[2] Their lovers did not approve of their laughing loud like men, they desired them to speak softly, as women speak.

When all the young warriors went to hoe the prince's cultivations each took his love with him. When they reached the cultivations they built a big hut for their captain and they set up a palsade around it. In this enclosure, filled with boys, otherwise was the captain alone. Then the youths began to build their little shelters adjacent to the hut of the captain, and they stretched far, crossing streams. But all their boys were in the enclosure they had erected for the captain. When it was dusk the boys scattered, each to the hut of his lover to kindle a fire there for his lover. Each went to kindle a fire in the hut of his own lover. Next morning they gathered together in the enclosure of the captain. No youth could enter there without permission. The captain gave them their meals behind the enclosure. Only if the captain felt well-disposed towards him might he summon one of the senior youths into the enclosure to share his meal with him. All the rest of them never entered the enclosure; they saw their loves at night. The youths hoed the cultivations till evening and then they returned to their sleeping places. Their loves had already made their husbands' beds and kindled fires for them in their huts.

Text (Evans-Pritchard 1962:16–17) was taken down from Ganga, one of King Gbudwe's captains of companies of warriors.

This is about how men married boys when Gbudwe was lord of his domains. In those days, if a man had relations with the wife of another the husband killed him or he cut off his hands and his genitals. So for that reason a man used to marry a boy to have orgasm between his thighs, which quieted his desire for a woman. If this boy was a good wife to his husband five spears might be paid for him, and for another as many as ten might be paid. A husband who was liberal to his in-laws, they would later give him a woman, saying that good for a boy, how much better for a woman; so if he married a girl his in-laws would greatly profit, and so they gave him a wife [girl]. This his boy, he did not abide seeing another near him; they would quarrel, and if they took the matter before [King] Gbudwe, Gbudwe told the one who went after the other's boy to pay him spears [in compensation] since he had gone after the other's boy. Also there were some men who, although they had [female] wives, still married boys. When war broke out they took their boys with them,[3] but they did not take them to the place of fighting; the boys remained behind in the camp, for they were like women; and they collected firewood for their husbands and plucked *nzawa* leaves [for the toilet] and they cooked meals for when their husbands returned from the fighting. They did for their husbands everything a wife does for her husband. They drew water and presented it before their husbands on their knees and they took food and brought it to them, and the husbands washed their hands and ate this meal and then recounted what had happened in the fighting to their boy-wives.

So far something has been said about male homosexuality. What about lesbianism? That also must be regarded as a product, like male homosexuality, of polygamy on a large scale; for if this precluded young men from normal sex, so in large polygamous homes it prevented the wives, or some of them, from receiving the amount of sexual attention they wished for from their common husband, who, moreover, might well have been elderly and not at the height of his sexual vigor. Though men have slightly different habits, it can be said generally that a woman who is one of three wives would not sleep with her husband more than some ten nights a month, one of six wives more than five nights, and so on. One of the many wives of a prince or of an important commoner in the past might not have shared her husband's bed for a month or two, whereas some of the dozens, even hundreds, of wives of a king must have been almost totally deprived of the sex life normal in smaller homes. Adulterous intercourse was very difficult for a wife in such large polygamous families, for the wives were kept in seclusion and carefully watched; death on discovery, or even on suspicion, would have been the penalty for both the wife and her lover.

It was in such polygamous families, Azande say, that lesbianism was practiced. Obviously I had no opportunity of knowing anything about it by observation, so that I can only tell what I was told (by males only, though women admitted that some women practiced it). Wives would cut a sweet potato or manioc root in the shape of the male organ, or use a banana for the purpose. Two of them would shut themselves in a hut and one would lie on the bed and play the female role while the other, with the artificial organ tied round her stomach, played the male role. They then reversed roles.

Women were certainly underprivileged in old Zande society, and it is a further indication of male dominance that what was encouraged among males was condemned among females. Zande men, princes especially, have a horror of lesbianism, and they regard it as highly dangerous, being more or less equivalent to *adandara*, a kind of cat born, it is believed, of women (Evans-Pritchard 1937:51–56). It would be fatal were a man to see one of these women suckling her kittens. I have heard it said that some of the great kings of the past—Bazingbi, Gbudwe, Wando, and others—died on account of lesbian practices between their wives, and it is alleged that in Gbudwe's home one of his senior wives, Nanduru, a wizened old lady in my day, executed several of his cowives for this offense. Some Azande have told me that lesbianism was much practiced by daughters and sisters of ruling nobles in whose homes they lived in an incestuous relationship. A ruler might give a girl slave to one of his daughters, who would anoint and paint the girl to make her attractive and then lie with her. Azande further say that once a woman has started homesexual intercourse she is likely to continue it because she is then her own master and may have gratification when she pleases and not just when a man cares to give it to her, and the gratification may also last as long as she pleases.

It would seem, if Zande statements are correct, that a lesbian relationship is often brought about in the first instance by a simple rite. When two women are very friendly they may seek to give formality to their friendship through a ceremony called *bagburu*, having obtained permission from their husbands to do so. A husband finds it difficult to refuse his consent for it would not normally mean that any sexual element was involved. One of the women makes a small gift to the other and the other makes a return gift. They then take a maize cob and divide it, and each plants the seeds of her half in her garden.[4] Later the women perform various mutual services and will from time to time exchange gifts. However, though a husband may give his consent he may do so with reluctance because Zande men think that this bond of friendship between women may be a respectable cover for homosexual intimacies.

Text (Evans-Pritchard 1963b:13–14) was taken down from Kuagbiaru.

> Among the Azande many women do the same as men. There are many of them who have intercourse among themselves as a husband with his wife. Lesbianism began with a maize the name of which is *kaima*, a maize with a cob red like blood. They take this cob and utter a spell over it in the same way as men utter a spell over the blood in making blood-brotherhood; and when that is done one of them [the two women] takes hold of the top of it on her side and the other takes hold of the bottom of it for her part and they break it between them. After this they should not call each other by their proper names, but they call each other *bagburu*. The one who is the wife cooks porridge and a fowl and brings them to the one who is the husband. They do this between them many times. They have sexual intercourse between them with sweet potatoes carved into the shape of a circumcised penis, with carved manioc also, and also with bananas. At the top it is just like the male organ. The husband dislikes her wife conversing with other women. She beats her wife just as a husband beats his wife for bad behaviour, such as going with a man. However, when Gbudwe was alive he was very much opposed to anything to do with lesbianism.

Text (Evans-Pritchard) was taken down from Kisanga, a man with a very wide knowledge of Zande customs.

> Women get together and one says to another "Oh my friend, you, why don't you like me mistress!" The other replies "O lady, my mistress, why should I bear you ill-will?" The first says "Lady, come the day after tomorrow as I have a little something to tell you." She replies "Eh lady, what is it that you do not now tell me? For unless you tell it to me now I cannot survive the night waiting to hear it!" So the one tells the other "Lady, I am greatly in love with you. O lady how shall we manage this horrible husband?"
>
> "Hm! Eh lady, do they keep all that watch on a woman lady!"
>
> "Ahe lady, let us play a trick. You come after my husband and we will make a pact of love-friendship (*bagburu*) between us and he will think it is just a friendship between women, and you lady can pleasure me." She adds "Early tomorrow you come with a little gift for him." Early in the morning she takes a gift, such as a

spear, and she comes to visit the husband in his home. She says to the husband:

"So, will you listen well to what I am going to say to you?"

"Lady, say what the lady has come to my home here for."

"Eh sir, sir it is about my friend, master. I said to myself sir that I would come to ask the prince about her; no man am I who could deceive you with a woman."

He says "O lady may be I shall consent."

"O sir by your head! O sir by your head! Let me have the woman sir. Sir I will grind her flour for her, and if she is sick I will gather her firewood."

"I must consult the oracles first lady, I must consult the oracles first. I think I must first consult the oracles."

"Eh sir, does one refuse with a woman? Is she a man?"

"All right my friend, you leave the spear and go home and I will think the matter over."

She wipes the ground before him [thanks him], saying "O my master I go about by myself among people sir!" Then she goes home. She sleeps two nights and then grinds flour and she comes with flour and porridge. When she appears on the path her lover runs to meet her on the path:

"O my love, O my friend, O lady have you not come today?" She puts down the flour and porridge at the side of the homestead. Her lover takes a stool and puts it for her to be seated. The husband sulks:

"You have come my friend?"

"Yes sir."

"Lady let me be, I am feeling chilly today."

They take his food and bing it. He is embarrassed: "Child pour water over my hands." His wife goes and takes water and pours it over his hands. He says "Lady that is good, lady, it is good." He breaks off one lump of porridge. He sulks and goes on sulking, telling his daughters "Now then come on and take it away and give it to the children."

"Ahe sir! A person brings her food and a man is not well—it should not be given away, it should be kept for him to eat at another time?"

"Hm! Eh woman, does one argue with a father in this manner!" They deceive him. "Oh no sir, I am not disputing anything sir."

"Mistress I do not feel well today, today is not a good day for me. I shall retire."

"He! Look at that spying husband of mine lady, what an unpleasant character!"

The wife puts water before her lover as though she were her [male] husband. She has her penis in her bag—she takes it around with her. They carve a sweet potato into the shape of a circumcised penis. The woman-husband makes a hole through the sweet potato and then ties it with cord through it to her loins so that she is like a male. She washes herself with water and anoints herself with oil.

Meanwhile the husband is eating his meal in the hut of his senior wife. He says to her: "O mistress since you have been a long time with me you have never done me ill. My wife, that which I have seen, do you see it too?"

"No sir, but I have an idea about it. I am not sure of things sir! Eh sir! As you are a man, in a matter of this kind why do you not hear what she has to say to satisfy yourself in your mind?"

He coughs: "All right, this death of mine they speak of, I will get to the bottom of it."

The two women get up to lie on the ground because their movements on the bed make a noise. The wife of the man says: "That spying husband of mine, he is nasty enough to try and trap people in a hut!"

"If he does he will die if he sees it. Madam do not weary yourself with thinking about women's affairs, you will see what happens."

"Let us do what we are going to do. Just stop talking about my husband." She makes her keep quiet by shaking her head at her while she takes her pleasure of her love. The husband comes and crouches in the porch and he hears the sounds of them in the hut; he hears the movement in the hut, as they say to each other "O my brother, O my darling, O my husband, O lady." He enters the hut and when they see him they rise from the ground. He seizes his wife and says (to the other woman):

"O my friend you kill me. I thought you had come to my home in goodwill, but it seems that it is my death you bring." Then he calls his senior wife:

"Mistress come here and see what evil has befallen me—this woman I have taken hold of together with her companion. . . ."

"Heyo! My husband, do you summon me to a woman's affair—your wives can be very malicious sir."

"Eh woman, we share a home with you in double-talk (*sanza*.) So you are all moved by wish for my death!"

"Hi! Leave off that talk with me—is it my fault that you went and entered the hut?"

Perhaps I should add in conclusion to this note that it is not of course being suggested that pederasty and tribadism are explained by social conditions such as those obtaining among the Azande. Obviously they are not. What is perhaps accounted for, given libidinous plasticity, are the institutional forms prevalent in Zande society and the (male) attitudes toward them.

Notes

[1] A man asking a girl's parents for her hand

in marriage gave them a spear or two as a first installment of bridewealth. In the case of boys, the acceptance of a spear likewise constituted a legal marriage.

[2] In preparing a meal for guests a Zande wife often kept part of it back before serving it so that her husband could have a second meal secretly when the guests had departed.

[3] Intercourse with women was taboo for warriors during periods of fighting.

[4] The rite corresponds to exchange of blood among men. That it is copied from the latter is suggested by the blood-red maize cob (Evans-Pritchard 1933).

References Cited

Czekanowski, Jan
1924 Forschungen im Nil-Kongo Zwischengebiet. Vol. 2. Leipzig: Klinkhardt & Biermann.

Evans-Pritchard, E. E.
1933 Zande blood-brotherhood. Africa 6:369-401.
1937 Witchcraft, oracles and magic among the Azande. Oxford: Clarendon Press.
1957a The Zande royal court. Zaïre 5:495-511.
1957b Zande border raids. Africa 28:217-232.
1957c Zande warfare. Anthropos 52:239-262.
1962 Zande texts: part 1. Oxford: Oxonian Press.
1963a Some Zande texts. Kush 11.
1963b Zande texts: part 3:1-43.
n.d. Vernacular text. Manuscript. Zande text collection. Oxford: Institute of Social Anthropology.

Junker, Wilhelm
1892 Travels in Africa. London: Chapman and Hall.

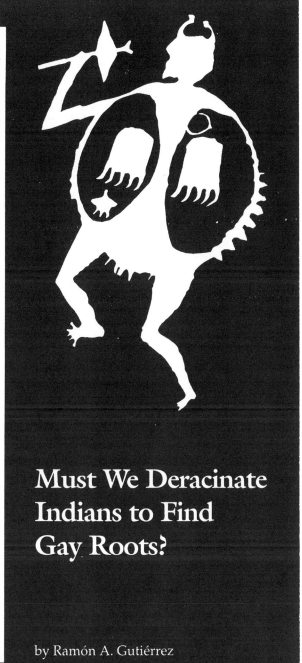

Must We Deracinate Indians to Find Gay Roots?

by Ramón A. Gutiérrez

WILL ROSCOE'S ARTICLE "The Zuñi Man-Woman," in the Summer 1988 issue of *OUT/LOOK* was an interesting cultural text. I was delighted to read that Will's "odyssey" into Pueblo Indian culture had been guided by my old friend Harry Hay. In 1978 I too met Harry Hay in Santa Fe. I was then a doctoral student at the University of Wisconsin and had returned home to write on Pueblo-Spanish relations in New Mexico's history. Harry befriended me, shared his library, and revealed the secrets of the berdaches to me, probably much in the same way as he befriended Will. The conclusions I reached about berdaches after ten years of research on the Pueblo Indians are very different from those Will Roscoe comes to. I wish to share some of the fruits of my research and offer a perspective very different from that found in the voluminous literature on the sex of the berdaches.[1] On pondering this essay readers will have to judge for themselves whether the berdache status in general, the Zuñi Indian We'wha in particular, really offers moderns an exemplary "gay role."

BERDACHE STATUS, that social arrangement whereby a man or group of men press another male into impersonating a female, forcing him to perform work generally associated with women, offering passive sexual service to men, and donning women's clothes, is widely reported historically throughout East Asia, in the Americas, in Islamic Africa, and is generally believed to have been diffused from these areas to Europe.[2] What we know about the Spanish American variant called *bradaje* (the Spanish word for male whore or prostitute) be it in New Mexico or Tierra del Fuego, comes largely from the narratives of the Spanish conquest and subsequent travelers' reports. Francisco Guerra recently collected all known references to *bradaje* in post-conquest sources in his book *The Pre-Columbian Mind*. The patterns of behavior which emerge from this compilation warrant our attention.

In every North and South American Indian group in which berdaches were reported after 1492, their numbers were always small; often only between one and six, and rarely more than twenty. Berdache status was one principally ascribed to defeated enemies. Among the insults and humiliations inflicted on prisoners of war were homosexual rape, castration, the wearing of women's clothes, and performing women's work.[3] Alvar Núñez Cabeza de Vaca said as much during his 1523-33 trek across New Mexico: "I saw one man married to another, and these are impotent, effeminate men and they go about dressed as women, and do women's tasks, and shoot with a bow, and carry great burdens...and they are huskier than the other men and taller."[4] That the berdaches were generally described as men who wielded instruments of war, who were stronger and taller than most, and who were forced to carry burdens, should lead us to warfare to explain their status. Wearing clothes, particularly women's clothing, among naked warriors, is another clue. When Cabeza de Vaca wrote the words cited above, he himself was naked and spoke of the nakedness of the Indian men. Why were the berdaches dressed when none of the other men were? To mark their status and humiliation among men.

RICHARD TREXLER proposes in his forthcoming book *Europe on Top: Male Homosexuality and the Conquests of America, 1400-1700*, that in the Old World and in the New, there was a rather universal gender representation of conquest: victors on vanquishing their enemies asserted their virility by transforming losers into effeminates. Enemies had to perform women's work and to wear women's clothes as a sign of vanquishment. We certainly know that heterosexual rape was a common habit of war. What we are only now starting to admit is that losing men were similarly treated and were forced to perform what were considered demeaning forms of sexual service. Thus, it does not matter much whether we examine male prisoners of war among the Zuñi and the Arawaks, Aztec and Inca male temple slaves, or those figures on pre-Columbian Moche pottery jars from northern Peru depicting male slaves in women's clothes being passively penetrated in homosexual intercourse, to see the status inversion marked through gender symbols that were so frequently associated with defeated men.[5]

Conquest narratives, travelers' accounts and ethnographies also indicate that the social status of the berdaches had meaning primarily in the socio-political world of men. Berdaches were reported as being under male ownership. They were frequently found in male social spaces performing activities associated with females during male rituals: fellating powerful men or being anally mounted by them. Through the long historical evolution of the berdache status, it appears that they gradually came to be regarded as temple experts or as shamans who fulfilled magical and cosmological functions.[6]

TO UNDERSTAND HOW these comparative ethnographic facts on berdache status square with Pueblo Indian culture, let us examine briefly the organization of space within pueblo life. Until quite recently, residential segregation by sex was the rule in every pueblo. Pedro de Castañeda, one of New Mexico's first explorers, observed in 1541 that the "young men live in the *estufas* [*kivas* or male ceremonial lodges]...it is punishable for the women to sleep in the *estufas* or to enter them for any other purpose than to bring food to their husbands or sons." Diego Pérez de Luxán reiterated this point in 1582, as did Fray Jerónimo Zárate de Salmerón when he wrote in 1623: "The women and young children sleep in [houses]; the men sleep in the *kiva*."[7]

Segregated from women in the *kiva*, men practiced the religious or political lore which kept the community at peace with itself and with its gods. Women's rituals, centered in the household, celebrated their powers over seed life and human reproduction. Their powers to bring forth life were immense and predictable. Men's magical powers over war, hunting, curing, and rain-making—the basic preoccupations of pueblo life—were always more unpredictable and precarious, and thus more elaborately ritualized. From men's perspective, women's capacity to produce, indeed to overproduce, was the problem that threatened to destroy the balance that existed in the cosmos between femininity and masculinity. Only by isolating themselves in ritual and placating the gods would men keep potent femininity from destroying everything. Women constantly sapped men of their energy—the men had to toil in fields that belonged to their mothers and wives, they had to protect the village from internal, external, natural, and supernatural enemies, and they constantly had to give semen to their voracious wives. Men got nothing in return from women in this agricultural society, for even if women bore children, until puberty those children belonged to their mothers.[8]

IT IS IN THIS isolated and fragile world of masculine political ritual that we must place berdaches or the *la'mana*, as they are known at Zuñi Pueblo. Male ritual was highly stratified. Men who became war chiefs, hunt chiefs or medicine men were persons with enormous political power by virtue of their physical strength, their knowledge of animal behavior, or their psychological acumen. It should thus not surprise us that the men who were pressed into berdache status were there primarily to service and delight the chiefs. Pedro de Castañeda, who observed a 1540 berdache initiation in New Mexico, noted that after the berdache had been cloaked in female garb,

> the *dignitaries* came in to make use of her one at a time, and after them all the others who cared to. From then on she was not to deny herself to any one, as she was paid a certain established amount for the service. And even though she might take a husband later on, she was not thereby free to deny herself to any one who offered her pay.[9]

Several centuries later, in 1852, Dr. William A. Hammond, the US Surgeon General, observed that the berdaches (he called them *mujerado*, literally "made into a woman") he met at Laguna and Acoma Pueblos, not far from Zuñi, were essential persons

The men who were pressed into berdache status were there primarily to service and delight the chiefs.

> in the saturnalia or orgies, in which these Indians, like the ancient Greeks, Egyptians and other nations, indulge. He is the chief passive agent in the pederastic ceremonies, which form so important a part in the performances. These take place in the Spring of every year.

Hammond added that when a man was transformed into a berdache,

> if he is a man occupying a prominent place in the councils of the pueblo, he is at once relieved of all power and responsibility, and his influence is at an end. If he is married, his wife and children pass from under his control, whether, however, through his wish or theirs, or by the orders of the council, I could not ascertain.

When Hammond asked if he could perform a physical exam on the Acoma berdache, it was Acoma's town chief who brought the berdache to Hammond and remained there throughout the examination. What these observations point to is the close association between Pueblo strong men or chiefs and the berdaches who offered sexual service. More important still is the status degeneration associated with these effeminates—they lost their social standing and family and were at the whim of any man who cared to use them.[10]

In Pueblo life, unmarried bachelors and junior men spent most of their time in the *kivas*. Ostensibly this was so that they could master religious lore, but in reality, also to minimize conflicts between juniors and seniors over claims to access to female sexuality which adult married men enjoyed. Sex with a berdache not only served a personal erotic need, but was also an assertion of power by these young men which served a religious (political) end. So long as bachelors were having sex with the berdaches, their village was not beset with conflicts between men over women. For as Hernando de Alarcón would note in 1540, berdaches "could not have carnal relations with women at all, but they themselves could be used by all marriageable youths." This may have been the reason why the Spaniards also called berdaches *putos* (male whores). European prostitutes initiated young men to sexuality and gave married men a sexual outlet without disrupting family, marriage or patrimony. Male prisoners of war pressed into prostitution in women's clothes were living testaments to their conqueror's virility and prowess. When berdaches were offered to guests as a gesture of generosity and hospitality, this too testified to the master's power. And like every slave historically, berdaches became economic assets when sold to other men—so that they could play out their fantasies of domination.[11]

THE VIOLENT MASCULINE WORLD of Pueblo Indian warriors is the cultural context within which we must place We'wha and the other *la'mana* that were reported at Zuñi Pueblo between 1880 and 1930. But bear in mind that conquest and annexation by the United States Army had, by these dates, totally constrained the ability of Pueblo men to wage war. What was left were the memories and rituals of war. In Pueblo religion, all ritual roles which are performed during ceremonials are believed to have supernatural antecedents or sanction. Will Roscoe correctly points us to the Zuñi myth "Destruction of the Kia'nakwe, and Songs of Thanksgiving," as the mythic explanation for the *la'mana*. I quote the myth here because it so poignantly elucidates the origins of berdache status.

The myth tells of war between the Zuñi gods and a group known as the Kia'nakwe. On the second night of what would be four days of fighting, the Zuñi Twin War Gods, U'yuyewi and Matsai'lema, were dispatched to Ko'thluwala'wa:

> to implore the Council of the Gods to cause rainfall, that the A'shiwi bowstrings, which were made of yucca fiber, might be made strong, and the bowstrings of the enemy, made of deer sinew, might be weakened. The A'shiwi secured their arrows for the engagement with the Kia'nakwe on Ko'yemshi mountain. The prayers of the A'shiwi brought heavy rains on the third morning, and again they met the enemy. This time their forces were strengthened by the Kok'ko, present at the request of U'yuyewi and Matsai'lema, who were now the recognized Gods of War. Again Ku'yapalitsa, the Cha'kwena [Warrior Woman], walked in front of her army, shaking her rattle. She suc-

SMITHSONIAN INSTITUTION, NATIONAL ANTHROPOLOGICAL ARCHIVES, NEG. 85-8666

We'wha

> ceeded in capturing four of the gods from Ko'thluwala'wa—Kor'kokshi, the first born of Si'wulutsiwa and Si'wulutsitsa; It'tsepasha (game-maker), one of the nine last-born; a Sa'yathlia (blue horn, a warrior god); and a Sha'lako (one of the couriers to the u'wannami (rain-makers). These gods succeeded in making their escape, but all were captured except the Sha'lako, who ran so like a hare that he could not be caught. The Kia'nakwe had a dance in which the prisoner gods appeared in celebration of their capture. Kor'kokshi, the first-born, was so angry and unmanageable that Ku'yapalitsa had him dressed in female attire previous to the dance, saying to him: 'You will now perhaps be less angry.'[12]

Matilda Coxe Stevenson, the anthropologist who transcribed this tale, explained in a marginal note that "in the Zuñi dramatization of the Kia'nakwe dance of thanksgiving for the capture of the gods the one personating the Kor'kokshi wears woman's dress and is referred to as the ko'thlama, meaning a man who has permanently adopted female attire." Elsie C. Parsons, another anthropologist, was told in 1916 that the reason the *la'mana* performed in the *kia'nakwe* dance was "because together with other *ko'ko* [gods] he [the *la'mana*] was taken prisoner by the *kia'nakwe*."

We know from other ethnographic sources that the person who personified Kor'kokshi during ceremonials not only wore female clothes, but also had blood smeared between his thighs. Matilda Coxe Stevenson and Elsie C. Parsons, the two persons who first observed this fact, as women, were predisposed to assume that a man dressed as a woman with blood between his thighs signified menstruation. Pueblo men greatly feared menstruating women and believed that they had the power to pollute male ritual. It thus seems highly unlikely that men would have represented a menstruating women in their rites. Rather, since the Kia'nakwe dance is about the capture and vanquishment of enemies, the blood might be explained more adequately as coming from a torn anus due to homosexual rape or castration.[13]

If we place We'wha and the other Zuñi berdaches in a larger comparative context, and in the thick description of the culture from which they were torn, does our understanding of them change? Matilda Coxe Stevenson described We'wha in 1904 as "the tallest person in Zuñi; certainly the strongest." During an 1890 fracas with American soldiers from Fort Wingate, We'wha was apprehended fighting alongside Zuñi's governor and members of the warrior society (the Bow priests). When Zuñi men staged their ceremonials, observed Elsie C. Parsons in 1916, the *la'mana* dressed like a woman, styled his hair like a woman, and then personified a woman in dance. Yet, when a *la'mana* died, the corpse was dressed like a woman except that "under the woman's skirt a pair of trousers are put on." *La'mana* were always buried among the men. Indeed, the Zuñi would say of We'wha and other *la'mana*, "she is a man." And while the berdaches may have performed women's work, and lived and dressed like women, their "behavior was not typical of Zuñi women," as Will Roscoe observes.[14]

GAY SCHOLARS HAVE been all too eager to cast the berdache as a gender role to which someone is socialized rather than as a social status a person was pressed into or assumed. American anthropologists on the other hand have been content to see the berdaches in the context of the Apollonian orderliness, peacefulness, and consensus that was once mistakenly imputed to Pueblo society. As for the issue of gender role or social status, let us squeeze the ethnographies a little harder. In 1904, Matilda Coxe Stevenson observed that "the men of the family...not only discourage men from unsexing [that is, becoming berdaches]...but ridicule them." Elsie C. Parsons wrote of Zuñi's *la'mana* in 1916, "in general a family would be somewhat ashamed of having a *la'mana* among its members." Of a Zuñi berdache named U'k, Parsons stated, "U'k was teased...by the children." During one of the *sha'lko* dances Parsons saw at Zuñi, the audience "grinned and even chuckled" at U'k; "a very infrequent display of amusement during these *sha'lko* dances," Parsons confided. After the dance ended, Parsons' Cherokee hostess asked her: "Did you notice them laughing at her [U'k]?...She is a great joke to the people..."[15]

How do we reconcile the ridicule and low status the berdaches had in Zuñi society with the high status and praise others lavish on them? For example, Roscoe writes:

> By all standards, We'wha was an important member of his community. Stevenson described him as "the strongest character and the most intelligent of the Zuñi tribe." The anthropologist Elsie Clew Parsons referred to him as "the celebrated *la'mana*."

The Pueblo Indians are well known for their aloofness toward outsiders, their general unwillingness to talk, and the secrecy with which they guard their esoteric knowledge and religion, even from their own young. We must thus ask why were berdaches like We'wha so eager to talk to American anthropologists in the 1890s? I suspect that as marginalized and low status individuals in the male political world, they were quite eager to tell their story to anyone willing to listen. Matilda Coxe Stevenson, Ruth Benedict and Elsie C. Parsons—all women who were themselves marginalized in the male academic world—listened to We'wha. As a result, We'wha was elevated greatly in social status in the eyes of all those whites who subsequently read about him. He quickly acculturated, and as Will Roscoe tells us, "We'wha was one of the first Zuñis to earn cash. After Stevenson showed him the bene-

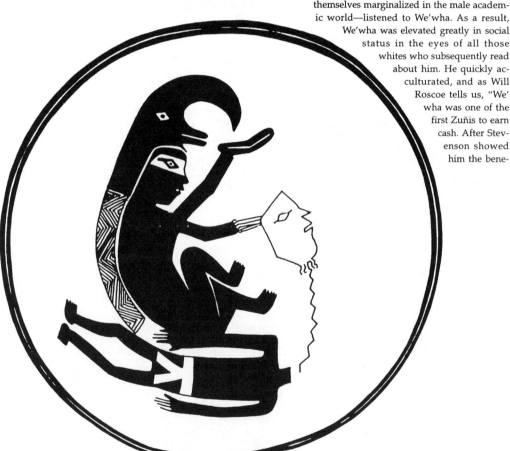

fits of using soap to wash clothes, he went into business doing laundry for local whites." And eventually We'wha even went to Washington, DC to mimic those caricatures of Indians which whites had created in their own minds.

In thinking about the meaning of berdache status among American Indians, we can profit by comparing it in different societies. It is equally important that when we pluck out an individual from his or her culture (be it We'wha, U'k or the countless other berdaches that once lived) that we place them in the context of those societies' hierarchies of gender. As for gays who seek a less rigid gender hierarchy in which to grow and prosper, the berdache status as a gender representation of power in war is probably not the place to find it. By finding gay models where they do not exist, let us not perpetrate on We'wha or U'k yet another level of humiliation with our pens. For then, the "conspiracy of silence" about the berdaches which Harry Hay had hoped to shatter will only be shrouded once again in romantic obfuscations. ▼

How do we reconcile the ridicule and low status the berdaches had in Zuñi society with the high status and praise others lavish on them?

[1]Those interested in this literature should consult J. Katz, Gay American History (New York, 1976) and C. Callender and L. Kochems, "The North American Berdache," Current Anthropology 24 (1963), pp. 443-70.

[2]Though the berdache status is reported for men and women, the male variant is best known. Harriet Whitehead does examine female berdache status in "The bow and the burden strap: A New Look at Institutionalized Homosexuality in Native North America," in Ortner and Whitehead, eds., Sexual Meanings (Cambridge, 1981), pp. 80-115.

[3]R. Trexler, Europe on Top: Male Homosexuality and the Conquests of America, 1400-1700 (forthcoming, Polity Press); C. Callender and L. Kochems, "The North American Berdache," Current Anthropology 24 (1963), pp. 443-70.

[4]"Naufrahios de Alvar Núñez Cabeza de Vaca," quoted in J. Katz, Gay American History (New York, 1976), p. 285.

[5]R. Trexler, Public Life in Renaissance Florence (New York, 1980).

[6]On berdaches as shamans see W. Williams, The Spirit and the Flesh: Sexual Diversity in American Indian Culture (Boston, 1986).

[7]G. Hammond and A. Rey, eds. and trans., Narratives of the Coronado Expedition 1540-1542 (Albuquerque, 1940), pp. 254-55; G. Hammond and A. Rey, eds. and trans., The Rediscovery of New Mexico 1580-1594 (Albuquerque, 1966), p. 178; Fray J. Zárate de Salméron, Relación (Albuquerque, 1967), paragraph 74.

[8]H. Haeberlin, The Idea of Fertilization in the Culture of the Pueblo Indians (New York, 1916); J. Collier, Marriage in Classless Societies (Stanford, 1988).

[9]Hammond and Rey, Narratives of the Coronado Expedition, p. 248.

[10]H. Hay, "The Hammond Report," One Institute Quarterly 6 (1963), p. 11.

[11]Hammond and Rey, Narratives of the Coronado Expedition. p. 147-48.

[12]M. Stevenson, The Zuñi Indians (Washington, D.C., 1904), pp. 36-37.

[13]Ibid., pp. 36-37; E. Parsons, "The Zuñi La'mana," American Anthropologist 18 (1916), p. 525.

[14]Parsons, p. 529.

[15]Stevenson, The Zuñi Indians, p. 37; Parsons, pp. 526, 528.

Ramón A. Gutiérrez is professor of history and a fellow at the Center for Advanced Study in the Behavioral Sciences in Stanford, California. He has written extensively on the Southwest and is the author of When Jesus Came, The Corn Mothers Went Away: Marriage, Conquest and Love in New Mexico, 1500-1846 *(forthcoming, Stanford University Press).* *This article was written while the author was a Fellow at the Center for Advanced Study in the Behavioral Sciences. He gratefully acknowledges the support provided by the Andrew W. Mellon Foundation.*

ON MALE INITIATION AND DUAL ORGANISATION IN NEW GUINEA

PER HAGE
University of Utah

A consideration of social organisation, culture and evolution in New Guinea suggests that male initiation rites which express sexual symmetry are not, as psychoanalytic interpretations maintain, based on unconscious relations of envy of female procreative powers but rather on perceived relations of analogy. They constitute a subset of possible magical acts designed to induce male growth. This subset is correlated with social structures based on dual organisation, or derived from it, and the entire set is congruent with a general type of social structure characteristic of New Guinea – one defined by a big man complex.

As a part of his psychoanalytic analysis of the bullroarer complex, Dundes (1976) interprets ritual homosexuality in initiation as an unconscious expression of male envy of female procreative powers. The New Guinea[1] societies adduced as examples are Marind (van Baal 1966) and Keraki (Williams 1936). Bettelheim (1962) in similar fashion interprets genital mutilation in imitation of menstruation among the Arapesh (Mead 1940; 1963) and Wogeo (Hogbin 1970)—so that there is anal eroticism on the south coast and urethral eroticism on the north coast. Not mentioned by either author is the displaced urethral eroticism, nose-bleeding in imitation of menstruation,[2] in the Highlands, e.g., Gahuku-Gama (Read 1952). Similar interpretations of these types of initiation rites have been made by Roheim (1949), Ashley Montagu (1937), Hiatt (1971) and Mead (1975). Sympathetic critics, such as Spiro (1955) and Aberle (1955), have pointed out that such arguments fail to explain the context in which these rites occur, while others, including Leach (1958) and Douglas (1966), have flatly rejected equations between primitive rites and neurotic behaviour. Dundes maintains that the 'ultimate test of [the] argument is not a matter of doctrinaire acceptance or rejection of Freud but rather how well or how poorly it succeeds in explaining the patterning of ethnographic facts' (Dundes 1976: 236). For New Guinea, and perhaps more generally, there is a simpler explanation based on morphological, cultural and historical-evolutionary considerations which accounts for both the context and the motives of rites based on forms of sexual symmetry. The purpose of this article is not to provide a general survey in the manner of Allen (1967) but to suggest a structural approach which tries to discern aspects of the logic underlying notions of gender and other cultural beliefs and social relations in New Guinea. The analysis here, and in a subsequent article by Hage and Harary (in press), attempts to combine features of the semiological and contextual treatments of

Man (N.S.) 16, 268–75

structure found in Lévi-Strauss and Douglas respectively, and incorporates some of the evolutionary speculations of Rubel and Rosman (1978) on New Guinea societies. The general aim is to contribute both to comparative work in New Guinea and to the elucidation of structures in *la pensée sauvage*.

As a symmetric corrective to psychoanalytic theory, Bettelheim (1962), on the basic of clinical and ethnographic data, proposed that corresponding to penis envy in women there is vaginal envy in men. The clinical data consisted of impromptu rituals of freely, self-induced bleeding in adolescent schizophrenic males, instigated by females, together with statements expressing envy of female sexual organs. The ethnographic data consisted of cases of genital mutilation equated with menstruation. The basic assumption is that the biological antithesis of the sexes in and of itself generates an envy of the opposite sex, some expression of which, as in ritual, promotes the development of an integrated, whole personality.

As an antisymmetric corrective to the relation between psychoanalysis and anthropology, Douglas (1975) proposed that such rites be interpreted in Durkheimian fashion as an expression of social morphology. The basic assumption is that 'Even the physiological differences between male and female can be masked by a categorization whose primary purpose is to reflect and sustain a particular social order' (Douglas 1975: 70). Thus in Arapesh and Wogeo, ritual penile incision, which is explicitly equated with the local conception of menstruation—the periodic discharge of bad blood as a condition of growth, is interpreted as a reflection of dual organisation: moieties which regulate feasting and initiation among the Arapesh and, in addition, marriage exchange among the Wogeo. More generally Douglas states:

> I would not argue that all rites of incision express the symmetry of dual social divisions. But if it is explicitly stated that the incision of the male genital organ is performed to achieve symmetry with the female reproductive system, then I would look for important dual social divisions whose symmetry I would suppose to be expressed in the ritual creating a symmetry of the sexes (Douglas 1975: 70).

If this proposition is generalised to include a variety of forms of ritual sexual symmetry, then it would account for the occurrence of the ritual analysed by both Bettelheim and Dundes in parts of the northern and southern coastal areas of New Guinea and also for their presence in certain areas of the Highlands and on the Papuan Plateau (see below). For the Sepik area generally, where dual organisation is common, e.g., Abelam (Kaberry 1941; Forge 1966), Iatmul (Bateson 1936), Banaro (Thurnwald 1916) and Umeda in addition to Arapesh and Wogeo, Gell (following Forge 1966) notes the 'elaborate cultural analogues of feminine reproductive activities (hence, e.g., penis-bleeding, 're-birth' ceremonies at initiation, etc.)' (1975: 277). On the south coast of New Guinea, in addition to the societies cited by Dundes (Marind, Keraki) there are others, such as Frederik Hendrik Island (Serpenti 1965), characterised by ritual homosexuality and dual organisation. Not only is the social organisation of the same basic type (namely, moieties which regulate feasting, initiation and in some case marriage, together with a rudimentary development of 'bigmanship' and competitive exchange and smallness of scale) but the initiation rituals as well are often similar and in some cases virtually identical in form, as can be seen by comparing the culminating ceremonies in Arapesh (Mead 1940; 1963) and Marind (van Baal 1966)[3] (see table 1).

TABLE 1.

Structural element	*Arapesh*	*Marind*
1. The supernatural tribal patron is:	*Tamberan*, a giant (androgynous?) male (who dwells in the sea and is 'tall as a coconut tree')	*Sosom*, a giant castrated male (who dwells in the sea and is 'tall as a coconut tree')
2. Whose voice is	a pair of male and female flutes which sound beautiful	a (phallic) bullroarer which inspires awe and anxiety
3. Whose mark is:	the imprint of his testicles and his anklets	piles of excrement and (reversed) footprints
4. Who is associated with:	a female cassowary initiator	male cassowary initiators
5. Who swallows the boys:	spitting them out 'plump and sleek'	excreting them 'stinking and disfigured'
6. The boys eat:	the good blood of the older men	the good semen of the older men
7. After seeing the patron the boys are	incised — to make them grow	sodomised — to make them grow

Rites of sexual symmetry, then, may have a common underlying structure and appear to be characteristic of a certain type of society. At the same time they can be regarded as alternatives in a larger set of practices, ubiquitous in New Guinea, whose basic aim is to induce male growth.

Langness remarks *à propos* of Bettelheim's argument that 'given Bena Bena beliefs about males and females in general, and about procreation in particular, I find it impossible to believe that in any meaningful sense men could be said to envy women' (Langness 1977: 13) since in Bena Bena and in the Highlands generally, 'women are considered in every way inferior.' Such objections pose no problem for psychoanalysis, which argues from biological givens and unconscious processes; indeed, they only manifest 'resistance.' A fundamental objection is Leach's (1958). He distinguishes between public symbolic behaviour, the concern of anthropologists, and private symbolism, the concern of psychoanalysis. The first refers to symbols connected with the social status of the actor where interpretation is a matter of elucidating recognised and shared conventional meanings. The second refers to psychological states of the actor where interpretation is a matter of elucidating repressed sexual wishes in the 'dreams and imaginings of individual psychopaths.' It is therefore false to equate the meanings of the obsessive behavior of neurotics with the rituals of primitives. If the interpretations of psychoanalysis and anthropology differ, they do not contradict and if they agree, they do not support one another.

Taking the high road then, it would be well to look at the actual meanings attributed to penile incision and homosexuality—to the traditional rationale offered by the natives (Dundes). In both cases, ethnography and sometimes mythology make it clear that the motive is quite simply and unequivocally to induce male growth. Some examples may be given. Among the Arapesh, penile incision is part of a complex of practices; in addition to food taboos a boy

> learns of the disciplinary and hygienic use of stinging nettles and actual bleeding with a sharpened bamboo instrument. He becomes the responsible custodian of his own growth; and the sanctions are all in terms of that growth. If he breaks the rules, no one will punish him; no one but himself will suffer. He will simply not grow to be a tall strong man (Mead 1963: 62–3).

Among the Keraki,

> More interesting is the rationalization of homosexual intercourse. The boys have to grow and the mothers are expected to be astonished at their sons having grown in stature when they return from seclusion. This alleged effect of sodomy is apparently parallel to the idea that prolonged cohabitation is necessary for pregnancy to be successful. The foetus must be built up through an accumulation of semen (van Baal 1966: 493).

Similar ideas prevail among the Marind where 'everywhere the act is seen as a necessary condition of a boy's physical development' (van Baal 1966: 494). There is also an interesting Keraki myth in this connection:

> *The beginning of sodomy.* Gufa, despite good feeding and attention, was a wretched undersized little boy, described as pot-bellied and constipated. He was the despair of his father until one day, ostensibly with the sole idea of promoting his growth, he conceived the idea of sodomising him. He took him apart from his mother during the night and put his idea into effect, rubbing semen over the child's body. The result was a miraculous increase in growth. The boy was instructed to keep this a dead secret from his mother, and when she next saw him she was delighted at the change but attributed it wrongly to the good food which Kambel [the father] must have given him, just as nowadays mothers are supposed to attribute the size of the initiates to the special feeding they have had at the *wara mongo* [seclusion] (Williams 1936: 308).

In general, the problem is really, to borrow Read's metaphor, an engineering one, and the solution is some form of imitation or analogy. As Read observes of Gahuku-Gama nose-bleeding,

> Informants unfailingly connect menstruation with a girl's physical growth. They point to its inevitable but unexplained advent and the concomitant signs of nubility, the increasing stature, the rounding and development of the bodily frame. It is a certain sign of her progress on the path to womanhood. But for the boy manhood and physical superiority are more a matter of chance and have therefore to be guarded, even engineered, in order to redress the balance of physiological inferiority. Initiation rites in consequence serve the same purpose for the male as menstruation for women. The one has been explained to me in terms of the other, and the same idea—the cyclical expulsion of blood—undoubtedly lies behind the men's ritual of nosebleeding (Read 1952: 15).

The preoccupation with male growth is not unique to Marind, Keraki, Arapesh, Wogeo and Gahuku-Gama, but is common throughout New Guinea. Therefore ritual bleeding and homosexuality should be viewed as part of a spectrum of magical acts, which in a certain type of society may involve some form of sexual symmetry, but in others may involve verbal spells, chants or cults of purification. It is worth noting here that the basic aim of Enga cults is the promotion of growth (and strength) (so that they might be more accurately termed 'growth' rather than 'purification' cults, to distinguish between their means and end):

> . . . bachelors as a category seek a generalized protection from females. They find this in the intermittent performance of *sanggai* rituals intended not only to cleanse and strengthen the actors but also to promote their growth and make them comely. Thus the more effective this magic is, the more attractive to young women the bachelors become, so that ultimately it procures wives for them and ensures that they will beget children for the clan (Meggitt 1964: 210).
>
> Most *sanggai* songs refer to plants and trees with desirable qualities, for instance certain mosses (*Lycopodium* and *Polytricum* spp.) are brightly colored and grow rapidly; the pine (*Podocarpus* sp.) has a smooth skin; the beech (*Nothophagus* sp.) is tall and strong (Meggitt 1964: 223).

Since these rites are common throughout New Guinea, they cannot be explained by reference to medical-hygienic factors—differential growth rates in different (Highland) societies—as some authors, such as Brown (1978) and Langness (1977), have suggested; and since they are not universal (are not found in Polynesia and Micronesia for example), they cannot be explained by reference to biological givens or innate psychic dispositions. The obvious answer is a structural one, namely that such rites are congruent with a basic type of society—one which emphasises competition and achieved status, one which is 'rampantly egalitarian,'[4] in short, one which in the ethnological and native vernacular has a 'big man complex'.[5] Literal and metaphorical bigness is here the precondition and sign of political success (and also of matrimonial success which the latter depends on), as opposed to situations in which status is theoretically determined by birth, as in the chiefdoms of Polynesia and Micronesia.

At the conclusion of his analysis, Dundes provides a synthesis of the anthropological theory of initiation rites—that they make men—and the psychoanalytic theory—that they make men into pseudo-women—by proposing that they make men by means of feminising the initiates. This is argued on the basis of the native equation between penile incision and menstruation and the passive role of initiates in homosexual rites. The ethnographic facts suggest otherwise: the relation between these rites and female physiology is based not on envy or identity but on analogy, that is, a perceived connexion between the onset of menstruation and growth, or on generalisation, that is, between initial and subsequent provisions of semen—if it induces growth in the foetus then it may also be thought to induce growth subsequently at adolescence. (In some societies a connexion may be made between mother's milk and semen.) They are magical acts which make a man more like a man; they put a (masculine) spring in his step and a gleam in his eye:

> The salutary effects of penile surgery are said to be immediately observable. The man's body loses its tiredness, his muscles harden, his step quickens, his eyes grow bright and his skin and hair develop a luster. He therefore feels lighthearted, strong and confident. This belief provides a means whereby the success of all perilous or doubtful undertakings can be guaranteed. Warriors make sure to menstruate before setting out on a raid, traders before carving an overseas canoe or refurbishing its sails, hunters before weaving a new net for trapping pigs (Hogbin 1970: 91)

As far as the presumed analogy between active and passive homosexuality and initiation is concerned, not only is libidinal satisfaction irrelevant to the culturally defined purpose of the act, but one could say that in the case of some societies, such as Kaluli (Schieffelin 1976) which define male/female on the basis of the opposition strong/weak, that the initiate is moved closer to the masculine pole and the initiator closer to the feminine pole as a result of obligatory and depleting provisions of semen.

Finally, on the subject of motivation, it should be noted that Dundes's emphasis on the secrecy of these rites lends no support to the sexual interpretation he advances (the sham sexual autonomy and therefore superiority of males) since initiation rites in general whether or not 'emulative of female procreativity' commonly involve secrecy. This can be taken as a formal expression of the superiority of one social group *vis-à-vis* another without any necessary reference to the specific content of the rites. In egalitarian societies, secrecy may mark off sex and age divisions and in stratified societies, class divisions as well, as the following example shows:

> Todd reported that the Huon Gulf initiation ceremonies, which form part of a secret male cult similar to that found in the eastern Highlands and in parts of the Sepik river area, were recently introduced into Möwehafen. The people, however, radically altered the rites by initiating boys and girls together and excluding all commoners. The operation of circumcision, which in the Huon Gulf area is a strictly guarded male secret equated with female menstruation, is performed shortly after birth by an old woman. During the course of the rites proper, which are performed some years after circumcision, the initiates, both boys and girls, are shown bullroarers and then remain secluded for a short period. The cognatic and socially stratified Möwehafen have thus transformed a ritual complex usually associated with a sex division into one associated with a class distinction between aristocrats and commoners (Allen 1967: 91).

In Rubel and Rosman's (1979) evolutionary taxonomy of New Guinea societies, the earliest and simplest type is one based on dual organisation which regulates the exchange of women, goods and ritual services. In the course of successive transformations based on an expansion in the Highlands and a concomitant increase in scale, the dual structures become separated, attenuated and eventually lost, being replaced by structures of multiple and cyclical exchange. The societies in the Sepik and on the south coast cited above are close to their prototype while those such as Enga represent the furthest evolutionary advance. It appears that Highland societies, such as Gahuku-Gama in the Eastern Central Highlands and Etoro on the Papuan Plateau, exhibiting ritual sexual symmetry, can be regarded as less evolved types which have retained some of the original dual structures. Etoro (Kelly 1977), for example, have implicit moieties which regulate marriage, and Gahuka Gama are organised into clan and sub-tribal pairs which exchange women and goods and hold joint rituals. The rites of the latter are similar to Arapesh and Wogeo: they involve a giant bird, *nama*, whose voice is a pair of flutes (age mates instead of male and female flutes) who comes to bleed the boys to make them grow. Geographically, then, there is a large area of ritual homosexuality on the south coast which reaches up to places on the Papuan Plateau and an area of ritual bleeding on the north coast which extends into the Eastern Central Highlands. The ritual and social resemblances suggest a common origin(s) and subsequent divergence from an *ur*-type. It should be a matter of considerable areal and theoretical interest to work out the general and specific transformations, following the lead of Rubel and Rosman, which would thus put into relation a large number of New Guinea societies.

To conclude: initiation rites of sexual symmetry are not based on unconscious relations of envy of female procreative powers but on perceived relations of analogy. They constitute a subset of possible magical acts designed to induce male growth. This subset is correlated with social structures based on dual organisation, and the entire set is congruent with a general type of social structure found in New Guinea—one defined by a big man complex. The interpretation advanced here does not deny that such rituals may express male dominance, superiority or solidarity. It only insists that their distribution must be explained and that their interpretation must be sought at the appropriate level—that social structure, native rationales and history must be taken into account.

NOTES

I wish to thank Dr Susan McKay for comments. This article was completed while I was a Visiting Fellow at Robinson College, Cambridge and a visitor at the Social and Political Sciences Committee, Cambridge University. I would like to thank both for their kind hospitality.

[1] 'New Guinea' is understood to refer to Papau New Guinea and West Irian.

[2] On the nose as an erogenous zone, functionally and structurally equivalent to the vagina, see the two volumes by W. Fliess (1897; 1902) which Paul Jorion has called to my attention.

[3] Summarised in a tabular form after Leach's (1972) analysis of Tongan myths.

[4] Forge's (1972) characterisation.

[5] Sahlins 1953.

REFERENCES

Aberle, D. 1955. Review of B. Bettelheim, *Symbolic wounds. Am. sociol. Rev.* 20, 248–9.

Allen, M. R. 1967. *Male cults and secret initiations in Melanesia.* Melbourne: Univ. Press.

Ashley Montagu, M. F. 1937. *Coming into being among the Australian Aborigines.* New York: AMS Press.

Baal, J. van 1966. *Dema: description and analysis of Marind-Anim culture (south New Guinea).* The Hague: Martinus Nijhoff.

Bateson, G. 1936. *Naven.* Cambridge: Univ. Press.

Bettelheim, B. 1962. *Symbolic wounds: puberty rites and the envious male.* New York: Collier Books.

Brown, P. 1978. *Highland peoples of New Guinea.* Cambridge: Univ. Press.

Douglas, M. 1966. *Purity and danger.* London: Routledge & Kegan Paul.

——— 1975. Couvade and menstruation. In *Implicit meanings.* London: Routledge & Kegan Paul.

Dundes, A. 1976. A psychoanalytic study of the bullroarer. *Man* (N.S.) 11, 220–38.

Fliess, W. 1897. *Die Beziehungen zwischen Nase und weibliche Geschlechtsorganen in ihrer biologischen Bedeutungen dargestellt.* Wien.

——— 1902. *Über den ursächlichen Zusammenhang von Nase und Geschlechtsorgan, zugleich ein Beitrag zur Nervenphysiologie.* Wien 1902.

Forge, A. 1966. Art and environment on the Sepik. *Proc. R. anthrop. Inst.* 1965, 23–31.

——— 1972. The golden fleece. *Man* (N.S.) 7, 527–40.

Gell, A. 1975. *Metamorphoses of the cassowaries.* New Jersey: Humanities Press.

Hage, P. & F. Harary in press. Pollution beliefs in Highland New Guinea. *Man* (N.S.) 16,

Hiatt, L. R. 1971. Secret pseudo-procreation rites among the Australian Aborigines. In *Anthropology in Oceania* (eds) L. R. Hiatt & C. Jayawardena. Sydney: Angus & Robertson.

Hogbin, I. 1970. *The island of menstruating men.* San Francisco: Chandler.

Kaberry, P. 1941. The Abelam tribe, Sepik District, New Guinea: a preliminary report. *Oceania* 11, 345–67.

Kelly, R. 1977. *Etoro social structure*. Ann Arbor: Univ. of Michigan Press.
Langness, L. 1977. Ritual power and male dominance in the New Guinea Highlands. In *The anthropology of power* (eds) R. Fogelson & R. Adams. New York: Academic Press.
Leach, E. 1958. Magical hair. *J. R. anthrop. Inst.* **88**, 145–64.

——— 1972. The structure of symbolism. In *The interpretation of ritual* (ed.) J. S. La Fontaine. London: Tavistock.
Mead, M. 1940. The Mountain Arapesh II: supernaturalism. *Anthrop. Pap. Am. Mus. Nat. Hist.* vol. **37** (3).
——— 1963. *Sex and temperament in three primitive societies*. New York: William Morrow.
——— 1975. *Male and female*. New York: William Morrow.
Meggitt, M. 1964. Male-female relationships in the highlands of Australian New Guinea. *Am. Anthrop.* **66**, 204–24.
Read, K. 1952. The nama cult of the Central Highlands, New Guinea. *Oceania* **23**, 1–25.
Roheim, G. 1949. The symbolism of subincision. *Am. Imago* **6**, 321–88.
Rubel, P. & A. Rosman 1978. *Your own pigs you may not eat*. Chicago: Univ. Press.
Sahlins, M. 1963. Poor man, rich man, big-man, chief. *Comp. Stud. Soc. Hist.* **5**, 283–300.
Schieffelin, E. 1976. *The sorrow of the lonely and the burning of the dancers*. New York: St Martin's Press.
Serpenti, L. M. 1965. *Cultivators in the swamps*. Assen: Van Gorcum.
Spiro, M. 1955. Review of B. Bettelheim, *Symbolic wounds*. *Am. J. Sociol.* **61**, 163–4.
Thurnwald, R. 1916. Banaro society: social organization and kinship system of a tribe in the interior of New Guinea. *Am. Anthrop. Ass. Mem.* **3**, 253–391.
Williams, F. R. 1936. *Papuans of the Trans-Fly*. Oxford: Clarendon Press.

1 Gilbert H. Herdt

Ritualized Homosexual Behavior in the Male Cults of Melanesia, 1862–1983: An Introduction

INTRODUCTION

Melanesia has long provided a rich stomping ground for anthropological studies of initiation rites, secret societies, sex-related principles of social grouping and, more recently, gender ideologies. The numerous studies of male/female relations and "sexual antagonism" (Brown and Buchbinder 1976; Langness 1967; Meggitt 1964; Read 1954; reviewed in Herdt and Poole 1982) alone distinguish Melanesia as a culture area. Considering this intersection of ritual and sexuality, it is puzzling how little has been written on the institutionalized aspects of eroticism in Melanesian societies, particularly since Melanesianists such as Haddon (1917:351) long ago argued that throughout New Guinea, "initiation ceremonies are not merely the promotion of the novitiates, but also their introduction to the sexual life." But even more puzzling is the virtual evasion of a psychosocial phenomenon that is of patent anthropological interest and one that now appears more common than once thought: ritualized homosexual behavior.

I reached this conclusion when summarizing a study of such sexual practices and their gender symbolism among the Sambia, a hunting and horticultural society of the Eastern Highlands, Papua New Guinea (Herdt 1981). In reviewing the Melanesian literature of the past 100 years or so, it surprised me that similar practices are more widespread and significant than one would ever suspect from contemporary Melanesian studies (e.g., Allen 1967).[1] Moreover, cross-cultural surveys of initiation and sexuality, which invariably draw upon Melanesia, ignore ritualized homosexuality (see, for example, Cohen 1964; Stephens 1962; Whiting et al. 1958; Whiting and Whiting 1975). By thus neglecting the data cited below, previous surveys and models of social and symbolic variation in initiation rites and relationships between the sexes and gender roles are lacking, and the incidence and meaning of ritualized homosexual practices in these groups remains obscure.

The aim of this introduction is to review the extant Melanesian literature and to explore the linkages between institutionalized homosexuality and certain sociocultural arrangements in Melanesia as a whole. My thesis is that systems that incorporate ritualized homosexuality can be seen as representing the extremes to which sexual polarity extends in a range of Melanesian societies. Rather than ignore homosexual practices as a tangential curiosity, we may look to their distribution, elaboration, and cultural meaning in helping to sort out cross-cultural variation in sexual behavior and gender ideologies in these groups. My review concludes with the possibility that there is a geographic-historical nexus of ritualized homosexuality between these Melanesian groups which is further substantiated by correlations of related sociocultural patterns among them.

What is the current state of the cross-cultural survey literature on homosexual behavior in Melanesia? The view outside of Melanesian studies is plainly muddled, a confusion that invites comment before sorting out the ethnographic texts. Opler (1965:121), for example, in a widely read textbook on human sexuality, denies the existence of institutionalized homosexual practices:

> Clubs and societies have on occasion been sex limited, as in Melanesia, but there is no reason to believe that this limitation has

> promoted homosexual behavior in these social, economic, or sometimes ritual settings—or indeed that such behavior exists at all in such instances.

Several years later, Minturn et al. (1969), in a Human Relations Area Files cross-cultural survey on sexual beliefs and behavior, coded homosexual behavior as being "absent" in New Guinea societies, but present in Australia. Yet Hiatt (1971:87), speaking in the context of Róheim's early accounts of Australian aboriginal rites, states, "It would be hard to find empirical grounds for representing these rites as 'guilty homosexual secrets.'" Where Australian and Melanesian materials bear comparison in this matter, Hiatt's view seems inadequate (see below). And as recently as 1976, Parratt, in a literature review of F. E. William's (1936*c*) Keraki work, writes:

> The trans-Fly Papuans appear to have been unique among Melanesian peoples in that novices were initiated also into the practice of sodomy, which was thought to contribute to the physical development of the youths.
>
> *(1976:65)*

Here we find homosexual practices either denied, coded as absent, or treated as unique. Why should scholars have developed such views?

There are several reasons. One is that many of the Melanesian references on ritualized homosexuality are skimpy, single-line allusions that do not inspire much confidence. Another is that sex remains one of the "taboo" subjects in anthropology (Marshall and Suggs 1971). Anthropologists, including Melanesianists, have not in general provided good descriptive accounts of sexual behavior, homosexual activity in particular. A third factor is a tendency for writers still to view homosexual behavior as universally deviant, unnatural, or perverse, not seeming to recognize that such practices are relative to particular cultural contexts and therefore invite analysis like any other form of social behavior.[2] Fourth is the related matter of "authorities" who have tended to regard only heterosexuality as prevalent or "normal." Malinowski is a case in point. In his early literature review on *The Family Among the*

Australian Aborigines, he paid no attention to ritual homosexuality, though he used Australian sources that had mentioned it (see especially 1913:262–269). Later, in his writings on the Trobriand Islands he denied the existence of homosexual activity except as "perversion" (1929:448–453, 468, 472–473), arguing that the *natives* saw "sexual aberrations as *bad* because a natural law has been flouted" (1929:468, emphasis mine). (He does not, incidentally, account for why Trobrianders should have a category for anal intercourse.) Elsewhere, he argued ironically: "Homosexuality is the rule among those upon whom white man's morality has been forced in such an irrational and unscientific manner," adding, however, that such indigenous "perversions" are "much more prevalent in the [nearby] Amphlett and d'Entrecasteau Archipelago" (Malinowski 1927:80; cf. Róheim 1950:174). Needless to say, no one has ever investigated that latter suggestion.

In his own day, when generalized to all of Melanesia, Malinowski's view was overdrawn. To illustrate, Havelock Ellis[3] (1936: Pt. II, 8–21), whose *Psychology of Sex* was widely read, cited various ethnographic examples of institutionalized homosexual practices in Melanesia and Australia. So did Westermarck (1917:459ff.) in another book of similar popular currency. Malinowski's teachers—Seligman (1902) and Haddon (cited in Ellis 1936:9)—also referred to such sources. Van Gennep in his classic study *Les Rites de Passage* (1960:170–171), specifically argued that the use of heterosexual coitus as a final "rite of incorporation" held "equally true for those of homosexual nature," and he quoted Parkinson's (1907) New Britain ethnography to make his point. Moreover, the early Freudians, always quick to exploit new ethnographic data, specifically compared the manifestations of ritualized homosexuality in Austro-Melanesian groups (e.g., see Reik 1946; Róheim 1926:70).

Since the days of such old-fashioned ethnological scrapbooks, other scholars have unsystematically used various works cited below. They have ranged from eminent sex researchers (Ford and Beach 1951:132; Money and Ehrhardt 1972:132–139), to cross-cultural psychiatrists (Foulks 1977:12–13), classicists (e.g., Bremmer 1980:280f.), the indefatigable German ethnologists (Baumann 1955:210–229; Bleibtreu-Ehrenberg 1980; Karsch-Haack

1911:92–115), Jungians (Eliade 1958:26–27), Freudians (Bettelheim 1955; Vanggaard 1972), social historians (Trumbach 1977:26–27), biologizers (Tiger 1970:126–155) and popularizers (Kottak 1974:287–288; Tripp 1975:64ff.). Each of these writers, in terms not altogether congenial to social anthropology, have variously argued for, and used, Melanesian materials on ritualized homosexuality to make one or another point about universals of normality and variation in human sexual behavior. Throughout this long period, however, no one ever systematically studied the phenomenon; the ethnological comments of Haddon (1936) and Layard (1959) are notable exceptions, and they appeared, unfortunately, in obscure places. Allen's *Male Cults and Secret Initiations in Melanesia*, still the chief source book on the area, only mentions ritualized homosexual practices (1967:96–99). Not until Dundes' (1976) discussion had an anthropologist studied and challenged this literature to interpret Melanesian sociocultural systems. In sum, there are ample reasons for non-Melanesianists to be confused about the Melanesian materials on ritualized homosexuality. The remainder of my chapter is devoted to clarifying both what we do and do not know about it.

To ensure the fullest measure of control over the ethnographic material, I shall only examine ritualized homosexuality in Melanesia, especially the island of New Guinea. This culture area involves an immense literature that is thick and uneven, with the older sources in several different languages, published in obscure and inaccessible, often defunct journals, and often referenced to outmoded ethnographic names; but this material I know best. Similar phenomena are reported from elsewhere in the tribal world; perhaps, beyond Australia, the Amazon Basin is closest to the Melanesian situation (see Keesing 1982).[4] Regretfully I cannot review the Australian Aboriginal material, which properly should be considered alongside of Melanesia, as Róheim (1926:70; 324–337 and passim) and later Van Baal (1963) have argued. Thus, I leave it to others to make sense of the following *explicit* references to ritualized homosexual practices in the Australian literature, especially on the Kimberley Mountains and Central Desert tribes (see Berndt and Berndt 1951:67; Hardman 1889:73–74; Kaberry 1939:257; Mathews 1896:334–335; 1900:635–636; Meggitt

5

1965*a*:183; Purcell 1893:287; Ravenscroft 1892:121–122; Róheim 1926:70; 1929:189; 1932:51; 1950:118–119, 122; 1974:243–244, 247–248; Spencer and Gillen 1927, 2:470, 486; Strehlow 1913:98–122).[5]

TERMS • Part of the difficulty in the anthropological literature on sex and gender stems from a plethora of confusing terminology which finds scholars arguing whether something is present or absent without first defining what that something is. The questions surrounding the Omani *xanith* (Wikan 1977) belong to this confusing morass (see Carrier 1980*b*). It is therefore crucial at the start to define the parameters of our subject as precisely as possible.

The subject of these essays is restricted to *ritualized* homosexual (RH)* practices and behavior. I myself prefer the adjective *ritualized*, despite its ambiguous and exotic connotations, over other imprecise terms such as *ceremonialized*, which is weaker and incidental. (Devereux's [1937] classic paper on Mohave homosexuality utilizes these modifiers and many more.) *Ritualized* as a modifier applies best to the Melanesian situation because: (1) homosexual practices are implemented usually through male initiation rites, having (2) religious overtones, as well as being (3) constrained by broader cultural rules and social roles, for which the full moral and jural force of a society, or a secret men's society, not only condones but often prescribes sexual intercourse among certain categories of males; and (4) various age-related and kinship taboos define and restrict the nature of this male/male sexual behavior. Ritualized homosexuality is thus a Melanesian type of institutionalized homosexual activity in the broader sense found elsewhere in the world.

Several other general points will help indicate the terms of the following review. First, the Melanesian literature advises that ritualized homosexual behavior is almost exclusively a *male* phenomenon (cf. Ford and Beach 1951). Institutionalized female homosexuality is very rare (cf. Hooker 1968:230), and little is known of the few reported cases (see below). Second, the males who are involved are usually of markedly different ages; they are

*I will at times use (RH) to indicate ritualized homosexual behavior or groups with such practices, to avoid too bumpy reading.

forbidden to reverse sexual roles (inserter/insertee) with *each* other, meaning, in effect, that they are in age-ranked, asymmetrical status relationships. Third, these homosexual contacts are culturally focused virtually everywhere on semen transmission. Fourth, as far as is known, Melanesian homosexual behaviors do not involve fetishistic cross-gender dressing or eroticized transvestism of any sort, individual or institutional (see Davenport 1977:155). Although nonerotic ceremonial transvestism is known from Melanesia, it seems infrequent and not strongly correlated with ritualized homosexuality,[6] (see Schwimmer, chap. 6 below). Nor is there any evidence that primary male transsexualism (Stoller 1968, 1975) is involved.[7] Fifth, in these societies males are involved in homoerotic contacts first as insertees, then as inserters, being often steadily involved, after initiation, for months or years. Yet in all known cases, they are later expected to marry and father children, as is customary. Their psychosexual involvement (to use a comfortably neutral term) does not make them into "homosexuals," in the sense that this noun connotes (life-long habitualized sexual preference for members of the same sex) in Western culture (Stoller 1980). In other words, to engage in initiatory or secular homosexual acts (behavior) does not necessarily mean that one is or becomes "homosexual" in habitual sexual motivation or sex object choice (identity). This analytic distinction is reviewed in my summary. Finally, if these acts are not performed by "homosexuals," then why use the adjective *homosexual*? It might be objected that their initial ritual context places these sexual contacts in a category different from that with which Westerners mark off "homosexual." While this objection holds truth in a sense, we should not forget that sexual acts, ritualized or not, always entail erotic arousal, at least for the inserter. Moreover, as a simple modifier, *homosexual* is preferable and more accurate than any other, since these societies permit sexual penetration and insemination between people of the same sex.* *Bisexual* is therefore inaccurate to describe these people or their homoerotic acts: typically, (RH) groups often forbid heterosexual contacts during the *same* period when boys

*Wherever possible below I shall use "ritualized homosexual behavior" or (RH) in this sense; where I slip into using "homosexuality" it is for stylistic economy, and it should be understood in the fuller sense.

are being inseminated by older males; and the younger insertees are strictly separated from females and are only allowed sexual contacts with superordinate males after initiation.

In these terms I thus exclude from this survey all of the following phenomena: individual (aberrant) or noninstitutionalized homosexual behavior; homosexual behavior as reported from acculturated settings such as plantations or prisons;[8] all fetishistic cross-gender dressing or eroticized transvestism; transsexualism; psychotic behavior or any other form of social deviance as defined by the natives. We shall only be concerned, then, with ritualized homosexual behaviors supported by customary sociocultural arrangements.

Finally, I wish to make it explicitly clear that I am *not* asserting (or even hinting) any of the following: that all ritual involves homosexual activity, latent or manifest, in Melanesia or elsewhere; that all Melanesians are prone to engage in homosexual activity; or, to reiterate, that these homoerotic activities make the practitioners into "homosexuals." The patterns of (RH) examined below are clearly known from only a small number—perhaps 10 to 20 percent—of all Melanesian groups that have been studied. What matters is not the gross numbers of these societies or their total populations but rather their psychosocial and symbolic meaning when viewed against broader trends of sexual polarity and gender ideology in Melanesia.

Because of its historical depth and unevenness, I have organized the literature review geographically, then by the date of ethnographic reportage and by cultural subarea (e.g., Eastern Melanesia, Western Papua, etc.). The unfolding survey may be read as a story—of increasing allusions followed by fuller accounts of ritual homosexuality, the accumulation of which provides understanding of the pieces of a puzzle widely scattered and still not entirely unscrambled.

Comparisons between these texts involve huge problems concerning the comparability of social units. In some ethnographic reports (e.g., Chalmers's [1903*a*] note on the Bugi, see below), tiny communities are described; in others, there are far larger populations (e.g., the Marind-anim [Van Baal 1966]), tribes whose total numbers run into the thousands, scattered over vast areas. Then there is the question of considering related social units as discrete and historically unrelated (i.e., Galton's problem). This issue raises difficulties in the entangled Melanesian literature. My solution is to be conservative: in doubtful cases of geographically close groups (e.g., the Bugi [Chalmers 1903*a*] versus Kiwai Islanders [Landtman 1927]) I will assume social linkage. When dealing with whole subregions (e.g., Southeastern Irian Jaya), I count groups as different (e.g., Marind-anim versus Jaquai) when there is evidence sufficient to justify their classification as separate units. But such classifications do not mean that these peoples necessarily belong to different subregional cultural traditions. We can thus identify a people both as constituting a separate *social unit* as well as belonging to a broader *cultural tradition* in a geographic subregion of Melanesia. In this survey we shall examine eight different subregions which vary in size and in the number of their constituent social units (see table 1.1). Then I shall briefly reconnoiter several questionable cases. Each subregion will be treated separately; clear statements about ritualized homosexual behavior is the organizing theme. Finally, I have tried also to assess the quality of these reports where possible and to substantiate early reports with later ones, either in the same society or elsewhere from the same cultural tradition.[9]

The ethnographic material from the earliest historical period is often thin, diverse, and difficult to interpret. It covers the widest possible geographic and ethnological spectrum, from Eastern Melanesia (Fiji, the New Hebrides,* and New Caledonia), the offlying islands of old German New Guinea, and the Papuan Gulf at the Fly River, to disparate parts of North and Southeast Dutch New Guinea (see endpaper map). It is also checkered, being an unreliable mixture of reports from travelers, missionaries, and early anthropologists. (Some early travelers' reports are fantastic—"a stimulus for jaded imaginations": Whittaker et al. 1975:271ff.)

EASTERN MELANESIA

FIJI • Our earliest hints of ritualized homosexuality come from the extreme easternmost part of Melanesia, Fiji, which was colonized before island New Guinea. These data suggest the presence

*The New Hebrides will be used here to conform to the older literature references; however, it covers the New Hebrides Archipelago, the Banks Islands, Torres Straits, and other islands now incorporated in the new nation of Vanuatu.

TABLE 1.1

THE DISTRIBUTION OF RITUALIZED HOMOSEXUALITY IN MELANESIAN GROUPS

Geographic Subregion	Social Unit (referred to in text)	Related social units (not referred to in text)	Language type*
I. Eastern insular Melanesia	1. Fiji		A
	2. New Caledonia		A
	New Hebrides:		A
	3. Malekula Island		
II. Northeastern insular Melanesia	4. New Britain		
	5. Duke-of-Yorks		
	6. East Bay		
III. Western Papua	Lower Fly River:		
	7. Kiwai Island (+ Bugilai)		N
	Trans-Fly Delta:		N
	8. Keraki	Karigare[1]	N
		Yarne	
		Kaunje	
		Wekamara	N
	9. Suki		N
	10. Boadzi		
IV. Southeastern Irian Jaya	11. Kanum		N
	12. Yéi-anim		N
	13. Marind-anim	Maklew-anim[2]	
		Yab-anim	
		Kurkari-anim	
	14. Kimam (Fr. Hen. Is.)		N
	15. Jaquai		N

	16. Asmat		N
	17. Casuarina Coast		N
V. Northeastern Irian Jaya	18. Humboldt Bay		N
VI. Great Papuan Plateau	19. Bedamini		N
	20. Etoro		N
	21. Kaluli		N
	22. Onabasalu		N
	23. Gebusi (Nomad River)		
VII. Anga (Kukukuku)	24. Sambia		N
	25. Baruya		N
	26. Jeghuje		N
	27. Other Highlands Anga groups	Usarumpiu	N
		Wantukiu	
		Aziana	
	28. Lowlands Anga groups	Lohiki[3]	N
		Kapau	
		Ivori	
		Mbwei	
		Yagwoia	
		Ampale	
		Langamar	
		Menya	
		Katje	
VIII. Northern Province	29. Ai'i		N
	Total: 29 societies	Total: 19 related societies	

* Austronesian = A
Non-Austronesian = N
[1] From Williams (1936c:208)
[2] From Van Baal (1966:maps)
[3] From Gajdusek et al. (1972)

of ritualized homosexuality, but they are highly questionable (see, for example, Seemann 1862:160–162, 169–170; and Waterhouse 1866:341, 345). Nonetheless, in the late 1920s, the authority A. M. Hocart speculated that "sodomy [anal intercourse] was once recognized between cross-cousins" among the hill tribes of Fiji (quoted in Layard 1942:491). Hocart linguistically compared the pertinent Fijian terms of address with those associated with anal intercourse in ancient Hawaii (cf. Remy 1862:xliii; and see below on Malekula Island). For Fiji, then, the case for ritual homosexuality is thin.

NEW CALEDONIA • Foley's (1879) report is the earliest definite mention of (RH). Comparing the New Caledonian villagers to the ancient Greeks, Foley states: "It is true that this military club is complicated by pederasty" (ibid.:606). Arguing that the warriorhood is opposed to "the uterine club," he also remarks, "Women are the enemies of pederasty" (ibid.). Collaborative sketchy reports can be found in De Rochas (1862:235) and in Jacobus X. (1893:330–331; 1898, 2: 359–360). New Caledonia is culturally similar to New Hebrides societies, where homosexual activities are much better described.

MALEKULA ISLAND (NEW HEBRIDES)* • The first major source for Malekula is A. B. Deacon, a Cambridge-trained anthropologist who carried out intensive fieldwork in Seniang district, South West Bay area, and who also collected valuable survey data on other Malekula communities (see map 2). Though the most elaborate forms of ritualized homosexuality occur in the northern districts, especially among the Big Nambas tribe, related elements of the same complex occur elsewhere on Malekula as well as on neighboring islands. The characteristics and possible interrelations of this complex are delineated in Allen's important paper below (see chap. 2). Outside the Big Nambas area, "homosexuality is apparently very rare" (Deacon 1934:156), though among prepubertal boys masturbation and heterosexual play are "common." In other, more northerly areas, male homosexual practices are "occasional and sporadic," whereas lesbianism is "com-

*I am very grateful to Professor Michael Allen for clarifying the ethnographic data provided in this section.

mon" (Deacon 1934:170).[10] Elements of the same ritual complex—including a belief in heads (both penis heads and mens' heads) as loci of male power, the use of elaborate headdresses to represent spirit beings, the symbolic importance of sharks, and the performance of painful initiation rites with long periods of seclusion—are found in varying combinations throughout much of the northern New Hebrides and Banks Islands (Layard 1942:493–494; Allen 1981).

The main features of the traditional North Malekula case can be roughly sketched as follows.[11] These groups tend toward chieftainship, the highest form being attained among the Big Nambas. Here, too, ritualized homosexuality is the most prominent. Layard (1942:489) describes the Big Nambas as "an extreme form of patrilineal culture . . . exceeding all other New Hebrides tribes in the very low status which they accord to women." Boys are initiated at an early age and thereafter stringently avoid women. Circum-incision* accords them masculine status; and it is positively correlated with "organized homosexuality" (Layard 1942:486–488). Thus, while homosexual contacts may have traditionally existed in other parts of Vanuatu, they are most highly elaborated among the Big Nambas, where circumcision is practiced (Allen 1967:96–97). Is demography a relevant consideration? Here as elsewhere in New Guinea, there is a sex ratio disparity (126 males per 100 females [Layard 1942:745]), exacerbated by the chiefly system, which enables the Big Nambas chiefs to hold a virtual monopoly of the women (Layard 1959:109). Is cultural belief related? Yes: the natives see homosexual intercourse as a way to strengthen the boy's penis (Deacon 1934:260–262)—which Layard (1942:489) believes to be a "transmission of male power by physical means"—for the penis is held in "high esteem" and the glans penis is accorded "extreme reverence."

Finally, the New Hebrides complex reveals a symbolic relation between living and dead kinsmen and male gender ideology. Homosexual partners refer to each other as husband and wife, the initiate calling his man-lover "sister's husband" (Deacon 1934:261; Layard 1942:488–489), terms that indicate the close affinal, sex-

*A rare and complex form of circumcision found here which Layard has described in detail and Allen (chap. 2) mentions below.

ual, and perhaps economic interrelation between these males. Layard speaks of homosexual anal intercourse as symbolizing "continuity with the ancestral ghosts in the male line," especially in areas, such as the Small Islands, wherein mystical anal penetration as a ritual hoax supplants actual homosexual coitus (Layard 1959:111). We see similar symbolic themes of spiritual insertion elsewhere in Melanesia (see Summary and Analysis). This same culture complex, minus circumcision and ritual homosexuality, is found in a wide area extending through Malekula, Raga, and the Banks Islands (Layard 1942:493–494). Deacon was so struck by the similarities between this cult and a structurally similiar initiatory complex (with circumcision, devouring ritual spirits, bullroarers, etc.) found in the Finschhafen area, near the Markham River on mainland New Guinea, that he argued for a historical connection through diffusion from a common source, most probably located in Eastern Indonesia (Deacon 1925, 1934:268–269).[12]

If Layard found mystical support for patrilineal descent in the New Hebrides, he also saw symbolic connections between homosexuality, marriage, and masculinity. Drawing speculative parallels between Malekula, Fiji, and Western Australia, Layard (1942:494) states: "Among the Big Nambas a man took as his boy lover a member of his wife's marriage section, and it was only later that this love-relationship turned into one of joking and mutual violence." Further, Layard (1942:489–490) advanced a rather sophisticated argument about the causes of (RH). He believed that social forms (sexual polarity, chieftainship, sister exchange), created by the religious rationalization of male descent and affiliation (e.g., circum-incision and ancestral "mythical homosexuality"), gradually resulted in homoerotic contacts "as an everyday practice." In other words, ideology and social structure historically produced ritual homosexual contacts that became as regularly institutionalized as heterosexual contacts. I shall return to this historicist argument in the summary.

NEW BRITAIN AND NORTHEASTERN MELANESIA

If we now look north (see map 1), we may trace a series of ethnographic cases including New Britain and the nearby Duke-of-York Islands (formerly German New Guinea), and East Bay.

NEW BRITAIN AND THE DUKE-OF-YORKS • The German ethnologist Richard Parkinson wrote a massive early text which, though in German and little read, remains the classic source on the area. He describes men's secret societies among the Tolai people of the Gazelle Peninsula area of New Britain island. Ritualized homosexual practices are present in the special Ingiet cult there.

> When candidates are admitted in the Ingiet, sodomy [anal intercourse] is committed before the eyes of all present. An older Ingiet leaves the *balana marawot* [cult house] and returns quite naked and smeared with lime from top to toe. He holds in his hand the end of a coconut mat, the other end he offers to one of the novices. The two of them scuffle around with it for some time, and then fall over each other and the abomination takes place. Each initiate in turn must submit to this procedure. In extenuation of this, however, I will remark that paederasty is no crime in the eyes of the native, who regards it merely in an amusing light.
>
> *(Parkinson 1907:544)*

Shortly later, no less an authority than Van Gennep (1960:171) used this passage as an example of homosexual "rites of incorporation" in *Les Rites des Passage.* It is unclear how widespread this practice was in the Bismarck Archipelago of that day, but it may have been restricted to the Ingiet secret society.

The lime-coated figure may here symbolically represent a "spirit woman," which Parkinson (1907:537) tells us the fully initiated elder can "turn himself into." If so, it would exemplify what Layard (1942:474) called a "mythical" symbolization of homosexual practices. Whether similar practices existed in the related Duk-Duk men's cult (Rickard 1891) is unclear, but Richard Salisbury (personal communication) thinks not. On the Ingiet cult, however, Parkinson pointedly (1907:544) reassures us that his sexual information is reliable.[13]

No further reports even mentioned ritual homosexuality in New Britain for almost seventy years.[14] Presumably, the practice is now long since abandoned. However, Epstein (1977:178–179) refers to fragmentary evidence indicating the traditional practice of anal homosexual intercourse among the Tolai. And Errington (1974), whose work on the neighboring Duke-of-York Islands is the first since Parkinson's (1907:545), has supplied important confirmation of ritualized homosexual practices in the wider New Britain area. In the contemporary context of initiation on the Duke-of-Yorks, he notes:

> One man, a volunteer, not otherwise important in the ritual, lay on his stomach without his waistcloth in order to expose his anus to the boy. An informant of sixty said that in the past a boy going to the *taraiu* for the first time had to perform fellatio* on one of the adult men. Another informant, a young man about thirty-five, was shocked when I asked about this practice. . . . [Errington here cites Parkinson. Thus, these practices suggest . . .] homosexual submission when a boy is separated from the society of women and incorporated into the society of men.
>
> *(Errington 1974:84)*

The New Britain material clearly indicates homosexual practices in secret initiation. But we do not know whether (RH) occurred after initiation in secular life. And in contrast to Malekula and Papua (see below), no evidence of native ideas about "growth" is evident. (I take up Errington's suggestion about "homosexual submission" later.)

No other definite reports are known from the off-lying islands north of New Guinea. The nearby island of Buka may be a candidate, "for homosexuality is actually found among these people, but is rare, and is regarded with intense disfavour" (Blackwood 1935:128). The channel islands and Vitiaz Straits groups, together with the lowlands' Northeastern New Guinea mainland communities seem similar in cultural form to New Britian and the Duke-of-Yorks, but again the relevant ethnographic materials, often collected by missionaries, are difficult to assess (e.g., Neuhauss 1911).

EAST BAY • The only new report of homosexual activity in an off-lying island society here is that of Davenport (1965, 1977).[15] Although he (1977:155–157) refers to "institutionalized male bisexualism" in an acculturated community, we may safely include East Bay in our sample.

*Note the presence of contrary sexual techniques—anal intercourse in the Ingiet society, and fellatio among Duke-of-Yorks—in such closely related areas. Cf. below on the Great Papuan Plateau.

It is particularly interesting that two contrary modes of homosexual relations exist side by side in East Bay. The first is *reciprocal* and egalitarian sexual satisfaction between peers (even "brothers"; Davenport 1965:199) or friends: each must please the other in return.

> As boys reach late adolescence, they may also engage in mutual masturbation, but in the switch away from masturbation they also may have anal intercourse with friends and trade off playing the active and passive roles. No love or strong emotional bonds are developed. . . . It is considered to be part of the accommodations expected of friendship.
>
> *(Davenport 1977:155)*

This type of homosexual contact between peers is apparently rare in Melanesia (but cf. below, and Hogbin 1970). It opposes the normative distinctions between inserter and insertee so common in (RH) groups. The other mode was *asymmetrical* homosexual contacts between East Bay men and boys, which is common.

> Another substitute for older men was young boys, and they did take boys as passive partners for anal intercourse. Before a boy could be induced into such a partnership, permission had to be obtained from his father.[16]
>
> *(Davenport 1977:155)*

It is not clear if transmission of semen is here involved in "strengthening" boys, but it seems a likely possibility because of traditional initiation rites. The boy would receive small presents in return for his sexual favors.

Essentially, Davenport (1977:155) sees asymmetrical homosexual activities as a substitute sexual outlet for heterosexual relationships before marriage (for adolescents) or during postpartum taboos after marriage (for men). Ritual homosexuality was also associated with male initiation (Davenport 1965:205–206), at least in its men's-house variety. Homosexual activities are sporadically engaged in for years, along with heterosexual contacts, even in adulthood. It is also unusual that two erotic modes (i.e., mutual masturbation and anal coitus) coexist in East Bay, while others (e.g., fellatio; see Davenport 1965:201) are considered "ridiculous." Much social change has occurred in East Bay. Homosexual practices, for example, are no longer secret. One wonders whether the more-or-less egalitarian mode of mutual masturbation does not represent cultural change. If so, it would help to explain the sexual mutuality of peers resulting from changes in the power relationships underlying customary asymmetrical (RH). Davenport (1977) has recently advanced an important idea about how "gender segregated communities" led to (RH) in Melanesia, to which I shall return in the summary.

WESTERN PAPUA

This area is vast and includes many different social groups that essentially belong to the same subregional cultural tradition. They were the first mainland New Guinea groups reported to have ritualized homosexuality.

THE LOWER FLY RIVER • Initial reports in this area came from the Fly River delta and Kiwai Island, which lies at its mouth. These small tribal groups were once fierce warriors. All males were initiated into a secret cult, the various forms of which extended west throughout the Morehead District. The status of women was low (see Landtman 1927; Williams 1936*c*). Beardmore (1890:464), a missionary, first mentioned that "sodomy [anal intercourse] is regularly indulged in" on the left bank of the Fly (see also Haddon 1890:315).

The next overt references came from James Chalmers, a better-known missionary, on two closely related peoples: the Bugilai, again of the left bank of the Fly (see Williams 1936*c*:32n), and the nearby Kiwai Islanders. Of the Bugilai, Chalmers (1903*a*:109) states: "At the initiation of young men, they practice sodomy, but not bestiality as some other tribes do." (No further explanation!)

On the Kiwai Islanders, Chalmers's often sympathetic view turned cold even when it came to their heterosexual life. "Fornication is rife, rife here and the old men are the greatest sinners" (quoted in Langmore 1978:22). (When Chalmers [1903*b*:123] alluded to heterosexual arousal in the *Journal of the Royal Anthropological Institute,* the editors placed the crucial passage entirely in Latin, presumably out of censorship.) And Langmore (ibid.), quoting

Chalmers's unpublished papers, cites him thus on ritual homosexuality:

> The festival which so incensed him was the *moguru:* the series of ceremonies which initiated the young men. Chalmers opposed it partly because it emptied his classrooms for four months of every year, but more fundamentally because of its nature. It was "abominably filthy" he wrote. "The lads are prostituted by the men for quite a long time and soon become so diseased* that they never recover."

Chalmers was heartened when they did "recover" from their heathen ways by dropping these cult ceremonies in around 1898 (ibid.).

Censorship is apparent again with Baxter-Riley's (1925:216, another missionary) work on Kiwai, for he obliquely refers to an "unprintable ritual" (cf. also Beaver 1920:158 on "sexual crimes," and Strachan 1888:148, 155). In such instances we see what was seemingly common censorship practice vis-à-vis ethnographic reports on sexuality, at least until recently; at any rate it is clear from Haddon that Baxter-Riley was referring to ritualized homosexuality.[17]

The richest ethnography of Kiwai came from the Finnish ethnographer Landtman. In 1917 he noted that anal intercourse, sanctioned by myth, was believed to promote the physical growth of initiates (see Landtman 1917:78–80, 293–295). Later, in *The Kiwai Papuans of British New Guinea* (quaintly subtitled "A nature-born instance of Rousseau's ideal community"), Landtman (1927:237) writes:

> In connection with the initiation of youths at Masingle [Kiwai village], these have to practice sodomy in order to become tall and strong. Mr. E. Beardmore, who stayed in Mawata in 1888, states that "sodomy is regularly indulged in". . . . I did not come across any traces of it at Mawata as a general or ceremonial practice, but think it quite possible that the customs of the people, changing as they are, may have altered in this respect since Mr. Beardmore's time.[18]

*Metaphorically.

In the Kiwai case, we see a set of cultural themes which extend throughout the Western Papuan Gulf: a ritual cult feeding into a warriorhood; ritual seclusion and separation from women; and homosexual practices instituted through initiation to spur boys' masculine development.

It is worth underlining in general effects of social change on sexual customs as illustrated by the differences between the reports of Beardmore and Landtman. By 1910, when Landtman first worked, some twenty-two years had elapsed since Beardmore's work: undoubtedly, after pacification and missionary activity, social change had led the natives at Mawata to drop ritual homosexual practices. It is certain that for decades a similar historical process has been at work elsewhere in Melanesia: by the time an anthropologist arrived on the scene, trailing behind government and mission, (RH) activity, which was traditionally secret and hidden from the uninitiated in many areas, had been abandoned or suppressed owing to European authorities. (For striking examples of the political suppression of such homosexual practices, see the rare reports of Parkinson [1907:530n, 543–544], on German New Guinea, and Van Baal [1966:492–493], on Dutch New Guinea.) Thus, its presence was actively hidden from the anthropologist (see, for example, Williams 1936*c*:158), and/or the practice was defunct and unknown to younger natives themselves, so descriptions had to be salvaged from oldster's memories (e.g., Errington 1974, quoted above).

THE TRANS-FLY RIVER DELTA • We have already examined early reports from the mouth of the Fly River. Beginning in the 1920s, government anthropologist F. E. Williams immeasurably added to the ethnography of this cultural tradition, which extends up to the Fly headwaters, throughout the Morehead district, and west beyond the international border. Williams's classic studies of the Purari Delta, Keraki, Elema, Orokaiva, and other societies provide rich material for an emerging ethnology of the Papuan Gulf and Southern Irian Jaya (cf. Haddon 1927, 1936; Parratt 1976; Wagner 1972; Van Baal 1966). The Lower Trans-Fly Keraki are also the most famous Melanesian example of ritualized homosexual behavior cited in cross-cultural studies (e.g., Ford and Beach 1951). Williams was usually careful to record notes on sexual behavior—along with his biases about them (see n. 2). Until recent years, the Keraki were also the best described Papuan case of ritualized homosexual (anal) intercourse (see Williams 1936*a*:33n; 1936*c*:158–159, 194, 202, 294, 308–309). They were but one of several small tribes, numbering only a few hundred people, whom he believed to be nearly identical in culture and social organization.

The following passage best illustrates the main features and context of Keraki homosexual practices:

> It was frequently maintained that *setiriva,* or bachelors, remained truly celibate until they entered upon sexual relations with their own wives. Without giving too much credence to this statement, we may note that the hospitable exchange above noted was nominally restricted to married adults. Some informants maintained that *setiriva* could secure the favors of married women at feast times, but it seems evident that this was not definitely sanctioned.
>
> The bachelors had recourse to sodomy, a practice which was not reprobated but was actually a custom of the country—and a custom in the true sense, i.e., fully sanctioned by male society and universally practiced. For a long time the existence of sodomy was successfully concealed from me, but latterly, once I had won the confidence of a few informants in the matter, it was admitted on every hand. It is actually regarded as essential to the growing boy to be sodomized. More than one informant being asked if he had ever been subjected to unnatural practice, answered, "Why, yes! Otherwise how should I have grown?"
>
> The ceremonial initiation to sodomy and the mythological antecedents to it will be spoken of elsewhere. . . . It is enough to note that every male adult in the Morehead district has in his time constantly played both parts in this perversion. The boy is initiated to it at the bull-roarer ceremony and not earlier, for he could not then be trusted to keep the secret from his mother. When he becomes adolescent his part is reversed and he may then sodomize his juniors, the new initiates to the bull-roarer. I am told that some boys are more attractive and consequently receive more attention of this kind than do others; but all must pass through it, since it is regarded as essential to their bodily growth. There is indeed no question as to the universality of the practice.
>
> It is commonly asserted that the early practice of sodomy does nothing to inhibit a man's natural desires when later on he marries; and it is a fact that while the older men are not debarred from indulging, and actually do so at the bull-roarer ceremony, sodomy is virtually restricted as a habit to the *setiriva.*
>
> *(Williams 1936c:158–159)*

These general patterns can thus be adduced on Keraki: Homosexual anal intercourse was (1) universal among all males, (2) obligatory, (3) implemented through ceremonial initiation, (4) secret and hidden from women and children, (5) culturally sanctioned by myth (Williams 1936*c*:194, 308–309), and (6) by the native belief that semen masculinized the initiate. The last notion is elaborated remarkably to the extent of fearing homosexual impregnation, which certain rites protect against (Williams 1936*c*; and cf. Meigs 1976). Trans-Fly homosexual contacts were also—as nearly everywhere else in Melanesia—(7) age graded and asymmetrical, so that bachelor youths inseminated younger males, who could not situationally reverse roles. (8) The Keraki initiate is inseminated by males of the opposite moiety, specifically his older cross-cousins (Williams 1936*c*:128), who have already been initiated and treated likewise by the initiates' older male clansmen (F E1.B., FB, FBSo). Hage (1981) has made much of this dualism (see my summary), following the important analysis of Rubel and Rosman (1978). It is likely, as Layard (1959:112–115) and Van Baal (1966:493–494) have argued, that this customary homoeroticism between groups that exchange wives—potential brother-in-laws—is a symbolic underpinning of semen exchanges between structurally related affines (see Herdt, chap. 4, and Lindenbaum, chap. 9, this volume). Finally, (9) Keraki homosexuality is practiced by unmarried males who eventually marry, as Williams noted above. These themes are discussed from a different perspective in Schwimmer's chapter 6.

Ethnographic data on other parts of the Fly River, Western Province, and eastern Gulf Coast are sketchy, but they should be mentioned here.* First, ritualized homosexuality is absent from the coastal Papuan societies east of the Fly River (Williams 1940*a*:428 n. 3), aside from the Ai'i and the probable exception of the coastal Anga peoples (see below). For example, the Elema people, in spite of symbolic and structural similarity to the Irian Jayan Marind-anim tribes, do not practice institutionalized homosexuality (Williams 1939:368 n. 3). (RH) also seems absent from

*I am greatly indebted to Professor J. Van Baal for information in the following two paragraphs and for many substantive remarks in the following section on Irian Jaya.

the Lake Kutubu area (Williams 1940*b*), as seems true for the eastern Motuan groups. Barker (1975), however, reports (RH) among the Ai'i, a people south of Orokavia, which Schwimmer discusses below. (RH) was absent from the Massim area, as noted above, and was probably absent from Normanby Island (Róheim 1950). And ritual homosexuality is not explicitly reported for any of the off-lying islands of the Papuan Gulf (see Haddon 1890, 1936). For the Torres Straits, there is a hint that Waiat cult leaders, impersonating spirits, may have on occasion perpetrated homosexual acts (see Haddon in *Reports* [1910, vol. 6], pointed out by Jeremy Becket, personal communication; see also Ellis 1936:9).

West of the Fly the situation is clear. Williams (1940*a*:492 n. 2) tells us that ritual homosexuality extended west throughout all villages of the left bank of the Lower Fly (e.g., including the Bugilai [Chalmers 1903*a*] noted above). Farther west the same practices are found. Culturally closely related to the Keraki are the most eastern tribes of the lowlands of Irian Jaya just across the international border. These include two distinct tribes, the Kanum peoples in the savannah east of the Lower Maro River, and the Yéi-anim (or Yéi-nan) of the Upper and Middle Maro River (see map 3). Their languages are closely related to those of the Trans-Fly. Information on the Kanum is very limited, though we know that some were yam-growers, that they are small in population, and that they practiced anal homosexuality, at least in the context of Sosom cult rites.* The Yéi-anim also live in small groups, and although sago-eaters like the Marind-anim, they consume tubers as daily food (like the Marind). The Yéi seem very similar to the Keraki: their totemism and moiety dualism match Keraki, and they identify the male sex with bull-roarer and *pahui* (ceremonial head-hunting clubs). More importantly, they practice quite similar anal homosexual intercourse, with young boys as insertees and bachelors (and some younger mature men) as inserters, for the purpose of "growing" the boys (Van Baal 1982).

To the north of Keraki, ritualized homosexuality of a like form has been reported from the Suki people on the Lower Middle Fly (Nieuwenhuijsen-Riedeman 1979), and from the Boadzi, a tribe

*In this area and among the Marind-anim peoples (discussed next), two elaborate and widespread ritual cults, referred to as Sosom and Mayo, utilized (RH).

inhabiting both sides of the international border where it meets the Fly River (see below). Farther to the north, recent anthropological work at the Fly headwaters, bordering the Telefomin area (see below), has revealed no ritualized homosexuality (Barth 1971).

IRIAN JAYA (formerly Dutch New Guinea)

The ethnography of Irian Jaya is not presently well integrated into Melanesian studies for several reasons, and since most ethnographic research there halted after Indonesia's annexation in the early 1960s, our contemporary knowledge is limited. Fortunately, we have Professor Van Baal's essay below (chap. 3) on the Marind-anim peoples, who are, next to the Keraki, the best known and probably the most flamboyant case of ritualized homosexuality known from Melanesia. Two areas of Irian Jaya are definitely known to have (RH): essentially the entire southern area, from the international border to Frederik Hendrik Island, extending north along the Irian Jaya coast in some groups; and in the extreme north, at Humboldt Bay.

THE MARIND-ANIM TRIBES • The Marind-anim groups numbered some 7,000 people (as of the most recent census; Van Baal 1966:33–37), dispersed in coastal villages, inland villages, and those on the Upper Bian River. They were sago-eaters, and though ecologically adjusted, they were demographically declining. Despite their relatively small numbers, they were unquestionably the fiercest headhunters throughout the Papuan Gulf (e.g., Beaver 1920:106ff.). They speak different dialects but are fairly homogeneous culturally. Linguistically, they are closely akin to the Boadzi, who also share in their traditions of head-hunting and ritualized homosexuality. Van Baal (1966:99–104) has shown affinities between the Boadzi of the Central Fly area around Lake Murray and the Marind-anim. Indeed, he (1966:214, 218) suggests the Middle Fly as the precursor cultural tradition of the Marind. Furthermore, as with the Marind, "sodomy has an important place in [Boadzi] life. The men indulge in it both in the men's house and in the bush" (Van Baal (1966:595). It had numerous magical functions in ritual, myth, and warfare.

First reports of the Marind came from Haddon (1891) and

others, but it is to Wirz (1922–1925) that we owe the first systematic study. Though published in German and not widely circulated, Wirz's dissertation contained rich mythological and ritual material on the Mayo and Sosum (bull-roarer) male cults of the Marind-anim. Wirz was cited by specialists (cf. Haddon 1927, 1936; Mead 1949:228–229; Williams 1936*c*), especially before Van Baal's (1966) work was available. Wirz (1922:39) noted, for instance:

> This is a secret society whose ceremonies consist, above all, of sexual orgies and end up with cannibalism.*. . . According to the natives, the abstinence of the novices from nutrition and administering of certain dishes that are garnished with sperm are supposed simply to excite the [sexually dominant] youth, in the usual *festivals,* so that the feasts get all the more obscene.

Some years later Haddon (1936:xxvi) summarized Wirz's data, in relation to ritual homosexual practices, thus:

> When a boy leaves the village and resides in the youth's house he comes under the care of the man to whom he is under complete obedience, and with whom he sleeps at night. There is sexual jealousy among the guardians, but when *Sosom* [spirit being] comes these proprietary rights vanish (as at ordinary feasts in the case of the women) and unrestricted sodomy prevails.

The Marind-anim material thus indicated the first glimpse of a widespread "homosexual initiation cult" (the phrase is Van Baal's [1963] extending from the Trans-Fly River tribes in the east to the Trans-Digul River Jaquai in the west.

The following general points will serve to introduce the Marind groups, which Van Baal's own essay below develops far more fully. The main point: ritualized anal homosexual practices are institutionalized on a widespread scale throughout the entire Marind area. They are associated with the Sosom cult, in particular, which is identified with the mythological figure of Sosom, an ancestral giant (Wirz 1922; Van Baal 1934, 1966:248). Homosexual anal intercourse is begun in male initiation for boys between the ages

*See Van Baal (chap. 3), who sees this cannibalistic act as a symbolic, rather than literal, practice.

of seven and fourteen years (Van Baal 1966:143–144). Afterward, boys live in the men's clubhouse for some six years, avoiding females and regularly engaging in anal intercourse. Initial promiscuous homosexual contacts, jealousies, and more extended liaisons are with members of the opposite moiety. Later sustained contacts are with the boy's appointed "mentor" or *binahor-evai*, who is usually his mother's brother (Van Baal 1966:113–115; 493). But, unlike with the Kimam of Frederik Hendrik Island (Serpenti 1965), there is no evidence at all that the *binahor* father—the (RH) inserter—cedes his daughter in sister exchange to the younger male.

As elsewhere, homosexual insemination here is seen as crucial to a boy's physical masculine development. Verschueren wrote early on: "In our studies of the notions underlying the [homosexual] practice F. Boelaars and I found that, everywhere, the act is seen as a necessary condition for the completion of a boy's physical development" (quoted in Van Baal 1966:494).

Compared to other (RH) groups, homosexual practices here are less secret, and women apparently know of their existence. This fact seems anomalous, considering the elaborate sexual polarity of Marind-anim society, a point pursued in my summary below. However, it may be, as Van Baal (1966:948ff.) argues, that the "phallic religion" of Marind symbolically concerns this oddity.

> The secret of the great cults is that the men must submit to the women, caught *in coitu*, powerless. . . . The source of all life, sperma, is effective only—at least, in principle—if produced in [heterosexual] copulation. These self-sufficient males need the females and they know it; only, they do not care to admit it.
>
> *(1966:949)*

Here is a very dramatic characteristic found only in Southern Irian Jaya: the efficacy of sperm used for certain (RH)-related activities must come from *heterosexual* intercourse. Homosexual activity is distinct from that, but as Van Baal (chap. 3) argues below, both types of sexual relationships must be seen as counterparts of each other.

The discrepancy between men's wanting to be self-sufficient yet needing women is associated with the act of head-hunting, which was so important in Marind-anim social reproduction. We know that head-hunting was the final incorporating initiatory rite of the Mayo cult (Van Baal 1966:740–742), and that it legitimized male adulthood. Van Baal (1966:949) goes beyond cultural facts, however, and sees a psychosocial dynamic in the men's ritual denial of women's power.

> In secret, in the celebration of the rites, they will allow their dependence and immediately afterwards go out headhunting. It is as if by that time their rage had mounted to such a pitch that they have to find an outlet for it. . . . It is fairly probable that these pent-up feelings of discomfort are, indeed, a major source of aggressiveness.[19] It is aggressiveness directed toward the innocent. Somebody has to be killed and there is no real motive for the act.
> *(1966:949)*

The Marind-anim were certainly regarded as among New Guinea's most ruthless headhunters from the earliest period of contact (see Haddon 1891; Baxter-Riley 1925; Wirz 1934).

Ultimately, Van Baal (1966:950–954) sees the meaning of Marind-anim ritual homosexuality as being caught up in the contradictions of their heterosexual relationships. Theirs was a society with an "ineffective" sexual segregation, with some freedom of marital choice nevertheless curtailed by sister exchange, and with promiscuity and wife-beating. And yet, "couples seem strongly attached to each other"; even in the male initiation rites, women took a part, while at other times, the sexes ceremonially battled. Other social facts inform, such as the kidnapping of children; and the associated "alarmingly low fertility rate of women. . . . [is] an indirect, but nevertheless convincing symptom of a serious imbalance in their sexual life" (Van Baal 1966:950). These conditions, in addition to the fact that men continue having homosexual intercourse throughout life, even into old age (unusual in Melanesia) suggest that "relations between the sexes are beset with [personal] conflicts and institutional controversies" (Van Baal 1966:949). The Marind-anim and related cultures thus show a complex system of variables that defy any simple causal explanation, psychological, ecological, or structural.

West of the Marind-anim, among groups occupying Frederik Hendrik Island, the north part of the Lower Digul River, and the Jaquai of the Mappi River basin, we are again confronted with ritualized homosexuality. In contrast to the Marind and Boadzi, however, who are organized in patrilineal clans and moieties, these are nonunilineal descent groups. In other respects they seem like the Marind.

First to the Kimam of Frederick Hendrik Island, who lie directly west of the Marind: Serpenti (1965) has already reported pronounced ritualized anal homosexual practices among them, and his chapter 7 below is an important addition to the literature. Here I will simply place the Kimam in a broader framework. Upon initiation, a boy was placed under the charge of an older youth, who "adopted" him as his "mentor" (Serpenti 1965:162). They regularly practiced homosexual anal intercourse. "This 'mentor' is usually a classificatory elder brother from the same *pabura* (village-sector)" (Serpenti 1965:162–163). But this remarkably close relationship was unusual; mentors were often mother's younger brothers or cross-cousins, too (biological brothers were excluded). At least some aspects of ritual homosexuality and initiation were secret (ibid.:171). The magical and medicinal employment of sperm here was central to cult activities: "Everywhere on the island sperm is believed to contain great powers" (ibid.:164). Sperm is rubbed all over an initiate's body, particularly into incisions made by his mentor, to make boys "big and strong" (ibid.:165n.). Serpenti compares Kimam to Marind-anim and Keraki in these respects (see also Landtman 1927).

Kimam culture reveals the clearest relationships between sister-exchange marriage and ritual homosexuality.

> For the purpose of arousing the sperm the "mentor" has to put his betrothed [wife] at the men's disposal.[20] Immediately after the betrothal the girl goes to live with her father-in-law. At the same time the boy goes to the [men's house], for he is not allowed to see the girl. Sometimes he does not even know who she is. At this stage, however, the girl is not yet sexually mature. The [mentor's] betrothed, on the other hand is mature, but the [mentors] are not allowed to have sexual intercourse with women. As a compensation for the use of his betrothed, the [mentor] has sexual claims on the [first-stage boy-initiate] for whom his betrothed is used [i.e., older men copulate with her to collect semen to anoint this boy's body, helping to strengthen him]. Only contact with women is considered dangerous at this critical period of their lives.
>
> *(Serpenti 1965:164)*

Here we see a complex exchange of: the right of the superordinate men to have sexual intercourse with the bachelor's betrothed woman; sperm collected from her through these contacts to "grow" younger initiates; and the bachelor-mentors' right of sexual intercourse with an initiate in return. (Wives are often MBD or FZD; Serpenti 1965:124–126.) Older men continue having homosexual relationships as well as heterosexual access to the bachelor-mentor's betrothed (ibid.:167). We shall see similar cases of structural relation between marriage and (RH) below.

Next are the Jaquai, reported on linguistically by Boelaars (1950:1, 60). They are linguistically closely related to the Marind but differ from them in social organization. The Jaquai (like tribes of Frederik Hendrik Island, the Asmat, and the Mimika) are organized in nonunilineal descent groups, the Marind in patriclans. They are separated by the lower Digul River area (see map 2). We can locate the Jaquai along an affluent of the Digul River north of its right bank, whereas the Marind-anim live at some distance south of its left bank. In spite of differences in social organization, though, among the Jaquai, (RH) is prominent. We are safest to quote Boelaars's (1981:84) most recent report:

> A father can order his son to go and sleep during the night with a certain man who will commit pederasty with him. The father will receive compensation for this.[21] If this happens regularly between a man and the same boy, a stable relationship arises, comparable to that between a father and son, *mo-e* or anus father and *mo-maq*, anus son (father = *nae*, son = *maq*). Such a boy is allowed to consider that man's daughter as his sister and she will be "awarded" to him as his exchange sister for his future marriage.

Here we have perhaps the most extreme instance of an (RH)/marriage correlation known in Melanesia: the insertee has the right to use his male partner's daughter for marriage exchange. In the marriage game, therefore, we can identify the Jaquai and the Kimam as being culturally very similar. Yet again, in significant aspects of social organization, both groups differ from the Marind groups even though all practice ritualized homosexuality.

What do we find north of these westerly Irian Jaya groups? The data are mostly useless. Along the western coast, only one group, the Asmat, is definitely known to practice homosexual activities.

But even here the situation is cloudy. Although the allusion is skimpy, Van Amelsvoort (1964:43) states of the Asmat: "Homosexual relationships are [present but] less institutionalized than among the neighboring Jaquai people." The same is probably true for the Casuarina Coast peoples. Nothing else is known, except that the northern neighbors of the Asmat—the Mimikans—do not practice ritualized homosexuality (J. Pouwer, personal communication to J. Van Baal; see also Pouwer [1955]).

Farther north and inland east, ritualized homosexuality is also absent. It is not found in the Wissel Lakes area among the Kapauku (Van Baal, personal communication). Farthest north at Vogelkop (the Bird's Head), Elmberg (1955:88) states that there is "no homosexuality" among the Mejbrat tribe. Likewise, at Geelvink Bay among the Waropen people, Held (1957:87–88) notes: "Among men anal sodomy also occurs, but according to my informants this only happens when they are drunk." All available information confirms that Held's statement refers to homosexuality being treated as a culturally standardized attribution of deviance (e.g., like madness) which should be taken on face value. The Waropen do not have *ritualized* homosexuality.[22]

Finally, Highlands Irian Jaya: It appears certain that ritualized homosexuality is completely absent here. Heider (1979:79) notes: "There is no sign at all of homosexual relations" among the Grand Valley Dani. In the Star Mountains to the east, extending to the international border, ritualized homosexuality is clearly absent (Hylkema 1974). (Here we see confirmation of the absence of RH in the adjacent Telefomin tribes, noted below.) Moreover, there is no indication of institutionalized homosexuality in the hill-dwelling tribes south of these mountains (J. Van Baal, personal communication).

NORTHEASTERN IRIAN JAYA • The only other reports of institutionalized homosexuality come from the northeastern part of the territory. The one clear and unequivocable report concerns the Humboldt Bay villages, due east of the Waropen. Ritual cult houses *(Karawari)* are prominent here. K. W. Galis confirmed older reports of ritualized homosexuality there:

> The boys [initiates] receive food once a day, at 9:00 P.M. They have to wait for it, and all the time they are teased. An important part

> is played by a boy's mother's brother. He has the right to let the boy take any thinkable posture and to let him stand that way. He also has the right to commit sodomy with the boy, which he does openly and apparently repeatedly. The act is, obviously, an important part of the initiation ritual (it is said, inter alia, that it is done to let the boys grow). Another pastime is that the older men walk around in the temple [the *Karawari* house] playing with their genitals [masturbating?]. The novices are forbidden on pain of death, to laugh.
>
> *(Galis 1955:190)*

Interestingly enough, Galis also noted that these ritual activities are necessary for the boys to learn how to play ritual flutes (see Herdt 1982*a*). The Humboldt Bay complex strikingly compares with that of other groups already described.

Yet, the combination of the Karawari cult houses and homosexual activity is limited to this group. Karawari houses are found as far away as the Sentani Lake area, much farther east. However, Wirz (1928) wrote that no form of homosexuality played a role in initiation there. The same is true of the Sarmi people, somewhat west of Humboldt Bay, whose Karawari cult houses are found as far west as the right bank of the Mamberao River (J. Van Baal, personal communication).

The Mamberamo River tribes are the only remaining Irian Jaya case. The situation in the early literature is murky. M. Moszkowski, an amateur explorer and ethnographer, lived for some eight months with the Kaowerawédj, one of the hill tribes of the Mamberamo River. Moszkowski (1911:339) claims to have seen the initiations, and he states that boys are initiated into the cult house at age ten. His astonishing report reads in part as follows:

> Unmarried men live together in the men's house. The origin of the men's house is apparently to be found in certain efforts on the part of the men to emancipate themselves from the tyranny of women. One immediate consequence of these efforts is that the worst orgies of a homosexual kind are celebrated in the men's house. The Papuans seem not to have the slightest modesty in this regard. Not only were obscenities uttered in our presence . . . but also mutual masturbation was directly marked and homosexual acts were indulged in.
>
> *(Moszkowski 1911:339)*

This paper and this particular passage, which has such an absolute ring of factuality about it, was cited by the old sexologists as fact (see Ellis 1936:20; Karsch-Haack 1911:528–529; Reik 1946:155). But Moszkowski's data, coming from one who *was* a popularizer (and who was probably stimulated by the earlier sensation of the Russian Mikloucho-Maclay's [1975] work), has never been confirmed.

Moszkowski's findings were disputed by J. P. K. Van Eekhoud who investigated the Kaowerawédj in 1939. The natives denied the occurrence of ritualized homosexuality not only among themselves but also among their friendly neighbors and enemies (Van Eekhoud 1962:50f.). Furthermore, in more recent, related work, G. Oosterwal has never mentioned ritualized homosexuality, neither east among the nearby Tor, a coastal people northwest of the Mamberamo (Oosterwal 1961), nor among the Upper Mamberamo villages (Oosterwal 1967). I think Oosterwal's report suggests the absence of (RH) here: he noted important facts such as the ritual use of transvestism (cf. the Mejbrat, Marind-anim, etc.) and the months-long supervision of initiates under their mother's brothers' supervision (Oosterwal 1961:241–242; 1967:184, 188). Although we cannot completely rule out the possibility that social change had eliminated homosexual activities in the area, the total evidence makes that unlikely. At the very least, then, Moszkowski's observations about male emancipation and female tyranny uncannily mirror the popular ideology of his day.[23] At the worst, his reports were fabrications. We may assume that (RH) simply does not here occur east of Humboldt Bay.

But how far east is it absent? Ritual complexes that seemingly parallel Humboldt Bay Karawari cults traditionally extended along the north coast of Papua New Guinea. Yet the occurrence of homosexuality is not known. Should not we expect historical and cultural continuities here, say, along the lines of Wurm's (1975:940–953) Trans-New Guinea Phylum migrations? Unfortunately, the concrete evidence for ritualized homosexuality must be culled from poor sources (e.g., Neuhauss 1911). And what of the Sepik River region? We shall later examine these questionable cases.

To summarize: Ritual homosexuality in Irian Jaya is a lowlands phenomena, concentrated along the southern coast. The related social units are numerous; they represent tremendous linguistic and cultural diversity. Yet, we are on safe ground in arguing that ritualized homosexuality, as part of a pervasive ritual complex, is virtually universal west of the Trans-Fly River, throughout the Morehead district, across the international border, to Frederik Hendrik Island, including the adjacent coastal fringe areas. Initiation rites and head-hunting (usually including cannibalism) were also pervasive among these groups. Though they can be defined essentially as culturally cognate societies, we cannot ignore differences among them. For instance, the Marind-anim: Van Baal (personal communication) believes they were "unique in Southwest Papua; that they have more in common with the cultures of Arnhem Land [Australia] than with others of New Guinea, except, possibly, the Elema of the Papuan Gulf" (e.g., see Williams 1940*a*). Again, this Australian parallelism has long been advocated (Van Baal 1963).[24] I shall later return to the diffusionist arguments for Melanesia. For the moment, let us ignore these infraregional cultural differences, however, and refer to this vast area as but one cultural tradition, the Southwestern New Guinea coastal fringe (or SWNG).

RECENT PAPUA NEW GUINEA WORK

The ethnography of the 1970s has revealed two new subregions in which ritualized homosexuality is prominent and probably universal. The Great Papuan Plateau (politically located in the southern Highlands Province of Papua New Guinea) saw anthropological work begin only in the mid-1960s. The plateau is relatively small, with small populations numbering only in the hundreds, who live in close proximity. They are "fringe-area" peoples, who hunt and exploit sago. These groups belong to one cultural tradition, however, and I think it may be argued that they should properly be considered cognate to the Southwestern New Guinea ritual complex (e.g., Boadzi, Marind-anim). The other new reports come from the Anga peoples (formerly called "Kukukuku"; politically located in the Eastern Highlands and Gulf provinces). They are diverse, with nine different languages and at least thirteen different tribal groups spread across a vast area numbering perhaps 100,000 people (see Gajdusek et al. 1972; Lloyd 1973). The Anga may eventually be seen as a cognate tradition of the SWNG systems too.

GREAT PAPUAN PLATEAU • On the plateau itself, four groups have been reported upon: Etoro, Kaluli, Onabasalu, and Bedamini. The Kaluli are best known from the works of E. L. Schieffelin (1976, 1982), who has written on their homosexual practices. The Etoro (Kelly 1976, 1977), are less documented in this regard. Thomas Ernst has not as yet published on homosexual activities among Onabasalu. Arve Sørum (1982) has mentioned homosexuality before on the Bedamini, and his chapter below is a new and important addition to the literature. Here, I shall examine the general relationship among these groups, highlighting the Kaluli in particular.

Raymond Kelly (1977) has provided a valuable schematic contrast between the Plateau tribal groups in terms of ritual and sexual techniques. I cite it in full:

> The Etoro, Onabasulu, and Kaluli culturally differentiate themselves from each other in a number of ways, but most particularly by their customs of male initiation. All three tribes share the belief that boys do not become physically mature men as a result of natural processes. Growth and attainment of physiological maturation is contingent on the cultural process of initiation, and this entails insemination because it is semen which ensures growth and development. According to the Etoro, semen does not occur naturally in boys and must be "planted" in them. If one does not plant sweet potato vines then no sweet potatoes will come up in the gardens and, likewise, semen must be planted in youths if they are to possess it as men (and indeed they do not possess it as boys). Moreover, all aspects of manliness are consequences of this acquisition. Although all three tribes share roughly similar views concerning the necessity of insemination, each differs from the others concerning the appropriate mode of transmission. The Etoro achieve this through oral intercourse, the Kaluli through anal intercourse, and the Onabasulu through masturbation and smearing of the semen over the bodies of the initates . . . (Ernst, personal communication, 1972). Inasmuch as the members of each tribe become men in different ways, they are preeminently different kinds of men, culturally distinct beings at the most fundamental level. The Kaluli are traditional enemies of the Etoro, and the Etoro particularly revile them for their initiatory practices which are regarded as totally disgusting. (The feeling is probably mutual.) The Onabasulu, on the other hand, are closer to the Etoro in this area of belief and some boys of that tribe have undergone initiation at Etoro seclusion houses. Ernst (personal communication, 1972) reports that the Onabasulu pre-

viously followed Etoro custom and have distinguished themselves in this respect only in recent generations.

(Kelly 1977:16)

The neighboring Bedamini also practice homosexual fellatio (Sørum, chap. 8), which is relatively rare (cf. below on Anga groups).[25] Cultural variation in these homosexual techniques is clearly related to the organization of ethnic identity, as Kelly hints. But it is not obvious how cultural arrangements and beliefs are functionally or symbolically correlated with such divergent homoerotic modes. Here is a research problem worthy of comparative study.

Both Kaluli and Etoro emphasize the need for boys to be inseminated to grow and become masculine. Yet they appear to vary considerably in the duration and cultural timing of these activities. Among the Etoro, "a youth is continually inseminated from about age ten until he reaches his early mid-twenties" (Kelly 1976:45). This long period follows from the belief that males do not "naturally" make semen and "moreover, all aspects of manliness are seen as consequences of this acquisition" (Kelly 1976:45).[26] Kaluli initiation and homosexual activities, in contrast, seem more truncated:

> Semen is also necessary for young boys to attain full growth to manhood. . . . They need a boost, as it were. When a boy is eleven or twelve years old, he is engaged for several months in homosexual intercourse with a healthy older man chosen by his father. (This is always an in-law or unrelated person, since the same notions of incestuous relations apply to little boys as to marriageable women.) Men point to the rapid growth of adolescent youths, the appearance of peach fuzz beards, and so on, as the favorable results of this child-rearing practice.
>
> *(Schieffelin 1976:124)*

Here we see that the duration of homosexual practices in the male life cycle of these two groups is quite different. We can certainly guess that the effects of this difference—years versus months of (RH) activity—would be significant, both in institutional and individual terms. (It is too bad neither ethnographer has addressed the meaning of this difference in comparative or regional study.)

What conclusions can be drawn from the Papuan Plateau case? Here again the ethnographers differ. While Kelly (1977:16) and

Sørum (1982) argue that homosexual practices should be seen as part of the "cultural process of initiation" in Plateau groups, Schieffelin (1982) has recently described the Kaluli context, the *bau a* ceremonial lodge, as an "alternative to an initiation program." He also says of their homosexual practices: "Certainly there is no ritualization about the act itself" (Schieffelin 1982:177–178), by which he seems to mean that the homoerotic acts are not framed by ritual or they occur also in secular situations. One fact that apparently supports this view is the nonobligatory character of homosexual practices: only certain males engage in them, and Kaluli stress choice in the matter. Here we have a distinct contrast with most groups reported on in this book, though I would argue that Kaluli are but a variant of the (RH) pattern.[27] In these groups, warfare also reinforces an aggressive ethos among men. Schieffelin's (1982) analysis sees hunting and homosexuality, and symbolic relationships to spirit beings, as interrelated elements in the social control of male transition from adolescence to the assumption of adult marital and sexual bonds in Kaluli society. He thus argues that "homosexual activity seems to have a certain aura of the profane or impure about it" (ibid.:178). On marriage, Etoro reveal a pattern strikingly similar to that of SWNG groups. "The ideal [homosexual] inseminator . . . is a boy's true sister's husband or her betrothed; brother and sister will then receive semen from the same man (ideally a FMBS) and be, in a sense, co-spouses to him" (Kelly 1976:52). (See also my summary, chap. 4, and chap. 9.) In Papuan Plateau groups, then, the male belief in the magical growth-power of homosexual insemination is stressed and symbolically elaborated in other domains, consistent with the above material on Southwestern Papuan groups.

Finally, the Nomad River area should be mentioned here. This region extends in both directions south of the Papuan Plateau, in the watershed of the Strickland gorge. Since it is geographically intermediate between the Plateau and the Upper Fly River area and has similar ecological parameters, we should expect to find similar homosexual practices. This area is still poorly described, though Shaw (n.d.) mentions "homosexual joking" among the Samo people. Nonetheless, it seems unclear whether actual homosexual contacts occur among Samo. Southwest of the Nomad area, however, Bruce Knauft describes widespread and obligatory male homosexual activity among the Gebusi people very similar to that of the Great Papuan Plateau,[28] for example, in the context of bawdy joking at spirit seances and ritual feasts (cf. Sørum, chap. 8). Homosexual fellatio "occurs for all males between 14 and 25 years of age." And Knauft explains: "The explicit reason for insemination is 'to make boys become big' *(wa kawala)*, so that they can be initiated. Indeed, this same term is the proper name of the initiation ceremonies, these being the public celebration of the 'bigness' the young men have attained." I expect that eventual publication of the Gebusi ethnography will confirm their similarity to cultural traditions of the Papuan Plateau, the Bedamini and Etoro in particular.

ANGA SOCIETIES • The Anga are a congeries of tribes spreading from the Papuan Gulf through the Eastern Highlands ranges of the Kratkes, east of the Lamari River. Some of these groups number into the thousands, and most of them are unstudied (see table 1.1). B. Blackwood (e.g., 1939) did the first ethnographic work in the Papuan hinterland near Menyamya in the 1930s; H. Fischer (1968) next worked farther inland in the 1950s. But the work of neither is well known. Colin Simpson, a flashy journalist[29]—wrote a popular account in the fifties (Simpson 1953). New Guinea folklore depicted the Anga generally as fierce headhunters, thieves, and homosexuals. Little else was known about this region[30] until the work of M. Godelier on the Baruya (1971, 1976), and my work on the Sambia, neighboring Eastern Highland fringe-dwelling groups, both immigrant groups from the Menyamya area who fled a great war, they say, some 150 to 200 years ago (Godelier 1969; Herdt 1981:22–23). Along with Lloyd (1973) and Gajdusek et al. (1972), I would argue that the Anga comprise many different social units of the same cultural tradition. They were all enmeshed in war; hunting and shifting tuber agriculture were pervasive; and initiation was obligatory.

Blackwood's early work on the Langimar and Nauti of the Upper Watut River* illustrates the complexities of superficial reports on sex in New Guinea and the difficulties in reinterpreting them. She

*Edited by Hallpike (1978).

described these groups as evincing "greater secretiveness" compared with the Buka whom she had previously studied (B. Blackwood 1935), adding that "sexual interests play a minor part" for Anga, "whose main concerns are food and fighting" (Hallpike 1978:153). Although Hallpike (1978:153 n. 62) approvingly footnotes Fischer's (1968) account of the Western Jeghuje—a neighboring people—in support of these views, Mimica (1981) questions its applicability to the Central Jeghuje (and, I would also add, to the Eastern Jeghuje, bordering the Sambia, based on my reconnaissance fieldwork there). Blackwood tried also to learn if homosexual practices occurred during the ritual seclusion of boys in the forest after initiation. Mimica (1981:226), in review of a relevant passage, derides Blackwood:

> Miss Blackwood was limited by her sex and bold naivety in approaching the matter of the male secret cult. The following immortal passage rather aptly expresses it: "In answer to the direct question, whether sodomy[31] occurred between the boys and their 'big brothers' while they were in the bush, they said that it did not" *(Hallpike, p. 127).*

Did these groups thus practice ritualized homosexuality? Mimica (1981) hints that they did. Hallpike (1978:127 n. 45) cites D. C. Gajdusek to the effect that "initiates" (groups unspecified) engage in homosexual practices because of prolonged periods of isolation from women. (Regarding the purely behavioral explanation of these practices, see the summary.) Yet Hallpike (1978:153 n. 62) later reaffirms Blackwood's remark about absent homosexuality, this time by citing Fischer (1968)—who has not reported it[32]—and concludes that Gajdusek's earlier report seems "uncharacteristic of the Kukukuku as a whole." No real evidence is thus cited in support of this claim. It is certainly false.

Godelier's work among the Baruya began in the late 1960s. In an important recent essay he describes social and sexual aspects of Baruya homosexuality:

> In the men's house, initiates live in pairs of different ages. They stroke each other, masturbate, suck each other; but sodomy [anal coitus] was unknown until the arrival of policemen and soldiers belonging to tribes that practiced it. Girls stroke each other, but

> we know little about what actually goes on among them.* Homosexuality apparently disappears after marriage.
>
> *(Godelier 1976:15)*

He describes further the intricate ideas and customs that inform reproduction and male/female relationships. The Baruya view heterosexuality as a force that potentially threatens the entire social order.

> Sex is dangerous, but the danger comes mainly from the woman, who constantly threatens to rob man of his integrity and above all of the synthesis of all his virtues which he calls strength. But the woman is dangerous too because, whether she likes it or not, she serves as a vector for the evil powers and hostile forces that populate the invisible side of the world. What is in fact threatened is the entire social and cosmic order. Sexual intercourse, therefore, is an evil under any circumstances, but a necessary evil, since homosexual relations are fruitless.
>
> *(Godelier 1976:20)*

How do these views of homosexuality and heterosexuality cohere?

Godelier's report provides important symbolic contextualization of homosexual activites in another Anga tribe. I would argue, however, that Godelier here blurs the natives' and observers' viewpoints on sexual contacts. It is true that homosexual contacts are "fruitless" in the procreative sense, since sperm does not create offspring in boys. But his observer model does not fully account for homosexual practices from the natives' point of view: they *are* fruitful given the belief in the magical power of semen to "grow" and "strengthen" boys, who will socially reproduce the village warriorhood in the next generation (Herdt, chap. 4; cf. Godelier 1982*a*). Given the symbolic power of male/male insemination in *facilitating* boys' reproductive competence, the "dangers" of women take on a new meaning. If we turn now to the nearby Sambia, certain contrasts will help fill out what can presently be said of the Anga case. Since my work is recent and sketched in chapter 4, I shall cover general themes here.

Among the Sambia, homosexual activities are believed vital to psychosocial and biological development. All males are initiated

*See also Godelier (1982*a*:80ff.).

into an age-graded secret society, coordinated with local patrilineal descent groups. Through prolonged homosexual fellatio, sperm creates growth and strength in males between ages seven through fourteen. Only older and younger unmarried males engage in homosexual intercourse, which is tied to the symbolic meanings of sacred flutes (Herdt 1982*a*). In this symbolic system, flutes are equated with mothers' breasts and penises, and semen is compared to breast milk. All homosexual contacts are asymmetrical, and boys must not situationally reverse roles. At puberty, they are elevated through initiation into the fellated-bachelor role, when they appropriately inseminate younger males until marriage in their late teens or early twenties. But after they have fathered a child, men are expected to give up homosexual activity, and most of them do so, preferring heterosexual activites with their wives (cf. Herdt 1980). Homosexual activities among females are unknown.

Several broad patterns link Sambia to other (RH) groups noted throughout this chapter. First, as an institutional complex, Sambia practice intitation as a means of sex-role socialization, and induction and recruitment into village-based warriorhoods. Warfare has been widespread and destructive within and between Sambia, Baruya, and their neighbors. Warfare and hunting are the chief secular contexts of public masculine performance. Initiation is the main sacred and secret context for demonstrating male "strength." Second, sexual polarity is intense and permeates virtually all social arenas and cultural domains. There is a concomitantly strict sexual division of labor. Third, residential arrangements separate all initiates from all females, initiates residing in men's houses, married men, women, and children living in women's houses (albeit divided into "male" and "female" spaces). Children are primarily socialized by their mothers and other caretakers until initiation (males) or marriage (females). Fourth, women have low social status, and men dominate public affairs. Fifth, Sambia emphasize patrilineality and patrifiliation at the expense of other kin and social bonds, which include all sexual relationships. All persons outside the natal hamlet are seen as potentially hostile. Hence, women are imported for marriage, and homosexual partners are from hostile hamlets. Sixth, men fear both depletion and pollution from their wives and, in general, from all reproductively active females. Seventh, sexual intercourse is carefully regulated and monitored through numerous taboos, institutional arrangements, values, and norms, including long postpartum taboos that result in prolonged mother/infant attachment bonds. Finally, semen is treated as a scarce resource that circulates in the population pool through both homosexual and heterosexual contacts. The "value" of semen thus rationalizes—"naturalizes" and "mystifies"—all sexual relationships (cf. Keesing 1982). Marriage and homosexual activities are therefore inseparably linked through semen exchange, in a manner paralleling that of Kimam, Etoro, and others (Herdt, chap. 4). Ultimately, the low population density of the Sambia and their warring relationships must be seen as the behavioral conditions that contributed to this cultural patterning of semen ingestion and (RH).

My impression is that this complex of factors applies in similar systemic relationship to all Anga groups of the Eastern Highlands, which includes many different tribes. Furthermore, this same ritual complex apparently occurs through the Menyamya area and probably extends south to the Papuan coast (although this latter suggestion must remain a conjecture for the present).[33]

QUESTIONABLE CASES

It seems clear now that ritualized homosexual practices are absent from the New Guinea Highlands, except among the fringe-area Anga groups just described. (Remember, though, that these mountain Anga groups are immigrants from the Papuan hinterland who should be seen as shareres in SWNG cultural traditions.) No homosexual activity is known from the Western Highlands or adjacent Chimbu areas, which encompass many different social units of different cultural traditions (see Lindenbaum, chap. 9). Likewise, it is absent among the Maring (Buchbinder 1973:85). K. E. Read (1980*b*), the key early ethnographer of Eastern Highlands groups, reported only ostentatious ritual masturbation in the context of nosebleeding ceremonies. More recently, he has questioned whether individual homosexual activity occurred among the Gahuku Gama; but it seems clear that it was not institutionalized (Read 1980*b*, app. I). He extends his observations and relates them to (RH) groups in a retrospective account below (see below, chap. 5). Meigs (1976) has noted a male ideology of male pregnancy and related beliefs among the Eastern Highlands' Hua, though no mention is made of homosexuality. Even among the Awa and Tairora groups bordering the west bank of the Lamari, near Anga groups, ritualized homosexuality is absent (Terence E. Hays, David Boyd, personal communications). The nearby South Fore may have secretly practiced (RH), though it is not reported anthropologically, so this suggestion remains doubtful.[34] (Keesing [1982:10], however, reports that one ethnographer in this central part of the Eastern Highlands has noted homosexual practices but has not published these data in respect of local people's wishes.)

The only report of *any* Highlands homosexual activity is from DuToit (1975), on the Eastern Highlands' Akuna.

> We do find a form of homosexual play. This is referred to as *iyer-anenu,* meaning simply "play," as children play with marbles or any other objects. In this homosexual play among boys, one will assume the active and another the passive role, while the first places his penis in the anus of the other. This seems to be relatively common among boys as they become increasingly segregated from their female age-mates, and informants explain that it usually continues until the sixteenth or seventeenth year of life. Among girls there is something similar, in which two girls associate intimately with one another caressing and petting the breasts and genitals of the other. In this homosexual play they assume the position of intercourse with one lying on the other. In neither case, it seems, is orgasm reached.
>
> *(DuToit 1975:220)*

We are informed that Akuna parents disapprove of homosexual play, which is regarded as "dangerous," though we are not told why. These activities occur out of sight of adults, who can only warn against them. Nothing else is said about their context or meaning. Nonetheless, if DuToit's report is taken at face value, it compares with that of East Bay (Davenport 1965, 1977) and indicates a form of homosexual activity that is an ad hoc, if illicit, pattern in Akuna sexual development. The Akuna are doubly aberrant because females also engage in homosexual activities (even if orgasm reportedly does not occur).

DuToit's report is anomalous; and Akuna homosexual practices are not supported by any institutional forces. This fragment thus reveals homosexual activity in Akuna but, until data are shown otherwise, not ritualized homosexuality.

No other Highlands instances are known, supporting the generalized and strong correlation between lowlands groups and ritualized homosexuality.

ADMIRALTY ISLANDS (MANUS) • The Manus Island case is dubious, but Margaret Mead's (1968) remarks are sufficiently suggestive to merit mention. Her data fall under the domain of what she called "variations of the sexual picture."

> Homosexuality occurs in both sexes, but rarely. The natives recognize it, and take only a laughing count of it, if it occurs between unmarried boys, in which cases it is sometimes exploited publicly in the boys' houses. Sodomy [anal intercourse?] is the only form of which I received any account.
>
> *(Mead 1968:126)*

This passage seems puzzling. For the natives to "recognize" homosexual practices and "laugh" at them (in public?) among bachelors—who nonetheless "publicly exploit" them—is somewhat inexplicable.

We can speculate about the historical context of such statements. Let us remember that Manus had sustained years of pacification and missionary activity well before Mead's fieldwork in the 1920s. Perhaps, then, seen as statements by acculturated natives to a European woman, the above passage might be interpreted as a means of admitting, yet simultaneously denying, homosexual practices, which were formerly practiced but then stopped (see below, on the Sepik Iatmul).

This suggestion remains purely speculative, however. No evidence suggests *ritualized* homosexuality. It is only the broader cultural pattern of explicit reports on (RH) in distant off-lying islands such as New Britain or the Humboldt Bay area that should make us question Manus Island in relation to Northern New Guinea as a whole.

THE SEPIK • The case for ritualized homosexuality in the vast Sepik River area is weakest of all. For others (see Keesing 1982:11n.) as for me, the great Sepik with its numerous anthropological studies for over sixty years remains an enigma in regard to the presence or absence of such practices.[35] Despite contemporary stories from New Guineasts[36] and the folklore of New Guineans themselves to the contrary, I have not been able to uncover a single clear-cut ethnographic report of (RH) from the entire area. Nevertheless, my doubts persist; so I shall here risk a reinterpretation.

Consider the following fragment from Bateson's (1958) classic *Naven,* which remains (along with the texts of Thurnwald [1916] and Mead [1935]) a well-known work from the Sepik.

> During the early period of initiation when the novices are being mercilessly bullied and hazed, they are spoken of as "wives" of the initiators, *whose penes they are made to handle.* Here it seems that the linguistic usage indicates an ethological analogy between the relationship of man and wife and that of initiator and novice.
> *(Bateson 1958:131, my emphasis)*

What does Bateson's observation suggest? My first question concerns the kind of data it represents. We know (Bateson 1932, 1958) that Iatmul initiation was gone by the time Bateson arrived; therefore, this passage must be from an informant's retrospective account. In the absence of ritual observations, then, should we interpret the boy's "handling" of the initiator's (probably MB) penis as an allusion to sexual, not merely symbolic, behavior? Perhaps; and here follows a speculative rethinking of the Iatmul case.

The *naven* ceremony itself, as is well known, concerned the mother's brother's "demeaning" act of "rubbing the cleft of his buttocks down the length of his *laua*'s [sister's son's] leg, a sort of sexual salute" (Bateson 1958:13). Such public displays required prestations in return. Does this act also represent or signify a homosexual component? Possibly: we know that sexual polarity and the subordination of women was marked in Iatmul society, that men were traditionally fierce headhunters concerned with maintaining a warriorhood and, through initiation, with instilling pride in the male ethos. We know also that boys had to stringently avoid women by hiding in capes after initiation (Bateson 1932:438). Furthermore, the fearsome gate to the initiation enclosure, represented by a crocodile jaw, was called "clitoris gate" (Bateson 1932:282), and men routinely referred to an "anal clitoris, an anatomical feature frequently imagined by the Iatmul" (Bateson 1932:279; see also Hauser-Schaeublin 1977).

A few years later, Margaret Mead described the Iatmul scene (from 1938 fieldnotes) in these ambiguous terms:

> In the men's group there is loud, over-definite masculine behavior, continuous use of verbs that draw their imagery from phallic attack on men and women alike. But there is also a very strong taboo on any display of passivity, and there is no development of male homosexuality within the society. The slightest show of weakness or of receptivity is regarded as a temptation, and men walk about, often comically carrying their small round wooden stools fixed firmly against their buttocks. A male child from any outside village or tribe becomes a ready victim, and Iatmul work-boys are said to become active homosexuals when they meet men from other tribes away at work. But within the group, the system holds . . . so that his capacity and temptation to introduce sex into his relationship with other males is very strong and yet kept closely in control.
> *(Mead 1949:95–96)*

How shall we view this report? Since Bateson has stated that the Iatmul male cult was in a state of "decay" by 1930, the men "fatalist" that "the mechanism of initiatory age grades had broken down" because "all the available young men had left the village to work for Europeans" (Bateson 1932:275), we wonder how Mead judged that there was "no male homosexuality." A possibility is that Iatmul had *secret* homosexual practices that were never revealed to ethnographers or had been already abandoned by the time Bateson and Mead arrived. Another problem is definitional: Mead ethnocentrically saw "homosexuality" as passive, effeminate, and deviant lifelong sexual contacts with the same sex.[37] On these terms one finds virtually no homosexual behavior anywhere in Melanesia. If the Iatmul practiced secret homosexuality, it almost surely did not take Mead's form.

The Iatmul may have thus practiced secret homosexuality in the context of traditional initiation (see also Layard 1959:107); moreover, there are two additional points made by Bateson (for other purposes) that support this view.

First, Bateson (1958:81–82) suggested that the structural and symbolic aspects of Iatmul marriage explained the "sexual gesture" in the naven act. Why should MB present buttocks to ZSo?

45

> Such conduct is of course not characteristic of a mother, but I have a casual mention in mythology of *a man who rubbed his buttocks on the leg of the man who was marrying his sister.* If we bear in mind the identification of a man with his sister, this conduct is comprehensible. . . . The man expressed his relationship to his sister's husband by ritually making a sexual gesture in which he identified himself with his sister. . . . For the sake of clarity we may state these identifications as if mother's brother were speaking, viz. "I am my sister" and "my nephew is my sister's husband." If now we consider these two identifications simultaneously it is perfectly "logical" for the *wau* to offer himself sexually to the boy, because he is the boy's wife. . . . Upon this hypothesis the *wau's* exclamation, "*Lan men to!*" "Husband thou indeed!" becomes understandable.
>
> *(Bateson 1958:81–82, emphasis mine)*

The subordinate position of being a prospective younger brother-in-law is converted via ritual action into a symbolic game. This game—the naven—denies the shame and submission of ZSo (Bateson 1958:270). Whether naven is merely ritual play seems debatable; but as Handelman (1979:181–182) argues convincingly, it seems like a superb mechanism for maintaining "the correctness of the complementary mode" between MB and ZSo. The wife-taker's shame-laden position is stressed in Bateson's (1958:132) remark, "Each of these elements of culture is based upon the basic assumption that the passive role in sex is shameful." I would go further than Bateson and argue, *mutatis mutandis,* that the symbolic structure of naven disguises the probability that the MB provides a wife for ZSo who, in the context of initiation, provides homosexual service to his "uncle." The shame-filled submission of that secret homosexuality is symbolically inverted and thereby expressed through the naven act in public. The *wau's* "sexual gesture" may be limited to the Sepik area, as Bateson (1958:82) thought. Yet the occurrence of homosexual service to the wife-givers by the younger initiate seems marked elsewhere (e.g., Kimam, Jaquai, Etoro, Sambia, etc.), in line with this reinterpretation.

Second, early on Bateson noted a cultural parallel that is germane to my reinterpretation. He believed that tribes of the Lower and Middle Sepik and of the Fly River all showed a "broad similarity of culture" (Bateson 1932:255). He names the Kiwai, the Marind-anim, and the Banaro,[38] suggesting parallels between because they all had large villages, were headhunters, initiated, and built great ceremonial cult houses. It is interesting to note that these groups (should we exclude the Banaro?) practiced (RH). In the summary, I will return to the Iatmul as a possible instance of "mythical homosexuality," in Layard's sense.

Elsewhere in the Sepik region, only two other groups are worth mentioning as questionable cases. Wogeo Island lies just off the Sepik mainland, and its ritual cult is similar to those of Iatmul, New Britain, and perhaps Humboldt Bay. Male initiation involved ordeals, sacred flutes, and spirit impersonations. Male fears of female menstrual pollution, with associated sexual polarity, were intense. In relation to these thematic features we are told:

> The popular attitude might well be thought to encourage homosexuality, especially as this is allegedly common among neighboring peoples of the [Sepik area] mainland.* Yet in fact homosexual relations, apart from mutual masturbation by pairs of youths, are rare in the village.
>
> *(Hogbin 1970:90)*

The extensiveness, meaning, or cultural context of such "mutual masturbation" is not clear from this report (nor from earlier Hogbin [1945–1946]). Is such reciprocal male/male sexual contact like the East Bay situation (Davenport 1965) noted above? We cannot know; so these fragments are insufficient to include Wogeo in our (RH) distribution.

One other Middle Sepik people, the Kwoma, merit a side note. Whiting (1941:51) states that they did not practice homosexuality, despite homosexual "games" and "teasing," which involved "very little genital contact" as such. In the same passage he remarks, "Sodomy [anal coitus?] is believed to be unnatural and revolting, and informants were unanimous in saying that anyone who would submit to it must be a 'ghost' and not a man." Presumably this was in response to Whiting's query. (Whom and what did he ask? The Sambia, incidentally, who practice fellatio, say the same thing about anal intercourse.) Whiting's statement raises further problems by his odd aside that "this sanction theoretically applied only

*Another ethnic attribution? What groups? Says who?

to *the person who played the passive role*" (ibid; emphasis mine). It is well known (e.g., see Sørum, chap. 7) beyond the Sepik that the sexual role of the homosexual insertee is frequently stigmatized in tribal societies, whereas the inserter role is seen as masculine and even honorable, not stigmatized (see Carrier 1980*a*). Here, as with the Iatmul, we may see a symbolic emphasis on the phallic fantasy of anal penetration, as opposed to actual homosexual relations. But this case is too vague and cannot be counted in our sample.

Explicit statements by other ethnographers nevertheless make it clear that homosexual practices are absent in other Sepik societies (e.g., Mead 1935:293 on the Mountain Arapesh and Mundugumor; Tuzin 1980:47 on the Ilahita Arapesh). Likewise it is entirely unreported from the Torricelli Mountains and the West Sepik area, the Upper Sepik, and, more distantly, both south and west, it is absent from the Telefomin area (Fitz John Poole, personal communication).

A HISTORICAL NEXUS?

What can be said of the historical-geographic relationship between Melanesian groups that practice ritualized homosexuality? Although I was initially opposed to speculative diffusionist arguments when I began this study, the data surveyed above suggest prehistoric cultural linkages among (RH) groups which have not yet been explicated and cannot therefore be ignored.

The accumulating evidence indicates that we are not only confronted in these Melanesian cultures with similar cultural and ecological systems; I propose that we are also faced with an ancient ritual complex that diffused through a vast area of lowland and fringe-area Melanesia, perhaps 10,000 years ago or less. Moreover, with the exception of some off-lying island societies of Northeastern Melanesia, all known cases of ritualized homosexuality are identified with non-Austronesian ("Papuan") languages (see table 1.1). These factors in turn are correlated with other regional attributes, the prehistorical and systemic bases of which we may consider.

Ritualized homosexuality is a lowlands phenomenon. The extant data show conclusively that these ritual practices, in one form or another, are confined to a few off-lying islands of Eastern Melanesia and the New Britain area, to the Ai'i, the lowlands of the Papuan Gulf, the entire Fly River basin, the Anga, the Great Papuan Plateau, Southeastern Irian Jaya, and the coastal fringe of Northeastern Irian Jaya. On the entire island of New Guinea, the only certain Highlands area with (RH) practices is the Anga (e.g., Sambia, Baruya), migrants from the Papuan hinterland. Both the Anga and the Great Papuan Plateau groups are marginal fringe groups adjacent to, but not typical of, the Central Highlands cordillera. The questionable cases, which I shall exclude from this review, are not exceptions to their geographic distributional pattern, aside from Akuna, which is too weak to utilize as an ethnographic case. New Britain, East Bay, New Caledonia, and Malekula should be seen as an island fringe that rings the northeastern and southeastern circumference of Melanesia. No Highlands examples of (RH) are otherwise known from Irian Jaya or Papua New Guinea, an extraordinarily large area with enormous populations well reported for decades.

Taken together, a general pattern emerges in the geographic distribution of these New Guinea lowland and island areas. Ritualized homosexuality is found in a fringe-area belt along the Highlands. We can trace this belt from east to west, or vice versa: it is merely a historical quirk of colonialism that ethnographic reports emerged initially from eastern-lying groups since the 1860s. Thus, from the extreme east to west, we can trace two main lines of this belt. (1) Fiji, the New Hebrides (and probably the Banks Islands), New Caledonia, East Bay, and then, to the northwest, parts of New Britain, the Duke-of-Yorks, and finally, leaving aside the uncertain area of coastal Northern New Guinea (including Wogeo and the Sepik), Humboldt Bay, the most westerly northern coastal case. (2) From southeast to southwest, the Ai'i, the Anga groups, the Fly River and the Morehead district, the Great Papuan Plateau and Nomad River, and the entire southeastern Irian Jaya area, including Frederik Hendrik Island, the Jaquai, and the southwestern coast north as far as the Asmat, people of the Casuarina coast probably being no exception (see map 1).

This vast belt encompasses about 3,000 miles from east to west. What areas aside from the New Guinea Highlands does it exclude? (RH) now seems absent from the Solomon Islands, Northern Papua New Guinea, the Massim area, the Markham River Valley, most of Eastern Papua to the Fly excluding the Ai'i of the Oro district and the Anga, the Telefomin area, and the Bird's Head and adjacent northwest Irian Jaya coastal areas (the Sepik River and adjacent areas, too, although again I would not entirely dismiss the possibility of ritualized homosexuality in these areas). Thus, there are vast parts of Melanesia without (RH). More importantly, the concentration of societies exhibiting this ritual complex are in Southwestern New Guinea and adjacent areas.

If we focus on southwestern coastal New Guinea on both sides of the international border, there is no longer any question that ritualized homosexualty is *universal* there. What this survey has added to the earlier areal arguments on SWNG by Haddon (1936), Van Baal (1963, 1966), and Wirz (1934), is the Ai'i and Anga material. Previously, a line of societies with (RH) could be drawn from the Fly River west. Now that line must be extended farther east, to include the Ai'i south of Orakaiva, the hill-dwelling Anga groups east of the Bulolo River, as well as Anga peoples in the lowlands and highlands ranging west to the headwaters of the Vailala and Purari Rivers. A new boundary can be further extended north to include the Great Papuan Plateau (and probably the Strickland River watershed), and the Lake Murray area all the way west into Irian Jaya. All middle or lowland groups west of the Fly practice ritualized homosexuality, as far north as the Mayo River hills, and as far west (excepting the Mimika) as the coastal Asmat.

For years various New Guinea specialists have argued for one or another kind of historical diffusion in this area (SWNG). Leaving aside the Anga groups for the moment, because they were unstudied until recently, scholars have argued for common origins and diffusion throughout this area. Haddon (1936) and Wirz (1933) both speculated that the Marind-anim, Trans-Fly Keraki, and Kiwai groups were cultural traditions resulting from a single migration/diffusion pattern, from west to east. They saw symbolic reflections of this prehistoric diffusion in myth, legend, and ritual customs (cf. Van Baal 1963). Many writers have also seen striking cultural parallels between SWNG groups (Bateson 1932; Haddon 1920, 1927, 1936; Landtman 1927; Rivers 1904:31; Serpenti 1965:171; Van Baal 1963:206; 1966:597n. and passim; Wagner

1972:19–24; Williams 1936*a*, 1936*c*; Wirz 1922). Wirz (1933), supporting his argument with legend and myth, saw the Kiwai as the "focal point" of a southeastern Marind-anim population stream that had prehistorically spread east. At the other end of the Fly River, its headwaters, Haddon (1920:244) saw the Sepik River as a great "cultural causeway" that had allowed diffusion from the Sepik to the Fly: "a convenient route for coastal cultures to reach the interior." This speculative river migration scenario seems plausible: it would enable contact points between the headwaters of the Fly and Sepik, the Great Papuan Plateau, Nomad and Strickland Rivers, and hence, the Morehead district, Lake Murray area, and the Irian Jayan southeastern hinterland and coast.[39]

I have alluded to certain cultural and ecological similarities and to symbolic and behavioral aspects of (RH) among these Papuan groups that link them to the other scattered cases reviewed herein, and I shall summarize these in the next section. But can other evidence be shown to support prehistoric connections between (RH) groups? Yes, though the only other support is linguistic, and here the evidence, while suggestive, is very speculative.

Wurm and his colleagues (1975:935–960) have developed several possible scenarios of Papuan language migrations in Melanesia, following upon Greenberg's (1971) "Indo-Pacific hypothesis" (i.e., interrelatedness between Papuan languages and those of the Andaman Islands and Tasmania). The details of Wurm's linguistic prehistory and postulated ancient migrations are complex and cannot be described here. What matters, for our purposes, is the hypothesis of an original west to east Trans-New Guinea Phylum migration that diffused language elements from insular Southeast Asia into island New Guinea 10,000 years ago or "even much less, with the time element probably greater in the case of the West Papuan and East Papuan Phyla" (Wurm et al. 1975:40).

In Wurm's reconstructed language migration of oldest Papuan elements, we can see a possible diffusionist basis for the regional and distributional relationships between groups that concern us.

> The languages of the Vogelkop Peninsula . . . as well as those in the northern part of the non-peninsular main portion of Irian Jaya, contain a common lexical substratum which extends to the south into the eastern part of the Irian Jaya highlands areas. At the same

> time, a substratum manifesting itself mainly on the structural and typological levels, i.e., in a prevalence of set II pronouns, an overt two-gender system, a tendency to prefixing in the morphology, number marking with nouns, verb stem suppletion and alteration in connection with object and subject marking and the absence of medial verb forms is, in varying degrees, mostly in evidence in the same areas (and reaches further east in the north), as well as in the south-eastern part of Irian Jaya, the adjacent southern parts of Papua New Guinea, and extends its influence, with interruptions, as far east as the Angan Family of the Trans-New Guinea Phylum whose speakers seem to have adopted an East New Guinea Highlands stock type language, though a few of the features mentioned above appear in the Angan Family languages as a substratum element.
>
> It seems tempting to suggest that this far-flung substratum which may have surviving primary manifestations in some members of the West Papuan Phylum . . . may outline the earlier presence in the New Guinea area, of an old language type which entered the area from west of northern Halmahera and the Vogelkop Peninsula and spread from there to the regions of its present occurrence, to be later overrun and reduced to substratum level by subsequent language migrations.
>
> *(Wurm et al. 1975:940–941)*

Here we see a speculative diffusionist basis of common linguistic origin for the so-called SWNG cultures.

We might speculate that along with some very old non-Austronesian linguistic elements, the migrants carried an ancient "root" ritual complex. Among the aspects of this structural complex was ritualized homosexuality. Perhaps a subsequent type II historical migration influenced and changed the eastern off-lying island world of Melanesia (e.g., New Hebrides), resulting in the interrelated East Papuan Phylum, before 3,000 B.C. (Wurm et al. 1975:941–943). This subsequent Austronesian influence thus resulted in the linguistic differentiation of the Eastern Melanesian group (New Caledonia, New Hebrides, East Bay) from the mainland non-Austronesian SWNG cultures. Yet, in spite of linguistic and probably other changes in their sociocultural systems, the "root" ritual structure of homosexuality among Eastern Melanesian groups remained. From the east, moreover, a major Austronesian migration about 5,000 years ago up the Markham Valley eventually influenced Highland peoples and the adjacent Angan groups of Papua (Wurm et al. 1975:947). Yet, again, we may hypothesize that these historical changes did not sweep away the (RH) practices associated with their ritual cults, at least among the non-Austronesian Angan stock-level language family[40] (see Wurm's language migration maps, ibid.:944–951).

In these speculative waves of language migrations, then, we find tentative support for the idea that a very old ritual complex was introduced by the earliest non-Austronesian speakers. It diffused over a vast area. Subsequent linguistic migrations affected language but not the element of ritual homosexuality. The exact time or geographic routes of these migrations is not my concern. But Wurm's migration scenarios do help explain why all groups evincing ritualized homosexuality are non-Austronesian speakers, excepting the Eastern Melanesian islanders, who apparently sustained later Austronesian influence. (This linguistic argument does not explain why other non-Austronesian or Austronesian groups do not practice ritualized homosexuality, an areal problem discussed in the summary.)

Once this old ritual complex permeated the Melanesian circle, as others have argued (e.g., Haddon 1920; Keesing 1982; Van Baal 1966), the great river systems, Sepik and Fly, may have served as a riverine causeway to adjacent lowland areas. Perhaps these migrants bypassed the Highlands, only touching its fringe areas. Or perhaps they settled early in some Highland areas, only to be pushed into the coastal areas by subsequent, and more numerous populations. We cannot know for certain. (To extrapolate further, perhaps this or a similar ritual complex spread across the Torres Straits: both Róheim[41] and Van Baal [1963] have argued for actual historical diffusion between the Papuan Gulf and Northern Australian cultures. But this speculation is far removed from my argument and need not concern us here.)[42]

One may reject these speculative diffusionist arguments altogether, while still acknowledging the impressive structural and symbolic parallels between Melanesian groups practicing ritual homosexuality. Nonetheless, we find recent precedents for diffusion as a contributing factor in the Austro-Melanesian literature (see Keesing 1982). Meggitt's (1965*a*) approach to the Australian areal aspects of Walbiri ritual is particularly attractive. He argues that an ancient ritual complex was introduced into Walbiri and then underwent successive regional, social, and ecological transformations in response to local group adaptations. Yet, the "deep" structure of ritual roles and symbols remained. This structure was necessary, but not sufficient in itself, to allow for the expression of the Walbiri ritual complex, which required other sociocultural elements to support its present institutional form and distribution. A comparable argument is made below for Melanesia.

Here, then, is a tentative *ultimate* causal view of the distribution of ritualized homosexuality in Melanesia. Arguments concerning various social structural and cultural underpinnings or concomitants of (RH) in different social units and subregional traditions may be seen as *proximate* transformational causes, discussed next. All these suggestions basically extend the interdisciplinary and scholarly work of others. Even so, I would not care to say more now: this rather shaky diffusionism leaves me, a social anthropologist, cautious and uneasy.

SUMMARY AND ANALYSIS

This survey shows clearly that ritualized homosexuality in Melanesia is more common than was ever thought, not to mention predicted, by contemporary surveys. Nor are its sociocultural forms and ecological distribution shapeless or random. I have argued that these customs belong to an ancient ritual complex manifested primarily in non-Austronesian-speaking groups of the western region of Papua and southeastern region of Irian Jaya and associated fringe areas, and some northeastern Melanesian island societies.

The range of ecological and social traits and institutions associated with (RH) is elaborate and rich. Sexual behavior, as much as or more than other human behaviors, is multivalent (Bateson 1972) in its antecedents and consequences. When one argues correlations, not causes, these factors can be catalogued and listed without concern for evolutionary or developmental sequelae or systemic interactions between environment, psyche, social structure, and culture. But when we choose to explain *systems* such as these, our task is more complex. Then we must seek a hierarchy of constraints (Keesing 1982) that systemically create and maintain the observed outcome: ritualized homosexual behavior.

To deal with systems that produce this outcome is indeed a complex matter. The task involves many variables: ecology; historical relatedness; warfare; population trends; social structure; homogeneity of local kin-based polities (the [1967] Allen hypothesis); cultural definitions of selfhood and personhood, sexuality, marriage, the nature of the sexes and gender development, including beliefs about the body, its orifices, fluids, and boundaries; residence patterns; descent ideologies; sexual morality and restrictiveness; initiation rites; warriorhood; definitions of homosexuality, bisexuality, and heterosexuality; the nature of the homosexual act (is it honorable, shameful, why and for whom?) and associated bonds; peer groups, age-groups; sexual dominance and the social status of women; gerontocracy; ceremonial impersonation, hoaxes, and symbolic communication with spirits; female pollution, semen depletion, and bloodletting; dual organization; secrecy; shame; postpartum taboos and sleeping arrangements; sex-typing; cultural attributes of masculinity and femininity that affect sexual contacts; identity, identification, sex-identity conflict and avoidance behavior, envy, conversion reactions, passivity, aggressivity, misogyny; and on and on. Another book would be required to treat these conceptual issues and associated theories in depth. In lieu of that (and with apologies for an already lengthy introduction), I shall here touch upon only the essential points raised in my survey.

INCIDENCE • The reader may wonder how frequent ritual homosexuality is in Melanesia, given this new distribution. I noted this problem in the preface. For Melanesia, in spite of this comprehensive review, the question is difficult to answer in a meaningful way. Not only is it difficult to convert the literature mess into statistical frequencies but our sample is certainly not random.[43] What ethnographic baseline do we select as our universe of phenomena against which to compare our data? (Highlands versus Lowlands? Austronesian versus non-Austronesian groups?) How do we count our sample? By cultural subregion or by representative social units? (The order of choice will affect tabulation.) For subregions, we could list as many as eight or as few as three—if one accepts the notion of a SWNG fringe area* (see map 1).

*These three subareas are: the SWNG area, including Anga groups; Humboldt Bay; and insular island Melanesia, including New Britain and adjacent areas, East Bay, and Eastern Melanesia.

When counting the total social units, the problems (due to Galton's problem) are greater. We may have as few as thirty-two groups,* or as many as fifty or so[44] (see table 1.1). Given the available Melanesian data, our survey conservatively results in between 10 to 20 percent of all Melanesian cultures having ritualized homosexuality as defined. Current information does not permit more precision.

ECOLOGY • The societies reported on in this book are, by and large, ecologically marginal populations associated with sago, yams, or taro, intensive hunting, and sparse populations. Shifting subsistence horticulture exists side by side with hunting and gathering in some areas. These peoples have "low intensity" agricultural regimes; mixed agriculture without single staple crops (e.g., sweet potatoes) is the rule (Brookfield and Hart 1971:94–124). Sweet potatoes are secondary crops among many SWNG groups; taro and yams, especially as feast crops, are prominent (cf. Watson 1965). Coconuts and pandanus are economically and symbolically important in most lowland and coastal areas. Hunting is prominent; and head-hunting, although not universal, is symbolically seen as one of its forms in some areas (e.g., Van Baal 1966; Zegwaard 1959; and see Van Baal, chap. 3 below). Moreover, the association between masculine prowess in hunting and exclusive male attachments is marked (Schieffelin 1982; Williams 1936*c*). By contrast, pig husbandry is of moderate importance (e.g., Marind-anim) or absent (e.g., Kaluli) from these groups. And none are involved in large-scale pig exchanges or ceremonial exchange systems in general (cf. P. Brown 1978; Rubel and Rossman 1978), which distinguishes these societies from those of the Highlands and the Massim area.

As elsewhere in Melanesia, there is a marked sexual division of labor in societies with ritualized homosexuality. Economic activities are identified with gender: hunting is masculine, certain forms of gardening are feminine; warfare is masculine, baby-sitting is feminine. Sex-typing and social status are thus linked, with male activities accorded higher status to the extent that (RH) groups

*Excluding all questionable cases, i.e.: Manus, Wogeo, the Sepik mainland, Iatmul (and all Sepik groups), Mamberamo River, Akuna, and all questionable adjacent areas of Irian Jaya and Vanuatu.

were called "men-admiring societies" by Layard (1959:108) and "comrad communities" *(genossenschaft)* by Wirz (1922:39–40). Brown and Buchbinder (1976) argue that these politicoeconomic patterns make the sexes complementary, not cooperative, with which I agree. Yet one wonders how far the emotional complementarity extended. Murphy (1959) has argued that sex antagonism—rivalry, ambivalence, envy—is generated in men working in close quarters and being dependent upon women as producers. Clearly, women are vital for the total reproduction of these socioeconomic systems (Donaldson n.d.; Keesing 1982), a fact that these male ideologies generally deny.

These groups, especially those of the SWNG, are demographically tenuous, too. They tend to have small populations numbering from a few hundred (Keraki) to several thousand (Marind-anim). Typically, villages are small, though among the Marind these could run into hundreds of people. Everywhere the man-to-land ratio is low, among the lowest in Melanesia, ranging from 4 or 5 persons per square mile upward to a limit of 40 per square mile (see Brookfield and Hart 1971:90ff., on Marind-anim, Anga, and others). By contrast, Highlands populations are dense, ranging from the Kuma (49 per m^2), to Mae Enga (160 per m^2), to Chimbu (225 per m^2) (see P. Brown 1978:106).

A related demographic factor is sex ratio at birth. Melanesian populations typically show a marked imbalance of males over females at birth (see Malcolm 1970). The data on this factor are uneven. However, Guiart (cited in Allen, chap. 3 below) showed a remarkable imbalance of 231 males over 115 females in his 1950 North Malekula census. Rates such as 120/100 males at birth for the Sambia (Herdt 1981) and 100/71 men over women (Bowers 1965:29) elsewhere are common (cf. Bulmer's 1971 survey). Was this overpopulation of males a factor in contributing to institutionalized homosexuality? It probably was, but how much of a causal role it played is unclear.

Male overpopulation must be seen in context. It is not simply the gross number of males at birth that matters, but how many survive into adulthood, and how women are reproductively controlled through marriage customs. Male deaths through warfare in Melanesia surely also affected the disparity. The role of misogyny, though, with chiefs (Malekula), elders, and war leaders taking several wives, must have exacerbated the shortage of women in these groups. The late onset of menarche among Melanesians probably also contributed to the female "shortage" (Buchbinder 1973:211; Malcolm 1968). It is safe to argue that male overpopulation did *contribute* to the institutionalization of homosexuality, for intuition tells us that a shortage of males would have made such practices less likely. However, correlation is not causation. The Tor of Northeast Irian Jaya had a very high rate of male overpopulation: Oosterwal (1961:38) reports that fully 47 percent of Tor males are bachelors at marriageable age. But adultery still occurs (Oosterwal 1959), and they do not practice (RH), as we have seen. A more detailed regional analysis is needed to clarify this factor.

Low fertility rates may be another contributing factor in these populations. Again, the data are thin. Yet in two areas, Southeastern Irian Jaya and the Great Papuan Plateau, groups practicing ritualized homosexuality were faced with low fertility rates and declining populations at the time of pacification. Van Baal has written of Marind-anim low female fertility, high vaginal irritations, and associated medical complications (due to ritual sexual promiscuity?), and birth-related diseases that precipitated kidnapping and/or purchase of children, which was a "dire necessity for continuity" (1966:31–32, and passim). Kelly (1977) argued that the Etoro declining population was exacerbated by their postcontact epidemics and by the fact that they "taboo heterosexual intercourse for 295 days during the year" (quoted in Kottack 1974:287). These factors, plus the cultural practice of homosexual contacts among young males, certainly threaten the viability of a small population. Yet we must again take care in reading correlation as causation. Other Melanesian groups have sustained low fertility and depopulation (see Rivers 1922), some of whom later thrived. And heterosexual avoidance behavior, expecially in the Highlands, seems marked (Meggitt 1964). Heider (1976), for instance, reports that the Dani of Highlands Irian Jaya have "low sexual energy" and practice extreme sexual abstinence for years at a time; yet the Dani do not practice ritualized homosexuality.

Left unchecked by Western pacification or colonialization, what would the long-term evolution of these marginal populations have been? Perhaps homosexual practices might have contributed to their extinction, but we cannot be certain of this possibility: if one accepts the assumption of ancient migrations and ritual practices, these groups had flourished for generations. But perhaps we look back at them as they were at their zenith, with groups like the Marind-anim having specialized to the point that "could not have lasted much longer" (Ernst 1979:52; Keesing 1976).

In short, (RH) cultures are fringe-area ecological groups whose subsistence and populations were generally tenuous. It seems likely that their peripherality is no accident. In their niches they have little economic competition. One wonders here the extent to which SWNG groups may have been displaced by larger, later migrations of more numerous Highlands peoples, forcing them over generations into fringe areas. This raises the general problem of warfare and warriorhood initiation.

WARFARE • Warfare occurred among all these peoples,* though its forms (e.g., intratribal versus intertribal fighting) and intensity varied from place to place. Why did war occur at all, given their peripherality? The full answer to this problem is complex and far-ranging and remains to be seen.[45] But given the small populations and lack of nearby competitors, a materialist explanation of war makes less sense here than it does for larger Highlands groups, for whom the data do not support it either (Keesing 1982; Sillitoe 1978). Among SWNG groups in particular, several patterns seem to hold true.

First, war was a fact of life that conditioned most cultural domains and social arenas in these societies. Warfare thus influenced the behavioral environment of child development, marriage and the family, gender roles, and sexual behavior (see Langness 1967; Mead 1935; Schwartz 1973).

Second, these groups generally recognized the difference between intratribal and intertribal fighting (Langness 1972). Their community-based warriorhoods did fight each other (though some did not, e.g., Marind-anim), but their real social concern was with intertribal fighting and war raids against enemies. These war raids took the form of head-hunting expeditions among many (Marind-anim, Kimam, Asmat, etc.), but not the Highlands Anga.[46] Indeed,

*I shall be speaking primarily here of mainland groups.

the association of heads (body and penis head, coconuts and pandanus) and male substance is symbolically marked in various (RH) groups (see Allen, Van Baal, and Serpenti below). Finally, we know that war raids customarily followed initiation cycles among groups such as the Marind-anim, the Kimam, the Sambia, and perhaps on the Great Papuan Plateau.

Third, (RH) groups tend to use initiation as *the* social mechanism for recruitment to their ritual cults and to the village-based warriorhood corps as well. Survival and social reproduction of communities depend upon the warriorhood, and initiation means introduction to homosexual activity. It also brings with it adult, masculine socialization, through successive ceremonies and related achievements. Thus homosexuality is linked to what are essentially military and age-graded organizations.[47] A number of important manifest and latent social functions stem from these military clubs.

INITIATION • What kind of initiation do (RH) cultures practice? They have initiations, not puberty rites, in Allen's (1967:5) sense: ceremonialized admissions to discreet groups "normally held at set intervals for a number of candidates simultaneously." These are all-male associations, with compulsory membership (but see Schieffelin 1982). Women are, in some places, involved (e.g., Marind-anim). Female initiation is usually confined to menarche or birth ceremonies (see Godelier 1982*a*), and the status and position of women is correspondingly low (cf. Van Baal 1975). Furthermore, initiation usually places boys in men's secret societies from which women and children are formally excluded. Ritual instruments, flutes and bull-roarers, are seen as hostile to women (Gourlay 1975; Herdt 1982*a*; Williams 1936*a*). (RH) ritual and political authority in general is vested in cult elders, compared with Highlands "big man" polities (Allen, in press; cf. Hage 1981).

An important and ignored aspect of initiation in (RH) groups is that it frequently occurs before puberty, often as early as middle to late childhood (e.g., Marind-anim, Sambia, Keraki, etc.). Elsewhere I have argued that this young age is psychologically necessary for the radical resocialization into, and eventual sex-role dramatization expected of, adult men (Herdt 1981, 1982*b*; cf. Mead 1949; Young 1965). A related and still poorly understood aspect is that of ritual secrecy, which has significant psychosocial consequences for gender formation (reviewed in Herdt 1982*a*; Schwimmer 1980). Separation from mother, household and playmates, ordeals and initiation traumas, the liminal stage of seclusion, fasting, and suspension of normal routines and relationships set the stage on which ritual homosexuality is begun.

Long ago Van Gennep suggested a view of erotic acts in initiation that merits renewed attention. In cultures where sex is seen as either impure or as holding magicoreligious danger, as in (RH) groups, Van Gennep (1960:169) suggested that a taboo on coitus would be present. Among such groups, "Coitus is 'powerful': that is why it is sometimes used as a rite of great efficacy. . . . The physical impact of the act—that of penetration—should be borne in mind" (ibid.). Following other initiation ordeals and seclusion, the sexual act becomes a means of effecting ritual transition change in selfhood. "Coitus as a final act in initiation ceremonies I interpret also as a rite of incorporation," which applies equally for heterosexual and homosexual practices (Van Gennep 1960:170–171). The homosexual act incorporates the boy into a new group, the ritual cult, with a new status and role. The boy's insemination coheres with the native view, universal in (RH) cultures, that the key (manifest) goal of homosexual contact is to get sperm inside the boy's body so he can grow.[48] This initiation principle is special. Some Melanesian groups lack initiation rites altogether. But among those who practice initiation, the insemination idea is unique to (RH) groups.*

Yet there are actually three interrelated parties to this homosexual act of incorporation. On the one hand, the boy (and others) may believe that this act will make him grow and strengthen. He is, in this sense, demonstrating his desire to be masculine, to act in accord with ritual ways, to be unfeminine.[49] On the other hand, his counterpart, the postpubescent inseminator, demonstrates his superordinate maleness by the homosexual act of masculinizing the boy (Herdt 1981:205). A third party is the ritual cult itself. The cult in turn is represented at three levels: through its concrete paraphernalia and cult house; through human agents (elders, cult leaders, father, and bachelors); and through spirit beings, who

*I exclude here insemination by analogy, i.e., sperm used in foods (see Schwimmer, chap. 6).

may be directly or indirectly personified through masks or dramatic impersonations. The paraphernalia becomes sacred stage, these authorities the audience (women a metaphoric audience for the men) which sanctify the homoerotic act, endowing it with the power of sacred tradition, the supernaturally blessed moral way of life. Thus, the ritual homosexual act serves here as a cultural sign, to self and others, of *submission* to ritual and spiritual authority (see Errington, cited above, and Tuzin 1980 in another context).

The question arises as to the nature of this submission. To what extent are the homosexual relations depicted in (RH) groups "real" or "mythical," in Layard's (1942:474) terms? Our survey is instructive, and it points to a new typology. Type I is represented by *symbolic* homosexual contacts. Actual homosexual penetration may or may not occur; or, as is likely with the Ingiet society on New Britain, it occurs but once only, in first initiation. Farces and hoaxes may be the genre of spirit impersonations. Actual homosexual contacts are not perpetuated thereafter. The person who inseminates the novice may be a spirit being impersonated by an elder. Homosexuality may also be symbolically projected in myth or folktales (see Schwimmer, chap. 6). Type II utilizes actual homosexual intercourse during initiation. It is usually with males who will copulate with the novice afterward. No hoaxes here; the boys' physical growth and the social effects of such for war and the marriage trade are serious business. Homosexual activity may go on in secular life for months or years. In our sample, Type I groups are few. (Does Iatmul belong in this group?) Type II groups are common, and they include all SWNG societies. Some societies, such as Malekula and the Marind-anim, seem to complexly utilize features of both types, with elaborate spirit impersonations and mythology buttressing actual homosexuality (Allen, chap. 2; Van Baal, chap. 3).

My guess is that Type II societies emphasize the actual physical penetration of the boy (in line with Van Gennep's idea). Here, real physical and psychological effects are expected from the male/male sexual act and implanted semen. Changes result, then, in "biological" maturation, which we may "read" analogically as also meaning changes in the boy's experience of self (see M. Strathern 1979) and in concomitant changes in his personhood (Read, chap. 5). In groups such as Kaluli, these actual homosexual contacts may occur late, in adolescence, and may last only a few months. In most SWNG and Eastern Melanesian groups, however, the actual contacts extend from childhood into adulthood on an exclusive and regular basis. (Perhaps, in this sense, they are "profane," not "sacred," the latter more characteristic of Type I groups; cf. Schieffelin 1982.) Again, we should not underrate the power of sexual submission to effect psychosocial changes in the boy's gender identity and role (Herdt 1982*a*; Vanggaard 1972) and societal variations in this power (cf. Allen, chap. 2). Such gender changes involve the boy's incorporation into warriorhood life. He may experience his homosexual contacts with fear, honor, shame, excitement, or all of these; but here, we confront individual thoughts and feelings, not merely cultural rules and ideals, a problem on which there is virtually no data. The initiate is coerced and expected to emulate his seniors, to identify with and probably compete with his peers. This psychosocial process eventuates in his internalization of the warrior role, ritual beliefs, probably misogyny, and behavioral conformity to cult rules and norms. Aggressiveness is inculcated. Again, we should reiterate that some SWNG groups follow initiation rites with a war-raiding party. For the newly initiated older bachelor, this raid is a confirmatory rite demonstrating his prowess, just as his newly achieved role as homosexual inserter to younger boys demonstrates his sexual maturity (Herdt 1981). Initiation rites and warfare thus interact with the inculcation of warrior identity. Homosexuality contributes, that is, as a latent social function in the maintenance of the cult, obedience to authority, and the development of aggressivity and eventual sexual antagonism toward women.

What about the erotics of ritual homosexuality? Let us underline the obvious: without erotic desire, arousal, and consummation, any sexual intercourse is impossible.* The conventional sentiment which I have heard expressed, by laymen and anthropologists, is that "these Melanesians are performing rituals, not erotics." Ethnocentrism aside,[50] it should be clear that these two modes are of one piece—experience—not opposed, in Melanesia. The Marind

*Excluding self- or other masturbation of course. The data show that masturbation to arousal is usually unnecessary here.

warrior who copulates with a boy may be aroused and still be conforming to or performing a ritual. The boy, in contrast, may be terrified or thrilled. But erection is necessary for the acts to take place, especially when they go on for a lifetime. The "sexual needs of bachelors" (Hiatt 1977:257) is involved, as are sexual segregation, suppression, and other factors already noted. Likewise, the social attributes of the role of homosexual partners must be taken into account. In most of these groups, the homosexual partners are in asymmetrical, age-graded older/younger relationships; but kinship, marital and ritual status, and other beliefs and rules about the function or purpose and outcome of the inseminating are contingencies. Secrecy, shame, and honor are probably crucial emotional factors (consciously and unconsciously) of sexual excitement here, too. A complex algebraic sum of all these things, as among the ancient Greeks,[51] produces the erotics necessary for ritualized homosexual behavior.

And what is the relation between these homoerotics and adult masculine identity? The essays below only touch upon this issue (see Van Baal, Read, and Schwimmer, this volume; cf. Herdt 1981). The question of sexual motivation, at all levels of awareness (e.g., conscious and unconscious), raise important issues on which we provide little direct data as such; and we are not satisfied to "read" individual motives and experience from customs. Clearly, the male role is problematic in many parts of Melanesia; perhaps this is true for both (RH) and other groups, as elsewhere (D'Andrade 1966). Yet, the involvement of males in homoerotic bonds in (RH) groups implies a kind of sexual and interpersonal fluidity of psychosexual development that may be a fundament of these Melanesian societies, in particular. Power relationships, both in the general sense of managing others and controlling public affairs, and in the delimited sense of dominance over others in everyday life, are germane here. Men in (RH) groups attempt a sexual and social control over all others, a control that is difficult to achieve and sustain, for instance, in the circumstances of domestic life (Rosaldo 1974). The attempt is supported by the nearly universal conscription of boys into warrior life via initiation. All males are thus involved in (RH), and their personal choice is, as we have seen, limited by many factors. The modifier *ritualized* with respect to homosexual behavior addresses this dimension of sexual orientation and identity formation. In spite of universal involvement in homosexual activities, however, no data indicate that these males become habitually motivated to same-sex contact later in life, or that the incidence of aberrant lifelong individual homosexuality, as an identity state, is greater in (RH) groups than elsewhere in the world. Homosexuality is the royal road to heterosexuality (to paraphrase Freud), but it is a temporary one. What remains unclear, however, is the effect of this early and transitional male/male sexual activity on the development or quality of male/female sexual bonds. In some, perhaps many, (RH) groups, men seem to view preinitiated boys as a composite of "feminine" and "masculine" characteristics. Homosexuality is designed, in this regard, to masculinize their selfhood and behavioral comportment in the direction of defined adult masculine roles. Yet, certain feminine characteristics may endure—to be expressed in secret male rites; is this why, perhaps, ritualized homosexuality itself is so often secret in Melanesia? No, (RH) does not make these males into what we Westerners call "homosexuals"; these data instead challenge our own views about what that category means, and what parts of nature and nuture it is made from. Perhaps we should now better look to understand how the fluidity of the human condition allows this Melanesian phenomena and what, in a general sense, bisexuality is all about.

SEXUAL POLARITY • The final set of interrelated conceptual issues may be grouped under the rubric *sexual polarity.* Though Melanesia has long been identified as a culture area with much "sexual antagonism," what does sexual polarity mean in cultures that ritualize homosexuality? Is its form different than in other Melanesian groups (see Herdt and Poole 1982)? I believe it is; and, when we examine the configurations of this theme here, we see how the differences inform, and are informed by, homosexuality. I will argue that sexual polarity takes its most extreme form in (RH) groups.

These are societies in which the gender and social roles of men and women are viewed not only as distinct, separate, and polarized but as hostile in many respects. I have noted this in the economic division of labor and in ritual cultism. To what extent do these differences extend into everyday social action, marriage, and intragroup relationships: not just a house divided, but one at war with itself?

The status of women is low in these cultures. (Social status is here indicated by women's low participation in public affairs; their low access to, or control of, their economic products; their lack of choice in marriage; beliefs about women's polluted bodies; negative images of women registered in idioms, myth, and everyday discourse; and the absence or peripherality of institutions such as initiation for women.) Women are described as being in a low or "degraded state" (William's 1936*c* term) among the Keraki, the Kiwai, the Marind-anim, the Baruya, the Sambia, the New Hebrides groups, and others, as shown in different ways in the chapters below. Ecological and economic factors are correlated with women's low status. The literature generally indicates that the larger the population, the higher the women's status (e.g., among Chimbu, Hagen, and Enga). Where economic exchange systems and pig husbandry are present, women play a crucial part which seems to provide higher status (Feil 1978; M. Strathern 1972, 1980). But these economic productive features are virtually absent from (RH) groups (cf. Lindenbaum, chap. 9).

These cultures are sexually restrictive. Sexual activity is fraught with rules and taboos, and in adulthood it is thoroughly ritualized through initiation and marriage customs. It is not clear to what extent premarital sexual play is forbidden in children among these groups, but it is strongly condemned among the Sambia and neighboring Anga peoples. Sex is morally charged: adultery and premarital heterosexual activity are generally considered shameful. Certainly rigorous taboos govern sexual contacts between men and women after male initiation occurs. One may argue that a similar situation exists throughout the Highlands, the Eastern Highlands initiatory systems in particular. Yet, (RH) cultures channel years-long male sexual development away from females toward males through homosexuality. *That* restrictiveness is unique to them. (Perhaps RH groups have more "prudes" than "lechers," in Meggitt's [1964] terms.) Sexual restrictiveness raises three related issues: gender differences, sex anxiety, and sexual segregation.

Gender differences are polarized in cultures with ritualized homosexuality. Adult masculinity and femininity are defined as essentially antithetical. The biological origins and cycles of males and females are seen as fundamentally different (Kelly 1977:16). Men's ideology views women as "naturally" competent throughout their developmental cycle (childhood growth, the menarche, childbirth), whereas males need a ritual push, as it were, through initiation (reviewed in Herdt 1981). Homosexual insemination is crucial for male growth and strength. Highlands initiatory systems show similar ideologies of gender differences, but they do not require homosexual contact. What does this difference imply? I think that a pervasive cultural principle separates Highlands from (RH) cultures here, and it has been discussed by Allen (chap. 3) below. (RH) groups focus on milk and semen as critical gender fluids. Eastern Highlands groups especially emphasize blood. Mother's and women's womb and menstrual blood is seen as contaminating and lethal to male development in the Highlands, so bloodletting rites are key initiation activities (see Read, chap. 5). Letting polluted blood is thus a sign of being masculinized (Herdt 1982*b*) there. By contrast, bloodletting is rare or absent in (RH) groups, except, that is, for Highlands Anga peoples, who undoubtedly imported nosebleeding rites from their Eastern Highlands neighbors. Aside from circum-incision in the New Hebrides, penis cutting is absent from (RH) groups. The differential principle seems to be this: in (RH) groups no distinction is made between male and female blood, and female contamination is not feared (excepting Highlands Anga); but mother's milk and semen are seen as fundamentally different, so gender ideology focuses upon homosexual insemination as a kind of later masculinizing-parturition process.

What accounts for this Highlands/(RH) difference? Population size and integrity are indirectly related (Lindenbaum 1972). The fact that SWNG groups do not generally marry their enemies is surely related (excepting Highlands Anga again). Perhaps these factors are contingent upon an even more important process: the early ritual development of gender necessary for later sex-role dramatization in *adulthood*. Remember that both bloodletting and semen-intake are practices bound to ritual, and ritual makes use of differentiation and contrast by analogy (among other processes). If Highlands' groups pinpoint femaleness in the menstrual act, (RH) groups focus it on breast-feeding; and in male rites, Highlands men emphasize bloodletting, whereas SWNG men emphasize homosexual insemination. Hage (1981) has criticized Dundes (1976) for interpreting these contrary ritual modes as "expressions" of (unconscious) envy, not of analogy. It is unfortunate that Hage sees these two processes as opposed, instead of complementary, as I think they are in this case (see Spiro 1982:168–171). At any rate, as Allen notes below (chap. 2), abundant evidence indicates that men exhibit envy of women's perceived "natural" powers here (cf. Van Baal, chap. 3; Read, chap. 5). Allen also suggests that two contrary images of women symbolically underlie these modes: "menstruating woman/reproductive mother" (Eastern Highlands, Wogeo) versus "wife/nurturant mother" (RH groups).

Does heterosexual anxiety enter in, and if so, to what extent? Sexual anxiety is difficult to measure (Stephens 1962). But it seems pronounced in Highlands groups (Meggitt 1964) and minimal for (RH) groups such as the Etoro (Kelly 1976), the Marind-anim (Van Baal 1966), and others, though I have suggested it is extreme among the fringe-area Sambia (Herdt 1981). Sex anxiety is correlated with the sexual restrictions of postpartum taboos, as Whiting et al. (1958) argue. The secrecy of childbirth, like that of homosexuality, seems related (Schieffelin 1976). Economic cooperation needed between spouses may exacerbate the sex anxiety (Murphy 1959), as does intermarriage with enemy groups, whereby a woman is seen as a potential enemy (e.g., Sambia), though among the Marind-anim such marriages do not occur since the Marind warred against distant enemies. From all these factors, sex anxiety and ambivalence toward women especially, the effects upon the father/child relationship must be significant (e.g., rivalry, jealousy, envy, aloofness, overcompensatory "protest masculinity"; see Whiting and Whiting 1975). Unfortunately, data on this topic in Melanesia are rare (but see Van Baal, chap. 3).

Sexual segregation is marked in (RH) and Highlands groups, and it is associated with the restrictive factors noted above, but here again there is a difference between the two cultural systems. In virtually all (RH) cultures there are men's houses or cult houses where men congregate. In groups such as the Marind-anim, men and women live in separate but close huts. Following initiation, boys usually have to avoid women and children for some period of time—months, years, as the case may be. Yet, in contrast to

Highlands groups, many SWNG societies customarily allow men and women to live together in close proximity. This may mean separate compartments of one long-house (Etoro, Kaluli), or separate male or female spaces in the same sleeping quarters (Keraki, Anga groups). Highlands groups, however, usually have strict sexual segregation in different houses, even in adulthood. In (RH) groups, the result may be a kind of divided (even tense) togetherness. In this regard one may thus characterize the (RH) attitude toward male/female proximity as enigmatic and ambivalent. One may hypothesize that years-long exposure to this ambivalence results in sex-identity conflict later for boys at initiation (cf. Herdt 1982*a*, 1982*b*; Schwimmer, chap. 6; A. Strathern 1970).

Sexual segregation must be counted as a key contributing factor to the institutionalization of homosexuality. When residential separation is added to sexual restrictiveness and socioeconomic polarity, homosexual activity as an acceptable sexual outlet seems likely. Davenport has argued this point:

> It should be noted that throughout Melanesian societies, where institutionalized forms of male bisexuality* are most frequently encountered, there is also a widespread tradition of separating men from women. So pronounced is this nearly everywhere, it can be regarded as a basic principle of social organization. . . . One can entertain the hypothesis that in the strongly gender-segregated communities of Melanesia, when the culture also imposes effective barriers to heterosexual intercourse, there is a likelihood that institutionalized male bisexual practices will result.
>
> *(Davenport 1977:156)*

While I sympathize with this view, a caveat is necessary. It seems a quirk that in the most "strongly gender-segregated" societies in Melanesia, the Eastern Highlands, ritual homosexuality is absent. Gender segregation is therefore a necessary but not sufficient cause of (RH). The other factors noted above must interact synergistically with segregation to produce this special outcome.

A final, and very important, factor remaining is marriage. Marriage in all these groups is customarily arranged. Sister exchange is a common form in (RH) groups. Infant betrothal and brideservice are uncommon but present. But bride-price marriage is

*Davenport uses this term in the same way I use ritualized homosexual behavior.

rare (e.g., among Marind-anim) and more commonly found in the Highlands. I suspect that sister exchange and moiety exogamy, as among the Marind (Van Baal 1966:122–127), are frequently correlated in (RH) societies; both are present in Irian Jaya, the Trans-Fly area, and Eastern Melanesia. Still, Anga groups such as the Sambia lack exogamous moieties, and intravillage marriage between closely related clans of the same phratry is common. Yet the (RH) inter-linkages between sister-exchange marriage and ritualized homosexuality are impressive. Since bride-wealth marriage is common in Highlands systems, we may see in sister-exchange marriage a structural pattern that distinguishes (RH) from Highlands cultures (cf. Collier and Rosaldo 1981; Lindenbaum, chap. 9).

The pattern that emerges in SWNG is one in which kin groups that intermarry are involved also in homosexual transactions. Women are controlled and traded as pawns by elders in the "marriage trade." Age differences enter in. Given several years' difference between brothers, older sisters, and even older sisters' husbands (as among Australian Aborigines), a woman's younger brother (biological or classificatory brother) is placed in a structurally subordinate position to his elder sister's husband, his brother-in-law (Serpenti, chap. 7). Yet the nature of this subordination is convoluted. Because of sister exchange, both parties are "wife-givers" and "wife-takers." The older man, however, takes his wife *first,* so he is, temporarily, beholden to his younger unmarried brother-in-law. The younger male, though, by virtue of his lower ritual and social status, is socially subordinate to the older man.

Now their kinship relationship enters in. They are not only in a "double" brother-in-law relationship (i.e., wife's brother is sister's husband) in Layard's phrase (1959:104), they can be matrilateral cross-cousins (Keraki), patrilateral cross-cousins (Sambia), or even, in the case of Etoro and Kimam, mother's brother and sister's son (real or classificatory). In (RH) groups that prescribe homosexual relations between these males, we have, in effect, a boy's parents giving his sister to an older male who becomes his brother-in-law and who will (with other members of his kinship group) inseminate the boy. The boy is being ritually "masculinized" into adulthood as his sister is being impregnated by the older man. The most extreme form that homosexual service takes in

(RH) cultures is, among the Jaquai, a rather extraordinary kind of bride-service:* a boy's parents, lacking a daughter to exchange, eventually receive from the older man who inseminated the boy (e.g., Kimam, Kunam) a woman for him to marry, a kind of sentimental gift. Thus, exchange of women and semen circulation go together in these groups (see Herdt, chap. 4).

Lévi-Strauss (1969:307) has suggested that the Nambikwara of the Amazon through polygamy create a "disequilibrium between the number of young men and the number of available girls," making homosexual relations a "provisional substitute" for marriage.[52] His point can be applied to these Melanesian groups, too. In a culture with strictly arranged marriages, male overpopulation, polygamy among older men, and extreme sexual polarity—sexual segregation and heterosexual restrictiveness in particular—ritualized homosexuality is a transitional alternative sexual outlet for males. (Certainly there is no evidence that it is a population control method, as Money and Ehrhardt ([1972:126] or Kottack [1974:287–288] suggest.) Yet it must be clear that this alternative seems to apply only in groups whose history, social structure, and other systemic factors make transitional homosexuality both necessary and sufficient for individual and societal coherence.

Hage (1981) has argued recently that ritual homosexuality in New Guinea is a product of some underlying structure of "sexual symmetry," also expressed in dual organizations, initiation rites, and a "big man complex" that is "rampantly egalitarian." He sees this underlying structure expressed, on the north coast and in the Eastern Highlands, in bloodletting rites, whereas on the south coast its form is (RH). To reiterate, contra Dundes (1976) he argues that it is not envy but this structural "sexual symmetry" that provides a "simpler explanation" of (RH), based on structural-evolutionary principles. Space does not permit a full review of these arguments, but several of his points are germane to my summary. First, the simplest "historical" explanation of homosexual customs is that they are distributed in relation to long-term transformational adjustments to the postulated migration-diffusion outlined above. In this regard, Hage's data are incomplete. Second, neither bloodletting nor semen-ingestion practices follow

*Or perhaps it is bride-wealth, if one views semen as a scarce commodity.

any simple structural or historical-evolutionary pattern, as I have argued elsewhere (Herdt 1980, 1982*b*). For instance, how would this theory accommodate groups such as the Sambia who practice *both* bloodletting and homosexuality?* Third, Hage's appeal to a probably nonexistent "big man complex" ignores the Western Highlands, where such political figures are most developed but whose societies (e.g., Melpa) lack both bloodletting and homosexuality. Here Hage has it backwards: it is in groups that lack the big man prototype that (RH) is more likely to be present. Fourth, as I noted above, not all groups that practice ritual homosexuality have marriage by exogamous moieties. It seems that such ethnological models will remain inadequate until researchers take the literature of Melanesia as a culture area more seriously.

To what extent can we argue that the ritual complex of homosexuality was caused by male gender ideology, as Layard (1942) argued? This chicken-and-egg problem cannot be answered on the basis of the extant literature, unless, that is, one regards the hypothetical ancient migrations as both a sufficient and necessary cause of (RH), which I do not. Clearly, these cultures exhibit marked sexual polarity; perhaps, and just as importantly, they show extreme ambivalence toward women (Van Baal 1966). These male misogynist ideologies described in this book contain a remarkable view of women, not as dangerous and polluting beings, but as valued and scarce sexual objects to be controlled and envied for their parturition capacities. Perhaps, then, given such ideologies, economic and sexual segregation led to ritual separation (Kaberry 1939), which evolved gradually into ritualized homosexuality.

Ritual homosexuality is a powerful symbolic structure that unites these cultures in a single pattern, in spite of their differences. It is too simple to say that one or another factor caused their customs. But when we combine the whole—the system of presumed migration history, ecology, and sociocultural structures with concomitant effects on personality and sex roles—the synergistic effect makes their form of sexual polarity understandable in time and

*No doubt another pseudoevolutionary "transformation" type can be invented to account for such variations.

place. Is not this complex image but one instance of the fact that humanness is complex?

The themes touched upon in this summary are empirically studied in the chapters that follow. And Professor Lindenbaum examines their theoretical underpinnings in her concluding chapter.

The comparative ethnography surveyed here presents such an embarrassment of rich interlinkages and ideas that I must end by expressing my bewilderment at an anthropology that has ignored their theoretical importance for so many decades. Undoubtedly, Western prudery and outmoded research conventions, which excluded sexual behavior from much of anthropology, were responsible. We hope that this book adds momentum to the growing interest in cross-cultural studies on sex and gender in Melanesia and elsewhere.

NOTES

Research funding for this chapter came, in part, from the Department of Anthropology, Stanford University, and I gratefully acknowledge its support. For careful and invaluable assistance in interpreting the ethnology of Irian Jaya I acknowledge with sincere thanks the help of J. Van Baal. I also wish to thank Michael Allen for reviewing this manuscript, especially on Vanuatu, as well as Shirley Lindenbaum, Stephen Murray, Fitz John P. Poole, Robert J. Stoller, and Donald F. Tuzin for their comments. Mark T. Janssen aided me in bibliographic work, and Thomas H. Baker assisted in translation, and I gratefully acknowledge their help. Responsibility for the final product is of course mine.

1. Such general cross-cultural surveys as those of J. Brown (1963), Burton and Whiting (1961), Cohen (1964), Stephens (1962), Whiting et al. (1958), and Young (1965), though they make use of Austro-Melanesian data, do not mention ritualized homosexuality. Allen (1967:96–97, 99) only mentions two island cases and does not review the New Guinea material.
2. See, for examples, Bell 1935–1936:185 and Hallpike 1977:36. Carrier (1980*a*:101) laments in a recent survey: "Data available on homosexual behavior in most of the world's societies, past or

present, are meagre." They are "complicated by the prejudice of many observers who consider the behavior unnatural, dysfunctional, or associated with mental illness, and by the fact that in many of the societies studied the behavior is stigmatized and thus not usually carried out openly. Under these circumstances, the behavior is not easily talked about. At the turn of the twentieth century such adjectives as disgusting, vile, and detestable were still being used to describe homosexual behavior. . . . In discussing sodomy with some of his New Guinea informants, Williams (1936*c*), for example, asked them if they 'had ever been subjected to unnatural practice.'" (See below, p. 21.) Eric Schwimmer tells me that F. E. Williams' relates in his unpublished diary how he discovered homosexuality by having been propositioned by a Keraki boy in the forest.

3. Remember that Ellis generously prefaced *The Sexual Life of Savages,* noting that "other students doubtless will be inspired to follow" Malinowski's lead (Ellis 1929:xi). Too bad that never happened.
4. On the Amazon see, for example, C. Hugh-Jones 1979:160–161; S. Hugh-Jones 1979:110; Lévi-Strauss 1969:307; and Murphy 1959.
5. Here is Kaberry (1939:257n.), for example: "Homosexuality amongst the men did exist. The youths of 17 or 18 who were still unmarried would take boys of 10 or 11 as lovers. The women had no hesitation in discussing the matter with me, did not regard it as shameful, gave the names of different boys, and seemed to regard the practice as a temporary substitute for marriage." Cf. also C. Berndt 1965:265.
6. I know of no reports of institutionalized transvestism from Melanesia in which males have lifelong cross-gender dressing and associated homosexual behavior comparable, for instance, to those of the Mohave *alyha* (Devereaux 1937) or the Tahitian *mahu* (Levy 1973); cf. also Whitehead's (1981) recent review of the *berdache.* Melanesian transvestite behavior is, apparently, nonerotic cross-dressing role behavior permitted only in restricted ceremonies (see Bateson 1932:277–278; Elmberg 1965:97, 110, 117; and Tuzin 1980:47n, 227; and other examples reviewed in Schwimmer, chap. 6).
7. Clinically, primary male transsexualism is defined as the conviction of biologically normal males that "from earliest childhood . . . they are really members of the opposite sex" (Stoller 1979:11). Data on this subject are virtually nil in Melanesia; the only report that seems appropriate to this category is still the old one by Seligman (1902), which is not associated directly with ritualized homosexuality. There are, however, folktales (Landtman 1917:293–295) or myths (Herdt 1981:255–294) that may be

hints of collective cultural projections related to transsexual fantasies.

8. There are scattered reports of individual homosexual behavior in acculturated settings such as sexually restricted plantations; see especially Davenport 1965:200–201; and examples in B. Blackwood 1935:128; Hogbin 1951:163–164; Mead 1949:90f.; and Mitchell 1978:160. See also Bulmer's (1971:150n.) comparative note in this context.
9. I used the following procedures in assessing (RH) reports: all reports of any kind available to me (including popular accounts) were read and compared; early allusions were contrasted to later accounts; sources from neighboring groups were compared; and whenever a case seemed questionable, I wrote to the ethnographer who reported, or, if that person was deceased, to another expert who had worked in the same or neighboring areas. I have omitted several early cases of reports by laymen that seemed dubious or were contradicted by subsequent ethnographers. Finally, several Melanesianist scholars have read this chapter, and their critical evaluations of certain sources have also been used in my final interpretations.
10. The only definite report of institutionalized lesbianism comes from Malekula Island in the New Hebrides. Deacon (1934:170–171), the earliest anthropological source, states: "Between women, however, homosexuality is common, many women being generally known as lesbians, or in the native term *nimomogh iap nimomogh* ('woman has intercourse with woman'). It is regarded as a form of play, but, at the same time, it is clearly recognized as a form of sexual desire, and that the women do it because it gives them pleasure. . . . From the Big Nambas [tribal group] alone, it is reported that lesbianism is common. . . ." (See also Godelier 1982*a*:82.) This puny material is, however, virtually all that has ever been published. (Barker [1975:150] has an unpublished report.) For questionable allusions, see Baumann 1955:228; and Harrison 1937:362, 410. We should be wary of this lack of data on lesbian behavior, though, since most Melanesianist ethnographers have been males who primarily studied males; whether lesbian activity existed elsewhere and was hidden will probably never be known. Cf. below for DuToit's (1975:220) anomalous report of Highlands female "homosexuality play." Inge Riebe mentions that "adolescent girls engage in homosexual relations" among the Western Highlands Kalam (quoted in Keesing 1982:10n.), among whom no (RH) is reported.
11. See Allen (1981) for the changing scene. For popular accounts attesting to the persistence of ritualized homosexuality among the Big Nambas, see Gourguechon 1977:62ff. and Harrison 1937:47–48, 409–411.

12. Haddon (1936:xxviii) reports that such mainland groups as the Tami and Yabim "did not have sodomy" (anal intercourse? his source is not cited) in initiation rites. Cf. also Bamler 1911:496 on the Tami.
13. Parkinson (1907:544) is worth citing at length on the general problem of ethnographic reliability of reports regarding ritual homosexuality: "It requires an acquaintance of many years and an absolute confidence in the interrogator before a native can be induced to divulge these things, not so much because he is ashamed of them, for all the natives do them, and do not think them wrong. . . . These observations are based on the exact, detailed statements of natives, and are confirmed by white missionaries and their colored teachers. . . . The Imperial authorities are now taking steps, at the instigation of the missions, to restrain the abuses. It is questionable whether the ban will have any effect; it is highly probable that what previously took place in public is now done in secret." (Cf. also the translator's note, ibid.:530.)
14. Chowning (1980:15) notes that the Sengseng of Southwest New Britain denied practicing "sodomy" (by which she meant anal intercourse), which also applies to their neighbors, the Kove (Ann Chowning, personal communication).
15. Davenport (1965:200–201) uses a pseudonym to protect the exact location of this group. But they belong in this culture subregion. Like me (Herdt 1981), he feared his informants would be placed at risk by disclosure of this data.
16. See Schieffelin (1976), and Boelaars (1981) quoted below, for examples of identical cultural rules pertaining to homosexual access to a boy.
17. Haddon (1936:xxxii), in his preface to F. E. Williams's *Papuans of the Trans-Fly,* chides the work of the "late Rev. E. Baxter-Riley (1925:201). . . . He does not refer to sodomy; but that proves nothing, as the publishers omitted [i.e., censored] a considerable amount of his manuscript." For discussions of censorship and other facets of ethnographic reports on homosexual behavior in New Guinea societies by the doyen of Highlands studies, see Read 1980*b*:183–188 and below (see chap. 5). Cf. also Carrier 1980*a*; Layard 1959:112; and Mead 1961.
18. Landtman lived with the Kiwai from 1910–1912 (see also Landtman 1954, his last report).
19. See Wirz 1922:39 quoted above.
20. The older men are jurally entitled to have serial intercourse with this woman for the purpose of collecting "fertile" sperm from her vagina after sex in order to anoint the initiates' bodies. This practice is found also among the Marind-anim (Van Baal, chap. 3), the Kimam (Serpenti, chap. 7), and is known from Thurnwald's (1916) study of the Banaro.

21. The structural position of the chief in Malekula (Deacon 1934:261) may be here compared to the Kimam father. See Allen's chapter 3 below.
22. Held (1957:87–88) continues: "Although this [anal intercourse] is not judged to be a direct violation of the manners established by the ancestors, it is considered highly ridiculous, so that it is a serious insult to say of somebody that he is a sodomite (*agho ri-roni*)." Held does not indicate if this derogatory term is applied to both insertee and inserter, but the evidence indicates nonetheless that ritual homosexuality was absent from Waropen, at least by the time of his (1957:156 n. 3) work. Still, as I have noted, there is a danger in reading negative attributions toward the insertee as a castigation of all homosexual behavior (i.e., the inserter role).
23. Here we have a vivid example of the Victorian heritage (e.g., Freud's *Totem and Taboo*) underlying early writings about Melanesia. Notions about prehistoric hominid hordes, patriarchal authority in the family, and the prehistoric preeminence of "matriarchy" over "patriarchy" are explicit in ethnographic pieces such as those of Moszkowski, Atkinson (1903), Layard (1942), Róheim (1926), and Thurnwald (1911). (For Australian studies, see Hiatt 1975.) See Herdt and Poole (1982), who consider these intellectual influences on the concept of "sexual antagonism" in New Guinea studies.
24. As early as 1926 we find Róheim, who was well read in the Melanesian literature, making the following statement: "The Morehead River natives are the neighbors of the Marind (Kaia-Kaia) and frequently suffer their raids. I intend to discuss the close connection between the Marind and the Central Australians in a separate paper" (1926:448 n.4). To my knowledge Róheim never published such a paper.
25. Gebhard (1971:215) flatly states: "Anal coitus is the usual technique employed by male homosexuals [sic] in preliterate societies. . . ." Although he cites no data in support of this claim, it generally holds true for Melanesia. The only certain groups practicing homosexual fellatio are the Etoro, Bedamani, Duke-of-York, and Highland Anga peoples. Anal and oral intercourse seem to be "mutually exclusive" (Read 1980*b*:185) in Melanesia, which is almost certainly related to cultural beliefs about growth and procreation, though no one has yet investigated this suggestion.
26. Kelly adds: "This is accomplished orally. The boy manipulates the man to the point of ejaculation and consumes the semen." (Cf. Herdt 1981, and chap. 4.)
27. Schieffelin's (1982) paper is significant both in arguing for a more complex set of distinctions than "initiation" or "no initiation," as well as in raising the issue of social constraints upon personal choice in institutional homosexual activities. Yet, interpretive

questions remain. Why do Kaluli differ so in both these domains compared with other Plateau groups? One factor may be the nature of Schieffelin's reconstructed material. Homosexual practices and the *bau a* complex were gone by the time he worked, the result of several forces, missionaries in particular. One wonders the extent to which Schieffelin's informants' accounts were idealized and tended to represent (RH) activities as open to more choice than actually existed. I offer this speculation not so much to criticize Schieffelin's fine account as to underline the complexities of interpreting *all* ethnographic reports in this book.

28. Personal communication from a field letter of October 27, 1981, quoted with the author's permission.
29. The Pharisee reports:

> [Government patrol officer:] "They say that if they don't get rid of their mother's blood [through initiation rituals] their skin will never become firm."
> [Simpson:] "And in a fighting society such as theirs a man needs to be a full man. Any pansies in the Kuk [ukuku] garden?"
> [Patrol Officer:] "Never heard of any homosexuality at all among them—though I don't say there isn't. We've been here less than two years, don't forget. There's still a lot we don't know" (Simpson 1953:139).
> How did the Australian folks back home view this sort of popular tripe?

30. In terms of long-term anthropological research. For fascinating accounts of early travels and medical contacts in these areas, see Farquhar and Gajdusek (1981), on Gajdusek's Anga patrols. Jadran Mimica, a student at the Australian National University, has done anthropological fieldwork nearby, but he has not yet published his findings.
31. Here, as in the other early quotations, we have another example of using vague terms that make ethnographic reports useless. The dictionary defines sodomy as "unnatural sexual relations," though we may speculate that Blackwood meant homosexual anal intercourse. (How else—through what Pidgin words—would one adduce "sodomy": *sutem as*?) One's questions and report must be precise. Again, were one to ask a Sambia or Baruya tribesman (who practice only fellatio) if they engaged in anal intercourse, the honest, and probably indignant, responses would be no.
32. Fischer has not mentioned homosexual activity, though we know he did not see important initiation rites (Fischer 1968:135). As with other cases mentioned above, Fischer should not be misconstrued to mean (RH) is absent. No wonder ethnologists have avoided topics such as sexuality in Melanesia; our literature is such an obstacle course.
33. I shall report elsewhere on these observations.
34. The Sambia, who interact with the South Fore, believe that the latter practice homosexual anal intercourse, but this proves noth-

ing since Sambia fear and hate the South Fore, and also regard anal sex as repulsive. We should remember that many ethnic groups make attributions, usually slurs about other groups, of this sort. However, Graham Scott (personal communication), the linguist, believes that anal coitus may possibly be practiced among the South Fore, and I have it on hearsay from several Fore myself that this is true. But again, these are only stories, and no ethnographer has mentioned (RH) there (e.g., see Lindenbaum 1979).

35. Several years ago a prominent anthropologist colleague who has worked in a Sepik basin tribe told me that he noticed homosexual illicit activities occurring quietly on the periphery of his village. He has never reported this because it is tangential to his research interests. I cannot help but wonder if other instances are not to be found; whether or not they are institutionalized remains open to question.
36. See the quotation below (p. 25) from Godelier, which belongs in this category. Many other examples are to be found in the literature. I would add—though again it is not published anywhere to my knowledge—that heterosexual anal intercourse is said to be acceptable practice in parts of the Sepik.
37. Here is a common example from Mead (1949:106): "When the fear of passivity is also present in the minds of the adults—that is, when homosexuality is recognized in a society, with either approval or disapproval—the fear is exacerbated. The parents begin to pick at the child, to worry about his behavior, to set him trials, or to lament his softness." Elsewhere Mead's equation of "homosexuality" with "passivity" and "inversion" was surprisingly consistent (see Mead 1930, 1935, 1949:73, 93, 107, 376, 378). Cf. Mead (1961), for more sophisticated views.
38. Thurnwald (1916) never mentioned homosexual activity among the Banaro, but see Baumann (1955). Nothing conclusive can be said, other than this; however, the 1916 work describes heterosexual activities in association with the magical use of semen, sister exchange, and the use of sacred flutes and spirit impersonations strikingly similar to that of the Keraki, Kimam (Serpenti, chap. 7, below), Kiwai, and others.
39. In a remarkable early passage we find Haddon (1924:vii) arguing: "Thus there seems to be but little doubt that the Tugeri [Marind-anim], or at all events one element in the population, migrated down the Strickland branch of the Fly and along the Merauke [Mayo River] to the sea."
40. Such a historical scenario implies that various groups who, in their social system, resemble Angan groups, may once have had ritualized homosexuality but abandoned it in prehistoric times, at the period of their Austronesian influence. The Elema of the Papuan coast might be an example. But another example which links

the eastern coast of mainland New Guinea with Malekula and New Hebrides is the Finschhafen ritual cults, which impressed Deacon (1925) in their similarity to Malekula (and cf. Bamler 1911; Haddon 1936:xxviii; Wirz 1933).

41. Róheim's (1926:324–337 and passim) elaborate speculative diffusions—minus the primal horde fantasy (Róheim: "Papuan degenerate survivals")—of archaic Malaya-Polynesian migrations into Indonesia, New Guinea, and hence Australia, may be partially vindicated. A landbridge probably traversed the Torres Straits at that time.
42. The explicit references to ritual homosexuality in Australia noted above should be emphasized again here. Of course, we can do no more than point to parallels between Australian and Melanesian systems, for there are many complex differences between these two culture areas. Nothing more can be said on the subject until a modern ethnology of these areas emerges. Will someone please move us beyond this crude state of affairs?
43. Anthropological studies in Melanesia are so uneven that it is difficult to draw up a complete list of the relevant social units, let alone to compare them on particular cultural patterns. Bulmer (1970:93–96) lists 138 ethnographic studies by writers just for Papua New Guinea, whereas Koch (1974:Map 4) lists 86 studies by professional ethnographers for the whole island of New Guinea. The number would be greater now, perhaps as many as 200 accounts, if one included all reports by all writers. But remember, we are dealing with a total universe of some 700 different cultures and 2,000 different languages in New Guinea and Melanesia. The choice of any of these subsets of the total will be arbitrary in one way or another.
44. Given the range of studies in note 43, we may devise these rough statistics: table 1.1 shows 29 distinct cultures definitely reported. (If we include adjacent groups among the Marind-anim, the Anga, and the Fly, the number would rise to about 48.) If our total baseline is 100 Melanesian societies, we have 29 percent; if 200 is selected, we have 15 percent. I would estimate between 10 and 20 percent as a reasonable estimate of frequency, given what we know.
45. Associated factors included cultural values that encouraged resort to violence and blood revenge as a part of public policy; the lack of redressive mechanisms for peacefully resolving wrongs or for inhibiting de-escalation (Koch 1974); and the range of societal scale, cultural rules, and armaments associated with levels of warfare (reviewed in Sillitoe 1978).
46. The general contrast: lowlands head-hunting (and/or cannibalism) versus Highlands war raids (but not head-hunting) holds for New

Guinea, and, moreover, for Highlands Anga versus Lowlands Anga (east of the Vailala River).

47. *Notes and Queries* (1951:109) had it right years ago: "In some societies with a strong military organization or with age-sets, homosexual practices are usual in certain grades before marriage, and are subject to conventional rules. Such temporary associations may not be regarded as detrimental to subsequent normal heterosexual development."
48. "The worry that boys will not grow up to be men is much more widespread than that girls will not grow up to be women, and in none of these South Sea societies does the latter fear appear at all" (Mead 1949:107). Such beliefs are widespread but not universal in Melanesia (e.g., the Massim). However, I believe that careful study will show systematic Melanesian variations in this belief system, with (RH) groups revealing that most intense form of such ideologies (see P. Brown 1978:155; Herdt 1980).
49. The situation is more complex than this statement suggests, at least among Sambia, but the complexity cannot be examined here. See Dundes' (1976) and Hage's (1981) arguments noted below.
50. It is as ethnocentric to deny eroticism among tribal peoples, i.e., reducing their eroticism to customs and rites, as it is ethnocentric to "read" eroticism into situations where none exists.
51. In spite of the great differences between the ancients and Melanesians, this much they share in common: "Homosexual relationships are not exhaustively divisible, in Greek society or in any other, into those which perform an educational function and those which provoke and relieve genital tension. Most relationships of any kind are complex, and the need for bodily contact and orgasm was one ingredient of the complex of needs met by homosexual eros" (Dover 1978:203).
52. Nambikwara call these homosexual relations "the loving lie"; they go on between adolescent boys who are cross-cousins. "That is to say, in which one partner would normally marry the other's sister and is taking her brother as a provisional substitute" (Lévi-Strauss 1969:307). He argues that the Nambikwara chief's extra wives support his position symbolically: "They are both the reward and instrument of power" (ibid.:307–308).

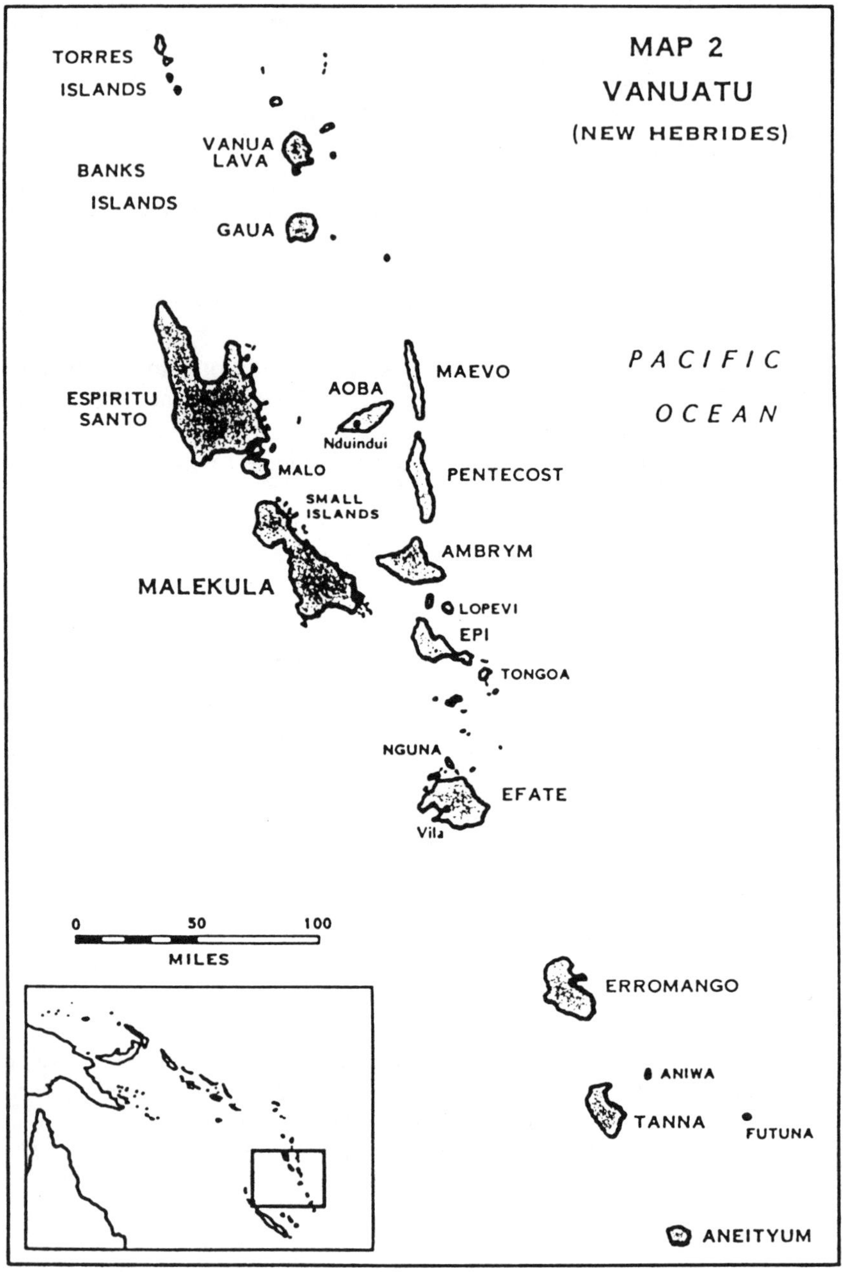
MAP 2
VANUATU
(NEW HEBRIDES)
TORRES
ISLANDS
VANUA
LAVA
BANKS
ISLANDS
GAUA
ESPIRITU
SANTO
AOBA
Nduindui
MAEVO
PACIFIC
OCEAN
MALO
PENTECOST
SMALL
ISLANDS
AMBRYM
MALEKULA
LOPEVI
EPI
TONGOA
NGUNA
EFATE
Vila
0
50
100
MILES
ERROMANGO
ANIWA
TANNA
FUTUNA
ANEITYUM

Reprinted from COLORADO ANTHROPOLOGIST, Vol. 1, No. 1, 1968

BERDACHE: A BRIEF REVIEW OF THE LITERATURE

SUE-ELLEN JACOBS

INTRODUCTION

Berdache may be defined as a term referring to one who behaves and dresses like a member of the opposite sex. According to Angelino and Shedd, the English word berdache comes from the French word bardash; furthermore, the French derived their term from the Italian berdasia, which was taken from Arabic bardaj; and the latter was borrowed from the Persian word barah: in all cases meaning a "kept boy" or a "male prostitute" (1955:121). The term was first used by the French explorers and travelers in the New World to refer to the Indian males who were passive homosexuals or those who played a passive part in sodomy. Angelino and Shedd use a quotation from Bossu's 1768 work, Nouveaux Voyages aux Indes Occidentales, to support this statement (1955:121-22). Bossu describes the Choctaws as being addicted to sodomy and gives a description of their dress.

John Lawson, in 1709, was traveling through the North Carolina area and wrote that sodomy was not practiced by the Indians of that area (Catawba, Cherokee, Monacan, Pamlico) (McNickle 1962:Map 1) and that they did not even have a word for "that beastly and loathsome sin" (Lawson 1709:48).

Denig used the term berdeches interchangeably with "hermaphrodite" (1850:58) and so did Maximillian (1906:354). Angelino and Shedd point out that Kroeber (1925, 1953) and Hill (1935) use the term "transvestite" and berdache as synonyms and, furthermore, these synonymous uses are found throughout the early literature on American Indians, all of which leads to confusion (1955:123). Some of the Indians did have expressions or words which showed the distinction between transvestite, hermaphrodite and homosexual (see Table 1). For example, the Navaho, who call berdaches nadle, distinguish between "those who pretend to be nadle" and the "real nadle" (Dorsey 1891:467, 516; Hill 1935:273). Lurie (1953:712) agrees with Angelino and Shedd that "berdache" should not be used interchangeably with transvestite or hermaphrodite, and that "berdache" should designate a person of a defined physical sex who assumes the role and status of the opposite sex and is viewed in this manner alone. Angelino and Shedd state that "while a berdache is a transvestite, a transvestite is not necessarily a berdache" (1955: 125). Stewart (1960a:13) agrees that berdache should be used in reference to homosexuals only and that transvestites and hermaphrodites should be called as such. But, in order to be able to gather data from the early writings that mention berdache among the American Indians, it is necessary to remember that the term has been used as a synonym for several types of deviation, "even though more is implied in role and status than occasional or even permanent cross-dressing" (Angelino and Shedd 1955:125).

Another term used in the past is found in Hay, who, in reviewing Hammond's report of 1887 on sexual impotence in the male and female, says that it is possible that the early Spaniards referred to berdache as mujer-hado, which means "man-witch-woman" (1963:20). Hammond gave the word mujerado as the term used by an Acoma berdache, which Hay defines as meaning "womanly."

Some Specific Incidences Noted

Kroeber said that berdache probably existed within all North American Indian tribes (1953:497; 1925:46). Driver was a little more conservative and said that it was probably present in all of Northern California (1939:405). In his study of this area several of the tribes investigated denied the presence of these people (see Table IV). The close proximity and status of cultural exchange in which these tribes lived suggests that they all probably did share this trait, but some simply refused to admit its existence. Lurie actually encountered this situation when she studied the Winnebago. She found in 1945-1947 that the Wisconsin Winnebago informants did not wish to speak of berdache and became embarassed when asked about it. Later, she learned that it was one of those things to be kept from whites (1953:708). The Nebraska Winnebago, however, were quite willing to speak about the subject. Possible reasons why this matter of denial has been found to occur when there is good reason for believing that the trait actually exists will be considered under the section dealing with tribal attitudes towards berdache.

There have been other studies besides Driver's of culture element distributions in California tribes, which showed berdache. Contrasting denial and admission in neighboring tribes was also found in these studies (Drucker 1941; Stewart 1941; Essene 1942; Harrington 1942; Voegelin 1942; Aginsky 1943; Gifford 1940). Lurie's work with the Winnebago showed parallels between Plains and Woodland Siouan practice. The only difference she found was in the terms which the Omaha and Ponca (Plains Sioux) and Winnebago used for berdache (see Table I).

Several authors agree that berdache was common among Plains Indians, but I found berdache reported only for several Sioux bands, Apache, Cheyenne and Shoshoni (Linton 1936:480; Honigmann 1954:278; Driver 1961:535). I was not able to find generalized statements on the incidence in other than these two areas (California and Plains). Other tribes are not spoken of by areal affiliation on this matter and should not be considered as representing traits common to their locale until further work can be done. (see Tables II and IV for these tribes; for tribes in which berdache was denied or not found, see Tables IIIa and IIIb)

POSTULATED REASONS FOR OCCURRENCE AND MANIFESTATIONS OF BERDACHE

The literature gives many reasons and origins for berdache. The expressed "cause" is probably determined by the society into which the berdache was born. Many tribes feel that a child is born with the condition. Lowie cites an incident in which a Crow berdache refused to follow the urgings of an Indian agent to dress like a man because it was "against his nature" (1935: 48). The man had been anatomically normal at birth, but grew up associating only with girls (49). Lowie later (1952) suggests that a berdache results from "the notion that a man as a result of a psychic experience must change his sex and thereafter fulfill all the duties of a woman" (181). He further asserts that this may or may not have religious associations in North America, and that the distribution of the trait was not definitely known in 1952. However, he does consider that the berdache "was a genuine male, mastered feminine accomplishments, often excelling in these, and indulged in homosexual intercourse. The Crow at one time had relatively many of these psychiatric cases...to them belong the task of chopping down the sacred tree of the Sun Dance" (244).

Among the Omaha, Lowie found the belief that berdaches resulted from the adolescent male's first vision quest. One case was reported in which a man tried to resist the vision and became so bound in the conflict that he committed suicide. "The Plains Indian berdache does not have a vision because he is an invert, for all the men in a generation who have visions only a handful are inverts" (1952:244). "The berdache phenomena are not the root of Plains religion, they pre-suppose its existence" (246).

Mead cites a case involving a boy, who she says was probably a "congenital invert" (1935:240), who grew up showing strong feminine characteristics and who performed women's tasks. He wore women's underclothing, but male outer dress (240).

An early preference for girls' company and women's work is mentioned as being present in quite a few groups. Many report that, in spite of parental efforts, a boy would begin in his early childhood to play and work with girls and refuse to have anything to do with boys. Examples are found among the Crow (Denig 1961: 187), Pomo (Gifford 1926:333), Zuni (Stevenson 1904:37) and the Omaha (Dorsey 1884:266). Among the Aleut and Tabatulabal, a boy might be deliberately raised as a girl and taught the work of women if particularly handsome (von Langsdorf 1817:345; Voegelin 1938:47). Among the California tribes, the Diegueno, Pima, Walapai and the Shivwits Paiute feel that some are "born thus" while others are transferred through a dream episode (Drucker 1941:154).

Dream inspiration has a wide distribution. Will (1906: 128) says that the Mandan berdache "follows this life by order from the spirits given to them in a dream." Bowers agrees with Will (Bowers 1950: 298) and points out that the dream determines a man's conversion. California Indians who give the cause as acting on a dream are the Achomawi (Voegelin 1942), Mohave, Cocopa, Maricopa, and Papago (Drucker 1941). Omaha, Pawnee, Chippewa, Navaho, and Winnebago berdaches are most often supported in their role by a dream conscription (Fletcher 1911:132; Dorsey 1940:108; Kinietz 1947:155-6; Hill 1935: 273; Lurie 1953:708). Driver (1961:535) indicates that the Plains berdaches were influenced by dreams.

Often, there are myths structured around the berdache giving support to their presence and function in the tribes. The Southern Okanagon of Washington blame the occurrence of berdache on the Coyote, who announced that such would occur when he left the Cougar's house disguised as a woman (Cline 1938:119). Tlingit mythology says they exist because a "half-man, half-woman" was reincarnated in a certain child because the woman of this child married the sun and had such a person as her 8th child (de Laguna 1954:178). There are many myths among the Navaho regarding berdaches. These stories often cite hermaphrodite cattle and sheep, as well as men, as possessing magical powers (Reichard 1950:140).

A white American explanation has been given by Benedict who feels that these people, as well as other social deviants, find personal value in this escape from the struggle with their culture (1932:4). Radin suggests that introversion of the Pueblo Indians, as a result of the pressures around them, caused the incidence of berdache to increase (1927:239). Linton observed that the Plains Indians provided a desirable alternate status to failure in the berdache (1936: 480), while Lowie (1952:244), like Benedict, refers to these berdaches in psychoanalytic terms: i.e., "these psychiatric cases."

A frequent occurrence in California is the procedure of testing for berdache. There are several means of doing this, but they all generally involve something similar to the following: A young boy is seated on the ground. On one side of him are placed the tools or weapons representing manhood, on the other side some implements of woman's work. The grass is set afire around the boy. As he flees from the burning grass, he will grab something from one side or the other. His selection will be the factor determining his future (Stewart 1960b:13).

Berdaches may fill a variety of roles, acting according to the demands of their culture. In some tribes, the berdache is considered in rather high esteem and is considered a vital member of religious rituals. In others, he is a shaman and a medicine-man. Yet, in still others, he is regarded as a good-for-nothing. Between these opposite poles there are berdaches who are required for special functions in funeral ceremonies and other special rites, such as in the Sun Dance of the Crow (Hays 1963:449). Table V lists only a sampling of the tribes under consideration, but gives an idea of the diversity of function.

The function of the berdache seems to correspond with the attitude their fellow tribe members have towards him. Perhaps it is that the function is due to the attitude. In any event, there is a correlation of extremes between these two.

ATTITUDES AND FEELINGS TOWARDS BERDACHE AND SIGNIFICANCE OF WHITE INFLUENCE

Even among the Southern Okanagon of Washington, who regarded the berdache as good-for-nothing, they still never ridiculed these men who dressed and behaved as women (Cline 1938:119). In many of the tribes mentioned herein, it is generally found that the berdache was never ridiculed. Stevenson (1904:37) reports that when a Zuni boy, at puberty, first assumed the dress and full-time work of women, the females teased him, but they looked on him with favor because they knew he would stay with them, helping them with their work. This same boy will, however, be discouraged and ridiculed by the men of the family until he has shown that in this chosen life he functions well in the community. Kroeber (1940:209-10) said that generally a berdache was not judged by his erotic life, but by his social status. "Born a male, he became accepted as a woman socially" (210). Driver (1961:535) agrees that they were accepted by their society, especially among the Plains Indians. In the Northeastern California tribes, Voegelin (1947:134) says that berdaches were regarded indifferently by the community.

Kinietz reports that the Chippewa berdaches were seldom despised or ridiculed and Hoffman says "they looked upon them as Manitous, or at least for great and uncomparable geniuses" (1891:153). Lurie notes that "at one time the berdache was a highly honored and respected person, but that the Winnebago had become ashamed of the custom because the white people thought it was amusing or evil" (1953: 708). By the time Dorsey had visited these Indians in 1889, there was already a certain amount of shame attached to the role.

Stewart (1960a:13) cites the case of a Minnesota Chippewa berdache who was "scorned, insulted, and greatly belittled by the American travelers who met him...." Lawson's report, referring to sodomy as a "beastly and loathsome sin" (1709: 48), indicates the idea that was often generated in treatment of these Indians by whites.

In earlier times, most berdaches dressed as women, unless of course, they were female homosexuals and these dressed as men. Denig again reflects the white attitude when he, as a result of observations of the Crow, says: "strange country this, where males assume the dress and perform the duties of females, while women turn men and mate with their own sex" (1961:199).

The former legal status of berdaches among the Navaho was the same as for women. "The blood payment for the murder of a nadle is the same as that for a woman, which is higher than that required when a man is killed" (Hill 1935: 275).

Navaho berdaches seldom dress as women now because they fear the ridicule of white people (Leighton 1947:78). Those who are so inclined have found, upon encountering white society, they are generally considered queer and referred to jokingly (Hill 1943:12). It is hard for the Navaho to understand this treatment, and an interesting observation by an old Navaho man at a ceremonial attended by a large number of tourists demonstrates a reason for their confusion: "There must be a great many more transvestites among the whites than among the Navaho because so many white women wear trousers" (Hill 1943: 12).

A Mohave berdache living in 1965 is regarded by the white people in the town where he lives as "something of a village idiot" (Waltrap 1965:6). He does not dress in women's attire, even though he likes the idea of being able to do so, because of the above fact. He makes jewelry and dolls, woman's work, and is considered an expert craftsman (9).

In the past, the berdache in the tribes listed have earned for themselves the reputation of excellent craftsmen and housekeepers, and it was once considered the highest compliment if a woman was told that her work was as good as a berdache's (Linton 1936:480). Often a male berdache also hunted with the men. If a man married so accomplished a berdache, he was ridiculed and accused of seeking a partner who would keep house and hunt for him. The berdache suffered no humiliation from this kind of union (481).

SUMMARY

The incidence of berdache among North American Indian tribes has been noted to have been quite widespread. The only areas lacking reference to berdache in the United States were the north-eastern, north-central, and east-central states' tribes. It is possible that the overt manifestations of berdache have diminished because of the imposition of white values on the Indian's way of life. Surely the fact that agents tried to force berdaches to change their ways with threat of punishment if they did not, and the fact that the berdaches were so ridiculed by white people, has influenced this diminution. In some cases however, the berdache existed amid ridicule and scorn, as with the Pima and Papago. These tribes considered a berdache a member of the backward group and he was required, in this instance, to use backward speech and action (Drucker 1914:218).

Formerly, a berdache assumed the dress of the opposite sex, as well as performing the latter's tasks. The evidence is that the dress is no longer changed, but the work of the opposite sex is very often still undertaken.

As with so many other institutions of Amerindian culture that served as means of social coordination by providing a place for even "deviant" members of the society, this position of berdache seems to have succumbed to the pressures of the white man. This pressure, in all cases, has forced the berdache into a position of a stigmatized member of society.

* * *

University of Colorado
Boulder, Colorado

Table I

Some Tribal Names for Berdache

Kalekau	murfidai (hermaphrodite), das	Ponca	mi^{n}-gu-ga
Mohave	alyha	Zuni	ko'thlama
Navajo	real nadle (hermaphrodite), nadle	Yuroks	wergern
Winnebago	šiáŋge	Pomo	das
Oglala	wi^{N}kte	Acoma	wujeroda
Omaha	mi^{n}-gu-ga	Chippewa	a-go-kwa

Table II

Some Tribes in which Berdache is Reported

- California
  - Round Valley Indians (Essene 1942)
    - Northern Pomo
    - Kalekau
    - Kato
    - Lassik
    - Yuki
  - Central California Coast (Harrington 1942)
    - Northern Castano
    - Southern Castano
    - Salinan
    - Chumash (Excluding Emigdiano band)
    - Shoshonean (Excluding Fernandeño band)
  - Yuman-Piman Area (Drucker 1941)
    - Digueño
    - Mohave
    - Cocopa
    - Maricopa
    - Pima
    - Papago
    - Walapai
    - Paiute
  - Northeastern California Area (Voegelin 1942)
    - Klamath
    - Shasta
    - Atsugewi
    - Achomawi
    - Wintu
  - Northwest California Area (Driver 1939)
    - Tolowa
    - Yurok
    - Hupa
    - Chilula
    - Mattole
    - Sinkyone
    - Yuki
  - Central Sierra (Aginsky 1943)
    - Yokuts
  - Others
    - Pit River
    - Tubatulabal
- Oregon
  - Klamath
  - Modoc
  - Shasta
  - Northern Paiute
- Washington
  - Okanagon (Cline 1938)
  - Quinault
- Idaho
  - Coeur D'Alene
  - Shoshoni
- Nevada
  - Paiute
- Colorado
  - Ute

Table II (continued)

Arizona
- Walapai
- Mohave
- Yuma
- Maricopa
- Pima
- Papago
- Navajo
- Zuni

New Mexico
- Apache
- Acoma
- Tewa (Hay 1963b)*

Texas
- Apache (Stewart 1960b)

Wyoming
- Shoshoni (Stewart 1960b)
- Cheyenne (Hay 1963b)

Montana
- Crow (Hays 1963)
- Flathead (Stewart 1960b)

North Dakota
- Hidatsa
- Mandan

South Dakota
- Sioux
- Oglala
- Ponca

Nebraska
- Cheyenne
- Pawnee
- Omaha
- Kansas

Minnesota
- Chippewa - Ojibwa
- Sioux

Iowa
- Iowa
- Oto

Wisconsin
- Menomini
- Winnebago
- Sac (Westermark 1906)
- Fox (Westermark 1906)

Missouri
- Osage

Illinois
- Illinois (Westermark 1906)

Alabama
- Choctaw

Georgia
- Creek

Florida
- Seminole (Stewart 1960b)

Canada
- Naskapi (Westermark 1906)
- Cree (Stewart 1960b)
- Tlingit

Alaska
- Aleut

Mexico
- Aztec (Stewart 1960b)
- Maya (Stewart 1960b)

* Whitman (1940:424) reports there is no homosexuality among the Tewa; Hay (1963b) mentions personal knowledge of berdache.

Table IIIa

Some Tribes in which Berdache Is Denied

Mono (Gashowu band)	Maidu
Chumash (Emigdieno band)	Nisenan
Akwa'ala	Chimarike (Driver 1939)
Shoshoni (Fernandino band)	Korok
Yaqui	Nongatl
Yavapai	

Table IIIb

Tribes Listed in the Human Relations Area File in which No Material Is to Be Found

Delaware	Comanche
Iroquois	Tiwi
Montagnais	Seri
Gros Ventre	Micmac

Table IV

Some Tribes in which Female Berdache Is Reported

California Area
- Northern Pomo
- Kalekau
- Kato
- Lassik
- Yuki
- Mohave
- Cocopa
- Klamath
- Shasta
- Atsugewi
- Achomawi
- Wintu
- Hupa
- Tubatulabal
- Yokuts

Other Areas
- Papago
- Crow (Denig 1850)
- Navajo (Hill 1935)
- Ojibwa (Landes 1937)
- Mohave (Winick 1956)

Table V

Role of the Berdache in 21 Tribes

Counted on for high spiritual ceremonies	Crow, Cheyenne, Dakota, Illinois
Shamans or medicine-men	Mattole, Tolowa, Yurok, Oglala, Coeur d'Alene, Sac, Fox, Creek, Navajo, Klamath, Flathead, Chippewa
Oracle	Winnebago
Special function at funerals	Navajo, Creek, Yokut
Good-for-nothing	Southern Okanagon

REFERENCES CITED

Aginsky, B.W.

1943 CULTURE ELEMENT DISTRIBUTION: XXIV. Central Sierra. Berkeley: University of California Press.

Angelino, Henry and Charles L. Shedd

1955 A NOTE ON BERDACHE. American Anthropologist 57: 121-125.

Benedict, Ruth F.

1932 CONFIGURATIONS OF CULTURE IN NORTH AMERICA. American Anthropologist 24:1-27.

Bowers, Alfred W.

1950 MANDAN SOCIAL AND CEREMONIAL ORGANIZATION. Chicago: University of Chicago Press.

Cline, Walter, Rachel S. Commons, May Mandelbaum, Richard H. Post and L.V.W. Walters

1938 THE SINKAIETK OR SOUTHERN OKANAGON OF WASHINGTON. Edited by Leslie Spier. General Series in Anthropology, 6. Menasha: George Banta Publishing Co.

de Laguna, Frederica

1954 TLINGIT IDEAS ABOUT THE INDIAN. Southwestern Journal of Anthropology 10:172-179.

Denig, Edward Thompson

1850 OF THE CROW NATION. Edited by John C. Ewers, 1950. Bureau of American Ethnology, Bulletin 151. Washington, D.C.:U.S. Government Printing Office.

1961 FIVE INDIAN TRIBES OF THE UPPER MISSOURI. Edited by John C. Ewers. Norman: University of Oklahoma Press.

Dorsey, George A.

1891 A STUDY OF SIOUAN CULTS. In Bureau of American Ethnology, 11th Annual Report. Washington, D.C.:

U.S. Government Printing Office.
Dorsey, George A. and James R. Murie
1940 NOTES ON THE SKIDI-PAWNEE SOCIETY. Field Museum of Natural History, Anthropology Series 27. Chicago: Field Museum Press.
Dorsey, Rev. J. Owen
1884 OMAHA SOCIOLOGY. In Bureau of American Ethnology, 3rd Annual Report. Washington, D.C.: U.S. Government Printing Office.
Driver, Harold E.
1939 CULTURE ELEMENT DISTRIBUTION: X. Northwest California. Berkeley: University of California Press.
1961 INDIANS OF NORTH AMERICA. Chicago: The University of Chicago Press.
Drucker, Philip
1941 CULTURE ELEMENT DISTRIBUTION: XVII. Yuman-Piman. Berkeley: University of California Press.
Essene, Frank
1942 CULTURE ELEMENT DISTRIBUTION: XXI. Round Valley. Berkeley: University of California Press.
Fletcher, Alice C. and Frances LaFlesche
1911 THE OMAHA TRIBE. In Bureau of American Ethnology, 27th Annual Report. Washington, D.C.: U.S. Government Printing Office.
Ford, Clellan S. and Frank A. Beach
1951 PATTERNS OF SEXUAL BEHAVIOR. New York: Harper and Brothers.
Gayton, Anna H.
1948 YOKUTS AND WEST MONO ETHNOGRAPHY, VOLUMES 1 AND 2. Berkeley: University of California Press.
Gifford, Edward Winslow
1926 CLEAR LAKE POMO SOCIETY. University of California Publications in American Archaeology and Ethnology 18:287-390.
1940 CULTURE ELEMENT DISTRIBUTION: XII. Apache-Pueblo. Berkeley: University of California Press.
Grant, Peter
1890 THE SAUTEUX INDIANS ABOUT 1804. In Les Bourgeois de'La Compagnie du Nord-Ouest, Volume II. Translated by L.F.R. Mason. Quebec: De L'Imprimerie Generale A. Cote' et Cie.
Hallowell, A. Irving
1955 CULTURE AND EXPERIENCE. Philadelphia: University of Pennsylvania Press.
Harrington, John P.
1942 CULTURE ELEMENT DISTRIBUTION: XIX. Central California Coast. Berkeley: University of California Press.

Hay, Henry
1963a REVIEW of *In the Beginnings* by H.R. Hays. New York: G.P. Putnam's Sons. *In Homophile Studies* 6:65-67.
1963b REVIEW of the Hammond Report. *In Homophile Studies* 6:1-21.

Hays, H.R.
1963 IN THE BEGINNINGS. New York: G.P. Putnam's Sons.

Hill, Willard W.
1935 THE STATUS OF THE HERMAPHRODITE AND TRANSVESTITE IN NAVAJO CULTURE. *American Anthropologist* 27:273-279.
1938 NOTE ON PIMA BERDACHE. *American Anthropologist* 40:338-340.
1943 NAVAHO HUMOR. *General Series in Anthropology*, 9. Menasha: George Banta Publishing Co.

Hoffman, W.J.
1891 THE MIDE'WIWIN OR "GRAND MEDICINE SOCIETY" OF THE OJIBWA. *In* Bureau of American Ethnology, 7th *Annual Report*. Washington, D.C.: U.S. Government Printing Office.

Honigmann, John J.
1954 CULTURE AND PERSONALITY. New York: Harper and Brothers.

Kelly, Isabel T.
1934 ETHNOLOGY OF THE SURPRISE VALLEY PAIUTE. *University of California Publications in American Archaeology and Ethnology* 31:67-210.

Kinietz, W. Vernon
1947 CHIPPEWA VILLAGE: The Story of Katikitegon. Cranbrook Institute of Science, *Bulletin* 3. Bloomfield: Cranbrook Press.

Kroeber, A.L.
1925 HANDBOOK OF THE INDIANS OF CALIFORNIA. Bureau of American Ethnology, *Bulletin* 78. Washington, D.C.: U.S. Government Printing Office.
1940 PSYCHOSIS OR SOCIAL SANCTION. *Culture and Personality* 8:204-215.
1953 HANDBOOK OF THE INDIANS OF CALIFORNIA. Berkeley: California Book Company, Ltd.

Landes, Ruth
1937 OJIBWA SOCIOLOGY. *Columbia University Contributions to Anthropology*, 29. New York: Columbia University Press.

Lawson, John
1709 THEY NEVER LOVE BEYOND RETRIEVING. *In* W.E. Washburn (ed.), *The Indian and the White Man*, pp.44-50. Garden City: Doubleday and Company.

Leighton, Dorothea and Clyde Kluckhohn
1947 CHILDREN OF THE PEOPLE. Cambridge: Harvard University Press.

Linton, Ralph
1936 THE STUDY OF MAN. New York: Appleton-Century-Crofts, Inc.

Lowie, Robert H.
1912 SOCIAL LIFE OF THE CROW INDIANS. Anthropological Papers of the American Museum of Natural History 9:179-248.
1924 NOTES ON SHOSHONEAN ETHNOGRAPHY. Anthropological Papers of the American Museum of Natural History 20:185-315.
1935 THE CROW INDIANS. New York: Farrar and Rinehart.
1952 PRIMITIVE RELIGION. New York: Liverright Publishing Corporation.

Lurie, Nancy Oestreich
1953 WINNEBAGO BERDACHE. American Anthropologist 55:708-712.

Maximillan, Alexander P.
1906 TRAVELS IN THE INTERIOR OF NORTH AMERICA. In R.G. Thwaites (ed.), Early Western Travels, Volume 22. Cleveland: Cleveland Press.

McNickle, D'Arcy
1962 THE INDIAN TRIBES OF THE UNITED STATES. New York: Oxford University Press.

Mead, Margaret
1935 SEX AND TEMPERMENT IN THREE PRIMITIVE SOCIETIES. New York: The New American Library.
1949 MALE AND FEMALE. New York: The New American Library.

Park, Willard Z.
1938 SHAMANISM IN WESTERN NORTH AMERICA. Northwestern University Studies in Social Sciences, 2. Evanston: Northwestern University Press.

Radin, Paul
1927 THE STORY OF THE AMERICAN INDIAN. New York: Boni and Liveright.

Reichard, Gladys A.
1928 SOCIAL LIFE OF THE NAVAJO INDIAN WITH SOME ATTENTION TO MINOR CEREMONIES. Columbia University Contributions to Anthropology, 7. New York: Columbia University Press.
1950 NAVAHO RELIGION: A Study of Symbolism. New York: Ballingen Foundation.

Simms, S.C.
1912 CROW INDIAN HERMAPHRODITES. American Anthropologist 4:580-581.

Skinner, Adamson
1912 NOTES ON THE EASTERN CREE AND NORTHERN SAUTEAUX. Anthropological Papers of the American Museum of Natural History 9:1-177.

Stevenson, Matilda Coxe
1904 THE ZUNI INDIANS: Their Mythology, Esoteric Fraternities and Ceremonies. In Bureau of American Ethnology, 2nd Annual Report. Washington, D.C.: U.S. Government Printing Office.

Stewart, Omer C.
1941 CULTURE ELEMENT DISTRIBUTION: XIV. Northern Paiute. Berkeley: University of California Press.
1942 CULTURE ELEMENT DISTRIBUTION: XVIII. Ute-Southern Paiute. Berkeley: University of California Press.
1960a HOMOSEXUALITY AMONG THE AMERICAN INDIANS AND OTHER NATIVE PEOPLES OF THE WORLD. Mattachine Review 6(1):9-15.
1960b HOMOSEXUALITY AMONG THE AMERICAN INDIANS AND OTHER NATIVE PEOPLES OF THE WORLD. Mattachine Review 6(2):13-19.

Swanton, John R.
1922 EARLY HISTORY OF THE CREEK INDIANS AND THEIR NEIGHBORS. Bureau of American Ethnology, Bulletin 73. Washington, D.C.: U.S. Government Printing Office.
1928 SOCIAL ORGANIZATION AND SOCIAL USAGES OF THE INDIANS OF THE CREEK CONFEDERATION. In Bureau of American Ethnology, 42nd Annual Report. Washington, D.C.: U.S. Government Printing Office.

Tanner, John
1963 DESCRIPTION OF INDIAN LIFE. Reprinted in Homophile Studies 6:21.

Teit, James A.
1930 THE SALISHAN TRIBES OF THE WESTERN PLATEAU. In Bureau of American Ethnology, 45th Annual Report. Washington, D.C.: U.S. Government Printing Office.

Tixier, Victor
1940 TIXIER'S TRAVELS ON THE OSAGE PRAIRIES. Translated from the French by Albert J. Salvan and edited by John F. McDermott. Norman: University of Oklahoma Press.

Underhill, Ruth
1936 THE AUTOBIOGRAPHY OF A PAPAGO WOMAN. American Anthropological Association, Memoir 46.

Voegelin, Erminie W.
1938 TUBATULABAL ETHNOGRAPHY. University of California, Anthropological Records 2:1-90.

1942 CULTURE ELEMENT DISTRIBUTION: XX. Northeastern California. Berkeley: University of California Press.

vonLangsdorf, G.H.
1817 VOYAGES AND TRAVELS IN VARIOUS PARTS OF THE WORLD DURING THE YEARS 1803, 1804, 1805, 1807. Carlisle: George Philips.

Waltrep, Bob
1965 ELMER GAGE: American Indian. One 13:6-10.

Westermark, Edward
1906 HOMOSEXUAL LOVE. In D.W. Cory (ed.), Homosexuality, A Cross-Cultural Approach, pp.101-138. New York: The Julian Press, 1956.

Whitman, William
1940 THE SAN ILDEFONSO OF NEW MEXICO. In Ralph Linton (ed.), Acculturation in 7 American Indian Tribes, pp.390-460. New York: D. Appleton-Century Co.

Will, G.F. and H.J. Spinden
1906 THE MANDANS: A Study of their Culture, Archaeology and Language. Papers of the Peabody Museum of American Archaeology and Ethnology 3:79-222.

SUBJECT HONOR AND OBJECT SHAME: THE CONSTRUCTION OF MALE HOMOSEXUALITY AND STIGMA IN NICARAGUA[1]

Roger N. Lancaster
University of California

THE SOCIAL CONSTRUCTION OF SEXUAL PRACTICES

In Nicaragua one encounters a folk category, the *cochón*. It can be given as either a male (*el cochón*) or female (*la cochón, la cochóna*) noun; either case typically refers to a male. This term is loosely translated as queer or faggot by visiting English-speakers. Educated Nicaraguans, if they are fluent in international terminologies, are apt to freely translate the term in the same fashion, giving gay or homosexual as its English equivalents. It becomes clear on closer inspection, however, that the phenomenon in question is markedly different from its Anglo-American counterparts of whatever shade. In the first place, the term is less clearly derogatory, although it can be derogative and usually is. It can also be neutral and descriptive. I have even heard it employed in a particular sort of praising manner by ordinary Nicaraguans; *viz.*, "We must go to *Carnaval*[2] this year and see the cochones. The cochones there are very, very beautiful."

Second, and more important, the term marks and delimits a set of sexual practices that overlaps but is clearly not identical to our own notion of the homosexual. The term specifies only certain practices, in certain contexts, and in certain manners. Some acts that we would describe as homosexual bear neither stigma nor an accompanying identity of any special sort whatsoever; others clearly mark their practitioner as a cochón.

If North American homosexuality is most characteristically an oral phenomenon, at least nowawdays, Nicaraguan homosexual practice is decidedly anal in preference. The lexicon of male insult clearly reflects this anal basic route of intercourse in Nicaragua, even as the North American lexicon reflects the oral route. But more is involved here than a mere shifting of the sites of erotic practice. With the exception of a few well-defined contexts (e.g., prisons), where the rule may be suspended, homosexual activity of any sort defines the North American homosexual. In Nicaragua, it is passive anal intercourse that alone defines the cochón. Oral or manual practices receive little social attention, and at any rate, nonanal practices appear far less significant in the repertoire of actually practiced homosexual activities.

The term cochón itself appears indicative of the nature of that status and role. None of my informants was certain about the origin of the term; it is a "*Nica*," or a word peculiar to Nicaraguan popular Spanish. Moreover, one encounters different pronunciations in various neighborhoods, classes, and regions, so there can really be no agreed-upon spelling of the word:[3] I have heard it rendered *cuchón*, and even *colchón*. The last suggests the probable origin of the word: colchón, or mattress. That is, as one of my informants suggested when prompted to speculate on the origin of the word, "You get on top of him like a mattress."

This summarizes the nature of that status as well as any phrase could but it also points to the question: "Who gets on top of him like a mattress?" The answer is not, "Only other cochones." Indeed, this type of relationship is relatively rare, and, where it occurs, is generally a short-term affair. It is typically a noncochón male who plays the active role in sexual intercourse: a *machista*, or *hombre-hombre*, a manly man. Either term designates a masculine man in the popular lexicon; cochones frequently use either term to designate potential sexual partners. Relationships of this type, between cochones and hombre-hombres, may be of any number of varieties: one time only affairs; purchased sex, with the purchase running in either direction (although most typically it is the cochón who pays); protracted relationships running weeks or months; or full-scale emotional commitments lasting years.

The last sort is preferred but carries its own type of difficulties, its own particular sadness. As one of my cochón informants related:

> I once had a lover for five continuous years. He was a sergeant in the military, an hombre-hombre. During this period of time he had at least fifteen girlfriends but I was his only male lover. He visited me and we made love almost every day. You have asked me if there is love and romance in these relations; yes, there is. He was very romantic, very tender, and very jealous. But he is married now and I rarely see him.

The actual range of sexual practices employed by cochones may be wider than sexual ideology would suggest. Many tell me that they are only really comfortable in the anal-passive position. Others alternate between active and passive roles, depending on whether they are having relations with an hombre-hombre (always passive) or with another cochón (passive or active). Very few report practicing oral sex at all and several of my informants--cochones and non-cochones alike--denied having any knowledge of such techniques. Many Nicaraguans express repulsion at the idea of either homo- or heterosexual intercourse of the oral sort. A series of (not necessarily sexual) aversions and prohibitions concerning the mouth seems to be involved here. The mouth is seen as the primary route of contamination, the major path whereby illness enters the body, and sex is quintessentially dirty (*sucio*). This conception is socialized into children from infancy onward. Parents are always scolding their small children for putting things in their mouths. This anti-oral outlook militates against the possibilities of oral intercourse.

The resultant anal emphasis suggests a significant constraint on the nature of homoerotic practices. Unlike oral intercourse, which may lend itself to reciprocal sexual practices, anal intercourse invariably produces an active partner and a passive partner. If oral intercourse suggests the possibility of an equal sign between partners, anal intercourse most likely produces an unequal relationship. But this anal emphasis is not merely a negative restraint on the independent variable (homosexuality); positively, it produces a whole field of practices and relations.

THE SPECIFIC ROUTES OF STIGMA

There is clearly stigma in Nicaraguan homosexual practice but it is not a stigma of the sort that clings equally to both partners. Rather, it is only the anal-passive cochón that is stigmatized. His partner, the active hombre-hombre, is not stigmatized at all and, moreover, no clear category exists in the popular language to classify him. For all intents and purposes, he is just a normal Nicaraguan male. The term "heterosexual" is inappropriate here. First, neither it nor any equivalent of it appear in the popular language. Second, it is not really the issue. One is either a cochón, or one is not. If one is not, it scarcely matters that one sleeps with cochones regularly or irregularly. Indeed, a man can gain status among his peers as a vigorous machista by sleeping with many cochones in precisely the same manner that one gains prestige by sleeping with many women. I once heard a Nicaraguan youth of nineteen boast to his younger friends in the following manner: "I am very sexually experienced. I have had a lot of women, especially when I was in the army, over on the Atlantic coast. I have done everything. I have even done it with cochones." No one in the group thought this a damning confession and all present were impressed with their friend's sexual experience and prowess.

For that matter, desire is not at issue here and it is irrelevant to what degree one is attracted sexually to members of one's own sex. What matters is the manner in which one is attracted to other males. It is expected that one would naturally be aroused by the idea of anally penetrating another male.

This is not to say that active homosexual pursuits are encouraged or even approved in all social contexts. Like adultery and heterosexual promiscuity, the active role in homosexual intercourse is seen as an infraction. That is, from the point of view of civil-religious authority, and from the point of view of women, it is indeed a sin (*pecado* or *mal*). But like its equivalent forms of adultery and promiscuity, the sodomizing act is a relatively minor sin. And in male-male social relations, any number of peccadillos (heavy drinking, promiscuity, the active role in same-sex intercourse) become status markers of male honor.

Nicaraguans exhibit no true horror of homosexuality in the North American style; their responses to the cochón tend rather toward amusement or contempt. The laughter of women often follows him down the street--discreet derision, perhaps, and behind his back, but the amusement of the community is ever present for the cochón. For men, the cochón is simultaneously an object of desire and reproach but that opprobrium knows tacit limits, community bounds. A reasonably discreet cochón--one who dresses conservatively and keeps his affairs relatively discreet--will rarely be harassed or ridiculed in public, although he may be the butt of private jokes. If he is very discreet, his status may never even be acknowledged in his public presence and his practices will occupy the ambiguous category of a public secret.

The stigma involved here is not at all the same as the stigma implied in the Western or North American concept of "the perverse," meaning "mis-use." It is certainly not the stigma of the fully rationalized, medicalized system of sexual meaning that elaborates a category, the homosexual, to identify both practice and identity. Rather, it is anal passivity alone that is stigmatized and it is anal passivity that defines the status identity in question. Moreover, the social definition of the person and his sexual stigma derive from culturally-shared meanings of not just anal passivity and penile activity in particular but passivity and activity in general. "To give" (*dar*) is to be masculine, "to receive" (*recibir, aceptar, tomar*) is to be feminine. This holds as the ideal in all spheres of transaction between and among the genders. It is symbolized by the popular interpretation of the male sexual organ as active in intercourse and the female sexual organ (or male anus) as passive.

Cochones are, therefore, feminine men, specifically, feminized men, not fully male men. They are men who are used by other men. Their stigma flows from this concept of use. Used by other men, the cochón is not a complete man. His passive acquiescence to the active drive of other men's sexual desires both defines and stigmatizes his status. Consequently, when one uses a cochón, one acquires masculinity; when one is "used" as a cochón, one expends it. The nature of homosexual transaction, then, is that the act makes one man a machista and the other a cochón. The machista's honor and the cochón's shame are opposite sides of the same coin. The line that this transaction draws is not between those who practice homosexual intercourse and those who do not (for this is not a meaningful distinction at all in Nicaragua's popular classes) but between two standardized roles in that intercourse. Machistas make cochones out of other men and each is necessary to the definition of the other in a dynamic sense that is very different from the way North American categories of the hetero- and homosexual define each other. While each is defined by his exclusion from membership in some normative category, the cochón is defined by his inclusion in the sexual practices of ordinary men, albeit in a standardized and stigmatized role, and the homosexual by his exclusion from the sexual practices of ordinary men.

This inclusive aspect of sex also has implications for the nature of the cochón status as a political concept, for that category lacks the theoretical independence attributed to Western homosexuality as a distinct category of activity and personal identity. A cochón requires ordinary men and his activity and identity can never be quite independent of them. Defined by its passivity, the status is ever a dependent one.

THE MAKING OF A COCHÓN

During my fieldwork in a working class barrio of Managua, I had the opportunity to observe over a period of several months the interaction of boys in the neighborhood with a boy, "Miguel," already labelled a cochón. This label was in very common use. Other children, including his older brother, teased him with the name and, on occasion, even adults would taunt him as such.

At the age of twelve, Miguel bore few characteristics that would distinguish him from other boys his age. He was unusually small, giving the impression of being a much younger child of perhaps eight or nine. He was also quite intelligent, and received good marks in school but not to such a degree that one could say he had thereby marginated himself from his peers. Quite mischievous and always getting into trouble, Miguel was by no means what one would think of as a sissy or "mama's boy."

A typical interaction between Miguel and the other boys would go as follows. They are all playing some game on the sidewalk out front or in the yard behind the house. The competition becomes acute and an argument develops. The argument eventually centers on Miguel versus some other boy or group of boys. Miguel's claim in the dispute is answered by the charge that he is a cochón. He insists, "*Yo no soy cochón*" ("I am not a cochón"), and fighting ensues, with Miguel typically throwing the first punches. The other boys eventually subdue Miguel and mimic sodomizing him.

In public, Miguel resists the label, in private he is less adamant. It is premature to say whether Miguel will in fact grow up to be a cochón. It appears that public opinion in the neighborhood is attempting to socialize him in that direction. But note that, unlike a North American counterpart labelled homosexual, the boy Miguel, labelled a cochón, is not thereby completely marginated from social activities among boys his age. He plays games and sports with them, fights with them, and at this stage the only thing that distinguishes him from the others is the fact that they call him cochón and pile on top of him in mock intercourse.

Of course, other readings of these actions are possible. Perhaps, seeing that he is small, and vulnerable, and fearing that he might grow up to be a cochón, the community is attempting to avert him from that dishonorable fate by punishing him whenever he shows signs of weakness, dependence, or passivity. It seems to me, however, that he was most likely to be punished by his peers when, as a small person, he attempted to assert his equality with much larger boys. At any rate, the argument is not that this particular case will indeed go on to become a cochón but that it exemplifies something of the rules of that status and its production.

We see this same sort of ambiguous status--stigmatized, yet not fully marginated--concerning adults. One incident in particular illustrates this. I was sitting in front of his repair shop and talking with "Carlos" one afternoon when a young man passed by on the street, riding in the back of a pickup truck that was hauling mechanical equipment. Carlos made obscene gestures at the other man, in effect offering to sodomize him. The man answered with his own gesticulations as the truck drove away. Carlos grinned and said, by way of explanation, that the man in the truck was a cochón, that he had fucked the man before, and that he would probably soon fuck the man again.

These obscene gestures, offers, and childhood games provide insight into the nature of the sexual practices in question and throw light on the social creation of the cochón. The cochón is but a necessary precipitant of the culture of machismo, or aggressive, competitive masculinity. One man offers to sodomize another, in effect, to make of him a cochón, or if he already is one, to use his services. Thus men desire to sodomize other men and fear being sodomized by them (Suarez-Orozco 1982). In the same manner, they desire to claim status and prestige and avoid being stigmatized. The routes of sexual use and pleasure thereby illuminate the pathways of male status and sexual power. Boys likewise exhibit their virility by labelling one of their members and mimicking anal intercourse with him. The object of sex/power is the same in either case. Those who consistently lose out in the competition for male status, or who can be convinced to dispose themselves to the sexual urges and status plays of other men, or who discover pleasure in the passive sexual role or its social status, are made into cochones.

It is most difficult to get reliable long-range material on the life cycles of cochones. Wrapped in an ambiguous public secrecy, they are both protected and maligned by community gossip. In practice, at the level of neighborhood rumors, this lends itself to both admissions and denials, accusations and defenses. Some men are clearly defined by that status, others are only slightly tainted with suspicion. Some apparently live out their entire life in that status, others successfully masculinize themselves by taking a wife and rearing children--though, in practice, they may (or may not) continue having covert affairs with men. Some develop longstanding covert relationships with particular men. Others become known in male gossip as someone to visit for sexual favors.

RULES IN THE SOCIAL CONSTRUCTION OF SEXUALITY

These processes in the production of sexuality do indeed bear some resemblance to North American practices, where male power and status are bound around sexual themes but the resemblance holds only up to a point. Both the homosexual and the cochón are objects in a sexual discourse whose real subject is sexual power. But the structure of that discourse, the meaning of its categories, and the language in which it speaks are decidedly different in each case. To the extent that these processes may be seen at work in our own culture, we may summarize that the object is to label without being labelled, but not to use without being used, for it is the homosexual act itself that is prohibited and not any particular role within the act. Some males, especially adolescents, in our own milieu do in fact attempt to label without being labelled and also use without being used. The difference is that in Anglo-American contexts this is seen as a breach of the rule (or, sometimes, an adolescent suspension of the rule), since homosexual desire itself, without any qualifications, stigmatizes one as a homosexual.

The nature of homosexual transaction in Nicaragua's popular classes seems to bear much greater resemblance to the sexual economy of North America's prison populations (Blake 1971) and, by extension, to the milieu of truckstops (Corzine and Kirby 1977) and public toilet (Humphreys 1970) encounters, where, for purposes of a deviant subculture, one may indeed both label without being labelled and use without being used. Similar rules seem to be in play in either context: passive partners are labelled and stigmatized; active partners are not. The act of intercourse assigns honor to one man, shame to the other. In North American prisons, sex between men becomes a means of exchange because it signifies simultaneously pleasure and power in the absence of access to either by other means. But while suggestive, this comparison should not be overstated or underqualified. Whereas the rules of prison sexuality represent a deviant and stigmatized subculture--that is, a suspension or even inversion of the normal rules--the rules of sexuality and stigma in Nicaragua represent the dominant culture of the popular classes, a normative rather than deviant set of rules and categories.

Thus, the dominant North American rule would read as follows. A man gains sexual status and honor among other men through and only through his sexual transactions with women. Homosexuals appear as the *refuseniks* of that system. In Nicaragua, the rule is built around different principles. A man gains sexual status and honor among other men through his active role in sexual intercourse (either with women or with other men). Cochones are (passive) participants in that system.

Again, similar to Northern stereotypes of the homosexual, the cochón is commonly ascribed (and frequently exhibits) such personal characteristics as effeminacy and flamboyance. Feminized by more masculine men, some cochones act out their role in the more extreme form of transvestism. Many more appropriate semitransvestic forms of dress: a shirt just a little too blousy, or pants slightly too feminine in color, fit, or texture. As a normal rule, transvestism and near-transvestism receive the reproach of the community. (I once saw a Nicaraguan girl throw out the dishwater on a cochón who passed by her house in just such a state of near-transvestism.) However, on the special occasions of certain popular religious celebrations, cochones may publicly exhibit their cross-dressing with the good will and even encouragement of the whole community.

These festivities represent a special niche in the religious life of the lower classes: like Bakhtin's (1984) carnival, they project the image of a libidinous popular insurrection (Davis 1978) through a spree of stylized rule-breaking. For these ritual occasions, the feminization of men semiotically corresponds to the themes of inversion and reversal that are the core of several popular religious festivities; men dress as women, people take on the costumes of animals, animals challenge human authority, lower classes challenge elite authority, and so on (Lancaster in press). In Masaya's *carnaval*, Managua's *Santo Domingo*, and other such rituals, the cochón is granted a reprieve from his secrecy and surreptition, given a political voice, and cast in a central role in popular religious festivities.

The popular imagination, then, takes up the cochón in an ambiguous way that imbues him with two different meanings. On the one hand, he is usually an object of amusement and contempt, a passive participant put to the use of others. On special occasions, though, the cochón becomes a subject who offers his parodical commentary on a whole array of social and sexual relations. Frequently taunting *machistas* and mocking civil-religious authority along the way, the transvestic cochón becomes the polysemic voice of discontent in these processions. In his inversion, object becomes subject, and silence bursts out with a voice that discerns the real powers of the powerless and the used. Through the alchemy of popular ritual, the cochón represents the larger point of view of the dispossessed classes in revolt against established authority.

Again, this points to a striking contrast with the North American homosexual. At his most politically-conscious, the homosexual organizes himself into a subculture, a subeconomy, a single-issue politics, all of whose logic is quite singular. The cochón, at his most political, represents a very different sort of thing: through the polymorphousness of metaphor, *carnaval* speaks to a multiplication of meanings and social entanglements, not to their compartmentalization and impoverishment.

Where Nicaragua's folk categories and sexual transactions most strikingly parallel Western European/North American rules is not in any deviant subculture of the present but, rather, in sexual categories and practices widespread in the past, before progressive rationalization in the institutions of religion, law, medicine, and psychiatry had refined a category--the homosexual--out of traditional folk constructs (Boswell 1980; Trumbach 1977; Weeks 1977). Like its traditional Western parallels of whatever shade (e.g., bugger, sodomite, faggot, etc.), the cochón represents a stigmatized sexual identity, as yet still minimally administered by the institutions of rational sexual categorization and control, still more or less under the rule of popular categories and controls. But even here the cultural tradition in which we encounter the cochón is different from its Anglo-European counterparts, whose folk-terms often designate the active, not passive, category of practice, identity and stigma. Even as a traditional or nonrationalized construct, the cochón lives in a different cultural stream than "buggers" and "sodomites."

COCHONES AND THE REVOLUTION

The Sandinista Revolution and its accompanying changes have clearly introduced a variety of contradictory changes in the culture's understanding of sexual practices. It may be that the image of *carnaval* captures and perpetuates the image of revolt so necessary in the imagination of the populace that would be revolutionary but the consolidation of a revolutionary state is anything but an extended carnival. Certainly, the revolution has produced a constraining effect on homosexual practice. The nature of socialist revolution, and perhaps particularly that variety influenced by liberation theology, entails a strong normative or corporatist component. The "New Man" and the "New Society" are envisioned as hardworking, diligent, and studious; pure and without corruption. The aspect of machismo that the New Man embodies is the self-sacrificing side, not the hedonistic one. The cult of the New Man, then, produces a cultural atmosphere in which homosexual practice (and sexual transgression in general) is at least publicly regarded as more suspect than before, tainted with the image of indulgence or corruption, and is perhaps even somewhat less readily available.

More concretely, the revolution has everywhere tried to strengthen the moral force of the community, especially through the Comites de Defensa Sandinista (CDS), the neighborhood defense organizations. Through such organizations and through the sensibility of revolution generally, the gaze of the community is particularly strong and the semiprivate, semipublic status of the cochón is rendered more problematic. Especially in areas of public morality and public order, a variety of activities, such as prostitution, have been actively curbed by the Sandinista Police and the CDS. On a much smaller scale than Havana, Managua once sported an elite and tourist-oriented night-life, including perhaps a dozen total assorted homosexual bars, exclusive gay clubs, drag shows, and male stripper acts. These serviced Managua's middle class homosexuals, some of its lower class cochones, and gay tourists from other countries. They are gone now and what remains is a small handful of much more discreet bars.

Such closures have affected the traditional cochón much less than the Western-oriented gay or homosexual of professional or middle class origins. As one Sandinista activist from a working class barrio (who alternately and in his mind synonymously described himself as a cochón, homosexual, or gay) put it, "It is true that there are fewer bars now but most of the ones that existed before served only the affluent, not the poor. You had to be rich to get into those nightclubs. It is not so much that they have been closed down by the police or the CDS, as that they have moved to Miami with the rich people."

Not all of the effects of the revolution on cochones have been restrictive. While maintaining a discreet sexual profile, many have participated in the revolutionary process, some rising to positions of great authority in the CDS, the FSLN, (Frente Sandinista de i Liberación Nacionál) and even the government proper. The informant cited above, for instance, had been elected Barrio Director, the highest position in the local CDS. Having fewer family responsibilities and dependents appears to have freed up the time of many politically-conscious cochones to work for the revolution. In the process some have gained recognition and stature in the community in a manner not unlike the charisma that priests derive from a life of celibacy and service.

In Nicaragua, the traditional categories remain the dominant popular ones but they are now coexisting and competing with a Western perception of homosexuality. Sexual education in the schools, social contact with *internacionalistas* from the United States and Western Europe, and greater access to international ideas and philosophies all facilitate the acquisition of Western sexual models, especially in elite segments of the populace; i.e., the urban, middle class sectors that look to the United States and Western Europe for educational and cultural values.

In some sections of Managua one now hears such terms as homosexual and heterosexual. For certain members of that narrow stratum of urban elites, these terms are not so misleading. But many of Managua's sexually-active youth, even some of working class origins (like the *Dirigente del Barrio* cited above), also now call themselves "homosexual," "bisexual," or "gay." New syncretisms are indeed slowly emerging but in practice the dominant logic of the sexual system remains traditional, native, and popular. The casual importation of scientific and even political sexual terminologies serves to confuse casual foreign observers in much the same way that the casual use of those terms in social science confuses issues and assimilates real differences. What a Nicaraguan means when he calls himself "gay" is very different from what a North American has in mind when he uses the same term, even though the two may find themselves in broad agreement on certain particulars. New words like homosexual and gay typically enter the popular vocabulary as synonyms for familiar categories and practices, rather than as new concepts in themselves. This is especially true in the popular classes; and many Nicaraguans, even in Managua, remain quite unfamiliar with these newly introduced words.

The remarkable conservatism of culture lies precisely in its ability to animate new words with old ideas. While it is doubtful that one could speak of a pure folk model anymore in Managua, it is clear that the traditional logic of sexuality remains intact for the massive lower classes. What would mark a real change in Nicaragua's sexual culture is not the importation of a new sexual lexicon--which might just as easily be imbued with archaic as with modern meanings--but, rather, the introduction of new terms, along with the proliferation of specialized bureaucratic instruments of sexual regulation to which those terms correspond (e.g., psychology) and the development of a homosexual subculture based on a wider variety of less stereotyped roles and practices. But these conditions clearly have not been met.

WHAT IS A HOMOSEXUAL?

Strathern (1981:682) uses the phrase, "No such thing as a woman," to stress certain theoretical points on the nature of gender studies. Here, I follow her lead and attempt to make similar points in treating the nature and construction of the traditional Nicaraguan folk category, the cochón. We may speculate that this category is the result of a syncretism between Iberian and indigenous sexual role systems. Moreover, based on my conversations with other Latin Americanists, it seems that the cochón exemplifies something of the sexual rules that are generally found in most Latin American countries, where the essential elements of the cochón appear under different names and with somewhat different definitions (Carrier 1976; Parker 1984, 1985; Williams 1986:147-151).

Labels such as homosexual or heterosexual, along with Northern European/North American presumptions about stigma, fail to account for the Nicaraguan sexual constructs that ultimately produce the cochón. Theoretically, this sort of difficulty crimps attempts at writing a general history or anthropology of homosexuality, for such projects must be hedged from the outset with a myriad of qualifications and circumlocutions. At every turn we are always running up against the unintelligibility of foreign practices to our concepts and categories.

But the cochón is by no means as exotic a phenomenon as the cross-gendered (Whitehead 1981) or gender-mixed (Callender and Kochems 1983) native North American berdache, nor are his practices as far from Northern European notions of homosexuality as are the homosexual initiation rites reported for parts of Melanesia (Herdt 1981, 1982). Indeed, it is his very similarity to the North American homosexual that makes the cochón appear at first glance readily interchangeable with him: both are adult males with a stigmatized sexual identity. Only on close inspection can we see that the process of identity- and stigma-production in each case is radically different, governed by different rules, producing a markedly different existential state. We could say, in Wittgensteinian terms, that machismo is a different game, governed by different rules; or we could say, in Marxian terms, that it represents a different sexual economy, a different mode in the production of sex/gender; or, in Foucauldian terms, we could say that Latin sexuality represents a radically different discursive practice than Anglo sexuality.

The necessity of drawing such distinctions is far from settled in the current literature. Herdt (1981:3, 321) finds "heterosexual adults" in the highlands of Papua New Guinea and Williams (1986) has more recently reiterated the old thesis that the berdache is an Amerindian gay in native drag. Nonetheless, anthropology has been becoming more or less sensitive to phenomenological differences when they exist at these great distances. Until now, though, the nuances that distinguish such phenomena as the cochón from the homosexual typically have been glossed under the misleading terminologies of the latter. Nash (1979:141) identifies persons who appear to be the Bolivian equivalents of Nicaraguan cochones as "men with homosexual tendencies" and Cuba's Santeria cult is sometimes given as a native niche for an otherwise unproblematic Cuban homosexuality (Arguelles and Rich, 1984:688). At best, modifications of that terminology have suggested themselves; e.g., "selective homophobia" to identify the stigmatization of the "passive homosexual" (Murphy 1984). (See also Brandes's [1981:232-234] discussion of the passive role in homosexual intercourse in Andalusia.)

Such terminology, even when modified, obscures more than it clarifies. Nicaragua's cochones are ontologically different creatures of culture than are Anglo-American homosexuals. Both are clearly stigmatized but they are stigmatized in different ways, according to different rules. Nor is it, as it is often maintained, that in Latin America homophobia is of substantively the same sort that one encounters in Northern Europe and North America, only more severe in its operations. It is not that homophobia is more intense in a culture of machismo but that it is of a different sort altogether. Indeed, the word "homophobia," meaning a fear of homosexuals or homosexual intercourse, is quite inappropriate in a milieu where men desire and actively seek homosexual intercourse. An altogether different word is necessary to identify the praxis implicit in machismo, whereby men may simultaneously desire to use, fear being used by, and stigmatize, other men.

If this criterion allows us to distinguish various systems of sexual signification and power, it may also allow us to generalize a limited number of systems based on the operation of similar rules. Nicaragua's sexual system, with its active-honor/passive-shame dichotomy, exemplifies rules governing male sexual relations not only for Latin America generally but also for cultures throughout the Mediterranean and the Middle East. Numerous and widely variegated subtypes no doubt obtain[4] in what we might provisionally call peasant sexuality, but with its series of dichotomous distinctions--penile-anal, active-passive, honor-stigma--it clearly stands opposed to what we might call the bourgeois sexuality predominant in Northern Europe and its offspring cultures, especially in the Anglophone world. While this latter type has undergone successive degrees of intensification and rationalization, its original peculiarity seems to rest on its blanket condemnation of all same-sex practices and, perhaps, especially active ones (Trumbach 1977). In general, bourgeois sexuality is susceptible to greater or lesser degrees of rationalization in socio-sexual control, whereas peasant sexuality is susceptible to greater or lesser degrees of severity in its prohibitions, constraints or stigmas.

This active honor/passive shame dichotomy recalls something of the logic of homosexual activity for the ancient Greeks, who divided appropriate roles into two age classes, adult activity and youthful passivity, as Foucault (1985:221) observes.

Hence the problem that we may call the "antinomy of the boy" in Greek ethics of aphrodisia. On the one hand, young men were recognized as objects of pleasure--and even as the only honorable and legitimate objects among the possible male partners of men: no one would ever reproach a man for loving a boy, for desiring and enjoying him, provided that the laws and proprieties were respected. But on the other hand, the boy, whose youth must be a training for manhood, could not and must not identify with that role. He could not of his own accord, in his own eyes, and for his own sake, be the object of that pleasure, even though the man was quite naturally fond of appointing him as an object of pleasure. In short, to delight in and be a subject of pleasure with a boy did not cause a problem for the Greeks; but to be an object of pleasure and to acknowledge oneself as such constituted a major difficulty for the boy.

Arguably, the same-sex initiation practices employed in certain Melanesian societies appear to represent a special instantiation of these active-passive rules: (oral or anal) adolescent passivity, (penile) adult activity. But in this case it makes little sense to speak of stigma and Melanesia clearly represents an independent type. The boy's social-sexual status is an absence of manhood; insemination is practiced to correct that, not to perpetuate or reinforce it. And these relationships, as in ancient Greece, ultimately take the form of generalized reciprocity; passive youths become active males vis-a-vis new youths.

Degrees of stigma may vary in both bourgeois and peasant contexts and the practice of labelling may or may not be stringent, depending on historical conditions. But it seems probable that all societies, save those in the Northern European cultural stream, elaborate some passive-active dichotomy for male homosexual practices and that the active role escapes both label and stigma. In none of these cases would we be justified to speak of a homosexual, although there is undoubtedly homosexual activity. In this model, transvestism appears, not as a separate type, as Trumbach (1977) argues, but as a residual one. It may be arrived at in either sexual system by different means or it may constitute a "third gender" (Whitehead 1981) belonging not to sexuality proper but to gender/labor relations more specifically. Unstigmatized and nonstereotyped reciprocal homosexual relations between adolescents may be informally countenanced in all systems save the most rationalized (bourgeois) modes or the most severe (peasant) ones.

The provisional models offered here say little about female same-sex practices. In Nicaragua, as throughout the peasant world, there is little folk interest in categorizing or regulating female same-sex relations and little exists in the popular lexicon to account for it. Surely, Nicaraguans can express censure over female same-sex improprieties but without the refined and specialized vocabulary through which they speak of the cochón. The culture of machismo, which speaks so directly to male practices, can only speak indirectly or inversely of female ones.

CONCLUSION

This paper differentiates apparent similarities in two sexual systems; it diagrams the rules that define the stigmatized Nicaraguan sexual category, the cochón, and contrasts it with the North American homosexual. The cochón is not just one refraction of a larger, universal homosexual category (embedded in nature--or perhaps, in unnature), nor is the English term "homosexual" an appropriate translation of that concept--which must, indeed, remain fundamentally untranslatable. This method of semiotic differentiation is in keeping with prevailing deconstructionist and Marxist (D'Emilio 1983:4) approaches in sexuality studies, but it also represents a straightforward application of basic Boasian principles on the terrain of sex: *viz.*, that what is meaningful about culture is internal, not external, and that cultural meaning rests in specific milieux, not in aggregations of cultures assembled in the light of unproblematic common sense categories. Thus, to study the cochón is also to deconstruct our own universalized category, the homosexual; an act may be called homosexual that involves two men, but what is significant and meaningful about that act lies beyond any *a priori* assumptions about the nature of homosexual activity.

Seen in these terms, the specific configuration of sex, power, and stigma traced in Nicaragua's popular classes is indeed jarringly dissimilar to the predominant North American configuration. But it is not dissimilar to other configurations. Our critical method need not lend itself only to the endless production of distinctions; it can also elaborate typologies based on the operation of similar rules. I have provisionally proposed: (1) Anglo-Northern European or bourgeois sexuality and (2) Circum-Mediterranean/Latin American or peasant sexuality.

This analysis of the cochón and the concomitant typology it draws differ from previous typologies on one significant account. Earlier typologies have classified same-sex practices in terms of simple variations on the repressive principle. For instance, Bullough (1976:25) accounts for the stark presence of role-differentiated homosexual activity in the Mediterranean by the relative absence of available heterosexual outlets. His logic is very simple: sexuality, like water, is an *a priori* force; dammed up in one outlet, it will invariably seek out another. In contrast to such simple hydraulic models of sexuality, our analysis of the cochón, and our elaboration of a broader cochón type, flows from our emphasis on a productive (not repressive) paradigm (Foucault 1978:3-13). That is, something in machismo other than scarcity of women (and certainly other than extreme homophobia) precipitates the cochón (as opposed to masturbation or abstinence), shapes his behavior, defines his identity. That something is a configuration of sex/power along the active/passive dimension. It renders certain organs and roles "active," other body passages and roles "passive," and assigns honor/shame and status/stigma accordingly.

This mapping of the body, its accesses and privileges, is at once a map of pleasure and power. And the relationship of the cochón to power, as to the grammar of sex, constitutes a different cultural ensemble than that configuration which we call the homosexual. The object-choice of the homosexual marginates him from male power, except insofar as he can serve as a negative example and thus mark off the circuitry of power; a breaker of rules, he is positioned outside the operational rules of normative (hetero)sexuality. That of the cochón casts him in the role of object to machismo's subjectivity; that is, it puts him in a stigmatized but by no means marginated relation to sex/power. Each is defined by a play of sex/power but the homosexual is a marginated subject, divested of power, around whom power flows, while the cochón-type is an object through whom power flows and who is therefore, paradoxically, the locus of power's investment in itself.

NOTES

1. An earlier draft of this paper was presented at the 1986, 85th Annual Meetings of the American Anthropological Association in Philadelphia. For their comments on earlier drafts, I am grateful to Marie Boutte, Sue Estroff, Robert Fernea, Byron Good, Richard Parker, Philip Pincus, Leonard Plotnicov, and Nancy Scheper-Hughes. Data for this article derive from fieldwork in Managua carried out in three periods totaling ten months, from December 1984 to June 1986. Funding was provided by the Center for Latin American Studies and the Tinker Foundation, a Graduate Humanities Research Grant from the Regents of the University of California, and three small grants from the Lowie Funds of the University of California Department of Anthropology at Berkeley. Write-up of these and other findings was generously supported by a stipend from the Institute for the Study of Social Change.

2. Called "the festival of disguises," Carnaval is a religious celebration held annually in the large agricultural market town of Masaya. It marks the climax of a series of religious festivals in that town, not the approach of Lent. An important presence among the elaborate masks and disguises of Carnaval is that of the cochones, who don female attire and parade alongside other participants in the day's procession.

3. My spelling throughout conforms to the only spelling I have ever seen in print, in a Nuevo Diario (6 December 1985) editorial.

4. For instance, some Middle Eastern cultures cast these active-passive rules in terms of active adults and passive youths (Trumbach 1977: 8).

BIBLIOGRAPHY

Arguelles, L., and B. R. Rich. 1984-85. Homosexuality, Homophobia, and Revolution: Notes Toward an Understanding of the Cuban Lesbian and Gay Male Experience. Signs 9:683-99 and 11:13-21.

Bakhtin, M. 1984. Rabelais and His World. Bloomington.

Blake, J. 1971. The Joint. New York.

Boswell, J. 1980. Christianity, Social Tolerance, and Homosexuality. Chicago.

Brandes, S. 1981. Like Wounded Stags: Male Sexual Ideology in an Andalusian Town. Sexual Meanings: The Cultural Construction of Gender and Sexuality, eds. S. Ortner and H. Whitehead, pp. 216-239. Cambridge.

Bullough, V. L. 1976. Sexual Variance in Society and History. Chicago.

Callender, C., and L. M. Kochems. 1983. The North American Berdache. Current Anthropology 24:1-76.

Carrier, J. J. 1976. Family Attitudes and Mexican Male Homosexuality. Urban Life 5:359-375.

Corzine, J., and R. Kirby. 1977. Cruising and Truckers: Sexual Encounters in a Highway Rest Area. Urban Life 6:171-192.

Davis, N. Z. 1978. Women on Top: Symbolic Sexual Inversion and Political Disorder in Early Modern Europe. The Reversible World: Symbolic Inversion in Art and Society, ed. B.A. Babcock, pp. 147-190. Ithaca.

D'Emilio, J. 1983. Sexual Politics, Sexual Communities: The Making of a Homosexual Minority in the United States, 1940-1970. Chicago.

Foucault, M. 1978. The History of Sexuality, Volume I: An Introduction. Trans. R. Hurley. New York.

_______ 1985. The Use of Pleasure: The History of Sexuality, Volume Two. Trans. R. Hurley. New York.

Herdt, G. H. 1981. Guardians of the Flutes: Idioms of Masculinity. New York.

_______ 1982. Fetish and Fantasy in Sambia Initiation. Rituals of Manhood: Male Initiation in Papua New Guinea, ed. G. H. Herdt, pp. 44-98. Berkeley.

Humphreys, L. 1970. Tearoom Trade: Impersonal Sex in Public Places. New York.

Lancaster, R. N. in press. Thanks to God and the Revolution: Popular Religion and Class Consciousness in the New Nicaragua. New York.

Murphy, M. D. 1984. Masculinity and Selective Homophobia: A Case from Spain. Anthropology Research Group on Homosexuality (ARGOH) Newsletter 5:6-12.

Nash, J. 1979. We Eat the Mines and the Mines Eat Us: Dependency and Exploitation in Bolivian Tin Mines. New York.

Parker, R. 1984. The Body and the Self: Aspects of Male Sexual Ideology in Brazil. Paper presented at the 83rd annual meeting of the American Anthropological Association in Denver, Colorado.

_______ 1985. Masculinity, Femininity, and Homosexuality: On the Anthropological Interpretation of Sexual Meanings in Brazil. Journal of Homosexuality 11:155-163.

Strathern, M. 1981. Culture in a Netbag: The Manufacture of a Subdiscipline in Anthropology. Man (N.S.) 16:665-88.

Suarez-Orozco, M. M. 1982. A Study of Argentine Soccer: The Dynamics of Fans and Their Folklore. Journal of Psychoanalytic Anthropology 5:7-28.

Trumbach, R. 1977. London's Sodomites: Homosexual Behavior and Western Culture in the Eighteenth Century. Journal of Social History 11:1-33.

Weeks, J. 1977. Coming Out: Homosexual Politics in Britain, from the Nineteenth Centurty to the Present. London.

Whitehead, H. 1981. The Bow and the Burden Strap: A New Look at Institutionalized Homosexuality in Native North America. Sexual Meanings, eds. S. Ortner and H. Whitehead, pp. 80-115. Cambridge.

Williams, W. L. 1986. The Spirit and the Flesh: Sexual Diversity in American Indian Culture. Boston.

A CULT MATRIARCHATE AND MALE HOMOSEXUALITY

BY RUTH LANDES
Department of Anthropology, Columbia University

MALE homosexuality occurs very widely, but the extent to which it becomes a social problem varies with the attitudes taken towards it by different cultures. One of these special attitudes is that which distinguishes sharply between the active homosexual and the passive. Either one or the other may be the object of strong social condemnation and hence must live as an outcaste, while the other is given a recognized role in society.

Among certain American Indian tribes of the last century, the *berdache* or passive homosexual was protected, encouraged to adopt the social and sexual roles of women, sometimes to assume sacred responsibilities, and, less often, allowed to cultivate with social approval the lewd conduct that we attribute to professional prostitutes. His " husband " was not considered as a homosexual but merely as a man who could make no more advantageous match. The active homosexual, however, who sought young partners, was an object of contempt. On the other hand, among the contemporary Tanala of Madagascar (communication from Ralph Linton), the passive homosexual arouses no comment at all provided he assumes the dress and occupations of a woman and eventually " marries " a man. In our own culture homosexuals have incurred disapproval whether they were active or passive; understandably enough, therefore, homosexuals are not so clearly differentiated into these two types as they are in cultures which distinguish sharply between them.

In the Negro community of Bahia, in northern Brazil, unusual circumstances encourage certain of the passive homosexuals to forge a new and respected status for themselves. Both individual and social changes have resulted which are important and easy to observe; but their special interest to psychology lies in demonstrating the way in which an outcaste group has made a new adaptation by taking advantage of changed circumstances.

In Brazil, condemnation of passive homosexuals puts them into the outcaste group while their partners pass unremarked and are often men of importance. Yet they are not hounded. The passive homosexuals solicit on the street in obscene whispers, and make themselves conspicuous by mincing with sickening exaggeration, overdoing the falsetto tones, and using women's turns of phrase. All their energies are focussed upon arranging the sexual act in which they take the female role. Rebuffed by a man they desire, they are said to drag themselves on their knees and plead sobbingly. They usually solicit normal men, who take advantage of them only when deprived of women. It is said that such men treat them most offensively. Solicitation, however, cannot provide a livelihood. They do not, like women prostitutes in Bahia, have a legal status, the right to claim a certain wage and to live in protected streets; rather, they are petty criminals hounded from the streets and with no right to claim pay.

It is this class, nevertheless, which has today provided leaders in dominant *candomble* cults of Bahia. In order to understand the change that is occurring, it is necessary to sketch the main features of these cults and the role they play in Bahia.

Bahia, also called Salvador, is the old capital of Brazil. It lies diagonally opposite the western horn of Africa and directly opposite the Angola coast. For centuries it was a teeming slave market, and a port of entry for freely migrating Negroes; today its population is preponderantly Negro and its folkways predominantly African. The lustiness of their life is everwhelmingly evident on holidays, when the sun beats down upon miles of gleaming streets packed with blacks swarming in from the outlying forests. The great squares are choked with people surging to insistent dance rhythms that are both mournful and lilting. At one point there is a deep hum as they sing, "Ah-h, Bahia, land of gold and luxury, land of *samba* and *candomble*!"

Candomble is an African fetish worship organized in some eighty cults and including in its membership most of the several hundred thousand Negroes of the city and its surrounding forests. Worship revolves around some ten West African gods; and each cult influences the whole lives of its followers. The greatest *candombles* today the Bahians trace to the Yoruba, the "Nagô" of Bahian speech, one of the greatest tribes of Nigeria and one which furnished many slaves in former days. These Nago priesthoods in Bahia are all but exclusively female. Tradition says baldly that only women are suited by their sex to nurse the deities, and that the service of men is blasphemous and unsexing. Although some men become priests, nevertheless, the ratio is hardly one male to fifty female priests. Most people feel that men should not be made priests, and so a man comes to this office only under exceptional circumstances. In any case he can never function as fully as a woman.

The principal fact in a Bahian Negro's world is the neighborhood in which he lives, and this is usually within sight and sound of some *candomble*. Everyone visits the cult house at least once a month, some several times a week. They pay social calls to the priestesses and bring the gossip of the outside world. Some come only to idle away the hours, but at one time or another all are obliged to consult the head priestess, called *iyalorixa* in Nago (Brazilian spelling) and meaning "mother in goodhood." The "mother," surrounded by the lesser priestesses, lives in the house of worship, both in order to be in the company of the gods she tends and to serve clients who need her intercession with the gods. Many are the sayings in honor of these cult women, famous throughout Brazil for their kindliness. A "mother's" sure speech and poised walk predispose her subordinates to obedience, at least in her own house and before her eyes. Under her guidance there flourishes a realm of peace and security.

The "mother" is aided by priestesses who are called her "daughters in godhood"—"daughters" because she has trained or "made" them over from creatures of common flesh to dedicated vessels for the manifestations of the gods. Clients usually need to be cured of an illness, for the people are always ailing; they come to the cult house to fulfill Catholic-like vows to the African deities or *orixas;* they come to fetch a magical remedy for disciplining an errant husband, an unwilling lover, an unfriendly employer; they beg strong measures for "despatching" rivals in love, business or friendship; they request ceremonial treatment to protect an unborn baby or an infant, or they want treatment for sterility. Any problem is brought to the "mother," whose fame thereupon spreads until some "mothers" are sought by highly placed whites. Some grow wealthy and justify the local belief that all experienced "daughters" of candomble are "rich."

Cult "daughters" are "made" for different reasons. A few

are made when still in the uterus because a priestess has dreamed so. Others are made in childhood to cure a disease. Sickness is often regarded as the castigation of a god, or as a god's way of putting his sign on a votary. The cult "mother" analyzes the situation by divining with African cowrie shells that have been treated ritually; besides, sometimes an elder "daughter" receives a dream from her god diagnosing the ailment. Most "daughters" are made, however, in adulthood with the hope of curing chronic headaches or stomach trouble; such votaries usually trace the beginnings of their ailments back to infancy, and explain that they delayed initiation or cure for economic reasons chiefly. Initiation requires a great expense of time and money, since it demands three months of absolute seclusion in the cult house, abstention from sex and rich foods and amusements, and charges of anything from fifty to a hundred dollars. Since money is hard to come by in Bahia, the large sums are paid off in various ways—in service, in kind, and in installments. After her formal release from the cult house, the novice observes awkward taboos for the remainder of the year; indeed, certain difficult taboos and proscriptions remain with her to her death, though in lessening severity. The taboos usually concern sex and foods, and exposure to heat and cold. The object is apparently to maintain the priestess in a removed half-ascetic state of diminished interest in fleshly affairs.

Occasionally little boys are "made" like girl children. Such a situation comes about because a child pledged before birth is born a boy, or because the illness of a boy child excites the sympathies of some priestess' god. These novices become "sons in godhood," but the mother of a Nago cult tries to avoid making "sons." She prefers instead an inconclusive ritual or cure called "seating the god," which confers no priestly status; and in fact she urges men to "seat" their gods so as to win divine protection for life. At the same time she fills the treasury of her house.

Boy "sons" may be called passive or inadvertent initiates in contrast with the men who persistently request initiation. A Nago "mother" hesitates before "making" men even after they have fallen into the ritual trance during which they dance possessed by a god who has entered them, and speak the god's message in his voice. She tries the man by traditional tests of fire and boiling oil, just as she tries a woman suspected of counterfeiting trance. Once I saw a " mother " eject a young man who habitually fell into trance, and she had this sharp notice pinned on the center post of the ceremonial room: " Gentlemen will kindly refrain from disturbing the rites or dancing in the space reserved for women "—and " women " meant the priestesses.

The Nago cults formerly had associated with them certain men who practised divination and sorcery but who were not cult heads. One or two such old men still operate in Bahia, and are called *babala.o* " father in godhood." They were consulted by the whole population, including the *candombles,* though sorcery is forbidden in Bahia. " Father in godhood " is as exalted as " mother," and, because of his claim to sorcery, may once have been even more powerful. When a " father " visits a cult ceremony today, he is received with deep bows and hand-kissing, the " mother " enthrones him by her right hand and calls him " brother," and the " daughters " call him " uncle." He may dance to honorific songs that are drummed out for him, but he dances wide-awake and alone. When he feels dangerously near to yielding to possession, as can happen when many of his god's songs are drummed and sung, he runs from the spot, fearing to profane the mysteries and unsex himself. The " father " is a dying institution now, and the two old men in Bahia unable to attract followers.

In very rare instances in the past men have acted as the heads of Nago cults, and then they too were called " father." Like the " mothers " they made few sons and many daughters, forbade male sacerdotes to dance with the women or to dance publicly when possessed, and debarred male novices from certain female mysteries. In comparison with the women, they were only partially initiated, and tolerated in view of certain anomalies. The more strictly a " father " observed the cult's restrictions, the more he improved his reputation, especially if he developed in the direction of a father-diviner. In cult affairs, as also in *babala.o* sorcery, a woman had to assist as " lesser mother in godhood," and eventually she succeeded the " father."

The cult structure requires men as *ogans,* " providers," " protectors." An *ogan* is expected to pay for the elaborate ceremonies, to keep the cult house in repair, and to help finance at least one of the priestesses in her ritual obligations. At times the *ogan* is obliged to defend the cult before the police. After he has been "confirmed" he is called "father" by all the women, who kiss his hand and beg his blessing, but he addresses the head as "mother" and usually stoops to kiss her hand and beg her blessing (as everyone does in greeting the Catholic *padres*), and the other priestesses he calls "daughter." A cult group tries to attract as many such "fathers" as possible, some even succeeding in ensnaring white men of means. This service by men who are in secular matters most patriarchically minded is striking; yet the situation bears a certain analogy to their own household arrangements in that each man is expected to take care of one woman, that is, of one priestess and her god. And the dominating "mother" is paralleled by the elder women who rule Brazilian families.

Among the *ogans* of each cult, three are charged with special duties. One supervises the three drums and drummers, which are fundamental in the rites, since "the voice of the drums calls the gods." One assists the "mother" in ritually slaughtering sacrificial cows, goats, cocks, chickens, and pigeons, being required to cut off and lay aside the genitals of male sacrifices; the third *ogan* assists him. Whenever these two approach the deep mysteries, they are subjected to the same taboos as are the priestesses.

Friction within the Nago cults is not due to masculine jealousy, for the men in the cult rarely complain of the authority and demands of the women, and more strongly even than the women they condemn grown "sons" as "sissies." The ancient *babala.os* are now negligible; instead, "mothers" are encouraged to take on their divining functions. When there is conflict within the Nago cults, it is usually the work of women ambitious to become "mothers," and it is due to such friction that new houses and small variations in ritual appear.

The most important rift appeared about a generation ago, when a Nago "mother" named Sylvina set up the so-called *caboclo* cult. *Caboclo* in this region of Brazil means an Indian-white mixed blood; Sylvina appropriated the term because she claimed to receive visions of ancient Brazilian Indians. She organized the worship of the first owners of the land, the Indian dead. Probably she had two or three sources for her inspiration: one, the Bantu practice of worshipping the ghosts of ancestors and ancient landowners; another, the Brazilian's romantic interest in Indian history, which is taught to every school child and which is especially interesting to mulattoes who prefer to describe themselves as *caboclos*; and a third, the ubiquitousness of European spiritualism and of "sessions" that invoke Indian "guides." Sylvina's schismatic ideas, immediately successful because of her prestige as a Nago "daughter," have resulted today in dozens of *caboclo* cults in Bahia. Nago gods still remain primary in *caboclo* ritual, and only after they are worshipped are the newer supernaturals invoked.

Caboclo cults have immensely relaxed the restrictions surrounding "mothers." A Nago "mother" must pass through at least seven years of strenuous training before her colleagues sanction her accession to office; as a rule she has gone through many more. There is also a tendency for a woman to inherit the office from a relative or close friend with whom she has served as assistant. *Caboclo* "mothers," however, assert the right to function without previous service, often without having been "made." They shape their shortcomings into a virtue, claiming that no human intermediaries placed hands on them in confirmation, but only the *caboclo* spirits themselves. They train novices in a very sketchy manner, requiring only seven days of seclusion, imposing few taboos for the remainder of the year, and so on. They visit the ceremonies of other cult houses far more frequently than the Nago priestesses, who in fact are warned against such gadding about, and it is believed that they eavesdrop to pick up portions of ritual knowledge. Their usual attitude is hostile and sulky, with the result that they have contributed notably to the Afro-Brazilian's collection of songs of defiance.

Their most radical departure from Nago tradition is that men may become *caboclo* cult-heads. In their rites, men abandon themselves like women to the pre-dance tremors and groans and to the final frenzied leaps. I am told of one *caboclo* house where men are in the majority, but the women in other priesthoods still far exceed the men. Although in one ceremony I saw five "sons" among ten "daughters," in another I saw only two "sons" among about a dozen "daughters." I never saw a *caboclo* ceremonial that did not include one or more "sons," a circumstance which is impossible in a Nago ceremonial.

Even though *caboclo* "mothers" still agree with the Nago in the dogma that no man should be made a "father," inevitably they defeat themselves in consequence of freely making "sons." In a partial enumeration made by a Bahian ethnologist, Edison Carneiro, the proportion stood:

	MOTHERS	FATHERS
Nago	20	3
Caboclo	10	34

This count is a fair sample. People claim that the *caboclo* "fathers" have appeared in numbers only in the present generation, an assertion substantiated by the fact that the non-Nago "fathers" are all under forty-five years of age and a large number in their early twenties.

The most facile explanation of this development in the non-Nago cults is that the men who play the role of priest are striving for oneness with the "mother" figure. Although an exposition of this sort is obvious, it does not go deep enough to explain why these *candomble* priests are all drawn from the outcaste homosexual solicitors of the Bahia underworld. Most of these *caboclo* "fathers" and "sons" are passive homosexuals of note, and were vagrants and casuals of the streets.

The relaxation of the strict taboos in the non-Nago cults, and especially the fact that the bars were let down to men, did not, however, obliterate the fundamental tenet that femininity alone could nurse the gods. All men considered normal in Bahia were, therefore, still debarred. Only one group fulfilled the requirements. The fact that they were a group which stood under the strongest social condemnation did not weigh against this basic tenet. When "sons" were made, they were made from among the solicitors, who in spite of their status were alone "feminine." Having made their entry into the influential *candomble,* as priests they have now a voice in all vital activities. They are supported and even adored by those normal men of whom they were before the butt and object of derision.

This metamorphosis has not taken place without changing both the men who have become *caboclo* priests and the *candomble* cults in which they now have leading roles. In contrast with the "mothers," the "fathers" seem combative and frustrated. They desire simple personal satisfactions usually, and rarely glimpse the social ends that are the stated goals of Nago fetishism. But as the voice of a hitherto voiceless group, they may be path-breakers to new institutions. They do not consider themselves rebels, "masculinists" to be grouped with our "feminists"; on the contrary, they aspire to a feeling of oneness with the "mother" tradition. The situation does not result in group solidarity, and the men are masters of slander. Least of all do they reflect the masculinity of the patriarchal culture in whose heart they live. They want one thing, for which the *candomble* provides widest opportunities: they want to be women.

Physically they have certain advantages, for many of the "fathers" are handsome in a boyish way, and all I have seen are mulattoes. *Caboclo* "fathers" and "sons" also have female mannerisms, emulating not the quiet authority and composed movements of the cult matriarchs, but the nervous coquettishness of the homosexuals. Instead, however, of soliciting affection and sexual satisfaction from casuals, they solicit and are approached by worshippers who are usually *ogans*; instead of meriting contemptuous talk and kicks, they are installed in comfortable houses, served by cult subordinates, and sometimes grow rich. Within the *candomble* they insist upon their womanliness and ritualize it in priestly trance; banking upon the prestige of Nago "mothers" and "daughters," they endow themselves with comparable titles of "fathers" and "sons." Passive homosexual fantasies are realizable under the protection of the cult, as men dance with women in the roles of women, wearing skirts and acting as mediums. One of the most conspicuous attributes of the prominent "fathers" is their style of dancing in the rites. This is stereotyped in the women's style, especially in being slow and sensuous *(dengoso)*, and is markedly different from the athletic forms cultivated by men in the secular dances. It makes a bulky man, like the famous "father" Bernardino, seem feminine, softening his bare back and shoulders, his bloomered legs and small naked feet into the body of a woman. They partially displace the women doing women's work; but they do not view themselves as women's sexual rivals. Simply, they care to *be* women, and constantly surround themselves with women priests. The "sons" increase in these surroundings, and one day may assume the major offices which are today in the sole hands of women.

Established "fathers" cultivate different types of behavior for the world of *candomble* and for the world outside. They confine their femaleness more and more to cult occasions, in secular life striving to imitate the actions of men. This conduct is part of the psychology of keeping cult activities secret. In public the

" fathers " wear trousers and roughen their gestures. Even in public they are protected by the cult, since they never venture forth without the company of some " sons " or *ogans.* Even so, they always have an air of challenge, of slight hostility.

Some " fathers " cherish friendships with important Nago " mothers " and " daughters," and a few strive to resemble them in priestly consecration. The ordinary " father " is interested solely in the opportunity for personal display, while the great " mothers " have primarily a tremendous pride in their office. To herself and to others, the " mother " is first and foremost the sacred head of African worship, and only secondarily the preening woman; but to himself and to others the " father " is first and foremost a sexual anomaly, and only secondarily the head of a cult. Yet the famous " fathers " Bernardino and Procopio worry about masking the cruder signs of homosexuality—though they never abandon its practice—and devote themselves to their mystical duties, like their women colleagues.

Most " fathers " are votaries of Yansan, the African goddess identified with the English St. Barbara. Psychologically this is an apt situation, for in African tradition Yansan is a masculine woman, or even a man. She is a warrior; at times she is the wife of the warrior-king, Shango, and at times she is his sister. Old wood carvings found in Bahia, made there or in Africa, represent Shango as a male figure and as a female. Yansan controls the wind and lightning; hence her emblematic colors of maroon, red, and blue. Shango lives in the sky ruling the thunder, and his colors are similar to hers—red, and red and white. Like male gods, Yansan wears trousers, and an abbreviated wide ballet skirt; " she is the man-woman."

Men have brought a hitherto foreign element into the atmosphere of *candomble,* a kind of terrorism expressed in their harsh and callous direction of the group, in their furtive but widely known use of sorcery, and in their actual whipping of priestesses. A " mother " knows how to use sorcery, and she owns a sacred whip or stick that hangs in the main altar room; but she uses neither instrument, for her simple command suffices. In resorting to violence, a " father " admits that though he has captured the office of " mother," he has failed to enter into its character. Because his purposes are different, he changes the nature of the office.

His terrorism derives in part from the diviner-sorcerer.

Bernardino, Procopio, and Cyriaco are the most noted "fathers" in Bahia, but their fame as priests is overshadowed by their fame as sorcerers *(feiticeiros)*. Their clients include distinguished white persons who protect them from the police, for the police occasionally round them up to be jailed and whipped.

Each father is an interesting variation of the prevailing type. A real psychological understanding is impossible without the intimate acquaintance that was closed to me as a woman; but a great deal could be gathered, and some observations that seem to block out the general situation are now offered.

The ten or so "fathers" whom I knew had come from the ranks of the street prostitutes and boy delinquents, and from the town's ruffians. Not all were natives of the city of Bahia; João, for example, came at the age of ten from the remote cattle land of the state, and lived in the town with the riff-raff of the streets. The place of birth is unimportant, for the same sorts of abnormal sex behavior characterize all parts of Brazil, and very few men have not been exposed to some one type. Naturally, as an outcaste João was a delinquent.

Some "fathers," like Bernardino, break their street ties completely and cultivate cult followers who are normal men dazzled by the mystery that surrounds a cult head. Others, however, like *pãe* João, retain the old ties along with the new. These contrasting attitudes towards the disreputable past are linked with other forms of behavior. Thus Bernardino struggles to hide his homosexuality, confining it to his home and the temple's terrain. He wears severe white clothes and shaves his woolly head. João, on the contrary, is quite unashamed, half mincing in the streets, writing love letters to the men of his heart, wearing fancy blouses whose color and cut set off his fine shoulders and skin—and he straightens his hair. Straightened hair, forbidden by Nago standards, is the symbol of male homosexuals.

"Fathers" are on the whole distinctly cold to women, a fact which is more conspicuous in Brazil than it would be in the States. But Bernardino and Procopio cultivate close professional and personal ties with important priestesses of other cult houses. In view of the bitter rivalry and mistrust normally existing among cult heads, their attitude is very striking. It is probably based on a peculiar kind of desexualized love and hero-worship; at the same time it guarantees the "father's" admission into a select small circle of leading priestesses. Bernardino likes to offer expensive gifts to these friends, but he also explodes into shocking abuse.

Men like João cultivate women prostitutes. He is famous for visting them in their houses and playing innocently. This habit of his recalls Wilhelm Stekel's interesting cases of homosexuals who derived their highest excitement from the company of easy women who had entertained the men they themselves desired.

Still others, like Vavá, are bisexual. He seems the most contained, and also one of the least interesting, of the group. Like João, he allows his cult grounds to be used for assignations, thus attaining for himself access to the men who visit there originally from heterosexual motives. At the same time he is happily married to an attractive white girl, having been married several times in his twenty-five years.

Others, like Cyriaco and Manuelzinho, are quite staid in their homosexual attachments. The first lives with three "sons," and the quartet is inseparable. The second, sunk in an apathetic adoration of the doll-like Vavá, never flirts in João's heartless fashion.

Some are shy and self-conscious, like Octavio; others are hostile and rude, like Bernardino and Procopio; others still are lewd like Vidal. Some are impudent, like Paím, and some are quite serene, like Cyriaco. Obviously homosexuality has different personal meanings to each of them.

"Fathers" are not equally devoted to their religious responsibilities. Procopio and Bernardino, like many "mothers," devote all their time to them. Vavá and João have white-collar jobs in the schools. Cyriaco operates a successful grocery. Others, like Paím, are wasters who have no other occupation, and who eventually lose prestige and their cult following.

It is clear, therefore, that when the bars were let down which had excluded men from cult leadership, the fact that the only group which qualified was made up of outcastes and vagrants did not militate against certain of these men playing the highest roles in *candomble*. It is clear also that *candomble* has been radically changed by their assumption of such roles. Many of the outcaste group of passive homosexuals who have become priests have broken with the outcaste group; all have persevered in the face of powerful hostility, taken over the roles of the priestly "mothers," and exploited the priestly offices to their own ends.

THE COMMUNITY FUNCTION OF TAHITIAN MALE TRANSVESTITISM: A HYPOTHESIS[1]

ROBERT I. LEVY, M.D.
University of California, San Diego

The role of the mahu, *a feminine role-playing male, has persisted in rural Tahitian villages since traditional times although there have been many other role and institutional changes in the 200 years since Western contact. It is suggested here that the role persists not primarily as an expressive outlet for men wishing to avoid masculine role playing, but primarily because it serves important covert needs for other members of the community. There tends to be one mahu in each village, the belief of villagers being that "it is natural" or "God so arranged it" that there should be at least one and no more than one. Tahitian sexual identity is undifferentiated in its contrast of maleness and femaleness in relation to Western expectations. It is proposed that the presence of the mahu helps stabilize this identity for men by providing a highly visible and exclusively limited contrast, implying for other men in the village, "I am a man because I am not a mahu."*

At the time of discovery by the West in 1767, Tahiti, like many other non-Western cultures, had an institutionalized form of male homosexuality. As James Morrison, left ashore in 1789 on Tahiti after the mutiny on the Bounty, noted,

> they have a set of men called mahu. These men are in some respects like the Eunuchs in India but are not castrated. They never cohabit with women, but live as they do. They pick their beards out and dress as women, dance and sing with them and are as effeminate in their voice. They are generally excellent hands at making and painting of cloth, making mats, and every other woman's employment. They are esteemed valuable friends in that way and it is said, though I never saw an instance of it, that they converse with men as familiar as

[1] Read in modified form at the 126th Annual Meeting of the American Psychiatric Association, San Francisco, California, May 11-15, 1970.

Dr. Levy is Professor, Department of Anthropology, University of California, San Diego, La Jolla, California 92037.

women do. This, however, I do not aver as a fact as I never found any who did not detest the thought (Morrison 1935: 238).

That the mahu did "converse with men as familiar as women do," was attested to by other observers. William Bligh, Morrison's captain, after noting in his journal that the mahus were "particularly selected when boys and kept with the women solely for the caresses of the men," goes on to note that "those connected with him have their beastly pleasures gratified between his thighs, but are no farther sodomites as they all positively deny the crime" (Bligh n.d.: 16).

Other early reports from explorers and missionaries added fellatio to the coital forms, the literature giving the impression that it was generally the mahu who performed fellatio on the partner (although there is at least one early report of the reverse).[2]

I spent twenty-six months (during 1961-1964) doing studies of various psychological and anthropological patterns in two Tahitian speaking communities in French Polynesia.[3] The mahu, as a social *type,* still exists. There was one in each of the two communities that I studied. In this paper I will briefly describe the mahu and his relation to others, and propose one of the dynamic factors in the maintenance of the role.

I will base this discussion mostly on the more rural and traditional of the two communities, "Piri," a village of about 300 people, with a mixed subsistence (horticulture and fishing) and market (vanilla and copra) economy, on the island of Huahine about 100 miles north-west of Tahiti.

In 1961 there was a sixteen year old boy in Piri, who was referred to sometimes by his personal name, sometimes as "the mahu." Although there were photographs of him proudly displayed in his foster mother's house showing him in girls' dancing

[2] There is a note from one of the early (1804) visitors to Tahiti, John Turnbull (quoted by M. Bouge in Journal de la Société des Océanistes, 1955 volume 11 page 147) that the mahu "eagerly swallows [the semen] down as if it were the vigor and force of the other; thinking no doubt thus to restore to himself greater strength." Contemporary Tahitians, describing similar acts, exactly echo Turnbull's incorporation-of-strength thesis to explain why some mahu are so "healthy looking."

[3] Some other reports on this work are noted in the references cited section.

costume, complete with brassiere, he wore male clothes ordinarily, favoring however the neutral sarong-like *pareu,* worn by both sexes, rather than the Western style trousers now worn frequently by men in the village. His speech and manner were somewhat feminine—resembling feminine style without exaggerating or mocking it. His feminine role-taking was made apparent to the villagers primarily because he performed women's household activities, and because his associations were of feminine type. He cleaned the house, took care of babies, plaited coconut palm leaves into thatching sections, and made decorative patch work quilts. He associated with the adolescent girls in the village as a peer, walking arm-in-arm with them, gossiping and visiting with them.[4]

There were two other men in Piri who had feminine mannerisms. It was sometimes said about them that they were mahu-like, but they were not said to be mahus. They had wives and children, and performed men's tasks in the village. There was also a man in his twenties who had been a mahu in Piri, when the present one was a child. According to the village reports he had given up being a mahu, had gone to Papeete to work, and was now living as an "ordinary man." Mahus were not defined by effeminate behavior alone; they also had to fulfill some aspects of a woman's village role, a role they could give up to become ex-mahus.

It also appeared that many people assumed that Tahitian villages usually had a mahu. Someone would say, "I don't know who the mahu is in X village." When asked, "Then how do you know there is one?" the answer would be something like, "There always is one," or "That's the way things are." When asked if there were ever two mahus in a village, the common answer was, "No, only one." One informant pressed on this said, "When one dies, another replaces him. God arranges it like that. It isn't the nature of things, two mahus in one place. Only one . . . and when that one dies, he is replaced." From what inquiries I was able to make about other villages, although there were periods without a mahu, as there had been in Piri itself, and occasionally two for brief periods, the supposition of "at least one, and

[4] The mahu in the other community that I studied, an urban enclave, in the major administrative center, Papeete, was in his fifties. He worked as a maid for a Chinese family. He was accepted as a semi-peer of a group of middle aged Tahitian women.

no more than one to a community," seemed to stand for an actual tendency. All but one of the villages on Huahine reportedly had one mahu at the time of my study.

Overt homosexual behavior was distinctly not an essential shared part of the community's idea of the mahu's role. The description on which everyone agreed was someone "who did woman's work."

All informants in Piri expressed generally positive feelings about the mahu in this aspect. First, they said he was "natural"; God (Tahitians have been Christian since the early 19th century) created him as a mahu—although this does not rule out a later, equally natural relinquishing of the role. Secondly, he was interesting. It was "wonderful" to see a man who had the skills to do women's things. Both men and women spoke with some pride of Piri's mahu's skill. Some men, however, expressed some discomfort about them—in spite of their adherence to a doctrine of approval.

As to his *overt* homosexual behavior there were a variety of suppositions and of evaluations. Some informants in the village said that most mahus did not engage in sexual activities. Others, mostly the younger men in Piri, stated that all mahus engaged in sexual activity with other males, although they tended to be discreet and secret about it. This latter was the opinion of the mahu in Papeete.[5]

For those who said the mahu did engage in sexual activities, there were differences in opinions as to how many of the village young men were involved with him at one time or another. From the most reliable reports it appears that only a small percentage were involved.[6] The type of sexual activity seems to be limited now (both in Piri and elsewhere) to fellatio, with the mahu being the active partner. Intercourse between the mahu's thighs, with its more clearly feminine sexual role-playing was not reported, and

[5] The mahu in Piri for various reasons, probably relating to village ambivalences about his sexual life and, thus, to the importance of discreetness, was one of the only two people approached in the village who refused requests for life histories.

[6] There were no reports of homosexual relationships between men if neither one was a mahu. Informants said that this "never" happened. In Papeete on the other hand these relationships did exist, and a new term *raerae* has been recently introduced to describe people who engage in preferential homosexual activities, but who are not necessarily mahus.

denied when asked about. Anal sodomy was known, but considered to be an unclean perversion introduced by the Europeans, and limited to Papeete.

Those men in Piri who had had contacts with a mahu (either in the village or on visits to Papeete) spoke about it quite openly in interviews. They portrayed the mahu as simply a substitute woman, and described the acts with much the same affect and evaluations that they used for describing casual heterosexual acts. Thus (from a tape recorded interview) an eighteen year old man, asked if he felt any shame or embarrassment over it, said, "No, one isn't ashamed. You don't put any particular importance on it. It is like feeding the mahu with your penis. You get more pleasure out of it than they do. . . . For you it is just the same as if you were having intercourse with a woman. You don't take it seriously."

Evaluations by those villagers who denied sexual contact with mahus as to the mahu's sexual behavior and evaluations of the mahu's partner were more complex than the acceptance of non-sexual parts of his behavior. While some villagers were tolerant, repeating that it was just like other kinds of sexual acts, some of the villagers, both men and women, thought that the acts were "disgusting," and that both the mahu and his partner should be ashamed—reflecting Morrison's pre-Christian "I never found any who did not detest the thought." No one, however, ever labeled the partner as a mahu, nor indicated that they thought he was any less manful for his "indecent" behavior.

It is evident that the existence of the mahu role serves various psychological functions. For the mahu himself it provides a legitimate identity congruent with some of his needs. (The one mahu whom I studied at any length had reported having a feminine self image from his earliest remembered childhood.) And similarly for the Tahitian men who had occasional physical relations with mahus a variety of motives, some quite culturally specific, were served.[7]

If we accept the proposition that mahu behavior represents a social role in Tahitian villages, one may ask about its functions, about the social or community purposes that it serves.

[7] I did not find any examples of exclusive or most-frequent contact of a male with a mahu rather than with women, although semi-legendary stories of men occasionally living with a mahu as a spouse were sometimes told.

The ideal of one and only one mahu to a village would imply not only that somebody was recruited for the role (recall Bligh's remark that mahus were "particularly selected when boys") but that other possible candidates were somehow kept out of the role. This limits the possible function of the role as an acceptable escape from the male role by men whose temperament or aberrant socialization ill-fit them for it. Not only are some candidates kept out, but I have seen in other Tahitian communities very young boys apparently being coaxed into the role where I had the impression that the clues, if any, to which the coaxers were responding were at most related to the possibility of the child playing a transvestite role and not to any strong inclination, and it is possible that the coaxers were acting with no clues at all.

A larger part of the population participated as partners, and this was also part of the use of the role. But for most people the essence of the mahu was his highly visible "doing woman's work" in its public aspects; the private and generally secret sexual acts were considered by some as a perverse aspect of this otherwise acceptable behavior.

I would suggest that the presence and the maintenance of the mahu role have as major aspects a cognitive and message function to the community as audience, particularly to the male members.

Sexual role differentiation has special features and problems for individuals in the communities which I studied. At the cultural level there is relatively little differentiation when compared to Western expectations. The Tahitian language has no grammatical index of gender, the majority of Tahitian first names are not differentiated sexually, there is a relative equality and similarity of much male and female role behavior. To the degree that they are differentiated there is a frequent crossing over in a number of the work roles when necessary, for example, because of the illness of one of the adults in a small household. There is an emphasis in doctrine on playing down sex differences, and this is striking in men's playing down of any special difficulties in women's experience (such as childbirth), or in giving women either any special distinctions or disabilities. The emphasis is on equality, and minimizing of differences.[8]

[8] There are clear anxieties underlying this equalizing, but they are not immediately relevant here.

On a more covert level, identity formation of children growing up in Tahitian households tends to be diffused. Generally the powerful caretakers include a network of older siblings and cousins in a system which is guided in a relatively exterior fashion by the mother, and to which the father is very peripheral except in unusual circumstances. The caretakers are mostly girls and young women, and this, and the fact that her eventual adult roles are those which she witnesses closely every day in the household, seem to make it considerably easier for girls to establish a sexual identity by modeling and role learning than for boys.[9] Some indication of the limited differentiation is given by a remark of Gauguin's that Tahitian men seemed to him "androgynous," and that, "there is something virile in the women and something feminine in the men" (Gauguin 1957:47). Similarly, Henry Adams remarked in a letter from Tahiti in the 1890's that, "the Polynesian woman seems to me too much like the Polynesian man; the difference is not great enough to admit of sentiment, only of physical divergence" (Adams 1930:484).

There is much homo-erotic play among boys, particularly related to the adolescent boys' life stage in which membership in the village peer group is of central importance. There is much body contact, occasional dancing together, occasional group masturbation, much darting out timidly into heterosexual forays and then a return for bragging and discussion to the peer group.

I propose that in the absence of strong internal shaping towards the self definition of manhood in its sense of contrast and complementarity to womanhood that there have been developed various external marks or signs which function to clarify that definition.

One is the supercision of the penis which all boys undergo in early puberty. An analysis of the symbolic aspects of this indicates that it marks (as has been often suggested for such rites) both separation from household-parent-child binding and special male status.

I believe that the mahu role, with its clear cut rules, its high visibility, its strictly limited incumbency, and its pre-empting of

[9] There is no *institutionalized* female homosexuality. There are some male role playing women in Papeete, but this is considered bizarre by the people in Piri.

homosexual behavior, also has a message function. It says "there, clearly, out in the open, is the mahu, the one man who has taken a female role. I am a non-mahu. Whatever feelings I have about men are no threat to me and to my eventual role as family head. I can see exactly what *he* is, and I am clear about myself in that I am not he."[10]

I suggest that the mahu is a carefully maintained role, building on pre-existing possibilities for a supply of candidates, which carefully presents a behavior complex that serves the important function, among other subsidiary ones, of defining and stabilizing a precarious aspect of identity by a clear negative image—that which I am not, and cannot be.

* * *

The orientation that some cultural forms, some (or aspects of some) roles, rites, myths and institutions (e.g. Polynesian adoption practices), have essential functions as messages for the community as audience, in addition to expressive and adaptational functions for the actors most immediately concerned, assumes that such forms act as maintenance systems for the stabilization of adult personality forms. Some theoretical background for this position is suggested in Levy (1969b).

The establishment of an identity through contrast and negation is only one of the possible types. The maintenance form may be *congruent* with an important major orientation. It is assumed here that the major orientation is conflictive or otherwise unstable, and that the maintenance form acts as a kind of ongoing rehearsal and reaffirmation of the orientation. (See Levy 1969b).

As to negative forms, it has been pointed out that *not* cannot be expressed directly in analogical language. (For example, see Bateson 1968). It may be indicated by expressing the feature to be negated in a positive form and indicating by the context that the positive form does not obtain. Thus a dog pretends to bite in a play situation, the context providing the statement, "This is the hostile relationship which I am *not* taking to-

---

[10] George Devereux (1937) in an article on institutionalized homosexuality of the Mohave Indians suggested that one of the functions of the practice was to create "an 'abscess of fixation' and [to localize] the disorder in a small area of the body social." This seems to be related to the thesis presented here.

wards you." Analogically, the visible presence of a mahu is necessary for the statement, "*this* is what you are not."

The assumptions made about the functional implications of "maintenance forms" based on the study of particular cultural cases have obvious consequences. In the case of a role (as opposed to other patternings which do not require training and recruits) the problems of filling it, or in the proposed mahu case of filling it and limiting its occupancy, should provide predictable tensions. Extra aspirants to the role should be forced out, new ones somehow recruited to empty slots. A sufficiently long period without the role being filled should produce adjustments and pathologies predictable from the functional assumptions concerning the role.

The mahu role is one of a limited number of dramatic cultural forms (others are adoption practices, supercision operations on male adolescents) which have persisted in Tahitian communities during a long period of acculturation in which much of the old culture, e.g., political superstructure, religion, amusements, has disappeared. These forms seem to be related to persisting aspects of organization involving values, structuring of everyday reality, philosophy, and aspects of personality, and to a clearly neo-Polynesian organization of introduced cultural materials. They seem to begin to breakdown when, under conditions of modernized economy and communication, the "acculturated" Tahitian community becomes a "modernized" sample of Western culture. The mahu becomes the raerae. This suggests that such forms when identified may be good indices to the absence of either breakdown or structural modernization. (c.f. Levy 1969d).

References Cited

Adams, H.
1930—Letters of Henry Adams. Boston and New York: Houghton Mifflin Company.

Bligh, W.
n. d.—The log of the Bounty. London: Golden Cockerel Press.

Bateson, Gregory
1968—Redundancy and coding. *In* Animal communication: techniques of study and results of research. T. A. Sebeok ed., Bloomington: Indiana University Press.

Devereux, G.
1937—Institutionalized homosexuality of the Mohave Indians. Human Biology 9:498-527.

GAUGUIN, PAUL
1957—Noa noa. New York: The Noonday Press.
LEVY, R.
1966—Ma'ohi drinking patterns in the Society Islands. The Journal of the Polynesian Society 75:304-320.
1967—Tahitian folk psychotherapy. International Mental Health Research Newsletter 9.
1968a–Child management structure and its implications in a Tahitian family. *In* A modern introduction to the family. E. Vogel and N. Bell eds., New York: The Free Press.
1968b–Tahiti observed: early European impressions of Tahitian personal style. The Journal of the Polynesian Society 77:1:33-42.
1969a–On getting angry in the Society Islands. *In* Mental health research in Asia and the Pacific. W. Caudill and T. Lin eds., Honolulu: East West Center Press.
1969b–Tahitian adoption as a psychological message. *In* Adoption in Eastern Oceania. V. Carroll, ed. Honolulu: University of Hawaii Press.
1969c–Personal forms and meanings in Tahitian Protestantism. Journal de la Société des Océanistes 25:125-136.
1969d–Personality studies in Polynesia and Micronesia, stability and change. Working papers 8, Social Science Research Institute. Honolulu: University of Hawaii.
MORRISON, J.
1935—The journal of James Morrison. London: Golden Cockerel Press.

CORRESPONDENCE

Fuzzy sets and abominations

As Mary Douglas (1966: 63) envisioned the division of labour, it is God's work to create order and, presumably, anthropologists' to reveal it. Witkowski, Brown and Chase (*Man* (N.S.) **16**, 1–14) again demonstrate that anthropologists perform this mission better with categories of life forms than for categories of social roles. In contrast to the positing of universals for the former, Carrier (*Man* (N.S.) **15**, 541–2) suggests that one of the most refractory of the latter, 'homosexual', be removed from the list of etic concepts (although, somewhat inconsistently, he projects an American view of 'transexual' onto the rest of the world).

Douglas's famed interpretation of the abominations of Leviticus (1966: 54–72) is premissed on the structural linguistics position that text reveals structure: 'The only sound approach is to forget hygiene, aesthetics, morals and instinctive revulsion, even to forget the Canaanites and the Zoroastrian Magi, and start with the texts' (1966: 63). This rejection of any relevance for comparative data is arresting in the course of a book presenting a cross-cultural theory of pollution and taboo (note the singular forms), and invites an ethnocentric bias even more than does reliance on dictionaries constructed by Western observers (see Murray & Arboleda in press). Douglas treats her own religious tradition as a privileged case—a subject that can therefore be a source of comparison but never an object to be explained by comparison. This ethnocentrism leads Douglas to explain variation in dependent variables with (unrecognisedly) invariant independent variables, namely, whereas there are always phenomena residual to any categorisation schema, what does not fit is not everywhere regarded with horror. Still less are attempts to exterminate what is anomalous to a classification schema universally made.

Mayr (1981) has interpreted the history of Western biological theory as a recurring clash between essentialisms (doctrines that maintain there are a limited, readily conceivable number of species characterised by essential, distinct features) and nominalism (doctrines positing an inter-breeding population of individual organisms grouped more or less arbitrarily by species names). Comparative ethnobiological work (in addition to Witkowksi *et al.*, see Berlin 1972; Berlin *et al.* 1966; 1968; Raven *et al.* 1971; Brown 1977; 1979; Bulmer 1967) has contrasted essentialisms, and found gross morphology universally employed to distinguish kinds of plants and animals.

Not only the ancient Hebrews noticed, 'In the firmament two-legged fowls fly with wings. In the water scaly fish swim with fins. On the earth four-legged animals hop, jump, or walk' (Douglas 1966: 70), and classified accordingly. Apparently there was a stage 4 classification in which 'wug' and 'animal' were not distinguished, but clearly contrasted to 'snake'. The Semitic (Amharic and Arabian), Cushitic (Galla) and Indo-Iranian (Pahlavi and Pashto) languages in Brown's (1979) survey of zoological classification systems are all stage 4 (as are more than a third of all those in the sample).

Aquatic crustaceans are usually classed 'fish'. 'True fish' are the prototype of this class (Hunn 1977: 250), and shrimp problematic, whether located in semantic space outside the 'wug' boundary or on the other side (that is, in the 'wug' class). There is no report of any ancient Semitic people attempting to exterminate shrimp, any more than peoples in Papua New Guinea faced with the difficulty of classifying cassowaries as 'birds' or 'mammals' (Bulmer 1967; cf. Herdt 1981: 131–57) have been reported to resolve the conceptual problem by eliminating cassowaries.

If there is any psychological reality to the 'horror' purportedly inspired by such classification difficulties, it is confined to anthropologists intent on eliciting complete and exhaustive contrast sets. As Goody (1977) suggested, fixing folk classification schemata into writing (as in tables of components or hierarchical tree diagrams) can *create* anomalous phenomena otherwise orally glossed over and not reflected upon. Kuhn (1962: 9) noted that even in 'science' there are *always* counterinstances: not everything that is unknown or does not easily fit received 'knowledge' is problematic. Anomalies are recognised with great reluctance, and attempts to construct a new paradigm (in the original linguistic sense from which Kuhn borrowed it) occur only after persistent failure to solve a problem produces a 'crisis' (Kuhn 1962: 144). With no felt problems and no widely-recognised failure(s), there is no rethinking of fundamentals. The psychological reality of the danger in *Purity and danger* (Douglas 1966) has not been demonstrated. The native-speakers, whom the theory would have one believe are driven by anxiety to proscribing and even attempting to annihilate what is not readily classifiable from the world, routinely operate with fuzzily-bounded categories and ignore the imperfect fit, rather than focus on it—as a taboo must (Searle 1975).

Folk theories implicit in everyday categorisation (for biology, see Raven *et al.* 1971) are not completely articulated logical sets of rules capable of generating clear answers to any question about any imaginable combination of 'essential' social features any more than of 'essential' features of life-forms. Anthropologists' concerns to the contrary notwithstanding, social categories are not designed to adjudicate boundary disputes to such conflicting answers as one is likely to elicit with questions such as, 'Is your mother's stepbrother's adopted son a "first cousin"?' This arcane genealogical creature may be classed with mother's brother's sons, or not, but it is unlikely there will be a separate named class for this infrequently occurring phenomenon.

Just as there are no exhaustive taxonomic slots for all plants or animals, or genealogical slots for each human individual, there are fewer roles than behaviours (in any culture). For instance, in cultures with labelled homosexual roles, there is homosexual behaviour in which neither participant enacts or defines himself by the role. (For Anglo-North America, see Humphreys 1975; Miller 1978; Weinberg 1978; Murray 1979; for indigenous North America, Whitehead 1981: 95; for Mesoamerica, Carrier 1975; Taylor 1978; Murray 1980; and for Tahiti, Levy 1973: 132).

The taboo on homosexual coupling is the part of the Holiness Code in the Old Testament that some social groups in the English-speaking world attempt to enforce on non-believers. Moreover, within living memory, it was the official policy of one state within Christendom to go beyond tabooing homosexual behaviour to exterminating those categorised 'homosexuals' (Steakley 1975; Lautmann 1980). This 'abomination of Leviticus' appropriated to legitimate policy in contemporary states is one Douglas (1966) did not treat. She extended her analysis from food taboos to bestiality but passed over contiguous passages in Leviticus dealing with same-sex copulation. Several followers (Vura 1979; Gorman 1980; Fry 1974; Plummer 1981), however, have extended her interpretation that 'Holiness requires that individuals shall conform to the class to which they belong. And holiness requires that different classes of things shall not be confused . . . keeping distinct the categories of creation' (Douglas 1966: 67), although homosexual copulation keeps the sexes distinct (as morphological, rather than functional classes) instead of mixing male and female 'classes'.

If taboos against homosexual behaviour were reaction formations against the anxiety provoked by classification difficulties where behaviour departs from the heterosexual, one would expect the taboos to be most intense in societies in which the most important distinction for the production and distribution of subsistence and wealth is male *v.* female. Yet precisely in the heartlands of sexual antagonism (Murphy 1959)—Melanesia and Amazonia—are societies in which protracted periods of exclusive homosexual receptivity is prescribed for would-be warriors (Kelly 1976; Schieffelin 1976; Herdt 1981; 1982; n.d.), or is pervasive, with the same lineage preferences as heterosexual marriage (Lévi-Strauss 1973: 313–14; C. Hugh-Jones 1979: 160–1; S. Hugh-Jones 1979: 110). In the more fully-documented Melanesian cases, as in ancient Greece (Dover 1979) and medieval Egypt (Murray 1981), a homosexual apprenticeship is regarded as masculinising. Homosexual coupling does not confuse anyone about the sex of the participants, for whom such relations do not signify cross-gender identities. Even in the native American cultures in which there was a role for men ordained (by visions) to do 'women's work', there was no confusion —except on the part of observers (as of Oman) —that 'berdaches' were men (Whitehead 1981: 90; Stevenson 1978 [1896]: 472–3). A man who did women's work and cross-dressed was 'thinkable', and so was a man who had sexual relationships with other men (whether or not either enacted the 'berdache' role generally).

Instead of cultures in which gender is the most salient criterion of social organisation with a rigid sexual division of labour, it is in cultures without that those defined by homosexual acts have been targeted for extirpation (notably during periods of rapid social change: see Perry 1980; Gerard 1981; 1982; Bullough 1976: 333–7). Goodich (1979) suggests one motivation in seizure of property. In addition to his examples (notably the Knights Templar), is Henry VIII's avuncular advice to James V, and later to the regent who succeeded him in Scotland, recounting his own earlier suppression of homosexuality in monastic orders as an exemplar of a more efficacious way to raise royal revenue than driving off subjects' sheep (quoted by Knowles 1959: 204–5). Perry (1980) suggests the diversion of unrest as another motivation for the spectacle of incinerating 'sodomites'. Hebrew prophets using prescription of temple prostitution to erect an ethnic boundary is another type of explanation (advanced by Devereux and Loeb 1943: 144–5 and supported by hermeneutic interpretations of the texts such as Bailey 1955; McNeil 1976; Boswell 1980). These seem more plausible explanations than horror inspired by difficulties in classifying the sexes or sexual actors.

To understand the 'abominations' of Leviticus and, even more, contemporary selective appeal to them for legitimation, the text does not suffice, because fitting nature into perfectly discrete categories does not appear to be how cognition operates (see Zadeh 1965; Kay 1978; Coleman and Kay 1981)—even for phenomena for which there are clear extra-linguistic standards to contrast with lexicon, such as colour (Kay & McDaniel 1978). Phenomena which are not prototypes of a category abound, whereas the alleged consequences of not fitting do not.

S. O. Murray

Bailey, D. S. 1955. *Homosexuality and western Christian tradition*. London: Longmans Green.

Berlin, B. 1972. Speculations on the growth of ethnobotanical nomenclature. *Lang. Soc.* **1**, 51–86.

———, D. E. Breedlove & P. H. Raven. 1966. Folk taxonomies and biological classification. *Science* **154**, 273–5.

——— 1968. Covert categories and folk taxonomies. *Am. Anthrop.* **70**, 29–99.

Boswell, J. 1980. *Christianity, social tolerance and homosexuality*. Chicago: Univ. Press.

Brown, C. H. 1977. Folk botanical life forms. *Am. Anthrop.* **79**, 317–42.

——— 1979. Folk zoological life forms. *Am. Anthrop.* **81**, 791–817.

Bulmer, R. 1967. Why is the cassowary not a bird? *Man* (N.S.) **2**, 1–25.

Bullough, V. 1976. *Sexual variance in history and society*. New York: Wiley.

Carrier, J. M. 1975. Urban Mexican male homosexual encounters. Thesis, University of California at Irvine.

Coleman, L. & P. Kay 1981. Prototype semantics. *Language* **57**, 26–44.

Devereux G. & E. M. Loeb 1943. Antagonistic acculturation. *Am. sociol. Rev.* **8**, 133–47.

Douglas, M. 1966. *Purity and danger*. Baltimore: Penguin.

Dover, K. 1979. *Greek homosexuality*. Cambridge: Univ. Press.

Fry, P. 1974. Homosexuality among Afro-Brazilian possession cults. Am. Anthrop. Assoc. meetings, Mexico, D.F.

Gerard, K. 1981. The tulip and the sodomite. Kroeber Anthrop. Soc. meetings, Berkeley.

——— 1982. The erection of the sodomite. Kroeber Anthrop. Soc. meetings, Berkeley.

Goodich, M. 1979. *The unmentionable vice*. Santa Barbara: Ross-Erikson.

Goody, J. 1977. *The domestication of the savage mind*. Cambridge: Univ. Press.

Gorman, M. 1980. A new light on Zion. Thesis, University of Chicago.

Herdt, G. H. 1981. *Guardians of the flute*. New York: McGraw-Hill.

——— 1982. *Male initiation in New Guinea*. Berkeley: Univ. of California Press.

——— n.d. Ritualised homosexual behavior in the male cults of Melanesia: 1862–1982. MS.

Hugh-Jones, C. 1979. *From the Milk River*. Cambridge: Univ. Press.

Hugh-Jones, S. 1979. *The palm and the Pleiades*. Cambridge: Univ. Press.

Humphreys, L. 1975. *Tearoom trade*. Chicago: Aldine.

Hunn, E. S. 1977. *Tzeltal folk zoology*. San Francisco: Academic Press.

Kay, P. 1978. Tahitian words for 'race' and 'class'. *Pub. Soc. Océan.* **39**, 81–91.

——— & C. McDaniel 1978. The linguistic significance of the meaning of basic color terms. *Language* **54**, 610–46.

Kelly, R. 1976. Witchcraft and sexual relations. In *Man and woman in the New Guinea Highlands* (eds) P. Brown & G. Buchbinder. Washington: American Anthropological Association.

Knowles, D. D. 1959. *The religious orders in England*. vol. 3. Cambridge: Univ. Press.

Kuhn, T. S. 1962. *The structure of scientific revolutions*. Chicago: Univ. Press.

Lautmann, R. 1980. *Terror und Hoffnung in Deutschland 1933–1945*. Hamburg: Rowohlt.

Lévi-Strauss, C. 1973. *Tristes tropiques*. New York: Atheneum.

Levy, R. I. 1973. *The Tahitians*. Chicago: Univ. Press.

Mayr, E. 1981. *The growth of biological thought*. Cambridge, Mass.: Harvard Univ. Press.

McNeil, J. J. 1976. *The Church and the homosexual*. Kansas City: Sheed, Andrews & McNeel.

Miller, B. 1978. Adult sexual resocialization. *Alternative Lifestyles* **1**, 207–33.

Murphy, R. F. 1959. Social structure and sexual antagonism. *SWest. J. Anthrop.* **15**, 89–98.

Murray, S. O. 1979. The art of gay insults. *Anthrop. Ling.* **21**, 211–23.

——— 1980. The 'species homosexual' in Guatemala. *Anthrop. Ling.* **22**, 177–85.

——— 1981. The status of women, acceptance of homosexuality and circulation of the Mamluke elite. Pacific Soc. Assoc., meetings, Portland.

——& M. Arboleda in press. Lexical inference. *J. of Homosexuality*.

Perry, M. E. 1980. *Crime and society in early modern Seville*. Hanover: Univ. Press of New England.

Plummer, K. 1981. *The making of the modern homosexual*. London: Hutchinson.

Raven, P. H., B. Berlin & D. E. Breedlove

1971. The origins of taxonomy. *Science* **174**, 1210–13.

Schieffelin, E. L. 1976. *The sorrow of the lonely and the burning of the dancers*. New York: St Martin's.

Searle, J. 1975. The logical stratus of fictional discourse. *New Literary History*.

Steakley, J. 1975. *The homosexual emancipation movement in Germany*. New York: Arno Press.

Stevenson, M. C. 1978 [1896]. A death which caused universal regret. In *Gay American history* (ed.) J. Katz. New York: Avon.

Taylor, C. L. 1978. El Ambiente, Thesis, University of California at Berkeley.

Vura, D. H. 1978. Legitimate intruders. Thesis, University of Arizona.

Weinberg, T. S. 1978. On 'doing' and 'being' gay. *J. Homosexuality* **13**, 1–11.

Whitehead, H. 1981. The bow and the burden strap. In *Sexual meaning* (eds) S. Ortner & H. Whitehead. Cambridge: Univ. Press.

Zadeh, L. 1965. Fuzzy sets. *Information & Control* 8, 338–53.

STIGMA TRANSFORMATION AND RELEXIFICATION: "GAY" IN LATIN AMERICA

by Stephen O. Murray and Manuel Arboleda G.[1]

In the past few years the term "gay" has diffused rapidly in urban Latin America, raising the question whether use of the term reflects changes from a "gender" to a "gay" organization of homosexuality. The latter was characterized by Adam (1979: 18) as one in which "people meet and form enduring social networks only because of mutual homosoexual interest , (2) there is a sense of peoplehood and emerging culture (Murray 1979a; Levine 1979), and (3) there is the possibility of exclusive (non-bisexual) and egalitarian (not role-bound) same-sex relations." In North American cities a shift -- albeit one that is not complete even now -- has occurred. Formerly, the man who took only the insertor role in homosexual coitus (termed "trade" in the homosexual subculture which preceded "gay community") was not identified and did not identify himself as homosexual. Only (some of) those regularly taking an insertee role ("queens") did (Reiss 1961; Humphreys 1975; Murray 1979b; Murray and Poolman 1981). Under the aegis of "gay", an agressively stigma-challenging label (Goffman 1963) without the negative connotations of "queer" or

---

[1]Earlier versions of this paper were presented at the 1982 Pacificic Sociological Association meetings in San Diego and the 1982 American Sociological Association meetings in San Francisco. The authors would like to acknowledge the encouragement of the session organizers -- resepectively, Wayne Wooden and William Devall -- and also that of Niyi Akinnaso, John Gumperz and Amparo Tuson.

"queen", a shift from what might be considered an exogamous system of sexual exchange in which those identifying themselves or fantasized by their partners as "straight" ("trade") were sought to an endogamous system in which both partners identify themselves as "gay" has occurred in Anglo North America. This change has brought ideal norms closer to behavior patterns (Humphreys 1971, 1979; Murray and Poolman 1981; Weinberg 1983; Wolf 1983) and ontogney has recapitulated phylogeny in this transformation to mutual definition by both partners (Miller 1978; Humphreys and Miller 1981).

When the word "gay" was unknown in Latin America, which was as recently as the mid-1970s, homosexual identification was analogous to the pre-gay pattern in Anglo North America: those whose homosexual behavior was confined to the *activo* (insertor) role did not consider themselves defined, nor even implicated by such behavior. Neither did their pasivo partners. *Activos* were simply *hombres* (men -- unmarked), quite regardless of the sex of the persons who received their phallic thrusts. Even those persons who switched roles tended to identify themselves by one role designation or the other and to attempt to constrain any publicity about the other, although there were terms -- *moderno* in Peru and *internacional* in Mesoamerica -- for such dichotomy-transcending conduct.

In Lima in 1976 the term "gay" was not used, and was known only to a very few Peruvians who had traveled to Europe or North America. By 1980, however, the term was widely-known and was

preferred above the previously standard term *entendido* (in the know) by most informants, both self- identified *pasivos* and *activos*. Although outside homosexual networks "gay" was an unfamiliar locution, in October 1980 the popular magazine *Gente* ran a cover story entitled "Los Gays Peruanos Son Libres" (Peruvian Gays are Free). The article itself oscillated between linking "gay"
with effeminacy and using it in the stigma-challenging sense common in North America, that it was used at all to refer to a group usually invisible in respectable publications and completely stereotyped in tabloids in Latin America (see Taylor 1978; Murray 1980a) was remarkable. By 1982 "gay" had entirely replaced *entendido* as a self-designation, but in some cases the spelling pronounciation (gai) was used rather than the phonetic realization borrowed from French or English (i.e., ge(y)).[2]

In Guatemala in 1978 two of five *pasivos* offered "gay" as a term for men who chose other men as sexual partners. The three *pasivo* informants who reported not having friends with similar preferences nor any involvement in settings where such persons congregated were not familiar with the term. Both those who identified themselves as *internacional* (and were much-traveled) used "gay" and remarked that the term was achieving ever wider currency in their country. Of the three *activos* from who lexical data were elicited, one did not know the word, one knew it

[2] Wooden (1982) reports the other solution to the problem of borrowing a word that is spelled in a way other than the one pronounced, i.e., changing the spelling, in Colombia and Venezuela.

TABLE ONE

Frequency of Conceptions of "Un hombre que prefiera los otros hombres" by Place/Time and Sex Role

LOCALE/ YEAR OF ELICITATION REPORTED ROLE	MODEL ONE	MODEL TWO	MODEL THREE	
Guatemala City,1978				
activo	1	1	1	
pasivo	3	2	0	
internacional	0	0	3	
Lima, 1979				
activo	4	2	2	
pasivo	7	3	1	
Mexico City, 1981-3				
	9	6	8	
pasivo	5	3	5	
internacional	0	0	10	
Lima, 1982-3				
activo	0	0	5	
pasivo	2	3	6	
moderno	0	0	4	
PERCENT TOTALS				(N)
activo	36	23	41	(39)
pasivo	43	28	30	(40)
moderno/internacional	0	0	100	(17)
late 70s	50	27	23	(30)
early 80s	24	18	58	(66)

but did not apply it to himself, and one both knew it and applied it to himself. [3]

Words that are borrowed do not necessarily retain the same meaning they had in the source language. For some of our informants "gay" seemed to be used as a fashionable (new and foreign) term that simply replaced *entendido* or *de ambiente* in an unchanged conception of homosexuality, i.e., relexification of the pre-existing conceptual order. For others, however, the new word seemed to reflect a new conception of homosexuality, paralleling the stigma-transformation involved in replacing "queer" and "homosexual" with "gay" in Anglo North America. Table One shows which of these models was held by informants varying in (self-reported) role preference.

Those who answered "No" to the ritualized cruising question, "?Eres activo o´ pasivo?", rather than one or the other, invariably considered those who are *activo* to be gay as well as those who are *pasivo*. For more than a third of those who identified themselves as *activo* and more than half of those who identified themselves as *pasivo* and who were familiar with the word, "gay" was a new word for the already existing conception of homosexuality. Interestingly, those who are stigmatized by this conception are less likely than those who seemingly profit in social esteem by it to embrace the wider conception of who is "gay." A number of explanations

---

[3] See Murray (1980b) for description of the elicitation procedures and social characteristics of this sample. Subsequent waves of repression in Guatemala prevented return fieldwork as well as driving underground a previously emerging subculture.

(including false consciousness, covert prestige among the stigmatized, cognitive dissonance and/or ambivalence on the part of heavily-involved *activos*) might be proffered, if this pattern holds up for larger samples. Here we are concerned with the more certain change over time observable among both *activos* and *pasivos* than with the tenuous differences by sex role.

Although we claim to have observed change in process,[4] it bears emphasizing that all three models in Figure One represent the conception of some men involved in homosexuality in Latin America. Some still use the old word(s), others have borrowed the word "gay" but simply replaced *entendido* with it in the same slot (relexification); but for some others, "gay" refers to a "new man" who can enact (*estar*) *pasivo* behavior without being (*ser*) *un pasivo.*

Although this change parallels the earler Anglo North American one (which is presumably the source of prestige for the label "gay"), some caution is in order before concluding that the development of a stigma-challenging gay community in Anglo North America provides a blueprint of stages that will be copied elsewhere in the world. Although homosexuality in Latin America has been gender-

[4]Although structuralist linguistic orthodoxy held that linguistic change is too slow to observe, Labov (1972) provided refutation. Generational differences in bounding "gay community" were found in the semantic work in San Francisco of Murray and Poolman (1981). The example of not merely observing but explaining linguistic change as reflecting significant social change which has particularly influenced the work presented here is Akinnaso's (1980, 1984) work on Yoruba naming .

defined, just as it was earlier in Anglo North America, residence patterns, censorship of materials that can be interpreted by invidual policemen or judges as politically subversive or incitements to vice, the absence of religious pluralism with its concomitant traditions (and freedoms) of voluntary associations, and other factors that may have been crucial to the history of gay institutional elaboration in Anglo North America but are quite different in Latin America (Taylor 1978; Murray 1980a, 1984; Lacey 1983) may shape different developments to different ends there (and elsewhere). Mexican liberation organizations eschew the term "gay" because their leadership do not consider Anglo gay culture to be what they aspire to emulate. They are also sensitive about "cultural imperialism" from the north and the elitism of expensive local replicas of Anglo gay bars. Moreover, cultures in which homosexuality is age-defined, such as Islamic, Amazonian and Melanesian ones (see Murray 1984, Herdt 1981, 1984) defy any scheme of unililiniear evolution to the "gay" organization of homosexuality even more clearly than the stirrings of change in Latin America (see also Wooden 1982; Kutsche 1983).

REFERENCES

Adam, B.D. Reply. *SGC Newsletter.* 1979, 18.8.

Akinnaso, F.N. The sociolinguistic basis of Yoruba personal names. *Anthropological Linguistics.* 1980. 22. 275-304. Akinnaso, F.N. Yoruba anthroponomy and the preservation of ritual knowledge. *Anthropological Linguistics.* 1984. 26. in press.

Arboleda, M. Gay life in Lima. *Gay Sunshine*. 1980. 42. 30.
Carrier, J.M. *Urban Mexican Male Homosexual Encounters,* Ph.D. thesis, University of California, Irvine. 1975.
---.Cultural factors affecting urban Mexican male homosexual behavior. *Archives of Sexual Behavior*. 1976. 5. 103-124.
Chauncey, G.W.Fairies, pogues and Christian brothers. Paper presented at the Among Men/ Among Women conference in Amsterdam, 1983.
Goffman, E. *Stigma*. Toronto: Prentice-Hall. 1963.
Herdt, G.H. *Guardians of the Flutes*. New York: McGraw-Hill. 1981.
Herdt, G.H. *Ritualized Homosexuality in Melanesia*. Berkeley: University of California Press. 1984.
Humphreys, L. New styles of homosexual manliness. *Transaction*. 1971. 38-65.
Humphreys, L. *Tearoom Trade*. Chicago: Aldine. 1975.
Humphreys, L. Exodus and identity. In M. Levine (Ed.) *Gay Men*. New York: Harper & Row. 1979.
Humphreys, L. & Miller, B. Satellite cultures. In J. Marmor (Ed.) *Homosexuality*. New York: Basic Books. 1981.
Itkin, M-F. On terminology. *Gay Sunshine*. 1971. 7.2.
Kutsche, P. Situational homosexuality in Costa Rica. *ARGOH Newsletter*. 1983. 4,4. 8-13.
Labov, W. *Sociolinguistic Patterns*. Philadelphia: University of Pennsylvania Press. 1972.
Lacey, E.A. *My Deep Dark Pain Is Love*. San Francisco: Gay Sunshine Press. 1983.
Levine, M.P. *Gay Men*. New York: Harper & Row. 1979.

Miller, B. Adult sexual resocialization. *Alternative Lifestyles.* 1978. 1. 207-233.
Murray, S.O. The institutional elaboration of a quasi-ethnic community. *International Review of Modern Sociology.* 1979. 9. 165-177.
--- The art of gay insults. *Anthropological Linguistics.* 1979b. 21. 211-223.
--- *Latino Homosexuality.* San Francisco: Social Networks. 1980a.
--- Lexical and institutional elaboration in Guatemala. *Anthropological Linguistics.* 1980b. 22. 177-185.
--- *Cultural Diversity and Homosexualities*. New York: Irvington Press, 1984.
Murray, S.O.& Poolman, R.C. Folk models of gay community. *Working Papers of the Language Behavior Research Laboratory.* 1981. 51.
Reiss, A.J. The social integration of "queers" and "peers." *Social Problems.* 1961. 9: 102-120.
Taylor, C.L. *El Ambiente.* Ph.D. thesis, University of California, Berkeley, 1978.
Weinberg, T.S. On "doing" and "being" gay. *Journal of Homosexuality* 1978. 4. 143-156.
Wolf, D.G. Growing Older Gay and Lesbian. MS. 1983.
Wooden, W.S. Cultural antecedents of gay communities in Latin America. Paper presented at the American Sociological Association meetings, San Francisco.

SENTIMENTAL EFFUSIONS OF GENITAL CONTACT IN UPPER AMAZONIA

In Northwest Amazonia, as in Melanesia (see Herdt 1982[1]), initiation, more than marriage,[2] is the central "passage from the asexual world of childhood to the sexual world of adults" (S. Hugh-Jones 1979: 110), as well as from family to society. According to Stephen Hugh-Jones (1979: 110),

From an outsider's point of view, one of the most noticeable manifestations of this is the incidence of joking sexual play among initiated but unmarried men. . . Missionaries working in the Pira-parana are frequently shocked by the apparent homosexual behavior of Indian men. However, the Barasana distinguish between this playful sexual activity and serious male homosexuality. This play, rather than coming from a frustration of 'normal' desire, is itself seen as being normal behavior between 'brothers-in-law' and expressed their close, affectionate, and supportive relationship

[1] Gilbert Herdt also called my attention to the Hugh-Jones books; Wayne Dynes to Gregor's..

[2] C. Hugh-Jones (1979: 160) did not consider marriage a signifcant event in the typical life-cycle, because, "Marriage was described as an event in another domain -- that of kinship and inter-group relations [the classic Lévi-Strauss position]. Although there is a sense in which marriage is obviously a life-cycle event, it is not ritualized like birth, menustration, Yurpary rites and death. The phsyiological possibility of a new generation has already been ritually recognized in initiation."

(emphasis on the rhetoric of explaining the observations away added).

He further avers, "Such play does not entail sexual satisfaction," although he does not explain how he concluded that. Lévi-Strauss, who had reported "reciprocal sexual services" by classificatory "brothers-in law" among the Nambikwara in 1943 (:407; also see 1948:95-6) suggested (in a personal communication cited by Hugh-Jones) that "it appears to provide unmarried men with an outlet for sentimental effusions. "Lévi-Strauss (1974:313) also remarked, "It remains an open question whether the partners achieve complete satisfaction or restrict themselves to sentimental demonstrations, accompanied by caresses, similar to the demonstrations and caresses chracteristic of conjugal relationships." Reading this "clarification", I wonder whether it is Lévi-Strauss who defines homosexuality out of the possibility of "complete satisfaction" and also whether "conjugal relationships" exclude ejaculations. Although maintaining that "the brother is acting as a temporary substitute" for his sister (314), he admits, "On reaching adulthood, the brothers-in-law continue to express their feelings quite openly" (314).

Hugh-Jones (1979:110) reports, "A young man will often lie in a hammock with his 'brother-in-law,' nuzzling him, fondling his penis, and talking quietly, often about sexual exploits with women."[3]

One is left wondering if fondled penises on occasion produce effusions more tangible than "sentimental", as they have been reported to do elsewhere in the world, and especially among young men who have little sexual experience, few approved sexual outlets, are "given over to personal display" and to talking about real or fantasized sexual exploits.

Similarly, one wonders how Altaschuler (1964:231) is so sure that young Cayapa boys he saw wrapped around each other on the floor or sharing hammocks confined themselves to homoeroticism in contrast to homosexuality when not observed by him.[4]

Murphy (1955: 82-3) challenged Lévi-Strauss's interpretation of Buell Quain's fieldnotes on the Trumai Indians, maintaining that liaisons could not be predicted along the lines of marriage rules; indeed, that a boy might seduce his own father. The boys made the advances to the men in general. In contrast, among the Yanomamo, "Some of the teen-age

[3] C. Hugh-Jones (1979: 160) similarly noted, "Boys approaching initiation are sometimes involved in homosexual teasing which takes place in hammocks in public: this play is most common between initiated but unmarried youths from separate exogamous groups." This suggests marriage is more important than her statement quoted in note 2 indicates.

[4] His credibility is further reduced by the argument based on Bieber that there could not be the "innovation" of homosexual intercourse, because homosexual behavior is based on feelings of inadequacy, and those who feel inadequate cannot innovate.

males have homosexual affairs with each other; [there too] the females of their own age are usually married" (Chagnon 1977: 76; corroborated by Johannes 1972: 55). In his 1967 dissertation, Chagnon wrote, "Most unmarried young men having homosexual realities with each other but no stigma attached to thise behavior. In fact, most of these bachelors joked about it and simulated copulation with each other in public" (pp. 62-3, note contrast of some/most). Alves da Silva (1962: 181) reported public mutual masturbation by boyrs, although officially, homosexuality only occurrs in the puberty rites for boys (p. 380).

Nimuenadju and Lowie (1938) reported formalized, intense, but apparently non-sexual friendships among another Gê tribe, the Ramko'kamekra. Wagley's 1939 salvage anthropology of the Tapirape, a Southern Amazon tribe with a Tupi-Guarani rather than Gê language were therefore likely pushed from the coast rather than being traditionally jungle dwellers prior to 1500, included reports

> of males in the past who had allowed themselves to be used in anal intercourse by other men. They were treated as favorites by the men, who took them along on hunting trips. There were no men alive in 1939-40 with such a reputation [there were only 187 Tapirape people alive by then]. Kamairaho gave me the names of five men whom he had known during his

> lifetime or about whom his father had told him "had holes." Some of these men were married to women, he said, but at night in the *takana* [men's house] they allowed other men to "eat them" (have anal intercourse). His father told him of one man who took a woman's name and did women's work. . . Older men had said that the "man-woman" had died because she was pregnant. "Her stomach was swollen but there was no womb to allow the child to be born." None of my informants had ever heard of a woman who had taken the male role or who preferred sex with another female (Wagley 1977: 160).

Even during the lifetime of Kamairaho's father, there were not very many Tapirape, so five is a considerable number to be known to be sexually receptive. There is nothing to indicate that these five were younger or judged to be less masculine than their partners; married men, of course, were judged fully adult, in any case. I do not know of any reports of Gê tribes with a "man-woman.' The acceptance of male sexual receptivity without such a role among the Tapirape is as notable as the memory of a the gender crosser.

Gregor (1985) added a muddled account of conceptions of homosexuality as (1) inconceivable, (2) situational, and (3) forgotten for the Mehinaku of the Xingu River. The evidence for inconceivable is the lack of a "term for the role of homosexual." As usual with such assertions, Gregor's is not accompanied by explanation of what role it was he attempted to elicit by what means. "Situational", the second line of defense (whether Gregor's or Mehinakus') is that young men from other villages "consorted with the white man [because] they wanted gifts. They had no sexual interest in him whatsoever. Admittedly, they were foolish to have participated, but no man really desires homosexual relations" (60). This rationalization (and its possible shaping by acculturative pressures) is passed on without comment by a Freudian ethographer! What he comments on in relating a myth about a man who got pregnant from having sex with his friend is the lack of elaboration in the tale. Gregor concludes his muddled account of Mehinaku conceptions by relating

> one historical instance. . . of a Mehinaku who, though uninfluenced by perverted [one does not know if this is supposed to be the Mehinaku view or is Gregor's own] outsiders, stepped beyond the boundaries of the masculine role. Tenejumine, "Slightly a Woman", as this person is referred to today, died more than forty-five years ago. . . grew up to assume the dress and role of a woman. . . [and] all agree that he formed special relationships with a few of the men that resembled those of lovers. The men, it is said, would get into the same hammock

as Slightly a Woman and "pretend" to engage in sex play. (61)

To preserve tribal honor, Tenejumine's partners are attributed the same rationalization used now: they only wanted presents. Gregor is struck that memories of Tenejumine are not clearer, though Tenejumine was two generations removed from Gregor's informants, who were not even descended from him.

In an earlier, less Freudian ethnography, Gregor (1977: 254) had written, "The villagers tolerate sexual deviance. Girls who experiment in lesbian affairs or men who participate in homosexual encounters are regarded as extremely foolish, but no one would directly interfere," and more calmly discussed the "mutability of gender" in Mehinaku myth and ritual.

Soares de Souza (1851 [1587]: 316) asserted the Tupinamba were "addicted to sodomy and do not consider it a shame... In the bush some offer themselves to all who want them."

In the upper Amazon, Tessman (1930:361) found, that

> While there are no homosexuals with masculine tendencies, there are some with extreme effeminacy. My informants knew of two such instances. One of them wears woman's clothing. . . [The other] wears man's clothing, but likes to do all the work that is generally done by women. He asked one member of our expedition to address him with a

woman's name and not with his masculine name. He lives with a settler and prostitutes himself as the passive patner to the settler's workers. He pays his lovers. He never practices active sexual intercourse.

Paul Fejos' (1948:106-7) ethnogaphy of a Uitoto-speaking tribe, included a description of a Yagua dandy. Either this description or personal communications led Ford and Beach (1951) to code Witoto as a tolerant-to-homosexuality culture. There is also a stray reference in Holmberg (1950: 169) to a man-woman among the Siriono of Eastern Bolivia. Among the depopulated Wachipaeri, Lyon (1984: 258) reported one enduring homosexual relationship.

A more extended description of widespread homosexual play and of fairly-enduring but "open" relationships is provided by Sorenson (1984: 184-8). He says, "Young men sit around enticingly sedate and formal in all their finery, or form troupes of panpipe-playing dancers" (185). Occasional sex is regarded as expectable behavior among friends; one is marked as nonfriendly --enemy -- if he does not join, especially in the youth "age group" (roughly 15 - 35). . . Homosexual activity is limited neither to within an "age group" nor to unmarried men (1984). Moreover, inter-village homosexuality is encouraged and some "best friends" relationships develop. That the "best friend" is more likely later to marry a sister of his "best friend" is implied in Sorenson's report (189).

At peripheries of what is considered "Amazonia" there are reports that do not attempt to argue away the sexual components of gender variance (see also the discussion of Araucanian shamans in this volume). Kirchoff (1948:486) reported homosexual relations to have been very common and publicly condoned among tribes north of the Orinoco River. Wilbert (1972) reported that among the Warao, who live in the Orinoco delta, male transvestites sometimes lived in union with other men. Among the tribes of north-central Venezuela, Hernández de Alba (1948:478) reported "sexual inverts" who "wore their hair shoulder length, were sodomists, practiced transvestism, avoided going to war, and carried on traditional tasks of women, such as spinning and weaving." Hill et al. (1956:29) reported one 40ish Warao transvestite who did women's work and another man "married" to three men younger than he. A Warao lexeme for the transvestitc role, *tiraguina,* was reported by Turrado Moreno (1945: 296).

Far to the south, Métraux (1948:: 324) used the term "Berdache" for such behavior, including explicit sexualization of the role, among a tribe of the Chaco. He reported, "Berdaches were very common among the Mbayá. They dressed and spoke like women, pretended to menstruate and engaged in feminine activities. They were regarded as the prostitutes of the village."

UPPER AMAZONIA

Male homosexuality among the Cagaba Kogi of Colombia was reported by Bolinder (1925: 114) and Reichel-Dolmatoff (1951: 290). The men of the neighboring Goajiro had (have?) a considerable reputation as lovers of men, including some cross-dressing men doing women's work (Bolinder 1925:114, 1957:61; Armosrong and Métraux 1948: 379)

Some of the denials that homosexual behavior among "my people" is "really homosexuality" say more about the observer than the observed. In other cases (Werner 1984: 130-1; and to some degree Gregor 1984), denials of what can be observed come from natives. In such cases, it is difficult to know whether the concern that imputations of accepting homosexuality will stigmatize their tribe are the result of Western acculturation or more venerable cultural concerns.

REFERENCES

Alves da Silva, Alcionilio B. (1962) *A Civilicação Indigena do Uaupés.* São Paulo: Centro de Pesquisos de Iauraté.

Alt.ꜞschuler, Milton (1964) *The Cayapa.* Ph.D. dissertation, University of Minnesota.

Armstrong, John M. and Alfred Métraux (1948) "Goajiro." *Handbook of South American Indians* 4:379.

Bolinder, Gustaf (1925) *Die Indianer der Trapishen.* Stuttgart: Strecker und Schröder.

Chagnon, Napoleon A. (1967) Yanomamo Warfare, Social Organizationand Marriage Alliance. Ph.D. dissertation, University of Michigan.

---(1977) *Yanomamo* . New York: Holt & Rinehart.
Fejos, Paul (1948) *Ethnography of Yagua.* Viking Fund Publication in Anthropology 1.
Ford, Clellan and Frank Beach (1951) *Patterns of Sexual Behavior.* New York: Harper & Row.
Gregor, Thomas (1977) *Mehunaku.* Chicago: University of Chicago Press.
(1985) *Anxious Pleasures: The Sexual Life of an Amazonian People.* Chicago: University of Chicago Press.
Hernández de Alba, Gregorio (1948) "The tribes of north central Venezuela." *Handbook of South American Indians* 4:478.
Herdt, Gilbert H. (1982) *Rituals of Manhood.* Berkeley: University of California Press.
Hill, George W. et al. (1956) *Los Guarao del Delta Amacuro.* Caracas: Universidad Central de Venezuela.
Holmberg, Alan R. (1950) *Nomads of the Long Bow: The Siriono of Eastern Bolivia* . New York: American Museum of Science.
Hugh-Jones, Christine (1979) *From the Milk River.* Cambridge University of Press.
Hugh-Jones, Stephen (1979) *The Palm and the Pleiades.* Cambridge University of Press.
Kirchoff, Paul (1948) "The tribes north of the Orinoco River." *Handbook of South American Indians* 5: 486.
Lévi-Strauss, Claude (1943) "Social uses of kinship terms among Brazilian Indians." *American Anthro.pologist* 45: 395-401.

--- (1948) "La vie familiale et sociale des Indiens Nambikwara." *Journal de la Société des Americanistes de Paris* 37: 75-96.

--- (1974) *Tristes Tropiques.* NY: Atheneum.

Lyon, Patricia J. (1984) "Changes in Wachipaeri marriage patterns." *Illinois Studies in Anthropologist* 14:248.

Magalães de Gandova, Pedro (1922 [1576]) in *Documents and Narratives Concerning the Discovery and Conquest of Latin America,* HRAF files.

Métraux, Alfred (1948) "Ethnography of the Chaco."*Handbook of South American Indians* 1:324

Murphy, Robert F. & Buell Quain (1955) The Trumai Indians of Central Brazil. *American Ethnol.ogical Society Monograph* 24.

Nimuenadju, Curt and Robert H. Lowie (1938) "The social structure of the Ramko'kamekra (Canella)." *American Anthropologist* 40: 51-74.

Reichel-Dolmatoff, Gerardo (1951) *Los Kogi.* Bofotá: Iqueima.

Soares de Souza, Gabriel (1851 [1587]) "Tratado descriptivo do Brazil em 1587." *Instituto Histórico e Geográfico do Brazil Revista* 14.

Sorenson, Arthur P. (1984) "Linguistic exogamy and personal choice in the Northwest Amazon." *Illinois Studies in Anthropology* 14:180-93.

Tessman, Günter (1930) *Die Indianer Nordost-Perus.* Hamburg: de Gruyter.

Turrado Moreno, Ángel (1945) *Etnografía de los Indios Guaraunos.* Caracas: Vargas.

UPPER AMAZONIA

Wagley, Charles (1977) *Welcome of Tears* . Oxford University of Press.
Wilbert, Johannes (1972) *Survivors of Eldorado* . New York: Praeger.

MISTAKING FANTASY FOR ETHNOGRAPHY[1]

by Stephen O. Murray

Informal communication among experts usually ensures that dubious work is ignored. So long as suspect results are not built upon nor enshrined as established knowledge, experts feel no need to pillory it in public (Barnes 1972: 287; Murray 1980). "Ignoring what is regarded as non-science is standard operating procedure in all scientific disciplines. Only when suspect work is taken seriously by some scientists is a need for public discussion felt," as Murray (1979:191) observed of another case of purported ethnography (see de Mille 1976, 1980).

Tobias Schneebaum's (1969) account of homosexuality and cannibalism in which he said he participated during 1956 among a heretofore undiscovered Amazonian tribe presents another case in which the informal professional dismissal of specialists need to be made explicit, since psychologists and sociologists in search of vivid examples have mistaken it for ethnography. Schneebaum provided the major example of culture-wide homosexual preference -- " in which all the men in an entire tribe maintain an ongoing predominant homosexuality" -- in Tripp's (1975: 64) widely- diffused (and for the most part

[1] Reprinted from the *ARGOH Newsletter*. The aid and encouragement provided by Richard de Mille are gratefully acknowledged.

sensible) book, was taken as exemplary by Mehan and Wood (1975: 27-31),[2] and used by Dover (1978:100) as authentic ethnographic evidence.

Schneebaum himself was careful to note, "There will be no pretense of objectivity here" (1969: 17), adding to the paperback edition a further disclaimer, "This book is not an attempt at an anthropological account of a tribe" (1970: viii), and reiterated the subjectivity of his writing (1979, 1980).

Anthropologists concerned with Amazonia did not take *Keep the River on Your Right* seriously. It was not reviewed in *The American Anthropologist* and has not been cited by anthropologists as a valid report of an Amazonian culture or typical behavior within an existing human group. An expert on Amazonia, Napoleon Chagnon, unequivocally stated, "What he described in this work can only be taken as a highly fictionalized account, a gross and inappropriate villification" (1969: 12). Since this judgment was registered in the 1969 *Book Review Digest,* it was readily available to anyone made suspicious enough by the unusualness of what Schneebaum described (or by the ripeness of his prose) to check whether the book was taken

[2] That both of what are regarded as exemplary ethnographies by the explicators of the "reality" of ethnomethodology are fiction fits perfectly with "Agnes" duping Garfinkel in the original *Studies in Ethnomethodology* (1967), could not be bothered by mere facts to revise his chapter; Stoller 1968, on the other hand, frankly admitted his earlier misdiagnosis).

seriously. T.R. Moore, an anthropologist who studied the same tribe with which Schneebaum stayed, reported

> *Keep the River on Your Right* is neither an ethnological study nor an accurate factual account, as Schneebaum himself makes clear. . . There is no evidence for Amarakaeri cannibalism. . . The character Schneebaum calls "Manolo" and reports beheaded and probably cannibalized [in 1956] was living in Ayacucho in the early 1960s. The sleeping arrangements and homosexual practices Schneebaum describes are not part of the Amarakaeri tradition (quoted in de Mille 1980: 74).

Travelers' reports predating scientific study of a culture cannot be ignored, but such reports must not be accepted uncritically -- especially when they include explicit disclaimers such as Schneebaum made, are wholly at variance with what is known about neighboring cultures, and are embedded in what seems to be wish fulfillment.

REFERENCES

Barnes, Barry (1972) *Sociology of Science.* Baltimore: Penguin.

Chagnon, Napoleon A. (1969) "Love among the cannibals."*Book World,* 21 September 1969, 3(38): 12.

de Mille, Richard (1976, 1978) *Castañeda's Journey.* Santa Barbara: Capra.

FANTASY

---(1980) *The Don Juan Papers.* Santa Barbara: Ross-Erikson.

Dover, Kenneth J. (1978) *Greek Homosexuality.* Cambridge: Harvard Univ. Press.

Garfinkel, Harold (1967) *Studies in Ethnomethodology.* Toronto: Prentice-Hall.

Mehan, Hugh & Houston Wood (1975) *The Reality of Ethnomethodology.* NY: Wiley.

Moore, T.R. (1980) *The White Peace of Madre de Dios.* Ph.D. thesis, New School for Social Research.

Murray, Stephen O. (1979) The scientific reception of Castañeda. *Contemporary Sociology* 8: 189-196.

---(1980) The invisibility of scientific scorn. In de Mille (1980).

Schneebaum, Tobias (1969, 1970) *Keep the River on Your Right.* NY: Grove

--- (1979) *Wild Man.* NY: Viking.

--- (1980) Realities loved and unloved. In de Mille (1980).

Stoller, Robert J. (1968) A further contribution to the study of gender identity. *International J.ournal of Psychoanlysis* 49: 364-369.

Tripp, C.A. (1975) *The Homosexual Matrix.* NY: Signet.

ROOTS

THE ZUNI MAN-WOMAN

by Will Roscoe

Will Roscoe has shown his slide-show on the American Indian berdache—the "Zuni Man-Woman: A Traditional Gay Role"—on both coasts. As coordinator for the History Project of Gay American Indians, he edited Living the Spirit: A Gay American Indian Anthology (St. Martin's Press, 1988).

ON A COLD December day in 1896, six great warrior-birds, the Sha'lakos, ten feet high with beaks that snapped and eyes that rolled in their sockets, descended from the southern mesas at dusk to the outskirts of the ancient village called the Anthill at the Middle of the World. That night they would dance in the six houses newly erected to receive them—for one night, all night—diving, bobbing, careening madly to the awe and delight of the onlookers. They would bestow their blessings of increase and health, and receive in turn the prayers of the people for snow and rain in the season to come.

There was little to distinguish the Sha'lako festival of 1896 from any other observed by the Zuni Indians from time immemorial up to the present day. The Zunis and their ancestors have occupied the same location in western New Mexico for two thousand years or more—long enough to view their homeland as the middle of the world. In 1896, however, one of the families selected to host a Sha'lako god included a "noted and prominent" Zuni named We'wha (WEE'wha). An accomplished artist and craftsman, an active participant in religious and ceremonial life, We'wha had served as a cultural ambassador for the Zunis when he traveled to Washington in 1886 and shook hands with the president. Six years later, he spent a month in jail for resisting soldiers sent by that same government to interfere in his community's affairs.

We'wha was also a berdache, to use the currently accepted anthropological term, or *lhamana* in the Zuni language, a man who combined the work and social roles of both men and women, an artist and a priest who dressed, at least in part, in women's clothes.

In 1896, We'wha had labored long and hard in preparation for the Sha'lako, carefully laying the stone floor in the large room where the bird-god would dance. Not yet fifty, he nonetheless suffered from heart disease, and, according to his white friend, anthropologist Matilda Coxe Stevenson, the effort proved too much. When the time came for the arrival of the god, We'wha could not attend. He was "listless and remained alone as much as possible." Stevenson, who refers to We'wha using female pronouns, joined her friend of over fifteen years in his final hours.

> We'wha was found crouching on the ledge by the fireplace.... Only a few days before, this strong-minded, generous-hearted creature had labored to make ready for the reception of her gods; now she was preparing to go to her beloved [Sacred Lake, site of "Zuni heaven"]....
>
> We'wha asked the writer to come close and in a feeble voice she said, in English: "Mother, I am going to the other world. I will tell the gods of you and Captain Stevenson. I will tell

them of Captain Carlisle, the great seed priest, and his wife, whom I love. They are my friends. Tell them good-by. Tell all my friends in Washington good-by. Tell President Cleveland, my friend, good-by. Mother, love all my people; protect them; they are your children; you are their mother...."

She leaned forward with the [prayersticks] tightly clasped, and as the setting sun lighted up the western windows, darkness and desolation entered the hearts of the mourners, for We'wha was dead.[1]

Among the Zunis, the death of the berdache We'wha elicited "universal regret and distress." Similar sentiments existed in as many as 130 American Indian tribes known to have had male and female berdache roles.[2] What is it that American Indians saw in these men and women who bridged genders that Western civilization has overlooked or denied?

I have focused on the Zuni berdache in order to study how this role fit into a specific cultural context, to look at all its social, economic, and religious facets as well as sexuality and gender. I cannot share here all that I've learned about We'wha and the Zuni philosophy of gender (I am writing a book to cover that!), but I would like to describe how I arrived at my interpretation of the Zuni berdache and why, in particular, I have abandoned the cross-gender model. In the process, I hope to explain why I refer to the Zuni berdache—or *lhamana*—as a "traditional gay role."

Life and Times of We'wha

By any standards, We'wha was an important member of his community. Stevenson described him as "the strongest character and the most intelligent of the Zuni tribe." The anthropologist Elsie Clews Parsons referred to him as "the celebrated *lhamana*." Robert Bunker, an Indian agent at Zuni in the 1940s, wrote, "We'wha, that man of enormous strength who lived a woman's daily life in woman's dress, but remained a power in his pueblo's gravest councils."[3] Today, nearly a hundred years since his death, Zunis still remember stories about We'wha.

SMITHSONIAN INSTITUTION, NATIONAL ANTHROPOLOGICAL ARCHIVES, NEG. 85-8666

We'wha

"We'wha, that man of enormous strength who lived a woman's daily life in woman's dress, but remained a power in his pueblo's gravest councils." Today, nearly a hundred years since his death, Zunis still remember stories about We'wha.

Born in 1849, three years after the United States seized control of the Southwest from Mexico, he lived to witness the influx of U.S. anthropologists, missionaries, Indian agents, traders, tourists, and settlers that threatened to disrupt Zuni life and overrun Zuni lands. He made important contributions to his tribe's response to these events. He helped develop commercial markets for traditional crafts, and he forged friendships with non-Indians who became advocates for Zuni interests.

Traveling to Zuni on a government-sponsored expedition, James and Matilda Stevenson met We'wha in 1879. Matilda Stevenson found the berdache well-qualified as an anthropological informant. We'wha "possessed an indomitable will and an insatiable thirst for knowledge"; he was "especially versed in their ancient lore."[4] We'wha became a key informant for Stevenson's exhaustive report on the Zunis, published in 1904.

Although We'wha wore female clothing, his masculine features seem obvious to us today.[5] Stevenson described him as "the tallest person in Zuni; certainly the strongest."[6] Still, for many years, she believed We'wha was a woman. Other visitors were told by the Zunis themselves that We'wha was a man. "It was the comments of her own friends, Zunis," noted one traveler, "that first made me 'wise' to the situation as to her sex."[7] When Stevenson did discover the truth, she wrote, "As the writer could never think of her faithful and devoted friend in any other light, she will continue to use the feminine gender when referring to We'wha."[8]

The Zunis, however, never ignored the fact that We'wha was male. As Stevenson herself observed, the Zunis referred to *lhamanas* by saying, "'She is a man'; which is certainly misleading to one not familiar with Indian thought."[9] In this usage, "she" connotes a social role, while in English "she" connotes biological sex. I use male pronouns in writing of We'wha to convey in English the same understanding a Zuni had: that We'wha was biologically male. In fact, Zuni berdaches underwent one of two male initiation rites, and they participated in the all-male societies responsible for portraying the gods, or kachinas, in sacred masked dances. In an 1881 census of the tribe, We'wha's occupations were listed as "Farmer; Weaver; Potter; Housekeeper"—the first two are traditionally men's activities, the last two women's.[10]

Like berdaches in many tribes, We'wha was a crafts specialist. He was known for his skill in both pottery and weaving. His early sales to collectors like Stevenson and the writer-lecturer George Wharton James prefigured a key development of the twentieth century—the emergence of commercial markets for native arts, an important source of economic independence for many Southwest Indians today. We'wha was also one of the first Zunis to earn cash. After Stevenson showed him the benefits of using soap to wash clothes, he went into business doing laundry for local whites.

In 1886, We'wha spent six months with the Stevensons in Washington, D.C. While Indian visits to the national capital were frequent in the nineteenth century, few Indians stayed as long or maintained as high a profile as the Zuni berdache We'wha.

In 1886, We'wha spent six months with the Stevensons in Washington, D.C. While Indian visits to the national capital were frequent in the nineteenth century, few Indians stayed as long or maintained as high a profile as the Zuni berdache We'wha.

According to Stevenson, We'wha "came in contact only with the highest conditions of culture, dining and receiving with some of the most distinguished women of the national capital."[11] He met Speaker of the House John Carlisle and other dignitaries. In May, he appeared at the National Theatre in an amateur theatrical event sponsored by local society women to benefit charity. According to a newspaper account, We'wha received "deafening" applause from an audience that included senators, congressmen, diplomats and Supreme Court justices.[12] In June, We'wha called on President Cleveland and presented him with a gift of his "handiwork."[13]

An article from a local paper illustrates the typical reaction of Washingtonians to the Zuni berdache:

> Folks who have formed poetic ideals of Indian maidens, after the pattern of Pocahontas or Minnehaha, might be disappointed in Wa-Wah on first sight. Her features, and especially her mouth, are rather large; her figure and carriage rather masculine.... Wa-Wah, who speaks a little English, and whose manner is very gentle, said that it took her six days to weave the blanket she wears.[14]

During his stay, We'wha demonstrated weaving at the Smithsonian and helped Stevenson and other anthropologists document Zuni traditions. He continued to follow Zuni religious practices, offering corn meal daily and making prayerstick offerings (normally a male activity) for the summer solstice, an important Zuni religious occasion. Despite his easy adaptation to Washington society, however, We'wha remained unchanged. His attitude towards the white world is conveyed in a story that Edmund Wilson heard at Zuni in the 1940s: "When he returned to the pueblo, he assured his compatriots that the white women were mostly frauds, for he had seen them, in the ladies' rooms, taking out their false teeth and the 'rats' from their hair."[15]

One incident from We'wha's life is especially revealing. In 1892, a young Zuni named Nick Tumaka was accused of witchcraft. Witchcraft—the anti-social use of tribal magic for revenge or personal gain—was the only real crime at Zuni. Nick came under suspicion because he had been raised by whites, spoke English, and rejected Zuni religion.

One night the Zuni governor gave Nick some whiskey. Nick got drunk and claimed to have witch-like powers. The bow priests—leaders of the warrior society—attempted to try Nick, which meant hanging him from the rafters of the old mission until he confessed. Nick called for help and was rescued by white friends who sent for soldiers from nearby Fort Wingate.

A small army detachment arrived to arrest the Zuni governor. At his doorway, however, the soldiers were met by the governor's "younger brother"—We'wha, one of the "tallest and strongest" members of the tribe. Lina Zuni told the story of what happened next to anthropologist Ruth Bunzel:

> [The soldiers] were going to take my sister's husband.... His younger brother, although he was a man in woman's dress, got angry. He hit the soldiers. When they were going to take his brother, although he pretended to be a woman, he hit them. He was strong. He stood, holding the door posts, and would not let them come in.[16]

The soldiers returned in full force—nearly two hundred men armed with guns and field artillery. The circumstances, and the potential for disaster, were similar to those at Wounded Knee, where three hundred Indians had been killed in 1890 by trigger-happy soldiers. We'wha, the governor, and the leading bow priest were arrested. We'wha spent a month in jail at Fort Wingate.[17] These arrests were an attack on the political and cultural independence of the Zunis. It was in this same period that the Pueblo Indian agent wrote to a school teacher at Zuni, "It is going to be quite a task to do away with their custom of the men wearing female dress, but I have made up my mind to make an effort to do so."[18]

The Puzzle of the Pants

We'wha's physical resistance against U.S. soldiers was uncharacteristic of Zuni men, let alone someone who had presumably crossed genders to become a woman. In fact, as my research proceeded, it became clear that We'wha was not crossing genders, but *bridging* or *combining* the social roles of men and women.

In terms of *religion*, for example, We'wha had been initiated into a male kiva society and fulfilled such male religious roles as reciting prayers on ceremonial occasions and making prayersticks. At the same time, he was knowledgeable in the religious lore of women—for example, the rites and observances that surrounded pottery making.

In terms of *economic* roles, We'wha participated in both male and female activities. He specialized in weaving and pottery, which were male and female crafts, respectively, in most pueblos. He apparently engaged in farming, too—another male role. At the same time, he helped manage his family's household, a woman's role.

We'wha bridged genders in terms of *kinship* roles as well. The Lina Zuni used the kinship term for "younger brother" to refer to We'wha. The part he took within his household, however, was that of daughter or sister.

Finally, in terms of *behavior*, We'wha's self-assurance and independence stood out from both men and women. He traveled widely in the white world at a time when few Zunis had ever left the reservation, and his resistance against the soldiers was particularly remarkable.

In short, although We'wha wore a woman's dress, he didn't "act the part."

Folks who have formed poetic ideals of Indian maidens, after the pattern of Pocahontas or Minnehaha, might be disappointed in We'wha on first sight. Her features, and especially her mouth, are rather large; her figure and carriage rather masculine.

BUREAU OF AMERICAN ETHNOLOGY

We'wha weaving belt

The inappropriateness of a cross-gender model is best illustrated in the rites observed by We'wha's family following his death in 1896. According to Stevenson, "After the body was bathed and rubbed with meal, a pair of white cotton trousers were drawn over the legs, the first male attire she had worn since she had adopted woman's dress years ago."[19] The body was carried to the cemetery in front of the old Zuni Mission. According to Zuni custom, men were buried on the south side of this cemetery, women on the north. Where was We'wha buried?

When Elsie Parsons asked a Zuni elder this question, he replied, "On the south side, the men's side, of course.... Is this not a man?"[20]

If We'wha had crossed genders to become a woman, as the gender-crossing model posits, why the pants, and why was he buried on the *men's* side? I call this problem "the dilemma of the dress" or "the puzzle of the pants."

If We'wha had crossed genders to become a woman, as the gender-crossing model posits, why the pants, and why was he buried on the men's side?

Zuni Gender: Raw and Cooked

Answers came from my study of Zuni philosophy and two key concepts in Zuni thought: the categories of the "raw" (*ky'apin*) and the "cooked" (*'akna*). "Raw" people include animals, natural elements, and supernatural beings. They are unfixed and can change form easily. They are powerful and, for this reason, dangerous.

The Zunis extend these concepts to human beings. "Cooking" is a metaphor for individual development. Newborn infants are "raw" because they are unsocialized. Adult Zunis are "cooked" because they have learned the forms of Zuni culture and have assumed adult roles in the social and religious life of the tribe. In Western terms, the "cooked person" might be described as "civilized" or "cultured."

"Cooking" is marked by a series of initiations which occur at key points in the life cycle. In these rites, individuals are identified with symbols of an ideal natural and social order. These include gender symbols which are relatively undifferentiated at infancy, but increasingly specialized as the individual reaches adulthood. The Zunis view gender as an *acquired* trait, an outcome of becoming a "cooked" person.

Of course, the Zunis are aware of the biological differences between males and females. The first religious symbol bestowed on the child is a perfect ear of corn. Male infants are given a single ear of corn; females a double ear, in which two ears have grown together. The "raw" material of both is the same, however—seeds of corn. And like seed, biological sex represents only a potential—it requires nurtur-

History Comes Home:

Gay Studies on the Rez

"I'M GIVING A slide show at Zuni!"

My San Francisco Indian friends were impressed but skeptical. Many had left reservations—the "rez"—to escape homophobia and sexism. Now I was about to take my slide show on Zuni berdaches back to the rez. "You'll love it!" one gay Indian assured me. "You're brave!" another warned.

For the past fifteen years lesbians and gay men, Indian and non-Indian, have been recovering the history of the berdache role in North America. But the connection between the sexual definition of gay identity in Western culture and the economic definition of berdaches typical of American Indians (individuals who do the work of the other sex) is not immediately apparent. Randy Burns, cofounder of Gay American Indians, declares, "These are our traditional gay Indian ancestors." But getting from there (dress-wearing men and warrior women) to here (urban gay lifestyles) has taken inquiry, reflection, and dialogue.

In 1986, I began presenting my research on the Zuni Indians of New Mexico in a slide-lecture, "The Zuni Man-Woman: A Traditional Gay Role." I argue that the berdache role included not only sexual, but social, economic, and religious dimensions, and that this multi-dimensional model can help us redefine our more limited category of "homosexuality." As the scope of my research grew, however, I felt the need to present my work to Zunis before I could consider my project complete. How to do this, however, eluded me until two anthropologists working with the tribe attended my slide show. They provided me with detailed advice on how to approach the tribe. "Zuni runs a little like Latin America," I was warned, "but in its own special way."

I began by writing to the tribal council requesting permission to present a lecture in the pueblo. I wanted to benefit from the reactions of a Zuni audience, I explained. My program would describe "key events and personalities" of the late nineteenth century. "I also have a good deal of new material on We'wha," I added, "a weaver and potter who spent six months in Washington in 1886, and the unique role he filled in the tribe."

The tribal council approved my request and referred the letter to the tribal archivist. By happy coincidence, I ran into her a few days later at the Museum of the American Indian in New York City. That personal connection helped the process that followed. We eventually scheduled presentations at both the tribal building and Zuni High School for November 1987.

The plane from Los Angeles to Albuquerque flew directly over Zuni. The village sprawled below us with Corn Mountain, the dramatic red and white mesa, to the south, and Twin Buttes to the north. Backtracking from Albuquerque to Gallup, the nearest white town and the nearest motel, took the rest of the day.

We arrived in Zuni the next morning. The first sight was encouraging: a bright red flyer announcing the event on the window of the arts and crafts shop in the tribal building. As soon as we had downed some black coffee and Zuni bread with the archivist, we were taken to meet the tribal council, beginning a round of introductions that continued throughout our stay. At two o'clock that afternoon, I gave my first talk to a Zuni audience—a crowded classroom of teenagers at Zuni High School.

How would the We'wha play on the rez? When Bradley Rose agreed to join me, we joked that his role would be to keep the car running while I talked.

In planning my slide-lecture for the Zunis, however, I knew I

COURTESY OF THE SMITHSONIAN INSTITUTION

could count on their interest in Zuni culture and history. I felt I could build a bridge to We'wha by placing him in the context of traditional society. I made the idea of "continuity-in-change" my theme, and I identified four traditional Zuni strategies for dealing with change, tracing them from prehistory through the European period. These were: friendship (forming alliances with outsiders), adapting (accepting new products and practices but integrating them into existing categories), adopting (transforming individuals and groups into Zunis by teaching them Zuni culture), and resisting (confrontation with outsiders). After introducing these strategies, I discussed how they were used by four Zuni leaders of a hundred years ago—and here I included We'wha, placing him on the same level as governors, war leaders, diplomats, and priests. If I was wrong about Zuni acceptance of berdaches and the high regard for We'wha, I would surely find out!

That my first presentation would be at the high school certainly added to my anticipation. My worst fear was that once the students saw pictures of We'wha they would start to giggle—and not stop. Adult Indians, of course, might simply denounce me on any number of grounds.

But my fears were unrealized. We'wha provoked giggles—but in the end, as I described his trip to Washington, D.C. in 1886 the laughs were on white society, so willing to accept the six-foot tall Zuni berdache as an "Indian maiden" and "princess." The public presentation that evening was also a pleasant surprise. Despite a variety of scheduling problems, we filled the room. When the archivist showed up with a tray of cheese and jars of punch I felt at home—food is always a part of successful Indian events.

After I spoke, members of the tribal council made closing comments. "This was a very good program," one of the councillors began, "and we thank Mr. Roscoe very much, *but…,*" Brad and I exchanged nervous glances. "But have our children seen this history?" To that, of course, the archivist and I could reply that his children had indeed seen the program, that afternoon.

Soon after our arrival, we were befriended by a young Zuni who became an unexpected source of introductions and information. Like We'wha, he had "an insatiable thirst for knowledge." The time we spent together driving around Zuni and the outlying countryside proved constantly interesting as he drilled us in our pronunciation of Zuni words and shared endless details about Zuni customs, places, and people. He took a particular interest in the berdache kachina. He xeroxed an illustration from an old anthropological report and took it to an older relative to learn more about the figure. We left Zuni excited by our new contacts and touched by the warmth shown us. ▼

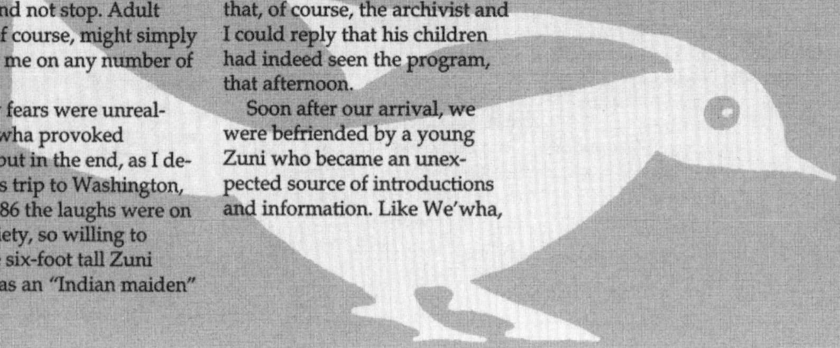

ing and cultivation before it will yield anything of social value. In the Zuni view, biological sex may distinguish male and female infants, but it does not make them men or women—that takes social intervention, "cooking."

Traditionally, until children receive a name at the age of five or six, they are addressed simply as "child," without reference to gender. Boys, to achieve adulthood, undergo two initiations. The first emphasizes the symbols of agriculture and the role of men as farmers. In the second, the initiates encounter fearful warrior kachinas who represent male roles in hunting and warfare.

With this insight into the Zuni philosophy of gender, it is possible to unravel the "puzzle of the pants."

Zuni berdaches receive the first male initiation "just like the other boys."[21] However, boys who manifest berdache interests do not receive the second male initiation. This means that, while they are eligible to participate in some male religious activities, berdaches were not eligible to participate in the male activities of hunting and warfare. The Zuni berdache, in Zuni terms, is an "unfinished" male—not an ersatz female.

These concepts explain the rites observed at We'wha's burial. At birth, in his raw state, We'wha was male. In the process of becoming a cooked person, however, he specialized in the roles of women, combining these with male roles. At death, he became raw again, returning to the spirit world the way he had arrived in this one, as a biological male. Therefore, he was buried on the male side of the cemetery. He was clothed in a woman's dress to symbolize his outward, social identity, with pants beneath the dress to symbolize his original state as a male.

We'wha was a specialist not just in women's work but in cultural work in general. Bridging genders meant drawing from the economic, social, and religious roles of both men and women to create a unique synthesis, neither male nor female.

In the Zuni theory of individuation, males and females begin from the same raw material. Gender arises through "cooking" and it becomes the basis for other specializations—work roles, social roles, kinship, and religion. At the same time, the Zunis recognized a danger in too *much* division of the sexes. The differences between men and women could become mutually exclusive, their interests at odds, the basis for mutuality undermined. The supernatural counterpart of the berdache, the kachina, Ko'lhamana, helps bridge this division.

Ko'lhamana (*lhamana*, or berdache, plus *Ko-*, the prefix for "supernatural"), appears in a key episode in the Zuni origin myth. The Zunis and their gods encounter an enemy god people and a war erupts. The Zunis are farmers, while the enemy gods are hunters. The Zunis are led by male war gods, while the enemies are led by a warrior woman. At first, neither side can win. Then, the enemy gods capture three of the Zuni kachinas, including Ko'lhamana, and they hold a dance to celebrate. But Ko'lhamana is unruly and uncooperative. The warrior woman puts him in a woman's dress and tells him, "You will now perhaps be less angry."[22]

While there are several variants of this myth, the outcome is always the same—the warring people merge, and balance is restored between hunting and farming, male and female. These events were commemorated in a ceremony held every four years. The enemy gods entered the Zuni village bearing freshly killed game. Ko'lhamana was the first of the captured kachinas.[23]

Ko'lhamana's costume symbolizes the economic and sexual themes of the myth. The mask is the same as that of the rain dancer and farmer kachina, Kokk'okshi. But Ko'lhamana also carries the warrior's bow and arrow. Normally, these symbols would never be combined, since the violence of warfare and hunting is inimical to agriculture. Ko'lhamana

"Cooking" is a metaphor for individual development. Newborn infants are "raw" because they are unsocialized. Adult Zunis are "cooked" because they have learned the forms of Zuni culture and have assumed adult roles in the social and religious life of the tribe.

We'wha was a specialist not just in women's work but in cultural work in general. Bridging genders meant drawing from the economic, social, and religious roles of both men and women to create a unique synthesis, neither male nor female.

also wears a woman's dress and, at the same time, a man's dance kilt over the shoulder. The hair is done half up in the female style and half down in the male style.

The ability to hold these opposites together is what makes Ko'lhamana supernaturally potent and, by extension, what makes the actual *lhamana* extraordinary as well.

The Problem of Terms

Harriet Whitehead has argued that the cross-gender features of berdache roles were society's way of constraining individuals to one or another role, by re-integrating variance into gender norms with the requirement that male berdaches pretend they are female. In this way, society prevents a potential opportunism—individuals who seek both male and female sources of prestige and power.[24]

The Zunis did indeed expect berdaches to contribute to the community—as all individuals were expected to do—but their contribution actually derived from their variance. They were valued precisely because they contributed something neither men nor women offered. Their variance was not ignored or disguised by the social fiction of gender crossing. The Zunis always acknowledged the biological gender of berdaches. At the same time, they looked for the positive potentials of berdache variance and encouraged berdaches to apply these potentials for the good of all.

We might conceptualize berdache status as a distinct gender. If we do so, we should talk of *four* genders, not three, since the many tribes with both male and female berdaches used distinct terminology for the two cases—a point that anthropologist Evelyn Blackwood stresses.[25]

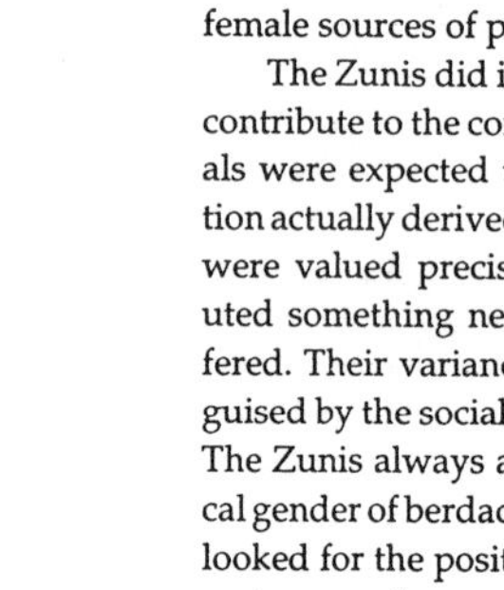

Why do I refer to the berdache as "a traditional gay role"?

Discussing alternative gender roles in the English language is difficult. The question is, what English words best describe Indian berdaches? The earliest European accounts called them sodomites or hermaphrodites. But these terms already force us to choose between sexuality and gender. In fact, in the twentieth century this same dichotomy has been perpetuated by the choice between homosexual and transvestite or transsexual.

The meaning of transvestite has been smudged by anthropologists. This term was coined in 1910 by the German sexologist Magnus Hirschfield to refer to men with an erotic desire to wear female clothing—an act usually performed in private by men who, in daily life, fulfilled normal roles. This is still the meaning of the term today as it is used by those who call themselves transvestites. Given this definition, we can see that We'wha's perfunctory cross-dressing does not qualify.

Was We'wha a transsexual? This is an even newer category, introduced in 1948 to refer to individuals who wish to change gender permanently. But if this were the motivation in We'wha's case, why didn't he attempt to act and look more feminine? As I've shown, We'wha's behavior was not typical of Zuni women.

Finally, there is homosexual. We do know that some Zuni berdaches married non-berdache men and that others enjoyed more casual relationships with men. In Kinsey's terms, this qualifies as homosexual behavior. Such contact was not pseudo-heterosexual, in the sense that berdaches were substitute women, because, as I've shown, the Zunis did not deny the biological gender of berdaches. The problem with homosexual lies elsewhere. In American Indian societies, berdaches were viewed in terms of their religious, economic, kinship, and social—not just sexual—roles. There are simply no Zuni equivalents for our single-dimensional categories of homosexual and heterosexual.

In short, we need a term which connotes *more* than sexuality and, for that matter, more

ADAM CLARK VROMAN / COURTESY OF THE SEAVER CENTER FOR WESTERN HISTORY RESEARCH, NATURAL HISTORY MUSEUM OF LOS ANGELES COUNTY

We'wha holding child

than gender variance—a term that refers to a multi-dimensional social role, not just a single dimensional trait. I believe gay is the closest equivalent in English. Even so, the berdache category was broader than any of our categories. Some of the individuals who once filled this role might today identify themselves as transsexuals, bisexuals, or transvestites—as well as homosexuals. However, even if the Zunis had had such a thing as transsexual surgery, they still would have had a berdache role, because the social, economic, and religious contributions of berdaches were unique, different from those of either men or women.

A second reason for my use of gay is the evidence I've found of continuity between traditional berdache roles and contemporary gay American Indians. By the mid-twentieth century, Zuni boys considered "berdache material" no longer adopted women's dress. According to John Adair, they often moved to Gallup and did "women's work" in the white world—cooking, cleaning, laundry, child care, etc.[26] At this juncture, Indian men who might have become berdaches begin to look and act like gay men in today's terms.

But the most interesting evidence regarding this transition is the testimony of Zunis themselves. While at Zuni recently, I was told that as the berdache role has changed, so has the Zuni word for berdaches. Instead of *lhamana*, people now say *lhalha*, and the word is used to mean "homosexual." Zunis discuss the subject among themselves all the time, I was told, but talking about it with Anglos is considered "dirty" or "pornographic"—i.e., sexual.

A final reason that I refer to berdache status as "a gay role" is the result of my conversations and dialogues over the past four years with gay and lesbian American Indians. I found that some knew about the berdache as a living tribal tradition, while others have learned about the role the same way I have—through research. But all affirmed a continuity between the berdache tradition and their own lives as gay Indians today. They never used the terms transvestite or berdache, and they disliked homosexual because of its narrow focus. All preferred gay.

For example, I asked Beth Brant, a Mohawk, "What does the berdache have to do with gay roles today?" She said, "It has everything to do with who we are now. As gay Indians, we feel that connection with our ancestors."[27] Randy Burns, a Northern Paiute and cofounder of Gay American Indians, told me, "We are living in the spirit of our traditional gay Indian people. The gay Indian person is probably more traditional and spiritual and more creative than his or her straight counterpart because that was the traditional role we played."[28]

Berdaches were not branded as threats to gender ideology; they were viewed as an affirmation of humanity's original, pre-gendered unity —a representation of collective solidarity that overcomes the division of male and female.

All affirmed a continuity between the berdache tradition and their own lives as gay Indians today. They never used the terms transvestite or berdache, and they disliked homosexual because of its narrow focus. All preferred gay.

Drawing from the wisdom of her Navajo background as well as a contemporary feminist perspective, Erna Pahe best explains the special contribution of the gay role—and her comments provide a fitting closing to this discussion:

> In our culture, in our little gay world, anybody can do anything. I mean, you find some very good mothers that are men. And you find very good fathers that are women. We can sympathize, we can really feel how the other sex feels. More so than the straight community. The straight community is so worried about staying within their little box and making sure that I look like a female when I'm out there, or that I really play the role of the male image.
>
> I think that society is ready for that kind of atmosphere where we don't have to compete against each other over sexual orientation, or we don't have to feel like the men play a bigger role in society than women do. I think it's time for that neutralness, where people can understand just how to be people....
>
> There's a lot of caring in gay people that is towards all lifestyles, from children, all the way up to grandparents. Society is getting used to it now because of this sensitivity. I think it might wear off after a while—we'll get everybody thinking like us. Even dealing in politics, we're a lot more aware of everything....We are special, because we're able to deal with all of life in general. It's very special.[29]

As Paula Gunn Allen points out, in seeking political and cultural recognition today lesbians and gay men are only restoring to America the gayness it once had. ▼

COURTESY OF THE NATIONAL ARCHIVES TRUST FUND BOARD

Sacred Dance Plaza of the Zuni, circa 1879.

References

A version of this paper was originally presented at The New Gender Scholarship conference, at the University of Southern California, February 13-15, 1987.

Harry Hay first drew my attention to the berdache in 1982, when he shared with me his extensive research and notes compiled thirty years earlier. In 1983, he arranged a trip to New Mexico, to explore its pueblos, ruins, villages, and people, inaugurating my love affair with that fascinating and beautiful land. Bradley Rose has also shared this odyssey and knows its joys and frustrations. Paula Gunn Allen, Clifford Barnett, Evelyn Blackwood, Randy Burns, John Burnside, John DeCecco, Sue-Ellen Jacobs, Erna Pahe, David Thomas, and Mark Thompson all deserve thanks. I cannot name them here, but I would also like to acknowledge the individuals and groups throughout the country that have sponsored my slide-lecture and shared their homes and hearts with me. I have benefited as well from my work with Gay American Indians of San Francisco. In 1987 I received a fellowship from the Van Waveren Foundation, and this made it possible for me to present my work at Zuni and begin writing a book. Finally, thanks are due to the tribal council and the people of Zuni.

1 Matilda C. Stevenson, "The Zuñi Indians: Their Mythology, Esoteric Societies, and Ceremonies," *Bureau of American Ethnology Annual Report* 23 (1904), 311-12.

2 See Will Roscoe, "A Bibliography of Berdache and Alternative Gender Roles Among North American Indians," *Journal of Homosexuality* 14, no. 3/4 (1987), 81-171.

3 Stevenson, "The Zuñi Indians" 20; Elsie Clews Parsons, "Notes on Zuñi," *Memoirs of the American Anthropological Association* 4(3-4) (1917):253; Robert Bunker, *Other Men's Skies* (Bloomington: Indiana University Press, 1956), 99-100.

4 Stevenson, "The Zuñi Indians" 37, 311.

5 One of the common misconceptions regarding berdaches is that they always or completely cross-dressed. A closer look at the evidence from many tribes reveals that berdaches often combined male and female clothing, or dressed in a unique (neither male nor female) manner.

6 Stevenson, "The Zuñi Indians" 310.

7 George Wharton James, *New Mexico: The Land of the Delight Makers* (Boston: The Page Co., 1920), 63-64.

ADAM CLARK VROMAN / COURTESY OF THE SMITHSONIAN INSTITUTION

Zuni pueblo, circa 1895.

[8] Stevenson, "The Zuñi Indians" 310. In fact, Stevenson used both male and female terms in referring to berdaches.

[9] Stevenson, "The Zuñi Indians" 37.

[10] Frank H. Cushing, "Nominal and Numerical Census of the Gentes of the Ashiwi or Zuni Indians," ms. 3915, National Anthropological Archives, Smithsonian Institution, Washington, DC. Weaving was a men's activity among most Pueblo Indians, although less strictly so at Zuni.

[11] Stevenson, "The Zuñi Indians" 130.

[12] *Evening Star* (Washington), 15 May 1886.

[13] Stevenson to Daniel S. Lamont, 18 June 1886, Grover Cleveland Papers, Library of Congress.

[14] *Evening Star* (Washington), 12 June 1886.

[15] Edmund Wilson, *Red, Black, Blond and Olive* (New York: Oxford University Press, 1956), 20.

[16] Ruth Bunzel, "Zuni Texts," *Publications of the American Ethnological Society* 15 (1933), 49.

[17] I have researched these events in Pueblo Agency Records, RG 75, National Archives, Denver and Records of the United States Army Continental Commands, RG 393, National Archives, Washington.

[18] Robertson to DeSette, 19 August 1892, Pueblo Agency Records.

[19] Stevenson, "The Zuñi Indians" 312-13.

[20] Elsie Clews Parsons. "A Few Zuni Death Beliefs and Practices," *American Anthropologist* 18 (1916):253; Elsie Clews Parsons, "The Zuñi La'mana," *American Anthropologist* 18 (1916):528.

[21] Parsons, "The Zuñi La'mana," 527.

[22] Stevenson, "The Zuñi Indians" 37.

[23] This ceremony lapsed when the caretaker of key songs and prayers died without an apprentice.

[24] Harriet Whitehead, "The Bow and the Burden Strap: A New Look at Institutionalized Homosexuality in Native North America," in *Sexual Meanings: The Cultural Construction of Gender and Sexuality*, ed. Sherry B. Ortner and Harriet Whitehead, pp. 80-115 (Cambridge: Cambridge University Press, 1981).

[25] Evelyn Blackwood, "Review of *The Spirit and the Flesh* and Beyond," *Journal of Homosexuality*, forthcoming.

[26] Personal communication, 29 September 1986. See also, Elsie Clews Parsons, "The Last Zuñi Transvestite," *American Anthropologist* 41:338.

[27] Will Roscoe, "Living the Tradition: Gay American Indians," in *Gay Spirit: Myth and Meaning*, ed. Mark Thompson, pp. 69-77 (New York: St. Martin's Press, 1987), 74.

[28] Ibid., 75.

[29] "Speaking Up: An Interview with Erna Pahe," *Living the Spirit: A Gay American Indian Anthology*, ed. Will Roscoe (New York: St. Martin's Press, 1988).

SEXUAL INVERSION AMONG PRIMITIVE RACES

By C. G. SELIGMANN,

M. R. C. S. ENG., L. R. C. P. LOND.

Superintendent of the Clinical Laboratory, St. Thomas' Hospital, London.

BUT few details of sexual inversion and perversion are known among savages, and it is commonly and tacitly assumed that abnormalities of the sexual instinct are the concomitants of Oriental luxury or advanced civilization. Too often merely the grosser forms of perversion have been looked for or noted, the condition described by Moll as psycho-sexual hermaphroditism, in which, while the psychical resemblance to the opposite sex colours the whole social life of the individual, there are also present traces of normal hetero-sexual instinct, being unrecognized or ignored. Among American Indians, from Alaska to Brazil, homosexual practices occur or occurred. Sodomy was prevalent among the Nahua (Aztec) and Maya nations* the latter tolerating if not systematizing its practice. Among savage races Bancroft, speaking of the Isthmian tribes of Cueba and Careba, says: "The caciques and some of the head men kept harems of youths who were dressed as women, did women's work about the house, and were exempt from war and its fatigues."‡ Again: "In the province of Tamaulipa there were public brothels where men enacted the part of women,"§ while the modern Omaha have a special name signifying hermaphrodite for the passive agent, whom they regard with contempt.|| Among the Aleuts of Alaska

*Bancroft, *Native Races of the Pacific Coast*, vol. II, pp. 467, 677.

‡*Ibid*, vol. I, p. 774.

§*Ibid*, vol. I, p. 635.

||Third Annual Report of the Bureau of Ethnology, p. 365, Washington, 1884.

certain boys, whom Holmberg* states were selected for their girlish appearance, are brought up as girls and decorated as women. Similar instances might be multiplied, but, apart from the last mentioned, which, according to Havelock Ellis, suggests the possibility of congenital inversion, they are all examples of the grossest forms of perversion, and no details suggesting that any of these are cases of congenital inversion are given. Similarly there is reason to believe that the pæderasty practiced by certain New Caledonian warriors, which is stated to constitute a relationship more sacred than blood-brotherhood, is resorted to for convenience and perhaps for Malthusian reasons,† as it is among some Papuans of the western district of British New Guinea.‡

A somewhat different condition of things prevails among the Tupi, a Brazilian tribe in a low stage of civilization to whom Lomonaco|| has devoted considerable attention. While noting that sodomy was prevalent in almost every local tribe, and that a class of men were met with whose function it was to lend themselves to the practice, he states that among the Tupi many women took no husbands, devoting themselves for the whole of their lives to perpetual chastity, and quotes Gandavo§ to the effect that there are some women among those who decide to be chaste who will not consent to know men even under threats of death. They wear their hair cut in the same fashion as the males, go to war with their bows and arrows, and take part in the chase. They frequent the company of men and each one of them has a woman who waits on her, to whom she says she is married and "with whom she communicates and converses like man and wife." It seems probable that here, among a people addicted to sodomy and in whom here is no strong feeling against homo-sexual relations,

*Quoted by Havelock Ellis and J. A. Symonds in Das Kontrare Geschlechtsgefühl, Leipsic, 1896.

†Foley: Bulletins de la Societe d'Anthropologie de Paris, 1879.

‡Beardmore, Journal of the Anthropological Institute, vol. xix, 1890.

||Sulle Razze Indigene del Brasile, Archivio per l'Antropologia e la Etnologia, 1889 Florence.

§Historia da Provincia de Santa Cruz, quoted by Lomonaco, *loc. cit.*

there is an element of true congenital inversion similar to that present in the sporadic cases among Papuans to be immediately described.

While with the Cambridge Anthropological Expedition to Torres Straits and New Guinea several instances were met with in the Rigo district of British New Guinea where, unlike the Fly river district, the habitual practice of pæd-erasty is unknown.* These cases occurred among a people practically still in their stone age and so uncontaminated by external influences that even white men's diseases had not yet obtained a footing among them. In the following notes the condition of the genitals is given on what is probably good authority, but in no case would it have been politic to have attempted to verify my informants' descriptions by actual examination. Three of the four cases alluded to were inhabitants of Bulaa, a considerable settlement built for the most part on piles in the sea. One of these had been dead for some time. In her, assuming the native diagnosis of sex to have been correct, there was maldevel-opment of the genitalia, while the remaining two Bulaa cases are probably pure instances of psycho-sexual herma-phroditism.

Hiro, a female aged about 30 years, is a daughter of one of the most influential men of the tribe. She is rather taller and her figure is less rounded than that of the aver-age Bulaa women. The skin over her breasts is somewhat wrinkled, but apparently the glands themselves are nor-mally developed. Her thighs and buttocks are tattooed in the usual female manner and her genitals are said to be normal and the mons hairy. As to previous history, as a little girl she preferred playing boys' games which by all accounts she played remarkably well; as she got older she still preferred boys as companions and avoided her own sex. For a long time she resolutely refused to adopt the usual girl's petticoat and at puberty was only compelled by threats to do so. For the next two years her conduct was not remarkable. Menstruation, which was said to be neither

*Cf. Beardmore, *loc. cit.*

irregular nor scanty, occurred and has since been normal in character. At about the age of 16 years she aborted; since then she has lived with her mother and has refused at least three offers of marriage. As far as can be ascertained she has never had a lover of her own sex and since the abortion has lived a solitary life or has at least carried on no intrigue of sufficient duration to arrest public attention. She is said to be more intelligent than the average woman and carries weights man-fashion on her shoulders instead of by a band round her forehead as other women do. In the garden she uses the heavy digging stick (*kai*) for turning over the soil, which is essentially man's work, women, as a rule, only weeding, planting, and digging yams.

An instance of pseudo-hermaphroditism occurring two generations ago was well remembered and appreciated. The subject who, since she had connection in that capacity, was considered a woman, was said to have possessed both penis and vagina; there was some doubt as to whether she had testes. It was stated that she menstruated and passed urine *per vaginam* and that her breasts were small. She wore a modified petticoat, consisting of a short tuft in front and behind, and spent most of her time among the men of the tribe, with whom she took part in any hunting or fighting that was going on.

Gima, aged about 30 years, is a "chief" much trusted by the government and very intelligent. He is thoroughly masculine in appearance and active, plucky, and energetic. Having become a man of importance and a firm supporter of the Government he now wears a jacket and short trousers. It is, however, a matter of common tribal knowledge that his thighs and buttocks are tattooed in the elaborate fashion peculiar to women, without which no girl is considered marriageable. His genitals are said to be normal. He is said to have previously taken the passive part in sodomy soon after puberty, later he married, but had no children, and divorced his wife on the score of infidelity. He has since lived as a bachelor, it is stated to avoid women, and to have, at any rate till very recently, habitually taken the passive part.

I am indebted to Mr. A. C. English, Government agent of the Rigo district, for notes of the following case, that of a man belonging to the Garia, an inland tribe which is gradually pressing down towards the coast from the foothills of the main range.

Unasé is aged about 50 years, unmarried, and is somewhat doubtfully stated to have abstained from intercourse since soon after puberty. His breasts are normally developed and there is hair on his chest; his genitals are normal and hairy; virile organ perhaps rather small; his voice is shrill. He habitually associates with women and accompanies them on their trading expeditions towards the coast, when he carries his "trade" slung by a band round his forehead as women do. He takes a woman's part in domestic and social life as well as in the work he does in the garden. In spite of this he has on one occasion joined a war party and bears on his back the tattoo marks which distinguish the successful homicide.

With these cases may be compared the following occurring in Sarawak among a people in the barbarous stage. At Sibu on the Rejang river, Budok, a Mahomedan Milanau,* probably suffering from elephantiasis, asked for medicine for swellings in both groins. He refused examination and it was noticed that he wore a veil† such as Malay women wear. His voice was soft, not shrill or treble; physically he was small-boned and of a somewhat delicate build, but not undersized, and on the whole masculine in appearance. He was said to have normal breasts and genitals, but not to care for intercourse, in place of which he took the passive role in sodomy. He sat with the women in the house and like them sewed and made clothes, baked cakes, and weeded the paddy fields. He wore women's clothes habitually and whenever possible.

*H. Laing Roth ("The Natives of Sarawak and British North Borneo," vol. I, p. 12) says: "The Milanaus are a quiet people, not Mahomedan, but dressing like the Malays and cultivating sago." Recently Mahomedanism has made considerable progress among them; there is, however, no reason to believe that it has led to or encouraged sexual perversion.

†Prostitutes at Kuching wore an exactly similar black veil.

Acknowledgments

Allen, Paula Gunn. "Lesbians in American Indian Cultures." *Conditions: Seven* 7 (1981): 67–87. Courtesy of Yale University Cross Campus Library.

Blackwood, Evelyn. "Sexuality and Gender in Certain Native American Tribes: The Case of Cross-Gender Females." *Signs* 10 (1984): 27–42. Reprinted with the permission of The University of Chicago Press, publisher. Copyright 1984 by The University of Chicago. All rights reserved. Courtesy of Yale University Sterling Memorial Library.

Broude, Gwen J. and Sarah J. Greene. "Cross-Cultural Codes on Twenty Sexual Attitudes and Practices." *Ethnology* 15 (1976): 409–429. Reprinted with the permission of *Ethnology*. Courtesy of *Ethnology*.

Callender, Charles and Lee M. Kochems. "The North American Berdache." *Current Anthropology* 24 (1983): 443–470. Reprinted with the permission of The University of Chicago Press, publisher. Courtesy of Yale University Sterling Memorial Library.

Carrier, Joseph M. "Cultural Factors Affecting Urban Mexican Male Homosexual Behavior." *Archives of Sexual Behavior* 5 (1976): 103–124. Reprinted with the permission of Plenum Publishing Corp. Courtesy of Yale University Medical Library.

Creed, Gerald W. "Sexual Subordination: Institutionalized Homosexuality and Social Control in Melanesia." *Ethnology* 23 (1984): 157–176. Reprinted with the permission of *Ethnology*. Courtesy of *Ethnology*.

Danielsson, Bengt and Marie Therese. "Polynesia's Third Sex: The Gay Life Starts in the Kitchen." *Pacific Islands Monthly* 49 (1978): 10–13. Reprinted with the permission of the Pacific Publications Pty. Ltd. Courtesy of *Pacific Islands Monthly*.

Devereux, George. "Institutionalized Homosexuality of the Mohave Indians." *Human Biology* 9 (1937): 498–527. Courtesy of Yale University Kline Science Library.

Dynes, Wayne. "Homosexuality in Sub-Saharan Africa: An Unnecessary Controversy." *Cabirion and Gay Books Bulletin* 9 (1983): 20–21. Reprinted with the permission of the Gay Academic Union, Inc. Courtesy of Wayne R. Dynes.

Evans-Pritchard, E.E. "Sexual Inversion among the Azande." *American Anthropologist* 72 (1970): 1428–1434. Reprinted with the permission of the American Anthropological Association. Not for further reproduction. Courtesy of Yale University Sterling Memorial Library.

Gutiérrez, Ramón A. "Must We Deracinate Indians to Find Gay Roots?" *Out/Look* 4 (1989): 61–67. Reprinted with the permission of *Out/Look*. Courtesy of Wayne R. Dynes.

Hage, Per. "On Male Initiation and Dual Organisation in New Guinea." *Man* 16 (1981): 268–275. Reprinted with the permission of the Royal Anthropological Institute of Great Britain & Ireland. Courtesy of Yale University Sterling Memorial Library.

Herdt, Gilbert H. "Ritualized Homosexual Behavior in the Male Cults of Melanesia, 1862–1983: An Introduction." in *Ritualized Homosexuality in Melanesia* (Berkeley: University of California Press, 1984): 1–82. Courtesy of Yale University Sterling Memorial Library.

Jacobs, Sue-Ellen. "Berdache: A Brief Review of the Literature." *Colorado Anthropologist* 1 (1968): 25–40. Reprinted with the permission of the *Colorado Anthropologist*. Courtesy of *Colorado Anthropologist*.

Lancaster, Roger N. "Subject Honor and Object Shame: The Construction of Male Homosexuality and Stigma in Nicaragua." *Ethnology* 27 (1988): 111–125. Reprinted with the permission of *Ethnology*. Courtesy of *Ethnology*.

Landes, Ruth. "A Cult Matriarchate and Male Homosexuality." *Journal of Abnormal and Social Psychology* 35 (1940): 386–97. Courtesy of Yale University Sterling Memorial Library.

Levy, Robert I. "The Community Function of Tahitian Male Transvestitism: A Hypothesis." *Anthropological Quarterly* 44 (1971): 12–21. Reprinted with the permission of the *Anthropological Quarterly*. Courtesy of Yale University Sterling Memorial Library.

Murray, S.O. "Fuzzy Sets and Abominations." *Man* 18 (1983): 396–399. Reprinted with the permission of the Royal Anthropological Institute of Great Britain & Ireland. Courtesy of Yale University Sterling Memorial Library.

Murray, Stephen O. and Manuel Arboleda G. "Stigma Transformation and Relexification: `Gay' in Latin America." In Stephen O. Murray, ed., *Male Homosexuality in Central and South America* (New York: Gay Academic Union, 1987): 130–138; Stephen O. Murray, "Sentimental Effusions of Genital Contact in Upper Amazonia" *ibid.* 139–151; Stephen O. Murray, "Mistaking Fantasy for Ethnography" *ibid.* 155–158. Reprinted with the permission of El Instituto Obregon. Courtesy of Wayne R. Dynes.

Roscoe, Will. "The Zuni Man-Woman." *Out/Look* (1988): 56–67. Reprinted with the permission of *Out/Look*. Courtesy of Wayne R. Dynes.

Seligmann, C.G. "Sexual Inversion among Primitive Races." *Alienist and Neurologist* 23 (1902): 11–15. Courtesy of Wayne R. Dynes.

Index

Achumawi Indians, 65, 276
Acoma, 274
"A Cult Matriarchate and Male Homosexuality" (Ruth Landes), 304–15
Adair, John, 367
Adam, B.D., 330
Adams, Henry, 322
Admiralty Islands, 233
Africa, 166–67
Africans
  in Bahia, Brazil, 305–15
Ai'i, 201, 212–13, 239, 240
Akuna, 232–33, 239
Alarcon, Hernando de, 178
Aleut Indians, 276, 371–72
Algonquian Indians, 69
Allen, Paula Gunn, 1–21, 35, 368
Altaschuler, Milton, 341
Alves da Silva, Alcionilio B., 342
Alyha, 138–43
  as shamans, 154
  courtship of, 151
  faked pregnancies of, 150–52, 159–60
  gambling skills of, 156
  initiation of, 144–48
  marriage of, 151–52, 156–57
  menstrual imitations among, 149–51
  occupations of, 151–52
  personality traits of, 155
  sexual etiquette of, 148–51
  and warfare, 155–56
Amarakaeri, 355
Amazonia
  cannibalism in, 353, 355
  homosexuality in, 327, 336, 339–51, 353, 355
Anal Intercourse
  in the Admiralty Islands, 233
  among the Akuna, 232
  Azande prohibit, 170
  among berdache, 176
  among the Baruya, 228
  among the Boadzi, 214
  in East Bay, 207
  in Fiji, 202
  among the Iatmul, 238
  among the Kaluli, 224
  among the Kanum, 213
  among the Keraki, 211–12
  among the Kiman, 218
  among the Kwoma, 237
  among the Marind-anim, 115, 214–16
  and Mexican homosexuals, 89, 99–100, 103, 105–7
  among Mohave Indians, 137–38, 145–46, 148–50, 152, 155
  in New Guinea, 208–9
  in the New Hebrides, 204
  in Nicaragua, 289–296
  in Tahiti, 320
  among the Tapirape, 342–43
  among the Tolai, 205
  in the Trobriand Islands, 194
  among the Yei-anim, 213
Anga
  ethnographic studies of, 227
  head-hunting practices of, 227
  housing patterns of, 259
  land ratio among, 247
  marriage practices of, 260
  premarital sex condemned among, 256
  ritualized homosexuality among, 227–31, 239, 240
  sexual polarity among, 257
  tribal groups of, 224
  warfare of, 249
Angelino, Henry, 273–74
Anthropology
  and the berdache, 61, 72–74, 75, 76–77, 83, 84, 179–80
  and comparative social categories of homosexuality, 326–27
  and cultural integration, 118

and feminism, 23
and homosexual studies, 111–12, 128, 298–99
and initiation rites, 121–22
and *Keep the River on Your Right*, 354–55
and negative constructs of identity, 323–24
and ritualized homosexuality studies, 184, 186, 191–96, 199, 214, 224, 244
and ritualized homosexuality studies in Melanesia, 210, 253–54, 263
and sexuality research, 41
and the Sepik area, 233–34
and the Standard Cross-Cultural Sample, 39
and the Tahitian mahu, 317
and transvestite studies, 366
and the Zuni Indians, 359–60
Apache Indians, 68, 78, 80, 82, 274
Arapaho Indians, 10, 34–35, 68
Arapesh, 182–85, 187
Arawak Indians, 176
Arboleda, Manuel, 330–38
Asmat, 201
head-hunting of, 249
ritualized homosexuality among, 219–20
Assiniboin Indians, 71
Athabaskan Indians, 82
Atsugewi Indians, 65, 66
Australia, 193–96, 204, 223, 260
Awa, 232
Azande, 168–74
Aztec Indians, 176, 371

Bahia, Brazil, 305–15
Banaro, 236–37
Bannock Indians, 66
Barasana, 339–40
Baruya, 201, 227
gender system of, 229
lesbianism among, 228–29
ritualized homosexuality among, 228–29, 239
sexuality beliefs of, 229
and wars with the Sambia, 230
women's status among, 256
Bazingbi, 172
Beach, Frank, 346
Beardmore, E., 209–10
Becket, Jeremy, 213
Bedamini, 116, 201, 224–25, 227
Bella Bella Indians, 68
Bella Coola Indians, 68, 70
Bena Bena, 184
Benedict, Ruth F., 180, 276
Berdache
adolescence of, 26, 78, 79, 275–76
anthropological studies of, 61, 72–74, 75, 76–77, 83, 84, 179–80
bisexuality of, 68–69
among the Chaco, 347
childrearing among, 30
contemporary lives of, 367
cross-dressing of, 33–34, 61–62, 65, 67, 72–73, 75, 76, 78, 79, 80, 81, 83, 84, 275, 277–79, 358–69
definition of, 61, 77, 83, 273–74
in different cultures, 175
disappearance of, 34–36, 61, 75, 78, 83, 84
distribution of, 274–75, 279, 280–82
and dreaming, 26
ethnographic studies of, 24–26, 27–28, 61, 73, 75, 76–77, 78, 80, 81, 82, 179–80
etymology of, 77, 82
frequency of, 62–65, 77, 78, 79, 81–82, 84
frequency of women among, 64, 73–74, 75, 76
gay scholars on, 179, 181
gender status of, 71–74, 366–67
as hermaphrodites, 62
historical development of, 176, 178–79, 275
and homosexuality, 61–62, 80, 81, 83, 84
initiation rights of, 27

and kinship, 77
marriage practices of, 30, 67–68, 176–77, 278–79, 304, 366
and matrilineal societies, 80, 84
among Mohave Indians, 139
mythical aspects of, 70
among Native Americans, 298, 327, 358–69, 372
negative attitudes toward, 35–36, 71, 73
in North America, 61–88
occupations of, 65–66, 72–74, 79–80, 83, 84, 275–79, 283, 360–62, 365–66, 367
ontogeny of, 69–71
as passive homosexuals, 304
among the Plains Indians, 32–35
postcontact changes in status of, 83
psyche of, 75
among Pueblo Indians, 175–81
rape of, 68, 179
ritual functions of, 71–73, 75, 78, 81, 84, 277
sexual practices of, 31, 67–69, 72–73, 78
slide shows about, 363–64
social position of, 63, 65, 71, 72–74, 75, 76, 277–78
sources on, 61, 67
Spaniards on, 175, 178, 274
spirit world of, 69–71, 71–74, 75, 76–77, 78, 80, 81, 83, 84, 275–77
suicide of, 275
tests of, 276–77
tribal names for, 280
violent behavior of, 67
and warfare, 66–67, 71, 72–74, 76, 77, 80, 81, 176, 178, 181, 365
and warrior women, 33
Harriet Whitehead on, 126, 366
whites attitude towards, 278–79
women hostile toward, 83
Zuni initiation of, 365
See also Homosexuals; Lesbianism
"Berdache: A Brief Review of the Literature" (Sue-Ellen Jacobs), 273–88
Bernardino, 312–15
Bettelheim, B., 183
Big Nambas, 202–4
Bisexuality, 197
among berdache, 68–69
among Mohave Indians, 139, 147, 158
in Bahia, Brazil, 315
in East Bay, 206
in Latin America, 330
of Mahu, 133
in Melanesia, 255, 259
in Nicaragua, 297
Blackfoot Indians, 33, 34, 73, 79, 83
Blackwood, B., 227–28
Blackwood, Evelyn, 23–38, 366
Bleibtreu-Ehrenberg, Gisela, 74–75, 83, 84–85
Bligh, William, 317, 321
Boadzi, 200, 213–14, 219, 224
Boelaars, F., 216, 219
Bolinder, Gustaf, 348
Bolivia, 299
Bowers, Alfred W., 276
Boyd, David, 232
Brant, Beth, 367
Brazil, 304–15
Broch, Harald Beyer, 75, 83, 84, 85
Broude, Gwen J., 39–59
Brown, C.H., 326
Brown, Judith K., 75–76, 82, 83, 84
Budok, 375
Bugi, 199–200
Bugilai, 208, 213
Buka, 206, 228
Bullough, V.L., 301
Bunker, Robert, 359
Bunzel, Ruth, 361
Burns, Randy, 363, 367
Burton, Richard, 166

Cabeza de Vaca, Alvar Nunez, 176
Caddo Indians, 64
Cagaba Kogi, 348
Cahuila Indians, 62

California, 62, 64, 274–77
Callender, Charles, 25, 36–38, 61–88
Cannibalism, 76, 353, 355
Careba, 371
Carlisle, John, 360
Carneiro, Edison, 311
Carrier, Joseph M., 89–110, 326
Carrier Indians, 63, 64
Castaneda, Pedro de, 176, 177
Castor, 79
Casuarina Coast, 201
Catawba Indians, 273
Cayapa, 341
Ceremony (Leslie Silko), 11–12
Chaco, 347
Chagnon, Napoleon A., 342, 355
Chalmers, James, 208–9
Cherokee Indians, 1, 77, 273
Cheyenne Indians
  berdache among, 65, 67, 68, 71, 74, 83, 84, 274
  cross-dressing among, 79
  women's status among, 79
Chimariko Indians, 62
Chimbu, 247, 256
Chippewa Indians, 82, 276, 277–78
Choctaw Indians, 64, 273
Christianity
  and acculturation of Native Americans, 3, 17–18
  and kinship, 7–8
Chumash Indians, 64
Circumcision
  ritual aspects of, in Melanesia, 203–4
Cleveland, Grover, 359, 360
Clothing and Sexuality Codes, 44
Coahuiltecan Indians, 64, 66
Cochiti Indians, 62
Cochon
  adolescence of, 292–94
  affected by the Sandinista Revolution, 296–97
  anal intercourse of, 289–296
  as a political concept, 292, 295–96
  cross-dressing of, 295
  definition of, 289–90
  feminine behaviors of, 295
  Managua night-life of, 296–97
  marriage of, 290, 294
  in Nicaragua, 289–303
  participation in religious festivals of, 295–96
  political activity of, 297
  and power relationships, 301–2
  sex role of, 290–92
  stigmatization of, 291–96, 298–302
  See also Homosexuals
Cocopa Indians, 24, 151
  berdache among, 26, 27, 67, 276
  homosexuality among, 164
Codes
  on cross-cultural sexual behavior, 48–57
  frequency scales of, 42
  present-absent model of, 42
  of sexual behavior, 39–59
Coeur d'Alene Indians, 62
Collier, Jane Fishburne, 17
Comanche Indians, 62, 64, 65, 82
Comites de Defensa Sandinista, 296–97
Courtship
  of Hwame, 153
  of Mohave Indian homosexuals, 151, 158
Creed, Gerald W., 111–30
Cree Indians, 68
Creek Indians, 62, 64
"Cross-Cultural Codes on Twenty Sexual Attitudes and Practices" (Gwen Broude and Sarah Greene), 39–59
Cross-dressing
  among the Aleuts, 372
  in the upper Amazon, 345–46
  anthropological studies of, 61, 366
  in Bahian Indian cults, 312
  of berdache, 33–34, 61–62, 65–69, 72–73, 75, 76, 78, 79, 80, 81, 83, 84, 175–79, 273–74, 275, 277–79, 327
  among Chaco berdache, 347

among the Cueba and Careba, 371
and gender systems, 300
among the Goajiro, 348
among the Mehinaku, 344–45
in Melanesia, 197–98, 222
of Mexican adolescents, 100
among Mohave Indians, 136–65
among New Guinea homosexuals, 375
in Nicaragua, 295
in Papua New Guinea, 82
in Polynesia, 132–35
prohibitions on, 64
in Samoa, 133–34
in Tahiti, 132–33, 316–25
among the Tanala, 304
in Tonga, 134–35
in Venezuela, 347
among the Warao, 347
among Zuni Indians, 358–69
Crow Indians
berdache among, 62, 64, 65, 66–67, 67, 68, 80, 275, 276, 277, 279
women's status among, 9–10
Cuba, 296, 299
Cueba, 371
"Cultural Factors Affecting Urban Mexican Male Homosexual Behavior" (Joseph M. Carrier), 89–110
Cyriaco, 314–15
Czekanowski, Jan, 169–70

Dakota Indians, 66, 67, 69
See also Santee Dakota Indians
Dani, 220, 248
Danielsson, Bengt, 132–33
Danielsson, Therese, 132–33
Datan, Nancy, 76, 83, 84
Deacon, B.A., 113–14, 124, 127, 202–4
Decline and Fall of the Roman Empire (Edward Gibbon), 166
Delaware Indians, 62, 64, 82
Denig, Edward Thompson, 273, 278
Devereux, George
on berdache children, 30
on berdache sexual practices, 31
"Institutionalized Homosexuality of the Mohave Indians," 136–65
on Sahaykwisa, 36
Dhegiha Indians, 69
Dictionary of the American Indian (Stoutenburgh), 79
Diegueno Indians, 276
Dogrib Indians, 82
Dorsey, George A., 278
Double Face, 79
Double-Woman, 66, 69
Douglas, Mary, 183, 326–27
Dover, Kenneth J., 354
Driver, Harold E., 274, 276–77
Duke-of-York Islands, 200, 204–8, 239
Dundes, Alan, 122, 186–87, 195, 258
Dynes, Wayne, 166–67

East Bay, 200
marriage and ritualized homosexuality in, 207
ritualized homosexuality in, 204–8, 232, 237, 239, 242
Effeminacy
as tool of European colonizers, 176
early childhood identification of, 100
of fa'a fafines in Samoa, 133
and homosexuality among Mohave Indians, 147
in Mexican urban culture, 89, 96–109
Egypt, 327
Elema, 210, 212, 223
Ellis, Havelock, 194, 372
Enga, 185–86, 187, 256
English, A.C., 375
Erdoes, Richard, 17
Ernst, Thomas, 224
Ethnography
on the Anga societies, 227
and the berdache, 61, 73, 75, 76–77, 78, 80, 81, 82, 179–80

and cross-gender roles, 24–26, 27–28
and genital mutilation, 184–86
and homosexuality studies, 113, 166, 205–6, 209, 344–46, 353–56
and Native Americans, 3–6, 9, 18
of Plains Indians, 33–37
and ritualized homosexuality studies, 126–27, 182–83, 214, 224, 225–26, 245–46
and ritualized homosexuality studies in Melanesia, 194–95, 198–99, 210–13, 263
and ritualized homosexuality studies in New Guinea, 231–32, 234–35, 238–44
and sexuality studies, 40–42, 111–12
Etoro, 201, 231
declining population of, 248
housing patterns of, 259
kinship system of, 122
lack of sexual anxiety among, 258
marriage practices of, 123, 128, 260
ritualized homosexuality among, 116–17, 126–27, 224–26, 227, 236
ritual sexual symmetry among, 187
witchcraft beliefs of, 117
Europe on Top: Male Homosexuality and the Conquests of America, 1400–1700 (Richard Trexler), 176
Evans-Pritchard, E. E., 168–74

Fa'a fafines, 133–34
See also Homosexuals
Fagatongo, Samoa, 134
Fakaleitis, 134–35
The Family Among the Australian Aborigines (B. Malinowski), 193–94
Fejos, Paul, 346
Fellatio
among berdache, 176
among the Bedamini, 225
on the Duke-of-York Islands, 206
in East Bay, 207
among the Etoro, 117, 224
among the Gebusi, 227
in Melanesia, 300
and Mexican homosexuals, 89, 105–7
among Mohave Indians, 137, 150, 152, 156
in Nicaragua, 290–91
in North America, 289
among the Onabasalu, 116
among Tahitian mahu, 317, 319
among the Sambia, 118, 123, 124, 230, 237
Fiji, 204, 199–200, 202, 239
Fineanganofa, Longosai, 134
First Man, 70
First Woman, 70
Fischer, H., 227
Flathead Indians, 34, 64, 65, 68
Ford, Clellan, 346
Forde, C. Daryll, 140
Foster, Stephen Wayne, 166
Foucault, M., 300
Four Bears, 79
Frederik Hendrik Island, 214, 217–18, 219, 223, 239
Frente Sandinista de i Liberacion Nacional, 297
Freud, Sigmund, 255
"Fuzzy Sets and Abominations" (Stephen O. Murray), 326–29

Gahuku Gama, 182, 185, 187, 231
Gajdusek, D. C., 228
Galis, K.W., 220–21
Ganga, 171
Garia, 375
Gauguin, Paul, 322
Gay American Indians, 363, 367
"Gay Studies on the Rez" (Will Roscoe), 363–64
Gbudwe, 170–71, 172
Gebusi, 201, 226–27
Gender

and the berdache, 25
definition of role of, 90
idealogical concepts of, 23–24
and sexual roles of Native Americans, 31-32, 35–38
and work roles of Native Americans, 28–30, 65–66
and work roles of Plains Indians, 32–33, 35
Gente, 332
Gibbon, Edward, 166
Gima, 374
Goajiro, 348
Godelier, M., 227, 228–29
Goethals, George W., 40
Goodich, M., 327
Goody, J., 326
Granzberg, Gary, 76, 83
Greece, 202, 254, 300, 327
Greene, Sarah J., 39–59
Gregor, Thomas, 343–45
Gros Ventre Indians, 64
Guadalajara, Mexico
adolescent homosexuals in, 101
crowded living conditions in, 95–96
homosexual joking in, 98–99
homosexual role preference in, 106
importance of manly behavior in, 91–92
male adolescent sexual activity in, 102
police harassment of homosexuals in, 109
See also Mexico
Guatemala, 10, 332–34
Guerra, Francisco, 175
Gutierrez, Ramon A., 175–81

Hage, Per
"On Male Initiation and Dual Organization in New Guinea," 182–89
on ritualized homosexuality among the Keraki, 212
on ritualized homosexuality in Melanesia, 261–62
on sexual polarity in Melanesia, 258
Hagen, 256
Haida Indians, 62, 64
Haile, Bernard, 16
Haisla Indians, 68
Hammond, William A., 177
Handbook of the Indians of California (Kroeber), 159
Handsome Lake, 4
Hanta yo (Hill), 69
Haqau, 163
Hare Indians, 75, 82, 83, 85
Havana, Cuba, 296
Hawaii, 202
Hay, Harry, 175, 181, 274
Hays, Terence E., 232
Head-hunting
among the Anga, 227
among the Iatmul, 234
among the Marind-anim, 216–17
in Melanesia, 246, 249–50
in New Guinea, 237
in the Irian Jaya, 223
Hera, 76
Herdt, Gilbert H., 117–25, 127–28, 191–272, 299
Hernandez de Alba, Gregorio, 347
Heterosexuality and Male Hegemony, 112
Hidatsa Indians
berdache among, 64, 65, 67, 71, 72
berdache marriage practices among, 68
berdache spirit world of, 69
Hill, George W., 347
Hill, Willard W., 273, 277–78
Hiro, 373–75
Hirschfield, Magnus, 366
Hivsu Tupoma, 159, 161, 164
Hocart, A. M., 202
Holmberg, Alan R., 346, 372
Holmberg, David, 76–77, 83, 85
Holy Women, 69
Homophobia
in Africa, 166
on Indian reservations, 363

in Nicaragua, 299, 301
in North America, 299
and passive homosexuals, 304–5
"Homosexuality in Sub-Saharan Africa" (Wayne Dynes), 166–67
Homosexuals
adolescence of, among berdache, 275–76
in East Bay, 207–8
in Melanesia, 113–27, 252–55
in Mexico, 99–101, 103
among Azande military companies, 168–74
in Bahian Indian cults, 311–15
cultural influences on, 90
gender roles among, 89, 96–109
Keraki sex roles of, 211–12
Managua nightlife of, 296–97
marriage of, among the Big Nambas, 204
among the Etoro, 226
among Mohave Indians, 141–51
occupations of, among Azande, 170–71
in Melanesia, 124
in the upper Amazon, 345–46
in Venezuela, 347
ritual functions of, 112–13
sex roles of, 304–5
in Latin America, 331–36
in Melanesia, 113–27, 196–98
in Nicaragua, 290–92, 299
in North America, 330–32, 334–36
suicide among, 275
and warfare, 140
among the Garia, 375
among the Sambia, 230–31
in Melanesia, 249–50
See also Berdache; Cochon; Fa'a fafines; Homophobia; Lesbianism; Mahu
Hopi Indians, 12, 66–67, 70, 78
Hua, 232
Hugh-Jones, Stephen, 339–41
Hultkrantz, Ake, 77, 82, 83, 84–85
Human Relations Area Files, 41
Humboldt Bay, 201, 214
ritualized homosexuality in, 220–21, 222, 233, 237, 239
Hwame, 138–43
as shamans, 153–55, 161, 163–64
and claims to children, 152–53
courtship of, 153
initiation of, 144–48
marriage of, 153, 156–57, 161–64
menstruation of, 148
occupations of, 161, 163
prostitution of, 147, 163
rape of, 157, 163
sexual practices of, 148–51, 152–53
warfare of, 156

Iatmul
head-hunting practices among, 234
ritualized homosexuality among, 234–37, 238, 252
women's status among, 234
Illinois Indians, 61, 67, 68, 69, 71
Inca Indians, 176
India, 316
Indonesia, 204, 214
Ingalik Indians, 68
Ingiet, 252
"Institutionalized Homosexuality of the Mohave Indians" (George Devereux), 136–65
Iowa Indians, 69
Irian Jaya
low fertility rates in, 248
marriage practices in, 260
ritualized homosexuality in, 214–23, 239, 240
Iroquois Indians, 79
acculturation of, 3–4
berdache among, 64, 66–67, 69, 77, 82, 83
economic position of women among, 74
gender system of, 75
Islam, 336
Israel-Nettle, Anna, 138
I'tcts'ity'i, 12
Iyetico, 12

Jacobs, Sue-Ellen, 77–78, 82, 83, 85
"Berdache: A Brief Review of the Literature," 273–88
on cross-gender roles, 38
Jalisco, 95
James, George Wharton, 360
Jaquai, 199–200
marriage practices of, 219, 261
ritualized homosexuality among, 215, 217–18, 219–20, 236, 239
Jeghuje, 201, 228
Joao, 314–15
Journal of a Voyage to North America (Charlevoix), 82
Journal of the Royal Anthropological Institute, 208
Junker, Wilhelm, 169–70
Jupiter, 79

Kaluli, 201, 246
gender system of, 187
Gisaro ceremony of, 116–17
housing patterns of, 259
hunters among, 120
ritualized homosexuality among, 116–17, 119–20, 126, 224–26, 253
Kamairaho, 342–43
Kamia Indians, 139, 165
Kaniagmiut Indians, 69
Kansa Indians, 69
Kanum, 200, 213
Kaowerawedj, 221–22
Kapauku, 220
Karankawa Indians, 67
Karsch-Haack, Ferdinand, 166
Kaska Indians, 24
berdache among, 26, 27, 63, 64, 69, 80
work roles of, 29
Keep the River on Your Right (Tobias Schneebaum), 355–56
Kehoe, Alice B., 78–79, 82, 83, 84, 85
Kelly, Raymond C., 116–17, 119, 122–23, 224–26
Keraki, 193, 200, 213, 214
adolescence of male homosexuals among, 211–12
bamboo pipe initiation among, 121
cultural origins of, 240
homosexuality among, 114, 115, 119–21, 123–2, 182–83, 185, 210–12, 218
housing patterns of, 259
male initiation among, 250
marriage of homosexuals among, 211–12
marriage practices of, 260
population of, 247
women's status among, 256
Keres Indians, 11, 12
Kickapoo Indians, 62
Kimam, 200, 231
head-hunting of, 249
marriage practices of, 260–61
ritualized homosexuality among, 216, 236
warfare of, 250
Kiman, 218–19
Kinietz, W. Vernon, 277
Kinship
among Native Americans, 2–8, 13–15, 28–30
among Mohave Indians, 30
berdache and, 77
and homosexuality among the Etoro, 117, 122, 226
and homosexuality in Amazonia, 339–41
influence of Christianity on, 7–8
and Keraki ritualized homosexuality, 212
and male gender ideology in the New Hebrides, 203–4
and ritualized homosexuality among the Sambia, 230–31
and ritualized homosexuality among Humboldt Bay villages, 221
and ritualized homosexuality among the Iatmul, 235–36
and ritualized homosexuality in Melanesia, 112–13, 127,

260–61
and ritualized male homosexuality among the Kiman, 218
and ritualized male homosexuality among the Marind-anim, 216
and subordination of women, 23
and Zuni berdache, 361
Kinugmiut Indians, 62
Kirchoff, Paul, 347
Kisanga, 172–73
Kiwai, 199–200
cultural origins of, 240–41
ritualized homosexuality among, 208–10, 236–37
women's status among, 256
The Kiwai Papuans of British New Guinea (Landtman), 209
Klamath Indians, 24, 26
berdache among, 27, 65, 68, 69
work roles of, 29
Knauft, Bruce, 226–27
Knobloch, Johann, 79, 82–83
Kochems, Lee M., 25, 36–38, 61–88
Kokk'okshi, 365
Ko'lhamana. 365–66
Korok Indians, 62
Kroeber, Alfred L., 34–35, 159
on berdache, 24, 273, 274, 277
on Mohave Indian alyha, 154
on Mohave Indian cross-dressing songs, 143
on Mohave Indian homosexual initiation, 144
Kuagbiaru, 170–71, 172
Kuhn, T.S., 326
Kuma, 247
Kunam, 261
Kutchin Indians, 82
Kutenai Indians
berdache among, 64, 67, 68, 69, 72
cross-dressing among, 33–34
deny existence of cross-gender women, 34
Kuwal, 145, 148, 153, 158–59
as shaman, 154
case study of, 159–61
on divorcing an alyha, 152
on Mohave imaginary children, 151
sexual practices of, 149
teasing of, 156
Kwakiutl Indians, 75
Kwiskwinay, 138
Kwoma, 237–38

Laguna Indians, 12
Lakota Indians
berdache among, 16–17, 35, 79–80, 82, 83, 84
women's roles among, 33
Lame Deer, John, 10, 17
Lame Deer: Seeker of Visions (John Lame Deer and Richard Erdoes), 17
Lancaster, Roger N., 289–303
Landes, Ruth, 33, 304–15
Landtman, G., 114, 209, 209–10
Langimar, 227–28
Langness, L., 184
Latin America, 298–99, 330–38
See also Cuba; Mexico; Nicaragua
Law and Homosexuality, 108–9
Lawson, John, 273, 278
Layard, J.
on mythical homosexual practices, 205
on homosexuality on Malekula Island, 113–14, 115, 127
on ritualized homosexuality in Melanesia, 195, 212
on ritualized homosexuality in the New Hebrides, 204
Leach, E., 184
Lesbians
among the Akuna, 232
among Azande, 168–69, 171–73
among the Baruya, 228–29
on Malekula Island, 202–3
among the Mehinaku, 345
among Mohave Indians, 138, 152–53
and cross-gender Native

Americans, 23–38
in Native American culture, 1–21, 279, 282
in New Guinea, 372–75
in Nicaragua, 300
rape of, 36
self perceptions of, 13
among the Siriono, 346
as Tahitian prostitutes, 133
absence of among the Tapirape, 343
among the Tupi, 372–73
verbal abuse of, 18–19
See also Homosexuals
"Lesbians in American Indian Cultures" (Paula Gunn Allen), 1–21
Les Rites des Passage (Van Gennep), 194, 205
Levi-Strauss, Claude, 261, 340, 341
Levy, Robert I., 316–25
Levy, Robert L., 133
Liberty, Margot, 79, 83, 84, 85
Lindenbaum, S., 125–27
Linton, Ralph, 276
London Missionary Society, 132
"Los Gays Peruanos Son Libres," 332
Love in the South Seas, 132
Lowie, Robert H., 9, 275–76, 342
Luiseno Indians, 68, 69
Lurie, Nancy Oestreich, 273, 274, 278
Luxan, Diego Perez de, 176
Lyon, Patricia J., 346

Machismo in Mexico, 91–92, 100
Madagascar, 304
Mae Enga, 247
Mahu
adolescence of, 132, 317–18, 320
anthropological studies of, 317
attitudes toward, 133, 318–21
disappearance of, 133
history of, 132–33
James Morrison on, 316–17
occupations of, 132–33, 316, 318–19, 321
sexuality of, 132–33, 319–21
in Tahiti, 316–25
village distribution of, 316, 318–19, 321
William Bligh on, 317
See also Homosexuals
Maidu Indians, 62
Male Cults and Secret Initiations in Melanesia (Allen), 195
Malekula Island, 200, 206
depopulation of, 127
homosexuality on, 113–14, 115, 126–27, 202–3, 239, 252
lesbianism on, 202–3
map of, 272
sex ratio on, 247
tribal social structures on, 203
Malinowski, Bronislaw, 4–6, 16, 193–94
Managua, Nicaragua, 292–93, 296–98
Mandan Indians, 66–67, 69, 71, 276
Manfred, Fred, 1
The Manly-Hearted Woman (Fred Manfred), 1
Manuelzinho, 315
Maricopa Indians, 24, 26, 155, 164, 276
Marind-anim, 199–200
cross-dressing among, 222
cultural origins of, 240–41
food consumption of, 213
gender system of, 216–17
head-hunting practices of, 216–17
housing patterns of, 258
importance of age among, 120
lack of sexual anxiety among, 258
low fertility rates among, 248–49
male cults of, 215–17
marriage practices of, 217, 259–60
pig husbandry of, 246
population of, 247
ritualized homosexuality among, 114–15, 119–20, 122–24, 182–85, 214–20, 223, 236–37, 252, 253–54
warfare of, 249–50
women's status among, 216–17, 250, 256

Maring, 231
Marriage
of Azande, 169–73
of Bahian bisexuals, 315
among Baruya homosexuals, 229
among berdache, 30, 67–68, 176–77, 278–79, 304
of the Big Nambas homosexuals, 204
and East Bay ritualized homosexuality, 207
Etoro patterns of, 123
among Keraki homosexuals, 211–12
among the Marind-anim, 217
in Melanesia, 247, 249, 255–63
of Melanesia homosexuals, 113–15, 117–18, 120–26, 197, 252, 254
in Mexico, 89, 92–95, 104–5, 108
among Mohave Indians, 140, 151–53, 156–57, 159–60, 161–64
among Native Americans, 6–8, 14, 23, 26–27, 29–31, 35, 65
among New Guinea homosexuals, 183, 374
of Nicaraguan cochon, 290, 294
among Sambia homosexuals, 230–31
sex outside of, 45–46
sex within, 43
and sister-exchange practices among the Jaquai, 219
and sister-exchange practices among the Kiman, 218–19
among Tapirape homosexuals, 343
among the Tanala, 304
of Tupi lesbians, 372–73
among Warao homosexuals, 347
and wife-sharing, 46
of Zuni berdache, 366
Martin, Kay, 38
Mastamho, 144
Masturbation, 301
among Amazonia homosexuals, 342
among Azande homosexuals, 169
among the Baruya, 228
in East Bay, 207–8
in Humboldt Bay villages, 221
among the Kaowerawedj, 221–22
on Malekula Island, 202
and Mexican homosexuals, 106–7
among the Mohave Indians, 137, 148
among New Guinea's Eastern Highland tribes, 231
among the Onabasulu, 224
and initiation rites in the Papuan Plateau, 116
among Tahitian boys, 322
on Wogeo Island, 237
Matavilye, 141
Maximillian, Alexander P., 273
Maya, 371
Mayr, E., 326
Mead, Margaret
on berdache, 275
on homosexuality in the Admiralty Islands, 233
on the Iatmul, 235
Medicine, Beatrice, 33
Mehan, Hugh, 354
Mehinaku, 343–45
Mejbrat, 220, 222
Melanesia
anthropological studies of, 191–96, 199
circumcision in, 203–4
disappearance of ritualized homosexuality in, 210
distribution of ritualized homosexuality in, 200–201, 245–46
ecology of societies with ritualized homosexuality in, 246–49
female initiation in, 250
gender systems in, 112–13, 119–29, 192, 198, 246–48, 250–51, 253–55, 255–63
Gisaro ceremony in, 116–17
historical diffusion of ritualized homosexuality in, 238–44

housing patterns in, 258–59
male initiation in, 250–55
marriage of homosexuals in, 113–15, 117–18, 120–26, 197
masculinity and hunting in, 246
Papuan language migrations in, 241–44
power relationships in, 254
ritualized homosexuality in, 113–29, 191–272, 298, 300, 327, 336, 339
sex ratios in, 247
sexual polarity in, 255–63
subregions of, 199–200
symbolic aspects of anal intercourse in, 204
warfare in, 249–50
women's status in, 246–48, 253, 255–63
Melpa, 262
Menstruation
and Chaco berdache, 347
and Melanesian women's development cycle, 248, 257–58
Mohave Indian beliefs about, 148–51, 153, 159, 161
Native American beliefs about, 9–10, 14, 73–74, 75, 77, 80, 81, 83, 84
among New Guinea lesbians, 373–74
Pueblo Indian beliefs about, 179
and ritual mutilation, 182–87
Wogeo Island beliefs about, 237
Metraux, Alfred, 347
Mexican National Institute of Housing, 95–96
Mexico
active male homosexuals not stigmatized in, 102–3
adolescence of homosexuals in, 99–101, 103
boy's feminine behavior discouraged in, 91–92
courtship in, 92
crowded living conditions in, 95–96, 102
cultural influences on homosexuality in, 96–105
disapproval of homosexuality in, 108–9
distribution of income in, 95–96
gender system in, 89, 91–92, 105–9
homosexuality and mass media in, 99, 101
homosexuality and mestizo culture in, 89–110
homosexuality in, 333, 336, 371
importance of machismo in, 91–92, 100
income distribution in, 103
influence of Indian culture on marriage in, 94–95
influence of migration on marriage in, 95
jokes about homosexuals in, 96–99, 101–2
legality of homosexuality in, 108–9
lifestyle of single men in, 95
male social networks in, 89, 93, 105
marriage and male sexuality in, 104–5
marriage of homosexuals in, 108
mestizo culture of, 90–96
prostitution in, 104–5
relative costs of male sexual outlets in, 103–4
sexual double standard in, 92–93, 105, 109
vocabulary of homosexuality in, 96–99, 101–2
women's status in, 89, 91–92, 104–5
Mexico City, Mexico, 109
Miami, Fla., 297
Miami Indians, 65, 67
Mimika, 220, 240
Minnehaha, 360
Missouri Indians, 62
"Mistaking Fantasy for Ethnography" (Stephen O. Murray), 353–56
Moche Indians, 176

Mohave Indians, 24
alyha among, 151–52, 156–57, 159–60
berdache among, 26–27, 30, 36, 37, 67, 68, 69, 70, 71, 72, 73, 74, 80, 84, 139, 276, 278
cross-dressing among, 136–65
cross-gender dreamers among, 26
determinants of homosexuality among, 138–43
dice games of, 140, 142–43
homosexual adolescents among, 137–39, 140–41
homosexual initiation among, 141–48
homosexuality and creation myths of, 139–43, 147
homosexuality among, 136–65
homosexual shamans among, 153–55
hwame among, 153, 156–57
lesbian sexual practices of, 31
masturbation practices among, 148
menstrual beliefs among, 149–50, 153, 159
name changes among, 147
pregnancy taboos of, 150–51
reservation conditions of, 136
ritualism of, 143–44
sexuality of, 136–37, 148–51, 156
suicide among, 157
and warfare, 155–56
witchcraft beliefs of, 143, 153–54, 161, 163–64
Mohawk Indians, 367
Monacan Indians, 273
Mono Indians, 65
Moore, T.R., 356
Morrison, James, 316–17, 320
Mortimer, George, 132
Moszkowski, M., 221–22
Mowehafen, 187
Murphy, Robert F., 341
Murray, Stephen O.
"Fuzzy Sets and Abominations," 326–29
"Mistaking Fantasy for Ethnography," 353–56
"Stigma Transformation and Relexification: 'Gay' in Latin America," 330–38
"Must We Deracinate Indians to Fine Gay Roots?" (Ramon A. Gutierrez), 175–81

Nacirema Indians, 76, 83
Nahwera, 139, 140, 141–43
Nambikwara, 261, 340
Nanduru, 172
Nash, J., 299
Natchez Indians, 64, 67, 83
Native Americans
acculturation of, 2, 3–4, 17–18
berdache among, 61–88, 273–88, 304, 327, 371
berdache warriors among, 66–67
berdache disappear among, 34–36, 61, 78
berdache marriage among, 278–79
community concept of, 2–8
conceptions of maternity among, 11
cross-dressing among, 33–34, 80, 81, 358–69
cross-gender females among, 23–38,
development of berdache among, 176, 178–79, 275
economic structures of, 24, 28–30, 32–33, 35
ethnographical study of, 3–6, 9, 18
European colonization of, 176
gender systems of, 13–14, 25, 28–30, 32–33, 35, 61, 66, 69, 71–78, 80, 81, 83, 85
homophobia among, 18–19, 363
homosexuality among, 136–65, 175–81, 358–69
kinship networks of, 2–8, 13–15, 28–30
lesbianism among, 1–21, 31, 279, 282

marriage practices of, 6–8, 14, 23, 26–27, 29–31, 35, 65, 67–68
menstrual beliefs of, 9–10, 14, 77, 80, 81, 83, 84
ostracization of berdache among, 35–36
sexual beliefs of, 31–32, 35–38
spirit world of, 2–4, 7–8, 10–12, 15–17, 26, 27, 66, 67, 69–74, 75, 76–77, 78, 79, 80, 81, 83, 84, 275–77
virginity codes of, 2
and white attitudes toward berdache, 278–79
witchcraft beliefs of, 16–17, 36
women's status among, 1–21, 73–74, 76, 78, 79, 80, 81, 84
women warriors among, 33
See also Plains Indians; individual tribe names
Nauti, 227–28
Nau'ts'ity, 12
Navajo Indians
berdache among, 62, 65, 66, 68, 70, 71, 72, 78, 80, 273, 276, 279, 368
religion of, 16
women's status among, 80, 279
Naven (Bateson), 234
New Britain, 200, 204–8, 233, 237, 239, 252
New Caledonia, 199–200, 202, 239, 242, 372
New Guinea, 85, 199, 204, 206
cross-dressing in, 82
gender system in, 82, 182–89
male initiation rites in, 182–89
ritualized homosexuality in, 116–17, 182–89, 208–14, 222–31, 239, 372, 373–75
semen and masculinity in, 185–87
sex ratio in, 203
social organization in, 187–88
societies without ritualized homosexuality in, 212–13
witchcraft beliefs in, 185–86, 188
women's status in, 184
New Hebrides, 199–200
circum-incision in, 257
kinship and male gender ideology in, 203–4
map of, 272
ritualized homosexuality in, 202, 239, 242
rituals in, 202–3
women's status in, 203–4, 256
New Zealand, 134
Nez Perce Indians, 64
Nicaragua
attitudes toward sexuality in, 290–91, 295, 298
cochon adolescence in, 292–94
cross-dressing in, 295
effects of the Sandinista Revolution in, 296–97
gender system of, 292, 295–96
homosexuality in, 289–303
lesbianism in, 300
religious disapproval of homosexuality in, 291
religious festivals in, 295
stigmatized homosexuality in, 291–96, 298–302
Western influence on homosexuality, 297–98
Nimuenadju, Curt, 342
Nootka Indians, 68
Normanby Island, 213
North America
homosexuality in, 294–96, 330–32, 334–36
Nouveaux Voyages aux Indes Occidentales (Bossu), 273
Nukaulofa, Tonga, 134–35
Observations and Remarks made during a Voyage to the Islands (George Mortimer), 132

Oceania, 5
Octavio, 315
Oglala Indians, 10
Ojibwa Indians, 14, 63, 67, 74
Okanagon Indians, 276, 277
Old Woman Above, 69

Omaha Indians, 62, 68, 69, 71, 73, 274, 275, 276, 371
Onabasalu, 116, 201, 224–25
"On Male Initiation and Dual Organisation in New Guinea" (Per Hage), 182–89
Oosterwal, G., 222
Orokaiva, 210
Ortner, Sherry, 9, 19
Osage Indians, 65, 66–67, 68, 69, 71
Oto Indians, 66–67, 69, 70, 71
Out/Look, 175

Pahe, Erna, 368
Paim, 315
Paiute Indians, 65, 66, 367
Pamlico Indians, 273
Papago Indians, 67, 69, 78, 276, 279
Papeete, Tahiti, 132–33
Parkinson, Richard, 205
Parsons, Elsie Clews, 179–80, 359, 362
Patriarchy and Suppression of Women, 2, 9, 12, 18
Paul, Lois, 10
Pawnee Indians, 69, 276
Perry, M.E., 327
Peru, 331–33
Piegan Indians, 74, 82
Pierson, Robin, 133–34
Pima Indians, 155
 berdache among, 62, 68, 69, 78, 276, 279
 prohibit cross-dressing, 65
Plains Indians
 berdache among, 32–35, 63, 64, 66, 68, 69, 76, 79, 83, 84, 274–76
 cross-dressing among, 79
 cultural development of, 32–33, 35
 disappearance of berdache among, 34–36
 ethnographic studies of, 33–37
 gender systems of, 32–33, 35
 nineteenth-century observers on, 34
 reluctance to discuss cross-gender women among, 35
 sexual categories among, 78–79
 social structure of, 24
 women's status among, 74, 79, 80
Pocahontas, 360
Polynesia, 132–35
"Polynesia's Third Sex: The Gay Life Starts in the Kitchen," 132–35
Pomo Indians, 276
Ponca Indians, 69, 274
Potawatomi Indians, 65, 66, 67, 71, 83
Powers, M.N., 79, 80
Powers, William K., 79–80, 82, 83, 84, 85
The Pre-Columbian Mind (Francisco Guerra), 175
Prisons and Homosexuality, 294–95
Procopio, 313–15
Prostitution
 in Bahia, Brazil, 305, 314–15
 and berdache, 304
 among Chaco berdache, 347
 among the Mohave Indians, 147, 153, 163
 effect on mahu of, 133
 in Europe, 178
 in Mexico, 92–93, 98, 102, 104
 in Nicaragua curbed by Sandinistas, 296
 by Tahitian lesbians, 133
 in Tonga, 135
Psychology of Sex (Havelock Ellis), 194
Pueblo Indians, 6
 berdache among, 65, 66–67, 69, 78, 80, 82, 175–81, 276
 controlling male sexuality among, 177–78
 dances of, 178–79
 menstrual beliefs of, 179
 religion of, 12, 176–79
 residential structures of, 176
 rituals of, 176–77
 and warfare, 178, 181
 women's status among, 80
Purari Delta, 210
Purity and Danger (Mary Douglas), 327

Quain, Buell, 341
Quapaw Indians, 64
Quinault Indians, 68

Radin, Paul, 276
Ramko'kamekra, 342
Rape
attitudes toward, 46–47
of berdache, 68, 176
of Cheyenne Indian women, 79
frequency of, 47
of lesbians, 36
of Mohave Indian hwame, 157
of Pueblo Indian berdache, 179
of Sahaykwisa, 163
and warfare, 176
Read, K.E., 231
Read, Kenneth, 111–12
Reichel-Dolmatoff, Gerardo, 348
Religion
in Africa, 166
in Bahia, Brazil, 305–15
and cross-dressing in Nicaragua, 295
and homosexuality in Latin America, 336
and homosexuality in Nicaragua, 291
in Melanesia, 251–52, 252
of Mohave Indians, 153–55
of Native Americans, 2–4, 7–8, 10–12, 15–17, 26, 27, 66, 67, 69–74, 75, 76–77, 78, 79, 80, 81, 83, 84, 139–43, 147, 275–77
of Pueblo Indians, 176–79
and taboos on homosexuality, 327
and the mahu in Tahiti, 318–19
of Zuni Indians, 358–59, 360–62, 365–66
"Ritualized Homosexual Behavior in the Male Cults of Melanesia, 1862–1983" (Gilbert H. Herdt), 191–272
Roheim, Geza, 154
Roscoe, Will
"Gay Studies on the Rez," 363–64
on Pueblo berdache, 178–81
"The Zuni Man-Woman," 175, 358–69
Rose, Bradley, 363–64
Rubin, Gayle, 31
Running Eagle, 34

Sahaykwisa, 36, 145, 158–59
appearance of, 147
case study of, 161–64
death of, 164
economic position of, 153
Salisbury, Richard, 205
Salmeron, Fray Jeronimo Zarate de, 176
Sambia, 192, 201, 227, 228
gender system of, 117–20, 230–31
importance of age among, 120–21
male initiation among, 250
marriage practices of, 260
outmigration of single men among, 127–28
pacification of, 128
premarital sex condemned among, 256
ritualized homosexuality among, 117–25, 127–28, 229–31, 236, 237, 239, 262
sex ratio among, 247
sexual anxiety among, 258
tribal councils of, 128
warfare of, 230–31, 250
women's status among, 230–31, 256
Samo, 226
Samoa, 133–34
Santee Dakota Indians
berdache among, 67, 69, 83
forced cross-dressing among, 62
See also Dakota Indians
Sarmi, 221
Sauk Indians, 67, 69, 74
Schieffelin, E.L., 116–17, 119–20, 224, 226

Schlegel, Alice, 80–81, 83, 84, 85
Schneebaum, Tobias, 353–56
Seligmann, C.G., 371–75
Semen
importance of to masculinity,
among the Baruya, 229
among the Gebusi, 227
among the Sambia, 230–31
in Melanesia, 112–19, 121–22, 125, 197–98, 251, 252–55, 257–58, 260–62, 300
in New Guinea, 185–87, 224–26
and Keraki masculinity, 212
and Kiman masculinity, 218–19
in Marind-anim rituals, 215–17
in ritualized homosexuality in East Bay, 207
"Sentimental Effusions of Genital Contact in Upper Amazonia," 339–51
Sepik, 233–40
Serrano Indians, 62
Sex, Culture and Myth (Bronislaw Malinowski), 4
"Sexual Inversion Among Primitive Races" (C.G. Seligmann), 371–75
"Sexual Inversion Among the Azande" (E.E. Evans-Pritchard), 168–74
Sexuality
anthropological studies of, 111–12
of Azande lesbians, 171–73
as basis for male power, 294–95
Baruya beliefs about, 229
before marriage, 44–45
of berdache, 31, 61–62, 67–69, 72–73, 78
coded cross-culturally, 48–57
codes for, 39–59
contemporary debates concerning, 80
and culture, 301
difficulties of researching, 40–41
ethnographic studies of, 40–42, 111–12
European perceptions of in Tahiti, 132
idealogical concepts of, 23–24
and impotence, 47
inversion of, 371–75
of Mahu, 132–33, 319–21
and male aggressiveness, 47
in Melanesia, 191–92, 251, 253–56, 258
in Mexico, 89, 92–93, 96–109
of Mohave Indians, 136–37, 158
multivalent aspects of, 244
Native Americans and, 31–32, 35–38
in Nicaragua, 290–91, 295–98
in North America, 294–95
outside marriage, 45–46
peasant and bourgeois forms of, 299–301
and politics, 112
in ritualized homosexuality, 253–55
social patterns of, 40
and society, 128–29
"Sexuality and Gender in Certain Native American Tribes: The Case of Cross-Gender Females" (Evelyn Blackwood), 23–38
"Sexual Subordination: Institutionalized Homosexuality and Social Control in Melanesia" (Gerald W. Creed), 111–30
Shaeffer, Claude E., 79
Shango, 313
Shasta Indians, 65, 66
Shedd, Charles L., 273–74
Shivwits Paiute Indians, 276
Shoshoni Indians, 64, 65, 68, 69, 77, 82, 83, 274
Signorini, Italo, 81–82, 84–85
Silko, Leslie, 11–12, 15
Simpson, Colin, 227
Sinkaietk Indians, 70
Sioux Indians, 1, 69, 79, 274
Siriono, 346
Slave Indians, 62, 82
Slave Woman, 75
Small Islands, 204
Soares de Souza, Gabriel, 345
Sorenson, Arthur P., 346–47

Sorum, Arve, 224, 226
Spain, 175, 178
Standard Cross-Cultural Sample, 39–41
Stekel, Wilhelm, 315
Stevenson, James, 359
Stevenson, Matilda Coxe
on berdache in Pueblo rituals, 179–81
on We'wha, 358–60, 362
on Zuni berdache, 277
Stewart, Omer C., 273–74, 278
"Stigma Transformation and Relexification: 'Gay' in Latin America" (Murray and Arboleda), 330–38
Strathern, Andrew, 82, 84, 85
Strathern, M., 298
"Subject Honor and Object Shame: The Construction of Male Homosexuality and Stigma in Nicaragua" (Roger N. Lancaster), 289–303
Suhuraye, 163
Suicide, 157, 275
Suki, 200, 213
Sun Dance, 79
Sxints, 70
Sylvina, 309–10

Tabatulabal Indians, 276
Tahiti
child-raising practices in, 322
cross-dressing in, 132–33, 316–25
development of masculinity in, 322–23
European perceptions of sexuality in, 132
gender system in, 133, 316, 321–22
homosexuality in, 132–33, 316–25
impact of modernization on social roles in, 324
lesbian prostitutes in, 133
mahu in, 133, 318–24
missionary activity in, 132–33
women's status in, 321–22
Tahitians, Mind and Experience in the Society Islands, 133
Tairora, 232
Tanala, 304
Tanner, John, 67
Tapirape, 342–43
Tcatc, 161
Tcuhum, 163–64
Teiresias, 76, 83
Telefomin, 220
Tenejumine, 344–45
Tessman, Gunter, 345–46
Teton Dakota Indians, 64, 66, 67, 68, 69, 73
Tewa Indians, 38, 78, 83
"The Community Function of Tahitian Male Transvestism: A Hypothesis" (Robert I. Levy), 316–25
"The North American Berdache" (Charles Callender and Lee M. Kochems), 61–88
"The Zuni Man-Woman" (Will Roscoe), 175, 358–69
Timucua Indians, 64, 64, 67, 71
Tipai Indians, 70
Tlingit Indians, 62, 69, 71, 81, 276
Tolai, 205
Tonga, 134–35
Tonto Indians, 164
Tooker, Elisabeth, 64
Tootsie, 76
Tor, 222, 248
Trans-Fly, 200
marriage practices in, 260
ritualized homosexuality in, 114, 115, 193, 210, 215, 223
Transvestism
See Cross-dressing
Trexler, Richard, 176
Tripp, C.A., 353–54
Trobriand Islands, 5, 194
Trumai, 341
Trumbach, R., 300
Ts'its'tsi'nako, 11–12, 15
Tumaka, Nick, 361
Tupi, 372–73

Tupinamba, 345
Turrado Moreno, Angel, 347
Tuscarora Indians, 62, 64

U'k, 179–81
Unasé, 375
Ute Indians, 69, 71

Van Baal, J.
 on ritualized homosexuality
 in Irian Jaya, 214–23
 among the Marind-anim, 114–15, 120, 122–24, 223
 in Melanesia, 212
Van Eekhoud, J.P.K., 222
Vava, 315
Venezuela, 347
Vidal, 315
Village-Old-Woman, 69
Voegelin, Erminie W., 277
Voorheis, Barbara, 38

Wachipaeri, 346
Wagley, Charles, 342–43
Waiat, 213
Walapai Indians, 62, 138, 276
Walbiri, 243–44
Wando, 172
Wappo Indians, 62
Warao, 347
Warburg, Bettina, 154
Waropen, 220
Westbrook, John T., 40
Wewha, 67, 68, 178–81, 363
 as Zuni intermediary with whites, 359
 confronts U.S. soldiers, 361
 death of, 359, 362
 occupations of, 360–62, 365–66
 and the Zuni Sha'lako festival, 358–59
 visit to Washington D.C. of, 360, 364
Whitehead, Harriet
 on different forms of homosexuality, 126
 on berdache, 25, 27, 32, 37, 366
Whiting, John W.M., 40
Wilbert, Johannes, 347
Will, G.F., 276
Williams, F.E., 114, 115, 119–21, 123–24, 210–13
Williams, W.L., 299
Wilson, Edmund, 360–61
Winnebago Indians
 berdache among, 65, 69, 71, 274, 276, 279
 forced cross-dressing among, 62
Wintu Indians, 66
Witchcraft
 in Bahia, Brazil, 308, 313–14
 among the Etoro, 117
 among Mohave Indians, 143, 153–54, 161, 163–64
 among Native Americans, 16–17, 36
 in New Guinea, 185–86, 188
 among Zuni Indians, 361
Witoto, 346
Wogeo Island
 genital mutilation on, 182–83, 185, 187
 ritualized homosexuality on, 237, 239
Woman Above, 69
Woman Chief, 33, 34, 65, 67
Women, Status of
 among the Azande, 171–72
 as female priests in Bahia, Brazil, 305–15
 among the Baruya, 229
 and berdache, 73–74, 75, 76
 among the Iatmul, 234
 on Kiwai Island, 208, 210
 among the Marind-anim, 216–17
 in Melanesia, 112, 119–26, 246–48, 250, 253, 255–63
 in Mexico, 89, 91–92, 104–5
 in Mohave Indian society, 150–51, 153, 155
 in Native American societies, 1–21, 33, 73–74, 76, 78–81, 84
 among Navajo Indians, 279
 in New Guinea, 184
 in the New Hebrides, 203–4
 and male homosexuality in

Nicaragua, 291
under patriarchy, 2, 9, 12, 18
among Plains Indians, 32–33, 35, 79
among Pueblo Indians, 176–77
among the Sambia, 230–31
in Tahiti, 321–22
threatening sexuality of, 120
among the Tupi, 372–73
in wife-sharing, 46
Wood, Houston, 354
"Work and Sex in a Guatemalan Village" (Lois Paul), 10
Wounded Knee, 361

Yankton Indians, 62, 69
Yanomamo, 341–42
Yansan, 313
Yavapai Indians, 62, 164
Yei-anim, 200, 213
Yellow Head, 67, 74
Yoruba, 305
Yuma Indians, 136, 151, 154, 155
alyha among, 160
berdache among, 37, 62, 64–65, 68, 78, 81, 82
homosexuality among, 144, 164–65
Yurok Indians, 64, 68, 71, 77, 84

Zeus, 76
Zuni Indians
berdache among, 66, 67, 68, 70, 71, 72, 74, 78, 175–81, 276, 277, 358–59
concepts of raw and cooked among, 362, 365
and confrontations with U.S. soldiers, 361
cross-dressing among, 358–69
gender system of, 361–62, 365–69
homosexuality among, 358–69
Ko'lhamana in origin myth of, 365–66
religion of, 12, 360–62, 365–66
reservation slide shows on berdache for, 363–64
Sha'lako festival of, 358–59
and strategies for dealing with change, 364
witchcraft among, 361